THE HISTORY OF NORTH RICHLAND HILLS

The History of North Richland Hills

WHERE FAMILIES LIVE, WORK, WORSHIP, AND PLAY

By George N. Green

SMITHFIELD PRESS, NORTH RICHLAND HILLS, TEXAS

**Smithfield
Press**

An Imprint of D. & F. Scott Publishing, Inc.
P.O. Box 821653
North Richland Hills, TX 76182

Printed in the United States of America

02 01 00 99 98   5 4 3 2 1

Library of Congress Cataloging-in-Publication Data

Green, George N. (George Norris)
   The history of North Richland Hills : where families live,
work, worship, and play / by George N. Green.
   p. cm.
   Includes index.

   ISBN 0-94-103779-7
   1. North Richland Hills (Tex.)--History. 2. North Richland Hills
(Tex.)--Biography. I. Title.
   F394.N67 G74 1999
   976.4'531--ddc21
                           98-58062
                           CIP

Cover design by KC Scott
Book design by John Baird
Index by Allied Editorial

Contents

Mural painted by Richland High School art students. Don Tipps, teacher.

The mural now hangs in the hall of the NRH Court Building

v

Foreword

In writing the history of North Richland Hills, I am indebted foremost to the enormous research efforts of the North Richland Hills Historical Committee. They are Polly Brinkley, Avis Crisp, Naomi Jones Cummings, Nancy Dowler, Jane West Dunkelberg, Mary Ruth Reeves Ellis, Evalyn Lochridge, Oscar Lochridge, Cheryl Cowan Lyman, Kenneth "Ace" Nace, Geraldine Orr, Aline Parker, Dorothy Lee Null Parker, Pat Nimmo Riddle, Mary Shilcutt, Billie Sommermeyer, Don Tipps, and Councilwoman JoAnn Johnson who first had the vision for this project and who has worked tirelessly to see it completed.

The George Green Family L/R Valerie, Deanna, George, (standing) Kathy

The family histories and interviews collected by the committee, as well as their research notes on Smithfield and on North Richland Hills businesses, city agencies, parks, schools, civic organizations, and other topics, were essential to the project. So were the clippings on Smithfield, Birdville, and North Richland Hills housed in the North Richland Hills Library, headed by Steve Brown, and in the *Fort Worth Star-Telegram* collection in the Special Collections Division, under Gerald Saxon, in the University of Texas at Arlington Library. The committee also unearthed various notes and records and many photographs from the Heritage Room, initiated by historian Duane Gage at the Tarrant County Junior College Library, Northeast Campus. My own interviews with several citizens in North Richland Hills were a delightful part of the research process. I also found Smithfield files at the Tarrant County Historical Commission, presided over with much hospitality by Dee Barker in the Tarrant County Courthouse.

Some of the historical committee had already written about the city. The history of the Birdville Independent School District, *School Bells and Chalk Dust*, by Don Tipps, Mary Ruth Reeves Ellis, Bette Nolen, and Ida Joe Reynolds and the historical booklet, *North Richland Hills, A Proud Heritage*, by Jane and Stephen Dunkelberg, are pioneering works providing considerable information and a vital framework for any history of North Richland Hills. Also useful were compilations of historical works on Birdville by Thelma Ray and by Arlita Hallam and on Smithfield by Hazel Lowrance.

Several members of the historical committee were informed by "experts" that the structure of our project was unworkable. Perhaps we'll send them a copy of the book. Finally, my wife Kathy and daughters Deanna and Valerie were very tolerant when I sequestered myself in my office for this project, and I am greatly indebted to them.

George N. Green, Ph.D

Professor of History, University of Texas at Arlington

Acknowledgments

JoAnn Johnson, council liaison to Historical Committee

In August 1996, NRH Councilwoman JoAnn Johnson invited a few people who had responded to a newspaper article and inquiry to meet for the purpose of discussing the possibility of writing a history of the city and early community. It was a vision and passionate desire of hers to see such a project accomplished. After being asked to chair this committee, I too caught the vision. After all, there were still many original residents in the NRH area plus "old-timers" in the Smithfield community that would give us a good start.

We have researched, interviewed, collected pictures, written material, typed, edited, proofed, and attempted to give some structure and continuity to what has been described as a "popcorn" community—additions and developments that popped up through the early years. We are sad to say there has been some loss of precious people and thus precious memories since this project began.

We extend our sincere thanks to the more than 300 families who responded to our plea for family stories and memories. However, because of the tremendous response to this portion of the book, the Historical Committee regrets having to edit the stories because of space limitations. A copy of unedited family stories and memories may be found in the reference section of the North Richland Hills Public Library and in the Heritage room at TCJC, Northeast Campus. Family histories were contributed by family members. The Historical Committee has made no attempt to verify the historical accuracy of their recollections.

Evalyn Lochridge, chair of NRH Historical Committee

Special thanks to Fran Burns for supplying us with two years of editions from the *North Hills News* for which she worked and for hundreds of negatives; to many early residents of NRH for all the information you supplied; to Bill Reeves for special family and Birdville history; Johnny Rumfield for his family, Smithfield Lodge, and Smithfield history; and especially Aline Shivers who was one of the first to respond. She not only supplied us with a great knowledge of her early settler family but also with wonderful family possessions for a future museum.

We owe a big "thank-you" to the NRH Library staff for letting us take over their boardroom during the last six weeks of this project. You've all been so kind to us, especially Steve Brown and Brenda Lewis who have helped in a myriad of ways.

NRH is so fortunate that our City Councils since 1996 have realized the need for a written history of our city and have been so supportive of this project. Thank you, former Mayor Tommy Brown, whose council supported us from the beginning, and Mayor Charles Scoma for seeing it to a conclusion. And heartfelt thanks to City Council members Lyle Welch, Mack Garvin, Mark Wood, JoAnn Johnson, Byron Sibbet, Linda Spurlock, Don Phifer, Cheryl Lyman, Matt Milano, Frank Metts, and Russ Mitchell.

There aren't enough words or ways to thank a wonderful committee of dedicated men and women who have made this dream a reality. Special appreciation to my husband, Oscar, whom I have told on many occasions, "Don't get up out of your chair—just type." He's had to eat lots of sandwiches and put up with my jangled nerves.

This committee has worked so hard. We thank our families for their support and understanding during these two years. We hope that all who read these pages will find the same enjoyment and pleasure with which we undertook this project.

Historians gather the past in anticipation of the future. We are not historians, simply a few who are interested in our history.

Respectfully,
Evalyn Wood Lochridge
Chair, North Richland Hills Historical Committee

North Richland Hills Historical Committee

Star-Telegram/Frank Stone

L/R-Nancy Dowler, Cheryl Lyman,
Mary Shilcutt

Row 1, L/R-George Green, "Ace" Nace, Geraldine Orr, Aline Parker • Row 2, Steve Brown,
Polly Brinkley, Naomi Cummings, Billie Sommermeyer • Row 3, Jane Dunkelberg, Dorothy Parker,
Evalyn Lochridge, Don Tipps, Mary Ruth Ellis • Row 4, JoAnn Johnson, Pat Riddle,
Oscar Lochridge

S P E C I A L   V O L U N T E E R S

Stephen Dunkelberg, Peggy Taylor

Front L/R-Bette Nolen, Brenda Lewis • Back R. A. Meek,
Ann Meek, JoAnne Betts

Historical Committee At Work

Naomi "Sis" Cummings, Aline Parker

Oscar Lochridge

Don Tipps, Jerry Orr, Mary Ruth Ellis

"Ace" Nace, George Green

Polly Brinkley, Evalyn Lochridge,
Billie Sommermeyer

Dorothy Parker, Steve Brown

Nancy Dowler, Polly Brinkley

Pat Riddle, Avis Crisp at "Make A Difference Day"

Mary Shilcutt, Jerry Orr, Pat Riddle

Pat Riddle, Jane Dunkelberg, Cheryl
Lyman, Mayor Tommy Brown in back

1 The Story of Our City

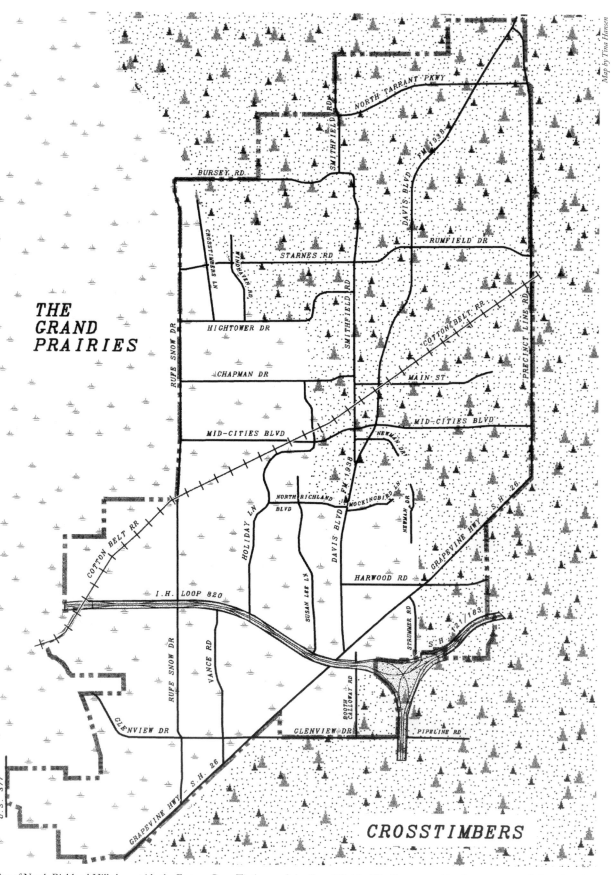

Map by Tina Hansen

The future site of North Richland Hills lay astride the Eastern Cross Timbers and the Grand Prairie. The future east side of town was wooded, with hills and sandy soil. The west side was flatter, black prairie land with clay and fewer trees.

EARLY BIRDVILLE TO THE BIRTH OF NORTH RICHLAND HILLS

Patricia Richards

North Richland Hills, Cross Timbers Region, current site of 100 Acre Park

EARLY INHABITANTS

The Americans who first rode into what is now Tarrant County in the 1840s encountered a pristine wilderness of rich, black soil, majestic hardwood trees, and flowing streams. The first settlers claimed that the prairie grass was "as high as a man on horseback." In less than a century the men and women of Tarrant County transformed it into a vast cityscape. Considerable internal variety marks the history of that transformation. This is a unique story of several communities that fused into one, North Richland Hills, whose colorful history is worthy of the county from which it sprang.

According to geologists, Texas was cov-

Patricia Richards

North Richland Hills, native prairie grass, current site of 100 Acre Park

ered by a great shallow sea a hundred million years ago, but through eons of time the waters receded toward the southeast. Sixty million years ago pressures from beneath the earth's crust pushed the land upward, and remnants of the sea drained rapidly into the Gulf of Mexico. The future site of Tarrant County sloped to the southeast from an elevation of more than a thousand feet in the northwest to less than half that in the southeast. Geological changes rippled through the area, creating four natural regions. From the west they were the Western Cross Timbers, with cliffs, waterfalls, and oaks, which gave way to the Grand Prairie, with its terraced effect and alternating layers of limestone and marl. Farther east were the Eastern Cross Timbers, with sandstone and more oaks. Finally the Black Prairie on the southeastern border was a gently rolling grassland with rich soil.

The future site of North Richland Hills lay astride the Eastern Cross Timbers and the Grand Prairie. The future east side of town was wooded, with hills and sandy soil. The west side was flatter, black prairie land with clay and fewer trees.

A rough line separating the timbers and the prairie can be discerned from old maps and recollections. Not all the following streets connect with each other, but from Bursey Road, trace a line south along Cross Timbers Lane, east on Starnes, south on Windhaven, east on Hightower, south on Holiday Lane and Susan Lee, east on North Richland Boulevard and

Fossil Creek, 1983

3

Little Bear Creek at Davis Boulevard

Mockingbird, south from Newman toward Strummer, west on 820, south on Booth-Calloway, west on Glenview, and southwest on the Grapevine Highway. West of that line was mostly prairie, except that Fossil Creek was forested and Calloway Branch somewhat wooded. More than three-fifths of the future city of North Richland Hills lay in the Cross Timbers. The names of modern subdivisions are not noted for accuracy, but those incorporating the names "oaks," "wood," and "tree" generally lie east of the line and recognize the land's original condition, while "richland," "richfield," and "meadow" are accurately deployed in the west and southwest of town. The oak and pecan trees of Fossil Creek, some of them hundreds of years old, stand as the best remnants of an earlier era.

Twelve rivers and major creeks drained the county, including four that flowed through the future North Richland Hills. Little Bear Creek and its tributaries course through the north side additions of Fair Oaks, Forest Glen, Green Valley, Cherokee, Shady Oaks, L. C. Tubb, Thornbridge, Holder Smithfield, Meadowview Estates, and Oak Leaf Park. Big Fossil Creek in the far southwest of town drains the Iron Horse Golf Course, Diamond Oaks Country Club, Diamond Loch Apartments, the North Hills and Diamond Oaks South additions, and Fossil Creek Park. In between, Calloway and Walker Branches drain innumerable subdivisions in the central city and join south of Hurst.

Fossils reveal that the creeks, springs, woods, and gently rolling prairies attracted wildlife in ancient times. A half-million years ago huge, shaggy mastodons and mammoths, with their spectacular tusks, roamed the North Texas area and shared the Trinity basin with early varieties of camels, horses, and bison. At the end of the Pleistocene epoch the drier climate reduced the forage necessary for the large grazing animals. A species of buffalo remained in the West, but the other animals were supplanted by speedy antelope, wolves, coyotes, and rabbits.

Most of the ancestors of American Indians reached North America by migrating across the Bering Strait when a land bridge connected the continents some 20,000 years ago. Some 30 species of large animals, whose numbers were depleted by climatic change, were hunted to extinction by the Paleo-Indians of north central Texas about 10,000 years ago. They were hunters and gatherers, who lacked bows, arrows, and pottery, but who used a throwing stick called an *atlatl*. Some of these prehistoric hunters were the ancestors of the Caddo Indians, a major woodland culture indigenous to northeast and north central Texas. The animals and the waterways certainly attracted them to the area. By the 1000–1500 A.D. period the Caddoan peoples had changed their way of life by acquiring bows, arrows, and knowledge of ceramics. The heart of the Caddo villages was in East Texas, but they made encampments in Tarrant County and its environs in search of buffalo and commerce. Perhaps the most disquieting feature of Caddo behavior was their custom of crying and wailing when they met strangers. A culturally related but enemy tribe to the Caddoes was the Wichita people, who migrated in the 18th century from Kansas into north central Texas, into the region between the Brazos and Red rivers. The Wichitas were stocky, dark, and extensively tattooed. The Wichitas also maintained agricultural villages centered around Spanish Fort in Montague County, as well as migratory encampments. The fearsome, migratory Comanches, with their buffalo horn head-dresses, also appeared in Texas in the 18th century, and attacked almost everyone who ven-

TCJC Heritage Room

Encampment of the Wichitas

tured onto the plains in search of buffalo. One of the Wichitas' trade encampments was in the southwest quadrant of current Mid-Cities Boulevard and Smithfield Road in the College Hill addition. A spring was once located there, and the Wichitas swapped tools and weapons with the Caddoes and Comanches when they weren't fighting them. Numerous flint clippings and arrowheads have been discovered there in recent times.

French trappers founded the trading outpost of Natchitoches on the Red River in Louisiana in 1714. The French journeyed to Indian settlements as far west as the forks of the Trinity in present Tarrant County. After France gave Spain the Louisiana Territory in 1763, a number of Frenchmen on this frontier offered their services to Spain. The Frenchman Athanase de Mezieres y Clugny (1719–1779) led several Spanish expeditions to the upper Trinity in the 1770s. His reports described the clear Trinity River abounding in fish, the lush river valley and forests, the fertile prairies of grass and wild grapes, and the astounding amount of game. He noted that the numerous creeks and springs could be used for irrigation and the timber for building materials, if Spain could develop the region. He visited the Caddoes, Wichitas, and others, attempting to forge an alliance with them and maybe even with the Comanches against the Apaches in the west and the possible future incursion of English traders from their American colony. Even as he maneuvered, however, the American Revolution was setting free the former colonists for a westward movement that was destined to overwhelm the Hispanic outposts in Texas in the 19th century.

THE ANGLO FRONTIER

Spain's empire succumbed to revolution in the 1810s. Texas became a province of Mexico, and Anglo-Americans were invited to settle in the region in the 1820s, providing they adopted Catholicism and Mexican citizenship. By the mid-1830s the Texans had won their independence from Mexico, and, lured by free land, were venturing into territory in central and north central Texas that was claimed by the Caddoes and Wichitas as well as by the Comanches and their Kiowa allies. Texas Gen. Edward H. Tarrant (1796–1858) commanded two expeditions into present Tarrant County in 1841. The Battle of Village Creek in present Arlington, along with other clashes in the area, discouraged the Indians from remaining in the area.

General Tarrant ordered Capt. Jonathan Bird of Bowie County to establish a military and civilian outpost in the area. In August 1841, with about 35 or 40 men, he chose a site on the north bank of the Trinity River, 10 miles downstream from the village later named for him. Bird chose a site inside the curve of a crescent-shaped lake on the north side of the Trinity River, one-half mile south of the present

Tombstone of Texas General Edward H. Tarrant, 1796-1858, commanded two expeditions into Tarrant County.

intersection of Calloway Cemetery Road and South Main in Euless. Republic of Texas President Sam Houston journeyed to Bird's Fort in August 1843, to attempt a council of peace, under the full moon, with all the Texas tribes. The Bird's Fort treaty line was agreed to in September 1843, extending from the hunting grounds north of present Tarrant County to present Menard and San Antonio. The irate Comanches never appeared, but Caddo, Wichita, and other chiefs agreed to remain north and west of the treaty line. Thus the farming-ranching frontier was thrust westward in the mid-1840s with the pacification of the upper Trinity basin.

By 1845 pioneers from Tennessee, Kentucky, and Missouri, supposedly holding valid Peters Colony property titles, settled in the northeastern sector of present Tarrant County. White family men were eligible for a section (640 acres) of free land and single men a half section. To obtain clear title the immigrants had to live on the land for three years, cultivate at least ten acres, and have the land surveyed and plainly marked. The company and the Texas government disputed ownership of various tracts, while many immigrants

Bird's Fort, established 1841 on the military road from Red River to Austin. Though no photos exist, it must have looked much like this replica of Fort Parker.

without connection to the company settled on company land. Land titles became confused and years of litigation followed, but most land claims were adjusted in the 1850s.

W. W. Wallace held the initial 1850s survey of the tract that included the original North Richland Hills addition and most of the southern half of the future city, though there is no evidence that Wallace ever lived in the area. The southern boundary of his land was the line that became Pipeline and Glenview drives, the western edge was Rufe Snow, the northern line was a latitude from near the point where the railroad tracks later crossed Rufe Snow to the Precinct Line Road-Cardinal Lane intersection, and the eastern boundary became Precinct Line Road. The survey line on the west was unusual in that it jogged to the east on future Glenview, then proceeded due south. A. G. Walker's (1807–1882) tract, including the future Jack Estes, Calloway Acres, and Parchman additions, was south

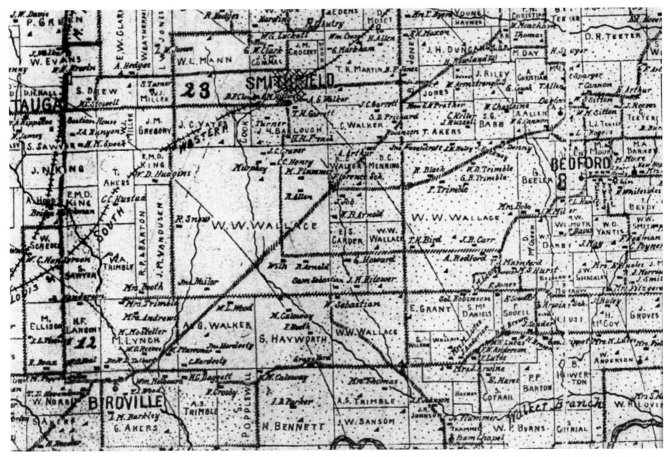

W. W. Wallace—held initial 1850s survey of the tract that included original North Richland Hills addition and most of the southern half of the future city of NRH.

of Wallace's, but their western boundaries lay on slightly different longitudes. Even today Rufe Snow jogs slightly as it crosses Glenview. At the northwest corner of the tract, Rufe Snow used to jog at the railroad tracks, but that has been reduced to a slight bend in the street.

Just west of Walker's land was the Mahala Lynch survey, which embraced current Richland Plaza and the additions of J. L. Autrey, Glenview Park, Nortex, Diamond Loch, Richland Hills West, and Diamond Oaks South. Just south of the present Diamond Oaks South neighborhood lay the original county seat of Birdville, the nearest community to the farmers, such as Walker, who were trickling into rolling prairie land that would one day be the southern half of North Richland Hills. The town was established after 1845 along Big Fossil Creek by various farmers and ranchers. The southwestern city limit of North Richland Hills comes to within a block of the site of the old courthouse, 6108 Broadway, where the Wiley G. Thomas Birdville Coliseum stands today.

One late-1840s settler who homesteaded in present North Richland Hills, perhaps the first, was Lewis W. James, but nothing is known about him. W. A. Trimble held an 1848 Peters Colony title to land included in the western ends of Glenview, Riviera, and Meadow Lakes drives. He apparently farmed there, and his widow still resided there in 1895, at the northern end of present Diamond Loch Street. Walker

A. G. Walker, 1807–1882, early land surveyor and Birdville civic leader.

surveyed his own land in present North Richland Hills and Richland Hills in the early 1850s and later moved to Smithfield.

In the 1850s Benjamin Franklin Andrews (1826–1894) and wife Mary Ray Andrews (1845–1868) moved to the area roughly between present Onyx Dr. S. and Glenview, west of Rufe Snow, and planted some 200 to 300 acres of bottomland in cotton, oats, and corn. He bought and sold land through the years. His brother Jabez Andrews (1837–1892) and wife Anna Burgoon Andrews (1840–1886) emigrated from Illinois in 1857 and farmed 100 or so adjacent acres.

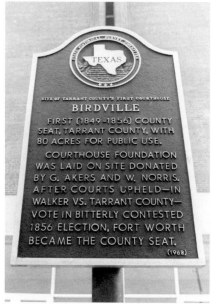

Birdville Historical Marker

The Birdville community in the 1850s, roughly defined, included the territory and people between present North Loop 820 and the Trinity River and between the western edge of present Haltom City and the western reaches of Hurst. Isaac Parker (1793–1883) bought a farm in the Birdville community in 1853 and built his domicile a mile and a half south of the present Calloway Farm-Richland Heights neighborhoods in North Richland Hills. Parker had served extensively in the Congress of the Republic of Texas and in the State Legislature. It was his niece, Cynthia Ann Parker (ca. 1825-ca. 1871), who had been seized at the age of 9 in a Comanche raid in 1836, the most famous of the American frontier kidnappings.

Parker's home was typical of the better ones of the period. It was a double log cabin separated by an open breezeway, the "dog run." One cabin was a kitchen and dining area, with a fireplace for cooking and heating, while the other section was the living room and sleeping quarters. The logs were notched and caulked, the floors puncheoned, and the roof built of handmade shingles. It is preserved today in Log Cabin Village in Fort Worth.

The area was roiled by political turmoil in the 1850s in the dispute over the location of the county seat and by Texas's drift toward secession from the United States. Tarrant County, with an area of about 898 square miles, had been founded in 1849 and named for Gen. Edward Tarrant. Land for a courthouse apparently had been donated or promised at the site that became Birdville and evidently promised at or near Fort Worth and other sites that lay within five miles of the surveyed center of the county. There was no town of Birdville or Fort Worth at the time, and the law provided that whatever site was selected would be called Birdville in honor of Jonathan Bird. The site that became Birdville was selected as the county seat on August 5, 1850, since, with about thirty families in the area, this site was closest to a plurality of the voters. The county was formally organized at the time of the election. The first county courthouse was on donated land where Thomas Coliseum now stands. The post office opened in November 1851, under Francis Jordan. But slightly less than six miles to the southwest, Fort Worth began to grow. The growth was triggered in 1853, after four years of military occupation, after every building in the abandoned fort was turned over to a civilian establishment. By 1855 Fort Worth town leaders began to lobby the Legislature to relocate the county seat.

Tombstone marker of Ben F. Andrews, who moved to NRH area in 1850s. Gravestone at Birdville Cemetery.

Parker Cemetery

Finally, the Legislature called for a special election, November 1856, to determine the county seat. Both towns engaged in vigorous campaigning, which meant, in those days, that barrels of whiskey were placed before the voters. Clowns, jugglers, and musicians performed in both communities on election day. Birdville's whiskey supply, however, hidden in an oak grove, was discovered and stolen by Fort Worth partisans on the eve of the election. Moreover, Wise County rancher Sam Woody, who had previously lived in Fort Worth, gathered 14 friends who mingled in town all day, remained sober, and were not challenged by Birdville observers when they voted late in the afternoon. The exact count is disputed, but the 15 votes from Wise County were more than the margin of victory for Fort Worth. Other shenanigans, probably on both sides, led to bitter feelings, and there were grave doubts by Birdville folks that there were as many male settlers in the county as had voted in the election. Brawls and several killings resulted.

One tragic incident involved Birdville-area resident A. G. Walker and Fort Worth's first notary public, John Jeff Courtenay. Courtenay was an early secessionist who established the county's first newspaper, *The Birdville Western Express*, in 1855 and was Birdville postmaster from January 1857 to November 1858. Despite the paper's location and Courtenay's postmastership, he favored moving the county seat to Fort Worth, where he handled most of his notary business. Walker farmed his land some, but was better known as a unionist and surveyor who had taken Birdville's case to the Texas Supreme Court in 1856. In the case of *Walker v. Tarrant County* the court upheld Fort Worth in ruling that the Legislature had failed to

Terrell's cabin in Birdville, believed to have served as first county seat. From *History of Birdville* by Thelma Ray

provide for this kind of emergency. Walker founded the *Birdville Union* in 1857 and continued to champion Birdville's cause. Personal and vicious editorials were exchanged between the two rivals until one day, according to some sources, the infuriated Courtenay stormed into the *Union* office, cursed Walker as a "Black, Abolition Republican," and fired his pistol at the enemy editor. Walker returned the fire and killed Courtenay instantly. Other accounts say they met on the street, drew on each other, and that Walker was fastest. Walker was tried for murder in Johnson County and found not guilty. Walker had already been elected to the State Senate, serving from 1857 to 1860, from the district that included Tarrant, Dallas, and eleven other counties, and fought to have the county seat election of 1856 overturned. The Legislature did establish a third and final election, held in April 1860, but Fort Worth was much bigger by then and triumphed easily. Birdville's population continued to decline. Walker, after serving as district clerk and county clerk during Reconstruction, 1867–1873, eventually moved to the community of Zion (Smithfield), four miles north of his original tract.

Historical events have permanent consequences. Had Birdville triumphed in the contest with Fort Worth, the cities of North Richland Hills, Richland Hills, Haltom City, and Hurst probably never would have existed. Judging from local history, it is likely that such a county seat town would have expanded into the territories later occupied by the four cities.

Mid-Cities News/Dallas Morning News

Mrs. Don Gibbons holding picture of her mother, Mrs. Laura Hardisty Barkley, descendants of early settlers of this area.

Land in three of these cities was once owned by the pioneering Hardisty family. Family chronicles note that Charles Hardisty (1836–1916) at the age of 16 was assigned by his family to depart the family homestead at the top of Birdville Hill, walk back to Kentucky, retrieve the family savings there, and walk back to Birdville. He made the exhausting journey back to his native Kentucky, toted the funds in a carpetbag, which served as his nightly pillow, and worked for several farmers on his way back. In the 1850s the money he secured bought parts of the three future cities of Richland Hills, Haltom City, and North Richland Hills, at 50 cents to a dollar an acre. His daughter Laura Hardisty (1868–1954) married Lon Barkley (1853–1928), son of Benjamin Franklin and Malinda Barkley, another pioneering couple. Lon lived on the square in downtown Birdville for years, then moved to Fort Worth when he became postmaster there in the early 1900s. Hardisty Street in Richland Hills commemorates Charles Hardisty's trek, while Tiffin Drive in the northeast quadrant of the Davis and Harwood intersection in North Richland Hills is named for Tiffin Barkley, Lon's grandson. Gibbons Court and Gibbons Drive are named for Mrs. Don Gibbons' North Richland Hills family. She was Lon and Laura Barkley's daughter. The story of these families is intertwined with the history of north central Tarrant County.

Meanwhile, in December 1860, on the eve of secession, a Texas Ranger raid on a Comanche encampment rescued Cynthia Ann Parker. By this time she was the "White Queen of the Comanches," married to Chief Peta Nacona, and did not want to return to Anglo civilization. Her son, Quanah Parker, was the last great Comanche chief. Captured

Quanah Parker, chief of the Comanches, son of Cynthia Ann Parker who was niece of Isaac Parker of the Birdville community.

with her daughter, Prairie Flower, she had lost much of her ability to speak English. Placed with Uncle Isaac Parker in his cabin in Birdville, she attempted to escape. After three months in Birdville, she was taken to her brother's farm in Van Zandt County, farther from the frontier, but she still yearned for the Indian way of life. Prairie Flower soon died, and Cynthia Ann never recovered from that or from Anglo captivity. She never again saw her Indian family, the only family she really knew. She died in 1871.

As the Civil War loomed, Tarrant County voted narrowly to secede from the Union, allegedly by 27 votes out of 800 cast. There were not many slaves in Tarrant County, and even some of the slaveholders opposed secession. Most Tarrant County farmers owned no slaves and hailed from border states that were divided on secession. But after the election of Republican Abraham Lincoln to the presidency, from a party that wanted to contain slavery, Texas voted more than three to one to secede, and even many opponents then supported the Southern cause. Ten companies of volunteers left the county for Confederate service. Those left behind suffered their share of the war in a sinking economy, privation, and Indian raids. Parched grain, okra seeds, and burnt okra served as a substitute for coffee. Many local governments, businesses, and schools in Tarrant County ceased to function, and the county population sank from about 6,000 to less than 1,000.

Dr. Benjamin Franklin Barkley (1822–1882), emigrating from Kentucky to Texas in 1855 with his wife, Malinda Barkley (1827–1917), settled in Birdville and practiced both law and medicine. The couple assisted struggling families, donated land for Birdville's first school, and fought to keep the town as county seat. Mrs. Barkley bought a slave in the Birdville auction house in the 1850s. The

Historical marker for Judge Benjamin Franklin Barkley, a physician who settled in Birdville in 1855 and practiced law and medicine throughout North Texas.

elderly slave woman was Aunt Nan, who was past useful-
ness as a field hand. The community was shocked when
Mrs. Barkley emancipated Aunt Nan. The Barkleys
achieved notoriety by denouncing slavery and secession,
but they kept an open house, feeding, lodging, and treat-
ing Confederate soldiers and their widows and orphans.
He was so active as county judge in the Reconstruction
process—conducting hearings on Ku Klux Klan activities,
for instance—that he became even more unpopular. He
had to be escorted by U. S. soldiers from his Birdville
home to his office in Fort Worth. Following the return of
state and county government to Democratic control in
1873, Barkley resumed his practice of law and medicine in
Birdville. He practiced all over Tarrant and surrounding
counties, toting his surgical instruments in his saddlebags.
He was buried on land that he had donated for Birdville

Historical marker of the Birdville Cemetery

Cemetery. Occasional Indian forays did not cease with the war. Samuel Cody (1861–1913),
born in Birdville, was attacked and wounded at his farmstead in 1874, near where the
Richland Plaza shopping center is today in North Richland Hills. He managed to hide under
some debris and crawled and staggered through the woods along the Trinity River for eight
miles to Fort Worth. Since his parents' bodies were not found in their burned-out farmhouse,
Cody believed the Comanches had carried them off and tortured them to death. His parents, however, had escaped and were living with friends but thought their son had died in the
attack. Several years later both parties discovered that everyone was alive. He became a cowboy and an owner of a Wild West show. Cody went on to fame in Britain as "Commander

"Bill" Cody, born in Birdville, pioneer aviator, first man to build and fly plane in Britain
in 1908.

Cody," the first man to build and fly an airplane in Britain, in 1908, and one of the
founders of the Royal Air Force.

Returning from service with Gano's
Confederate company, Jabez Andrews
resumed his farming. Benjamin F. Andrews'
wife died after the war and he married
Caroline Burgoon (1836–1929) in 1869. Both
the brothers died in the early 1890s. It was
Caroline Burgoon Andrews who was living in
the home place at the western end of present
Harmonson Road, as shown on Sam Street's
Tarrant County map in 1895.

The other great landowning family at the
southern tip of present North Richland Hills
was the Reeves clan. George Franklin Reeves
(1831–1886) and wife Carolyn Brewer Reeves
(1836–1908) migrated from Virginia via
Georgia and arrived in Tarrant County in 1866
or 1867. He built a cabin in front of where the
Montgomery Ward store was later located in

Birdville School, 1907, land for first Birdville school donated by Dr. (Judge) Benjamin Barkley.

Richland Plaza. For a time they farmed some 300 acres, including land between the Grapevine Highway and present Baker Boulevard in Richland Hills, all of present Richland Plaza, and most of the land south of current Richland Plaza Dr., east of present Tourist Dr., and north of Broadway. The couple moved to Handley before 1895 and left the estate in the hands of their son, William O. Reves, who dropped one "e" from the family name.

Schooling in Birdville probably dates back to 1855, though records are incomplete. In 1858 English prohibitionist William Hudson helped establish the Birdville Academy, a well-known institution at the time, paid for by donations from Birdville Independent School District citizens. It was on present Walker Street, a little northeast of the BISD tax

Birdville School, two-story brick building erected in 1920.

Birdville School, 1924–25

office. Hudson taught in the area for years. Two teachers were needed by 1864, when Mr. Hudson taught the upper grades. Students' tuitions paid the teachers' salaries.

One winter day in 1875 at the Birdville School, it was so cold that most students were absent. Miss Mattie Steele's class was huddling around the stove and got a real scare when an Indian on horseback peered in the window. Everyone became silent and still for several min-utes. Finally the teacher opened the door, by which time the Indian had ridden away. One pupil was 6-year-old T. Ernest Cloud (1869–1955), brought from Missouri in 1870. Cloud lived much closer to Zion (Smithfield) than Birdville, and the boy gave up the horseback commute to Birdville when the Zion school opened in 1876.

FARM, SCHOOL, AND BUSINESS LIFE

William O. Reves (1869–1924) and wife Mary Pelley Reves (1872–1950) continued farming his father's estate. They built a white, two-story house a block off Broadway and Carson streets in Birdville and used the cabin in which W. O. had been born for the storage of hay. Reves served as county commissioner for a time. After his death in 1924, Mary Reves, with the help of various rela-tives, continued raising oats and wheat and main-taining a dairy. Grandson E. F. Crites recalls the

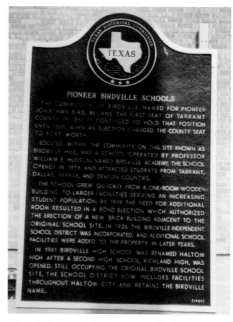

Historical marker—Pioneer Birdville Schools. First school, Birdville Academy established 1858 and the site is still in use by the Birdville ISD, housing many facilities for the school district.

Downtown Birdville-In 1930, the population was 107. In the 1930s, there were two grocery stores, owned by Lonnie Adkins and M. H. Portwood, a blacksmith shop by Earl West, a garage by Chester Brooks, and a telephone exchange—all located on Broadway Street, 1927

time when he and his cousins were playing around some old machinery at the farm and he cut the end of one finger off. He ran to the house and "Granny" Reves put his finger in a can of coal oil, then wrapped it in a coal oil rag. It eased the pain and apparently promoted the healing. One of his occasional assignments was to capture pigeons in the loft of the barn so that Granny could make pigeon pie.

Another farmer who made a name for himself in the Birdville community was Rufus (Rufe) Snow (1867–1957). His father had migrated from Missouri in 1860 and opened a blacksmith shop in Birdville. His parents were married in Birdville in 1866, and he was born the next year some 200 yards from the Birdville School, which he attended a few years. In 1888 he inherited 375 acres, which he developed into a model stock farm. He farmed for decades, served as a School Board trustee, and from November 1913 to January 1918 was a county commissioner. The orphans' home, city-county hospital, and county criminal court building were built during his tenure. He was affiliated with the Smithfield Odd Fellows Lodge and the Baptist Church. He remained engaged in the community, e.g. School Board activities, long past the time when he had any family involvement at stake. His

Old grain separator, much of it wood—owned by Packy Harlow, Denison, Texas.

Rufus Snow (1867-1957)

name was attached to the Birdville-Watauga Road late in his lifetime, and his home was there, in the present southeast corner of Rufe Snow and Shauna drives, across the street from North Richland Middle School. His porch extended all the way across the front of the house, and there were three front doors. His stock farm included much of the current Skyline Homes Addition. He and Jessie Melbourne Snow (1870–1942) had five children who lived to adulthood.

Hattie Arwine Anderson, at the grind stone sharpening plow blade.

The state called for the establishment of school districts in the early and mid-1880s, and presumably Birdville drew its district lines at that time. By then, the exact location of the school, probably a new building, was apparently just south of the old one, at the northeast corner of Carson and Belknap. A black school was also established nearby in the 1880s. In 1902 the two-room frame schoolhouse burned and was replaced by another. By 1905 the Birdville School had four teachers. School trustees began horseback rides through the district in 1916 to begin rounding up support for a school bond package. As a result a new, two-story, brick building was erected in 1920, with 156 students that fall and a capacity for 180. There were five staff members. There were four classrooms upstairs as well as down, and an auditorium upstairs as well. The PTA was organized in 1925.

While the school district thrived, Birdville itself did not grow. The post office closed in 1906, when the community's population was reported at 107. The same population was reported through 1940. Most of the farmers and ranchers who lived in the southern third of present North Richland Hills were attached to Birdville through the schools and several stores.

James M. Anderson (1860–1936) migrated from Indiana to Texas in 1883, married Hattie Arwine (1868–1960) from a prominent Hurst family, and gradually acquired a group of farms. He was a civic and community leader both in Hurst and Birdville. The place that he bought around 1903 was bounded by Lynn Terrace Road on the west, Bedford Road on the north, Walker Creek on the east, and Pipeline on the south. For years Hattie A. Anderson rang a bell every day at 11:30 A.M., to call in Jim and others from the fields for lunch. The bell could be heard for miles. Everyone in the extended family was expected to pitch in regularly to help harvest and share in the proceeds of the wheat and cotton and one-acre vegetable garden. The garden produced ample amounts of peas, beets, okra, corn, etc. The family might put up 500 cans of vegetables for the winter. The front pasture was where Chili's is today on Bedford Road; the main house was a quarter mile to the south.

James Mordecai and Hattie Arwine Anderson with their ten children. They were civic and community leaders in early 1900s in the Birdville and Hurst areas. A portion of their farm and pasture land is now Restaurant Row on Bedford-Euless Road and the North East Mall area.

Kate Calloway, person standing unidentified

Mrs. Elmer James

"Hog killin' time" was still a big event on the farms in the 1920s and 1930s. The techniques had not changed much since pre-Civil War days, but there were now more by-products. Lye soap was made from the remains. And the bladder was washed, dried, and filled with air for the children to play ball with.

Anderson used Red Mule Chewing Tobacco and saved the little red mules in the packets for his grandchildren, including Mary Ruth Reeves (Ellis). The children sometimes tired of their quotas in the cotton fields. Niece Hattie Belle Reeves (Cribbs) once placed a good-sized rock in her cotton bag, which gave her an impressive weigh-in. She soon confessed to the crime.

Christmas was a favorite season. The house was filled with relatives and sumptuous meals were prepared. The children always received an apple, an orange, and a five-cent package of firecrackers in their stockings. The fruit was quickly devoured, except that the orange peels were dried and saved for consumption at a later date.

A number of farmers in the area took up dairying in the post-World War I era. Expanding and prosperous American cities were consuming more milk and cream. The Anderson farm was in part a dairy operation. Another large one was Bill Mackey's farm, with its deep well used by many neighbors. It was north of old Pipeline, west of present Vance, and east of current Rufe Snow Drive, including the present Hillview and southern section of Skyline Homes additions around Briley Street. Will Snow (1890–1961), Rufe and Jessie's eldest son, built a house and dairy on the Grapevine Pike around 1919. The homestead land is now the location of a Diamond Shamrock station.

West and south of the Anderson place were an eventual 2,100 acres of farms owned by Marsh Calloway (1869–1945) and wife Catherine (1876–1951). The land stretched from the Rock Island Railroad tracks about where they intersect current Loop 820 to the current site of the North Hills Mall. He was so impressed with the Reves house in Birdville that he built a near duplicate in the late 1910s or the 1920s, adding extensively to the house that his grandfather or father had built in the late 19th century. The fourteen-room house was two or three blocks

Marsh and Kate Calloway home

18

south of the present 7400 block of Baker Boulevard in Richland Hills. Marsh Calloway was a little man who walked peculiarly after falling from a water tower and breaking his back and legs. Along with Frank Booth and some of Billy Hurst's clan, he dealt in cattle. They would turn cattle loose in the Trinity bottoms for a time to fatten them up, then sell them to Swift and Armour meatpackers in Fort Worth. Calloway owned some of the bottom land and sold the gravel in it to the Fort Worth Sand and Gravel Company. A large washing plant, com-

Courtesy of W. W. White

Harmonson Road looking south, 1956

plete with steam Monoghan draglines, was erected in 1929 near Walker Branch and Precinct Line Road. Calloway quickly discovered that he needed to hire a gravel checker to count the five-yard buckets on the Monoghan.

Ben Andrews' son Charles continued to live on the northeastern part of the old family tract and brought in a well in 1909, which overflowed from 600 feet. (It was the site of the metal water tanks at Glenview and Rufe Snow today, except the water table has been drained through the decades and is now 3,000 feet down.) Probably around 1900 Ben Andrews' daughter Lucille and her husband Jack Eaton moved into the old Andrews house at the western end of present Harmonson Road. They kept a sizable garden as well as chickens and cows. Much of the old estate and perhaps Jabez Andrews' as well was gradually sold, and a sparsely settled neighborhood called Andrews Gardens developed in the 1920s. Charles' well served as the Andrews Gardens well, and the homes were generally located west of present Rufe Snow Drive and between present Harmonson and Glenview.

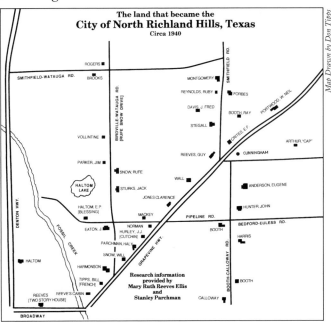

Map Drawn by Don Tipps

The land that became the
City of North Richland Hills, Texas
Circa 1940

Research information provided by
Mary Ruth Reeves Ellis
and
Stanley Parchman

Grapevine Hwy - Rufe Snow corridor

Willie and Juanita Anglin moved to the Andrews Gardens neighborhood in 1934. She maintained a garden, with fruit and pecan trees. She raised chickens, horses, cows, and reg-

Harmonson Road and Rufe Snow street sign, site of the home of Charles Andrews, son of Ben Andrews.

istered rabbits and sheep. The gas lights in the ceiling would often be snuffed out by a puff of wind. Heat was provided by a pot-bellied stove. Mrs. Anglin later recalled that, "Ben and Nora Harmonson bought the water rights and changed the name from Andrews Gardens to the Harmonson Addition."

Mr. Rufe Snow was located at what they considered to be the far northern end of the road not yet named for him, where North Richland Middle School is now. The southern end of present Rufe Snow, south of the Grapevine Pike, was just a horse trail and was known in the com-

19

North Richland Hills, Cross Timbers region, current site of 100 Acre Park

munity as "Lover's Lane." There was a little commercial development on the road, especially in the 3700–3900 blocks. The Anglins, who owned a radiator shop in Fort Worth, opened an auto repair business at 3745, a site that is still being used by a light truck and auto repair business. Joe Waller moved into the community in 1939 and opened a grocery store on present Rufe Snow.

Even bumper crops were no assurance of prosperity during the hard times of the Great Depression of the 1930s. Cotton that would not even pay the cost of ginning would be dumped beside the road. Birdville area farmers would haul their cantaloupes and tomatoes to the Fort Worth market for the weekend, but so did many others. The market was the full length of Jones Street in downtown Fort Worth. They would try to sell cantaloupes for a nickel a bushel and tomatoes for thirty-five cents a peck. Often there were no takers, and the farmers would haul the produce back and feed it to the hogs.

Many old-timers recall that no one locked their doors in those days, since there was no crime, but that was not quite the case. In between one of the Andrews houses and Rufe Snow's house on current Rufe Snow Drive was Jim Cavender's place. Cavender was murdered in 1930 and placed in his barn, with a granary full of oats, and covered with oats. He was dead three or four days before being discovered. The murderers were never apprehended. Fort Worth radio stations warned one morning in 1934 that Texas Rangers were chasing the bandits Clyde Barrow and Bonnie Parker in the Birdville-Smithfield area. Bonnie and Clyde had spent at least one night in a clump of trees on Fossil Creek near the current coliseum. Mrs. Anglin stayed home the next morning rather than take her usual drive through the area. The Rangers found only Bonnie's cigar butts and a smoldering fire.

Birdville High School, Bidistrict Champions 1939–40, Birdville's first football championship: Back row: Glenn Thomas, Arthur Parr, James Cheatham, Marvin Harris; Front Row: Joe Hatcher, J. W. Sinclair, Roy Jenuine, Junior Rudd, Troy Pennington, James Cate, Marvin Mackey.

Birdville moved from a common school district to an independent one in 1926. Now the school district rather than the county could collect Birdville school taxes, disperse funds, keep its own books, and sell its own bonds. A $10,000 addition was constructed in 1926, with four classrooms and a superintendent's office upstairs and a new auditorium below. A walkway on the second floor connected the two buildings. The old auditorium was converted into a study hall and library, which had very few books. Short, stocky W. T. Francisco (1896–1944) arrived in 1924 as teacher and principal, and soon became superintendent as well. Into the 1920s nine grades were usually offered, so the last two would have to be taken at Central or North Side High Schools in Fort Worth or Handley High School, if they were taken at all. But by 1932–1933 the final (eleventh) grade needed for a complete high school education was added, and nine graduated, including W. G. Thomas Jr. The professional staff had grown to 13. Black students were transferred to Fort Worth in 1931 and paid for by the Birdville District.

Girls basketball team, Birdville High School, about 1925

Entertainment in the 1920s and 1930s included Birdville High's softball and basketball games with other area villages and 4-H Club products and livestock to be entered in the Fort Worth Fat Stock Show each winter. Witnessing "declaiming" was a grand event within schools and at county competitions. Each student would recite a poem, which would be judged not only for accuracy but also for expression. Every October the Texas State Fair in Dallas and the Grapevine Community Fair attracted Birdville area residents. During the era that betting was allowed on horse racing, 1933–1937, some residents would slip away to Arlington Downs. Brief entertainment was provided by O. B. Guynn in the 1930s, who was dared to take his Shetland pony up to the second story of the school house and did so.

The girls' basketball team did not always enjoy games in Keller, since the basketball goal was attached to the rock wall of the gym. Players often ran into the wall. Businesses sponsored

Aerial view of Birdville School, 1939

girls' basketball teams that played all over Texas. Dorothy Snow Clopton, Elizabeth Reeves, and Mary Angle played for the Lucas Funeral Home team called the "Embalmers."

The Birdville mascot was chosen after much discussion in the early 1930s. The girls preferred "Bees," while the boys wanted the more fearsome "Buffaloes." There were more girls enrolled than boys, but some of the boys convinced the girls to change their votes. Buffalo football was played for the first time in 1935, with an opening victory at Grapevine. Apparently the only defeat in seven games was against Justin. It was not bad at all, since prior to the games nobody at the school had ever picked up a football, and the quarterback rarely passed. Coach O. H. Stowe sent in defensive back Eldred Echols before the half at Grapevine and wondered why he did not intercept nearby passes. At half-time Eldred rushed over and asked, "Say, Coach, is there any reason I can't catch some of those they are throwing?" There were no stands or places to sit, and parents rarely attended the games.

Suddenly, on April 7, 1936, the School Board fired Francisco. The next day the students went out on strike in protest, marching out in the midst of a school day and parading with placards in downtown Fort Worth. Fewer than 30 of approximately 400 students remained in the classrooms. Seventeen-year-old Arlene Sanders led the strike. "We want Fran" was not only inscribed on signs and banners but also on high school walls and other buildings in Birdville. The students also held a pep rally in downtown Birdville.

Board chairman R. M. Reeves claimed that Francisco had been uncooperative in efforts to audit the school's financial records and accused a Francisco partisan on the board of giving the school's insurance business to his brother. The School Board also fired three teachers as well as a janitor, who had told Reeves that he was neutral in the controversy. Considerable bedlam ensued. Reeves narrowly lost control of the board in somewhat violent elections. Francisco was offered his job back, but he declined in the interest of harmony. O. H. Stowe, who had been teaching at Birdville School since 1934, was selected as superintendent. A new teacher who joined the staff in 1937 was Wiley G. Thomas Jr.

Mrs. A. B. Earle led a movement in the fall of 1936 to move away from the controversy and the financial problems by taking the Birdville District into Fort Worth's, and Fort Worth was poised to take it over. Earle needed to secure one-fourth of the total 430 voters on a petition to establish an election. The effort fell through in January 1937, after 119 signed, but 52 of them withdrew their names. Had Birdville community pride not been asserted, the district surely would have been swallowed up by Fort Worth, and the Fort Worth ISD would have been in place for North Richland Hills in 1953. A few dozen people made a fateful choice.

The School Board passed a rule in 1937 providing that any woman school teacher who married during the school year would be suspended without pay for the remainder of the year. If she married in the summer her contract was nullified. It is not known whether the controversy the year before had any bearing on the new policy, but in any event it appeared that the board was clinging to the one-sided morality of the day, attempting to keep the work force docile and trying to curb the turnover in low-paying teacher jobs.

Meanwhile, enrollment began dramatically increasing as both Fort Worth and the Birdville area began growing shortly before and during World War II. The Birdville School District lines reached north almost to Four Points and took a northern turn to include the current Holiday West addition and the current Industrial Park. To the west it extended to the Beach Street area, to the south the Trinity River, and to the east the present Loop 820 area.

A bond election to erect more buildings was approved in February 1938, by a vote of 177 to 28. In the spring of 1938 there were 150 in the high school and 300 below that level. In the fall of 1939, some 200 enrolled in high school and 325 in the lower grades. A new $100,000 high school was built in 1939, with the other buildings remodeled, and the twelfth grade added in 1943. Enrollment reached 838 in 1944.

After Stowe joined the Coast Guard in 1942, Francisco replaced him but passed away a year and a half later. His former student, Mr. Thomas, was named superintendent in 1944. During the war the school shop was utilized by the students to make model airplanes for the Navy, and pupils learned Morse Code in General Science. Huge Army convoys carrying personnel, artillery, and equipment of all kinds rolled down the Grapevine Highway, sometimes non-stop for eight or ten hours. Students would go to the highway and cheer them during the day.

A village school superintendent had to be a jack-of-all-trades. In the summer of 1945 Superintendent Thomas and the custodian, using lumber salvaged from the school shop, built the tables and benches to be used by the students when the first school cafeteria opened in the fall. The National School Lunch Program was implemented in 1946. The shop, which had no teacher, was converted into the lunchroom. A tile building was completed in the fall of 1945, with a federal grant paying for half of it, creating several new classrooms. It is still part of the present Shannon Learning Center. In the summer of 1946 taxpaying voters agreed to dramatically raise the school levy from $1 to $1.50 per $100 valuation of property. The area north of Birdville was still rural during and after the war, but suburban development and lifestyles were creeping up on it.

Gene Anderson handled most of the old Jim Anderson farm after his father's death in 1936. His children, attending Birdville School in the 1940s and 1950s, were sent there with their home-cooked biscuits, home-cured ham, and thick pies. They were delighted to trade them for the junk food that some of the Birdville kids had. On many Sunday afternoons after church the Anderson boys and friends played softball and baseball near present-day Chili's. Chicken wire was used for the backstop, and old plow disks were the bases.

Georgia Anderson's older sister, Willie Hazel Anderson (1900–1969), married Guy Reeves (1897–1983) in 1918 and farmed in the area for years. In 1944 they moved to Four Points and kept a dairy farm there until 1958, just northwest of Jim Anderson's old farm. The Reeves farm extended to present Holiday Lane on the west, Maplewood on the north, Riviera on the south, and the Grapevine Road on the east. It is now bisected by Loop 820. Mesquite Hill lay at the west end of the property. From there you could see the country for miles around. It is the current 4800 block of Holiday Lane. Willie kept a vegetable garden as well as an extensive iris and rose garden that delighted passers-by at Four Points for years. Guy was a member of the Birdville School Board during the 1940s and 1950s. Four Points was the common name for the intersection of Smithfield Road (now Davis Blvd.), Bedford-Euless Road, and two directions of Grapevine Highway.

Courtesy of Mary Ruth Ellis

Willie Hazel (Anderson) Reeves in garden at Four Points, now site of Hudiburg Chevrolet.

Courtesy of Gary Starnes

Aerial view of service station at Four Points where Smithfield Road, (now Davis Boulevard), Grapevine Hwy. and Bedford-Euless Road join.

North of the Reeves place, J. M. and Lila Stegall farmed 150 acres west of present Davis Boulevard, embracing the current neighborhoods around Lola and Susan Lee streets, extending to Holiday Lane. Stegall was a Fort Worth attorney, too old for the draft, but he wanted to do something to help the war effort. They moved to the farm in 1943 to raise food to assist the U.S. in the war, and stayed with it afterward. Their home was 100 yards or more south of the present Davis Memorial Methodist Church. The Stegalls produced huge quantities of corn, peas, beans of all kinds, and other vegetables. Old-timer Ray Booth, in his straw hat and gold-rimmed glasses, was astounded by it. Booth had once owned the Reeves and Stegall farms as well as the J. Fred Davis place north of Stegall's, and had never seen such production. The crops were so prodigious that Stegall just invited everyone to help themselves. A friend was allowed to plant an acre of irises, which constituted a stunning sight for about two weeks out of the year, but were a pain for young Don and Bill Stegall who had to pull out weeds and Johnson grass the rest of the year.

The Stegalls also rented some land on the Birdville-Watauga Road (present Rufe Snow) to run cattle, and visited the site, in the present Skyline Homes Addition, late one evening around 1945. There

Courtesy Mary Ruth Ellis

Aerial view of the intersection of Belknap Street and Carson, showing Birdville School and the O. B. Guynn general merchandise store and meat market. Probably taken in the late 1930s or early 1940s

was an ancient house there that hadn't had a coat of paint on it in decades. An old man emerged, wearing old overalls and an old hat. To young Don Stegall it looked as though he were being greeted by Father Time. It was Rufe Snow, who welcomed them to the neighborhood and told them, among other things, that he had lived in the house for 55 years. In his old age Snow was sometimes seen hoeing his garden in his long underwear.

Old J. E. Flory home, photo taken 1997

Evalyn Lockridge

Folks all over the area often bought groceries, gasoline, and/or feed at Bert Starnes's (1908–1965) or Andrew and Delia Rumfield Cunningham's stores at Four Points. Guy Reeves leased a Four Points Texaco station to Tiny Anderson then to Ralph Wade in the 1940s and finally to Starnes, who arrived in 1949. Starnes also operated a feed store and a tractor rental business. Gary Starnes delivered feed for his father and mowed lots for people with a Ford tractor with a five-foot brush hog behind it. The Cunninghams had no children and seemed to delight in all the children from near-by farms. He sold fresh meat and cheese that he would slice for customers on a big wood chopping table. Edward L. Rogers recollects of Cunningham's country store, "It had one gas pump outside, a screen door to go inside, and all manner of snacks, ice cream, candy, and all of the delights that kids enjoyed during the unbearably hot, non-air-conditioned summers of the fifties." They kept the store open six and a half days a week. There was only a limited choice of fresh fruits and vegetables, since most customers had their own gardens.

Four Points was equidistant from Smithfield and Birdville. It was at the southern edge of the Smithfield school district and rural mail route, but the Reeves' owned much of it, and their connections were more in the direction of the Anderson farm and Birdville. Much of the commercial and civic orientation among folks in the area, even those geographically closer to Smithfield, e.g. the Stegalls, was southward toward Birdville and Fort Worth.

Gasoline, groceries, and other commodities were also available at Portwood Grocery and Feed or Fisher Drugstore or O. B. Guynn's in Birdville. Guynn's parents had opened the general merchandise store and meat market in 1930 at the corner of Belknap and present Carson. They advertised "home killed meats our specialty" and sold bottled milk and but-ter from their own small dairy. They bought pro-duce from farmers and sold them to other cus-tomers. But folks also often kept on going south to Cowtown for serious shopping and diversified activities. Major shopping was accomplished at Leonard Brothers' Department Store in down-town Fort Worth. It was frequently an all-day family activity, since Leonard's had everything from clothing and toys to farm and ranch sup-plies and baked goods. Most movie theaters were located in downtown Fort Worth, too.

A few more businesses opened on future Rufe Snow Drive in the 1940s. Luke Davis opened a

Guy and Willie Anderson Reeves home, built of native stone from the Hurst area and custom designed by Willie, who never dreamed that in scarcely 22 years progress would replace it. Their home was located at Four Points and is now the site of Hudiburg Chevrolet.

Courtesy of Mary Ruth Ellis

garage in the 3800 block, and a Mr. Ford established a grocery store next to it at 3812. Angela McGowan Renfro remembered that a nickel could buy a nice amount of candy. J. E. Flory and family moved to 3741 Rufe Snow in 1941. Flory started telegraph and teletype schools and a woodwork shop at his enlarged house after World War II. He also installed his own water system, with a large overhead water storage tank, the only one in the area.

The documented history of the area began changing during the war also. Thelma Ray began teaching in the Birdville schools in 1942. She is remembered for keeping extensive records and scrapbooks. Her book, *The History of Birdville*, set the standard for future histories of Tarrant County communities. History, meanwhile, was about to bring dramatic changes to the old Birdville community, more than the Snow, Anderson, Reeves, Stegall, and other families in what is now North Richland Hills could have imagined during World War II. When Willie and Guy Reeves built their dream home at Four Points in 1944, they did not dream at the time that the stone house with the three gables and large garden—a landmark in the area—would last scarcely 22 years.

THE BIRTH OF NORTH RICHLAND HILLS:
FROM FARMS TO SUBURBS

The Harmonson Addition, usually defined as bounded by Dawn, Glenview, Rufe Snow, and Harmonson streets, grew during the war. Several families lived on 1.25 acre lots off Honey Lane and Glenview, but most were smaller homes, complete with outhouses. There was no police or fire protection, but Ben Harmonson provided water and gas service for the tranquil area. The settlers became accustomed to seeing the Cotton Belt and other rail-

Fort Worth Star-Telegram

9/3/45-Two bombers crashed in Birdville where present Richland Plaza is today. Smoke from burning wreckage of one of the two B-24 Liberator bombers that collided in midair over Birdville about 7 A.M. Friday and crashed to earth about two miles northeast. This plane broke in two and dropped in a brush-filled creekbed. The other dived into a wheat field a mile away.

roads haul troops, tanks, and cannons through the countryside. And B-24 Liberator bombers practiced flying in close formation overhead.

The customary serenity was broken early on the morning of September 3, 1943, and the war came closer to home. Two Liberators collided in midair above a pasture, which is now Richland Plaza. The planes had been in formation and were practicing flying blind. The seven dead crewmen lay in and around where the shopping center is now, while one plane crashed close to the creek and the other south of where Montgomery Ward was later located in Richland Plaza.

There were at least twenty families south of Harmonson and west of Rufe Snow by the late 1940s, and they too were generally considered part of the Harmonson Addition. All the children from this area, of course, attended Birdville School, but the school had become somewhat crowded by the late 1940s, and an incident occurred that alarmed the community about the safety of the school.

The new Birdville School building caught fire in January 1947—a gas heater exploded in the gym—and there was no water system for fire fighting. Seventeen classrooms remained in other buildings for 1,025 students. A new building was ready for occupancy in the fall of 1948. The citizens of Birdville, meanwhile, had little desire to incorporate as a city, but the school fire helped convince them to accept merger with a neighbor.

Fort Worth jeweler G. W. Haltom purchased 1,100 or more acres near the Denton highway in 1932, where he built a park and community building. Just west of downtown Birdville, the development may have been an effort to move the town closer to the junction of the Denton highway and Belknap. Few moved, but Haltom City incorporated in

Courtesy of Bell Helicopter

Bell Helicopter, Hurst Plant assembly line.

Naomi Jones Cummings

Opening of Haltom Bank—Mr. and Mrs. Clarence Jones, Mr. and Mrs. Guy Cummings, and Mr. and Mrs. Cullen Turner

1944. The name of the town was chosen in an election, though many residents voted for "Birdville" and were bitter about losing the old community name to an upstart name. Considerably larger than Birdville due to wartime growth, it annexed the older community in July 1949, and, of course, provided fire protection. At the time it was annexed the town of Birdville had about 200 people with five businesses, but there were thousands more in the Birdville School District.

Birdville community farmers and countryside dwellers on the east side, between Big Fossil Creek and Grapevine Road, were not included in the Haltom City annexation. Much of the land there had been purchased by the J. B. Baker Sr. family, whose mail and express nursery business dated back to the early 1900s and served Texas as far west as Abilene. Baker dug wells and built a plant nursery in present Richland Hills in 1929. The Bakers had developed nursery tracts into residential areas before, and in 1946 they began developing a 900-acre tract on the southeast side of the Grapevine Highway (then State Highway 121). They erected four stone homes in an effort to start an addition. His company had to finance the homes because Fort Worth bankers said they were too far out in the country. The first settlers had to drive to Birdville to use the telephone. The development caught on, and the citizens voted 34-1 in the autumn of 1950 to incorporate as Richland Hills. Bess Barker, company secretary since 1912, suggested the name of the 250-person community based on the rich soil and the rolling land.

No single event triggered the encroachment of suburbs into northeast Tarrant County, but some had noticeable impacts. In March 1951 the Bell Aircraft Corporation announced that it would build a helicopter factory valued at more than $3 million in the southern part of Hurst. The plant at 600 East Hurst Boulevard opened in 1953 and hastened the inevitable boom in the mid-cities. Old Highway 183 and Hurst and Baker Boulevards were paved with concrete at this time and that opened up the area. The opening of Amon Carter Field in 1953, on the east side of Euless, brought airline professionals to the area as well.

Birdville community folks on the northeast side were not included in the Haltom City annexation either. One was short, chunky Clarence Jones (1895–1966), who had owned a lumber company on the 4000 block of East Belknap (the Grapevine Highway) in Fort Worth since 1931. Jones and some other businessmen were instrumental in 1951 in organizing the Haltom City State Bank located at 28th Street and Belknap. He became president of the bank in 1952 and moved it to the 4000 block of East Belknap in 1965. He

Courtesy of Jack and Lynn Starr

Aerial view of Haly Parchman home and farm on left; Wade Cutchin home on right across Vance Road, fronting Grapevine Highway; Bill Mackey dairy farm upper left, mid-1940s

had also maintained a stock farm for a decade in the area north and west of Pipeline (Glenview Drive) and Grapevine Highway. Jones had development in mind from the beginning, and in 1952 it seemed time to begin subdividing some of his farm. H. L. Arnold's construction company, which had helped the Bakers develop Richland Hills, was the main builder. Eighty new homes were built in the first half of 1952, out of 182 lots platted for initial development.

The Birdville School District hastened to keep pace with area growth. The National School Lunch Program of 1946 benefited numerous children. During the 1949–1950 school year the first school nurse and first high school counselor were hired. The first two school buses were purchased, one to transport black students to Fort Worth, the other mainly to fetch Watauga students who had been added to the Birdville District. Plans for the first school on a separate campus were made, with the purchase of a site in southern Haltom City, and a $225,000 bond

Courtesy of Jack and Lynn Starr

J. J. Hurley/Wade Cutchin home, Grapevine Highway and Vance Road, mid-1940s

Courtesy of Naomi Jones Cummings

1955, Greater Richland Center, corner of Grapevine Highway and Blaney Avenue

issue was voted. It was just the beginning of a continuous building program that barely kept pace with the explosive population boom. Superintendent Thomas was often asked why campuses were not started sooner or built larger. He always replied that most of the buildings were launched before the money was available and bonds were sold annually on a basis that the tax rolls would support.

INCORPORATION AND THE CIVIC LEAGUE

Clarence Jones at first assumed that his development, bounded by Briley on the north, Vance on the west, and the Grapevine Road, would be annexed by Richland Hills. In 1952 the *Fort Worth Star-Telegram* referred to the area as Richland Hills North. In February 1953 the residents in Richland Hills North petitioned Richland Hills for annexation, but there was no immediate response. It was not certain that Richland Hills, barely developed itself, really desired to take on still more dwellers in need of paved streets and other services.

A "citizens committee" including Arnold, Jones, and George Henry met February 28, 1953 and decided to call for citizens' opinions on whether to form a private organization to deal with problems of common interest, or incorporate as a town, or both. By late February this trio evidently favored both approaches and had cooled on the desirability of joining Richland Hills. They apparently printed and mailed handbills calling for a meeting on March 6 at the Arnold Construction Company office, 7305 Grapevine Highway, where an office building stands today. Close to 40 people attended the meeting, sitting on boards supported by nail kegs. A decision to form a private organization, the North Richland Hills Civic League, passed 28 to 8. Its purpose was to foster cooperation, good government, and the social welfare of the community and to serve as a forum for the full and free discussion of all matters of public interest. Annual membership dues were $1.00. W. G. Tripp, a big, blustery title company researcher, served as chairman.

There was more discussion about incorporation. Proponents of a move to join Richland Hills claimed that the costs of necessary government could be reduced by eliminating duplication of municipal functions, such as fire and police protection, maintenance of parks, etc. These entities were already in place in Richland Hills. Those who favored incorporating as a separate village averred that Richland Hills had done nothing that residents of North Richland Hills could not do also, perhaps better. They also asserted that there was no real evidence that costs of municipal government decrease generally when the size of the city increases. Jones announced that an election would be held April 25, 1953, to determine if those qualified voters (with paid-up poll taxes) who had lived in the addition six months desired to form an incorporated village. If incorporation

Clarence Jones, Chairman of the Board, Haltom City State Bank, 1952

failed, it was explained, the area would probably remain as it was for a time, but could be annexed at will by Fort Worth, Haltom City, Richland Hills, or Hurst.

By late March the Civic League's greeting committee (to meet and welcome new residents) counted just over 300 residents and 90 occupied houses, 48 of which had been built at least six months previously. Other estimates hold that there were 110 occupied houses and some 350 people. A constitution and bylaws were adopted by the League at its April 10 meeting, and officers were elected. Among them were Tripp, who became president, and K. B. "Ace" Nace, an airline pilot, who was elected vice chairman. Clarence Jones was appointed chairman of the street-paving committee, and painting contractor J. W. Watson was selected vice secretary. Arnold's office, which had the only telephone in the community, was used continually.

Courtesy of Naomi Jones Cummings

Clarence Jones home, corner of Grapevine Highway and Glenview Drive, current site of Greater Richland Shopping Center.

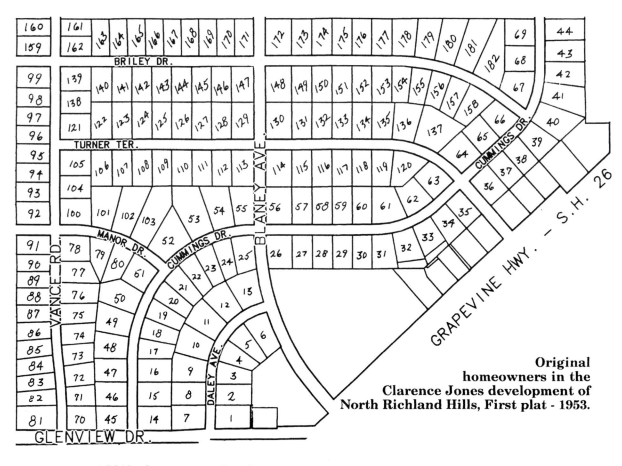

Original homeowners in the Clarence Jones development of North Richland Hills, First plat - 1953.

1. Mulder, C.	38. Ryan, D.	75. Walker	112. Bogart	148. Davis, C.
2. Kindler, R.	39. Messersmith, G.	76.	113. Simmons	149. Coker
3. Wirtanen	40. Hughes	77. Holton	114. Scroggins	150.
4. McEachern, J.	41. Pritchard	78. Peavler, F.	115. Gerard, R.	151. Harral, O. L.
5. Lokey, B.	42. Yaeger, L.	79. Johnson, E.	116. Jones, W.	152.
6. Parton	43. Henry, G.	80.	117. Hill, F.	153.
7. Wilson, O.	44.	81. Roberts	118. Berrier, B.	154.
8. Christopher	45.	82. White, S.	119. Massey, C.	155. Gandy, P.
9. Sims, E.	46.	83. Foster, L.	120.	156. Miller, D.
10. Tripp, W.	47. Mayberry	84. Griffin, J.	121. Brimmer	157.
11. Burnett	48. Walker	85. Houston	122.	158. Butcher
12. Tice	49. Lambert, R. F.	86. Smith, E.	123. Fuller, B.	160. Cobb, J.
13. Tittle	50. Cates	87. McMahon	124. Goodale	161. Caram, A.
14.	51. Smith	88. Hays, B.	125. Digiovanni	162. Liscomb, P.
15.	52. Roe, C. B.	89. Gower, J.	126. McCarthy, W. T.	163. Parker
16. Rodgers	53. Denney, D.	90. Davis, D. W.	127. Nace, K.	164. Knowles, B.
17. Van Summer	54. Cherry	91.	128. Richardson, M.	165. Wood, H.
18. Williams, W.	55. Watson, J.	92.	129. Kinnaird, C.	166. Baker, B.
19. Miller, G.	56. Green	93.	130. Scott	167. Nelson
20.	57. Graner, S.	94. Reynolds, A.	131. Baird, M.	168.
21. Dunleavey	58. Ray, B.	95. Williams, B.	132. Scroggins	169.
22. Ward, A.	59. Miller	96. McGuire, P.	133. Wester, C.	170. Merritt
23. Kutilek, P.	60. Clemens	97. Evans, V.	134.	171. Grelle
24. Dreiling	61.	98. Ragsdale	135. Steele, C.	172.
25. Goss, L.	62. Ray, C.	99. Lewis	136.	173. Woody, J.
26. Koenig, F.	63. Williams, S.	100.	137. Hill, G.	174.
27. Cooper, A.	64. Jordon, M. R.	101. Robinson-Hagler	138. Kennedy, C.	175.
28. Rutledge, J.	65. Norman, J.	102.	139. Wood, C.	176.
29.	66. Hill, A.	103. Smith, E.	140. Green, F.	177. Knaur
30.	67. Brooks, R.	104. Craine, J.	141. Brooks, B.	178. Riddle, C.
31.	68. Kronheim, H.	105. Elliott, G.	142. Emmett, E.	179. Carrithers, P.
32. Jones, C.	69. Goedeck, E.	106. Filbert, J.	143.	180. Guynn
33.	70.	107.	144. Wallace	181. Neyland, C.
34. Halmontaller	71. Brooks	108. Kruger, Bud	145. Cummings, S.	182. Secord, C.
35. English	72. Eddleman, K.	109. Ellenburg, N.	146. Blevins, R.	
36. Baker, S.	73. Frost, H.	110. Jones	147. Gray, H.	
37. Kelly, F.	74. O'Henry	111. Weaver		

Compiled by Evalyn Lochridge and Don Tipps

The League favored incorporation, but some in the community circulated a petition requesting annexation to Richland Hills. At a special meeting of the League on April 23, J. D. McEachern, chairman of the Civic Affairs Committee, led a detailed discussion concerning the advantages and disadvantages of incorporation. Richland Hills already had a tax structure, which many were determined to stave off as long as possible. But North Richland Hills had wretched streets, and area residents would soon have to pay for paving them under one town government or another. It was decided that if incorporation passed, the petition would be destroyed. If it failed, the League would consider the petition at its next meeting.

The turnout was very light. As in many American towns, quite a few citizens were unaware that an election was even occurring. Moreover, Jones and his allies feared incorporation would fail, and they deliberately tried to discourage voting. By state law two public notices had to be posted. One was on a sign which somehow wound up face down in mud, and another was on the back of the Arnold Construction Company door, which, when opened, was out of sight. North Richland Hills was incorporated by a vote of 24 to 23! The name was retained because of the widespread assumption that the two towns might yet merge. Jones' farm of 268 acres was included in the new city.

J. W. Watson's friends talked him into running for mayor, but before his candidacy was generally known, Jones tried to talk him out of running.

Herbert and Maude Arnold. Maude served as the first "unpaid" city secretary. Herb was co-developer along with Clarence Jones. Their office, located at 7305 Grapevine Highway, was the first meeting place of the Civic League.

New Village Gets Officers Tonight

Tarrant County's newest village North Richland Hills, will have its first set of officers after installation services at 8 p. m. Friday.

J. W. Watson will be sworn in as mayor of the village at the home of one of the new aldermen R. F. Lambert, 4117 Cummings Dr., E. County Judge Gus Brown is slated to swear in the officers at a party sponsored by the North Richland Hills Civic Assn., according to W. H. Tripp, chairman of arangements.

Other aldermen sworn in are J. T. Norman, N. A. Ellenburg, Paul Kutilek and T. S. Christopher. Robert Hays will be town marshal.

Swearing-in of first North Richland Hills aldermen

Jones ran his own candidate against Watson in May 1953, but Watson won. Five city councilmen were elected at large. The Civic League sponsored an inaugural celebration for the mayor and council.

Anxious to avoid taxation, the town government and the League's Paving Committee immediately launched a door-to-door campaign to interest residents in paying $1.25 per foot of their frontage on the roads to be paved. The lots were large, and this was a particular expense to those with corner lots, but $5,600 had been collected by July. A paving contractor was selected from submitted bids. A few residents refused to participate, so parts of various streets were not paved.

The streets in the first subdivision were mostly named for Jones family members. Cummings and Turner were his daughters' married names. Daley, Blaney, and Briley were other family names. In the second building phase, extending north from Briley to Riviera, Jones had run out of family names. He visited Kinnaird Brothers Motor Company and picked out the names of seven 1950s cars, e.g. Riviera, Victoria, and DeVille. Still others were soon named for prominent men in the community, e.g. Harmonson, Starnes, and Arnold.

J. W. Watson, First Mayor of NRH, with family, 1953

Home of Ace & Dayle Nace, 7105 Turner Terrace, 1952

The Blossom Battalion was also born in 1953. It started as the Civic League's Garden Beautification Committee under Margaret Lambert and soon became a Garden Club with its own officers and regular meetings. It later changed its name to the North Richland Hills Garden Club. Mrs. Bea Elliott and Mrs. Laura Ray were among those who served on the Welcoming Committee, a group of six people who watched for moving vans and newcomers to the neighborhood. They called on new neighbors and helped organize the Garden Club and Bridge Club. They were active in the openings and early Christmas celebrations in Greater Richland Center and in the North Richland Hills Shopping Center.

Home of Clyde "Corky" & Evalyn Wood, 4408 Vance Road. Intersection of Vance & Briley, northwestern corner of NRH, in 1953, prior to street paving.

All the town's public officials were members of the North Richland Hills Civic League and/or attended its early meetings, and both groups were absorbed with the needs of the community. Both groups constantly discussed livestock restrictions, building restrictions, building permits, traffic signs, garbage collection, sewage systems, road problems, transportation of students, and (by December 1953) the annexation of other neighborhoods. The Civic League minutes constitute a serious and sober record of the early history of the city, although the secretary did note on the occasion when refreshments were first served, the November 13, 1953 meeting, that upon adjournment the members discovered that the coffee and cookies had been largely consumed by the secretary.

The initial garbage collection was made in an open trailer truck by a hog farmer. Much of what was collected became litter as the open truck bounced along the mostly unpaved roads. In October 1953 the O'Rourke Garbage Collection Service began backdoor service twice weekly for $1.50 per month, but could not guarantee specific days of the week.

Like other new local governments at the time, the town could exist for awhile with no taxes, with no revenue other than the utility franchise fees and building permits

Street signs for Turner and Cummings

The popular Rapid Mart grocery owned by Tully Angle and Stanley Parchman.

(collected by Maude Arnold at the construction company). The Civic League was always there as a backup and shadow government. When the Town Council adopted ordinances concerning the keeping of animals and street patching, state law required the town to advertise them. The city treasury was virtually penniless, so at the December 1953 Civic League meeting, four members—Arnold, Jones, Tripp, and League Parliamentarian and City Councilman T. S. Christopher—dug into their pockets and came up with the necessary $15.00.

Very few businesses were located along the North Richland Hills segment of the Grapevine Highway during the first two years after the village was incorporated. The most memorable was the Rapid Mart grocery at 6959 owned by Tully Angle and Stanley Parchman. Haly and Gladys Parchman had owned 13 acres on the highway since 1925. Thirty years later Haly and son Stanley built the Rapid Mart on Parchman land at the Vance Road intersection and operated the business for several years. The store was best

Early business owned by Parchmans, located on Grapevine Highway and Parchman Street.

Haly Parchman built the first swimming pool located off Grapevine Hwy. and Parchman.

known for top-quality meat, doubtless in part because Haly had worked for Armour for more than 40 years. Free delivery twice a day, at 11 A.M. and 4 P.M., also endeared the owners to area housewives. In the late 1950s Southland Corporation built a 7-Eleven nearby and Parchman thought he was in for stiff competition. But the 7-Eleven soon closed its doors and posted a sign saying, "OPEN BY MISTAKE." Parchman later discovered that the Rev. Robert Young, minister of Richland Hills Methodist Church, had encouraged everyone he came in contact with to support local business people. The burgeoning town had a sense of community.

The Parchmans also built a Dairy Kreem Drive-In and rented it. It was the first drive-in in the area and specialized in hamburgers and malts. In February 1956 Parchman announced to the Civic League his plans to build a swimming pool on his property behind the Dairy Kreem, accessible from the side street. He leased it to the YMCA for several seasons as well as to others. Many area youngsters learned to swim in this pool.

Mason's Hobby Lobby, established in 1953, is the oldest, continuously operating business in North Richland Hills. Moreover, it is at the same site and in the same family's hands today. Contractor-builder Paul Mason (ca. 1907–1977), a big, quiet man from Bushyhead, Oklahoma, built the shop next to his home (later his office) at 6905 Grapevine Highway. He built it for his wife, Juanita, "to give her an outlet for her art interests." He made frames for her and her many customers, and she taught art classes in the store. She worked closely with the Birdville schools through their arts and crafts classes. Mason built 58 of the homes in the original North Richland Hills tract, with Juanita as the designer

Mason's Hobby Lobby, established in 1953.

North Richland Center Grand Opening 1955, (later renamed to Greater Richland Center)

and interior decorator. For years Mason, doubtless remembering his hard times during the Depression, loaded his station wagon with toys on Christmas Day and gave them away to children he spotted in poorer neighborhoods.

The Haltom City State Bank helped finance aspiring homeowners and businesses. Indeed, if Clarence Jones favored someone or took an immediate shine to him or her, a person could obtain a loan without even signing a note. The document showing the amount loaned was simply inserted into Jones' desk—"drawer paper," it was called—and there was no interest charged. It was perfectly legal. Some whom Jones had never met just walked in and secured loans.

The twelve acres surrounding Clarence Jones' house and barn were set aside for the North Richland Shopping Center (soon changed to Greater Richland). Jones moved his colonial style house north to 4324 Cummings Drive, just behind the center. The barn was demolished and replaced by Berry's Super Market (soon bought out by Buddies). Mott's Variety store was also completed in the initial building phase. After two years of construction, the first community activity was the cosponsorship of the Civic League, Garden Club, and North Richland Hills Merchants' Association of the 1955 community Christmas Tree on the site of the newly completed shopping center. During the 10-day formal opening many businesses contributed goods and services, a new Chevrolet was awarded as a grand

"BUDDIES" in North Richland Shopping Center, 1955

Joe J. Hicks bought land from Haly Parchman in 1956 and built a 24-hour, full-service station at 6955 Grapevine Highway.

prize, and Santa Claus landed in a helicopter.

Clarence Jones could often be found in the afternoons, drinking coffee and visiting in the North Richland Cafeteria, which had a seating capacity of 260. Charles Morrison's North Richland Hills Barber Shop quickly became a center of masculine conversation. Morris Bloodworth's North Richland Drugstore was the only pharmacy in town for two years. The Pillow-Rush Medical and Surgical Clinic offered convenient medical assistance. The fifteen upscale shops and offices constituted one of the most complete and modern shopping centers in the Southwest.

Ace Nace, a slender, mustachioed airline pilot, bought a new Sinclair station around 1953, run by Lewis Crawford. It burned to the ground in 1955, and Ace moved on to a Mobil station, where Eckerd is now. After some three years Ace was more than ready to unload and sold out to Crawford. L. C. Akins opened a full-service Humble station at 7101 Grapevine Highway, at the intersection with Daley, July 30, 1955. It was still open land. For several years Akins could watch a man plow the corner field across from his station. Joe J. Hicks bought land from Haly Parchman in 1956 and built a 24-hour, full-service station at 6955 Grapevine Highway. It was a Premier station in the 1950s. Located between Rapid Mart and Dairy Kreem, Hicks sold gasoline, oil, sporting goods, and fishing supplies. The station also had a

WANT IT UNDER YOUR TREE?--Some lucky shopper will be driving this beautiful new 1956 Chevrolet by Christmas. It will be given away by the merchants in North Richland Shopping Center, December 23 at 8:00 p.m. in a drawing to be held in the huge parking area. An oversize Christmas tree, Christmas music and personal appearances by Santa Claus are other highlights of the big month long Grand Opening Celebration of Fort Worth's newest shopping center.

Grand prize of a new Chevrolet given away at the newly opened North Richland Shopping Center in 1955.

wash rack, a grease rack, and a mechanic. Don Andrews opened a Gulf station in 1955 at Grapevine Highway, Pipeline, and Blaney. He was there for two years, mostly marked by gas wars. His price on regular sank to a low of 14.9 cents per gallon. In 1957 he moved southeast two blocks, ran a Texaco for six months, went broke, and abandoned the service station business altogether. All were full-service stations where attendants checked the oil and other fluids, checked the tires, cleaned the windshield, and filled the gas tank.

The Richland Bowl at 6601 Grapevine Highway opened in 1957, a $300,000 facility advertised as the first modern bowling alley in Tarrant County and the only one with a country club flavor. Four thousand people streamed in on opening day to see the automatic pin-setting machines, the teleview scorers that projected bowlers' scores overhead, and the underlane ball

Richland Bowl, interior, about 1957

return. Friends had warned prominent builder Ray Lofland that he'd make a big mistake if he built a bowling alley in an area that was legally dry, but Lofland knew that the Holiday Skating Rink near the Birdville School marked a success for wholesome recreation. Having three sons of their own, Ray and Ethel Lofland wanted a wholesome place. There were few sites for teenagers to hang out, but now they could bowl or play billiards. Moreover, a room was set aside for a "teen canteen," where youngsters could dance and fraternize. Dancing was not allowed in the Birdville schools, so the teen canteen was an enormously popular site. The young people had a slate of officers, strictly enforced rules, and parents who chaperoned all activities. Richland Bowl instantly became the social center of the suburbs.

Courtesy of Ethel Lofland

Richland Bowl located on Grapevine Hwy., about 1957.

Courtesy of Naomi Jones Cummings

Texaco Service Station and North Richland Auto Service, 1955 - Corner Grapevine Hwy., Turner Terrace

The red brick building also housed Johnny Nobles' Cleaners, the G and H Barber Shop, Cullen Turner's terrazzo floor business, and Everett Truelove's Sportsman's Store. Nobles was a well-known area sportsman and longtime coach at Birdville High School. John Garner and James Hankins knew that opening a shop inside the Richland Bowl would make them vulnerable to much kidding about "bowl haircuts," but they were undaunted and were open seven days a week. Turner supplied the Botticino terrazzo floors for Richland Bowl and for many buildings in the area.

The energetic Clarence Jones remained involved in the community. He was one of the founders of Richland Lodge 1348 of the Masonic Order, along with H. L. Arnold and Claud Griffith, and donated the land where the building was located. Chartered in 1954, the lodge was erected the next year at

Richland Lodge 1348 of the Masonic Order, at 7115 Glenview

7115 Glenview, just off Blaney and the Grapevine Highway. It was part of the original Jones farm. Jones paid for paving Blaney out of his own pocket, or else worked one of his many deals to get it paved.

Other landowners beside Jones now knew that development could not be avoided.

As urbanization encroached during the 1950s, Guy Reeves sold off his farm in pieces. Bill Mackey's dairy farm was developed in 1955. Gene Anderson could also see the end of an era coming in the late 1950s.

Early in the 1950s, J. M. Stegall began to

Cornerstone of Richland Hills Lodge 1348 leveled by The Grand Lodge of Texas A.F. & A.M. June 10, 1955, George Moffett, Most Worshipful Grand Master.

think about subdividing the land, but he knew he would have to have water and he knew nothing about drilling wells. Then he received a call from a friend, O. P. Leonard, one of the owners of Leonard's Department Store in Fort Worth. Leonard wanted a favor. He was trying to buy a tract north of Stegall's to drill water and begin installing the Smithfield water system, but he balked at paying $3,750 for a quarter acre of land. Leonard suspected that the owner was trying to hold him up because of his known fortune and wondered if Stegall might buy it for him in Stegall's name. Stegall told Leonard that if he would drill the well on his farm, he would give Leonard the necessary little tracts. They consummated the deal the same day, looking over the land from Mesquite Hill. Stegall's land increased in value, and he sold off the eastern half, the current Davis Boulevard Baptist Church and additions between Maplewood and Lola, to the Centex Development Company in 1954.

Guy Reeves plowing the garden at Four Points in the mid-sixties with grandchildren Deana and David Ellis enjoying a ride on the plow horse.

THE EXPANDING TOWN

In a growing area, new towns have to expand or be absorbed by towns that are also expanding. As a general law town in the 1950s North Richland Hills could annex contiguous, unincorporated tracts if they were no more than a half mile wide and if the owners petitioned for it. General law charters were not designed for expansionism, but North Richland Hills and other newly incorporated suburbs did not have the population base to become home rule cities.

Mayor Watson was traveling 50,000 miles a year for an industrial painting firm and concluded he had no time for the mayorship. He stepped down and Donald Denney was elected mayor in April 1954, with three new councilmen. Denney apparently had no opponent and won with 44 votes. The mayor and council launched a vigorous annexation program. They started with the neighboring Parchman Addition to the south in February 1955. Four additions were annexed by majority petition in their neighborhoods in April 1955: Lynnwood and Richaven, where Loop 820 later crossed the Grapevine Highway, and Harmonson and Richland Hills West between Harmonson and Onyx streets.

First street light at Grapevine Highway, Blaney, and Pipeline Road (now Glenview Drive)

O. P. Leonard's Smithfield Water Company had changed its name to Tarrant Utilities, already served about 65 water customers in North Richland Hills as of January 1955, and wanted to serve the town. Mayor Denney and the council were not quite ready to link up with a company that had yet to turn a profit and was having to raise rates. Council discussion in July 1955, centered on what to do about a peeping tom lurking in the area.

The annexation movement continued to be promoted by Mayor Denney and ongoing councilmen Ace Nace, N. A. Ellenburg, T. S. Christopher, and Paul Kutilek, all of whom were reelected in 1955 and 1956. Their motives in the annexations were largely defensive, that is they were creating buffer zones against other cities. As they saw it in the early years, they really did not want a city. Clarence Jones and his faction were more development-oriented. The annexation movement to the west and southwest was relentless in 1955 and 1956, and eventually clashed with Haltom City's eastward drive. In the confusion of a compromise agreement the families in three houses on Tourist Drive discovered they could vote in both cities' elections and proceeded to do so. The not-so-affluent Harmonson Addition was taken as well as the more posh North Hills neighborhood around Tourist Drive, eventually populated mostly by professionals. Some of these annexations were illegal since it was a violation of state law for a town to annex land that constituted more than ten percent of its land area.

The southernmost limit was reached on February 6, 1956, with the annexation of a tract that reached to Broadway Street just east of the former village of Birdville. Continuing westward, it was one of Birdville's main streets and was known as the Old Fort Worth-Birdville Road. Landowners here included branches of old-line Birdville families—Boaz, Portwood, Angle, and Reeves, among others—who petitioned to be part of North Richland Hills. So did Hardy and Nora Reeves Rumfield, who had moved from Smithfield.

The need for a civic center was obvious, as a meeting place for the city government, the Civic League, Boy Scouts, the Garden Club, and other private organizations. The cost of the desired lot in the recently added Hillview Addition, at the corner of Glenview and Morgan Circle, was $1,500. The League's building committee requested citizens to donate their water refund checks to the building fund. The fund drive took in $1,300 and League members made

NRH Civic League building became 1st City Hall, currently Dan Echols senior center, Glenview Drive and Morgan Circle

up the difference in their April 8, 1954 meeting. With the lot secured, fund-raising intensified for the center, beginning with a car raffle that netted over $2,800. Kinnaird Brothers Motor Company donated the car, while H. L. and Maude Arnold provided concrete at cost for the foundation of the building. Boyd and Laura Ray of Ray Steel Company donated the steel. For the next year other fund-raising activities included bowling tournaments, bake sales, bingo nights, chili suppers, carnivals, used paper drives, and a campaign for new Civic League members.

Plans called for a brick building of 2,400 square feet, expected to cost about $7,000. Money was slow in accumulating, but the need for the center was increasing, so in the summer of 1955 League trustees signed a note for the $3,500 needed to complete the building. The Civic League held its first meeting in its new building in October 1956, although there were no doors or windows and a cool breeze was blowing. The building was finished by the time the City Council first met there, April 12, 1957. The North Richland Hills Garden Club landscaped the area.

Ever alert in forestalling taxes, Mayor Denney and the City Council established an auxiliary police force in July 1956. It was a volunteer effort to assist the appointed town marshal, Robert Hays. Also, Marvin Shelton had served as a private security man even before incorporation; residents and businesses who wanted his services paid him a dollar or more per month. The Civic League resolved in 1956 that there was no need for a paid police force at the time. The 21 volunteers in the auxiliary did fend off the need, or at least the implementation, of a professional force for four more years.

By April 1955 the annexations of some 15 additions had increased the population to 2,000 people. At one point in 1956 the average construction going on throughout the state amounted to $17 per capita, while North Richland Hills' per capita construction was $1,587. In April 1957 the Bureau of Business Research at the University of Texas reported that North Richland Hills, "a satellite community on the east fringe of Fort Worth is the top Texas spot in construction."

The growth was so prodigious that by the winter of 1957–1958, with the population estimated at 4,500, the Clarence Jones faction grew more fearful of higher taxes, zoning restrictions, and other appurtenances of city life. They challenged the dominant faction that was somewhat more amenable to

Volunteer Police Dept., 1956

zoning ordinances and, if necessary, levying taxes. Denney was stepping down, but Ace Nace represented those who favored a more active city government against challenger Cullen Turner, who was Jones' son-in-law. Veteran Councilman Kutilek was challenged by Maude Arnold. It would not be accurate, however, to portray the 1957 elections as battles between slates, because Ellenburg had no challenger, and the other three council races featured independents not wholly identified with any faction. Indeed, the policy differences may have been secondary to the differences in personality, styles, and friendship networks. Several of Nace's group accused Jones of trying to control the town, and Jones publicly threatened to sue Nace and five of his allies, including outgoing Mayor Denney.

Gertrude Tarpley, center, at work at the Chamber.

Nace defeated Turner 207 to 187 and Kutilek beat Arnold 208 to 173. Once in office Mayor Nace and Councilman Kutilek hinted that street maintenance and the apparent need for a professional police force might bring on the first city taxes. The Civic League was doubtful and asked city leaders not to levy taxes without first submitting the issue to the voters. Nace and Kutilek did not push the issues, and there was no public consensus for taxes or a police force.

Gertrude Tarpley, a local journalist, and Jack Bean, vice president of First Container Corporation in Richland Industrial Park (in Richland Hills) put together a list of 75 civic leaders in Bean's kitchen in November 1957. The population and business boom all over the

Cynthia Orr in front of her dad's pharmacy October 1958. The building was originally a short-lived 7-Eleven store.

43

area prompted them to promote the establishment of the Greater Richland Area Chamber of Commerce on December 23, 1957. Business leaders from North Richland Hills, Richland Hills, Bedford, Smithfield, and Colleyville attended the initial meeting. The name was soon changed to the Haltom-Richland Chamber of Commerce, and the annual membership fee was $25. Bean served as the chamber's first president, and Tarpley served as executive director for 23 years. Seventy-five corporate and individual memberships were sold, and a thirteen-member board of directors was selected. H. L. Arnold, Joe Hicks, and Paul Mason were on the board from North Richland Hills and sand and gravel magnate Foy Abbott from Smithfield. Charles Morrison, Tully Angle, Ray Lofland, L. C. Akins, and Ace Nace signed up as members. The 7200 block of Grapevine Highway was the Greater Richland Center. As in the case of many conglomerate chambers, internal tensions were destined to cause major disruptions. Indeed, Colleyville delegates walked out before the first meeting had concluded.

Ace Nace's work took him out of town several days each week, so as mayor, 1957–1958, he was on the run while in town. He remembers many a meal eaten with fork in one hand and telephone in the other. The council authorized rental of a small, two-room office in what was known as the Richardson Center. Marvin Richardson, who advertised "All kinds of Real Estate and Air-Conditioned Office," let the town use the spare office either rent free or close to it. Since Nace was away so often, a city secretary, Mrs. Laura Ray, was hired in January 1958 to keep the office going, at a salary of $25 per week. Philip E. Orr Jr. opened Orr's Pharmacy in the Richardson building in 1957. Nace found the mayor's post was distracting him from his work as a pilot, and he surrendered his political career after one year in office.

The annexations to the west took in existing businesses along Rufe Snow Drive. Willie and Juanita Anglin's auto repair shop was still there as well as Luke Davis' garage at 3810, Fort's Grocery and Market at 3812, and perhaps other old businesses. Henry's Superett, advertised as an "old-fashioned meat market," was established at 3900 and had also been in place for years. A Pak and Save convenience store is there now.

The annexations also picked up Raymond and Hazel Anderson's furniture store at 6608 Harmonson Road. Anderson's Furniture, later North Richland Furniture, was founded in 1954. They also operated a moving and storage business at the same location. After their uninsured furniture store burned to the ground a few years later, the Andersons depended on the moving and storage business to support the family until they could get the furniture store rebuilt. Low overhead in the countryside permitted them to offer very competitive prices. Raymond Anderson was a born "horse trader" who loved dealing with people. He was known for saying, "If you find what you want, I'll make you a good deal today."

Churches were organized to keep pace with development. Richland Hills United Methodist

Furniture store founded in 1954 as Anderson's Furniture, later renamed North Richland Furniture, located on Harmonson Road near Rufe Snow Road. Store is still in business in 1998.

Gilstrap Photography

Richland Hills United Methodist Church, early 1970s

Church was organized with 89 members in July 1953 and by 1959 had moved into its permanent site at 7301 Glenview Drive, purchased from the Calloway family in North Richland. Robert Young served as pastor, 1953–1962. North Richland Hills Baptist Church traces its beginnings to services held in the North Richland Elementary School (now Mullendore) on February 26, 1956. Forty-one people accepted membership that first Sunday. The church was chartered on May 20, 1956, the date of the first meeting in the newly built auditorium. Charter members numbered 115. The Rev. James Hester served as pastor from 1956–1959. Civic clubs also made an entrance. The Northeast Optimist Club was established in 1952, with Bill Blessing as the key leader. The Kiwanis Club of Northeast Fort Worth was founded in 1957.

Expansion and growth also included development of schools. Glenview

North Richland Hills Baptist Church, top picture of first facility, May 1956, and bottom photo of sanctuary.

45

Elementary, which opened in 1954, served the original North Richland Hills addition; it was and is a few blocks down Glenview Drive on the Richland Hills side of the street. (Pipeline had already been changed to Glenview in Richland Hills and Haltom City, and was so changed in North Richland in 1960.) Successful bond issues were continuous. North Richland Elementary (later Alliene Mullendore) at 4100 Flory opened its doors in the fall of 1955 on land that had been part of the Mackey dairy farm. In 1958, the same year the school district administration building was completed, a $4.5 million bond issue was voted to finance a program that included three elementary schools (Snow Heights at 4801 Vance Road being one), a third junior high school, and a new senior high school, Richland, at 5201 Holiday Lane East. By 1958 there were 6,867 students in the district and more than 300 staff. Suburban growth almost overwhelmed the district. Richland Junior High, 1956, had to serve the entire district east of Big Fossil Creek. The junior highs were so overcrowded in the 1950s that "STOP" and "GO" signs were used to direct student traffic during class changes.

Basketball remained popular in the district, and from the mid-1940s through the mid-1950s Johnny Nobles' teams won 11 district championships in 12 years. Three teams played Christmas tournaments in Pampa, and one was almost snowed in on the roads. The football field was still up on Birdville Hill near the present Shannon Learning Center. One side of the field was on an incline, and those who ran out of bounds might roll down the hill. The referees knew to call time out until players could climb back up and resume their positions.

By 1958 the Smithfield annexation question came to the forefront in North Richland Hills. It involved a neighboring town whose history was almost as old as Birdville's, but Smithfield had become a deeply divided community.

Aerial view of Birdville Stadium between Broadway and Grapevine Highway/Belknap Street, Dec. 1965

SMITHFIELD

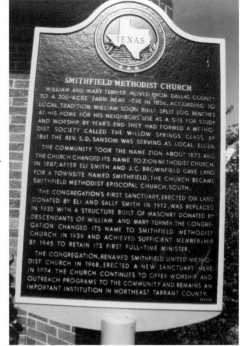

William Turner (1803–1878) and his wife Mary (1819–1906) were among the tens of thousands of immigrants streaming into Texas after it entered the union in 1845. Arriving from Virginia in 1846, the Turners migrated to the Tarrant County frontier in 1856, establishing their home and blacksmith shop on the south side of Watauga Road (present Mid-Cities Boulevard) near the current intersection with Smithfield Road. Their 300 acres stretched toward the current site of the Fort Worth Christian School. The immediate farming area was evidently considered by some to be part of the Willow Springs community. Willow Springs Methodist Church was located two-and-a-half miles west in present Watauga. There are also references to the area as Bethel.

The Turners in the late 1850s attended the Willow Springs Methodist "Class," a Methodist institution which was a small, local substitute church in a sparsely settled area, visited whenever possible by itinerant preachers. Desiring services in the immediate community, Turner bought a class leader book, printed by the Methodist Church, constructed split log benches at home, and invited friends into his home for services in 1858. They may have clung to the "Willow

Historica Marker of the Smithfield Methodist Church.

Springs" name for awhile, but probably the congregation called itself Zion and established that name for the community that grew around the area. Or perhaps the church that was eventually established, the Zion Methodist Episcopal Church, South, founded around 1866, took its name from the community.

Zion Methodist Church founded around 1866, probably first called "Willow Springs."

Courtesy of Smithfield United Methodist Church

A. M. Hightower, Pernelis Hightower (second wife)

Other early settlers included William and Elizabeth Smith and their three young sons. They migrated from Missouri to Fort Worth in 1859, camped for a year within the present site of Trinity Park, then moved to the community of Zion. Two of the brothers, Dave (1845–1920) and Eli (who was born in Golden Grove, Missouri, 1848), eventually owned land in and around the village. Eli kept some of the first shorthorns in the area.

Alfred M. Hightower (1825–1897) and his first wife, Sarah Hightower (1824–1878) reached Tarrant County in 1858 and entered the cattle business. Hightower was born in Tennessee but was raised on a farm in Illinois. Like many in Texas' north-central tier of counties near the Red River, Hightower was bitterly opposed to secession, but nonetheless served the Confederacy in battle and as a recruiting officer. At 6 feet, 3 inches and 300 pounds he cut an imposing figure for the time. Not until 1880 did he permanently settle in the Smithfield area, where he raised crops and cattle on 200 acres. He and Sarah had six children.

Historical Marker—Alfred Madison Hightower, a man though bitterly opposed to secession fought in many battles for the Confederate Army. This marker is located in the Smithfield Cemetery.

Still another early settler was L. W. Jones (1817-1895), who hailed from Kentucky and Illinois, and homesteaded 284 acres in Bethel, as he called it, in 1852.

The high prairie grasses in Tarrant County helped cloak small Indian raids. Apparently on several occasions from the 1850s into the 1870s Zion's men slipped out to the north Tarrant County countryside and exchanged gunshots with a few raiders. On such occasions women and children would take pallets and hide in the corn fields and stay there until the men returned. Excitement was actually meager on the Texas frontier, and was more typically confined to such activities as those enacted by some of Zion's women—dipping snuff and spitting on the little pot-bellied stoves just to hear the hot iron sizzle.

Over 100 years later, tall prairie grasses continue to grow along the nature trails of NRH 100 Acre Park off Starnes Road. Photo taken 1998.

Zion may have had two stores by the early 1870s. A general store, with drygoods and groceries, may have been opened that early by the Reverend Sam Durrell Sansom (1816–1894). The local Methodist minister took one of his sons, S. J. D. Sansom (1861–1913), into the business with him. A hardware store was reputedly operated by Wesley Prather for a time and (perhaps the same store) by James E. "Jimmy" Turner (1842–1917), son of William and Mary. Turner, a Confederate veteran, also maintained a blacksmith shop on his nearby farm for 30 years. He farmed 239 acres in 1890. Turner may have maintained his smithy in town for a time, and a Mr. Holt reputedly had one as well.

Sansom moved from Tennessee to the Republic of Texas in 1837, served as a mounted Ranger in 1839, and ministered various East Texas circuits after becoming a Methodist Episcopal pastor in 1851. His young wife, Sarah King Sansom (ca. 1824–1861) passed away after bearing nine children. Sansom relocated as an elder in the Willow Springs church and married 20-year-old Sarah Thomas (ca. 1842–1934) of Illinois in 1862. Having served the Confederacy, he took the Oath of Amnesty in Fort Worth, September 26, 1865. He became pastor of the Zion congregation when it was established after the Civil War.

Courtesy of Smithfield Masonic Lodge

S. J. D. Sansom Jr.; First Master of Grand Prairie Lodge and Smithfield merchant.

Historical Marker—Smithfield Masonic Lodge No. 455, A.F. & A.M. Lodge was organized July 13, 1875.

Many Methodists also belonged to the fraternal order of Masons, which organized the Grand Prairie Lodge in Zion on July 13, 1875. It was named for its geographical location, along the margins of Texas' Grand Prairie backland and the Eastern Cross Timbers. Two Master Masons were named in October, 1875, Eli Smith and Dan Hightower, son of Alfred M. and Sarah Hightower. Both were young, but were veteran settlers and community leaders. The Rev. Sansom and Felix G. Bransford, for whom the nearby village was named, were also officers. Lodge meetings were held on Saturdays, "on or before the first full moon in each month." The meetings would commence in the early afternoons and continue into the night. Lengthy meetings and full moons were necessary since many members had to drive for miles in slow buggies and wagons.

EARLY SMITHFIELD, 1876–1900

In 1875 or 1876 Eli and his wife, Sallie (Hightower), Alfred and Sarah's daughter, and perhaps Dave Smith as well, donated part of their cleared land to the community for a Methodist meeting place, cemetery, and/or additional space for the village to grow. The community's first church building was the Methodists' small, white frame structure, which was also used as the public school and for early meetings of the Masonic lodge. Reverend Lewis White was evidently the Methodist pastor at this time, but he also served other congregations on his circuit. The donated land is the site of the present day care center at 6700 Smithfield Road. The village of Zion changed its name to Smithfield, undoubtedly honoring Eli and Sallie's contribution, and perhaps Dave's. Attorney D. W. Smith (1845–1920), Dr. H. C. Gilbert (1850–1932), former senator A. G. Walker, Jimmy Turner,

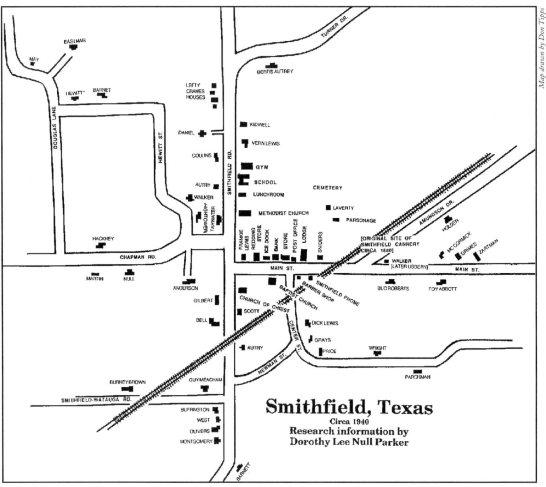

Map drawn by Don Tipps

Smithfield, Texas
Circa 1940
Research information by
Dorothy Lee Null Parker

Map of old Smithfield

A. C. Brown, and D. B. Brown chartered the town of Smithfield in 1876; the original charter included some 57 to 60 acres.

The Smiths had already buried two of their infant children in the cemetery when Eli became ill in the winter of 1878–1879 and died on January 27, 1879. He was laid to rest beside his children in the Smithfield Cemetery with the Grand Prairie Masonic Lodge conducting the funeral. More than 1,000 early settlers and descendants lie in the cemetery, including numerous Civil War veterans. The oldest three acres lie just east of the original Methodist Church lot.

Not everyone qualified for burial in the Smithfield Cemetery. James Autrey, whose Georgia plantation was wiped out by the Civil War, migrated to Texas in 1867. He lived about a mile north of the present Smithfield Elementary School with two old former slaves who stayed on after emancipation and helped with the

Smithfield Cemetery, oldest marker is dated October 13, 1872.

Historical Marker of Eli Smith is located in the Smithfield Cemetery.

farm and the 12 children. There was no black cemetery, so when the couple died they were buried in an apple orchard in the southwest quadrant of Smithfield and Starnes roads.

A succession of doctors—Barkley, already mentioned, Jeremiah Cloud (1821–1878), John Boatner (1845–1904), Lilburn H. Colley (1843–1924), and Henry C. Gilbert—practiced in and around the community in the late 19th century. One could not necessarily make a living just practicing medicine in that era. Dr. Gilbert farmed 242 acres in 1890. He lived on Smithfield Road just south of the Church of Christ in a big two-story house with a huge front yard.

In the spring of 1876 the Masons built their own two-story frame lodge building, about one-fourth of a mile west of the present Masonic Lodge. Skilled craftsmen among the members earned $1.50 per day erecting their building, common laborers $1. The total cost was $412.36. At one point, to help pay for the building, the lodge took out a $23.37 loan from the Zion Church Missionary Society at 12 percent interest. The Smith and Beddo mercantile firm leased the lower floor in 1878 for $5 a month on condition that they "agree not to sell or give away any intoxicating liquors." Portions of the lower floor were rented to storekeepers through the years, including Sansom and Hightower, who opened another general store.

Dr. Henry Gilbert's old home on Main St. in Smithfield, Summer 1975

By 1877 Smithfield definitely included the Methodist Church (though it kept the "Zion" name until 1885 or 1887), the Masonic Lodge, at least one smithy, and a store separate from the ones housed in the Lodge. The separate store may have been Louia Brown's (1857–1939), who began his business career as operator of the town's drugstore.

Before the Post Office was established, Dan Hightower served as unofficial postmaster for a time. For awhile in 1876–1877 the Birdville postmaster allowed Hightower to pay 20 cents a trip to youngster T. E. Cloud, who would carry the mail on his pony once a week to Birdville, more than five miles to the southwest, and bring Smithfield's mail back. The mail was probably distributed at Hightower's store. A young Mason, John G. Walker (1854–1879), built a frame post office east of Brown's store in 1878. He served as first postmaster, from February 1878 to

Grand Prairie Masonic Lodge in Smithfield

October 1879, when he unexpectedly died. It was a fourth-class post office where farmers and villagers congregated to fetch their mail. All had to obey postal regulations, so the offices could not become "the resort for loungers or disorderly persons or the scene of dispute or controversy." The weekly Pony Express was replaced by a regular mail carriage in 1879. The first hack line went from Fort Worth to Birdville to Smithfield to Bedford to Grapevine

Second Building, Smithfield Methodist Church

and back again. Albert G. Walker Jr. served less than three months as postmaster, then Jerry W. Johnson held office for two years, January 1880 to January 1882. Louia Brown served two stints, January 1882 to August 1889 and May 1893 to November 1897. Daniel LeBow tended the office from August 1889 to May 1893, and Tom Garrett (1835–1919) from November 1897 to June 1905.

The school still met in the Methodist Church and numbered 54 students in 1877. Birdville and Willow Springs were the other two "community" schools in Tarrant County. The Zion Community School counted 38 students in 1879, and when its name was finally changed to Smithfield School in 1880–1881 there were 82 "scholastics," ages 8 to 13, enrolled and three teachers and one assistant. The school year was only five months long.

Smithfield United Methodist Church, Summer 1975

Meanwhile, the Grand Prairie Masonic Lodge 455 endured the usual struggles of fraternal organizations, some of whose members could not adhere to the rules. Several members were tried by the lodge for intoxication. In one trial a member was accused of being "beastly drunk, falling off his wagon and being unable to right himself and return to his wagon." The defense maintained that the member had climbed down from the wagon and was adjusting the harness when the horses spooked and knocked him in the side, rendering him breathless and unable to get up.

Some organizations were more oriented toward political and economic action than the churches and fraternal lodges, but little is known about their local activities. L. W. Jones (1817–1895) was apparently active in the 1870s and 1880s in the local chapter of the Grange, which spoke out for family farmers against middlemen, such as the railroads and grain elevators. S. J. D. Sansom was a member of the Knights of Labor Smithfield Assembly 4770, established December 12, 1880. The Knights included farmers and small-town mechanics who wanted working people to be able to accumulate a greater share of the national wealth, while the railroads and other corporations would have some of their powers curbed.

Smithfield farmers raised berries, grapes, plums, peaches, corn, and cotton, especially on the east side of the community, on the sandy land. Wheat, oats, and cattle were located more on the west side, and cotton on the blackland prairie. It took them a day and a half to haul their produce, including wood, eggs, and hens, to downtown Fort Worth. Frequently two old plow horses pulling wooden wagons would slip and slide through the deep ruts of the old Smithfield Road, going south. Often they would set out about noon on a Friday and make it as far as River City (present Riverside) that night, where they slept in or beneath the wagons. Saturday morning they would go the rest of the way. With the money from the produce they sold—minus whatever was spent in barbershops, saloons, the notorious Hell's Half Acre and such—they would fill their wagons with store-bought goods to take home. Dan Hightower was reputedly the talk of the town when he returned once with a pair of red-topped boots with brass toes on them.

John R. Crane (1848–1914) and wife Mary Ann (1847–1914) bought and sold different farms in the area where they raised beans, corn, and fruit and sold tombstones. Smallpox took their first child, Laura Elizabeth, at the age of four in 1873, and the family had to be placed under quarantine. Neighbors brought food and placed it on the gatepost, to help the family as much as possible. From 1875 to 1881 the Cranes owned a 120 acre site northeast of town, from the James Harrell survey, east of Precinct Line and north of Shady Grove Road in the Bransford community, which they purchased for $480. In 1894 Crane swapped land near Canton for over 38 acres on the northeastern edge of Smithfield, north of the railroad depot, where Crane built a two-room log cabin with a boxed "lean-to" attached. This property, embracing some of the North Tarrant Parkway area today, was worth about $750 at the time.

Cotton was the cash crop of the Smithfield area, as it was in most of Texas and the South. A cotton gin, run by an old steam engine, was erected in Smithfield in 1885. It was apparently west of town three quarters of a mile, on the south side of what is now Chapman Road, in the Fox Hollow addition. The gin lacked the capacity to handle all the area's cotton, so some farmers continued transporting their crops to Fort Worth or Birdville to have it ginned. Buyers at the gins represented large companies that compressed the bales into still smaller cylindrical shapes for easier shipping. These smaller bales were sold to the mills that made it into thread or cloth.

Settlers continued trickling in and putting down roots in the community. Ozias Rumfield (1842–1919) and his wife Mary Jane (1844–1883) migrated from Ohio and filed for 72 acres of land in 1873. The Rumfield clan lived on the brow of a hill in a log cabin they built on the southside of the present intersection of Rumfield Road and Kirk Lane, east of the Stoneybrooke Addition. William Henry Harrison Meacham (1839–1894) and his wife Martha Ann (1839–1914) moved their family of six children by covered wagon to the Smithfield area in 1879. Settling on a farm, their house stood where the Holiday Heights School now stands on Lola Drive. Their son Will (1863–1925) married Catherine Hightower (1865–1948) and eventually settled on the southwest corner of Smithfield Road and Mid-Cities Boulevard where the La Casita Mobile Home park is today.

One of the grandest events in Smithfield's history was the arrival of the St. Louis, Arkansas, and Texas Railroad (the Cotton Belt) in 1887. Watching the work train lay

Early Texas Train, photo taken 1938.

tracks constituted much of the excitement of the day, as men and boys would run down to Big Bear Creek for weeks to take it all in. After the tracks finally reached town, some boys would walk to Bransford, its new site being slightly less than three miles up the tracks, just to pay a dime to ride the train back home. The railroad fare from Smithfield to Fort Worth was thirty-five cents, and the trip took about an hour to cover the eighteen or nineteen miles in good weather. During storms the same trip took three or four hours.

For a time the railroad, which had 679 miles of track in Texas and had been recently absorbed by the Jay Gould system, stopped twice a day, at 10:10 in the morning going southwest to Fort Worth and at 10:10 at night going to points east such as Plano and Greenville. Mail bags would be tossed off or passengers could climb aboard or detrain. The morning stop in particular attracted townsfolk who would gossip and collect news from the conductor. The tracks bypassed the Smithfield business district by about a quarter mile. Undaunted, storekeepers and others moved their buildings southward, closer to the depot, and a new business district was established.

About the time of the arrival of the railroad Louia

Mr. Moody Walker at Smithfield Station

Brown bought out Dan Hightower and put up a new building filled with general merchandise, including drugs, hardware, implements, buggies, and wagons. Some of the doctors practiced on occasion in the store's back offices. Brown retired from the mercantile business in

1898 and moved to his 350 acre farm, roughly including the area that today lies between Mid-Cities Boulevard, Rufe Snow, Chapman, and Smithfield Road—the North Park and Fox Hollow additions.

A common saying of the day was that the Cotton Belt railroad began nowhere and went nowhere, but it opened up potential commercial development, and in the late 1880s Smithfield received its first real industry. Louia Brown put up $500, as did Dave Smith and Birdville entrepreneur Richard Boaz (pronounced boze), to build the Smithfield Canning factory near the depot alongside the tracks, at present 8201 East Main. Smith was the manager and employed twenty to thirty women and children, who canned tomatoes, corn, peaches, and peas grown by area farmers and shipped the tin cans out by railroad. John Brown's berry farm, a mile to the southeast, north of what would become Mangham Field, supplied part of the fruit. Successful for a time, the cannery closed after four or five years because local farmers started getting higher prices at the market in Fort Worth.

Courtesy of Aline Shivers

The train enabled John Thomas Shivers (1855–1923), who emigrated from Alabama to Texas by covered wagon in 1871, to follow through on his plans. He bought, on credit, 240 acres of timberland for $13 an acre in the present Thornbridge Addition off the 8300 block of Davis Boulevard. He hauled the logs to the depot and shipped them north to pay for his place. He built a log house, later framed, and

Aerial view of James & Mabel Shivers' farm, circa mid-40s, in the 8300 block of Smithfield, now Davis Boulevard.

remained there on the far northeast outskirts of the Smithfield community.

Other churches were founded as the community grew. Members of the Church of Christ evidently met in Tom Garrett's home for a time, then erected a one-room, frame building facing Smithfield Road at the corner of Main Street, across Smithfield Road from the current Church of Christ. The lot was obtained for $5 and the first service was October 23, 1888. Later a ferocious storm twisted the building on its foundation. The men of the congregation decided that it would be easier to twist it all the way around so that it faced Main Street rather than to return it to its original orientation.

Twelve Smithfield Baptists, including Dr. Gilbert and John R. Crane's son, J. D. Crane (1878–1957), met in the summer of 1895. Tired of traveling to Birdville for services, they agreed to form a local congregation. They were accepted for membership in the Tarrant Baptist Association, which provided pastors. The Baptists were assigned certain days to worship in the Methodist Church. The Smithfield Methodist "Charge," meanwhile, counted 400 in its flock in 1889, scattered among White's Chapel, Oak Grove, Keller, Roanoke, Elizabethtown, Fossil Creek, and Smithfield itself. The Rev. J. I. Lavender served the seven congregations. In 1893 the Smithfield congregation purchased a lot 187 feet square for $275 on the west side of Smithfield Road, across from the property given by Eli Smith, which they intended as a site for a parsonage. The Charge, or most of it, (293 members) was absorbed by the Fort Worth District in 1894.

Protestant campground preaching was popular throughout the nineteenth century. A large campground was set aside in the 1860s, about where Cortland, Mickey, Odell, and Cross streets are today, where the faithful would gather in their covered wagons from miles around.

Those from outside the Smithfield area would bring bedding and food and might camp for three or four weeks during the summer months to hear old-time gospel preaching. Beds of straw were spread at the altar to soften the ground for sinners' knees. One of the fiery orators was H. S. P. "Stump" Ashby (1848–1923), a Methodist preacher as well as an easy-money, antimonopoly spokesman for the Texas Farmers' Alliance. He was a leader in

Smithfield Baptist Church, founded 1895

the independent political movement in Fort Worth, which succeeded in the midst of the Great Southwest (railroad) strike in 1886 in electing the mayor of the city. While living in Grapevine in 1888 he was apparently defrocked from his itinerant ministry for his criticism of the church's failure to support reform and for his alleged fondness for the bottle. It was said that once he had indulged in too much intoxicating cider, he could "talk hair on a cue ball." His effective oratory gave him his nickname, "Stump." Many members of the Farmers' Alliance and the Knights of Labor founded the new Populist Party in 1891, and labeled the Democrats and Republicans as hopeless pawns of the railroads and hard-money bankers. Stump was one of the founders of the Texas branch of the Populist Party in its Dallas convention in 1891 and was state party chairman in 1892 and 1894, unsuccessfully challenging the dominant Democrats. He lived in Smithfield for a time; in 1895 his place was just south of Little Bear Creek in the current Cherokee addition, about where Ember Oaks and Fireside Drive converge. In 1902 he attended the Texas state Populist convention as a delegate from Smithfield for the purpose of blocking a prohibition plank in the party's platform.

Dr. Gilbert of Smithfield, wife, and granddaughter, Maurine Pruitt, who now is Mrs. Maurine Shaw.

Rainwater cisterns supplied the community since water from shallow wells was so foul that even the stock did not like to drink it. Cisterns, however, supplied inadequate amounts of water during hot, dry summers and the water was suspected of causing various illnesses. People in Hurst had found water at 400 feet, so Dr. Gilbert and Louia Brown drilled a water well on the school grounds around 1890 and it spared the inhabitants from hauling water from the Trinity River, Fort Worth, Hurst, or the springs in Watauga.

Halcie Brown, grandmother of Shirley Brown Newman and Kay Brown Alread

Wagons with water barrels could soon be seen coming and going from the initial well and others, carrying drinking water to various homes.

The railroad stimulated commerce, but the old steamers also tossed out sparks that set dry grasslands or corn crops on fire. Usually railroad officials would reimburse the farmers for their losses. Smithfield had no firewagons, but the residents would come running with buckets of water and wet burlap feed sacks to fight the fires. A major fire struck Smithfield in 1890, burning almost all the business district, but the town rebuilt. The Masonic Lodge survived the blaze and in 1894 the lodge building was moved a quarter-mile eastward, toward the railroad tracks—a tedious task that took weeks, using horses and log rollers—to a lot adjacent to the present lodge at 8013 Main Street.

Louia Brown, grandfather of Kay Brown Alread and Shirley Brown Newman

The school year was lengthened to six months in the 1890s. A local school tax election was held, January 28, 1893, and the property owners approved by a vote of 22 to seven the tax rate of 20 cents per $100 evaluation of property. It was a typical southern starvation level appropriation of the era. The local tax provided about $136 in revenue in 1896–1897, while the state sent $436, and local tuition and transfer fees provided some $78—all for the purpose of educating some 74 boys and 50 girls. P. M. and Mattie Heltzell were the teachers, 1895–1901. P. M. earned some $50 to $60 a month, while Mattie received some $30 to $40.

A NEW CENTURY

At the turn of the century Smithfield numbered 137 people. By the early 1900s the Woodmen of the World had built a lodge on Main Street and sponsored a brass band, the pride of the village. The first auto came to town, a chain-propelled vehicle with lever steering driven by J. D. Crane. Children and horses ran from it. By this time Dan Hightower's

Courtesy of Smithfield Masonic Lodge

Downtown Smithfield circa 1920s. Masonic Lodge on right.

son, L. A. Hightower (1875–1961) had bought Louia Brown's store. Dr. Gilbert's office was in back of the store. John Shaw had a blacksmith shop and a Mr. Elliot a lumber yard. The W.O.W. lodge rented its lower floor to J. B. Little for a grocery store. Calvin Gillis (1866–1949) opened a sorghum syrup mill in Smithfield before 1915, and his son C. A. Gillis recalled that his father "sold the syrup on halves." The Gillis farms were located astride present North Tarrant Parkway, in the McKee, Shady Oaks, and Forest Glenn additions.

Courtesy of Smithfield Masonic Lodge

Grapevine Band visited downtown Smithfield, early 1900s.

Shortly after the turn of the century J. D. Crane and L. A. Hightower bought a downtown "gin lot," a site for a second cotton gin, though it is not certain that the first one was still operating. It was north of the railroad, just east of present Davis Boulevard. A large water well was dug to provide water for the boiler to operate the gin, but it proved insufficient. Another well some yards away seemed inexhaustible, so a hand pump was installed in it and Crane's sister, Mary Lou Ellie Crane (1874–1961), was hired to operate the pump. The value of cottonseed was now recognized, so it was often accepted in payment by the ginners. J. D. bought a two-acre tract near the gin lot in 1905 and built his house there.

L. A. Hightower succeeded Tom Garrett as postmaster for seven months, June 1905 to January 1906, then John R. Crane maintained the office until his death in December 1914. His daughter, Mayme Crane Scott, then served as postmistress until 1923. Meanwhile, rural free delivery spread like a prairie fire through the countryside at the turn of the century. Bob Curry, who had just returned from the Battle of Manila Bay (1898), was the first, or one of the first, rural mail carriers operating out of Smithfield, and another was Seth Turner. Farmers quickly grew attached to the home delivery service, which conveyed highly-prized Sears and Roebuck catalogs as well as letters. By 1911 two rural routes emanated from the Smithfield office.

Farmers had long been obliged to maintain the roads near their spreads, but this chore became more onerous in the 1910s with increased usage by mailmen and others in their automobiles. Farmers were threatened with the loss of mail service if the roads deteriorated too badly. Farmers and postmen were among the leading lobbyists for federal road construction, and in the late 1910s the government began building the rural post roads. The military favored it also, especially as the nation edged toward war in 1916 and 1917.

John R. Crane's grandson, John Frank Crane, a substitute rural mail carrier in Smithfield, was killed late in World War I (September 23, 1918), while serving with the 315th Engineers, 90th Division, and is buried in Arlington National Cemetery. Guy Meacham (1893–1978) was on his way to the front with the 324th Field Artillery when the Armistice was signed November 11, 1918.

Smithfield Baptists were able to construct their own building in 1902. G. W. Gunter, a carpenter and member of the congregation, bought nine lots for $40 and donated two of them to the church. The two lots were located on the corner of Main and Center, the same

site the church occupies today. Gunter supervised the construction of the $1,000 building. Baptists and Methodists donated much of the labor. Smithfield Baptists supported area missions and maintained a Sunday School and the Woman's Missionary Union. But the church did not quite have the necessary numbers to survive. Banker Jimmy Jarvis donated coal to the hard-pressed congregation in February 1920, but the church had to shut down in 1925. The Methodist "Charge" numbered 290 in 1910, served by four preachers. The church building was evidently rebuilt in 1912. Some 407 members were claimed in 1913.

The farmers who lived in what are now the suburban neighborhoods along North Tarrant Parkway, that portion of present North Richland Hills north of Little Bear Creek, were considered part of the Bransford community by the late 1880s. The

Arthur Guy Meacham

creek was a center for fishing and swimming. Felix G. Bransford opened his general store in 1870, near the current Pleasant Run-Grapevine Highway intersection, about two miles east of the present NRH city limits. Mr. Bransford served as postmaster until he left the area in 1876, and there were a few houses nearby. The site was abandoned in 1888 when the St. Louis

Southwestern railroad built through the nearby village of Red Rock. The Bransford post office and store moved about a mile northwest to Red Rock, which adopted the name Bransford. In its heyday in the early 1900s Bransford had four general stores, four doctors (including L. H. Colley), two blacksmiths, and a livery stable. The local school enrolled 117 students and employed two teachers during the 1905–1906 term. In 1903 the area between Little Bear Creek and present state road 1709 was designated the Bransford voting precinct, which contained some 124 families in 1910. Most were farmers, but there were also a half-dozen rail-

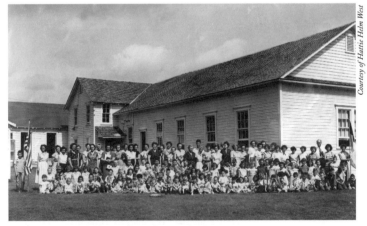

Smithfield Baptist Church Vacation Bible School, circa 1952.

road employees. The Bransford Lodge Hall, erected in 1911, was shared by the Odd Fellows, Farmers Union, Woodmen of the World, and the Knights of Modern Macabees. In April 1913 the Bransford post office was moved to Smithfield. A young Bransford storekeeper, Walter Crouch, was anxious to start his own business, and in October 1914, paid Dr. Lilburn Colley $50 for two acres and a small house about a mile southeast of Bransford, near the Grapevine road, near the original site of the village. The doctor had something in mind with

Dr. and Mrs. Lilburn H. Colley, Colleyville named for Dr. Colley, 1915

his generous offer. He asked Crouch to give the doctor's name to his store and the area around it. Colley, a Union army veteran, also lent his name to the community by practicing in the area for 40 years. Colley's house was just southwest of Bransford, close to the tracks. The Colleyville name was in use before the doctor died. For decades Crouch's store—complete with coal oil, harnesses, and 300-pound blocks of ice—was the biggest store between Grapevine and Birdville. Meanwhile, John R. Webb, a section foreman for the railroad, opened a general merchandise store in Bransford in 1914 and closed it, the last store in the village, in 1925. Dr. Colley was buried in Smithfield Cemetery in 1924. In 1956 most of the old Bransford community was absorbed by the growing village of Colleyville.

By 1904 the school term lasted seven months. By 1905 there were more than 150 students. A count showed that library holdings had risen from 21 books in 1903 to 50 in 1906. A two-story Smithfield "grammar" school was built around 1916 on the site that the elementary school occupies today. John Autrey (1853–1939) served as a water boy during construction. There were four classrooms and an upstairs auditorium. By this time the school was in session eight to nine months, and Smithfield usually offered eight to nine grades. Sometimes schools started late because cotton picking was continuing and was deemed more important.

The boys dressed up when they wore their knee-length trousers with a row of three buttons on the outside seam at the knee. Their legs were covered by long, ribbed stockings. Usually, of course, they wore work clothes—blue denim overalls and a bandana around the neck to keep from sunburning. All underwear was made from muslin flour and feed bags from nearby Bewley's Mill. The company slogan was "Bewley's Best," which invariably showed up on the garment itself.

Louia Brown's daughter-in-law, Mrs. Walter H. Brown (1895–1976), writing decades later, recollected that in the early 1900s, "Two teachers of some renown were Misses Kate and Elizabeth Gillis, who lived in Smithfield and taught there, 1903–1912, before going to Fort Worth, where they taught until their retirement. Their outstanding Christian influence left its mark on the lives of all with whom they made contact." Anywhere from eight to eleven grades were taught there before World War II, when eleven grades were all that was required for a high school education and diploma. There were no bathrooms, no running water, and no lunchroom in the 1920s. The Mothers' Club, a forerunner of the PTA, provided students with hot soup on cold days. On one occasion in the early spring of 1926 the school ran out of money and shut down in the midst of the academic year.

Nancy Scott

Building of Smithfield School, 1916, on site of present Smithfield Elementary School.

The Johnstride provided dangerous recreation on the school grounds. Mattie Belle Lewis Borden recalls that it was a pole with chains attached at the top and little bars on each chain to hold on to. You would run to gain altitude and speed, and others would pull you and push you. She was zipping around at the height of the pole when her gloved hands slipped off. She fell onto the frozen ground and broke her nose.

The students also played hide and seek, red rover, spin the tops, and marbles. The lunches they took to school might well include biscuits and sausage, baked sweet potatoes, and fried pies. They were required to take ink pens, bottles of ink, and paper to school. The big boys could get out of classes occasionally to carry coal to the coal house at the northeast corner of the building. Another evasive tactic was to volunteer to dust the erasers. Some walked to school for several miles, others rode horses, and a few arrived by automobile.

Getting peaches ready for market.

Spelling bees and dramatic plays were presented at the school. There was a large 4-H Club, which entered animals in state fair competitions each year in Dallas. Recreation was also provided by the Cotton Belt Railroad, which continued to stop at the depot twice daily and was a particular attraction to young couples on Sunday afternoons. The Cotton Belt coaches would stop at least once daily going to Fort Worth and one arriving from Fort Worth in 1911. It would stop again, both coming and going if flagged.

Farmers would sometimes market their own produce, and John Henry Davis (1882–1957) was one of the best at it. He and his son Howard, born 1915, would hitch mules to their wagons loaded with berries, peaches, and plums and haul them to the courthouse square in Fort Worth. They would sleep overnight on cots near the mules. Once he had acquired a truck in the early 1920s, Davis would also tour neighboring towns—Roanoke, Justin, Keller, Ponder, Haslet—ringing a bell and announcing "John is here." His fruit was big and plump, irrigated by eight wells on his place. Davis owned 27 acres about two miles north of Smithfield School, toward where Green Valley Raceway later stood (in the present Green Valley, Bathman, Martin Oaks, and Bridlewood additions). Young Howard liked to help, but was not always successful. In 1920 at the age of four he set fire to some paper on the end of a fishing pole to burn a wasp nest. The nest was burning when his mother called him in, and while he was thus diverted the entire barn burned down.

Courtesy of Dorothy Mize, Granddaughter

J. D. Crane was another superior farmer. On at least one of his farms, about where the Thompson Parks Estates addition is now, at the southern end of Crane Road, Crane grew large honey ball cantaloupes and sold them to restaurants. He made prize winning sorghum and molasses, which he exhibited at the state fair in Dallas.

While most everyone farmed, some supplemented their incomes by doing other things. Early in the century, on occasion Louia Brown, Jess Turner, and Will Meacham provided the school with supplies, Brown and J. R. Crane provided insurance, and J. D. Crane painted the school or provided paint. Walter Autrey (1883–1965) guarded convicts for the county and did road work. Turner, William and Mary Turner's grandson, served as postmaster from 1920 to 1937, delivering the mail in a Model-T in the 1920s. B. C. Redding (1902–1985) discovered after World

Roy Jenkins Farm Located at Watauga Rd. and Smithfield Rd.

War I that plumbing was much more profitable than growing tomatoes or milking cows, although he did continue with farm and dairy work.

During Prohibition, 1919–1933, as in many rural communities, the wooded areas and creekbeds around Smithfield, especially to the north and east, were off limits to most citizens because of extensive, illegal distilling of whiskey. A number of farmers were more noted for their stills than their tomatoes. In an era when cotton was sometimes dumped on the side of the road because the price was so low that it would not pay to have it ginned, farmers had to survive however they could. Young men might earn $10 a night hauling mash in ten-gallon cans from the barrels, where it was fermented, to the stills. The whiskey sold for $10 a gallon. Pigs and chickens would root in the woods, sometimes get drunk on the sour mash they discovered, and stagger out in comical fashion.

In 1919 Smithfield got its first bank, with Jimmy Jarvis as president, but rural banks were vulnerable during the hard times on the farms in the 1920s. Four men attempted to rob the First State Bank of Smithfield in early March 1929. The combination apparatus was knocked off the

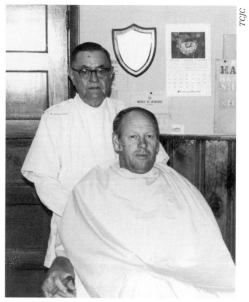

TCJC

"Barber" Clarence Cobb cut hair in Smithfield for nearly 55 years, customer is Ford Reynolds, picture taken July 8, 1975.

lock to the vault, but the would-be burglars were unable to open the safe, which contained only $40. The bandits were responsible for other robberies in the area but were captured and charged in late March by the Dallas and Fort Worth sheriffs. The bank had disappeared by 1930.

Clarence G. Cobb (1901–1986), a 1918 graduate of a barber school in Birmingham, Alabama, got off the train when it stopped in Smithfield, November 11, 1920, liked what he saw, and decided to stay. He walked down Main Street to the barbershop owned by D. Q. Brown, asked for a job, and was hired. The barbershop was one of the central meeting places in town, especially on Saturdays. Some would wait three hours for their 20-cent haircut. Many were from neighboring towns that lacked barbers and many were women, in an era before beauty shops entered the area.

George Fry (1883–1952) and wife Bunie (1892–1975) opened a small grocery store just west of the old white post office in the 1920s. They lived in the store. Louia Brown's old store that had become L. A. Hightower's drugstore early in the century was purchased from Hightower in the early or mid-1920s by a rich oilman from Iowa Park, John T. Overbey (1859–1927). He replaced the old building with a new one of 5,000 square feet in 1926. Overbey died in 1927 and I. C. Snider (1874–1940) of Tennessee opened his general store in the building in 1929. It was crammed with clothes, agricultural implements, kitchen ware, hardware, medicines, and a wide variety of groceries and commodities, e.g. candy and snuff. It became the town meeting place, where neighbors would gather on the porch and chat over current events or play dominoes. The Sniders lived in the store for a time. Their son, Sam (1900–1971) inherited the place in the 1930s.

Old-timers and youngsters tried to enhance their quality of life during fairly hard times. Cotton and corn prices slumped after World War I ended in 1918, and many an American farmer barely eked out a living; Smithfield area farmers, like most others, entered into the Great Depression years even before the stock market crash of 1929. Moreover, the village was relatively isolated. The only route into Fort Worth was down Smithfield Road, with its sharp "S" turn south of the tracks on to Grapevine Highway then down Belknap, but there were no movies, parks, or retail outlets along the 13-mile stretch into the big city. (There was only a filling station at Four Points, the intersection of Bedford Road, the Grapevine Highway, and Smithfield Road). Veteran settlers coped in part by launching annual Smithfield reunions in 1919. Among the hymns sung at these gatherings was The Old Gang of Smithfield. School kids during the academic year, as well as in the summer, played basketball, volleyball, softball, and baseball against teams from Keller, Grapevine, Birdville, and other villages, but all were miles away and transportation was not always readily available. Smithfield's children and teenagers competed with each other more often. Girls concentrated on basketball more than the other sports.

Ocie Green, one of the town's three telegraph operators in the 1920s, submitted columns of daily events, which were printed with a Smithfield dateline, to the *Fort Worth Star-Telegram*. Travel was so unusual that even a trip to Fort Worth was reported, or guests coming to spend a weekend from as far away as Weatherford or Grapevine.

The main thoroughfares in the 1920s, all of which dated back to the 1870s or 1880s and very few of which were yet paved, included Main Street, which journeyed due east from the Smithfield Road to the Grapevine Pike, as it was often called. The Smithfield-Bear Creek Road led straight north to about the present Bridlewood Addition, then followed a stairstep pattern to the northeast, in a rough parallel with present Davis, to the Keller-Grapevine Road, intersecting slightly closer to the village of Keller. The Smithfield Road went due south from town, with the "S" jog, to Four Points, from which the Bedford Road wound north of Hurst into Bedford. Also from Four Points the Grapevine Pike led northeast to that community, but past its intersection with Main Street (which may not have borne that name outside of Smithfield), the paved Grapevine Road traveled a much more meandering path than today. From Four Points it traced almost its current course southwest to Fort Worth, except that it followed Broadway through Birdville before turning more to the southwest. Three-fifths of a mile north of Four Points the Old Dallas Road moved eastward to Bedford and took on the name Harwood in later years. The Watauga Road a half mile south of town cut a straight line from Smithfield Road to the village of Watauga. The Birdville-Watauga Road (later Rufe Snow) stretched from the Grapevine Pike north to present Hightower. The present Amundson-Precinct Line-Glade Road course was known as the Colleyville-Smithfield Road until it reached the Grapevine Pike. The Grapevine Pike and the Denton Highway through Watauga and Keller were macadamized (small rocks rolled solid) "cardinal" roads, while the rest mentioned here were graveled "post" roads. There were other unimproved "lateral" roads in the area, including one that went south of town along present Davis and east-southeast on current Cardinal Lane to the Grapevine Road. All of these had been wagon trails, but two had not existed in the 1890s: the Colleyville-Smithfield Road and the stretch of the Old Dallas Road between Smithfield Road and the Grapevine Road. Downtown Smithfield Road was hot-topped in the late 1920s or early 1930s, but had plenty of potholes.

G. R. Montgomery, whose home occupied the site where the North Richland Hills Post Office now stands at 6501 Davis, was a first grader in 1930, and by then a few changes were detectable in toilet facilities and lunchtime destinations. The students still had two 20-minute recesses and an hour for lunch. During these times they were now expected to use the outhouses that had been installed some 75 yards away. The boys' facilities were on the northeast corner of the grounds, the girls' on the southeast. They were unheated, of course, and infested with wasps and spiders. Some students walked home for lunch, while others bought nickel hamburgers from Snider's new store. G. R. took his lunch, which was often fried rabbit and biscuits. The recesses and lunch hour were also used for kite-flying, mumblety-peg, yo-yos, jacks, jump rope, and hop scotch.

FIRE AND DEPRESSION

The winter of 1929–1930 was a harsh one. Lone Star Gas ranked it the coldest in 30 years. The average temperature that January was 33 degrees. G. R. Montgomery's family had just moved to the area, but decades later he could not recall another winter like it. "They drove cars on Lake Worth. My daddy milked cows, and bottles of milk beside the bed froze and pushed the corks out." The weather put a strain on heating equipment and may explain Smithfield's second great fire. It occurred February 18, 1930, when an oil stove exploded in the back part of a building that served as a home for the W. D. Quinn family. The front part was the telephone exchange, complete with switchboard and "crank" telephone system. Lora B. Buckworth, a 76-year old invalid, may have accidentally kicked over a kerosene lantern to trigger the blaze and explosion. She was burned to death. Also burned was her son-in-law, Quinn, and a dinner guest, Fort Worth oilman Charles Parrot, both of whom rushed into the burning room in an effort to save Mrs. Buckworth. Ed Walker (1870–1954), proprietor of the filling station next door, ran over when he heard Mrs. Buckworth scream and was also burned. The blaze quickly consumed the telephone exchange building, Walker's service station, a blacksmith shop, Brown's barbershop, and the town's only electric lighting equipment, two Delco systems, all lined up on the north side of Main Street. The bank, made of brick, checked the rush of flames, though its wooden parts were burned. Those buildings east of the bank on the north side of Main were saved: Fry's grocery, the post office, the Masonic Lodge, and Snider's store at the end of the street, the current address of 8021 Main. The only available water supply was the artesian well at the school that furnished the town, not far from the telephone office, but a hastily

Picture taken 7/3/87 of the G. R. Montgomery home, the present site of NRH Post Office.

formed bucket brigade, which included many school boys, was unable to prevent the flames from spreading across the street to the Woodmen's Lodge. The Woodmen and Odd Fellows had been meeting in separate rooms on the second floor for three decades, and Verne Lewis' (1887–1946) and Darthula Lewis' (1891–1963) grocery had occupied the

Ed and Moody Walker standing in front of Walker's Service Station, Main Street, Smithfield.

first floor for several years, succeeding J. B. Little's grocery. The lodge and grocery burned down. Telephone communication was cut off, and a messenger was dispatched to the Riverside Fire Department. The firefighters were hampered in their efforts by fear that the flames would cause the explosion of the gasoline tanks at the filling station. About half the business district was destroyed. The Red Cross helped out in the emergency.

Evidently undaunted, as they had been 40 years earlier, Smithfield's citizens rebuilt most of their community. "Barber" Cobb bought the box building across the street, painted its wooden posts in the traditional barbershop red, white, and blue, and continued practicing his profession there for over five more decades as his own boss. Verne Lewis relocated his grocery in the bank building. Grand Prairie Masonic Lodge 455 survived the fire, but in

The Ed Walker Family—L/R-Earl, Moody, Guy, Baby Ella (on bicycle), Ed, Clara, Mattie (mother)

1937 the building was found to be so unsafe that it required extensive repairs. The upper floor was lowered, and the building was turned around to face south.

By the 1930s, of course, the Great Depression had set in, and the town had considerably more spirit than it had cash. A band of burglars seized the safe from the post office in November 1932, and looted Postmaster Turner's confectionary store. The half dozen men, evidently intent on cleaning out the town, were attempting to break into Fry's grocery next to the post office when F. M. Kirk was awakened by the barking of a dog. Kirk, a garage owner, lived about a block away. Impulsively, he ran out into the street and fired his shotgun long range at the men. They returned the fire, while jumping into two automobiles and driving in Kirk's direction. Kirk blasted again at the speeding cars, which roared through town. A third car, loaded with Turner's merchandise, was abandoned in front of the post office. Evidently the gangsters could not get it started. A posse of aroused citizens chased one car into a blind road, and the occupants fled on foot into the woods. The safe, loaded in the one car that successfully got away, contained post office records, but no money or stamps. Eight Fort Worth police officers and two deputy sheriffs directed the search. The strongbox was found near the Trinity River the next day, its bottom torn out, but no documents were missing. A lumberjack coat peppered with buckshot was also discovered. The robbers evidently escaped. Their take was 75 cents from Turner's cash register.

The community, none too prosperous to begin with, was too hard hit by fire and the

Ed Walker house at Amundson and Main, Smithfield, 1914

Depression to completely rebuild or improve. The Delco lighting system, which supplied only a few buildings, would fizzle out occasionally. Most people used kerosene or gasoline lamps and stayed home after nightfall. The water supply remained inadequate since the old school well was tapped only by a half-inch water line. As Foy Abbott (ca. 1909–1996) recalled 50 years later, "If you were number one on Saturday to take a bath, you were lucky, but if you were the last one, you didn't get a bath." Dry cleaning was unavailable in town, so folks had to journey to Art Way Cleaners in Haltom City. Barber Cobb still charged 20 cents for a haircut when he could get it, but often took in eggs, chickens, fruit, and vegetables in lieu of money. It was inexpensive entertainment for mothers to take their children to Cobb's shop and stay all day. Magdalene Wright made dresses for her twin girls out of feed sacks. Her hus-

B. C. Redding, Bobby Atwood, "Barber" Cobb, Dec. 3, 1980

band John always had to buy two identical sacks of feed so the girls could dress alike.

President Franklin Roosevelt's New Deal programs eventually lent a helping hand. Free government food for those in dire straits (worse off than Don Wiseman, see pioneer family story), was available at Snider's grocery and general store. Pete Dunlop (ca. 1890s-1965) and others worked on government construction projects. Foy Abbott had just sold a number of pigs for $3 each, and the government, which was buying cows and pigs by the thousands, granted him $5 each for all the pigs he had already sold. The Agricultural Department slaughtered cows and pigs in a successful effort to raise prices for farmers. Abbott's farm was one of the sites where the animal carcasses were burned.

School life, at least, improved during the Depression. The school rooms continued to be heated by large, pot-bellied coal stoves that belched dirty smoke, but by the 1930s there were outdoor drinking faucets that came from the town well and a tank tower behind the school. In the spring of 1935 C. C. White stepped down after eight years as superintendent of the Smithfield School. He noted that 11 grades were offered that year and that student enrollment had grown since 1927 from 125 to 220 and the number of teachers from four to seven. The local Parent Teachers' Association was begun in 1935, with Mrs. Ed Walker (1873–1948) as first president. Teachers often rented rooms from Mrs. Quinn at the telephone exchange. She prepared lunches for them, which Mr. Quinn delivered to the school.

Tommy Abbott and Foy Abbott

That year's graduating class, as part of their vocational training, erected a new building on the grounds. It housed first and second graders for a couple of years, then became the school lunchroom. One new Ford bus was purchased in 1936, to the relief of many who walked for miles to secure an education. An 86-foot-by-78-foot, $15,000 gym was built north of the school in two months in 1936 by some 60 workers, who were on the payroll of the Federal Emergency Relief Administration. Work relief was a key feature of President Roosevelt's effort to ease the suffering of the Depression. The FERA also provided some of the money for materials, but most was raised by the sale of school bonds in Smithfield. The gym contained two small basketball courts, a stage, and two club rooms. Democratic precinct meetings and other political gatherings were also held in the gym. Despite the eleventh-grade graduation of 1935, however, Smithfield School offered only eight grades most of the time before and after that year.

Not all New Deal programs involved material matters. Geraldine Hall remembered that in the summer of 1937 federal workers were brought into the classrooms to tell stories to the children. That is how she heard Snow White and the Seven Dwarfs for the first time.

Churches coped with the hard times. In 1934 the Methodists razed their old sanctuary, "the little brown church in the vale," after holding a grand reunion presided over by the veteran circuit preacher J. T. Ferguson. The old structure was replaced in 1935 with a masonry building, donated by William and Mary Turner's grandchildren. Two members had planned for some time to be married in the old building (which was white most of the time), but when it was torn down just before their wedding, Sam Snider and Marguerite Crane went to the home of the ailing Methodist minister, the Rev. J. Matthew Scott, who had preached in the area for more than half a century. Scott married the couple March 17, 1934, and died two weeks later.

First and second grade play, Smithfield Elementary, 1948–49

Ferguson died the next year in an auto accident. The Baptist Church was inactive for 10 years until it reopened its white frame building in 1934. Mrs. H. C. Gilbert (1862–1946) was the sole surviving charter member at the time. In 1937 the young voting members of the church, to the consternation of several elders, called 21-year-old Charles Johnson to the ministry. The ladies of the congregation provided weekly food contributions to the Johnsons.

Fay Ballier recollects the baseball games played every Sunday in warm weather. People brought chairs and spittoons and cheered the players. Local berry farmers paid a penny for picking a pint box; kids would often pack 10 of them in order to buy a double-dip ice cream cone at the Gulf filling station in town. She remembers that each teacher had a ruler, a razor strap, and a board with a hole in it and that parents' views toward punishment were not even considered. Discipline was seldom a problem. She does not romanticize the past, since she remembers all too well that, "You sliced your own bread, churned your own butter, milked your own cow, cut your own wood, cranked your own car, oiled your own lamps, gathered your own eggs, quilted your own quilts, picked your own corn, shelled your own peas, and sewed your own clothes."

One highlight of the decade was the emergence of the community from the kerosene age to electric lighting. The Texas Electric Service Company was undertaking rural electrification in Tarrant County and took its power lines into Smithfield in late November 1936. Some 500 persons attended a gala celebration in the recreation center (gym). Company officials noted that surrounding farms would soon also be served. (It took them about five years, however, to reach the Wiseman farm a mile north of town and Walter Autrey's a half mile south of it.) School board chairman John Crane was especially happy with the lighting of the school.

Rail service was still available to the community. Southbound freights left Smithfield at 5:35 A.M. daily and a train with mixed coaches and freight cars departed at 1:15 A.M. if it had been flagged to a stop. Northbound freights departed the old town at 7:44 P.M., while a mixed train left at 9:55 P.M. if it had been flagged.

James Harold "Stormy" Mangham (ca. 1907–1974), who bought land southeast of town in 1932 to pasture his horses, was also delighted by the new electric service. Stormy taught himself to fly in a World War I jenny in the 1920s. He flew a lighted sign for Mrs. Baird's Bakery and flew for the Internal Revenue Service to spot stills from the air during Prohibition. In 1928 he latched on with Texas Air Transport, the forerunner of American Airlines, and flew for American until he retired in 1966. On his property east of Walker Branch and west of present Cardinal Lane he designed his home in 1938 in the shape of an airplane. It was one of the first houses in the area with an all-electric kitchen. The white stucco exterior was later replaced with brick.

Americans were more trusting in pre-World War II times. Bart May was working in Smithfield in 1940 and renting land some distance out of town for his cows. Driving back from feeding them, he picked up a man who, in the course of casual conversation, stated that he had a little farm in Smithfield that he wanted to sell. May observed that he had two houses in Poly that he was willing to sell. The stranger proposed that they swap without either party seeing any of the properties. May agreed, shook the man's hand, and drove on to the courthouse in Fort Worth, where the two closed the deal. The Smithfield farm was fenced, with a house, windmill, and barn, and it was a perfect home for the cows.

Perry Booth—played baseball for Birdville, 1920.

One new citizen, however, did not always inspire trust. Henry Clay Allison was born in Hood County in 1896, served as a private in the U.S. Army in World War I, briefly attended a chiropractor school in California, and settled in Smithfield in the mid-1930s. He presented himself as a doctor. He opened a chiropractic clinic in Fort Worth and the so-called Smithfield Springs Health Farm near his homestead just south of present Starnes Boulevard near Century Drive in the Century Oaks addition. He launched the village's first newspaper in 1939, the weekly Smithfield Springs Bulletin, in which he made endorsements in the Democratic primaries, ran columns about the area's history, and carried ads from area merchants, e.g. Walter Fitch's grocery in Bedford (which asked 68 cents for 24 pounds of Bewley's Best Flour). For a time he broadcast news, northeast Tarrant County school programs, and miscellaneous programs every Sunday on radio station KFJZ, claiming that it gave Smithfield widespread publicity. He bought houses and lots in the area. He instigated the Northeast Tarrant Civic League in 1941.

The newspaper was titled Smithfield Springs because that was the name of the "health farm" Allison operated. The spring on the grounds reputedly had healing waters that aided those who were ailing, who needed to get away from it all, and who had good prospects for recov-

Dr. H. C. Allison

Allison's Enterprises

ery. There were hiking paths, playgrounds, and a herd of registered Jerseys to provide milk and milk products for the patrons. This public image differed somewhat from the reality, which was that many of the participants were mentally ill, while others were alcoholics, and that there was no tangible program to cure them. Their presence was assured by a high fence and by county subsidies. A common threat by parents who were angry at their children, from at least the late 1930s into the 1950s, was to send them to "Dr. Allison's Crazy House." Whether he had a license to operate it is not known.

In 1941 he launched a maladroit campaign to rename the town "Smithfield Springs." The name "Smithfield," he asserted, was often confused with "Smithville," in Central Texas. Moreover, every community that is famous is known for something, he thought, and the healing waters of the Smithfield Springs health "resort" would put the place on the map. The radio broadcasts and newspaper emanated from Smithfield Springs. Allison believed he should be running the community, but most of the old line families in the 1930s and 1940s resented his pushiness.

All parties tried to get along. Old-timer G. M. Autrey (1863–1946), who had lived in Smithfield since 1870, was interviewed by the Bulletin. Home Demonstration Club meetings were advertised. Snider's Grocery and Market advertised its Gold Chain Flour and fresh meat. But it was an uneasy relationship from the beginning. Allison's paper referred to opponents of the Civic League, and the selection of Mickey Hurley to head it, as "back-biters" and "stumbling blocks." The February 7, 1941, issue labeled those who opposed the community name change as "sullen and sulking" in their "obstinacy" and as "aristocratic ladies" trying to block progress. It was an ill omen for the future.

WAR AND POST-WAR GROWTH

Smithfield's population in the 1930s remained at about what it had been at the turn of the century, but World War II stimulated a spurt of growth in town. The Texas Almanac estimated that Smithfield's population increased from 137 with nine businesses in 1936 to 250 with 15 businesses in 1941–1942. The population numbered 350 or more, if one counted the Smithfield community as a whole. And now there were available jobs nearby that paid more than farming, e.g. working at Fort Worth's Consolidated Vultee Aircraft (later Convair, General Dynamics, and Lockheed-Martin). Better known at the time as the "bomber plant," the factory near Lake Worth opened in April 1942 and built some 3,000 B-24 Liberators and other aircraft. Eagle Mountain Air Base and Fort Worth Army Air Field (later Carswell) also employed hundreds of civilians and purchased food and supplies from area farmers and businessmen.

Charlie Ed Turner (1916–1992), two years out of high school, succeeded his father as postmaster. He was called into the Army, so his wife Imogene and his father ran the post office. One day his dad was calling out the names of those in the building who had received mail when he received a telegram himself. The Army notified him that Charlie Ed was missing in action with the 30th Infantry Division in Europe. It was a sad day for the town, but Charlie Ed was a prisoner of war who returned in 1945 and resumed the postmastership. Others who served included E. E. Parkman, a Seabee with two tours of duty in the South Pacific, J. C.

The Smithfield Home Demonstration Club members contributed to the community with programs on canning, sewing, etc.: First row-Mrs. Maggie Gilbert, Mrs. Louise Brown, Mrs. Sis Whisenand, Mrs. T. C. Bell, Mrs. Halcie Brown, Mrs. Ina Turner, Mrs. E. C. Montague; Second Row-Mrs. Jessie Scott, Mrs. Nancy Scott, Mrs. Imogene Gilbert, Mrs. Aline Shivers, Mrs. Dick Lewis, Mrs. E. F. Crites; Third Row-Mrs. Lahawn, Mrs. Edna Hightower, Mrs. Oleta Lewis, Miss Maria Lahawn, Mrs. Etta Shivers.

Parkman, a B-17 pilot with some 40 missions over Germany, and Leon Wiseman, who took Army ski training at a time it looked like Norway might be a second front. Johnny Rumfield served in the Army Air Corps and was known as "Rumfield from Smithfield."

B. C. Redding enlisted but was rejected for service because an old injury from a plumbing job made one leg slightly longer than the other. B. C. bought the old blacksmith shop, remodeled its hull into a grocery store, and set himself up in business. He also helped build airplanes for a time at the bomber plant. Crusty, witty, "Uncle Burney," as many knew him, was also a noted repairman.

Other Smithfield entrepreneurs who benefited were Foy Abbott and Earl Newman. During the war Foy turned from hauling gravel to searching for it by walking the hills and creeks. There was a huge demand for concrete, and Foy formed his own company in 1944. In 1947 he merged with his friend Newman and organized Abbott and Newman Sand and Gravel. They eventually maintained two plants and employed more than 50 workers before selling out to Gifford Hill Concrete in 1961.

Free weekly movies were shown in Smithfield during the war years and perhaps before and afterward. They were shown outdoors in the evenings. People brought quilts and sheets to sit on. Mostly westerns, they were financed by the sale of popcorn and candy. Leonard Brothers Department Store in Fort Worth provided the movies and owned the concessions.

The ninth grade was restored in 1943, and the tenth in 1944, by which year the school had about 135 pupils and five teachers. The students were active in the wartime efforts of the day. The school's older boys, aided by men in the community, brought in 40 tons of scrap iron one Sunday after church. The school helped the community oversubscribe its $10,000 quota in the

Mrs. Edna Hightower, Mrs. Jessie Scott, Mrs. E. F. Crites, Mrs. Etta Shivers, Mrs. Ina Turner, Mrs. Maggie Gilbert (seated)

Courtesy of Ella Walker Turner

Ed Walker's Filling Station on Main Street in early Smithfield

fourth war loan by setting as a definite goal enough bonds to buy a jeep, 25 hospital beds, and other equipment. Students canvassed every house in the community for scrap paper, collecting more than 2,000 pounds. They gathered up nine hundred pounds of scrap rubber and more than two hundred worn out tires to ship to the reclamation station. Smithfield School was commended for its war participation record by the state superintendent of schools, but in the 1950s it was reduced to six grades.

Lunches were fifteen cents a week in the 1940s. Dorothy Null Parker recalls that "Some of the girls helped make sauerkraut by mashing up the cabbage in large wooden barrels with a baseball bat. What fun the FDA would have with that today." Extensive repairs were required on the school in 1945, but the gym was big enough for all classes to move into. Those who were able to complete high school usually went on to Birdville or Carter Riverside, whichever had room for the Smithfield kids.

Charles (1908–1976) and Martha (1913–1968) Null moved to a farm three-fourths of a mile west of town in 1937, on what is now the Fox Hollow addition in the southwest quadrant of Smithfield Road and Chapman Road. This was the site of the 1885 cotton gin, and the well was 16 feet across and fed by three springs. Through most of the 1940s modern conveniences had not yet arrived. Light was provided by coal oil lamps. The weekly wash was performed at the well in a huge cast iron pot with water hand drawn from the well and heated over a wood fire. The detergent was a concoction of lye, grease, and ashes. The iron for the clothes was heated on the coal oil stove in the house. The concrete foundation slabs for the old gin are still there on a vacant lot.

Courtesy of Myrene Montgomery Sanders

The Walter N. Autrey family of Smithfield, 1943; Back Row–Ruby Lee, O. S., Billie Louise, Cantrell, May Jean, Mary Helen, Mildred; Front Row–Etha Mae Autrey (mother), Walter Johnson Jr. (Ruby Lee's son) and Walter N. Autrey (father).

The Cotton Belt, now part of the Southern Pacific system, kept on running for a few years after the war. As late as 1947 three southbound trains, some with as many as 56 cars, stopped daily. One was the Blue Streak, which departed at 9:01 P.M. every night. Two northbound trains stopped every evening, though one had to be flagged. But scheduled service ended after 60 years. By 1949 the connections were irregular and soon thereafter disappeared. The automobile culture took over.

Many families hung onto their farms, but sent members into Fort Worth to secure paying jobs. Dozens worked at Convair aircraft. A connection was made between the plant and Smithfield by a Convair personnel manager, L. E. Adams. L. E. and Beth

Courtesy of Hattie Helm West

Quilting Bee 1940s; standing-Faye Hudler, Hattie West, Mae Turner, Mrs. O'Dell, Imogene Gilbert, Kathryn (Morrow) Autrey; seated-Virgie Estill, Pat Baldwin, Billie Wolf, Pauline Morrow, Mary Johnson.

Adams led the revival singing at Smithfield Baptist Church even before they decided to move to Smithfield after World War II. He was naturally disposed to hire many of his friends and neighbors in Smithfield as the plant expanded during the Cold War-Korean War era of the 1950s. Convair and other paying jobs brought a prosperity that the area had never known, visibly demonstrated as area farmers began taking vacations and buying cars and refrigerators. The Adamses also had a positive impact on attendance and money at Smithfield Baptist Church, until they and their followers left after a factional dispute in 1956.

Barber Cobb remained on the job, cutting everyone's hair straight up the sides and rather short. He was in the cattle business, too. People would drive up to the shop with a cow or two in a trailer, wanting to sell. Cobb might leave a customer in a chair, half finished, and go out and dicker with the seller for several minutes. If a deal was struck, Cobb would pull out a wad of cash, pay the seller, and tell him to deliver the animals to his lot in town.

The Masonic Lodge almost lost its charter in 1946 because of declining membership and the neglect of its building. The lower floor was rented out to help defray expenses, first as a general store, then as a garage. But an influx of new membership helped revitalize the civic group. In 1947 the lodge received permission to change its name from Grand Prairie to Smithfield, keeping its number, 455. Most lodges bear the name of their hometowns, and, of course, the existence of the nearby town of Grand Prairie made it confusing for the lodge to use that name. The building was remodeled in 1958 with the addition of a kitchen, dining room, and bath; air-conditioning and heating were added years later.

The population growth of the early war years was not sustained. It leveled off at about 250 until the mid-1950s. The number of businesses actually declined to nine in 1943–1944, then to four for the next decade. Perhaps more importantly, after the harsh challenges of the Depression and war, the community seemed to lose some of its closeness after 1945.

A COMMUNITY OR A TOWN?

Dawson Davis, a lawyer, and his family moved to Smithfield in 1947 and was immediately consulted by many in the community about the antiquated, "crank type" telephone sys-

Courtesy of Johnny Rumfield

B. C. Redding Store-Johnny Rumfield and Jimmy Ray Scott, Spring 1947

tem. He helped replace the old system with "city telephones." A group of residents also consulted him about the water situation, since many families were still hauling it from the school well. A mass meeting was held in the school gym, during which Davis and Joe Rady, an engineer, explained that the community would have to hold an election to incorporate, which was necessary to achieve power of contract with water companies.

Incorporation was approved in the community, October 20, 1951, by the less than overwhelming margin of 41 to 36. A petition to incorporate was approved by the County Commissioners' court, November 1, 1951, signed by many of the old-line families in Smithfield, e.g. the Sniders, Usserys, Meachams, Bells, Reddings, Abbotts, and Zartmans. For a couple of years the city governing body met in the homes of various members, then a modest city hall was constructed on Main Street with voluntary donations and labor. Charles Zartman (1895–1976), an Ohio oilman who had moved to Smithfield in 1928, was the first elected mayor, and Davis was the town attorney.

On Thanksgiving Day, 1952, a huge fire blown by a north wind swept an area five miles long and a mile wide, including the hill on which Northeast Tarrant County Junior College now stands as well as the University Plaza and Richland Oaks neighborhoods. Volunteers from Smithfield, Birdville, and Hurst rushed over with buckets of water, wet tow sacks, and house brooms. The wind ceased at nightfall, and the fire was finally doused. Smithfield, never completely rebuilt after the 1930 blaze, was now determined to take action. The next month about twenty people met in the school gym, and B. C. Redding and railroad worker Jack Gray were among those who took the initiative in organizing the Smithfield Fire Department. It was officially established in January 1953, with the Haltom City fire chief as advisor.

Community donations of $2,250 purchased a 1941 Ford fire truck from Olney, Texas. It was an old Army truck with a 500-gallon-per-minute pumper. "Old Red" was impractical

Smithfield Lodge, pictured on left. Smithfield Feed & Seed on right, 1975

to use in fighting grass fires, but it would carry the bucket and tow sack brigade to the scene. "Old Red" was vital in dealing with bigger fires; the pumper helped extinguish one fire that started on Amundson Street, burned one house, and spread almost to the Baptist Church.

Street picnics helped bring newcomers into the community and paid for most of the cost of buildings, trucks, and maintenance. The Smithfield band would preside over dancing, and various contests enlivened the festivities. The biggest picnic was a barbecue and political rally June 12, 1954. Twenty-nine candidates, including Jim Wright waging his first congressional campaign, spoke in front of the partially constructed, two-story city hall and fire house. The building on Main Street was soon finished, and two more trucks were added in the next five years. Only one truck was partially paid for with tax money, and that was less than $2,000. The last truck was literally put together bit by bit over a 13-month stretch by volunteers who worked nights and weekends for about a third of the cost of a similar factory-built truck.

Jack Gray was elected chief of the volunteer, unpaid group of firefighters. A button in Redding's store could set off the siren in the fire station, while a committee of women were given firemen's telephone numbers to call. Upon pushing the siren button, Redding, who served the Fire Department 23 years, would race to the station, leaving any poor customer who might be shopping in charge of the store. The Smithfield Firemen's Ladies Auxiliary would take coffee and sandwiches to the men if the fire was of long duration. The auxiliary also constituted a pumper team itself, in case no men were available when fire broke out.

Watauga and Chapman roads were still gravel in the early 1950s, but the other main arteries had asphalt by then. One sign of encroaching civilization was the establishment and paving of FM Road 1938 from the Keller-Grapevine Road to the Grapevine Highway in 1956–1957. This was dubbed the Smithfield Highway (named Davis Boulevard in 1960), which supplanted the old unnamed dirt road that ran by the Shivers and Rumfield farms, intercepted and replaced old Smithfield Road just south of its crossing with Watauga Road, straightened out the old "S" curve, and terminated at Four Points. Growth resumed in the mid-1950s. The 1954–1955 Texas Almanac estimated that Smithfield had 350 people and eight businesses.

One surprising development was the building of a private airfield southeast of town. Stormy Mangham opened his airport

Smithfield Feed & Seed, store front, 1975

in 1954, between Cardinal Road and Walker Branch. It was a commercial operation, but also a place for him to store his airplanes. His wife Clara and son Charles were also fliers, and Charles was the airport manager. A hangar was built for a hundred planes and sometimes twice that number were on hand.

Courtesy of Vera Abbott Redding

The First Pumper Team, Smithfield Volunteer Fire Department, Roy Buck Hewitt, Melton Rhine, Andy Knight, R. W. Koonze, Chief Jack Gray and Marvin Crane in 1953.

Five men who were members of the Church of Christ, interested in Christian education and somewhat fearful of growing secularization, formed a corporation in August 1957, for the purpose of establishing a Christian school and donated a campus site free of charge. Foy Abbott, Earl Newman, R. H. Banowsky, Clint Price, and Huey Northcutt, through their corporation, took an option on a 212-acre tract west of Smithfield Road and south of Watauga Road (present Mid-Cities Boulevard). Donating 40 acres to the school for its campus, the men planned a residential development on the remaining land. The idea was that some 400 to 500 Christian families would live close together as one community. The corporation even turned over its profits from the sales of the lots and houses to the school. The campus was built, and grades one through eight opened in the fall of 1958. Grades were eventually added through the junior college level. In addition to secular studies, students were required to study the Bible each day and attend daily chapel services. The school offers classes from kindergarten through high school today. The homes were slower to be erected than the campus, since they had to await utilities and general improvements, but the College Hill Addition began with W. A. Ledbetter's house in 1958.

Meanwhile, Mayor Zartman, Councilman Foy Abbott, Fire Chief Gray, Secretary-Treasurer Martha Gray, town attorney Davis, and perhaps others, decided in 1956 and 1957 to expand Smithfield's tax base out into the countryside to the north and west, to start building a larger and more populous community, and avoid being annexed by nearby Hurst. There was no one among them, of course, with the expertise and experience of a modern city manager, and their reach exceeded their grasp. Some of the farmers who signed on were not qualified voters. Some may have been placed on the tax rolls prematurely.

Annexation by Hurst was, in fact, a very real possibility in some strips north of town. Indeed, in February 1957, residents of a two-mile wide area petitioned Smithfield for annexation to prevent becoming part of Hurst. One of the leaders of the move, Mrs. Carl Goerte Jr., lived three miles north of Smithfield. She noted that Hurst could not provide utilities for

At the time NRH annexed Smithfield, the volunteer firemen who personally owned the fire equipment would not let NRH have their equipment for "nothing" and parked the fire trucks in Zartman Park.

the area and that "we go to church in Smithfield, we take our dry cleaning there, and some of our neighbors work in stores there." Smithfield and most other towns in northeast Tarrant County were general law towns that could annex territory only by petition of a majority of property owners in the area. But Hurst, like Fort Worth and Haltom City, had become a home rule city (in December 1956)—it could take over territory without permission of the residents.

THE BATTLE OF SMITHFIELD

The mid-cities border wars revolved mostly around Hurst, whose city officials were naturally upset that their anticipated southern expansion had been blocked by Fort Worth's elongated extension to Greater Southwest Field (later Amon Carter field). Hurst moved rapidly, but Euless reacted with its own annexations. Bedford incorporated in 1953 out of fear of being swallowed up by Hurst or Euless. Southlake hastily incorporated in September 1956 to stave off Hurst. Grapevine, Southlake, Colleyville, and North Richland Hills, as well as Smithfield, were petitioned by residents who, because of proximity, preferred one of them to Hurst. Some of the petitioners' lands had been annexed by Hurst. Rising tensions prompted a conference of nearly a hundred officials from 13 neighboring towns, which convened in February 1957, to work out the difficulties. In the midst of the turbulent gathering, Hurst Mayor W. E. Vincent, a real estate developer, presided briefly and blamed Fort Worth for beginning the encroachments. Then the mayor added, "That's right, another greedy city to the west of us acted first, and . . . " Laughter drowned out his words. After Vincent asserted that Hurst was not grabbing land but just trying to protect everyone's interests, he was bombard-

Fort Worth Christian School Campus. The campus was built, and grades one through eight opened in the fall of 1958. The College Hill Addition began with W. A. Ledbetter's house in 1958.

ed with a wave of moans. Bedford Mayor David Sloan shouted, "How does that shoe taste by now? You've had it in your mouth all night." When Vincent stood fast on Hurst's annexations, the representatives of 12 towns stormed out of Hurst's First Baptist Church, denouncing the Hurst officials. By 1958 Hurst, which had attained a respectable size, reversed its untenable policy, and deannexed several disputed areas.

Regarding the tracts north of Smithfield, Hurst City Attorney Rex McEntire announced that Hurst would probably give up any territory that it had claimed under first reading if another community wanted it. Actually, Hurst had accidentally included a portion of Smithfield in its claim; if Hurst had not cut across Smithfield's boundary, Hurst could have ignored Smithfield's desires. As it was, Hurst agreed to release the tracts to Smithfield.

Smithfield also annexed land and farms south, east, and west of the old town. Davis estimated that Smithfield's population had grown to 2,500 or 3,000. But many citizens on the north side came to the conclusion in a few months that the threat from Hurst had either never existed or had become negligible. Many formed the Rural Rights Association, retained a lawyer, and filed a deannexation suit. The RRA was established in July, with J. C. Carroll Jr.

Courtesy of American Airlines

Grand opening of Greater Fort Worth International Airport/Amon Carter Field, 1953. Later Greater Southwest International Airport.

as president. The lawsuit was filed in his name and that of fifty-two others, most of whom lived in the Keller School District.

At this point H. C. Allison strode into the public limelight again. His 177-acre farm had been annexed. Having long since abandoned the Smithfield Springs Bulletin, he relaunched his newspaper career with the Smithfield Signal in the autumn of 1957. His avowed purposes were to support the RRA, disincorporate Smithfield entirely, and restore a virtually tax-free country life for the local citizenry. He noted that North Richland Hills had ready cash from building permits and utility service assessments but had no city tax.

The 48th District Court upheld Smithfield's annexations in October 1957, but Smithfield's leaders came to the conclusion that the irate northside farmers were a threat to the community. Allison delighted in observing that the RRA's protests had reached the point that on December 9, 1957, the Smithfield City Council forced itself—unanimously—to deannex four half-mile country areas to the north and west of town to rid themselves of the RRA's hostile voters. He compared the town's machinations to Huey Long's political machine in Louisiana. The town's big-shot bosses, he charged, were cutting their losses and were now desperately trying to stave off abolition of the town government. While Allison blew it out of proportion, it was all true, except there is no proof of Allison's additional charge that the town deliberately collected some countryside taxes, knowing that they were illegal.

Allison made some valid points in the December 1957 issue of the Signal:

"Suppose a farmer, leaving a small village, drives through . . . four miles . . . of open farmland to get to his farm home, and learns that he cannot build a residence on his own farm without first obtaining permission of a half dozen citizens of that village and, further, that permission is not obtainable unless the proposed residence has 'a livable area' (exclusive of closets, hallways, etc.) of more than 750 square feet because of a 'law'—what happens to that man's respect for law?"

Allison was identifying a problem, of course, and an ongoing conflict that had long plagued American towns and farmers. Most towns grandfathered those being annexed, tolerating otherwise outlawed practices for the lifetimes of particular dwellers, but some towns were more adroit at it than others. Smithfield's town fathers hadn't thought it through and were making needless enemies.

Five years of taxes, Allison charged, had resulted only in part of a fire truck and an unfinished jail. Keller, Colleyville, and North Richland Hills had no taxes, Richland Hills had only a $ .25 per $100 valuation of property, while Smithfield had a one-dollar tax.

The incumbents running for their third terms defended their record in a mailing, signed by others so that it would look as though it came from supportive voters. The taxes helped support the water system, streetlights, and some of the money for fire trucks. Fire insurance rates had been lowered, they claimed. A garbage disposal service was in place. And the curfew ordinance and speed limits had reduced mischievousness. There was a hint that the volunteer firefighters might walk out if the city charter was abolished. But as Allison and others promptly noted, most in Smithfield still depended solely on well water, and fire insurance rates declined only if one lived within 500 feet of one of the few fire plugs. Most of Smithfield was without streetlights, and the $9 a month lighting bill could be paid for from utility revenues. The city marshal supposedly enforcing curfews and speed limits faced a hopeless task in the sprawling village, Allison argued, and the garbage disposal service was private and was not a city service. And true community volunteers would not threaten to walk off their posts.

The incumbents would have done better to sign their own letter, make note of the unpaid years of service that most of them had contributed, and try to educate the voters about the justification for building codes and the inevitability of towns and services in the Dallas-Fort Worth area, which they could try to slow down and control. They needed to better advertise the efforts of Dawson Davis and Fred Ross, the founder of the Smithfield

Civic League, who put in many unpaid hours just trying to persuade a water company to enter the town. They needed something a little more catchy and relevant than their supporters' campaign pitch printed in the Northeast Times, March 29, 1958: "Any dead fish can swim downstream; it takes a live one to swim upstream."

A five-person "people's ticket," vociferously backed by Allison, challenged the old leadership in the April 1, 1958, town elections. They pledged to abolish the salaries of the city marshal and city secretary-treasurer, fire the town attorney, repeal the tax ordinance, and get rid of the jail. What the candidates wanted, and what Allison promised everyone they could have, was the virtual abolition of the town. If the "people's" slate won, the town government could be scaled back and the current town charter retained. If the incumbents retained their offices, Allison wrote, the 270-voter petition requesting the county judge to call an election to abolish the city charter would be submitted—but not until a plan was in place to reincorporate Smithfield into a quiet, nontaxable village that could not be annexed by any other town.

One of Allison's problems was his extreme rhetoric. "Boss" Davis headed the little coterie of "evil minds." Mayor Zartman "spews his venom . . . like a snake that has been injured." The "corrupt" regime was compared to the Communists overseas. Another opponent was compared to cannibals.

School taxes were also a topic of much conversation in 1957. Allison noted, probably correctly, that school taxes in the tiny Smithfield district were about the same as Birdville's, but that the Birdville school was far superior in equipment and instruction. The Smithfield school had lost its higher grades, and the School Board had contracted with Birdville to educate Smithfield's high school students for $75 per pupil, but obviously Smithfield was vulnerable to a change of mind on the part of the Birdville School Board. Consolidation with Birdville was the only solution, but, Allison said, the "smug and defiant" Smithfield board was holding off. In another article in the same issue of the paper, Allison claimed the Smithfield board realized the problem, and was willing to call a merger vote. Also, Allison charged, the schools were being dragged into politics since one teacher, Jack Gray's wife Martha, was also the town's secretary-treasurer. Tax money, he observed incorrectly, was "being paid to the same person from two sources: the school and the city." Smithfield citizens did in fact vote, June 14, 1957, to abolish their own district and join Birdville's by 194 to 14. Two weeks later a bond issue was approved, raising school taxes from $1.10 per $100 valuation of property to $1.20. (Teachers, by the way, still drove school buses. Some math classes tried to stay very quiet so that Mr. Smoot, tired from waking early to drive the bus route, would doze off.) The school district merger was handled smoothly, without any constructive help from Allison.

In the city elections, however, poor Smithfield faced a choice between good-willed incumbents of marginal competence in governing abilities but with a vision of an urban future, who clearly bungled their arguments on behalf of preserving the township, and good-willed challengers who mistakenly thought they could preserve their country lives and were led by a demagogue who had his own secret plan for Smithfield. The bunglers won. Out of 380 votes the "people's ticket" lost all five contested races, albeit by narrow margins.

Immediately thereafter Allison, after denouncing the election as rigged, presented a petition to the county judge. Containing the signatures of far more than the required 100 eligible voters, it asked for an election on May 24, 1958, to dissolve the town. The Smithfield Signal assured its readers that the vote to abolish would return the town to a quiet and peaceful rural community. He admitted that the Richland Oaks neighborhood, far south of town on the Bedford Road, east of Davis, wanted to be annexed to North Richland Hills, but the rest of Smithfield would retain its name and its lifestyle. He said nothing about his repeated appearances at the meetings of the North Richland Hills Civic League.

The opposition Northeast Times, which Allison denounced as a "city-sponsored rag," warned that "if the city of Smithfield is abolished, the community can be annexed by a home rule city." The Times was published bimonthly for awhile, from the east side of Snider's store, by Dolores Fuchs and Frances Smoot, both of whom had husbands who were members of the volunteer Fire Department.

In this second campaign, Allison appeared to lose control. The volunteer firefighters were labeled as "fanatic fire worshippers," and the community needed to remain "attractive to white citizens wanting to live and rear their children in an all-white community." Finally, Allison charged, "The principles of AMERICANISM have recently been challenged in Smithfield as in many other communities since Communism has infiltrated into the churches and some other organizations." His opponents, he railed, "are infected with the Communist idea. They will deceive, lie, cheat, and murder when the end warrants."

Smithfield voted 201 to 193 to disincorporate. Allison changed the next issue of his paper to the North Richland Hills Signal. There was no more blather about the Smithfield name or a plan to stave off annexation, but he continued to lash out at the Communist infestation in Smithfield's "city government, fire department, churches, and other organizations."

Allison soon transferred his energy to working with the North Richland Hills Civic League in persuading folks in the southern reaches of old Smithfield, in half-mile swathes of territory, that they should petition to join the burgeoning town to the south. It would increase land values, he argued, including his own, and the annexations did in fact increase the value of property in Smithfield.

At this juncture in local history, as late as 1957, if Smithfield had come up with able political leaders, offering political leadership comparable to the economic leadership of L. E. Adams, it might be a town today. By linking with burgeoning North Richland Hills, Smithfield soon put aside its deep community division and eventually became an integral part of a city destined to become the third largest in Tarrant County. The two towns were a natural fit in that Smithfield needed the dynamic leadership and the police protection (established in 1960) of North Richland Hills, while North Richland Hills needed Smithfield's Fire Department, the railroad right-of-way as a possible industrial tax base, and its countryside for expansion. Smithfield was unable to handle its own expansion, and, as events later proved, North Richland Hills was almost unable to handle it either.

Early Homes of North Richland Hills, 1920s to 1940s

Hightower/Autrey house at 6725 Smithfield Road. Jimmy Hightower probably built this house for his son, L. A. Hightower, around 1880. This was the home of L. A. Hightower until 1918 when the Bud Autrey family purchased it. This house is one of the oldest in the Smithfield area. Photo taken 1998.

Shivers home, Smithfield Road, 1925, presently Davis Boulevard.

Smathers home/Holiday Lane and Chapman Road, 1940s.

Owned by E. P. Haltom, later by W. A. and Ruth Blessing on Glenview Drive, across the street from current Linda Spurlock Park.

Native rock house located on Scruggs Drive and Harmonson Road. Built by Jack Holder, Tiny Anderson, Herbert Walker, Finas Buckingham, and Jackson Himes in the late 1940s.

THE BOOMING, BUSTLING CITY
GROWING PAINS

In 1958 Thomas McFarland, an entrepreneur, edged Clyde Zellers, an insurance man, in the mayor's race, 122 to 118. No incumbents were defeated, but only Paul Kutilek was left on the council from the men who had launched the expansion of the town. Clarence Jones favored McFarland, but North Richland Hills factions seemed united on the leading issue of the day—absorbing Smithfield. The city government and residents were also united in delight that the state was widening and resurfacing the Grapevine Highway and Texas 183. Both roads, as the Richland Review put it in August 1958, would "provide speedy access to downtown and other sections of Fort Worth as well as to the North Side and Love Field districts of Dallas." No city administration in Northeast Tarrant County at that time had any inkling of its future transportation problems. The speedy access was about as short-lived as the Richland Review. The North Richland Hills city government was divid-

ed physically. The City Council rented the civic building at Glenview and Morgan Circle for its meetings, while city secretary Laura Ray and Mayor McFarland, 1958–1959, continued to maintain their offices at the Richardson Center on Grapevine Highway.

Mayor McFarland and the council in 1958 were the first to be presented with a large-scale request for a professional police force. Jack Bean (president of the Haltom-Richland Chamber of Commerce), Paul Mason, Ray Lofland, and Jim Norman (Birdville School Board president) spoke for some fifty citi-

First paid Police Department with Mayor Clyde Zellers, 1960

zens in calling for the establishment of a police department. Henry Allison spoke in opposition, averring that there was no real need. The administration took no action.

North Richland Hills city officials were determined to keep growing through annexation. The population had surpassed the 5,000 mark, which meant that the city could legally dispose of its original general law charter and adopt a home-rule charter. Annexations would no longer require consent from the parties being annexed and would not be limited to half-mile strips. On February 25, 1959, Mayor McFarland appointed Lloyd Reeder as chairman of a charter writing committee, which included Clarence Jones, Haly Parchman, Cullen Turner, John Hay, and Clyde Zellers among its members. But the move was temporarily derailed by political problems.

Englishman Sir Ernest Benn once defined politics as the art of looking for trouble, finding it everywhere, diagnosing it wrongly, and applying unsuitable remedies. It seemed for a time as if North Richland Hills was determined to live down to Sir Ernest's definition. The disincorporation of Smithfield triggered lawsuits, 1958–1960, but North Richland Hills began annexing half-mile strips of land that had traditionally been considered part of the Smithfield community. The second, third, and final readings for three half-mile strips were accomplished in one council meeting, November 10, 1958. Many Smithfield residents, led by Allison, supported taxless North Richland Hills, abandoning Smithfield and its property tax. Others embraced North Richland Hills reluctantly, preferring it to Hurst. Others held out.

Henry Allison apparently believed he could dominate North Richland Hills much as he had Smithfield. He began by attempting to establish financial support for his newspaper, with the idea of making himself a media and political star. Knowing that the Civic League appreciated his services in the Smithfield annexation, he blithely proposed to the League in February 1959 that it appoint a committee to solicit advertising in order to support a nonprofit North Richland Hills newspaper. After some discussion a committee was established, not to solicit ads but to study the basic issue of becoming involved in the newspaper business (and embracing Allison). At the next meeting the committee recommended that the League "not venture into an enterprise too controversial for a civic association." The League was already gifted, or afflicted, with enough would-be leaders and saw no reason to anoint the erratic Allison.

Never one to be put down easily, Allison then filed for mayor in the April 7, 1959 election, against Bill Perry, who was backed by Clarence Jones and other established leaders in North Richland Hills. Perry defeated Allison 347 to 129. Fifty-three voters cast write-in ballots for Mayor McFarland, who had made it clear that he was not a candidate.

Allison probably could not have taken office even if he had won. The annexation of the heart of Smithfield was challenged by 226 of the old town's residents in April, 1959, and Smithfield did win a court decision holding that its annexation was illegal. North Richland Hills was staved off for a time, but Smithfield citizens feared that their unincorporated village would again be annexed and felt they had no choice but to petition for incorporation. In another close election at the fire hall, the community revealed that it was still deeply divided. In this final battle, February 1960, incorporation failed 107 to 94. On April 18, 1960, upon petition of over half the registered voters in the last two half-mile strips in Smithfield, the remainder of the old town was annexed. (The action added some 1,200 to 1,500 persons to the official 1960 North Richland Hills population of 8,623, but the census deadline was April 1.)

Had Allison been elected and somehow seated in office, political tumult would doubtless have continued, but that is what happened anyway with the election of Perry. Some city matters, however, were handled in a normal manner during the Perry administration.

In August 1959, Walter Smith was awarded a license to operate a night patrol, providing the town with two night watch patrols. But at almost the same time newspapers published unfavorable articles about the town's other security operator. A citizens' delegation appeared before the City Council and asked for J. M. Shelton's removal, describing him as unnecessarily rough and verbally abusive. Several witnesses charged him with carrying a gun, driving a car with police insignia, and stopping and harassing drivers, although he lacked authority to do any of these things. Shelton was a fearless little man with a checkered background who yearned to be police chief. He was placed on probation in August and was criticized again at the September council meeting. One of his few defenders stated that since he employed Shelton and the critics did not, that they had no right to complain, and added that most teenagers needed pushing. Sheriff H. "Punch" Wright had recommended to a group of councilmen that they name Shelton as their police chief. Perhaps to make amends, the sheriff's office placed a full-time deputy in town, for which the Civic League sent a letter of thanks. Shelton died in October.

In December 1959, with the annexation of Smithfield seemingly complete, North Richland Hills purchased the old town's fire fighting equipment for $6,000. The city pledged that the money would be expended for civic improvements in Smithfield and that a fire station would always be maintained in the Smithfield area. In protest to the annexation, Smithfield's volunteer firefighters held the equipment hostage for several days in Zartman Park. In the council minutes the primary assets are simply listed as 1940, 1948, and 1955 Ford Fire Trucks, but that hardly did justice to them as a rolling fire museum. The 1940 vehicle had begun as a three-quarter-ton military weapons carrier, and for a time it had to be pushed off before it would start. The 1948 vehicle was a converted Falstaff Beer truck, and the 1955 Ford had been a hearse. Smithfield's part-time volunteer force continued to man the department for years.

Tarrant County Water Supply Corp. receipt dated 6/23/61

Primarily, the Perry administration was marked by unusual conflict. Only in office a few weeks, Perry began refusing to entertain motions from council members. With relations strained, and in the absence of the mayor, the council voted in October 1959 to purchase the Tarrant Utility Company, then join with neighboring towns in forming the nonprofit Tarrant County Water Supply Corporation. The city was allying with others in northeast Tarrant County to form a new water-sewage facility, but Perry and Clarence Jones were bitterly opposed. Fear of too much expansionism and ultimate higher taxes appears to have been their main motive. The three majority councilmen, led by Clyde Zellers, overrode Perry's two allies by parliamentary procedures, and also made their displeasure with Perry manifest in other ways. In March 1960 one councilman resolved that city funds be withdrawn from (Clarence Jones') Haltom City State Bank. It passed three to zero, after Perry's two allies walked out of the chamber. There was still city money there eleven months later when $10,000 was transferred to Fort Worth National.

Perry's allies on the council were defeated in the April 1960 election, by margins of about 450 to 250 in each case. From the faction opposing the TCWSC, only Perry was reelected. The mayor was legally obliged to act as a director of the fledging TCWSC, but

Old Smithfield Fire Department, now North Richland Hills Fire Department, 1975

Car dropped in open ditch in front of 5021 Nancy Lane

instead, without council consent, he filed suit in district court to have the corporation declared illegal. Perry not only lost the case, but also removed council minutes and records from city files that pertained to the TCWSC. Meanwhile, the city water supply was unstable, and by June 1960 a water rationing plan was implemented.

Other charges came to public light in Perry's impeachment trial, May 28, 1960, at North Richland Elementary School (now Mullendore). Perry had also filed questionable travel expenses, and had moved the mayor's office to the civic center and hired a part-time clerk without council consent. The prosecutor was Tom Christopher, whom Perry had tried to replace as city attorney. Christopher resigned as city attorney in May, when he moved out of town, but he accepted appointment as special counsel for the trial. The immediate result of the trial was that Mayor Pro Tem Clyde Zellers, and the City Council removed Perry from office. Ironically, while Perry's motives and tactics may not have been justified, his belief that the water supply corporation was not in the best interests of North Richland Hills was embraced by the city a decade later.

At the impeachment trial Zellers announced that an election to fill the vacancy would be called within a month. Zellers won the mayorship himself, defeating write-in candidate Carroll Morrow, 409 to 255, at the three voting boxes at the Civic Center, Starnes' service station, and a model home at Orient and Tourist Drive. All the new councilmen elected in the spring of 1960 were pledged to "progressive development," while the defeated incumbents had promised "no new taxes." While many voters did not object that their town was the only one of any size in the state without a city tax, it looked as though North Richland Hills no longer appreciated its designation as the largest town in Texas without a professional police force or fire department. Greater Richland Chamber of Commerce President Ray Lofland warned that the town was a "sitting duck" for costly fires and crime and that he was ashamed that North Richland was "sponging" off Richland Hills and Haltom City for fire and police protection. And also, as Mayor Zellers noted, "When you start breaking your axles as you drive down the streets in North Richland, you finally start thinking of ways to get some city services." Zellers also observed in a speech to the Greater Richland Hills Junior Chamber of

Perry's impeachment; Bill Perry-center-seated at table.

Fort Worth Star-Telegram

88

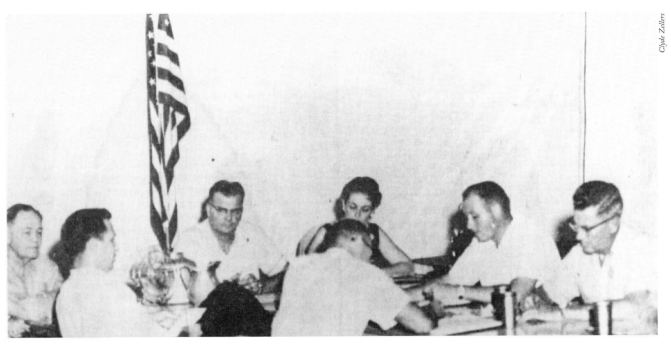

Clyde Zellers

City council members of NRH announced the city's tax program.

Commerce that if the city had instituted taxation five years earlier, "the citizens would now enjoy satisfactory programs of street and drainage improvements."

In the summer of 1960 North Richland adopted its first property tax. The rate was $0.35 per $100 valuation, based on Birdville Independent School District evaluations and collected by the BISD. Recently annexed Smithfield was exempted for a year. The tax raised $57,000 the first year and was spent on the establishment of a six-man police force with two patrol cars, a municipal court, and a fire department. Prisoners were hauled to the Richland Hills jail, which charged North Richland $1.75 per head per day. George Coe of Virginia was the first chief and lasted less than six months, until mid-January 1961, when the council and Mayor Zellers, after secretly meeting in the mayor's home, pressured him to resign for reasons unknown. The City Council meetings moved around occasionally, but the lease with the Richardson Building could not be broken. Glenn Goodnight was appointed city attorney.

The new levy did not raise enough money to deal with immediate street and drainage problems, so Mayor Zellers and the council put together a $1,350,000 bond issue, $1,220,000 of which would be plowed into street and drainage improvements. Construction of a city hall and fire station would receive $80,000 from the bonds, and $50,000 would go into parks. The street bonds came closest to passing, being crushed by a three to one margin, 1,199 to 397. The city hall-fire station request lost 1,252 to 338 and the parks 1,362 to 222. The 1,602 votes cast in the October 26th election was an all-time high. Mayor Zellers and the progressive development leaders had read half the signals correctly—people did want better services but not so desperately that they would actually pay for them.

The vote did have the effect, at least, of uniting old Smithfield, the heart of the opposition. The bonds lost in all the boxes, but the margin at the Smithfield fire hall was 20 to 1. The opponents were led by none other than Henry Allison, who monopolized the October 10th City Council meeting with a defamatory harangue. His extreme ridicule of city councilmen and Mayor Zellers predictably prompted threats of slander suits. Smithfield's streets were not as bedraggled as the rest of the city's and opposition to taxes was more deeply ingrained.

In the early months of 1961 Mayor Zellers made two of the shrewdest moves of his life. One was to call upon articulate citizens' committees to carry the burden of civic education to the voters. In January 1961 he convened a meeting of 26 members of the previously appointed Citizens' Committee for Permanent Street and Drainage Program. The mayor announced that he had tried to select a cross-section of the city for the committee, including presidents of the Jaycees, Lions Club, PTA, and other leading civic organizations (not just the old Civic League.) The mayor considered it obvious that the city needed a permanent street and drainage program rather than the constant but temporary patching of holes. Assessing all individual landowners for paving and maintaining streets along their property was discussed, but while commercial and vacant property could be assessed without the consent of the owner, homeowners could not be forced to pay. Contractors submitted higher bids when dealing with an assessment plan than a bond program because under the former the contractor could not be certain of payment. The contractors could try to foreclose on the homeowner, but it was a messy, drawn-out process.

For some weeks there were debates within the community and various appointed committees on how best to raise money for paving and repair of streets and building up the police force. The General Chairman of the Citizens' Committee, Burl Daniel Jr., a pharmacist, worked closely with the mayor and council, as did Steering Committee Chairman Jack Smith. The four study groups were Drainage and Paving, Bond Study, Assessment Study, and Tax Study. Finally around early March 1961 the Citizens' Committee revealed a preference for the bond issue route rather than front-foot assessments. They suggested city improvements that would cost an estimated $827,581, over half a million dollars less than the failed effort five months earlier. If the bonds were approved, it would mean an additional $ .17 tax per $100 valuation to back up the bonds.

Burl Daniel's committees pushed hard for the bonds, working in tandem with Mayor Zellers and the council. They noted that the increased tax rate would still be only $ .52 per $100 valuation, the lowest tax rate of any city in the county. Mayor Zellers, possibly anticipating what was coming, made his second shrewd decision in March. He quit North Richland Hills politics and entered the ministry; he announced he would not run for reelection in April. The Taxpayers League led by Joe Blake denounced the new bond effort as another attempt at needless expenditures. The educational effort had an obvious impact, but the bonds failed by the very narrow margin of 733 to 727.

Believing now that momentum was with them, the Citizens' Committee petitioned for another vote and it was called for April 15. Blake denounced it as another example of "highhanded, reckless spending." Meanwhile, bond opponents organized a slate for the mayor's post and the two open council seats. They claimed that they could make repairs on the worst streets within the current budget and without the bonds, that the bond issue was unfair since all would pay the tax increase but only a few would reside on improved streets, and that the bonds amounted to a 30-year mortgage on everyone's home. The mayoralty race was decided on April 4, and John P. Hunter was elected over four opponents on a platform opposing the bond issue. His slate won, too. Actually, the candidates who favored the bond issue garnered 300 more votes than those who were elected, but in general law towns there are no runoffs. Whoever received the most votes won the election, and the bond proponents had scattered their votes among too many candidates. It was an omen, and in the mid-April balloting the bonds were flattened 925 to 551.

North Richland Hills was paying the price for its aggressive leadership. Some of the aggressive leaders themselves, notably Clarence Jones and others like J. D. McEachern, had turned against the taxes that were seemingly necessary to support an infrastructure. Also, Smithfield had been swallowed but could not be digested. Indeed, during the bond campaign in March and April 1961, old Smithfield spokesmen led by John Hay petitioned for deannexation of everything north of Watauga Road. Hay claimed, with some justification, that it would be years before city sewage and natural gas could be brought to Smithfield and that it was a long reach for the tiny police force. Aware that a deannexed Smithfield would then be gobbled up by a neighboring town, Hay proposed that a ten-foot buffer zone around Smithfield be retained by North Richland Hills. The ubiquitous Allison, who had almost coerced Smithfield into joining North Richland, now embraced deannexation. (Allison felt so strongly about it that he voted absentee as well as in person. In their last meeting, April 10, 1961, the Zellers council voted unanimously that the city attorney prosecute Allison in county court.) The council refused the deannexation request, but ordered a committee of six to study the situation, three elected by Smithfield residents and three appointed by the council. The fierce taxpayers rebellion from within the original North Richland Hills neighborhoods, and the presence of Smithfield, which was beginning to look like a Trojan Horse, appeared to bring North Richland Hills to the verge of dismemberment.

Even its name was shaky. In the summer of 1962 Mayor Hunter appointed a committee to study the idea of changing the name of North Richland Hills. The idea had been kicked around for a decade, since North Richland Hills and Richland Hills were sometimes confused with each other. A spokesman from Richland Hills observed, "We would be very happy to see North Richland Hills get another name." Some North Richland Hills residents were unhappy that adverse flood publicity in Richland Hills affected property values in North Richland Hills. But the Greater Richland Area Chamber of Commerce was opposed because of the expense involved for businesses, schools, and churches that used North Richland Hills in their titles. A nonbinding vote was held April 2, 1963, and it was voted down 525 to 277.

Adding to the confusion of the period was the June 29, 1961, termination of the police dispatcher and one patrolman, and the July 28 dismissal, at 3 A.M. of Police Chief Johnnie Wise and his only captain. No reasons were cited except "deficiencies."

The existence of the North Richland Hills Civic League was in jeopardy, but its last act was of considerable benefit to the city. Attendance at Civic League meetings began to wane by late 1959, since the city government, complete with tax structure and open council meetings, could assume many of the League's functions. In June 1961 the League offered to sell the community center to the city as a city hall for $2,029. The city accepted on October 1, since it was practically a gift. There was a proviso in the deed that if the building ceased to be used for city offices, it would revert to the sellers. The building soon housed all city offices. After donating the remainder of its funds to the city library, the North Richland Hills Civic League disbanded.

Zoning is an ongoing challenge in nearly all communities, and North Richland Hills was no exception. The City Council adopted a comprehensive zoning ordinance in January 1958 with five general land use classifications or districts. Very few plats at that time were zoned commercial, industrial, or multifamily dwelling. Most of the city was zoned for single-family dwellings or left with an agricultural classification. There was no city planning and zoning committee, so the council was besieged by local and out-of-town developers with requests for apartment or retail designations, which are more profitable to them than single-family houses. The resulting discord was typical of newly incorporated towns, with councilmen having to hear lengthy zoning presentations and emotional pleas by neighbors who were opposed.

The home rule issue was resurrected in the winter of 1962–1963. The City Council, in a split vote in 1962, decided not to allow citizens to vote on the issue. Early in 1963 Mayor John Hunter was doing nothing for the home rule cause and was certainly no exponent of tax-and-spend policies, having been elected two years earlier in opposition to the street bonds. But the faction that opposed higher taxes and home rule distrusted him and tried to defeat him for reelection. Hunter brushed aside the challenger, but the faction did elect a new councilman.

The council implemented extremely tight financial policies that summer of 1963 by easing City Director Bill French from his position. He had been promoted to the post a year before, but now he was gone and the position's salary was slashed. City Secretary Laura Ray, a six-year veteran, had her pay cut from $400 per month to $325. And despite vocal appeals to fix the streets, the council, with Alvis Dowell dissenting, voted to hold the $ .35 per $100 valuation tax rate. The council also received the dismaying report that a bawdy house might be operating in the town, but that they could not legally pass an ordinance banning them. Anyone arrested in town and accused of operating such a house had to be turned over to the district attorney.

The council's frugal policies drove the volunteer firefighters into rebellion. For several months Fire Chief Frank Cook and others pressed the council to pay insurance coverage as well as the continuation of the usual $10 per month expense account (mostly for gasoline) for each firefighter. Some volunteers also urged the city to hire some full-time paid firemen, since the city covered about 24 square miles with 12,000 people in the fall of 1963. Councilmen finally agreed to seek insurance coverage but noted that the payments for premiums would probably come out of the $10 allowance. Beginning September 28, the volunteers refused to drive the fire trucks even in emergencies, but would fight fires if the city furnished drivers. Mayor Hunter announced that some firemen were trying to "dictate" to the city, and he asked policemen to drive the trucks until the issue was settled. Several grass fires broke out, and policemen did drive the trucks. On October 1 in a special meeting the council announced that it had always intended to provide insurance coverage as well as expense payments, thus ending what the council termed a "misunderstanding."

Sporadic water supply was a problem that could not be ignored. In 1963 the city was supplied by wells operated by the Tarrant County Water Supply Corporation, but the town's Water Supply Planning Board reported that surface water was vital for town growth. Mayor Hunter, who had stated that "I don't believe we should ask for federal aid for anything we can do ourselves," did not object when U.S. Sen. Ralph Yarborough announced a grant of some $37,000 to the TCWSC to aid it in constructing a water line to the four cities that owned the corporation—North Richland Hills, Azle, Lakeside, and Richland Hills. The council also approved a contract that would allow the TCWSC to buy water from Fort Worth.

Petitioners forced the City Council to allow a vote on home rule, November 19, 1963. Voters would also select the 15 members of the Home Rule Charter Commission. With an estimated population of 12,000, North Richland Hills was easily the largest town in the county without home rule. Enhanced annexation power was obviously one motive for adopting it, not just making it easier to incorporate new territory, but also as a method of attracting industry. New businesses could be lured by tax benefits under a home rule city's ability to deannex land and then reannex it under "first reading." Land under first reading pays no city taxes (and usually receives no city services in return).

City Council policies remained financially restrictive in 1964. Hunter pointed out the need for street repairs, but the council was unmoved. The mayor defended Laura Ray's original salary in vain, and she resigned as city secretary that summer. One of the new councilmen, L. B. Falcone, wanted to strip Hunter of his appointive powers but was informed by City Attorney Glenn Goodnight that the action would violate state law. Falcone challenged the ruling, but the matter was tabled. Fossil Creek Park, the city's first, was partially developed in 1964 but by the Jaycees rather than the city. Civic leader Alan Hamm asked the council to begin considering a thoroughfare system for the city, but he might as well have been speaking in Chinese.

The mayor and council did develop better relations with city firemen. Evidently beginning in 1964 the part-time volunteer firefighters, mostly from old Smithfield, were reimbursed. Their pay was raised October 1, 1964 from $0.65 to $0.75 per hour. Two full-time firefighters, who worked from 7 A.M. to 5 P.M., were hired the next year. The volunteers were on call the other hours.

Upon presenting its draft of a city charter to the council in 1964, the Charter Commission discovered that the council would not call an election. The commission dragged the city administration into the 48th District Court, which ordered the council to hold the election for a new charter. The council appealed the decision, using taxpayers' money. Mayor Hunter went on record as being opposed to the election. The appeal collapsed and a new city charter was adopted November 3, 1964, by a vote of 1,682 to 1,273. Of the four boxes, it lost only in Smithfield, 563 to 420. Mayor Hunter went on record as asserting that home rule was the greatest event in the city's history.

But at the November 9 council meeting, Councilman Alvis Dowell could not even secure a second for his motion to accept the vote. Instead, a petition with some 216 names was presented with the claim that the signees had never received the city charter that was supposedly mailed to everyone. Councilman Dowell immediately established, through two

NRH fire equipment and Station No. 2 in the 1970s

citizens in the audience, that at least two of the signatures were forgeries. The petitioners, who presumably had not voted, were not numerous enough to affect the outcome of the election anyway. The council reluctantly accepted the vote, three to one, with Falcone dissenting. Home rule was inaugurated January 9, 1965, with an enlarged City Council of seven, a city manager, John Hall, and a new city attorney, Marion Massey.

Alvis Dowell was a safety engineer, seeking affordable housing, who moved to the Smithfield section of North Richland in 1961. He believed the city was allowing developers to build substandard streets and inadequate two-inch water mains serving the fire hydrants. Promising stronger codes, he served two terms on the City Council, then ran for mayor in April 1966. Dowell finished ahead of Calvin Luper, 476 to 453, but under the home rule system Asa Short's 120 votes caused a runoff between the top two contenders. In a tense runoff in May with Luper, the owner of Homestead Mobile Homes, Dowell recollected that opponents put sugar in his gas tank and threw rotten eggs at his wife's car. The returns showed him with 357 votes and Luper with 358. One election judge had been tipped off that Luper's campaign manager, Ray Sprinkle, would attempt to vote, but no longer lived in North Richland Hills. At the polls Sprinkle was asked twice if he still lived at the address on Cummings Drive as shown on the poll list, and both times replied that he did. Actually he had lived on Cavender Street in Hurst for 15 months. Sprinkle's defense was that he owned his former North Richland home and was voting in the precinct where he was registered. The City Council, which did not want Dowell as mayor, decided that it was powerless to change the result, as in fact it was.

Courtesy of Jerry Anderson

Mayor Luper and the council asked the public to approve the issuance of three bonds. Some $4.38 million would be spent on streets and drainage, $200,000 on the acquisition and development of parks, and $420,000 for municipal facilities for the city administration, library, and police force. The street bonds were approved in April 1968 by a record turnout of voters who voted 1,413 to 801 in favor of the proposal, but the other two were voted down by about 57 percent to 43 percent. Luper and the council then took the additional political risk of calling an election in 1969 for the adoption of a 1 percent city sales tax.

Aerial photograph of North Richland Hills/Hurst Area, 1959, showing loop 820 marked and Airport Fwy.

LEGEND	
(1)	Grapevine Hwy.
(2)	Current NE Mall
(3)	Current North Hills Mall
(4)	Present Hwy. 10

The voters, perhaps surprisingly, approved it, 350 to 205.

The Fire Department hired its first full-time chief in 1968, Ray Rhine, from the Smithfield section of town. The four-man force began providing 24-hour protection in 1969. One firefighter would be on duty 24 hours and off 48. They maintained the city hall fire station at Morgan Circle and Glenview as well as the old Main Street station in Smithfield. The volunteers worked out of the Smithfield station and provided vital manpower on fire scenes. Various funeral homes still answered emergency calls. Fistfights occasionally broke out between firefighters and those funeral home employees who were intent on keeping their company's business thriving. Their real money was made from hauling deceased persons rather than conveying live, injured ones to a hospital.

URBANIZATION AND MERGERS

A Planning and Zoning Commission was established under the new city charter. After 18 months of studying other cities' zoning ordinances and holding a joint public hearing with the City Council, the new commission recommended a revised zoning ordinance and a map drawing the city into eleven land-use districts. The new zoning master plan was adopted by voters in November 1967, replacing the old 1958 zoning ordinance. The streets had become so defective that the citizens approved $4,380,000 in street bonds by a vote of 1,413 to 801. It even barely carried in Smithfield, 489 to 481. The $200,000 bond issue for parks was turned down, 1,267 to 921, and for a municipal center, 1,247 to 951. Higher property taxes were implemented in the next few years for bond retirement. An urban mindset had not yet arrived, but attitudes were beginning to change.

For veteran Smithfield citizens some of the sting of the transition was alleviated by the 1960 election of Vern and Darthula Lewis' son as County Commissioner of Precinct Three. Dick Lewis (1911–1975) and Mattie Belle Quayle Lewis had been raised in Smithfield. Mattie Belle's parents farmed 13.5 acres where the Sunny Meadows Addition is now, around Newman Street, and the couple made their home on part of that land near the present intersection of Davis and Mid-Cities Boulevard. Many folks in Smithfield, and North Richland Hills as well, knocked on doors to elect Lewis, who was particularly interested in doing something about the terrible condition of the roads in the area. As commissioner for 18 years, he did preside over many road repairs. He also helped to create the junior college system, worked for the passage of the bonds to build the Dallas-Fort Worth

First NRH post office located on Blaney, 1955

Courtesy of Naomi Jones Cummings

Airport, and helped establish the Tarrant County Convention Center.

In 1969 a post office was built at the intersection of Grapevine Highway and Blaney, but it was simply the Richland Hills Branch of the Fort Worth Post Office and the zip code of 76118 was on the Fort Worth list. In 1976 it moved to 7800 Bedford-Euless Road and was known as the Greater Richland Area Branch of the Fort Worth office.

Individual farmers, whether they desired to or not, had to give up their way of life and sell for handsome profits. They could not afford to pay city taxes on extensive acreage. The last 12 acres of Guy Reeves' farm were sold in 1966 to Hudiburg Chevrolet, which still occupies the site. Gene Anderson in the early 1960s presided over the demolition of the old Anderson homestead, the center section of which was a log cabin, and the sale of the farm to the Texas Highway Department to make way for the Loop 820-Airport Freeway interchange. Helen

Fort Worth Star-Telegram

Calvin Luper with K. H. Hudiburg, breaking ground for the new Hudiburg Chevrolet.

Catherine Calloway, representing the fourth generation of her clan in the area, closed the Happy Hollow Golf Course and sold the land where the North Hills Mall is today. Those who were farther from the highways naturally held on longer. From the 1940s into the 1970s Frank Vollintine farmed about 250 acres on the west side of Rufe Snow where the railroad tracks cross the road. Vollintine, who once served as director of the Tarrant County Soil Conservation District, had a heart attack and died while driving his tractor on the farm. The old farm is now part of the Industrial Park.

THE BUSINESS SIDE

After Loop 820 was opened for traffic in the mid-1960s, the two corners south on Rufe Snow were quickly purchased by corporations. A Mobil station was built on the southeast corner, and a Humble station (now Exxon) on the southwest corner. A Stop and Go convenience store opened next door to Humble. It is now the site of a Jones Blair Paint store. Rufe Snow north of the loop was just a gravel road through the countryside.

Farther south on Rufe Snow, the old businesses in the 3800–3900 blocks remained in place. Luke Davis, in his auto repair garage at 3810, was a patient man who loved to teach neighborhood boys about mechanics. One of them, Bob McGee, seemed to be a natural mechanic. When Davis announced his plans to move to Arkansas, William A. "Mac" McGee bought Davis' place in 1959 and ran the garage for decades thereafter. Bob's specialty was motors, while brother Bill worked with all the electrical jobs.

The Haltom City State Bank continued to help develop North Richland Hills. After

McGee Garage at 3810 Rufe Snow. One of the city's oldest continuously operated businesses.

Clarence Jones passed away in 1966, his widow, Ruth Jones (1900–1983) became chairman of the Board of Directors from 1966 to 1982.

A group of Tarrant County businessmen began working early in 1961 to organize a home-owned bank in North Richland Hills. They recruited Charles Brinkley, first vice president of the First National Bank in Weatherford, to serve as president of the new operation. The charter was approved in the summer of 1961, and Brinkley began working on the organization in an office in the Richardson Center at 7109 Grapevine Highway. Ten acres were purchased for $10,000 from the Wade Cutchin estate at Grapevine Highway and Vance Road. Northeast National Bank was the first bank located in North Richland Hills, officially opening on June 14, 1962. Opening day deposits totaled some $700,000. One depositor, Elmer Spurgeon, arrived at the back of the building on horseback.

Expanded facilities, including four drive-in windows, were completed in 1967. One of the directors, golfer Byron Nelson, cut a ribbon of $5 bills with a five iron. In 1971 four new drive-in windows were built across the street in Richland Hills, and Spurgeon rode his horse in to make the first deposit. By then Northeast had almost $31 million in assets. The next year the stockholders voted to form Northeast Bancorp Inc., a holding company that could acquire other

Courtesy of Charles Brinkley

Northeast National Bank, corner Grapevine & Vance Rd., following expansion

Artist rendering of Richland Plaza

banks. In 1976, before any acquisitions, Northeast had 67 employees and officers, making it a major employer in North Richland Hills.

During the political wars of 1960–1961 the city transferred its holdings from Haltom City State Bank to Northeast Bank. But in January 1969 Mayor Calvin Luper and the council were concerned that a million-dollar deposit at Northeast sat for a month before it was invested. In a 6-1 vote January 27, 1969, that apparently attracted no public attention, the council voted to transfer the money to Haltom City State Bank. Northeast claimed that City Manager Stephen Shutt had taken a month to provide instructions for investment, but the council believed the bank was at fault. Councilman Harold Daley had to defend his vote for the majority because he was Mrs. Jones' nephew and she was still chairman of the board of the Haltom bank. The city, of course, had a direct financial interest in Northeast Bank in that it paid more than $5,000 in city taxes to North Richland Hills in 1968. Northeast later was named the sole depository again.

Businesses continued their kaleidoscopic march along the Grapevine Highway. Joe Hicks' station changed to Shell around 1960, then in 1964 Hicks sold it as well as others he owned elsewhere, to Pioneer Oil Company. A gas station is still in operation at this site.

Billboard advertising Richland Plaza, July 1967

Akins stayed on at 7101, and watched his business signs change from Humble to Enco to Exxon, but his friendly and helpful manner never changed. In 1959 Philip Orr purchased the barely used 7-Eleven store and moved his pharmacy to that location in the middle of the 7000 block. He operated under the name Bench and Orr Pharmacy. The Dairy Kreem closed and fruit stands later occupied that site.

The Richland Bowl was in its heyday. Owner Ray Lofland was a burly, crew-cut man who believed that bowling was a therapeutic sport. Bowlers sometimes had to wait two hours to play so Lofland expanded the alleys from 16 lanes to 24, then to 32. He considered it "an investment in our town, our area." By the 1970s, however, his business had slowed because of the availability of other attractions and the general retail decline at the southern tip of the city.

Half a mile down the street the Richland Plaza Shopping Center opened amidst considerable fanfare August 2, 1962. Officials from

Seniors meet for morning coffee in the Mustard Jar Restaurant of North Richland Drug—later Town & Country Drugs.

neighboring cities, the chairman of the board of Montgomery Ward, and representatives from many stores were on hand amidst a throng of nearly 1,000 shoppers. Touted as Northeast Tarrant's first regional shopping center, the $4.5 million mall was supposed to create a great crossroads of commerce at Grapevine Highway and Texas 183. A deluge of rain caused Fossil Creek to flood some of the stores, which were forced to hold flood sales on opening day, but the rains did not slow down the crowds.

North Richland Drug owner, Alan Hamm, is shown with employees Eva Evans, left, and Marie Erskine, right.

Meanwhile, the older, more centrally located Greater Richland Shopping Center continued to thrive. There were 20 tenants, no vacancies, and 76,000 square feet of floor space occupied. By the late 1960s Mott's variety store had doubled its annual sales after five years of operations and increased its original space by two-thirds to 10,000 square feet. The medical clinic had started with two physicians and now had four.

Anchoring the northeast corner was North Richland Drug, purchased by Alan and Nancy Hamm in 1959. With its small restaurant in the rear, named the Mustard Jar, along with its family charge accounts, delivery service, and employees who knew customers by name, it became the social center for the community. A couple of dozen retirees were usually waiting for the doors to open at 9 A.M. Children in the area grew up knowing all the traditions and friendliness of the store and its employees. The fountain area received the Mustard Jar name from young Greer Phillips in a contest. The Phillips family were regulars at

North Richland Drug Mustard Jar employees are Shirley Massingale, left, Glenda Akins, circa Fall of '91.

Shown at North Richland Drug—then Town & Country Drugs—during its closing days in the fall of 1991 are, L/R-David Hamm and daughter Ashley, Carolyn Hamm DeGuire, Alan Hamm (store owner), Dustin DeGuire, Nancy Hamm, and Jean Anne Hamm.

the popular eatery, and the place was famous for its old fashioned hamburgers cooked by Shirley Massingale and Dorothy Hollum. Greer's prize for winning the contest was 25 free hamburgers, which he recalled, "went quickly." The Hamms bought other store sites and named the chain Town and Country Drug, though customers still referred to the original store as North Richland Drug.

The North Richland Hills Barber Shop in the same center was another favorite. Don Parker and Bill Otwell bought the shop from the original owner, Charles Morrison, who opened it in 1955. It was a gathering site for males and their conversations about sports, politics, and personal matters. Charlie Morrison hired Bill Otwell in 1957 and Don Parker in 1961, and many young men got their first haircuts from one of these three. Parker and Otwell bought the shop from Morrison in 1968.

Mangham Field housed a flight school, 1964–1986. Airplane and helicopter pilots trained on a 2,500 foot concrete landing strip and could obtain ratings in various types of craft. There were also two maintenance shops, five airplane rental companies, a second runway, and a fuel depot, but no control tower. Several accidents occurred through the years. Senator and astronaut John Glenn landed there when he came to speak at TCJC. Stormy Mangham had a heart attack while flying a plane, crashed, and died in Luling, Texas, in 1974.

Four Points has been a busy intersection since the 1930s and was the commercial heart of the area between Birdville and Smithfield. With Hudiburg Chevrolet replacing Guy Reeves' farm and a Safeway Grocery replacing Cunningham's, Four Points

Mangham Field, 1986

remained busy in the 1960s. A giant earthmover widened the intersection in the 1960s, and it is being reconstructed again in the 1990s so there will be a Davis-Grapevine Highway ramp onto Loop 820. Given the businesses still there and their proximity to the Loop, Four Points' place in the commercial history of the region seems to be permanent.

MORE POLITICS

In 1970 North Richland Hills had the hottest of Tarrant County suburban elections. Mayor Calvin Luper ran for reelection, heading a slate of council candidates who were perceived as being oriented toward the attraction of industry and apartment complexes. They also put the city sales tax into effect in January 1970 (sent to the state by businesses and reimbursed to the city by the state). Former City Attorney Marion Massey headed a slate that seemed to want to rein in the developers, restrict apartment zoning, and establish a city library. Massey ousted the incumbent mayor, 1,147 to 562 and the rest of his slate won by similar margins. Three incumbent councilmen were defeated.

Charles Brinkley and Mrs. James Free (Lois) led a successful year-long effort to involve the community in founding a city library, and on April 30, 1971, Mayor Massey cut the ribbon to open the facility at Richland Plaza. Mrs. Mildred Clinger was named the first head librarian.

Zoning questions popped up occasionally. Councilman M. E. "Gene" Riddle complained in 1971 that the north end of town was becoming a junkyard. He was referring to the 8300 block of Odell in old Smithfield, where a wrecking yard was established near people's homes. The owner of the business promised to erect a fence, but at least one homeowner wanted the business kicked out of the neighborhood.

All-Around Cowboy. Chamber of Commerce presentation, Andy Kulaga, president, at left

The Tarrant County Water Supply Corporation, the intercity water and sewer service established in 1960, formed from Tarrant Utilities and others, was administratively clumsy, limited financially in making improvements through the years, and plagued by water pressure problems through the system. By the late 1960s North Richland Hills wanted to take charge of its own water-sewer system in order to better control development and costs as well as water pressure. After Gene Riddle became acting city manager, he noted that North Richland owned 93 percent of the corporation and had 25 percent of the say. Azle and Lakeside seemed to waver on the matter of taking control of their own water-sewer systems, and Richland Hills resisted. Richland Hills had few water pressure problems and evidently regarded the status quo as most cost effective for their largely built-out community. When the other three towns made it plain that the intercity effort was ending, the Richland Hills council voted to help retire the bonds, and the corporation was dissolved in the spring of 1971.

North Richland Hills then proceeded to prove that water bills could be dangerous to one's political career. Mayor Massey's "independent slate" won four races in the spring of 1972, and placed two candidates in runoffs. An opposing slate, which was critical of a growing controversy at City Hall, won two council positions, and placed two in runoffs. But one candidate, Bell Helicopter employee Lloyd McKinney, who defeated incumbent William Ratcliff 720 to 624, on April 4, 1972, was denied his seat because of an overdue $9.60 water bill, discovered by Ratcliff. A three-to-three tie council

Charles Brinkley, on left, chairman of the NRH Library Board and city manager, Jack Russell, show the one-year rent free lease for new library to be located in Richland Plaza Shopping Center.

Four Points revisited in 1998. Four Points has been a busy intersection since the pioneer family days; the four points are made up of the intersection of Davis Boulevard, Bedford-Euless Road, and the two directions of Grapevine Highway.

Courtesy of Sean Hughes

vote was broken by Massey, who ruled that McKinney did not meet a stipulation in the city charter that requires candidates not be in arrears of any bill owed to the city. A special election was called on May 16 to fill Place One, while Ratcliff was temporarily seated. It is probably superfluous to note that McKinney was an opponent of Massey's slate.

The outraged McKinney retorted that his $10 water deposit offset the bill, so there was no "liability due the city." Also, the charter language did not specify whether any debt had to be paid by the time of filing, by election day, or at the time of taking office. (McKinney apparently had paid by the latter date.) The city's political arena temporarily moved to the water billing office, where on any given day there were as many politicians as city employees plowing through back records. At least two councilmen had previously been tardy with payments but not during campaigns. There was a public backlash, some of it orchestrated, against the perceived nit-picking. Public pressure prompted Massey and others in his faction to consider resigning. McKinney was seated.

There was additional pressure on the council to divulge why so many city employees were mysteriously disappearing through unexplained resignations and terminations. The mayor and council decided to disclose

Getting ready to open the new library at Richland Plaza Shopping Center on May 2, 1971.

what they could in a special meeting on April 17. It was revealed that former City Manager Jack Russell, who had abruptly resigned to become city manager in Corsicana, had recommended the dismissal of the city's first professional librarian (no reasons were specified) and also the termination of the city secretary because of "inefficiency and inability to account for city funds." No comment was made over the termination of five Water Department employees because an investigation was still under way. There was no cover-up, just an effort to spare various former city employees and their families any more embarrassment. The political dust settled for awhile. The high jinks had overshadowed the election of the first woman to the council, JoAnn Goodnight.

In February 1973 a $1.2 million bond election was called for March 20. Mayor Massey and the council believed it was past time to fund construction, equipment, and site acquisition for a municipal building, including a city hall and library, and a third fire station (which would also provide Police Department quarters) for a burgeoning city of some 20,000 people. City Hall as well as the Police and Fire Departments were still housed in the civic building at 4101 Morgan Circle acquired in 1961, though it had been expanded several times to about 9,000 square feet. The roof leaked badly. The city library, housed in donated space in

Richland Plaza, would soon be forced out because of expansion of the shopping center. No increase in the $1.20 per $100 ad valorem tax rate would be necessary for repayment of the bonds. Having learned from crushing defeats in the past, the mayor and council carefully scheduled three public forums to lay the plans before the voters, explain the need for the facilities, and answer questions. In fact, expanded facilities were going to have to be provided at some time, and with land prices escalating constantly, future costs would be much greater.

The three public forums drew a total of 25 persons. The $1.1 million municipal building proposition failed 492 to 290. The $100,000 fire station proposal died 447 to 335. The 782 voters represented about 9 percent of the electorate. Ironically, by August 1973 the city government was awash in cash. City Manager Riddle had discovered 18 businesses in the city, with Fort Worth mailing addresses, whose city sales tax revenues were flowing to the wrong city. Many were along the Grapevine Highway and were chain operations, which had home offices elsewhere and were unfamiliar with boundary lines. Texas Electric Service Company, Montgomery Ward, Firestone, Buddies, Piggly Wiggly, Ward's Drugs, and Mott's were among them. The state confirmed that North Richland Hills would receive some $200,000 in back sales tax revenues. Six more stores that would soon be audited would bring still more revenue. The city could expect from the 18 businesses during the next fiscal year some $100,000 in sales tax revenue.

A-Kay Betts receives check and congratulations for naming Richfield Park in 1973. B-Richfield Park, 1998

Mayor Massey commented that North Richland could now easily build a city hall, but he and the council prudently went along with a tax decrease instead.

The Parks and Recreation Board began functioning in the early 1970s, and land for Norich and Richfield parks was donated and developed in that period. Richfield, filled with athletic fields, was the first park north of Watauga Road. Twenty-six acres were added to Fossil Creek Park, giving it a total of some 430 acres, and development of it commenced. Twenty-nine acres were donated for Northfield Park, but it was not developed at this time.

Veteran Councilman Dick Faram, a medical services representative for Parke-Davis, was elected

NRH City Councilman Norman Ellis, Park and Recreation Committeeman Warren Connelley, City Manager Gene Riddle, and Haltom City Manager Pat Moffatt reviewing plans for Fossil Creek Park, May 31, 1973.

mayor in 1974, apparently with a slate or at least a group of supporters on the council with him. In March 1974, a month before Faram's election, the North Richland Hills Firefighters Association began circulating petitions asking for a citywide collective bargaining election. City Attorney Tim Truman ruled that there were not enough signatures to force an election, but he was overruled in June by Judge Harold Craik of the 96th District Court. Two days after the judge's writ of mandamus ordering the council to accept the petitions, FFA president, 21-year-old Bob Harvey, was fired at the instigation of City Manager Riddle. Riddle announced that the dismissal was not related to the association's campaign for collective bargaining. Actually the 1973–1974 council seemed to have a tough time meeting at all; the cancellation of the July 1974 meeting was the sixth in a year due to lack of a quorum. A plethora of court hearings followed. In August, two more firefighters left the department, one of whom had been voted "Fireman of the Year" in 1973 by his coworkers. More court hearings and City Council flurries followed, but the city had to hold the election. Rex McEntire was named city attorney in mid-1974.

In the campaign Mayor Faram and six of the seven councilmen denounced collective bargaining as a means by which the union could make demands on the city, secure a binding agreement, and thereby compel a tax increase. Furthermore, the seven argued in a mailing, the city would have to hire labor-management experts. Councilman Tom Newman did not sign the letter. Firefighters retorted that local administrators and firemen could certainly handle their own negotiations among themselves and that the union, which had no right to strike, had no means of forcing "demands" on a city. They also argued that the city needed at least twice as many firemen, that 16 people could not continue protecting a city of 20,000. Collective bargaining for firefighters was beaten 515 to 259 in mid-November 1974. Why the mayor and council stalled the election is incomprehensible, since any referendum on unionism in most any Texas city would have been defeated two-to-one at any time of the year.

Six-year department veteran Stan Gertz named fire chief in 1975.

With unionization's demise, the firefighters came to the conclusion that the police force's earlier call for civil service was the next best option. Various citizens and councilmen agreed. The city charter was substantively amended in June 1974, with the establishment of a Civil Service Commission. Indeed, it was already in place, but not yet in action, at the time of the collective bargaining vote. It was a compromise that appeared fair to all parties. The commission was empowered to hear appeals from aggrieved city employees. Its five unpaid members were appointed by the mayor and council. Acting as an impartial body, the commission interpreted gray areas in city employment and benefits rules and prepared a recommended hourly wage scale and benefit program for City Council consideration. One other innovation dates to 1974—city offices were provided with computers and told that reports were to be put on something called a "floppy disk."

Six-year department veteran Stan Gertz was named fire chief in 1975. At that time North Richland still qualified as a "bedroom community" with much countryside. There were not many commercial buildings, and the firefighters seldom had to put on their breathing apparatus. When people in the Smithfield part of the city called a police dispatcher, they listed their address by route and box number. Policemen had to know people in the area, so they could turn to them easily and repeatedly to secure directions. As late as the early 1970s, if vacations and sickness claimed a few men, an officer could end up on duty by himself for North Richland Hills.

By 1975 Mayor Faram and the council had amassed federal and state funds along with some of the city budget surplus. They built the new City Hall and library complex at 7301 Northeast Loop 820 for some $650,000. The

City's first ambulance, 1978 Pontiac Station Wagon, picture taken in 1978.

library's floor space expanded from 500 square feet to 11,000, while City Hall floor space doubled to about 15,000.

Faram and his council were challenged by a slate in 1976 headed by retired management

1967 Chevrolet Pickup, picture taken in 1976; originally "Dog Catchers" truck transferred to Fire Department in 1976.

analyst Tom Newman. The Newman slate talked about geographical diversity and the inadequate parks system much more than the incumbents. The incumbents apparently all lived south of the Loop and at least three lived in the Snow Heights Addition. Of course, some three-fourths of the population lived south of the Loop at that time, and the proximity of council members was not by design, but it left some of the incumbents vulnerable. Councilwoman Dorothy McClure, former owner of the Green Valley racetrack, worked hard for her neighbor Newman, and both benefited from a heavy northside vote and from firefighter sympathizers.

Newman edged Faram 879 to 835 and carried two or three councilpersons with him. But Newman found himself surrounded by Faram supporters, one of whom was city secretary Winnie Barclay. He charged that the secretary secretly taped some of his phone calls, and she resigned in May 1976. Newman was disgusted by North Richland Hills politics and got out. Only one of his council followers survived the next election in 1978, when Faram reclaimed the mayor's post.

Ollie Godsey had been collecting stray animals for the city since about 1964, evidently having replaced Bill Taylor, but the official Animal Services Division began in 1978 with the hiring of Pam Burney. She was given a desk in the breezeway of the Police Department, a 1967

One of RYA's first softball teams, 1964; in the excitement of getting to play softball, the team, coached by Dub Crisp, ordered basketball uniforms instead of softball uniforms.

RYA Girls' Softball, Roadrunners Softball Team, 1971

pickup with hand-built wire cages, and a dog pole with a couple of ropes on it. The Richland Hills shelter housed animals that were impounded. Also in 1978 a paramedic-staffed ambulance system was established within the Fire Department, eliminating the undertakers from ambulance runs.

Fossil Creek Park was enlarged again and further developed in 1978–1979, and it remains one of the city's prime natural areas. The Richland Youth Association has served as the hub for athletic activities at Fossil Creek and other parks since the 1960s. Dennis Horvath was hired as the first Parks and Recreation Director in 1979. The city awarded the Cable TV franchise to Black Hawk Communications (later bought out by Marcus Cable) for a 15-year period.

The sales tax bonus did not last, of course, and by the late 1970s the city suffered a cash-flow problem. Under the civil service section of the city charter, employees had to receive raises equal to the current cost of living, a 14.3 percent raise, and 13 new employees were added—these moves added $2.5 million to the budget. The costs of Social Security and workmen's compensation payments also rose. Moreover, the projected 18 percent increase in sales tax yield from the new North Hills Mall for 1980–1981 was considered a disappointment. Mayor Faram and the council reluctantly raised the tax rate from $1.02 to $1.25 per $100 valuation.

In 1980 Rufe Snow Drive was a two-lane country road with a string of potholes, widely regarded by drivers as the world's worst street. An $8 million utility bond issue was approved that year, and once agreements between the City Councils of North Richland Hills and Watauga were reached, road construction and widening proceeded in record time. The improvement of the road triggered considerable development, especially at corners where major east-west roads were built, paved, and/or widened. The development was also spurred by the fact that water lines were put into place in 1980. Once the city controlled its own water-sewer systems, it could take gambles. The council estimated that the line would attract business and the city would get its money back, which it did. Rufe Snow turned into a five-lane thorough-fare from the Loop to the railroad tracks by 1982. By 1983 the widening of Rufe Snow from the Cotton Belt tracks to the Foster Village Addition between Hightower and Starnes was nearly completed.

A water distribution system connected to the Trinity

City of NRH

Rufe Snow Drive improvements, July 1982

106

River Authority was also completed. The dangerous dry weather crossing on Onyx Drive across Fossil Creek was finally replaced by a bridge in 1978, but repeated floods began damaging the bridge. There were 17 or 18 men in the Public Works Department by this time, and it was hot, hard labor putting in streets and bridges and erecting water storage towers. North Richland Hills still had a lot of countryside, however, and several stock tanks were

Fran Burns

available to crew personnel for cooling off on hot summer days. Dr. J. L. McGlasson was named police chief in 1982 and began enlarging and organizing the force to reflect different specializations. A quarterly newsletter regarding these projects and other city affairs was mailed with everyone's water bill.

By the early 1980s the zoning ordinances of the late 1960s were considered too old and too general. The old code's provisions for local retail zoning allowed 62 different types of business to be built on the same tract of land. Some developers took advantage of the vagueness by building apartments in areas where adjacent single family dwellers expected a small shopping center. Landscaping was often minimal. The zoning changes implemented in 1983 removed apartments from the list of "businesses" that could be built in areas zoned for local retail.

City Manager, Rodger Line, tenure 1982–1995

Pyramid zoning was beginning to be phased out. Landscaping requirements were enlarged in almost all zoning categories. Local retail zoning required 15 percent of the lot to be landscaped, while offices needed 20 percent. Large trash containers had to be screened from public view and from adjacent property.

Unfortunately, with the price of land rising rapidly, new zoning requirements for more space in neighborhoods drove up costs to homebuyers. And a builder with J. B. Sandlin Homes questioned the ordinance's proviso that homes be a minimum 1,400 square feet. City employees and young couples would be priced out. A 1,400 square-foot home at the time cost approximately $75,000, requiring an income of around $33,000, which most young couples in the early 1980s did not have. The American median income of $24,000 could only carry a $59,000 house. City Manager Rodger Line observed that North Richland could wind up with a city population of old folks, costing the city its strength and vibrancy. Planning

Sean Hughes

Aerial view of Loop 820 and Rufe Snow Drive, looking north, 1997 and Zoning Committee Chairman George Tucker predicted that in five years a 1,000-square-foot home was all that people would be able to afford. (Tucker noted that even smaller homes could be erected only with brick or be required to have a certain type of roof or no prefabricated parts.) Not everyone viewed these predictions as problems. Some citizens believed it was legitimate and appropriate to create a city constituted only of the wealthy. From the vantage point of the late 1990s the predictions look off target. Two-earner households, enhanced incomes, and low interest rates have rendered some of the old debate anachronistic.

Also in 1983 Mayor Faram, City Manager Line, and Assistant City Manager Dennis Horvath headed another treasure hunt that discovered many businesses incorrectly listing themselves with Fort Worth addresses, which meant their city sales tax revenues would go to Fort Worth, not North Richland Hills. The sales tax bonanzas led to a $630,000 refund covering the previous several years. City sales tax revenue had increased three and a half times in four years. Despite ongoing bond retirement in 1983, the city cut its tax rate from 57 cents to 50 cents, the second year in a row for a decrease.

Meanwhile, about the time he retired from office in 1974, former mayor Massey formed a behind-the-scenes political alliance with his old friend, Charles Brinkley, founder, president, and chairman of the board of the Northeast Bank. Various businessmen and landowners were invited to join the North Richland Hills Civic Association. Unlike the defunct Civic League, the Civic Association collected political action money from its members, conducted quiet hearings for incumbents and challengers, and endorsed a slate of city candidates through newspaper advertisements, newsletters and such. The contributions did not go to the candidates themselves. The CA endorsed Faram and his allies on the council, beginning in 1974.

The CA's existence became more public when Les Harper wrote an article about them in the Northeast Extra edition of the *Star-Telegram*, March 23–24, 1983. It was revealed that the CA had spent almost $2,000 for its slate the year before. No individual candidate had spent more than $750 the year before, and most not nearly that much. James M. Walker, general manager of Walker Construction Company, had contributed $300. Ex-councilman W. N. Ratcliff, who no longer lived in the city, contributed $250. He still owned property in North Richland.

At the La Quinta Motor Inn on March 7, 1983, each council candidate was given about 10 minutes before the CA's Steering Committee, chaired by Massey. Former councilman Sid Cavanaugh was on hand, challenging an incumbent, and credited his single term, 1978–1980, to his CA endorsement. He recalled that he spent only $26 on his campaign, while his opponent spent $500, but Cavanaugh rode in on the Civic Association campaign on his behalf. He was rejected by the CA in 1980 because he fought with Faram on the council too much. Predictably rejected again by the CA in 1983, Cavanaugh asserted that the screening committee's minds were made up before the screening. Massey denied that, but in fact the CA already had the group it wanted and endorsed all incumbents in 1983. Only 911 votes were cast in an extremely light turnout in 1983—that was less than 5 percent of the electorate—and all four incumbents won by wide margins.

Massey stated that the Civic Association was a loose-knit group of 30 or 35 businessmen, with no formal membership, who were looking for dedicated people and simply wanted to preserve orderly growth and a high quality of life. Brinkley had no political ambitions nor did Massey after retiring as mayor. Others regarded the CA as a power center of two people who, along with their business cronies, wanted to pick the candidates. The reality is that these two concepts are not mutually exclusive, and most American cities are more or less run or heavily influenced by businessmen and bankers. Also, public officials can generate their own following. Mayor Faram, according to several accounts, was certainly not hostile toward the CA, but he was not particularly beholden to it either. The CA as a group was only active during campaigns and did not make any demands on officeholders.

In January 1984 city authorities asked the State Highway Commission for $25 million of relief from traffic congestion near North Hills Mall, an area that racked up 179 accidents in 1983, 20 percent of the city's total. The intersections of Loop 820, the Grapevine Highway, and Davis generated such traffic volume that it was difficult to exit off the Airport Freeway out of Hurst onto Davis or Grapevine Highway. Eastbound motorists on the Loop had to cross several lanes of traffic, if they dared, to get on the eastbound Airport Freeway.

The city was about 40 percent developed in 1983, and some 14,000 of its estimated 32,000 people lived north of Loop 820. Its tax base was heavily homeowner and retail, but there were some light industries, e.g. Tandy Advanced Products, Walker Construction Company, and Graham Magnetics. The Birdville Independent School District was the largest employer with 1,500, while Walker and Tandy each employed about 400. Only 21 percent of North Richland citizens who were employed worked in the city. The University of Texas at Arlington's Institute of Urban Studies issued a report on Texas cities in 1984, showing North Richland Hills as one of the top five cities in the state in quality of housing. For cities of less than 50,000, it was third behind Duncanville and Carrollton. Only three-tenths of one percent of homes in North Richland Hills did not have complete indoor plumbing. In those few houses, there may have been running water but no toilet. About 75 percent of North Richland residents owned their homes, another high mark according to the study. The new zoning required homes to be 75 percent brick or stone, which allowed the city to preserve the overall beauty and flavor of the community. There were four parks, and a million-dollar construction project was launched at Northfield Park late in 1983, with playgrounds, softball fields, tennis and basketball courts, etc. It was a bright picture, and with new zoning in place, traffic congestion being addressed, the tax rate going down, and the city's bond rating improved from a to A, 1984 promised to be a good election year for incumbents. It wasn't.

Managing a city calls for continuous and courteous contact with constituents and is a constant balancing act between commercial and residential development. A mayor and City Council can lose support before they know it. Dan Echols, a dean at Tarrant County Junior College, challenged Mayor Dick Faram. Virginia Moody, a housewife and farm manager from the Smithfield section of town, took on a veteran pro-Faram councilman who had become vulnerable. Two ghost candidates, who did not campaign, who spent nothing, and who may not have even been eligible to vote, filed against two other veteran councilmen, both of whom were Bell Helicopter managers.

An anti-developer sentiment had taken hold of the electorate (or at least the tiny minority who voted)—there seemed to be too much commercialism, too few parks, and too many developers draining their property into neighbors' yards and overloading utility lines in several neighborhoods. Echols demanded quicker action on a master plan for the city. Also, an arrogance of power, or the projection of arrogance, may have infected a few officeholders in their dealings with citizens. Mayor Faram tried to turn Mangham Airport into an issue. Echols, who was a flier and head of the safety committee at the private airport, had hoped to eventually transform it into a general aviation airport like Addison's (an idea first discussed in 1973, when Greater Southwest Field closed). A livelier airport would have angered area residents on the east-central side of town. But as Echols noted in the campaign, the sale of the airport to E-Systems was going through, so there was no issue. Had there been a "toss them out" slate, it would have carried the day. As it was, Echols defeated Faram 815 to 596, Moody won easily, and even the unknown ghost candidates received around 550 votes each against the two incumbent councilmen, who each received about 800.

During the year under both mayorships, a series of town hall meetings were held, involving citizens, city staff, and the Planning and Zoning Commission. The idea was to come up with a master plan, following up on the zoning ordinance and zoning map adopted early in the year. Planning what the rest of the city should look like seemed prudent for a city of less than 35,000 that might eventually top out at 90,000. So the housing restrictions were part of the master plan, as it evolved, and so was long-range zoning. One unseen benefit of the master plan was to eliminate much of the land speculation that plagued cities such as Euless, where speculators bought land after Dallas-Fort Worth Airport was built. When Euless did not bloom, the land lay fallow for years. The North Richland land-use plan informed speculators that only residential zoning would be allowed in certain parts of the city, so there was no purpose in buying relatively cheap land there in expectation that it would be zoned commercial.

Integrated street planning was part of the master plan. Planning and Zoning Chairman Tucker observed that subdivision builders must now align their streets with other subdivisions, which had not been required until this time. "East of Rufe Snow, you turn on a street and it's like a rat's maze," Tucker said. "You can go around and around and never find your way out. We've got streets like Starnes that skip. They jump whole sections of land and pick up. That confuses the Fire Department. They don't know which end of Starnes to go to." The prospective interchange at Davis, Grapevine Highway, and the Loop was viewed as crucial to relieving congestion and preventing the demise of the southeastern section of the city.

Mayor Echols pushed for North Richland Hills to join the cities of Northeast Tarrant County, a revived group trying to persuade cities to work on mutual traffic problems, e.g. poor east-west access. Certainly the lack of east-west thoroughfares contributed to the congestion on Rufe Snow and Loop 820. (Rufe Snow was the super hot commercial developing area at the time.) The master plan called for Watauga Road to become a major artery, border to border.

The next step was to sell the voters on a bond issue in 1985. More than $31 million would be expended for streets and drainage, to make Watauga Road a six-lane thoroughfare, to widen Davis and Rufe Snow south of the Loop, and to rescue 900 homes from flood plains. Some $5 million would be spent on purchasing the Richland Hills Church of Christ complex as a new library and on a new recreation center. Over $3.5 million would go to new police and fire fighting facilities. The tax rate would climb some 11.5 cents per $100 valuation over a six-year period. No organized opposition arose, and in September the city of some 38,000 people voted to approve the five propositions by an average tally of 1,450 to 319 on each one. After the vote there were a couple of $75,000 surprises when the city discovered a hole in the roof of the church and asbestos in the building, but the city still saved millions by buying the complex rather than building a new library.

The library's grand opening was September 26, 1987, featuring a chili cook-off and other festivities. The library included an auditorium and children's theater. State and federal funds put some personal computers in the building, and elementary school teacher Hazel Lowrance moved her Adult Basic Education classes—especially reading, math, and English as a second language—into the new facility. Including the recreation center, there were 85,000 square feet.

Until 1988 the police had been crammed into the Municipal Complex, so that the crime scene detectives housed the tools of their trade in what used to be a broom closet. With the new police station built onto the City Hall's west side, floor space was almost four times as large. The firefighters received a fourth station (in burgundy brick, early American style), central offices, and a fire training center. The Watauga Road station, with ten stalls, was designed to serve the growing northwest quadrant of the city. Fighting fires was more difficult than it had been just 15 years earlier. The city's density had increased, especially with commercial buildings, and many structures were built with materials that gave off caustic fumes. Firemen frequently had to don their breathing apparatus. The department also received an aerial ladder truck with a 100-foot ladder capable of reaching the top of a seven-story building.

North Richland Hills opened its own Animal Services Division at 7200B Dick Fisher Dr. South in 1987. By now, some in the city were also involved in a quest for identity. North Richland Hills had an identity in the 1950s—even after development established more and more subdivisions—and Smithfield had an identity. Between them they represented a few thousand folks, many with some acreage, who lived a quieter, simpler life than folks in Dallas, Fort Worth, and Arlington. The country feel, with cities nearby for entertainment and shopping, seemed ideal, and virtually everyone felt that it was a good place to raise kids. The country feel was still there in the 1960s and 1970s but was obviously disappearing. By the mid-1980s there were still livestock grazing near some homes, but the era was vanishing fast.

North Richland Hills had become a city of young professionals who commuted to the big cities. The rural environment was no longer the lure, nor cheap housing. Rather it was the mid-cities location, the quality of housing, and the cost of housing compared to Dallas and Fort Worth that were the biggest draws. They did not particularly identify with the city of North Richland Hills. People get a sense of identity from what they see, feel, and experience, but North Richland had lost the countryside community feeling and had not replaced it with anything—no downtown core or skyscrapers or historical district or any distinctive place or characteristic. The lack of identity explained some of the lack of civic participation and poor turnout in elections, though it must be noted that most American cities—even those with long histories and lively downtowns—face the same challenges. The problem was compounded in North Richland Hills by transiency. It is difficult to achieve identity with any community if one is in it only three to five years before moving on with the next promotion. Some shrugged it off as unimportant. Civic participation and turnout were invariably dismal, but voters would turn out if they felt threatened by city affairs. Low turnout might just equate with contented voters. Others yearned for a community identity and searched for one or more items that might provide it. Many facets of identity cannot be created, but distinctive characteristics are a facet that can be built up in a community. Professor Joel Goldstein of UTA observed that even ten 50-foot flagpoles in North Richland would be something distinctive. By the mid-1980s the search was on.

In the mid- and late 1980s, the search for identity and a sense of community involved holding public town hall meetings for bond proposals and charter amendments, cable TV broadcasting of city news, a drive for a new post office with an appropriate North Richland Hills name, central location, and North Richland Hills zip codes, city newsletters and pamphlets explaining issues to be decided at the polls, and changing the town's name to something that sounded less like neighboring Richland Hills.

Partial success was soon achieved on the post office matter. The Smithfield and Bedford Road stations shut down and were replaced by an office at 6051 Davis that did at least carry the North Richland Hills name. But it was still just a branch of the Fort Worth system with a Fort Worth zip code, 76180. It was disconcerting for commercial and industrial clients thinking of relocating to North Richland who could not even find the zip codes for the city.

The danger of establishing closer communications with the people is that city literature might appear to advocate one side of an issue that is destined to be decided at the polls, and that would violate Texas election laws. The danger in abandoning a town's name is that a more appealing substitute name must be on hand. Thirteen proposed city charter amendments, to be decided by election on November 3, 1987, included one that would change the name of the city to North Hills and another that would lengthen City Council and mayoralty terms from two years to four. The city pamphlet that summarized the effects of a name change stated, "Persons who spoke in favor of this change pointed out that our city has an identity problem because of the close proximity of Richland Hills and the fact that many persons identify the two cities as being one and the same." Charter Committee member Dr. Tommy Duer, a local veterinarian, asserted that no residents at the public hearings on the matter spoke in favor of the change. Duer suggested that the title of one newsletter article was not neutral: "Election to Open Door for Changes in City Name, Mayor-Council Terms." Duer and Charles Brinkley were concerned about language in a city pamphlet where no mention is made of reasons against lengthening terms of office, but it does say, "The annual elections provide an element of distraction that would be lessened by the biennial elections." Those who want to influence elections always prefer shorter terms of office but so do many other voters, and the critics may have had a point in this case. What constitutes campaign literature is a gray area in the law, but the city seemed to be leaving itself vulnerable to a lawsuit.

The name "North Hills" was actually already used by many smaller businesses, which liked the shorter, simpler name and who believed that it differentiated the community from Richland Hills. The cost of a name change to the city was estimated at only $20,000, but the cost to businesses would have been more, and some businesses opposed it for that reason. Some opponents thought it looked as though the city was naming itself for the shopping mall. Others were willing to vote for a name change to "Smithfield," but not North Hills. The name change was voted down 3,663 to 1,654.

Four-year terms were approved by a wide margin, but more than a few voters considered the wording on the ballot obscure. If you voted for holding elections every two years for half the council, rather than annually, you were voting for a four-year term, but the phrase "four-year term" did not appear on the ballot. No one involved in the wording of the ballot would admit that it was deliberately obscured, but voters easily could have been given a choice printed on the ballot of four-year terms or two-year terms. The outcome likely would not have been what the advocates wanted, since few American voters prefer four-year terms for City Councils. The four-year term champions almost pulled it off, but they could not have anticipated the immediate and widespread post-election voter protest. City Hall was virtually overrun by people who shouted that the "two years" they voted for meant two-year terms. It was sufficient to persuade the City Council not to canvass the proposition, which was of dubious legality, but which in effect killed it. Mayor Echols, who had favored both proposals, was probably relieved to be able to announce a month after the election that improving roads and drainage would be the top priorities for the city the next year.

Echols declined to run for reelection in the spring of 1988. He was actually willing to serve again but was persuaded that his utter inability to keep track of receipts and document his minor expenditures on city-financed trips would erupt as a major scandal in a reelection effort. He threw his support to two newcomers in the city elections, both of whom won. One was the former owner of B and B Pest Control, Tommy Brown, who defeated veteran councilman Jim Ramsey for mayor, 773 to 679. Ramsey at one point in the campaign had to state that he was not against development, he just did not think that taxpayers should pay for all development. Brown was close to developers and seemed to have their support as well as the Civic Association's.

Overlapping three mayorships was a set of events that benefited the city, beginning with a bit of bad news received by the Rostland Corporation, the developer of the Meadow Lakes subdivision. Late in 1981 Rostland directors were informed by a newly hired engineer that most of the land they owned in North Richland and Haltom was in a flood plain. If it were possible to reclaim the land, which it was not, it would cost about $5 million, which was a lot of money in 1981. Bob McMullin, who was in charge of Meadow Lakes at the time, abruptly left the room for about five minutes. As director Bob Frank recalled, "He told us later that he went to the restroom to throw up." Establishing a golf course seemed a possible solution, but through six years no fewer than nine private, potential developers failed to deliver.

Early in 1988 Rostland representatives, having concluded that no one was going to construct a golf course, visited with City Manager Rodger Line. They showed him a plat, which indicated that much of the property, which had been tentatively set aside for the golf course, could be utilized for residences. Line urged them to give the city a chance to develop the golf course instead. The company gave the city six months to acquire financing and some additional property that would be needed. Former Hurst Mayor C. A. Sanford had been hired to head the city's first economic development department the year before, and Line gave him full time to spend on this project. The city met all the conditions with a week to spare, and Rostland donated the land to the city.

Sanford's and Line's dedication was crucial, especially in the face of the virtually unanimous opinion of golf developers that it was impossible to build an upscale municipally owned golf course that would pay for itself. Marty Streiff's Recreation Services Ltd. thought it was possible and secured the contracts to construct and manage the facility. Line and Sanford as well as Mayor Brown and the 1988 City Council were willing to take a political risk for something they felt would really

Fossil Creek flood over road at Glenview Drive, 1988 or 1989

enhance the community. In May 1989 a tremendous flood all but destroyed the course, but all parties persevered and the Iron Horse Golf Course opened in the spring of 1990.

THE SOCIAL SIDE

The Methodist Church, the Church of Christ, and Baptist churches of the Smithfield community have celebrated their centennials, the Methodist Church in the 1960s and the others in the 1990s. All three outgrew their old buildings and erected new ones. Growth and expansion marks the history of the newer churches as well. The outreach programs are particularly impressive. Some are religious, of course, e.g. conducting missionary work, while others are broadly social, e.g. materially assisting the less fortunate. Many North Richland Hills congregations are directly involved in contributing food and volunteers to the North East Emergency Distribution, undertaking home repairs for the elderly, and establishing child care centers.

The Greater Fort Worth Christmas Pageant is sponsored by the North Richland Hills Baptist Church and involves more than 600 area volunteers. The pageant is held at the Tarrant County Convention Center.

Probably the most spectacular annual church event is North Richland Hills Baptist's Greater Fort Worth Christmas Pageant. It was launched at Richland High School in 1973 with two performances. Since 1980 it has been produced and staged at the Tarrant County Convention Center, and the number of performances had increased to six by 1998. By the 1990s more than 600 volunteers, some from other churches, were responsible for everything from props to making costumes to acting. Several million dollars' worth of props and costumes are housed in a warehouse, and are rented out to various organizations. This production became a reality because of the vision of Hal Brooks, former pastor of North Richland Hills Baptist, and Paul Paschall, the present minister of music. According to the Convention Center it is consistently one of the best-attended regularly scheduled programs featured at the theatre, and thousands more view the pageant on television.

The civic clubs are similarly active. Smithfield Masonic Lodge No. 455 continued operating in its historic building through 1982; some of the structure dated back to 1876. The members moved into their new building next door in 1983. Hoping the old structure could be preserved, the lodge gladly accepted a $700 offer by accountant Charles Mayberry to move it to Baker Boulevard in Richland Hills and remodel it as

Building is original Grand Prairie-Smithfield Masonic Lodge, moved to 6600 block of Baker Boulevard, Richland Hills, 1983, presently in use as office building, 1998.

Richland Hills Mayor Paul Daniel and NRH Mayor Clyde Zellers

his office. He planned to restore some of the original look, but the building is not in good shape at this time. The lodge still aids the widows of members and gives a scholarship each year to a deserving senior selected by the Birdville Independent School District. The membership still meets monthly, but is no longer dependent on the full moon for travel. The lodge will celebrate its 125th anniversary in 2001. Richland Lodge No. 1348 survived 42 years at its Glenview-Blaney site, while the members annually granted college scholarships to the two seniors of Richland High who had shown the greatest improvement during that year. The building was torn down in 1997 to make room for additional parking for a newly built Walgreen Drugstore, and the lodge relocated to Richland Hills.

The Northeast Optimist Club has been particularly active in sponsoring baseball and softball teams for young boys and girls in Northeast Tarrant County. They also disburse funds to needy families, scout organizations, and charitable groups, and make loans to college students. The Northeast Lions Club, chartered with 24 members in March 1963 in the cafeteria at Richland Plaza, is noted for its expenditures on eyeglasses for the needy and other projects regarding sight, and also for dispersing clothing, toys, and food to needy families. The Rotary Club of North Hills, organized by independent businessmen in 1981, has supported international immunization projects, planted over a thousand trees in the community, and awarded vocational scholarships to area students.

"Service Above Self," the Rotary motto, seems to apply to the citizens of North Richland in general. The city has not needed to be much involved in antipoverty programs because of the extraordinary effort of the churches and the service organizations. Veteran Councilwoman JoAnn Johnson, the first woman mayor pro tem, has represented North Richland Hills at the National League of Cities, and she informed the delegates at one conference that she had little to report regarding city-financed social programs since North Richland churches and private organizations take care of those programs. Her tidings caused a stir, since it is such a rare situation.

The Cornerstone Assistance Network (CAN) is a charitable organization begun by the members of the North Richland Hills Baptist Church in 1992. It is committed to

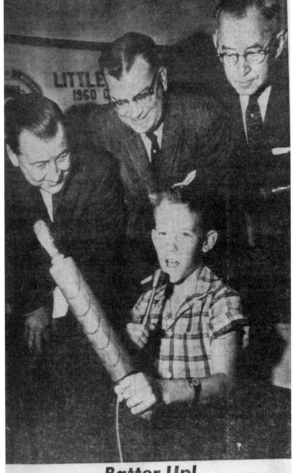

Batter Up!

Ten-year-old Gary Pewitt, 4117 Flory, makes like an auctioneer with a rolling pin instead of the bat he swings as a Little Leaguer. The auction was part of a fund-raising drive by Northeast Optimists, sponsors of the team that went to the Little League World Series last year. Looking on are, left to right, Mayors Paul Daniel of Richland Hills, Clyde Zellers of North Richland Hills and J. C. Gunter of Haltom City.—Press Staff Photo.

Gary Pewitt at auction sponsored by Northeast Optimists fund-raiser

115

being involved in the lives of people in the community by meeting their physical and spiritual needs. Clothing, furniture, and other property are distributed through shelters and churches. Case management is offered to the homeless and others in transition, and counseling is available for adoption planning and parenting. Housing is provided for single men and women in transition, e.g. coming out of prison. Similarly, the Community Enrichment Center (CEC) is a charitable organization begun by the Richland Hills Church of Christ. It provides free food for people in need in Northeast Tarrant County and relief for victims of famine and natural disasters around the world. About 300 homeless families were provided with homes in the 1990s. There is a children's home and a ministry for abused women and their children. A counseling ministry provides help for approximately 50 people per week. Both the CAN and CEC have transcended their original churches and are supported by hundreds of churches, businesses, and volunteers throughout Tarrant County.

Delinquency and drugs are not major problems in North Richland Hills, at least compared to most other cities, but after researching the effects of unsupervised youth after school, the city took action in 1994. The Teen After School Program, known as THE EDGE, has been implemented at several schools and serves 150 or more teenagers daily. The city funds a variety of activities between 3:15 P.M. and 5:30 P.M. during the school year. Free of charge, students may engage in intramural sports, drama, arts, dance, computer classes, science club, and Helping Hands Social Service Club among others.

Medical services are another facet of community life. Glenview Hospital was established in North Richland Hills in May 1961, a $350,000 structure at Glenview and Pipeline headed by six family doctors. It had 50 beds and a 24-hour emergency room, but not a lot of space on which to expand. Twenty years later Glenview was purchased by Hospital Corporation of America, which needed to expand. The four-story, 160-bed HCA North Hills Medical Center opened in December 1983 at 4401 Booth Calloway Road. It more than doubled the space of the old facility. Glenview in its last year, 1983, averaged 75 patients a day, while North Hills averaged 95 the next year. The new hospital, with some new equipment, staunched the outflow of patients to Fort Worth and Dallas. Over the next decade or so, the hospital added a state-of-the-art surgical laser system, opened a cardiac catheterization lab and open heart surgery suite, and purchased the latest mammography equipment. It became Columbia North Hills Hospital in 1995.

There is a rising national need for assisted living facilities, and Mayor Brown and the council approved two new facilities in 1995. Some 6.8 percent of the city's 50,650 residents in 1990 were older than 65. Meadow Lakes Retirement Community with 120 units is on Meadow Lakes Drive, and Good Place, with 80 beds, is on North Richland Boulevard just west of Davis.

The voters of Tarrant County organized the Tarrant County Junior College District in a

Aerial view of the Northeast Campus of Tarrant County Junior College, 1982. The Tarrant County Junior College District was created by a county bond election in 1965, and by 1982 the Northeast Campus was nationally recognized and attracting over 12,000 students to academic and vocational programs which reflected the diversified activities and interests of the booming area.

bond election, July, 1965. The northeast campus, located partially in North Richland, opened in 1968. It offers the usual array of survey courses for potential transfer to senior colleges as well as such specialized, professional ones as fashion merchandising, real estate, nursing, medical training, and composite bonding classes (teaching a skill required for making the skin that covers Bell's V-22 Osprey). By the time of the 1990 anniversary celebration of its 25th year (since the county vote authorizing its construction), TCJC had enrolled some 300,000 students, about half of whom were and are the first in their families to attend college. Half the students take university parallel courses, which are accepted at the University of Texas at Arlington, 12 miles to the south, and other universities. The Heritage Room in the TCJC Library, along with the Tarrant County Historical Commission in the county courthouse, have been instrumental in preserving the area's history. The northeast campus is the site for most of the College for Kids classes, launched with six courses in 1982. By 1992 some 324 three-week-long sections were taught to third through eighth graders interested in summer education, often in subjects not found in most schools, e.g. astronomy and backyard paleontology.

TCJC Clock Tower, a visual landmark added to the Northeast Campus in the early '90s.

Because the student population had reached 9,000, the construction of the Birdville Independent School District's second high school began in 1960. To the shock of many, it was built in a cow pasture far from any homes, at present-day 5201 Holiday Lane E. Loop 820 had not yet come through, of course, but the School Board was appropriately taking account of the northward population movement. No one wanted the school names to be Birdville High North and South, so shortened versions of city names seemed the best recourse. Richland High was the name of the new school, which opened in 1961, while Birdville High's name was changed to Haltom High. A number of alumni were upset over the old school's name change, but were somewhat pacified by the retention of Birdville as the district's name.

Old ties with the Birdville community persisted at Richland High. Ruth Metts and Bette Nolen supplemented their biology teaching materials from outside sources. The butcher shop at Guynn's store provided them with beef eyes, sections of bone, and organs for study.

Five more schools were built in the 1960s, three of them junior highs, and the pace has continued. Four new campuses were established in the 1970s, three in the 1980s, and four in the 1990s. Along the way the Birdville district earned a reputation for being innovative. Carrie F. Thomas Elementary at 8200 O'Brian Way, named for the teacher who was W. G. Thomas' wife, was the first elementary designed with a central library and the first and only one on a floating foundation. After Thomas was occupied in 1979, light fixtures and ceiling tiles plunged to the floors below, some walls separated from the foundation, and the building had to be demolished and replaced. Green Valley Elementary at 7900 Smithfield Road is the first school in Texas to be entirely heated and cooled by geothermal energy from a ground source heat pump. The third high school, named Birdville in 1998, was designed by architects who consulted district teachers and staffers. It is planned to be in operation fall of 1999. It features an oak grove in the center, and all the windows in the building look out on it. The selection of the old name "Birdville" ensures its permanent place in the community and reflects a sensitivity to the area's heritage and community self-confidence that perhaps was lacking during the school name change in 1961.

A few school bond issue defeats have been shrugged off. In the 1970s some homes were not yet air-conditioned, and many parents remembered that they had survived schooling without air-conditioning, so bonds for that purpose were voted down. A severe heat wave prompted some 2,000 petitioners to call for another effort, and in May 1977, air-conditioning passed. In March 1992, while the Legislature debated the Robin Hood Plan that might cost the Birdville district money, a $72.5 million bond package was voted down by some 300 votes. But between 1986 and 1996 three bond programs totaling almost $200 million were adopted.

Issues that caused controversy in some districts never reached white-hot status in the BISD. The busing of black students to the Fort Worth schools was gradually phased out. Beginning with the first grade at South Birdville Elementary in 1963–1964, these students were slowly integrated into the system. The use of tobacco and drugs and the wearing of shorts were forbidden. Birdville teacher Libby Conant once detected the smell of liquor in class, but could not locate the source until a student toppled out of his chair to the floor. Teachers' dress codes were an issue also. Some employees in the 1960s considered leaving the district when women were granted permission to wear pantsuits.

Some teachers were burdened with courses outside their fields in the 1960s and 1970s or with an unseemly variety of courses. Birdville Superintendent W. G. Thomas might ask a prospective teacher, perhaps one who could not carry a tune, if she could teach elementary music. In order to secure the job, the prospective teacher could get away with admitting that it would not be her favorite thing to do but had to hastily add that she could do it and would try to do anything else he assigned. Thomas often faced teacher shortages since the jobs paid little and doubtless sometimes had to take what he could get. If the classroom mismatch was too bizarre, the teacher might escape it in a year or two or might well resign. More than a few teachers had five different preparations in the 1960s and 1970s, an unimaginable burden to a later generation of teachers, and rightly so.

High school sports events are as popular in North Richland as in any Texas community. In 1987 the Haltom Buffaloes stampeded to the second round of the state football playoffs before losing to Denton. That same year, Richland High's volleyball team won the district's first state championship.

Through much of the post-World War II period the Birdville District was perceived as a low-income district, with its better schools in the northern sector and an attitude that condoned the status quo. There is a kernel of truth therein, but a more accurate appraisal would include the fact that the district was of necessity preoccupied with growth. With the $43 million bond issue in the late 1980s and the dramatic relocation of Haltom High, the image of the district began to improve and so did the TAAS scores. The board hired Dr. Bob Griggs as superintendent in 1993 with a mandate to renew emphasis on academic programs. The Northeast Tarrant Chamber of Commerce named the school district "Industry of the Year" in 1994. In 1995 the Birdville Board of Trustees was named one of the top four boards in the state by the Texas Association of School Administrators. By the 1994–1995 academic year, Green Valley Elementary was awarded exemplary status, while 12 schools received "recognized" status. No district in Tarrant County had more schools in those combined categories.

The Green Valley neighborhood also once had a different image. Bill and Dorothy McClure moved a little over a mile north of downtown Smithfield in 1948 and maintained a dairy farm on some 250 acres of the 400 they purchased. In 1960 they turned part of the farm into the Green Valley Raceway, which became a major stop on the national drag racing circuit. A small, wiry, race car driver, Bill Hielscher, bought the 150 acres containing the track in 1972 and hosted some major events. By the late 1970s, however, there were an increasing number of homes in the area, and some owners began complaining about the noise and traffic. The City Council adopted a targeted ordinance, of uncertain constitutionality, prohibiting more than 500 people from gathering more than eight consecutive hours. Willie Nelson appeared after a day of racing in 1977, but North Richland Police Chief Hamp Scruggs enforced the ordinance and riled the crowd by pulling the plug after Willie's second song. Irate concert fans tore up the concession tents and ripped down a fence in front of the stage.

Chamber of Mary Mabry

Green Valley Raceway

Hielscher persevered. Evel Knievel once wowed a crowd of 35,000, jumping over a dozen Mack trucks on national television. But the growing number of neighbors complained about the noise and the crowds. In 1981 a free drag-racing program and rock concert attracted 55,000 fans, twice the population of North Richland at the time. Twelve were arrested for intoxication, and two police officers were slightly injured. The police estimated that 40 percent of the crowd was drunk. Twenty-five traffic accidents resulted, and the traffic was backed up four miles all afternoon.

Five hundred citizens packed the next meeting of the City Council, demanding action against the raceway, and they got it. A far more restrictive public gathering ordinance was passed that night, requiring special permits for events attracting more than 500 people, and a city lawsuit was soon filed. Hielscher fought the rule in court for more than a year, and got an injunction that allowed the track to operate in violation of the ordinances until the suit was settled. The track was expanded in 1984 for the Texas Challenge. Now there were six turns, including a hairpin at the end of the 1,400-foot straightaway that started the race. Temporary grandstands were erected. But by 1986 Hielscher faced legal costs of up to $100,000, $100-per-day property taxes, high land values, and a court order to end the races. Finally, after the last race in July 1986, Hielscher completed the two-year sale process to developers. Green Valley Elementary School, which opened in 1992, occupies nine of the acres, while the remaining 141 are the Forest Glen West subdivision. Dorothy McClure also sold in the late 1980s, except for 18 acres of wooded flood plain at the intersection of Cherokee Trail and Davis. She donated the acreage to a youth organization, the First Texas Council of Camp Fire, which named their new campsite Camp McClure.

Trudging through flood plains was all in a day's work for some city employees. Reading water meters was still something of an adventure in the still developing town in the 1970s, as reported by Chris Johnson in 1979. He was one of three meter readers at the time who kept tabs on 11,253 meters. To reach the meters sometimes required traipsing through tall grass, through ants, chiggers, or mud. While gas and electric meters were mounted above ground, water meters were subsurface and often surrounded by snakes, lizards, birds, spiders,

Fossil Creek flood east of Birdville Football Stadium, view from Belknap

frogs, or scorpions. One was filled with horse manure every month as a playful prank. Johnson reported that he really liked his job. In 1993 North Richland became one of the first cities in the country to begin purchasing an automated water meter reading system. The new meters emit radio signals picked up by a city-operated van. One person can now get an accurate reading of every meter in the city in one and a half days.

But community and identity were lingering issues in old Smithfield. In 1975 a *Fort Worth Star-Telegram* reporter visited the new Glenann Addition, east of old Smithfield between Amundson and Main, wondering how the residents identified themselves. They lived in North Richland Hills, paid Birdville school taxes, had a Fort Worth telephone listing, and a Smithfield address. The local post office at 6716 Smithfield Road still bore the Smithfield (Branch of Fort Worth) name, to the consternation of North Richland Hills officials. In an unscientific survey of fifteen families, fourteen expressed no confusion—they knew they lived in Smithfield. One family had recently discovered that they lived in North Richland Hills. Former Smithfield Mayor Charles Zartman groused that local residents joined North Richland Hills with the idea of escaping taxes, but since that time taxes had continually risen. His lament was literally true through 1973, but taxes were rising throughout the Metroplex and would have risen had Smithfield remained incorporated. North Richland taxes had actually decreased for two years before Zartman's interview. Zartman also complained that the

The country lifestyle still is enjoyed in some parts of NRH but is rapidly vanishing.

Glenann Addition was the former site of two ponds where he used to take his children fishing. Like many rural dwellers who suddenly found themselves in the suburbs, Zartman was having difficulty adjusting to continual development and the demise of old Smithfield. He was not alone. As late as 1980 a newspaper account of the opening of the First United Bank referred to its primary service area as Richland Hills, Watauga, North Richland Hills, and Smithfield.

The country lifestyle was being rapidly supplanted in the 1970s, so the transition from countryside to suburb took place in less than a generation. Ruth Coppock arrived as principal of the Smithfield School in 1976 and found a village elementary school of 350. There were empty rooms in the old building. Fifth graders adjourned one day to watch a calf being born in the pasture next to the playground. The event would have been so commonplace

that the class diversion would have been unnecessary a few years earlier, so rural sensibilities were already beginning to yield. Three years later when Coppock left, the school population had doubled, and all rooms were full. The pasture was part of a subdivision, which precluded any more neighborly natural science lessons.

It was in the 1970s that the wet-dry issue, a staple in Texas politics since the 1850s, reached North Richland Hills. State law declares Texas wet unless cities or justice of the peace precincts vote dry, which many have done, especially in west, north, and east Texas. The rural Justice Precinct Three in northeast Tarrant County voted dry in 1941. By 1973 Justice Three included two-thirds of North Richland, everything north of Loop 820 and east of Rufe Snow, as well as neighboring towns to the east and northeast. The other third of North Richland had also long been dry territory.

With the opening of the Dallas-Fort Worth Airport, however, hotel chains informed the chambers of commerce, local politicians, and other interest groups that they were not going to build at a dry airport, that there would be no convention trade. Suddenly in July 1973 the "wets" slipped up on the "drys" in Justice Precinct Three, and petitioned for an election that would legalize the sale of beer off premises and the sale of mixed drinks. There was an immediate reaction by dry forces in full-page ads, denouncing the liquor interests for corrupting the area. The wets slipped by the drys in most of the 15 voting precincts. The sale of off-premises beer won 6,383 to 5,998 and mixed drinks won 6,227 to 6,077. Restaurants and liquor stores could now dispense beer and hard liquor, though their locations were subject to city zoning laws. By the time the dry forces had mustered for a second election, 12 supermarkets and convenience stores sold beer for off-premises consumption and Steak and Ale Restaurant sold mixed drinks. In April 1977, the drys triumphed in a much lighter turnout in Justice Precinct Three by a six-to-five margin, averaging 1,458 to 1,230 on each of the two separate votes regarding the sales of beer and mixed drinks. Unfortunately for the drys, the petitions that had persuaded the county commissioners to call the election were filled with hundreds of signatures that were signed by other people, were ineligible voters, or who gave their addresses as Fort Worth

Courtesy of American Airlines

Aerial view of an American Airlines terminal at DFW Airport, 1983

121

or Smithfield—among other glitches. District Judge Charles Murray voided the election. The drys forced another election, August 9, 1977, in Justice Three, but lost the two issues by a total of 4,548 to 3,089.

Thus only a third of North Richland remained dry, and even that did not last. Birra Poretti's restaurant, being constructed in North Hills Mall, requested a liquor license in 1985 and was informed that the mall lay in the dry portion of North Richland Hills. But the restaurant's attorney noticed that the August 1977 ballot and the canvassing of votes by the county stated that the election pertained to North Richland Hills, not to Justice Precinct Three. Because of this 1977 election snafu, the county district attorney determined in July 1985 that the whole city was wet. It has been so ever since.

Most merchants regard the sale of liquor and beer as essential to recreation and tourism.

Red Lobster, one of the anchors of Restaurant Row

Adding to the recreational milieu is the Tarantula Corporation's steam locomotive, built in 1896 that began running on the old Cotton Belt tracks in 1996. The corporation takes its name from B. B. Paddock's 1873 map that depicted Fort Worth as a blob in the center with the legs of future railroads and stagecoach lines radiating in various directions. The Tarantula train runs between the Fort Worth Stockyards and Grapevine's historical district, and stops for water in North Richland Hills near the municipal complex. Some local entrepreneurs hope that a plan may be devised someday whereby the train will stop for a longer, more substantive period in North Richland Hills. The Iron Horse Golf Course has adopted the nickname of the old steam engines.

The year 1986 marked a distinctive celebration and two closures. It was the last hurrah of the Texas Sesquicentennial, which honored the Lone Star State's 150th birthday. Pioneer days were recreated by a train of 150 wagons and hundreds of horsemen, who camped at Green Valley Raceway June 30–July 2. Tens of thousands visited the North Richland campsite for free entertainment and presentations. The caravan ended its 3,000-mile journey at the Fort Worth Stockyards July 4. The Green Valley Raceway and Mangham Airport closed their doors that same year, both considered a nuisance by the city and both squeezed out by development. The racing track and runways were demolished.

Georgia (Anderson) Ward and niece, Mary Ruth (Reeves) Ellis enjoying the wagon train festivities during the Sesquicentennial celebration in NRH.

122

BUSINESS IN THE 1980S AND 1990S

The Haltom-Richland Chamber of Commerce held a groundbreaking for its new, expanded headquarters in May 1982, at 5001 Denton Highway in Haltom City. Some 250 people gathered on a tract that was still infested with varmints living in the high grass. Charles Brinkley recalls, "Being a country boy from Weatherford, I knew what that meant. So I told the crowd that I was going home and take a bath with a half-cup of ammonia in my tub. Some laughed, but apparently there was a run on ammonia at local drug-stores. One fellow even sprayed himself with Windex." The chamber quickly recovered from the chigger blunder and during the next 10 years it took its current name of Northeast Tarrant, adopted a new logo featuring four stars, and planted an oak tree in each of the four member cities: Watauga, Haltom City, Richland Hills, and North Richland Hills. Despite the death of veteran director Gertrude Tarpley in 1994, it was in the 1990s that the chamber renewed its programs to assist member businesses, especially small businesses, market their goods and services. Change is the chamber's constant companion, and given the new influx of technology firms, it may be that work-force education will be a focus of the chamber's efforts.

Courtesy of Tommy Brown

Mayor Tommy Brown worked during his ten-year term to bring NRH to the national and international economic forefront. Because of his efforts today the City of NRH is known and respected by State and National officials. Tommy and Sue Brown with President Bill Clinton.

The face of the Grapevine Highway is another story of constant change since the mid-1950s. The Rapid Mart property was sold to Revco, and then to Eckerd Drug, but it remained the "Rapid Mart" corner to many in the community. The Eckerd closed in 1997, and the North Richland Hills Baptist Church now owns the property. The fruit stands at the old Dairy Kreem site were demolished and the lots cleaned off in 1996. Parchman's swimming pool, surpassed by others, was filled in. After 25 years in the service station business, L. C. Akins sold his Exxon franchise to Shorty Hall in 1980. The building now houses Richland Cleaners. The Hobby Lobby stands at the same site; Paul Mason passed away in 1977, but grandson John "Tripp" McGuffin has managed the store since 1985.

The North Richland Hills Barber Shop has operated on three sites within the Greater Richland Center, and Don Parker and Bill Otwell have changed its name to Pro Barber Shop, but it remains a popular meeting and greeting place in the community. In March 1998 Don Parker gave the first hair-cut to ten-month-old Derek Wheeler, the fourth generation of Wheelers to receive haircuts from Parker. Paul Wheeler, 75 in 1998, first visited the shop in 1962, followed by Robert Wheeler, 45, Jason Wheeler, 24, and Derek. They are part of a tradition worthy of barbershop conversation. PRO Barber is one of the oldest, continuously run businesses in the city.

Traditional meeting places eventually die and perhaps the saddest demise in North Richland Hills was that of Town and Country Drug in the Greater Richland Center. Modern drugstores are not usually a site for childhood memories,

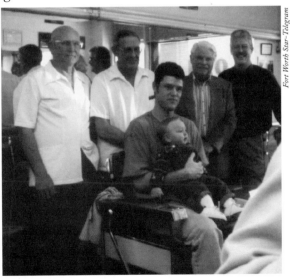

Fort Worth Star–Telegram

4 generations of the male-side of the Wheeler family have received haircuts from Don Parker at PRO Barber Shop in NRH.

weddings, and baby showers, family charge accounts, employees who know customers by name, or even hamburgers, but all were characteristic of Alan and Nancy Hamm's original store in the Town and Country chain. The 14 stores were sold to Eckerd in 1992, which closed the Greater Richland store because it was too close to the Eckerd at Grapevine Highway and Vance Road. Longtime employees like Eva Evans, Marie Erskine, and Thelma Town cried and reminisced, as did many of their customer friends who had been patronizing the place for 20 or 30 years. Eckerds would have done far better to reverse the closings, since the Vance Road store was shuttered five years later and two new ones were built in the area, but national chains have no roots in any community. Commendably, Eckerds and the Hamms worked out job opportunities for everyone, but the veteran workers scattered, and Eckerd's store policies are set by national standards rather than local family-style practices.

The Richland Plaza shopping center was dealt another blow in 1979, when North Hills Mall opened at the intersection of Loop 820 and Grapevine Highway. As development moved northward, Richland Plaza's tenants declined to renew their leases. Tandy Corporation leased a large section for a time for an assembling center for computers. Thrift Town kept its business at Richland Plaza for years. So did Montgomery Ward, which pulled out in 1997. Pancho's Mexican Restaurant remains, and there is an office furniture store, resale shop, barber shop, karate school, tax assistance service, and an auto repair facility currently doing business, all on the east side, facing Grapevine Highway. The west portion of the mall is vacant and all the stores along the open interior of the mall are boarded up. Thrift Town kept its business at Richland Plaza for years. The rusty, graffiti-covered water tower on the backside of the Plaza parking lot was demolished in 1996, though the old tower was much stronger than the wrecking crews anticipated. The city's Environmental Services Department held a community outreach event for Texas Recycles Day, November 17, 1997, an apt event for a center that needs to be recycled. Fort Worth developer Richard Bates set out to do just that. He bought Richland Plaza and is redeveloping it into an office center, which should meet the city's goals for the area.

The nearby Richland Bowl continued to operate, but ran into harder times. Bowling itself had lost some popularity, but Ray Lofland continued to believe that, "I can count on my fingers the number of kids who bowl that have gotten into trouble." Lofland did not give up easily. He renovated every few years and finally, in dismay, added a video games parlor. But he closed his bowling alley in 1993 and died the next year. Thrift Town then purchased the building from the Lofland family for about $200,000, intending to spend $350,000 on renovations. But the roof needed replacement rather than repair, and the walls had to be torn down and rebuilt. The project ended up about $350,000 over budget, and Thrift Town, as manager James Reid noted, was clearly making a long-term commitment to the city and the area. After 21 years at Richland Plaza, Thrift Town moved into its greatly renovated building in the mid-1990s. As Dave Lieber noted in his Northeast Beat column in the *Fort Worth Star-Telegram*, "Somebody has finally picked up Ray Lofland's commitment from decades before."

Northeast Bancorp, the parent company for Northeast National Bank, acquired the First State Bank of Bedford in 1977 and named Clyde Wood, a resident of North Richland Hills since 1953, as president. Other subsidiary banks were acquired and a six-story tower was completed in 1978 as Bancorp's headquarters. It was the first high rise building in North Richland Hills, and the Fire Department was concerned about how it would handle a fire should one occur. Locally owned banks began disappearing in the United States, and Northeast Bancorp, after changing to Texas United Bancorp, was itself acquired in May 1984 by Allied Bancshares of Houston. Allied was purchased by First Interstate in 1989, which in turn was bought by Wells Fargo Bank of Los Angeles in 1996.

At the same time, some 60 North Richland Hills residents and city officials and Haltom-Richland Area Chamber of Commerce representatives attended the grand opening ceremonies officially welcoming the First United Bank—Richland. A ribbon of dollar bills was cut on July 21, 1980 at the bank's new facility, 6100 Rufe Snow Drive, about a mile north of Loop 820. The 5,000-square-foot bank (now a Nations Bank), complete with drive-in, was built by Walker Construction Company of North Richland Hills. Rufe Snow was so sparsely developed at the time that many observers wondered why it was built so far out from anything, in the plains wilderness north of the railroad tracks. President Robert Harrison had lived in the community for more than 30 years and was well aware that the rebuilt Rufe Snow Drive would generate considerable and rapid development.

And in the early 1980s business establishments, also anticipating the growth of suburbs to the north of Loop 820 on Rufe Snow, began building in the direction of the bank. One of the first was a McDonald's near the northeast corner, which also appeared to be in the wilderness at the time. By 1984 the outlet mall named Richland Pointe, several more fast food restaurants, Pippins Restaurant (later Tippins), and a strip center just north of these businesses were beginning to flourish. Also on the east side of Rufe Snow near the Loop, Minyard's Grocery opened its 54th store with fanfare, in the summer of 1984, with Chairman of the Board M. T. "Buddy" Minyard in attendance. An adjacent two-story building housed several retail, service oriented, and office businesses. This site became known as Northwood Plaza. The second phase of this center became home to the area's first Wal-Mart in late 1984. Rufe Snow Village in the southeast quadrant of Rufe Snow and Watauga Road (Mid-Cities Boulevard) featured a Kroger Store with almost 50,000 square feet.

In 1981 only eight businesses were counted on Rufe Snow, but by 1983 there were more than a hundred. When the sales tax revenue from them was added to that generated by the North Hills Mall, Grapevine Highway businesses, and various strip centers, North Richland had a sales tax income envied by most of its neighbors.

Light industry added to the picture. Walker Construction employed some 500 people by 1984, Sanger Harris 325, and the $7 million Graham Magnetics plant 260. Graham, a computer tape manufacturer, was the first industry to locate in North Richland (1980) under a nonprofit industrial corporation chartered by the City Council in the late 1970s. Under the program the company could receive tax free, low interest revenue bonds to purchase existing buildings or construct a new building within the city.

Raymond Anderson continued operating North Richland Furniture until a few years before his death in 1994, and Hazel Anderson has continued to run the store since that time. The old advantage of low countryside overhead expense has vanished, but this is probably the second oldest business in North Richland Hills. The Andersons have sold furniture to three generations of some families.

Similarly, McGee's Garage on Rufe Snow has been in business continually since 1958 or 1959. Bob has continued working on motors. After William McGee developed health problems, he had to give up the electrical work and devote full time to the administrative end of garage work. In later years "Mac" was at work every day in a wheelchair. Mac died in 1997, but Bob continues operating the garage, and his mother Roberta has assumed Mac's duties.

Clarence "Barber" Cobb was presented with a plaque in 1970 by North Richland residents, mostly from the old Smithfield area, in celebration of his 50 years of barbering in the community. While he remained full of stories and conversation, he continued to enforce the house rule that politics and religion could not be discussed. Well into his eighties, in the early 1980s, Barber Cobb continued to cut hair in the old frame shop six days a week, from 7 A.M. to 6 P.M. He was still uninterested in adjusting to the times, so there were no magazines in the shop and there were no shag cuts or layered cuts. He retired from cutting hair shortly before his death in 1986. Marvin Smith, a lifelong resident of the Smithfield area who remembered Cobb's stories and his handing out nickels to children for soft drinks, rebuilt Cobb's dilapidated shop in brick, where it still stands at 8000 Main, marked with Smith's historical plaque. The building now houses Nail Perfection and Morning Donuts.

The first public inkling of the single most important economic development in the history of the city occurred on August 26, 1977. Mayor Newman and the City Council met in emergency session to approve a plat for a site in the 7600 block of Texas 121. Only minutes before the meeting, the Planning and Zoning Commission unanimously approved plats for the proposed site. Sanger-Harris would soon commence building a 170,000-square-foot store that might anchor a Federated Department Stores' shopping center. Within days, Federated, which owned Sanger-Harris, confirmed that construction of the mall would begin after Sanger-Harris had been open about a year, in October 1978. The Walker Construction Company of North Richland Hills excavated the site and did miscellaneous metal work and caulking and waterproofing. Sanger's was joined by Cox's as an anchor store and by 55 specialty shops for the grand opening of North Hills Mall, September 12, 1979. It is considered a "boutique mall" because of its design, decoration and the preponderance of independent shops rather than chain operations. One of the decorative highlights is the ten-foot high bronze sculpture, "Kids in a Tree," by G. Pat Foley of Houston. A third anchor, Mervyn's, and more than a dozen new stores were added in 1985. Malls receive face-lifts periodically, and North Hills installed brighter floors, new restrooms, and a more easily accessible food court in 1993. The mall creates almost a thousand jobs and has been a vital contributor to North Richland Hills' tax base. Since the mid-1990s, North Hills Mall has been challenged by construction on the Loop and the opening of Grapevine Mills mall in October 1997. But much of the construction interference ended in 1997, and sales tax revenues increased in 1997–1998 despite the new competition from Grapevine Mills. North Hills faces the massive renovation of the North East Mall across the Loop in 1998–1999, but North Hills Mall is expanding also, and there appears to be room for all in the Metroplex.

The North Richland Hills City Council organized the Economic Development Department in 1987, designed to aid existing businesses, to attract new business, and to promote tourism. Tax abatements were part of the strategy, and helped the city land the four-story AEGON (now MEGA Life and Health) Insurance Center in 1989. The abatements helped motivate Tecnol (now Kimberly-Clark) to expand its facilities in 1992.

A well-known bedding producer, Sealy Mattress Manufacturing, and a regional box manufacturer, Bates Container Inc., are other major firms that have maintained a corporate presence in North Richland Hills for several years. A sizable industry that entered the city in 1998 was H and M Foods, a major manufacturer of pizza toppings and custom-made foods. It began shutting down its Fort Worth plant and consolidating all operations in its North Richland Hills center, which is undergoing a $17 million overhaul and expansion.

North Hills Hospital's $26 million renovation and expansion illustrate how tax abatements can help both community and corporation. After agreeing to abate the real property improvements, $16 million in value, of an announced $20.8 million hospital expansion, the city began realizing a return on its investment when the hospital announced plans to add two additional floors to its medical office building and open a pediatric day surgery facility. Besides adding another 50 or so jobs, the additions increase the project's value by $5.2 million, all of which is taxable.

As Texas Business magazine pointed out in 1995 when its editors selected North Richland Hills as one of the state's five "Cities to Watch," the city "is perfectly situated to benefit from both Alliance and Dallas/Fort Worth International airports" and has "good economic development packages available." A few years later North Richland became the fourth city in Tarrant County to reach the $2 billion level of appraised property value, making it, in the words of the *Star-Telegram*, a "prominent player."

REFLECTIONS ON THE CURRENT SCENE

For North Richland Hills, the largest city in Northeast Tarrant County, attaining its own post office and zip code was a key step toward achieving identity as a major city. Finally in 1992 at the Davis Street station the North Richland branch of the Fort Worth system was changed on the front sign to "U.S. Post Office, North Richland Hills, Texas." Postal officials were so proud of the sign that they took a couple of photos and mailed them to Mayor Brown. They addressed the letter to "Mayor Tommy Brown, Fort Worth, Texas 76180." C. A. Sanford recalled, "Tommy said he can't win."

Traffic congestion and potholed streets remained ongoing, leading issues in the 1990s, of more concern to most citizens than a search for identity. The Four Points-Loop 820 area and the Rufe Snow corridor have generated the most complaints, and many drivers can barely remember when they were not under construction. After purchase of a new truck and patching equipment in the spring of 1991, the Public Works Service Center announced it would repair any pothole pointed out by any resident and do it within 48 hours. During the program's first two weeks 100 callers reported 100 different chug holes, but the Pothole Patrol was able to keep to its 48-hour timetable. After three months the calls had slowed to one or two per day. In an interview in 1991 Mayor Brown stated, "Within five years I hope we have most of the road problems cleared up." Much like a fast pitch thrown by a Texas Ranger hurler, this may have been an idle thought tossed out by the mayor, which he wanted to retrieve immediately.

In any case, the continuing road construction in the early 1990s did look promising. The completion of Industrial Park Boulevard already gave some motorists an alternative to Rufe Snow, and the widening of Bursey Road, commencing in 1992, promised to do the same. But the $12,000,000 widening of Rufe Snow itself (from five to seven lanes from Loop 820 to Mid-Cities Boulevard), over half of it paid with federal grant money, did not get under way until 1999, causing some restiveness among voters. Meanwhile, the first phase of the 10-year project to revamp the Loop 820-Grapevine Highway interchange was completed and celebrated in April, 1997, with the opening of six lanes on 820 and turn lanes on Grapevine Highway. But neither the 1994 bond program for street repair nor the city's ongoing street overlay program provided enough money to keep up with North Richland's growth and traffic.

Besides streets, the city has also been concerned recently about tourism. In hopes of competing for the tourist trade, special projects manager C. A. Sanford unveiled a $1.2 million

127

plan, in October, 1997, for a banquet center to be added to the clubhouse at Iron Horse Golf Course. The banquet hall would seat about 300 and would be styled as a turn-of-the-century railroad depot. Mayor Brown noted that there were hundreds of church, civic, and regional groups that needed such a rental facility, especially on the western edge of Northeast Tarrant County.

The seemingly endless cycle of more taxes and more streets has prompted some to embrace mass transit as an alternative. An inexpensive interurban line once ran between Fort Worth and Dallas and other area cities in the early years of the century, and mass transit is returning to the area. DART is proving its value in Dallas today and its joint venture with the "T" in Fort Worth, with a stop in Richland Hills, partially revives the interurban. North Richland Hills and the other area cities whose boundaries are not touched by the tracks can benefit nevertheless. But mass transit will not displace the car culture. Suburban life is not possible without a car. To be a suburbanite is to be almost always on the road—traveling to work, school, supermarkets, and soccer games. The sheer number of destinations in the average suburbanite's day overwhelms any other form of transportation. There are now more cars than there are drivers in the suburbs, doubtless including North Richland Hills. The cycle of taxes and streets will go on.

City environmental consciousness arose in the 1990s. The Consumer Health Division, which had to add staff, inspected mobile food trucks, waste hauling trucks, grocery stores,

Courtesy of Sean Hughes

Ribbon cutting at Adventure World in June, 1994, a playground in the City's 100 Acre Park, located north of Starnes. L/R Mark Wood, Linda Spurlock, Mayor Tommy Brown, Congressman Pete Geren, JoAnn Johnson, Cheryl Lyman, Bob Watkins, Ann Perchard, Jay Jenson, Kathy Graves, Avis Crisp

convenience stores, foster homes, and swimming pools. Its ozone awareness and household hazardous waste programs helped place the city as a finalist for the Governor's Award for Environmental Excellence in 1996 and won several grants from the state. Urban forestry efforts within the city are notable too, such as the Trophy Tree program, the preservation of bluestem prairie grass at the Hundred Acre Park, and the transplanting of prairie grasses from fields that are being developed.

Parks and recreation are invariably postponed longer than other city projects in burgeoning communities, but in the 1990s North Richland caught up. Mayor Brown and the council thought the time was right, and on August 8, 1992, 52 percent of the voters approved an additional half-cent city sales tax (a third to a half of which was expected to be paid by non-residents) for new parks. Bonds were sold before the year was out in order to secure coveted land in various areas of the city. In the five years since the extra half-penny sales tax was added, it has generated about $3,500,000 annually, and another $9,000,000 has been acquired from state and federal grants.

A water facility was the first priority in the city's long-range master plan for parks and recreation. Residents had long wanted more pools. Construction began in 1993 on the Family Water Park, NRH2O, which opened in 1995. The city invested some $8 million in bonds for the water park, a debt being paid off with money from the special half-cent sales tax. The Green Extreme, which carries raft riders uphill at 19 feet a second, cost $2.5 million, financed through bonds paid off by park revenue. Some 200,000 people come annually to frolic in the wave pool and other segments. The revenue has averaged more than $2 million per year during its first four years and has increased every year.

Acquisition of a hundred acres for a centerpiece city park north of Starnes also commenced immediately after the bond sale. Land for the Hundred Acre Park was donated by Gary Starnes and Mr. Walter Wolff. Adventure World playground within the Hundred Acre park is designed to accommodate creative play for children of all ages. It is one of the largest totally accessible playgrounds in the country. The Adventure World project was completed with the combined efforts of the city, school district, and community volunteers. The city of NRH provided the infrastructure, Birdville ISD provided an opportunity for children to submit design plans (Local students submitted drawings of the ideal playground and top drawings were selected as part of the plan for Adventure World), and the community built the playground. There is also a fitness course. Native trees and grasses were consciously conserved. Fund-raising projects were held over the course of two years, and on the first two weekends of May 1994, the community came together to actually build Adventure World. No matter the age or skill level, there was a place for everyone. A Richland High School child development class coordinated the childcare for volunteer workers and local restaurants provided food and refreshments. By the end of the second weekend, Adventure World was built. In

Community members building the playground at Adventure World.

June 1994, a large party was held for the official grand opening. Hundreds of adults and children were a part of the celebration. Finally the dream had become a reality.

The extra half-penny tax has allowed the Parks and Recreation Department under Jim Browne and the park board under Don Tipps to put together an astonishing number of projects for a city the size of North Richland. One unique effort is a joint enterprise with the Birdville School District. The BISD donated a 33.5 acre tract northeast of Richland High for a sports complex—with tennis courts, soccer fields and more—which the city and school share.

Roger Brooks, raised on a farm at Rufe Snow and Watauga Road, once interviewed a fellow old-timer from the area who recollected his amazement about the last sixty-some-odd years. Asked if he had seen a lot of changes, the old-timer replied, "Yep, and I've been against almost every one of 'em." While there is no turning back, perhaps we can do more than sympathize with what has been lost or relive history in books.

The city government must maintain a flexibility about the master plan and zoning, and it seems to be doing so. A "neo-traditional" development has been proposed for about 330 acres north of NRH2O along the west side of Cardinal Lane. It is a proposed back-to-the-basics community where people live, work, and play without being a part of the car culture around them. It would be an old-fashioned type of community, with different sized homes, where children walk to the grocery store to buy bread and where merchants live above their places of business. Nearby ice rinks and performing arts venues are part of the proposed site. But if the rare, back-to-basics neighborhood and pedestrian-friendly site for visitors becomes a reality, it will certainly add to the identity of North Richland Hills.

Another innovative development that required rezoning is the 252 unit, upscale, multi-family townhouse complex for families and professionals who work at home. Western Rim Investors erected the rental units, The Villas on the Green, at Emerald Hills Way and Grapevine Highway. A six-foot masonry wall marks the frontage on Grapevine Highway. There's a computer-laden business center, with fax machines and copiers, a day-care center, hiking and picnic areas, and sports facilities.

Before the spring 1998 elections, the city seemed to show less flexibility in regard to a zoning question in a rural part of Davis Boulevard in the far north of the city. A developer wanted to build storage warehouses that would back up to Steeple Ridge, where homeowners were worried about crime if the facility was open around the clock, large parking lots, and lights that would be lit all the time. They feared the dense commercial look of South Davis. The zoning would have to be changed from agricultural to commercial, but Davis is already designated as a commercial corridor in the city's land use plan, so the city intended to follow through and allow the warehouses. One reason a city has a zoning plan is to prevent battles for variances from taking up all the time in planning and zoning committee meetings and City Council sessions. A good plan should be adhered to, and as Mayor Brown noted, the building codes today are tighter than those prevailing when much of South Davis was developed. Lights would be pointed away from homes and a six-foot masonry fence would buffer any developments next to homes. Since warehouses required a special use permit, the city had the option of stipulating hours of operation. But nearly 200 residents in the area were not appeased and asserted that Colleyville and Southlake had stricter standards. Whether this was truth or merely some citizens' perception of truth is not known, but the issue generated strong feelings leading up to the election.

The dispute did not affect Mayor Brown personally or politically because he had already decided to bow out. Despite recent complaints about streets and zoning, which have plagued every city administration, Tommy Brown had sufficient accomplishments to serve an unprecedented 10 years as mayor, and he retired undefeated in mayoralty contests. Charles Scoma made it a point in his successful mayoralty campaign in 1998 to call for more citizen involvement in zoning and ordinance reviews. After the election the City Council unanimously rejected the mini-warehouse plan and seemed poised to speed up the already planned reexamination of zoning corridors in general as well as landscaping and sign ordinances.

North Richland Hills is perhaps 75 percent built out as of 1998, which gives city authorities a rare opportunity to ponder the most recent trends regarding urban sprawl. In the late 1990s, calls for "smart growth" in metropolitan areas are coming not just from traditional environmentalists and liberals, but also from conservatives trying to preserve the character of their communities. Increasingly, just as there is no Democratic or Republican way to pave a street, the same is true for saving greenbelts and open space. The slow-growth movement has become potent in several western cities and states. The idea is to steer local government money away from subsidizing development. The slogan is "let growth pay for growth," meaning that if developers want to put in new subdivisions, they should also pay an appropriate proportion of the costs, not just of roads and sewers but also nearby schools and fire stations. Even more sweeping are "urban growth boundaries" modeled after a Portland, Oregon, plan (and neighboring communities) that restricts development to an area inside a specified line to protect the open spaces or woodlands beyond it.

Many commuters returning home from work, taking the Holiday Lane or Rufe Snow or Grapevine Highway exit, probably regard North Richland Hills as just another name for their exit off the highway. It is just their access to the malls and the airport and their schools and grocery stores. Hopefully that is changing. With NRH2O, the Iron Horse Golf Course, the 100-acre centerpiece park and other delightful parks, perhaps a few unique neighborhoods, the opportunity to preserve more greenery, and maybe a greater appreciation of its historical heritage, North Richland Hills has just about found that long-sought identity.

North Richland Hills Homes of the 1940s to 1990s

Inez and H. M. "Mc" Howes' home, built by Joe Womack in the late 1940s, which is now the site of Bursey Senior Center.

Bursey Senior Center - 1997

The 12 acres, surrounding the Clarence Jones' home were set aside for the North Richland Shopping Center. Since Jones colonial-style house sat on this property it was moved north to Cummings Drive. The home was later bricked.

Lacy Stewart home, 1989.

Area Homes Circa '60s to '90s

Area Homes Circa '80s to '90s

2 Government

MAYOR, COUNCIL, AND ADMINISTRATION STAFF

North Richland Hills operates under a "council-manager" form of government. The city manager is responsible for the day to day operation of the City. The seven member City Council is responsible for all policy matters. The mayor participates in the discussion of all matters coming before the council and shall be entitled to vote in case of a tie. During its 45-year history, NRH has had 14 men occupy the office of mayor.

MAYOR AND COUNCIL

The city's first council meeting was June 23, 1953.

1953–Council

T. S. Christopher
J. T. Norman
N. A. Ellenburg
Paul Kutilek
R. F. Lambert
Secretary: R. F. Lambert

MAYOR J. W. WATSON was elected in 1953, becoming NRH's first mayor. He served a one year term. The city was established as a legal entity operating under a general law system.

1954–1956 Councils

1954

Mayor Pro Tem Boyd E. Ray
K. B. "Ace" Nace
W. T. MacCarthy
N. A. Ellenburg
Robert Hays

1955

Mayor Pro Tem: T. S. Christopher
K. B. "Ace" Nace
N. A. Ellenburg
Boyd E. Ray
W. T. MacCarthy

1956

Mayor Pro Tem: T. S. Christopher
Council Members:
James M. Williamson
Paul Kutilek
N. A. Ellenburg
K. B. "Ace" Nace

MAYOR DONALD F. DENNEY 1954–56. With no city hall, the City Council often met in the Denney living room. The first land for a park was acquired.

1957–Council

Mayor Pro Tem: Clyde Wood
Council Members:
Wayne Franklin
Paul Kutilek
Bill Putnam
N. A. Ellenburg

MAYOR K. B. "ACE" NACE served in 1957. A small, two-room office in the Richardson Center was rented for city offices.

MAYOR THOMAS McFARLAND JR., 1958. NRH increased greatly in size when the Smithfield area was annexed.

1958–Council

Mayor Pro Tem: Paul Kutilek

Stanley Graner

Harden Rowe

Wayne Franklin

Bill Putnam

BILL PERRY became mayor in 1959-60. This was a very turbulent period politically for North Richland Hills. Mr. Perry was removed from office in June 1960.

1959–Council

Mayor Pro Tem: Paul Kutilek

Stanley Graner

Clyde Zellers

Harden Rowe

Wayne Franklin

MAYOR CLYDE ZELLERS: In a special called election in August 1960, the unexpired portion of the former mayor's term was filled by acting Mayor Clyde Zellers who was elected mayor. He decided not to run for reelection.

1960–Council

Mayor Pro Tem: Clyde Zellers until special election, then Stanley Graner

Kenneth E. Johns

Herbert Campbell

Kenneth Bell Jr.

Herb Owens

MAYOR JOHN P. HUNTER, April 1961 to April 1966. During Mr. Hunter's administration, population rose to more than 8,000 residents and the city received its home-rule charter in 1964.

1961–1965 Councils

1961

Mayor Pro Tem: Herbert Campbell
Claude White
W. T. Terrell
Kenneth Bell Jr.
Kenneth E. Johns

1962

Mayor Pro Tem: Herbert Campbell
Kenneth E. Johns
Kenneth Bell Jr.
Claude White
Granville L. Edwards

1963

Mayor Pro Tem: Herbert Campbell
W. B. "Bill" Leffingwell
Joe Barnett
Alvis Dowell
Kenneth E. Johns

1964

Mayor Pro Tem: Don Roberts
L. B. Falcone
T. C. Stevens
Joe Barnett
Alvis Dowell

1965

Mayor Pro Tem: Alvis Dowell
P. M. "Tex " Dodson
Harold B. Daley
Dick Faram
Dick H. King
John B. Sandlin
Fred Chester

In 1965 NRH became a home rule city, which required seven council members elected to council places one to seven.

MAYOR CALVIN LUPER, 1966 to 1970. The city's first bond issue was passed.

1966–1970 Councils

1966–67

Mayor Pro Tem: Fred Chester
Council Members:
P. M. "Tex" Dodson
James R. "Buck" Hubbard
Harold B. Daley
Dick Faram
James F. "Jim" Cato
John B. Sandlin

1968–70

Mayor Pro Tem: J. R. "Buck " Hubbard
Council Members:
P. M. "Tex" Dodson
Harold B. Daley
Dick Faram
J. F. "Jim" Cato
John B. Sandlin
Morris E. Riddle

The north side of Grapevine Highway had previously had its name changed to North Richland Boulevard; the south side of the street however, which was inside Richland Hills city limits, continued to be named Grapevine Highway. Merchants on the north side of the street petitioned to change the name back to Grapevine Highway. The city agreed and the two sides were reunited as Grapevine Highway.

MARION MASSEY, 1970–1974.
The first library was opened in 1971.

1970–1973 Councils

1970–1971

Mayor Pro Tem: J. R. Hubbard
M. E. Riddle (resigned 5/24/71)
W. N. Ratcliff (7/23/71)
Dick Faram
W. F. "Bill" Poister
Tom E. Newman
J. F. "Jim" Cato
Charles L. Owen

1972–1973

Mayor Pro Tem: Dick Faram
Lloyd McKinney
Norman Ellis (5/2/72)
Walter Smith
Tom E. Newman
J. F. "Jim" Cato
Mrs. Glenn (JoAnn) Goodnight

MAYOR DICK FARAM served eight years as
mayor, but not consecutively. First elected in
1974, he was mayor until 1976, and then served
again from 1978 to 1984.

1974–75 Councils

Mayor Pro Tem: Dr. Norman Ellis
James T. "Jim" Wood Jr. (5/7/74)
Mrs. Bill (Dorothy) McClure (7/12/75)
George Conant Jr.
John Lamond III
Tom E. Newman
J. F. "Jim" Cato
Mrs. Glenn (JoAnn) Goodnight

TOM E. NEWMAN was mayor for one term,
1976–77. During his term the library moved to
larger quarters in the City Hall building. NRH
had the greatest number of housing starts in
northeast Tarrant County during this period.

1976–77 Councils

Mayor Pro Tem: James F. Cato
Denver Mills (5/8/76)
Mrs. Bill (Dorothy) McClure
George Conant Jr.
John Lamond (5/8/76)
Walter Smith
JoAnn Goodnight (resigned 1977)
Dave Freeman (2/9/77)

DICK FARAM'S second term as mayor ran from 1978 to 1984. North Hills Mall opened. Council members' terms were staggered after 1982, with the mayor and Places 2, 4, and 6 being elected in even years and Places 1, 3, 5, and 7 in odd years.

1978–83 Councils

1978–1979

Mayor Pro Tem: James F. Cato
Denver Mills
Lena Mae Reeder
James T. Wood (5/3/78)
John Michener Jr. (5/3/78)
Sidney A. Cavanaugh
Dave Freeman

1980–1981

Mayor Pro Tem: Dave Freeman
Jim Kenna
Sharyl Groves
James T. "Jim" Wood (resigned 1/25/82)
J. C. Hubbard (5/10/80)
Wiley Thomas
Bob Brady (resigned 12/80)
Jim Ramsey (4/13/81)

1982–1983

Mayor Pro Tem: Jim Ramsey
Marie Hinkle
Jim Kenna
Richard Davis
J. C. Hubbard
Dick Fisher
Harold Newman

MAYOR DAN ECHOLS 1983–87. In 1985, postal authorities assigned the city its own zip code.

1983–1987 Councils

1983

Mayor Pro Tem: Jim Ramsey
Marie Hinkle
Jim Kenna
Richard Davis
J. C. Hubbard
Dick Fisher
Harold Newman

1984–1985

Mayor Pro Tem: Richard Davis
Marie Hinkle
Jim Kenna
Virginia Moody (4/28/84)
Dick Fisher
Jim Ramsey
Harold Newman

1986

Mayor Pro Tem: Richard Davis
Marie Hinkle
Mack Garvin
Virginia Moody
Dick Fisher
Jim Ramsey
Harold Newman

1987

Mayor Pro Tem: Dick Fisher
Marie Hinkle
Mack Garvin
Richard Davis
Virginia Moody
Jim Ramsey
Linda Spurlock

1988–1997 Councils

MAYOR TOMMY BROWN 1988–98, NRH's longest tenured mayor during the first 45 years of its history. The population of the city had grown to more than 55,000 residents, making NRH the third largest city in Tarrant County.

1988
Mayor Pro Tem: Richard Davis, Dick Fisher, 5/88–7/88, Richard Davis

Marie Hinkle (resigned 8/88)
Lyle E. Welch (8/15/88)
Mack Garvin
Virginia Moody (8/15/88)
Byron Sibbet
Linda Spurlock

1989–1990
Mayor Pro Tem: Richard Davis
Lyle E. Welch
Mack Garvin
Frank Metts Jr.
Charles Scoma
Byron Sibbet
Linda Spurlock

1996
Mayor Pro Tem: Mack Garvin
Lyle E. Welch
Mark Wood
JoAnn Johnson
Don Phifer
Byron Sibbet
Linda Spurlock Sansoucie

1991 Council L/R Back - Lyle E. Welch, Mayor Tommy Brown, Byron Sibbet, Mark Wood. Front - JoAnn Johnson, Mack Garvin, Linda Spurlock, Charles Scoma.

1992-1995 Council L/R Back - Lyle E. Welch, Mack Garvin, Mark Wood, Mayor Tommy Brown. Front - Linda Spurlock Sansoucie, Byron Sibbet, Ray Oujesky, JoAnn Johnson
Mayor Pro-Tem: 1992 - Byron Sibbet, 1993 - Lyle E. Welch, 1994 - Mark Wood, 1995 - JoAnn Johnson

1997 Council L/R Back - Cheryl Lyman, Lyle Welch, Mack Garvin, JoAnn Johnson, Don Phifer. Front - Frank Metts, Jr., Mayor Tommy Brown, Byron Sibbet.

1998

Mayor Pro Tem: Don Phifer

MAYOR CHARLES SCOMA, 1998—NRH's current mayor is Charles Scoma, elected in May 1998. The project to record the city's history was completed during Mr. Scoma's term as mayor when the historical committee published *The History of NRH, 1953—1998.*

1998 City Council. L/R Standing - Frank Metts, Jr., Mayor Charles Scoma, Lyle E. Welch, Russ Mitchell, Mayor Pro Tem Don Phifer. Seated - Cheryl Lyman, Matt Milano, JoAnn Johnson.

Administration Staff

NRH City Managers

John Porter Hall 1965–67
C. W. Adcock (Acting) 1967
Stephen K. Shutt 1967–70
Jack Russell 1970–72
Gene Riddle 1972–78
Stan Gertz (Acting) 1978
Tom Paul 1979–80
Charles "Chuck" Williams 1980–82
Dennis Horvath (Acting) 1982–83
Rodger Line 1983–94
C. A. Sanford 1994–97
Larry Cunningham 1997–present.

On July 21,1997, the City Council appointed Mr. Cunningham to the position of City Manager. He became the city's manager after the retirement of C. A. Sanford. He joined the City of NRH from Lubbock in March of 1993 as director of finance. He had worked his way up from an administrative intern to city manager, a position he held for 16 years. Mr. Cunningham served as assistant city manager in NRH since 1994.

Larry Cunningham

He and his wife, Julie, have three children: Kim, Kril, and Kristen.

Lisa Daugherty, executive secretary to administration staff

James D. Saint, Assistant to the City Manager, 1997

Randy Shiflet

Randy Shiflet, deputy city manager, has worked for the City of North Richland Hills his entire career. Mr. Shiflet joined the City of NRH as a police cadet in 1973. In 1979 he became a captain, and was promoted through the ranks to assistant police chief in 1992. The following year, he became the assistant city manager, and in 1997 he was named deputy city manager.

Ron Ragland

Assistant City Manager, 1998-Ron Ragland has been assistant city manager from 1998 to the present. Mr. Ragland came to NRH with over 18 years of experience in local government. This includes almost ten years combined experience as City Manager. Mr. Ragland has received the "Award for Program Excellence—Citizen as Customer" from the International City Management Association in 1991.

Patricia Hutson, 1996 to present

NORTH RICHLAND HILLS CITY SECRETARIES
Laura Ray (first paid) 1960–64
Ida Reagan 1964–65
Rita Jane Clower 1965–66
Evalyn (Reed) Huston 1966–71
Donna Parish 1971–72
Anna Lee Caudry 1972–75
Winnie Barclay 1975–76
Jeanette (Moore) Rewis 1976–96
Patricia Hutson, 1996–Present

City Attorney Rex McEntire, 1976-Present

CITY ATTORNEY
Thomas Christopher 1954–62
Glenn Goodnight 1963–64
Dawson Davis 1964–65
Marion Massey 1965–68
Dennis Morrow 1968–72
Tim Truman 1972–76
Rex McEntire 1976–Present

CITICABLE NRH

1981 to 1998

In 1981, working with CBS Blackhawk, Citicable NRH was created and mandated by the city to maintain a 24-hour cable casting of public messages and video programs in order to keep its citizenry informed. From 1981 to the present, Citicable programming has been cablecast over CBS Blackhawk, Sammons Cable Television, and presently over Marcus Cable Television.

The City's cable channel is now known as "Citicable NRH." From 1981 to the early 1990s it was known as "Citicable 36." It is currently located on cable channel 7 on the converter boxes in North Richland Hills. Today there are more than 9,000 cable TV subscribers.

Cable Department: Back - cable director Greg Odenburg and Mark Fisher
Front - George Comin and Michael Clark

Cable Crew working with Metlife on a high school football game

Citicable NRH produces community television material focusing on the education, cultural, civic, and recreational needs and interests of the community. Programming goals for Citicable NRH are to create a television channel for the purposes of disseminating information and events to provide quality programs.

In 1990 Citicable NRH and Birdville ISD formed the media technology classes for teaching broadcast journalism at the high school level. The early classrooms were started at the Citicable studio and in 1992 moved to the Shannon Center. To date more than 250 students have completed this program.

ECONOMIC DEVELOPMENT DEPARTMENT

North Richland Hills is perfectly situated to benefit from both Alliance and Dallas/Fort Worth International airports and has good economic development packages available. It is surrounded by nine of Tarrant County's 10 major business centers. In less than 50 years North Richland Hills has come to be known by the companies it keeps: a major division of Kimberly-Clark (Tecnol), a well-known bedding producer (Sealy Mattress Manufacturing) and Home Depot, Bates Container, Inc., MEGA Life & Health Insurance, Sam Pack's Five Star Ford.

The insurance agent for members of the National Association for the Self-Employed; (MEGA Life & Health Insurance)

Mr. Hardy Sanders, owner of Bates Containers, a regional box manufacturer

H&M Food Systems (one of the largest producers of pizza toppings in the world), also lead the list of firms that have maintained a corporate presence here and chosen to expand their NRH operations in recent years.

As a result of such growth and investment, NRH recently became the fourth city in Tarrant County to reach the $2 billion level of appraised property value—making it (in the words of the *Fort Worth Star-Telegram*) a "prominent player."

NRH operates an aggressive economic development department, organized by the City Council in 1987. C. A. Sanford was the city's first economic director. When C. A. was

The five sons of Lois and George Phillips L/R-Greer, Gavin, Gary, Grant, and Greg were among the first depositors at Northeast National Bank in 1961.

The grown Phillips boys, now dads, are owners of NRH Tropical Greenery and are teaching their own children the value of saving in 1988. Reba McMinn is the Northeast Bank teller with Greer, Gavin, Gary, and Grant, pictured with their families. Greg Phillips is deceased.

Construction on a six-story tower addition to Northeast National Bank began in 1977. This was the first multistory building in NRH.

moved to assistant city manager, Bob Mill became director. The current economic director is Marty Weider. The department works to attract new business and promotes tourism development.

NRH's Economic Development Department recently celebrated a decade of dynamic development by helping bring about the largest single-occupant construction project (North Hills Hospital's $26 million renovation/expansion) and the largest manufacturing expansion (H&M Foods $16.9 million) in the city's history. Both projects were started in late 1997.

In February 1998 representatives of two investment companies will renovate the existing Richland Plaza complex creating the "Richland Business Centre."

NRH has more than 500 stores and restaurants, including tenants of North Hills and Richland Pointe

North Hills Hospital

Malls. Earlier this decade, developers completed construction of the retail power centers—which feature retailers Barnes & Noble, Old Navy, Garden Ridge, and Circuit City—and restaurants like Don Pablo's, Applebee's, and TGI Friday's.

Since the half-cent sales tax for parks referendum's passage, NRH has opened NRH2O Family Water Park, a 16-court tennis center, a nine-field soccer complex and the largest known handicapped-accessible playground west of the Mississippi River, and the construction on a new girls' fast-pitch softball fourplex.

Developments such as these have complemented NRH's private recreational enterprises (such as Mountasia Family FunCenter immediately south of NRH2O), as well as attract other business (Texas Indoor Speedway and Laser Quest) and lodging amenities (Country Inn & Suites).

In 1999, the beginning steps of a ten-year development program were taken by Raytheon-E-Systems Trust, creating an NRH town center. The center is located on almost three hundred acres between Mid-Cities Boulevard and Grapevine Highway.

Liberty Bank opened for business Dec. 5, 1985, at 5801 Davis Blvd.

Bank of North Texas is located on a wedge of NRH land between Bedford-Euless road and Airport Freeway. Photo 1980. Now Wells Fargo Bank

Northeast Fence Co. built its business on land purchased by Delma Phillips from G. R. Montgomery.

J. B. Sandlin Homes has grown into a huge corporation since Johnny Sandlin first began building homes in 1956. Sons Terry, Mike, Scott, and son-in-law, Matt Speight, are now all part of the business.

Environmental Service
Animal Services/Consumer Health

What began in 1978 with a woman, a desk in the breezeway of the Police Department, a 1967 Ford pick up truck (with hand-built wire cages), and a dog pole that consisted of a couple of ropes and a metal pole has grown to include a staff of 13, two state-of-the-art Animal Services vehicles, and 2 divisions (housed in two separate buildings).

The Animal Services Division began in 1978 utilizing what was at the time the basic equipment needed for a city "dog catcher," and used the Richland Hills animal shelter to house the animals that were impounded.

In 1980, the city began an agreement to house animals in the shelter used by the Tarrant County Humane Society. By this time a second animal control officer's position had been added, and by 1985 there was a staff of three, two animal control officers and one supervisor.

The NRH Animal Services Center located at 7200 B Dick Fisher Dr. South opened in January 1987 at a cost of $430,000.00. At that time, "Oscar Ray Leonard," a black and white cat that had numerous battle scars and was surviving on food from the dumpster of McDonalds on Rufe Snow, was its first "guest." "Oscar" died in 1998, donating eight years as a "city employed" pet therapist.

The shelter was designed to break the stereotype "dog pound" with programs such as "Warm Hugs on Wheels," which is a pet therapy program that utilizes trained shelter animals and volunteers that visit local senior citizen assisted care facilities as well as cancer treatment centers for children. When the program began in 1989 the therapy animals were "Oscar Ray Leonard" and a yellow Labrador named "Kasey".

"Bear Hugs" is another program that the shelter started as a way to ease the trauma of children involved in animal attacks. Stuffed bears, donated by local businesses, are dressed

Animal Services Center at 7200 Dick Fisher Dr.

in a small T-shirt that has the shelter logo on it and are given to children on the scene of a severe bite, and at children's hospitals.

The shelter was expanded and an additional 2,300 square feet was added in 1992. Because of new regulations, and a lack of available landfill space, a crematorium was added to the shelter in May 1993.

The Consumer Health Division was born out of a move by Tarrant County to try to force cities to pay a contract fee to the County Health Department in exchange for inspections on establishments that they held no enforcement power over. Mayor Dan Echols spearheaded the creation of the Environmental Services Department, one that would assure the citizens of NRH that along with the inspection, went the power to make certain the violations were corrected, and to have more local control in matters of consumer health.

The "two-woman" Consumer Health Division began in 1988 in the Animal Services Center. From there, they were officed in the new Fire Administration building that had been built in front of the Animal Services Center. The division began taking on more tasks that included mobile food trucks, waste hauling trucks, grocery stores, convenience stores, foster homes, group day homes, plan reviews and by 1993, had also taken on the responsibility for inspection of public and semipublic swimming pools and spas.

First American Savings, which was located on Bedford Euless Road, donated the building, and it was moved to its current site at 7200 C Dick Fisher Dr. and was ready for occupancy in the spring of 1993.

A countywide Household Hazardous Waste program has operated the busiest collection site since 1994. This activity allowed us to apply for, and receive, a grant from Texas Natural Resource Conservation Commission for $23,000 to purchase a mobile collection unit that will be operated at different city locations throughout the year.

As a result of some of the programs that have been started, the city was a finalist for the Governor's Award for Environmental Excellence in May 1996. Pam Burney has served as director since its beginning.

Renovated First American Building for Environmental Service offices

FIRE DEPARTMENT
By Sean Hughes

Not many opportunities to document history have the source of so many people to assist with the collection of facts and dates. The primary source for 28 years of history in the North Richland Hills Fire Department is retired Fire Chief Stan Gertz.

Chief Gertz began his career as a patrolman with the Police Department and moved to the Fire Department, also serving in the capacity as acting city manager. Chief Gertz replaced Chief Ted Castleberry, who held the position for 1970–1972. Chief Castleberry took over the department from E. Dean Holland, and Chief Holland assumed the duties of fire chief from Chief Ray Rhine, the city's first paid fire chief.

Fire service to the residents of NRH actually entails the history of two departments: the Smithfield Volunteer Fire Department and the NRH Fire Department. During the mid-1940s fire service to the residents of Smithfield was changed by the war effort which took many of the town's men. B. C. Redding, the town's fire chief and local grocer, recognized the need to continue the response to fire in the area. The biggest threat of fire at that time was grass fires. Chief Redding, upon hearing of a grass fire in the area, would drive around town and pick up the women of the town and with the use of burlap sacks and water carried in the back of the chief's station wagon, they would extinguish the fire. For structure fires the city of Smithfield and the undeveloped NRH area would rely on the cities of Richland Hills, Haltom City, and Tarrant County for fire protection. In 1948 the Smithfield Volunteer Fire Department built a fire station across from the town's barber, Mr. Cobb. This single bay fire station was built from cinder blocks recycled from the Smithfield Elementary School gym, which was destroyed by a tornado. Additional bays were added for a total of three bays, two vehicles deep.

Former Chief Stan Gertz with Former City Manager Rodger Line receiving congratulations.

When the city of North Richland Hills incorporated in 1953, it relied on volunteer firefighters as well as surrounding cities fire departments. In 1958 the annexation of the town of Smithfield created the issue of ownership of the fire equipment. This became a heated debate due to the fact that the Smithfield volunteers personally owned the equipment and were not appreciative of having their fire vehicles just "assumed" in the annexation. As a show of their ownership privileges, all of the Smithfield fire vehicles were parked at a site located near Amundson and Main Street. This action caused the City of NRH to purchase, at a total cost of $2,500, eleven fire response vehicles. Many of these vehicles were "converted," meaning they had been designed for some purpose other than fire fighting, but were trucks nonetheless.

1998 Fire Administration: Front (from left to right) Jonathan Brown, Charles Goggans, Mike Rawson, Sean Hughes • Back (from left to right) Pat Hughes, Danny Taylor, Jocelyn Whitener, Chief Andrew A. Jones Jr., Charlotte South, Mike Duncan, Kirk Marcum

In 1965 the City of NRH hired the first two paid firefighters, Ray Rhine and Gene Butler. Ray Rhine was to later be fire chief from 1969–1970.

In November 1969 the city hired the fourth paid firefighter and began providing 24-hour fire protection to the citizens. A firefighter worked 24 hours and was off 48 hours. This shift schedule continues today.

In 1977, the city took over providing emergency medical services to the residents. Today medically trained personnel will arrive in an average of 4.3 minutes and an ambulance for transport to the hospital arrives in an average of 4.8 minutes.

Station #2 after relocation to Rufe Snow near Glenview.

Fire Station Three

The opening of Fire Station Three on July 9, 1980, located at 5301 Davis Blvd., carried mixed emotions for the Fire Department. The summer of 1980 was one of the hottest summers on record in Tarrant County, with temperatures soaring above 105 degrees for many days straight. Senior Fire Lieutenant John Shelton, 28, had worked for the Fire Department for 11 years. After responding to a dumpster fire, Lt. Shelton was speaking with another lieutenant on the phone and collapsed. Despite immediate attention by his fellow firefighters, he later died at North Hills Medical Center. Lt. Shelton was the first NRH firefighter to die in the line of duty, and that station is dedicated in his memory.

On February 28, 1986, Fire Station One was relocated to 8300 Starnes Road. The relocation of Fire Station One was necessary for two reasons: first, the poor condition of the old original Smithfield station building; second, the growth in the northern section of the city required placement of fire equipment in the northern part of the city.

Fire Station One

Fire Station Four

Fire Station Four was opened on April 22, 1988 and incorporated a number of advancements for the department: administration and fire training, the emergency management office, fire prevention, fire marshal's office, and two classrooms for training of all types. Integral to this facility was the five-story training tower for all weather training of on-duty companies.

160

The NRH Radio Amateur Civil Emergency Service (R.A.C.E.S.) group was formed to fill the need for early warning and detection of the dangerous weather situations. Approximately 25 volunteers, all experienced amateur radio operators, contribute many hours to their community. These volunteers mobilize with the onset of severe weather and risk their vehicles to hail and water to be the eyes and ears of the Emergency Management Division.

The NRH Radio Amateur Civil Emergency Service

Today in 1998 the NRH Fire Department employs some 78, with Andy Jones Jr. as fire chief, who assumed the position on January 26, 1998 after the retirement of Chief Gertz.

LIBRARY

The North Richland Hills Public Library grew out of the volunteer efforts of community residents. Before NRH established its library, residents primarily used the Richland Hills Library. For several years, NRH had been paying $3,000 per year to Richland Hills to help support access for its citizens. When Richland Hills asked for $5,000 in 1967, the city balked, and withdrew from the arrangement. Several citizens began dreaming of starting their own library.

NRH City Library, 1998

The first organized effort to establish a library for NRH began in 1970, when Mrs. W. F. Polster called a meeting at the Smithfield Fire Station on June 9, 1970 to discuss the formation of a Citizens' Library Association. About 25 interested citizens turned out and the CLA was organized. Mrs. Polster was acting president until officers could be elected. At the second meeting Mrs. Lois Free was elected president. The CLA sold individual memberships for $1 per year, and family memberships for $2.

City officials offered cooperation and appointed an official Library Commission in July. The first members of the Library Commission were Charles and Polly Brinkley, J. Fred Davis, John Scully, Mrs. Bill Clinger, Mrs. Thad Biard, and the Rev. Don Hazlewood. Polly Brinkley has served continuously on the Board from the beginning.

Both the Library Commission and the CLA worked together to raise funds and collect books. Mary Shilcutt volunteered to serve as librarian during the summer months. Mrs. Bill Clinger later resigned from the commission to accept the part-time position as librarian, and Mrs. Shilcutt was appointed in her place on the commission.

Marilyn Ellis, who would later become the second employee of the library and served for 27 years before retiring, was treasurer of the Citizens Library Association. She also helped organize the membership campaign.

NRH Library childrens area

161

The first location for the fledgling library was at Richland Plaza Mall, which offered a vacant storefront rent-free. On February 22, 1971, the City Council approved a lease for the storefront, paving the way for the library to move in. Volunteers got to work making the space suitable.

The library officially opened with a celebration on Sunday, May 2, 1971, less than a year from the first organizational meeting. In that first year, city funding for the library totaled $18,235.35.

Early in 1972 the city hired Laura Prewitt as its first full-time professional librarian. That year the City Council also instituted an innovative way of helping fund parks and libraries: asking residents to pay a voluntary fifty cents per month donation along with their water bills.

In 1975, following the failure of a bond issue to build a new municipal complex for the city, the City Council nevertheless found a way to fund the needed facilities. The new City Hall at 7301 Loop 820 included the library. It relocated to its new quarters early 1976, with about 9,200 square feet.

Dawn Anderson, current reference and adult services supervisor, first joined the library staff as the children's librarian in March 1978. In 1981 Tiffany Nourse became director. Library hours were again expanded to 46 hours per week.

In 1982, Arlita Hallam joined the library as adult services librarian and in 1985 replaced Tiffany Nourse. Also in 1982, Citicable 36 was established by the city as a function of the library, with Jeff Jones becoming the first cable coordinator.

The library closed on February 4, 1985, for two weeks to make the transition to a computerized system for cataloguing and tracking the lending of books.

But the greatest changes were yet to come. The library quarters in City Hall, which had seemed so vast in 1976, had long since been outgrown. Other city departments were feeling the strain of rapid growth too.

The city proposed a $40 million bond package, and on September 10, 1985, voters approved the plan by a nearly 4-to-1 margin. Included in the plan was $5 million to buy the old Richland Hills Church of Christ and convert the complex into a library and recreation center.

When the work was complete, a grand opening celebration was held on June 4, 1987. The library opened in its cavernous new quarters with about 50,000 volumes. The conversion of the church into a modern library was featured in Texas Library Journal.

In 1987 a partnership with the Fort Worth Independent School District brought basic adult education, ESL (English as a Second Language) and GED classes to the library.

Wynette Schwalm became library director in late 1992. She won a grant to greatly expand the business collections of the library to support the information needs of businesses in the area.

Mark Gretchen served as library director from September 1994 to Fall 1995.

Steve Brown, current director, joined the library in 1996.

By the close of 1998, the NRH Library had become one of the best midsized libraries in Texas. Open 65 hours per week, the library lends over 400,000 volumes per year to about 225,000 visitors. The library's collections, still growing, have yet to catch up with demand. The Library is rapidly reaching the limits of its capacity to serve the city.

Once again the library faces the challenge of developing a new master plan to serve the citizens of NRH. The library's future, like that of the city it serves, is a blank page, on which its citizens have the opportunity to write their vision of community.

Municipal Court

The Municipal Court of North Richland Hills was established November 9, 1964. City Hall was located at 6801 Glenview Drive at that time and the original judge for the court was H. Edward Johnson. The court was called the "Corporation Court" but was renamed when the State of Texas changed its name to the Municipal Court. The first court clerk also held the position of city secretary and hired Ann Cannon as the deputy court clerk. Bobbie McCorkle replaced Cannon in January 1968.

When City Hall moved from Glenview Drive to its current location on N.E. Loop 820, the Municipal Court moved with it. After the death of Judge Johnson, the city appointed Judge Glen Eakman to replace him.

Judge David Casey replaced Judge Eakman and remained in the position of Municipal Court judge until 1986. In the 1980s NRH began to grow and so did the need for establishing building codes, planning and zoning of land areas, animal control (which was handled by the police department through the means of an animal control officer), and traffic control. Rufe Snow Drive was a two-lane road at the time with a stop sign at the inclined railroad tracks. Managing the flow of traffic through NRH had become a formidable task.

Citations were issued by the Police Department, but were processed by the Municipal Court. As the number of citations increased so did the need for additional court employees to process them and a division to serve warrants. In 1983 the NRH Municipal Court hired Dennis Nelson as its first Marshal. Nelson was given the duties of compiling and serving warrants for the almost 8,000 citations issued each year.

In February 1987 the court moved to its current location at 6701 N.E. Loop 820, the former Richland Hills Church of Christ building purchased by the city. With the relocation of the court came its change to a Municipal Court of Record. The Court of Record kept all initial trials heard by the City Judge and gave original jurisdiction for all Class C misdemeanors to the court with the exception of juvenile issues.

The Court of Record required that certain processes be in place and the operation of the court changed in 1989. A full-time court reporter was hired and continues to the present day recording transcripts of all trials conducted at the Municipal Court. The judge is required by state law in a Court of Record to be an attorney and at this time must be elected to the office. In 1989 Judge Charles Thorn became NRH's first elected Judge, serving until 1995. Judge Ray Oujesky was elected in 1996 and is NRH's current Judge.

Dealing with teen issues had become important to the Municipal Court. Judge Thorn was successful in establishing a Teen Court and the first coordinator was a volunteer, Susan Hunt. The judge and all attorneys for Teen Court were volunteers. Judge Cleveland "Scotty" Scott volunteered to be the Teen Court judge as part of his commitment to the teenagers. The first paid coordinator of Teen Court was Nancy Kirkland, with Bruce Auld and David Casey volunteering as judges.

The price of a citation has also changed over the years. When the court began in NRH State Court costs were $2.00 as compared with today's cost of $49.25. A speeding citation for speeding 10 miles over the posted limit cost $17.00 as compared to $80.00 today. The few hundred citations issued per year in the late 1960s have become 22,000 citations issued for 1997–98. The court currently employs one city prosecutor, 11 full-time judges, including the municipal judge, and two part-time employees. Approximately 6,500 warrants are issued each year and most of them are served by the Court. The Municipal Court's job is to assist the quality of life in NRH, while offering an unbiased ruling on violations, city ordinances, and complaints.

PARKS AND RECREATION DEPARTMENT

The mission statement of the North Richland Hills Parks and Recreation Department is, "To enrich the lives of the people of NRH through the stewardship of our natural resources and the responsive provision of quality recreational, cultural, and educational experiences." Though the Recreation Commission formally incorporated that mission statement in 1991, that was evident when the City Council established the Parks Department in 1959 only a few years after incorporation.

The Parks and Recreation Board really started to become active in 1971. In 1989, Don Tipps was elected as chairman by the board and remained chair until 1998, when Rick Work was elected following Tipps' resignation, culminating 19 years of volunteer service.

Dennis Horvath was hired as the first Parks and Recreation director in 1979. David Petika was hired in 1984, and was replaced by the current director, Jim Browne, who has served the city as Director of Parks and Recreation since 1988.

The original 10 acres of land for Fossil Creek Park, near Onyx Drive, became the city's first park. It was purchased from Progressive Development for $10 in 1961 and developed in 1964.

Land for Richfield Park was donated in 1972 by Cambridge Companies Development Corporation. The park was developed in 1973. Richfield Park was named by sixth grader Kay Betts in a citywide contest for which she received a $500 scholarship (which she later used at Texas Tech University).

Linda Spurlock Park

Twenty-nine acres of land were donated in 1973 by Bost and Montgomery for Northfield Park, which was developed in 1983.

NRH2O North Richland Hills Water Park

"Are you ready for a party?" ask Vi Lehnert and Marlin Miller. The Dan Echols Senior Adult Center was opened in 1991.

The year 1991 proved to be significant in the history of the city's park system. The City's Comprehensive Park and Recreation System Master Plan was updated for the first time in nearly a decade. Many needs were identified through citizen feedback and projects were prioritized. In the summer of 1992, the voters of NRH approved a one-half cent sales tax to help finance the development of the park system as identified and prioritized in the recently approved Park System Master Plan. The referendum passed, and collection of the dedicated sales tax began in January 1993.

The NRH Trail System Master Plan was approved by the City Council in November 1993. The plan provides long-range direction for a trail system that will serve the needs of pedestrians, bicyclists, and equestrians.

In December 1992, the Parks and Recreation Department acquired 300 acres of parkland. The inventory of the parkland and public open spaces more than tripled from 135 to 435 acres. Today, the park system includes more than 600 acres of parks and facilities.

Design for the 100-acre (yet to be named) city park is currently under way with Phase I construction to begin in the fall of 1998. Plans include baseball fields, equestrian trails, nature trails, multi-use trails, playground, picnic areas, pavilions, and preservation of several significant environmental areas.

In addition to the aggressive park and recreation facility growth that occurred during the 1990s, the programming and special event functions within the department experienced tremendous growth. NRH became a leader in Tarrant County by implementing one of the first comprehensive "youth at risk" programs in the city's middle schools. "The Edge," as it was named by the participants, has become a model program for addressing the needs of unsupervised youth after school hours.

The first department budget totaling $22,100 was approved for the 1972–73 fiscal year. Today's annual budget (1998) totals approximately $8 million. The history of parks and recreation in NRH is full of the stories of individuals and groups coming together, forging partnerships, identifying and acting upon opportunities. And while the history has been exciting, the future is still ours to create!

Leon and Morgan Lopez attend "Daddy-Daughter Valentine Dance," one of the award-winning events which also includes "Head for the Hills" Festival and numerous other innovative programs and activities.

Alice Scoma and Mayor Tommy Brown giving out Yard of the Month awards, also a part of the Parks Department.

IRON HORSE GOLF COURSE

In early 1981, Rostland Corporation, which owned and developed the Meadow Lakes subdivision, decided to build a golf course after being informed that most of the remaining land they owned in NRH was in the flood plain. According to engineers it would cost approximately $5 million in drainage work to bring the property out of the flood plain and suitable for home development. They visited with NRH City Manager Rodger Line who wanted the city to have a chance at developing this property as a golf course. Rostland agreed to give NRH six months to acquire financing and additional property to the north of Loop 820. This was done with a week to spare.

Under the direction of C. A. Sanford, a request for proposal was sent to a number of

James Ray Photography

A foursome to be dealt with.

companies asking for their opinions on ways to develop an upscale, municipally owned golf facility. Almost every company, with the exception of one, said it was impossible to develop an upscale course that would pay for itself. It was felt that the fees would be higher than residents were willing to pay, and that the city would need to subsidize debt service for construction. A proposal was received by a company called RSL (Recreation Services, Limited) whose owner, Marty Streiff, felt that it was possible for NRH to operate a course that could also pay for itself. His company was small and did not have a track record for the type of facility desired. However, the courses that he managed and/or leased for other municipalities were doing well and looked as good as possible. The company awarded Marty Streiff two contracts. One was to supervise construction. The other was to manage the golf course upon its completion. The architect used was Dick Phelps from Colorado. Nothing went smoothly with the construction of the golf course. There were constant delays.

The facility that exists today is testimony to the collaboration of many dedicated individuals and to Rodger Line's faith in giving C. A. Sanford time to spend on this project. The Mayor and Council were willing to be at risk for something that they felt would really enhance the community. Employees such as Bob Miller made the construction of this course a labor of love.

Dallas Morning News

In May 1989 a tremendous flood in NRH all but wiped out the new golf course. Work began with the planting of grass and the course was able to reopen in early 1990. The course struggled for the first year or so trying to get a healthy fairway and green system. This was accomplished after much effort. Iron Horse proved to be the success that a number of people felt it would. Under the direction of president Mike Lohner and resident pro-manager Mitch Harrell, Iron Horse has become one of the premier courses in Texas.

C. A. Sanford scoping out the land of Iron Horse.

Through the year 1998, Iron Horse was used as a benchmark to other communities who developed above-average golf courses.

Today Iron Horse pays for itself though green fees. The taxpayers of NRH have not been left with the burden of subsidizing a golf course.

POLICE DEPARTMENT

The Police Department is currently operating with an authorized strength of 88 sworn police officers and 36 civilian employees.

In order to trace the history of law enforcement in the area that is now known as North Richland Hills, we must go back some 137 years to the year 1856 when L. W. Jones was selected as justice of the peace of the area. Shortly after his selection, he was called to serve in the "War Between the States." However, his service was short-lived because the community was able to have Mr. Jones released from service in the war to fulfill his duties as justice of the peace, to help maintain order in the area, and assist the families whose men were off fighting the war. In 1876, during Mr. Jones' tenure, the northern end of what is now NRH had been known as Willow Springs, Bethel, and then Zion. These names were rejected by the post office when they attempted to charter themselves as towns because there were already communities in and around Tarrant County with the same names. So, the community of about 60 acres chose Smithfield for its name and was chartered as the town of Smithfield. Mr. Jones must have been quite popular because the records indicate that he served in this capacity until 1886, some 30 years. He died nine years after leaving office.

After the incorporation of NRH, Robert Hays was appointed town marshal. This was required of all incorporated towns. In addition to Mr. Hays, J. M. Shelton was licensed by the city as a night watchman to provide protection during hours of darkness. Each family was assessed a small monthly fee to pay for this service.

In July 1956, Mayor Donald F. Denney and the council approved and installed an Auxiliary Police Force. The force was all volunteers appointed to assist the town marshal. Knowing how expensive a paid police force would be, the Civic League, which appeared to exercise great control over the City Council, resolved to the City Council that there was "no need for a paid police force at this time."

In June of 1959, Walter Smith was also given a license to operate a night patrol in NRH. This created two night watchman patrols for the town. In September of this same year, Mr. Shelton was reprimanded by the City Council after it received complaints from citizens as to his cursing, manhandling of teenagers, driving without lights, and carrying a gun without authorization. Two months later Mr. Shelton died. During this period, talk of a paid police force was growing. In July of 1960, the council hired George Brazton Coe of Virginia as the first police chief. A property tax was passed to pay the chief and five officers as well as establishing a city court. The population of the city, according to the U.S. Census, was 8,662 residents. Chief Coe organized the newly formed department and designed the first police uniforms. However, on January 16, 1961, the City Council voted 5–0 to give the mayor authority to suspend the chief. Chief Coe submitted his letter of resignation and was commended for his efforts in setting up the department.

During the 1960s, the department was headed by two other chiefs, Chester Lewis and James Barnett. In April 1968, Chief Lewis was meeting with police employees at the Richland Plaza Shopping Center to discuss the City Manager's meddling into the Police Department's business. During the meeting, the City Manager and James Barnett walked

Police Department, 1979

in. After a discussion between the manager and Chief Lewis, all but two of the sworn officers walked off the job. James Barnett was appointed chief and ran the department with the two sworn officers and reserve officers. Eventually, some of the officers who had walked out returned, and the remaining positions were filled with new personnel.

In the 1970s, Chiefs J. R. Price, H. S. Scruggs, Charles W. Williams, and G. W. Williams were appointed to and served in the position of chief. The 1970 U.S. Census indicated that the population of NRH was 16,514. In 1971 departmental photographs indicate that the police force consisted of fourteen officers, six civilians, and one animal control officer (also a sworn police officer). In 1974, NRH was exposed to what was the beginning of perhaps the most revolutionary concept in the police profession. A computer was delivered to the dispatch office, and personnel were told that someday all police department records and reports would be computerized on something called a "floppy disk."

By 1980, the city had grown to 30,952 residents, and Jack Long was appointed police chief, a position he held for about a year. In 1982, Dr. J. L. McGlasson was appointed police chief. Under his guidance and leadership, the agency has grown to the third largest police force in the county with a total of 134 sworn and civilian officers. Animal control became its own department in the mid-1980s. During this period the agency also enhanced its functions and services. Some of the expanded services include crime prevention/community services/D.A.R.E., a full-time crime scene search unit, polygraph services, a traffic section, around-the-clock records technicians, a fully staffed detention facility, and an automobile impound facility. The agency has sought to recruit and retain the most qualified applicants, resulting in a more efficient and effective professional organization.

Officer Sid Johnson helping at a Bike Rodeo

The police department was able to move into the physical facility that has become the envy of many other agencies and officers who have visited. In addition, the new building is equipped with state-of-the-art equipment in every area. The records section is now completely automated with offense and incident reporting directly into the department's own computer system.

Police van at NRH2O

In 1991, mobile data terminals were installed in criminal investigation vehicles and the D.A.R.E. program was expanded into the middle schools. Video cameras have been installed in all patrol vehicles. Thomas R. Shockley became Chief of Police in December 1998 with 25 years in law enforcement. He joined the NRH police department in 1989. Greater emphasis will be placed on community services and neighborhood crime watches as we attempt to become more interactive with the community and citizens.

PUBLIC WORKS

The unsung heroes of the city are the men and women who repair the streets and water lines, clean out the drainage ditches, and unclog sewer lines at all times of the day and night. Three long-time employees tell their personal stories as city employees as well as the story of the Public Works Department: Larry Jones, Jimmy Cates, and David Smyth.

Public Works employees preparing the street for patching.

On October 16, 1982, I began my employment with the City of North Richland Hills where I worked my way up. During the past 14 years, I have witnessed constant growth and numerous changes within the City of NRH Utility Department.. A summary of the most significant items is as follows:

1983–Davis Blvd. 2.0 M.G. Elevated Storage Tank constructed, 1987-Public Works Service Center constructed (Municipal Complex -7200 A. Dick Fisher Dr. S.), 1989-Iron Horse Golf Course constructed, 1990-Amundson Dr. 1.5 M.G. Elevated Storage Tank constructed, 1991-College Hills 5.0 M.G. Ground Storage Tank constructed, 1991-Stanley Keller Booster Pump Station constructed.

1993-Implementation of Construction Division, 1994-NRH Water Park (NRH2O) constructed. 1996-City Hall Expansion, and in 1996-the sale of Watauga Water & Sewer System.

Larry Jones Public Works Superintendent/Utilities

My first day of employment started on June 27, 1978 as a Maintenance Worker 1. Pete Pistole ("Pistol Pete," as some people called him) was the superintendent of streets, Ray Britton was the director of Public Works, and Dick Faram was the mayor. We had approximately 17–19 employees in our department and a wide variety of equipment. Our Public Works shop was located at 4001 Rufe Snow Drive, close to where the big water tower is located today. Fire Station No. 2 replaced our old facility several years ago.

During the late '70s and early '80s our city had a lot of rural-type areas which were very enjoyable to work in. Several stock tanks were available for crew personnel to swim in on very hot summer days. We would work very hard on the streets and then Pete would come by and check on us, then tell us to hit the water tank. A good reward for a hard day's work. Our favorite stock tank was the one on the south side of Starnes Road, where Cottonwood Court is located now.

On Friday evenings, some of the employees would meet at the Green Valley Race Track to watch street car racing. This was about the only type of entertainment we had for young people in the early '80s in NRH. Concerts were also held at the Green Valley Race Track. There are several historical events that happened during my tenure. The Texas Wagon

Train of 1986 passed through our city in celebration of 150 years of independence from Mexico. The wagon train set up camp at the Green Valley Race Track for several days and then finally made its way down Rufe Snow Drive in route to the Fort Worth stockyards. At age 26 I became Public Works Superintendent. In 1992-93 a closed loop system was installed for traffic signals on Rufe Snow Drive from Lewis Lane to Starnes Road. This system was the first to be installed in our city. The system allows us to monitor and optimize the traffic signals from our traffic division office.

Growth within our division has been slow. In 1978 the Street Division of the Public Works Department had 17–19 employees. We currently have 23 employees and more than 200 miles of streets to maintain.

Jimmy Cates: (Public Works Superintendent/Street Division)

I started with the city in March 1986, as Maintenance Worker 1 in the Utility Department. John Moody was the utility superintendent at that time. I was promoted in May 1994 to my present position of construction superintendent.

The Utility Department and Streets and Drainage Department were located in separate buildings until 1987 when Utility, Streets and Drainage, and Support Services all moved to the present location of 7200 A Dick Fisher Dr. South. In 1992 a Public Works Construction Division was approved by Council. Larry Jones was appointed superintendent of construction at its inception. Though we take for granted the fact we have telephone, electric, gas, and water, getting these utilities to our homes for the first time took work on the part of dedicated city officials.

NRH Water Tower, Home of the Rebels

David K. Smyth (Public Works Superintendent/Construction.)

SPECIAL MEMORIES OF RUFE SNOW

From Former Assistant City Manager Dennis Horvath

I was hired by the City of North Richland Hills in June 1979 as the first director of Parks and Recreation and also was subsequently promoted to assistant city manager (the city's first) and then to deputy city manager (the city's first). In early 1980 the voters of North Richland Hills approved a $4 million bond issue. The main promise of the issue was that the city would reconstruct Rufe Snow. At that time it was the world's worst road, a two-lane "county type" road—one big pothole patch. It was awful, to say the very least.

At that particular time NRH's relationship with Watauga was terrible. Politically the problem was this—NRH had, and still has, a very good, enforceable assessment policy. (If we improve your street you pay for your fair share of the improvements based on your frontage.) Watauga did not have that policy—and they certainly didn't want NRH to assess their property owners. We (NRH) also had kind of a "dumb" policy: We didn't want to buy right of way, we wanted it donated.

Much like the traffic on Rufe Snow the political posturing was at a standstill. Absolutely nothing was agreed upon and the parties involved were downright disagreeable. The situation was so bad that the city had completed preliminary plans to move Rufe Snow east of its current location. It was being seriously considered. Sometime in mid-1980 I went to Mayor Dick Faram, and after a few drinks (which was not uncommon at that time) I convinced him that the politics were really screwed up and could I have a try at getting things off of dead center. He agreed.

That afternoon I called Robert Harrison, then the president of First United Richland Bank. He had just finished constructing the new bank on Rufe Snow (currently the drive-in facility of Nations Bank). Robert and I agreed that a neutral ground would be the best for a meeting of the minds and egos. He offered us the use of his bank office for the meeting. Two evenings later Robert Harrison, Mayor Faram (NRH), Mayor Anthony (Watauga), Mac McCumber (city manager of Watauga), Roger Brooks (the largest Watauga property owner fronting Rufe Snow in Watauga), and I met at the bank. In a very few short hours we all had eaten a little crow, repaired our egos, and had an agreement. And more importantly we all left as friends, each with our interest protected.

In the following weeks I made two presentations to the Watauga City Council obtaining their approval of the agreement, and Mayor Faram obtained an agreement from our council.

The right of way was then purchased in record time, and, thanks to the great work of contractors, the road construction also proceeded in record time. With Rufe Snow widened, development went absolutely wild. I'm not sure we ever really got caught up.

Thank the Lord, Rodger Line showed up to become NRH city manager within the following months to help us cope with the growth that came our way as a result of this project.

I have many fond memories of my 14 years at NRH. The Rufe Snow project is certainly one of them.

3 Churches

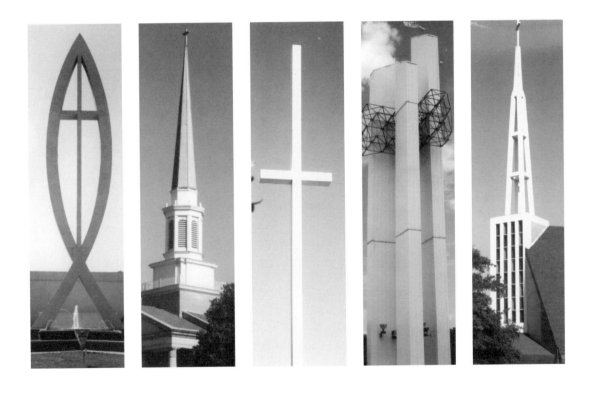

CHURCH OF JESUS CHRIST OF LATTER-DAY SAINTS

4401 N.E. Loop 820

The Church of Jesus Christ of Latter-day Saints (Mormon) was formed in 1830. The national headquarters are in Salt Lake City. The church has been in Texas since 1843. Texas contains the sixth largest Latter-day Saints population in the United States. The building on Loop 820 in North Richland Hills is one of their stake centers consisting of three wards. When a ward gets to a certain size, the church forms a new ward. Only three wards can meet in one building, then a new building is constructed.

The church operates through a huge, unsalaried ministry. There are no paid positions in the church. All are called, not elected, usually for five years. Each ward has a bishop who is also called.

Every member is assigned two or three families to visit monthly and help in any needed area. By fasting two meals each week and giving the corresponding monies to the church, welfare funds are secured for needy families. Once each year the church members do hands-on voluntary chores for the community: washing a dog, yard work, cleaning a house, etc.

Church of Jesus Christ of Latter-day Saints

The Hurst Texas Stake Family History Center located on the church property on Loop 820, is a branch of the Salt Lake City Family History Library. The family history center was once in Hurst, but when the church and center moved to North Richland Hills, the center kept its name to avoid confusion. The Hurst Family History Center is open to church members and visitors interested in genealogy. Seventy to ninety percent of the people using the center are not church members.

COLLEGE HILL CHURCH OF CHRIST

7447 College Circle

On March 31, 1963, under the oversight of the Richland Hills eldership the College Hill Church of Christ was founded with 70 persons meeting in the auditorium of Fort Worth Christian College. From an assembly of 148 persons at that first worship service, the congregation grew to more than 500. On May 26, 1963 four men were ordained as elders of the College Hill Church of Christ. They were Jesse Holmes, Raymond Bullard, Ed Usrey, and Bill Stalnaker.

Evangelist Elmo Hall was the first minister of the church. College Hill Church of Christ
During his service the congregation built its first facilities on the present five-acre church site at 7447 College Circle in North Richland Hills and moved from its temporary worship quarters on May 23, 1965. The circular structure was designed so that no member of the audience would be more than 40 feet from the speaker. The completed structure offered a beautiful plant for the congregation to use as a base of service to the community of North Richland Hills and the Fort Worth Christian College campus.

In 1969 the church completed a second addition which provided 15 classrooms, expanded nursery facilities and expanded auditorium seating. In 1984 and 1985 a major interior renovation was done so the auditorium could accommodate 150 more persons.

A close bond between Fort Worth Christian College and the College Hill Church of Christ existed from the beginning. That tradition has continued as the college closed and the campus developed into a fully accredited academy.

Many families purchased residential lots from the Fort Worth Christian School and built homes to be near College Hill Church of Christ and the Fort Worth Christian School.

The church purchased three additional acres and is in a position for continued growth. Increased parking now allows for entrance to the building from two sides.

The College Hill congregation has always maintained a strong commitment to teaching the Bible, spiritual development of the children and young people, strong emphasis in families and their missionaries in "going with the gospel."

COLLEGE HILL CHURCH OF CHRIST MINISTERS

Elmo Hall	1963-65
Kenneth Green	1965-70
Eugene Gilmore	1970-72
Preston Cotham	1972-77
Larry Calvin	1977-81
Rick Andre	1982-84
Robert Waller	1985-Present

Davis Blvd. Baptist Church, organized April 18, 1954

DAVIS BOULEVARD BAPTIST CHURCH
5201 Davis Boulevard

The Davis Boulevard Baptist Church was organized Easter Sunday, April 18, 1954. The church began with 36 charter members with the leadership of Rev. Jack Taliaferro. Members met in a home for a while then erected a tent. On June 8, 1955, the church voted to pay a full-time salary of $75 a week to Pastor Taliaferro.

A small frame building was built at a cost of $6,000 at 6540 Pipeline Road (presently known as Glenview Drive), where the new church was dedicated March 7, 1957. Charter Member J. L. Autrey, who donated $500 for the land, witnessed several times to an unsaved young man named Oscar Huston who later became one of the church's pastors.

On August 3, 1958, the church voted to join the Southern Baptist Convention. In 1959 the church changed its name to West Richland Hills Baptist. In August 1959, the church joined the Tarrant County Baptist Association.

On August 23, 1967, the church voted to buy 3.11 acres at 5201 Smithfield Road (presently Davis Boulevard). Groundbreaking ceremony at the new site took place September 28, 1968. The church sold its property on Pipeline Road and built on the new property. The church changed its name to Davis Boulevard Baptist Church, effective January 1, 1969, when the finished building was occupied.

The membership voted to begin the "Together We Build" building program for an educational building for $120,000. The new educational building was completed October 25, 1981. This addition also included a kitchen and fellowship area. Both the sanctuary and the new educational building loans were paid off November 18, 1983.

On July 29, 1990, the membership again voted to begin another "Together We Build" program for an additional education space and a new office building; both were dedicated August 9, 1992. With this addition, all buildings were connected.

The membership is very supportive of NEED (North East Emergency Distribution) with food and volunteers.

Davis Boulevard Baptist Church is committed to reaching families for Christ. Our ministries are biblically based and family oriented. In the future, there will be a strong emphasis on our children, youth, and young families. As a new generation of God's children takes the reins of Davis Boulevard Baptist Church, there is a strong foundation to build for our future. The faithful members of our history are combining their efforts to reach another generation for the cause of Christ.

PASTORS	DATE
Jack Taliaferro	1954–57
J. D. Lundy	1957–59
Joe Stewart	1959–60
James A. Copeland	1960–69
John D. Sherman	1970–73
Steve McKown	1973–75
Oscar J. Huston	1975–88
Michael L. Wyatt	1989–92
Charles Wright	1993–93
Ewell Humphreys	1994–97
R. Mitch Randall	1998-

DAVIS MEMORIAL UNITED METHODIST CHURCH

5301 Davis Boulevard

About 50 people began meeting July 26, 1959, in a cattle barn on the farm of J. Fred Davis Sr. to establish Davis Memorial United Methodist Church. Many stories are told about that memorable first service. Ted Spencer, the first minister of Davis Memorial, wrote in his memoirs of the church's early history that a lot of people with shovels and tractors met on Saturday afternoon before the initial Sunday service to clean the barn. Someone shouted, "We've got a problem. There is 10 feet of manure under us." About 20 men frantically spread lime over the manure. They knew if they didn't do something quickly, no one would ever come back because of the odor in the barn. The next morning, when prospective members came to worship, one lady asked, "Where did you get such a soft and pretty carpet?"—not knowing what was really under her feet. Davis Memorial was formally organized on September 13, 1959.

The church was erected on 5.2 acres of land donated by J. Fred and Maude Davis. Ground was broken (using a helicopter, piloted by Lou Hartwig, to raise buckets of earth) in 1960 to begin con-

"Memorable first service was held in a barn."

struction of the first building and the first service was held in the newly completed sanctuary on January 15, 1961. The site fronted on what was then Smithfield Highway; the name of the street was changed to Davis Boulevard in 1960 at the request of Rev. Spencer. The church was dedicated as a living memorial to the Reverend G. V. Davis, father of J. Fred Davis Sr. and a Methodist minister for more than 50 years.

Fort Worth Star-Telegram

During construction of the church, the congregation met in various locations in North Richland Hills.

The $90,000 building of granite and stone, the first unit of the church, was dedicated in January 1961. Designed in a modern gothic style, the church had eight stained glass windows on the sides and a circular stained glass window on the front that was a gift to the congregation from Clarence Jones. The sanctuary could seat 300. At the time of its dedication, membership stood at 265. On May 19, 1968, groundbreaking services were held to add a 3,000-square-foot facility for Sunday school rooms and a fellowship hall.

In 1986, an 8,000-pound, 70-foot cross was erected in front of the church and the church sanctuary and educational facilities were remodeled. In addition, a foyer and an office wing were added, and the kitchen and parking lots were expanded.

Contractors erected an 8,000-pound, 70-foot cross

The growing congregation of Davis Memorial is involved in service to our community by its support of programs such as NEED. Also, youth summer mission trips where young people have opportunities to help less fortunate people, are supported. The women's groups support a variety of outreach programs including the Salvation Army's Christmas drives.

MINISTERS	YEARS SERVED
Reverend Ted Spencer	7/59–2/64
Reverend Charles Chadwick (Interim)	2/64–5/64
Reverend Robert L. Robertson	6/64–6/67
Reverend W. C. Taylor Jr.	6/67–6/70
Reverend Don Hazelwood	6/70–6/77
Reverend John McDaniel	6/77–6/82
Reverend Claude Davison	6/82–6/84
Reverend Dean Posey	6/84–6/90
Reverend Wesley Howard	6/90–6/95
Reverend Grady Brittain	6/95–present

FIRST BAPTIST CHURCH, SMITHFIELD

The Long Shadow of the Collective Heart

Standing on the black asphalt parking lot of the church at the corner of Center and Main in old Smithfield, one can watch the shadows lengthen as the sun finally drops behind the trees that hover protectively over the west side of the building. The cream-colored brick walls form an L-shaped structure. At this hour, the children's playground is empty; swings turn listlessly with the first hint of a late afternoon breeze.

Lulled by the relentless drone of the cicadas, the mind wanders, and a different scene shimmers in the wonderful realm of memory. The weather is still oppressively hot, but the stillness is shattered by the shouts and cries of happy children clambering up on wooden risers to practice their song for the revival. They all wear little white tin pins attached to their clothing. The pins say, "Booster Band," and they have earned them because they have perfect attendance for the week. "Jesus loves the little children"; the words hang in the breathless air as the crowd begins to gather for the service under the stars. Cardboard fans are placed in the seats of the straight-backed chairs. Moths lazily start to circle the yellow lightbulbs illuminating the side yard of the church. Afterward, there will be a homemade ice cream supper.

The first services were held in the new 500-seat auditorium on Mothers Day, 1962.

With a vision extending into the next century, twelve Baptist believers living in the tiny settlement of Smithfield, called as their first pastor a missionary named George Washington Greene.

The little congregation met in the Methodist Church building until 1902. A member named Gunter donated two lots to the church as the site for a permanent building. Aided by the labor of men from the Methodist Church, they saw the small frame structure take its place at Center and Main, where the modern church stands today.

The neophyte church struggled, but it doggedly survived. In 1917, a membership of 39 gave $75 for the pastor's salary. In 1924 the church was meeting once a month. At least once during this time, services were held at the Methodist Church because there was no "stove up" in their own building. Demonstrating their determination to continue during this trying period, the congregation purchased a piano and three dozen hymnals. Records are scant for the next several years. Evidently the little group had lapsed into inactivity. Then in 1934, an article in the *Fort Worth Star-Telegram* detailed the reopening of the white double doors on the small frame structure. The people had gathered to reorganize their church. Since that date, those doors have not closed again.

In 1937, the church called Charles P. Johnson as pastor. He later became director of libraries at Southwestern Baptist Theological Seminary.

New converts were baptized in a nearby creek or at a sister church. Windows were opened in warm weather to catch any breeze, but they also let in flying insects and community noises. Many a small child's attention was diverted from the long sermon by the antics of a June bug flying by. Seldom could an adult resist taking a swat at a pesky mosquito.

In the mid-'40s, a two-story educational building was added on the west side of the existing structure also had two restrooms. Members lined up to use the "indoor plumbing" between Sunday school and church.

By the mid-'50s, remodeling of the sanctuary included side extensions, which increased the seating capacity. Window air conditioners were purchased and installed. A beautiful baptistry was added. Space for a choir was created, raised, and divided from the rest of the auditorium by a low wall. In front of the choir, upholstered chairs and a new carved pulpit were placed on the carpeted platform. In 1954 the church sponsored a mission, Shady Grove, which became self-sustaining the next year. It remains today on Precinct Line Road, a testimony to its parent church.

Property west of the church was acquired with a new sanctuary in mind. Floyd Amos was the builder-pastor. Under his direction, the church erected a new auditorium, seating

500. The bricks were bought for 8 cents each in a churchwide "Buy A Brick" campaign. The first service was held in the new building on Mother's Day, 1962. There was even an organ to go with the piano. In January 1968, the church, now under the leadership of Lawrence Hammond, dedicated a new two-story brick Educational Building. A new parsonage was built on Douglas Road. In 1973, the youth of the church ventured all the way to Nebraska on a mission trip.

Jim Eager served the church longest as pastor. He led the congregation two different times, nearly fifteen years in all, resigning the second time in 1990. New property was added to the existing campus, extending the west property line to Smithfield Road. The budget for 1980 was more than a quarter million dollars. The staff was enlarged to include directors for senior citizens and children's worship. By 1989, the church was debt free. A Mother's Day Out Program was added in 1991.

In 1995, the church was awarded historical status and a plaque was unveiled during a dedication service. It has been a compelling presence in the community for more than 100 years.

More than 32 men of God have led this stalwart church during the last century. Eighteen men have been ordained and licensed to preach the Gospel by this body. Nearly one hundred deacons and countless other workers have directed the fellowship across the years.

There is an awesome feeling that nearly overwhelms one as the pages of the church history are slowly turned. Space limits the writer to mentioning just a few of the many, many strong dedicated people whose names grace those pages. Those names, long forgotten, leap off the pages, to become, once again, vibrant dear people who influenced so many lives over the decades.

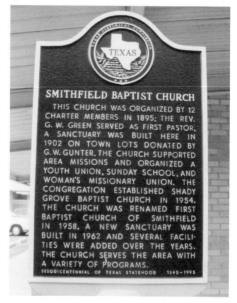

Historical Marker dedicated to 100 years of service

Shadows lengthen, swallows circle overhead, and I turn, retracing my steps to the car. Has the wind picked up, or do I really hear the beautiful voice of Grace Garrison singing . . .

Precious memories,
How they linger
How they ever flood my soul
In the stillness of the midnight,
Precious sacred scenes unfold.

Submitted by Dorothy Null Parker
Member First Baptist Church of Smithfield
1943–1964

Grateful acknowledgment for the use of the book, *On Jordan's Stormy Banks, A History of the First Baptist Church of Smithfield*, by Doris Hudler Shipman.

FIRST CHURCH OF CHRIST SCIENTIST

7318 N.E. Loop 820

In August 1955, a group of five Christian Scientists met to discuss the need of a Christian Science Church in this rapidly growing area. They felt the need of a local church, which would provide a convenient Sunday school for the children. They met in various places in Richland Hills until May of 1963 when they purchased property at 7904 Bedford Euless Road in North Richland Hills. It was an older building, which was completely renovated. The first service was held on Sunday, February 2, 1964. Dedication services were held on Sunday, November 23, 1975.

First service held February 2, 1964.

In August of 1995, the membership purchased property at 7318 Northeast Loop 820, which is the present location.

The unique stained glass window in the church was given by a member, who found it in a back storeroom of an antique store. It was all in pieces. The member had it restored long before the church was built. It was from a slave chapel, which was on a plantation between Marshall and Jefferson, Texas. The design of the cross and crown in the stained glass are sealed trademarks of the Christian Science Board of Directors, registered in the United States and other countries.

The church has no ministers. The membership elects readers who read from the King James Version of the *Bible* and *Science and Health With Key to the Scriptures* by Mary Baker Eddy for a Sunday morning service and a Wednesday evening testimony meeting.

The membership is confidential, but several charter members still remain.

HOLY TRINITY CHARISMATIC EPISCOPAL CHURCH

(CEC OF NORTH AMERICA)

4900 Cummings Drive

Easter Sunday, April 3, 1994, was the beginning of this body of believers with the first minister, The Reverend Canon Michael Serra Cumbie.

Inquirers meetings were held at the North Richland Hills Community Center. From there they moved to the home of Gerald and Sally Cope (Bedford) and after two months moved to the Day Care Chapel of the First United Methodist Church of Bedford. Two months later, with a membership of 18, the parish

First service held Easter Sunday, April 3, 1994.

was able to assume the loan on the 4900 Cummings Drive property. The congregation tripled in size within the first three weeks (probably due to the excellent exposure on N.E. Loop 820). The parish continues to flourish, and plans to expand are under way.

MINISTERS
Father Ralph Dodd
The Reverend Canon Michael Cumbie
The Reverend Gerald Cope (Deacon)
The Reverend Bob Tomlinson (Deacon)

The parish has founded two other mission works in its short two-year history—one in Fort Worth and one in Dallas.

The Charismatic Episcopal Church is not affiliated with the Episcopal Church U.S.A. or the Orthodox, a Roman Catholic Church.

IMMANUEL EVANGELICAL LUTHERAN CHURCH

7321 Lola Dr.

The first service was held November 2, 1969, at 7109 Grapevine Highway with 16 people present. Mission status was announced on May 3, 1970, and the church was organized on May 17, 1970, at the home of Pastor and Mrs.

Organized May 17, 1970, at the home of Pastor Walter Diehl in Dallas.

Walter Diehl in Dallas. The Buerger, Neubauer, Stabell, and Walton families were present.

On September 13, 1970 Myrl Wagenknecht was installed as Immanuel's first and (to this date) only pastor. Pastor Wagenknecht, his wife Marcy, and two sons, Daniel and Steven, moved to Texas from Huntsville, Alabama. A parsonage was rented for them on Brown Trail in Hurst and most weekday meetings, Vacation Bible Schools, and Lenten Services were held at the parsonage.

Following an extensive door-to-door canvass of 2,280 houses in August 1971, it was determined that North Richland Hills was the prime area. In January 1971, the church rented space in the shopping center at 5249 Davis Boulevard. The church worshipped at this site for 18 months. Lutheran Pioneer Train #296 was chartered on February 26, 1972.

In December 1972, six acres of land (including the creek) at 7321 Lola Drive was purchased for $12,150. Building plans for a new unit were delayed when the Wels Mission Board informed Immanuel that a doublewide, portable chapel was available. This mobile home was used from July 1, 1973 to June 1975. The move of the portable chapel from Houston, Texas was plagued with 18 flat tires! It also took two winch truck wreckers to pull the unit onto Immanuel's property, when one unit got stuck in a muddy ditch.

Immanuel Lutheran Elementary School was begun in the back third of the portable chapel in September 1974. Mrs. Fred (Annette) Wulff was the first teacher. The school year began with nine students.

Groundbreaking for the present worship/fellowship building was held on January 12, 1975. Robinwood Construction Co. was selected to draw plans and construct the 4,000-square-foot facility for $64,000. Construction began on January 27, 1975, with dedication on June 1, 1975. Pastor Wagenknecht preached with an attendance of 111. Membership at this time was 92, with 58 communicants.

The portable chapel was disassembled and driven to Trinity Lutheran Church in Temple, Texas. This time the unit only had seven flat tires! However, while it was parked on the side of Highway 77, an 18-wheeler drove past and caused one unit to tip over. Fortunately no one was injured, and the damage was repairable.

In October 1981, a "100-year rain" caused neighboring Calloway Branch Creek to flood. There was extensive flood damage to a large part of the church. Members hauled out water and vacuum dried as much as possible.

In 1983, Immanuel transferred members to Flower Mound, Arlington, and southwest Fort Worth to help start missions in these areas. In April 1988, members decided to build a new education building, began work on April 21, 1989, and finished the building "dried in" on August 11, 1989. The four-classroom facility is used to educate children Pre-K (4 years old) through eighth grade. Following another flood in September 1990, new carpeting was installed in the entire church building. Mary Martha Society remodeled the kitchen area and soon after, playground equipment was donated.

Construction for Calloway Branch bridge widening, plus street and creek drainage improvements on Lola Drive closed the east access to the church and school from June 1993 to April 1994. This project took the buildings out of the flood plain.

On March 26, 1995, 26 thirteen-foot pews replaced the original 18 eleven-foot pews. This increased seating capacity in the sanctuary to about 200.

Outstanding community involvement and service includes working with the Carter Blood Mobile and NEED (North East Emergency Distribution).

Mission Statement: The continuing purpose of our congregation, as a gathering of Christians, is to serve all people in God's world with the Gospel of Jesus Christ on the basis of the verbally inspired and unerring Word of God, the Holy Scriptures, the Holy Bible.

Minister: Pastor Myrl Wagenknecht has served since September 13, 1970.

MAPLEWOOD BAPTIST CHURCH
7708 Maplewood Dr.

The church building at 7708 Maplewood Dr. was up for sale when Della Gillespie called Rev. Charles R. McClure and asked if he would come and consider beginning a church in the old building. He responded and preached the first Sunday of September 1970. After much prayer the church was incorporated in February of 1971.

In 1973 the church bought three acres of land behind the church and later built a new 450-seat sanctuary, church offices, and nursery.

Maplewood Baptist Church

The church is involved in many community services: the Boy Scouts and Girl Scouts and Texas Clown Association, which works with children's hospitals. The Puppet Ministry works in churches and traveled to Mexico last year on a mission trip.

Rev. McClure retired in 1993 after 23 years as pastor.

Rev. Tony Colburn served as pastor from 1994 to 1998.

Rev. Kevin Barke began serving as interim pastor in June of 1998.

NEW BEGINNINGS BAPTIST CHURCH
6540 Glenview

In January 1989 a group of Baptist ministers recognized the need for a Black church in the Hurst, Euless, Bedford, and North Richland Hills area. After much consecration and prayer our church was formed the first Sunday in May 1989. Our meeting place was 625

Moved to new location in March 1998.

W. Pipeline Road at the Bellevue Baptist Church. Bellevue, which was currently housing a Chinese and Korean Mission, had agreed to open its doors for a Black mission, pastored by Rev. Don Rogers. The first Sunday that we met there were nine people in attendance, and one united with the church. At this time we were called Bellevue Black Mission.

With the assistance and direction of the Tarrant Baptist Association, Baptist General Convention of Texas, and a few other local pastors, the church became a thriving entity within the Hurst, Euless, Bedford, and North Richland Hills communities.

In October 1991, our church chose the name Mid-Cities Baptist Church. The church continued to grow and we began to have a full church schedule, Sunday school, morning worship, Wednesday night Bible study, and evangelism meeting.

Under the direction of our pastor and being led by the Holy Spirit, in June of 1995 we changed our name to New Beginnings Baptist Church, still meeting at Bellevue Baptist Church, where we had begun to outgrow our meeting place. After months of searching for a facility of our own, in March 1998 we purchased a building located at 6540 Glenview Drive, which is our new church home. Our church has grown from 0 members to well over 100 members. Our church stands as a beacon of light in this community, holding true to our purpose, which is to share the love of Jesus Christ, Him crucified and resurrected.

New Life Outreach Church.

NEW LIFE OUTREACH CHURCH
6100 Davis Blvd.

In 1950 Rev. James L. Barnes established and built an Assembly of God church at 3900 Scruggs Drive in North Richland Hills. There were other ministers after Rev. Barnes left. In 1970 Rev. Charles O'Neal took over the church with only 10 members. The church relocated to 6101 Davis Blvd. in 1990 and was renamed New Life Outreach Church. It is now an interdenominational church with 500 members. The church is involved in working with Metro Ministries of Fort Worth and Dallas, going into the projects and working with drug addicts. Approximately 150 to 200 attend New Life Outreach Church regularly.

NEWCHURCH CHRISTIAN FELLOWSHIP
7300 Smithfield Road

NEWCHURCH Christian Fellowship is a nondenominational church founded by Gary D. Kirksey and Larry Ford on February 10, 1991, with the mission of glorifying God by carrying out the commands of Jesus in the power of the Holy Spirit. The vision of NEWCHURCH is to be a church that offers an opportunity for people in the Metroplex and around the world to know God intimately.

NEWCHURCH began in a home, moved to a leased facility in Hurst where it stayed for 21 months. As NEWCHURCH continued steady growth, and as various ministries

NEWCHURCH Christian Fellowship

began to be raised up, there was a need for more space. During June 1992 leaders submitted a bid of $330,000 to the Resolution Trust Corporation for a 4.9-acre tract located in North Richland Hills. NEW-CHURCH won the bid and secured the property valued at approximately $1 million.

The newly acquired property contained a 42,000-square-foot shopping mall that consisted of a shell building and a concrete pad. The membership put in uncountable hours cleaning the land of debris, tearing down walls, sweeping, and cleaning. Between July and November, $240,000 was raised to create the worship center, children's education space, and staff offices. When NEWCHURCH moved to its new 13,000-square-foot facility on the first Sunday in November 1992, there were approximately 200 people attending.

During 1993 Sunday morning attendance grew to more than 300, and the need for additional space was becoming apparent. Funds were raised once again for a 4,500-square-foot addition.

A 4.1-acre tract of land across Starnes and northeast of the current facility was obtained in January 1995. Development of the east-west wing began during the summer of 1995. New staff offices, a large fellowship hall, and additional educational rooms were added.

Gary Kirksey resigned in April 1998 to take the pastorate of Trinity Church in Lubbock, Texas, and Ronnie Matheny currently serves as senior pastor.

Through the blessings of God some 700 or 800 people now call NEWCHURCH their family. Home groups form the core of adult and youth ministries and are essential to integrating members into meaningful relationships.

Our first service was held at the YMCA on Davis.

NORTH HILLS ALLIANCE CHURCH
8224 Grapevine Highway
North Hills Alliance Church, originally known as the Alliance Bible Fellowship, was organized in 1984 with the Rev. John Mechtly as first minister. Our first service as a church was held at the YMCA on Davis Blvd. Over the next few years we met in various places: a daycare on Rufe Snow, a hotel on Baker Blvd., and a rented store front on Hurst Blvd. Finally in 1993 we purchased our present building on Grapevine Highway. This was originally a chiropractic office. We completely gutted and rebuilt the inside. We now have a small but very attractive church building. All of the remodeling was done by our church people of all ages and genders. Land has been purchased in North Richland Hills for a future building program.

The church has had four ministers:

Rev. John Mechtly	1984–88
Rev. Mitch Schultz	1989–92
Rev. Richard Rutherford	1992–96
Jeffrey Wheeler	1997 to present

First services held in this building Sept. 1972.

NORTH PARK BAPTIST CHURCH
7025 Mid-Cities Boulevard

North Park Baptist Church had its beginning in the minds and hearts of a group of people who met in the living room of Dr. Chapmond Davis in early November 1970. A total of seventeen people were present for that meeting. The YMCA on Davis Boulevard in North Richland Hills was secured for later meetings. This facility was used until property at the present location was purchased, and a building was erected. The first services were held in this building in early September 1972. At the first service, an attendance of 150 was recorded.

Dr. Davis acted as missionary pastor until April 1973, when he resigned to go to Israel as a foreign missionary. Dr. Curtis Coleman became the pastor and remained until August 1975. From August 1975 until September 1977, Rev. Wayne Pope led the new church. From 1977 until May 1988, Dr. Bob Lane served as pastor. At that time, Dr. Gene Edwards became the senior pastor and continues to lead the church today. The church has grown from the original three families to more than 1,000 members. The church is located on three and one-half acres of choice property with an estimated value of $2.5 million.

North Park Ministries constitutes not only the field of worship but also consists of a child care center, academy, inner-city ministry to disadvantaged youth and children, world-wide missions, and the only Messianic Ministry in Tarrant County, led by the founding Pastor Dr. Chapmond Davis. The church's ministries make up an annual budget in the vicinity of $1 million. North Park has grown numerically, spiritually, and in mission outreach ministry. As the church has grown, the average attendance has now reached more than 300, with steady increase in the number of people who worship with us each Lord's Day.

The church was originally organized under the efforts of the Baptist Missionary Association of Texas. It became expedient for the church to realign itself in the Southern Baptist Convention in 1990. This was done in order to facilitate both physical and spiritual growth for the next millennium.

At this time North Park looks forward to a great period of service to our Lord Jesus Christ by serving those in this community with the glorious gospel of Christ and its transforming power, until He shall return to receive us unto Himself.

Presented by Bettie Hinkle

NORTH RICHLAND HILLS BAPTIST CHURCH

4001 Vance Rd.

North Richland Hills Baptist Church (NRHBC) had its beginning on February 26, 1956, with services being held in the North Richland Elementary School (Mullendore Elementary). It began as God impressed members of the Richland Hills Baptist Church with the need for a mission church in the fast-growing area of North Richland Hills.

Growth was phenomenal from that first Sunday when 41 people became members. Four lots on Vance Road were purchased from the A. L. (Roy) Freeman family for the first building. The mission church was self-supporting by the time they held their first meeting in the new $32,000 building on May 20, 1956. Chartered on that date with 115 members, James Hester became the first pastor of NRHBC.

Present sanctuary completed in 1974.

First building occupied May 1956.

In June 1958, ground was broken for a new $60,000 auditorium to seat 600. The building contained additional space for staff offices. Four small houses on Vance Road and one on Parchman Street were purchased for a parsonage and more nursery and educational space.

In April 1959, with the membership close to 600, Rev. W. Hal Brooks became pastor and served for the next 24 years. A parsonage on Reynolds Road was later purchased for the Brooks family.

Jack Terry became minister of education, music, and youth in March 1963 and served until August 1966. Dr. Terry later became dean of religious education, then vice president of institutional advancement at Southwestern Baptist Theological Seminary. He and his wife, Barbara, continue to make their home in NRH.

In June, 1964, two acres on the corner of Vance Road and Glenview Drive were purchased. In November 1966, God united the hearts of the people to establish a building fund to begin a new venture that became known as "Building by Faith." The goal was a 1,200-seat auditorium, library space, and offices that would be entirely paid for when completed.

Rev. Paul Paschall became the new minister of music and youth in 1967. By the mid-1970s, the church had begun production of an annual Christmas Pageant under the direction of Paul Paschall. The pageant outgrew the Richland High School auditorium where it had been held for seven years and in 1980 moved to the Tarrant County Convention Center Theatre and, with more than 10,000 in attendance, has grown from two performances to six. The pageant was named the Greater Fort Worth Christmas Pageant and in 1998 will complete its twenty-fifth year of presenting the Gospel in drama and music.

Greater Fort Worth Christian Pageant celebrates its 25th year, December 1998.

Groundbreaking services for a new sanctuary were held Easter Sunday, March 29, 1970, and the church celebrated its 15th anniversary with outdoor services on the new concrete slab in May 1971. The facilities were filled for dedication services in 1974 with the membership achieving their "Building by Faith" goal.

The Tower of Truth, a 75-foot sculpture, has become a point of direction to the community. It was designed by Hal Brooks, and each part represents a symbol of God's Word to man. The shape of the tower is the fish, the ancient symbol of Christianity. The cross within the fish is the symbol of Jesus Christ, Him crucified and risen. The base, in the shape of the Star of David, containing a fountain, symbolizes the foundation of God's Word and the fountain of water is the symbol of the Holy Spirit, flowing in the life of believers.

In 1983 Hal Brooks resigned after 24 years, and the church called Phillip E. Simmons. After a courageous battle against cancer, Dr. Hal Brooks died in April 1987. The "Hal Brooks Memorial Prayer Chapel" was dedicated in October 1987. In 1985, NRHBC repeated what had been done for them 30 years earlier when they sent members to begin a mission church on the northern border of NRH. Northwood Baptist Church met for the first time Sept. 15, 1985.

Under the ministry of Phillip Simmons, NRHBC broke ground on April 2, 1989 for a 42,000-square-foot Family Life Center and Education Building. With the building of the Family Life Center, all of the small houses purchased years before were moved off the property to make room for parking space. In 1988, Rev. Simmons led the church in establishing the Cornerstone Assistance Network (CAN) ministry with offices located on the corner of Glenview and Parchman.

In January 1994, the church celebrated Pastor Simmons' tenth anniversary—a bittersweet occasion, as he had learned earlier he had brain cancer. He died March 1994 at the age of 52.

The church called Joe McKinney as pastor in the fall of 1994. Its leaders encouraged the church to become debt free by the end of 1996, which was accomplished. Rev. McKinney resigned in July 1997.

On July 26, 1998, North Richland Hills Baptist Church called Dr. Tommy Teague as pastor. At the time he was called, he was serving as senior associate pastor of First Baptist Dallas. NRHBC's current membership is around 3,535 members and the annual budget is $2.8 million.

Because of the sacrifice and service of all its predecessors in the faith, NRHBC has had the opportunity to share Christ's message with Northeast Tarrant County and beyond. The congregation is excited about the future as they seek new ways to serve God and meet the needs of the community.

One of those ways is the Cornerstone Counseling Center. In 1988, Pastor Phil Simmons began the procedures for creating the Cornerstone Counseling Center with David Dickerson as Clinical Director.

OUR LADY OF MOUNT CARMEL ROMAN CATHOLIC CHURCH
3900 Scruggs Drive

The first traditional Latin mass in many years was celebrated in Fort Worth in May, 1986. Father Peter Philips, associate priest of the Society of St. Pius X, was the celebrant, the server was Nick Novelly, and the location was the home of Mr. and Mrs. A. F. Tatarko in River Oaks. Approximately 20 people were present.

This was the beginning of Our Lady of Mount Carmel Catholic Church in North Richland Hills. On the first Sunday in July 1986, the traditional Latin mass was again celebrated at the Metro Center Hotel in downtown Fort Worth. Father Philips, a Hungarian, was assigned to our mission as pastor. Jerry Oberg was appointed coordinator, and Dorothy Tatarko, treasurer. Father Philips named the new mission "Our Lady of Mount Carmel."

Our Lady of Mount Carmel Roman Catholic Church

Each Sunday thereafter, the Oberg family transported from their home items required for mass, until a nearby storage room was made available. In March 1987 the church moved to the Holiday Inn on the West Freeway at University Drive. However, a storage area was not available on the property. So again mass furnishings were transported to the site. Needing additional space, the church moved to the Hugh M. Moore Funeral Home in Arlington in November 1987. Hallelujah! Storage area for mass furnishings was available.

In the summer of 1992 property and church buildings were purchased at 3900 Scruggs Drive in North Richland Hills. The first mass in the new church was celebrated on August 30, 1992. Remodeling of the church building included many parishioners working many months of Saturdays and evenings. Furnishings were purchased for the church.

The church is affiliated with the Society of St. Pius X, a worldwide organization. The United States headquarters is located in Kansas City, Missouri. Traditional Latin mass is celebrated every Sunday at 8:30 A.M. with confession and rosary before mass. The church has a circuit priest who flies in Saturday afternoon and leaves Sunday. He also does masses in Wichita and Little Rock. The priests are headquartered in St. Mary's, Kansas. This church differs from traditional Catholicism in that Latin is used in the mass and differs in spiritual practice.

PRIESTS WHO HAVE SERVED:

Father Peter Philips
Father Peter Lemay
Father Kenneth Novak
Father James Buckley
Father Jaime Pazst

RICHLAND HILLS CHURCH OF CHRIST
6300 N.E. Loop 820

To begin a new church in the growing area, the Birdville Church of Christ purchased three lots in 1954 on the Grapevine Highway at Popplewell, in Richland Hills, at a cost of $5,500.

The first service was January 22, 1956, when 187 people met in the Glenview Elementary School in Richland Hills. Worship services were held in the cafeteria and children's classes in the hallways. Mid-week evening services were on Tuesdays at the Birdville Church of Christ

New $8.5 million building occupied Nov. 1986

in Haltom City. This continued two years. The church selected Berlin Cummings and Royce Blevins to serve as elders and Walter Burch as first pulpit minister. A house on Manor Drive in North Richland Hills was purchased for the use of Minister Walter Burch and his family. Later that same year the church began printing a weekly bulletin of news and teaching. It was titled The Richland Hills Echo.

After meeting for two years in the Glenview school, our first building was constructed at 7060 Grapevine Hwy. at a cost of $85,448. Church members did much of the work themselves and secured the loan with individual guarantees. As members worked on the building in the evenings and on Saturdays, close friendships and fellowship resulted. A spirit of love and harmony has always prevailed, and through the years there have been no divisions or splits in the congregation. Our first service in the new building on Grapevine Highway was in February 1958.

Houses on Cummings Drive, Manor Avenue, and three houses on Hardisty were purchased for church use as it grew.

The first mission work was the purchase of a half-ton pickup for missionary Eldred Echols to use in Africa. One hundred dollars per month was given to help in his support. Eventually, the Birdville church relinquished his full support to Richland Hills. Mr. Echols has been supported by this congregation since that time.

During heavy rains in 1957, '58 and '59, Fossil Creek flooded many houses in Richland Hills. The church helped flood victims by stacking furniture, taking children to safety, providing lodging, cleaning up, and serving sandwiches and drinks to workers.

This church accepted the oversight of "Exodus/Bay Shore," in 1961. This was a massive effort of up to 70 families who left their jobs, sold their houses, and moved in the summer of 1963, to Long Island, N.Y., to establish a church. It gained publicity in *Time* magazine, which sent reporters to our services to find out who we were and what we believed.

Due to the church's rapid growth, 10 acres in undeveloped North Richland Hills land was bought at the intersection of the proposed Loop 820 and Rufe Snow Drive for $25,000. Attendance reached 600 for the first time in February 1963. At an all-day retreat in June 1963, plans for a new building on the Loop 820 site were discussed.

An architect was engaged in 1967 to draw plans for the building that would seat 1,000 in the auditorium, with comparable classroom space. Construction was begun on the building with an official groundbreaking April 13, 1969. At the time the land was purchased plans were to begin another congregation, but later it was decided the church should stay together and all move to the new location.

Interior-Atrium

The building was occupied in August 1970.

A children's television program, Carpenter's Children, was begun by this church on Dec. 16, 1973, on Channel 5, in Fort Worth. It had approximately 50,000 viewers each Sunday morning. It continued for 10 years.

A period of rapid growth ensued giving us an average Sunday morning attendance of more than 3,300 with a weekly budget of $74,500 by 1979. In that year, $750,000 was given on one Sunday for construction of a Family Life Center and classrooms adjacent to the church. A residence on Corona Street was also purchased in 1982 to house the benevolence work.

A tract of 54 acres was purchased in April 1984, on Loop 820 and the proposed extension of Meadow Lakes Drive. On May 20, 1984, members pledged $8.5 million toward the new building. Another building across the street on Meadow Lakes was to be built to house the benevolence and counseling ministries. Groundbreaking for a 178,000-square-foot building was held Sunday, Dec. 2, 1984 and was occupied Nov. 11, 1986. The City of North Richland Hills purchased the property at Loop 820 and Rufe Snow for a Library and Recreation Center.

The Richland Hills Church of Christ has an outstanding history and strong commitment to community and world ministries and services. The Community Enrichment Center meets the needs of tens of thousands of people in northeast Tarrant County and is assisted in this work by numerous businesses, civic organizations, and individuals. Many volunteers provide countless hours of labor for this ministry.

Other programs the church participates in are The World Bible Translation Center, Open Arms, a ministry to abused women and their children, Christ's Haven Children's Home, Counseling Center, and Bread for a Hungry World, a disaster relief organization.

PULPIT PREACHERS WHO SERVED:

Walter Burch	1956–58
Ralph Starling	1958–66
Lanny Henninger	1966–71
Darrell Rickard	1971–77
Jon Jones	1977–89
Rick Atchley	1989–present

RICHLAND HILLS UNITED METHODIST CHURCH
7301 Glenview Drive

Organized July 26, 1953

In 1953, a canvass of the neighborhoods of Richland Hills was conducted by the following men: Del Barron, Dan McKee, A. C. Metts, Alan Adams, Howard Patterson, Herman Duncan, Buck Dysert, and Mike Compton. As a result of this survey, Richland Hills United Methodist Church was organized with 89 members on July 26,1953, in the Richland Hills Civic Center building under the leadership of the Reverend Robert E. Young. Membership increased so rapidly, that property that had been purchased on Reeves Street in Richland Hills was termed inadequate, and five acres were purchased at 7301 Glenview Drive in North Richland Hills, its present site. Del Barron and Dan McKee purchased the property from the Calloway family.

Services were held in Richland Elementary School beginning in September 1953. Charter membership was closed October 25, 1953 with 215 persons forming the church. Morning worship services continued at Richland Elementary and then Glenview Elementary Schools until February 1955. Many evening services were held in the open air on the church lot next to the parsonage, which was located at 6624 Reeves Street.

The present sanctuary on Glenview was consecrated in July 1959. Our current 1,070 membership roll totals 500 families.

PASTORS WHO HAVE SERVED:

Robert E. Young	1953–1962
Gilbert Ferrell	1962–1967
Michael Patison	1967–1972
Don Pike	1972–1976
Bob Briles	1976–1979
John Dowd	1979–1983
Joe Saylor	1983–1988
Randy Wild	1988–1994
Don Scroggs	1994-present

Fort Worth Star–Telegram

The Church moved into its new building in 1955.

Members of the Richland Hills Methodist sponsored the formation of Watauga United Methodist and Davis Memorial United Methodist churches.

Many persons have felt the call to full-time Christian service in the congregation. Those who pursued or are still pursuing this call are the late John McDaniel, Clyde Zellers, Janice Kreitner Cane, Joseph Dee Faram, Paul Bailey, Steven Ramsdell, and Wesley Byas. We have two diaconal ministers, Jeannie Trevino-Toddlie and Greg Loving and many others who carry the ministry of the laity as lay speakers and heads of the various committees and commissions.

This congregation has a long history of community involvement in keeping with the Wesleyan tradition. Some of the endeavors of the members included a tutoring program for children of low-income families known as North East Community Action Program (NECAP). We presently make sandwiches for the Presbyterian Night Shelter and support NEED (North East Emergency Distribution), Mid-Cities Care Corps, Tarrant Area of Community Churches, and several Community Centers. We have sponsored families for Cuba, Vietnam, and Ethiopia. We have a strong youth group. They have shown their care and responsibility by going on mission trips. For the last three summers they have helped build and repair churches in depressed areas and make repairs on homes for elderly and handicapped persons. Several of our members are involved in Habitat for Humanity. Another of our community services that we are most proud of is our day care. In May 1982, the church opened the day-care center to help meet the needs of working parents.

Since we built our sanctuary in 1959, we have added classrooms and a covered walkway that connects our fellowship hall (Reeves Hall) and the main sanctuary. We also have added a new wing, which contains adult classrooms and an office complex.

We are most proud of our music program. Jeanene Petrie has been our choir director for many years and has developed several children and youth choirs in addition to the regular adult choir. She has sponsored three bell choirs, which have provided music on a regular basis, and we also have a brass ensemble known as the Richland Brass and a lovely flute choir under the direction of Janice Spooner. We also have been most fortunate to have a multitalented organist, carillon bell choir director, and musician in the person of Tim Scholl.

This past year we completely redecorated our sanctuary and were gifted with a beautiful grand piano by Byron and Myrtis Gray.

Between Reeves Hall and the sanctuary, two trees were planted in memory of Robert Scott and Pat Hill. From this a Memorial Garden is being developed with the help of Jack Binion, Mary Beth Kugle, Andy Dobson, Marion Johnson, Ruth Hays, Don Hamilton, and Ward and Kathryn Anderson. A dove statuary honoring Georgia Duncan was given by the Fidelis Class and placed in a raised stone bed surrounded by seasonal plantings. Next to Reeves Hall, a patio with three concrete benches with landscaping has been built.

The attractive church building with the two towering steeples in a prominent location on Glenview between the two local shopping malls has attracted many to visit and join the church. The church is a popular choice for weddings. The Christmas Eve candlelight service is well attended by church members and friends in the community.

SHADY GROVE BAPTIST CHURCH

8241 Precinct Line Road
On January 2, 1955, Reverend John Streater, pastor of First Baptist Church in Smithfield, called to order the meeting that would constitute and organize the Shady Grove Baptist Church. Mr. S. L. Bailey presented a statement of purpose and called for the reading of the names of the 31 charter members that desired to enter in the new fellowship.

James Lafferty asked the new congregation to stand and read the Church Covenant after which he presented the articles of faith from the New Hampshire Confession of Faith.

New auditorium, early 1970s

The Advisory Council that recommended the church be constituted consisted of:

Rev. John Streater,	FBC Smithfield
Rev. E. D. Vison,	Mount Gilead Baptist Church
Rev. Boyce Evans	Pleasant Run Baptist Church
Rev. Bill Williams	Carroll Road Baptist Church
Rev. Elton Hinze	Springdale Baptist Church
Rev. Miles Walsworth	Florence Baptist Church
Rev. S. R. Garrison	Broadview Baptist Church
Rev. Leroy Gaston	Shady Grove Baptist Church
Mr. Charles McLaughlin	Superintendent of Missions of the Tarrant Baptist Association

The first offering received by the church was $30.55 for World Missions through the cooperative program.

Over the intervening years Shady Grove has built several buildings and developed ministries to reach their community. As the community began to change and new ideas and innovations were introduced to the congregation, membership and attendance rose and fell. A succession of pastors attempted to bring stability to the group of folks who remained faithful to the cause of reaching northern boundaries of North Richland Hills and the surrounding areas of Colleyville, Keller and Southlake.

In the early 1970s the church grew to the point of having to build a new auditorium. Departing from the traditional wood-frame, white, country church, an imposing A-frame structure was built using the latest technology and innovations. During the late '80s pastor Roger D. Eakin, writing his doctoral dissertation for Southwestern Seminary, produced a book entitled *Leading a Church in a Transitional Area to Establish and Adopt Plans Necessary for Revitalization and Growth*. Soon after, with much uncertainty about the future, the church reached its lowest ebb. Pastor Eakin moved on, and the church fell on hard times.

In 1993 a new focus regarding the explosive growth of the community surrounding the church property, and the addition of varied ministries designed to reach the new demographics are still being implemented on a consistent basis.

In the spring of 1998, ground was broken for a new $250,000 education/activity center, to be followed by a 500-seat auditorium and educational space to match. New landscaping, signage, and the opening of a major thoroughfare (Precinct Line Road) have added to the excitement that mirrors that of the 30-plus folk, who, in 1955, envisioned a place where men and women, boys and girls, could come to faith in Christ and grow in maturity in spiritual things.

The little church located on a dead-end road, deep in the country, has become a vibrant congregation situated at a major intersection. The $30 offering to missions has become thousands of dollars given each year through the cooperative program and to local folks in need of assistance. Some of the goals of the first 30 members have been reached through

such current ministries as a food pantry for the needy. We have parenting seminars for those who need help raising children, all encompassed by a Bible study program, which moved from the simplest of truths to the deeper walk with Christ.

SMITHFIELD CHURCH OF CHRIST
6525 Smithfield Road

Smithfield Church of Christ was first located on Main Street and was obtained for $5.

The Smithfield Church of Christ first met on October 23, 1888 in a small building that was located just across Smithfield Road from our present location. The original congregation consisted of families from the surrounding farming and ranching communities who came to church on horseback or wagon.

That early-day church occupied a lot on Smithfield's Main Street, which was obtained for $5.00. Originally the building faced Smithfield Road, but during a bad storm the building was twisted on its foundation. The men of the congregation decided it would be easier to twist it all the way around so it faced Main Street than to put it back in its original orientation.

By 1960 they had outgrown the building, so a new 530-seat building was constructed. The new $80,000 building was located on a two-acre site across the street on Smithfield Road. This structure was a contrast to the one-room frame building that housed the small group of ardent leaders of faith who founded the church in 1888. They had their first worship service in the new building on a Sunday evening December 1960 during Evangelist Bob Barnhill's ministry. Church Leaders were Elders W. S. Couch, E. F. Abbott, and Olen Goldsberry. Deacons were J. C. Harston, Elbert Lindley, and Marvin Shockey. From that time on fellowships were held under a large live oak, which flourished behind the building. The old fellowship tree survived until it finally fell during a great storm in 1995. Thankfully, in 1980 the present fellowship annex was added to the building and is now used for classroom space, fellowship, and community outreach programs.

Bill Paxton came as pastor to Smithfield Church of Christ in 1994. As a result of Pastor Paxton's interest in foreign mission work in India, Smithfield is supporting several preachers, congregations, and an orphans' home in that land.

The mission of the Smithfield Church is to prepare for works of service so the Body of Christ may be built up, to strive for unity in the faith, and to proclaim the truth. Our goal is to love the Lord with all our heart, mind, and soul and to go and make disciples of everyone in the world so that all may have the promise of eternal life.

SMITHFIELD UNITED METHODIST CHURCH
6701 Smithfield Road

The early Methodists of the present Smithfield community attended the Willow Springs Class (church) that was located approximately two and a half miles west of the present location. It was in existence in the early 1860s, but the exact date is unknown. The earliest date recorded is in the 1865 quarterly conference records of the Dallas

The Smithfield United Methodist Church Sanctuary built in 1974

District of the East Texas Conference held at Minter's Chapel. According to Methodist history, a "class" was a unique Methodist institution and was organized locally to enforce discipline with a hierarchical structure. It supervised the itinerant preachers with a strong efficiently organized central authority. According to the 1867 class records of the Willow Springs Class, the class was part of the Indian Creek Circuit of the Dallas District of the Trinity Conference (North Texas Conference today).

The first class services in the community were held in the home of William and Mary Turner. William Turner was a native of Virginia and came to Texas in 1846. According to the quarterly conference records, Mr. Turner was a steward in 1866 in the early Willow Springs Class. The first pastor was Rev. William L. Carleton.

Later a church was organized as part of the Methodist Episcopal Church South. Since the town was called Zion, the church took the name Zion Methodist Episcopal South Church. Upon organization of the church, a building was erected. The land, which was approximately one and a quarter acres, was given to the church by Eli Smith. The first building was small but served the community as a public school as well as a church.

Historical marker dedicated 1993

In 1887, the name of the town was changed to Smithfield so the church changed its name to Smithfield Methodist Episcopal South. According to the 1889 quarterly conference records, there were 400 churches in the circuit.

In 1894, Smithfield became part of the Fort Worth District of the Northwest Conference. By 1913 the Smithfield charge (membership) had increased to 400 church members. In 1928–1936 the Smithfield Church became part of the Forest Hill charge. This charge consisted of Forest Hill, Birdville, and Smithfield with a church membership of 220.

In the year 1935, the second of the two frame buildings was built. Charles E. Turner of Mineral Wells, Texas, gave the masonry materials in memory of his grandparents William and Mary Turner. The Rev. J. T. Fergerson was the pastor.

In 1939, the Methodist Protestant, Northern Methodist, and Southern Methodist united to form the Methodist Church, and the church name changed to Smithfield United Methodist Church.

By the year 1945, the church's membership had about 204 and it retained its first "station" minister, the Rev. Gilbert Ferrell. A "station" church meant that a church had enough membership to have both its own pastor and parsonage. Another building was constructed in the year 1952 under the leadership of Rev. Richard Millsap. The masonry materials for this building were furnished by Harold Dennis of Mineral Wells in the memory of Charles E. Turner, a friend and business partner. The Sunday school enrollment was 160 and the church enrollment was 241.

In 1965 further growth of the church required better educational facilities. Under the leadership of Rev. Burt Gillis, a new structure was built across the street from the original Smithfield Methodist Church, with plans for a new adjoining sanctuary.

The new parsonage located at 7801 Owens Drive was completed in the year 1968 under the leadership of Rev. Norman Purvis. Rev. Purvis also started the Lord's Acre Day.

In 1968, Texas Methodists were host to the General Conference in Dallas. At this meeting, the Methodist Church and the Evangelical United Brethren Church merged to form the United Methodist Church. This marked the fourth time the Smithfield United Methodist Church's name had changed.

In 1974 the present sanctuary was constructed under the leadership of Roy Bassett. In 1976 Rev. Walter Black served as pastor until June 1982, at which time he retired from the ministry for health reasons.

Rev. James Olney served our church as pastor from June 1982 until June 1983. During his leadership, the church continued to grow in membership and added two new Sunday school classes. Groundwork was initiated for a Mother's Day Out program.

During the leadership of Rev. Mike Phillips the Mother's Day Out program was started in September 1983 with four children enrolled. The program expanded, and by 1986 there were 60 children enrolled, and the program had changed its name to Discovery School. In 1987 the present adult/youth educational building and church parking lot were built, and the church offices in the educational wing were remodeled.

Rev. John McKee served as pastor from June 1987 until June 1990. During his leadership an adult Sunday school class was added due to church growth. The church purchased a new Allen Digital computer organ.

The Rev. Kyle Glenn became pastor in 1990. Under his leadership the church continued to grow with a membership of 649.

Our church reaches out to many families in this area through Discovery School (129 enrolled), NEED (Northeast Emergency Distribution), the annual Harvest Festival (Lord's Acre), and Vacation Bible School. Also a senior citizens group meets monthly in the church's fellowship hall. We have active United Methodist Women and United Methodist Men groups that meet regularly.

Rev. Dr. Richard Reed became pastor in 1993.

St. John the Apostle Parish
7401 Glenview Dr.

St. John the Apostle Catholic Church was founded in 1964. St. John's is now the second largest Catholic church in the Fort Worth Diocese. The parish was formed from a part of St.

George Catholic Church and is located on Glenview Drive in North Richland Hills. The parish had approximately 600 families. Msgr. William J. McCoey was assigned by the bishop to serve as first pastor. He held the first mass on August 15, 1964 in Glenview Elementary School.

In June of 1965, two small buildings were purchased to be used as school buildings. Religious education classes were held in a building on the Grapevine Highway, directly behind the parish property. Three hundred and forty-eight children were taught religious education by volunteer teachers, a practice still used in St. John's Parish.

Founded 1964, it is now the second largest Catholic Church in Fort Worth Diocese.

Construction on the permanent school building for grades one through eight was completed for the school year 1966. It was the first Catholic school in the United States to begin teaching without nuns.

The first Christmas mass was celebrated in the Richland Plaza Cinema Theatre. In 1965, masses had to be moved to Richland Junior High because of the growth in the parish. Actual construction on the church began in 1966. The church is highlighted by unusual stained glass windows. The windows depict the 13 apostles in the main church and scenes of the sorrowful mysteries of Christ in the windows of the chapel.

The first mass celebrated in the new church was on Christmas Eve in 1966. The formal dedication of the church and school was on April 8, 1967. In January 1967, the first wedding was performed in the church.

A group of about 450 volunteers organized to run the concessions at the Fort Worth Convention Center in return for a percent of the profits in 1969. This money was applied directly to the mortgage on the church. By 1977, the earnings of the Convention Center group had reached the quarter-of-a-million-dollar mark.

Fr. Robert Wilson came to St. John's in 1970 to replace Msgr. McCoey as pastor. Shortly after Fr. Wilson came to St. John's a preschool was added to the school program. The preschool building was built in 1971 and paid for by the sale of bonds. Another building was needed for offices by 1975. Another sale of promissory notes paid for the construction of St. John the Apostle Administration and Resource Center. By this time, St. John's was the largest parish in the Diocese of Fort Worth, with 1,400 families.

In 1977 the Diocese divided St. John's parish and formed a new parish in Bedford. This shifted about 250 families out of St. John's to the new parish. Fr. Leon Flusche replaced Fr. Wilson as pastor in 1982. St. John's had grown to 2,250 families by this time. Fr. Albert Tyl came in 1985 as pastor.

Another parish was formed to the west, in Keller. St. Elizabeth Ann Seton took about 600 families out of St. John's parish in 1985. A 22,000-square-foot Family Life Center was built in 1987. This building housed a childcare center, gym, meeting rooms, dining room, and kitchen. Also at this time, four more classrooms were added to the school. The school had 451 students at this time.

Msgr. Charles King came to St. John's as pastor in 1988. By 1991, St. John's now had 2,562 families, with 1,200 children in religious education and 484 children in the school.

By 1991, St. John's had 2,901 families, so another parish was formed in Colleyville taking another 300 families from St. John's. Another four classrooms were added for the school and Religious Education.

1994 brought more changes to St. John's. Plans were made to renovate the church and the school and to add much needed parking space. At the time these plans were being made, the Schick-Shadel Hospital directly behind the school became available on the market. The Diocese approved the purchase of the facility for St. John's. It is a 22,000-square-foot building with four acres of ground. This building was made into administration for school and religious education, classrooms for religious education for 1,600 children, a youth center, and one wing will be renovated for a three-and four-year-old preschool program.

The parish day school currently has an enrollment of 617 children from preschool through eighth grade. Four more classrooms have been added to accommodate this added growth. The school is fully accredited and its student body today includes students whose parents received their educations there. Graduates of the school have gone on to a wide variety of careers and to serve their communities in many diverse ways.

St. John's always has been known for its volunteers. Approximately 1,500 volunteers now are involved in one or more ministries. The church is active in 20 different family life programs, a Social Service coordinator, helping several hundred a month with food, gas, rent, utilities, and medicine. They have a liturgical director planning all liturgical celebrations for 3,181 families, and more than 90 organizations make up the very active Christian Community of St. John the Apostle Parish. This makes St. John's a leader in church ministry in Northeast Tarrant County and to be the fourth largest Catholic congregation in Tarrant County.

ST. PAUL PRESBYTERIAN CHURCH

4517 Rufe Snow Dr.

In October 1961 the Central Texas Presbytery placed the Rev. John H. Brannon in the newly created St. Paul Presbyterian Parish as its evangelist. The first preliminary meeting was held November 19, 1961. During the intervening months Rev. John Brannon visited in community homes of North Richland Hills, Richland Hills, and Haltom City east of the Denton Hwy. He conducted services in various homes and in the manse at 7017 Marilyn Lane.

On November 3, 1963, at North Richland Junior High School, a petition was signed to organize a church. There were more than 100 charter members representing 39 families. Rev. Brannon became the church's first pastor. The first worship services were held in the Civic Center on Vance Road in Richland Hills. Sunday church school, youth meetings, and adult groups as well as the pastor's study were located in a leased house at 7063 Dover Lane. Fellowship and study hour were held at the manse, 7017 Marilyn Lane.

St. Paul Presbyterian Church

A beautiful tract of land near North Richland Junior High School at 4517 Rufe Snow measuring 4.85 acres was purchased for the parish by the Presbytery in 1964. Ground was broken for the church building on Rufe Snow January 1965. The building was dedicated Sept. 26, 1965. The building consisted of sanctuary seating for 150 persons, eight classrooms, pastor's study, church office, and kitchens. The attractive stained glass sign on the street that announces the name of the church was a three-year project of love led by James Black. The present sanctuary, together with a classroom and restrooms, occupies a building that was completed in 1970 and dedicated on October 11 of that year.

St. Paul Presbyterian Church provides the facilities, programs, and services to meet the needs of its parishioners and the community. We are a member and participant in Northeast Emergency Distribution (NEED) activities as well as providing sandwiches and counseling for residents at the Presbyterian Night Shelter. We provide meeting space for many activities including Boy Scouts, Girl Scouts, Weight Watchers, and various government elections. We sponsor nursing home bingo, dress dolls and bears, and fill stockings for the Salvation Army at Christmas, as well as help with Habitat for Humanity house projects.

Paul's charge to the church:

"I wish you peace
Let your life be worthy of the Gospel of Christ.
I want to hear that you stand in one spirit
One mind, striving for the faith of the Gospel."

LIST OF CHURCH PASTORS:

John Harvey Brannon	1961–67
Jerry Walker	1967–72
Charles H. Fox	1973–76
Cynthia Campbell	1976–77 (Interim)
David L. Northcutt	1977–81
George Adams	1981–82 (Interim)
Richard Schmidt	1982–present

4 Schools

BIRDVILLE INDEPENDENT SCHOOL DISTRICT

The roots of the Birdville Independent School District have been firmly planted in Northeast Tarrant County from the time of the county's earliest settlement. The Birdville Academy, which attracted students from a wide area, including Dallas, Parker, and Denton counties, opened in 1858. Professor William E. Hudson operated the school until the mid-1860s. The Academy was financed by student tuition.

The first public school financed by taxes was established in 1882. In 1919, a building site located at East Belknap and Carson streets was purchased, and the district's first brick school building, which opened in 1920 with four teachers, was erected. That location is still the heart of BISD.

The Birdville Common School District was incorporated in 1926 and became the Birdville Independent School District under the direction of Superintendent W. T. Francisco, who served from 1925 until 1935.

The class of 1933 was the first to graduate from Birdville High School. Among the nine members of the graduating class, one, who had been enrolled in the Birdville School since first grade, would return to the school after college to become the longest tenured employee of the BISD. Wiley G. Thomas Jr. was hired in 1933 as the sixth-grade teacher. He remained an employee of the district as teacher, coach, principal, superintendent, and consultant (with the exception of a one-year hiatus during the 1942–43 school year) for the next 46 years. The Birdville ISD W. G. Thomas Jr. Coliseum is named in his honor.

From the 1950s to the present, growth has been the constant condition faced by those in charge of education in Northeast Tarrant County, and their task has been to equip the district to handle it successfully. The superintendents following Mr. Thomas were Billy H. Smith, 1979–84, Joe Bill Fox, 1984–92, and Dr. Bob E. Griggs, 1993 to the present. Their leadership, along with that of School Board members, has enabled BISD to plan and carry out future needs of the district.

The district has grown from the single campus on Birdville Hill with 747 students to the 30 campuses with an enrollment of more than 20,000 students. Along the way, BISD, as an established and experienced school district, was asked to assume educational responsibility for children moving into the fast-growing adjacent towns: Smithfield, North Richland Hills, Richland Hills, Watauga, Haltom City, and part of Hurst.

The future of BISD looks bright with promise. In 1995 the Birdville Board of Trustees was named Texas's Outstanding School Board, and in 1996, Dr. Bob Griggs was selected Outstanding Superintendent in Texas. Board members are Charles Yates, Kelly Hancock, John D. Spicer, Wanda Strong, Dolores Webb, Calvin White, and Fred Wilson. The board is currently overseeing construction of a new high school for the district. The new school, perhaps in an attempt by the district to hearken back to its roots, will be named Birdville High School.

ALLIENE MULLENDORE ELEMENTARY
(FORMERLY NORTH RICHLAND ELEMENTARY)
4100 Flory Street

Principals: Lane DuBose, John Parish, Alliene Mullendore, Richard Richeson, John Fanning.

Alliene Mullendore Elementary

Alliene Stephens Mullendore grew up in Fort Worth and graduated from Polytechnic High School at 15 years of age. She began her teaching career when she was 17 years old at Blewett, a rural school district in Uvalde County in Southwest Texas. After three years at Blewett, she taught at Avondale, a one-teacher school near Saginaw. She came to a rural Birdville School District as a teacher in 1943. She served as a teacher, dean of girls, assistant principal, consultant, and principal during her tenure with the Birdville ISD before retiring in 1972. She was also the first woman elected to the Birdville School Board of Trustees, winning the post by a landslide. She was the first teacher hired by Superintendent W. G. Thomas Jr. at the beginning of his 34-year tenure as top administrator in BISD. He once said, "I may have done some things wrong during my life, but hiring Mrs. Mullendore was not one of them."

Smithfield Elementary

SMITHFIELD ELEMENTARY

6724 Smithfield Road

Principals: William Walts, Marvin Fuller, Ruth Coppock, Joe Max Wilson, Wanda Strong, Jolene Armstrong, Pat Gaffney.

SNOW HEIGHTS ELEMENTARY

4801 Vance Road

Principals: Billy Smith, John (Jake) Richards, Johnny Sandlin, Jack Peterson, James Rodgers, Sue Martin, Georgene Mais, Janelle Bourgeois, Suzanne Nickel.

Snow Heights Elementary

RICHLAND HIGH SCHOOL

5201 Holiday Lane East

Principals: Billy Smith, Ben Shilcutt, John Rice, Ray Williams, Gary Clark, Annette Keller, and Randy Cobb.

Richland High School opened its doors in the fall of 1961. Some people talked about the "foolish idea of constructing a new high school in the middle of a muddy pasture where there would never be any homes." Some said there would never be enough students to start school much less fill the building. Construction began during the 1960–61 school year.

The saying, "Just build it and they will come" was certainly true. The north wing of the new high school was incomplete, but classes began the first day of school with 740 students. Teachers had to adjust to the inconveniences and reminded each other that some day they would laugh about it all. Rowena Ballew held homemaking classes in the teacher's lounge, George Virgili's band played enthusiastically in the hall. His choir class wrote the school fight song. Even though band uniforms had been ordered early, they did not arrive in time for the first game; however, "plan B" worked well and dark trousers and white T-shirts were worn by the marching band. The gym wasn't finished, so pep rallies were held outside.

The Richland "Rebel" theme had been chosen, "Dixie" was the school song, "Johnny Reb" the mascot, and David McCombs, son of Joe and Estelle McCombs was the first

Johnny Reb. The Confederate battle flag was chosen the school symbol. Blue and gray was chosen as the school colors.

Theo Rigsby went to Richland as head coach. The following years would prove him to be a highly respected coach and gentleman both on and off the football field. He built a staff of coaches second to none—Dub Stewart, Bobby Prince, Bobbie Lambert, and others. Dub Stewart spent the rest of his career at RHS, retiring in 1989.

Sean Hughes

Richland High School

A group of 42 girls organized the Rebelettes in 1961 and made their first appearance at the November 10, 1961, football game and the Veteran's Day parade the following day. Lt. Noel Morrow was drill team instructor. Jane Reddell (Curtis) organized the Dixie Belle girls drill team in 1964. Joyce Baker remembered helping design and make the first uniforms. There was a real problem with the length of the skirt—it had to be short enough to dance and march in, but not so short to cause the group to fall out of favor with the public.

Events in the world affected the curriculum in the schoolroom. If this country hoped to remain the leader in the military arms race, then students must be educated to become engineers and scientists. In 1961 the highest level of mathematics offered was trigonometry, but by 1968 the students of Ron Tillery were the first class to finish analytical geometry. The 1970s had added classes in elementary analysis I and II, calculus and pre-calculus, and a second year of chemistry and physics taught by Ruth Metts.

Vocational education became an important part of the curriculum in the 1960s. Several work-study programs quickly came into favor with RHS students. Vocational health, office education, child care, industrial training, cosmetology, drafting, general mechanical repair, and auto mechanics each placed students in work-related jobs to correlate with their classwork.

Evelyn "Dell" Parrent started Reading Improvement in 1969. It became so popular that she stopped teaching English and taught five classes of reading. It was one of the first programs of its kind in the state.

During the 1960s and years following, each school began staffing counselors, nurses, speech therapists, and resource teachers. In the beginning some of these staff members traveled to two or more different campuses.

A highlight of the year for Minerva Kimbell's Spanish classes was a trip to Mexico for advanced students during the Easter holidays.

Horst Krause began teaching classes in German in 1967, and in just a few years it became a four-year program. The German Club became the largest organization on campus.

The Music and Drama departments of RHS have always been outstanding. The stage productions of these combined groups evoke many memories—*South Pacific*, *Bye-Bye Birdie*, *Oklahoma*, *West Side Story*, *Music Man*,—the list goes on and on.

Dub Fisher, Paula Brooks, George Virgili, Owen Phillips, Terry Sinclair, David Hall, Patricia Neighbors, and many others helped in all these success stories.

The Rebellaires singing group was formed in 1966. Members were chosen from the best voices in school and their reputation as a fine vocal group has continued through the decades.

In 1971 in the school cafeterias, hamburgers, stew, and chili and beans cost 25 cents. Vegetable soup cost 20 cents. In 1974–75 competitive girls' sports were approved.

In 1976 Krause's German program and the Spanish program of Minerva Kimbell were recognized among the five best foreign language departments in the state of Texas.

In October 1978 Wiley G. Thomas retired as superintendent of BISD effective Feb. 1, 1979. On Feb. 22, 1979 the coliseum was renamed W. G. Thomas Jr. Coliseum.

Another Richland tradition was begun in the 1977–78 year—selecting a distinguished alumnus to be presented at the homecoming pep rally and game.

Year Honored	Distinguished Alumni	Grad. Year
1998-99	Tim McClendon	1968
1997–98	Debbie Tribble	1971
1996–97	Alan Baker	1972
1995–96	Kelly Hancock	1982
1994–95	Mark Howe	1973
1993-94	Mark Brooks	1979
	Cynthia Spencer Brooks	1973
1992–93	Richard Rigsby	1970
1991–92	Randy Moran	1968
1990–91	Richard Davis	1974
1989–90	Mike Skipper	1973
1988–89	Mona Nolen Kerby	1974
1987–88	Dr. Fred Murphy	1968
1986–87	Gary Morris	1967
1985–86	Mark Wood	1973
1984–85	Tommy Duer	1973
1983–84	Gary Johnson	1968
1982–83		
1981–82	Charles Mayberry	1970
1980–81	Mike Brinkley	1970
1979–80	Richard Norman	1965
1978–79	Lanny Basham	1965
1977–78	Lori Smith	1976

Courtesy of Giltrap Photography

Richland High School in the 1980s

The 1980s saw sweeping changes to Richland High's traditions. The school was receiving pressure to change the Rebel flag symbol. Students were very opposed, arguing it was a spirit symbol only, representing school heritage and nothing more. In recent years, however, many of the Richland traditions have experienced change.

The '80s presented several other issues to occupy time and energy of teachers and staff: to change or not to change from junior high schools to middle schools; earrings "yes" or "no" for male students; changing Birdville ISD's name; religious meetings at school; disruptive students; school prayer; the dress code; competency testing for teachers and administrators.

Richland High was the object of a huge new building program in the mid-'90s which, along with many other changes and much added space, created a new large building now facing south instead of west.

The burgeoning enrollment at RHS will receive some relief when the new Birdville High School opens for the 1999–2000 school year.

Joyce Baker

Fran Burns

Fran Burns

Fran Burns

Fran Burns

Kristy Robichaux

Joyce Baker

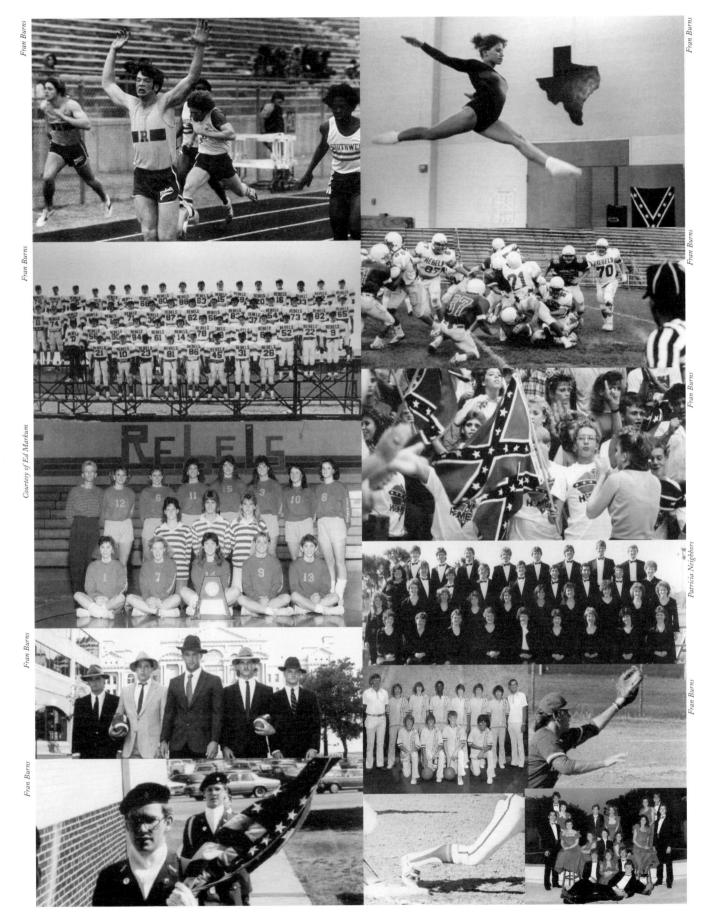

North Richland Middle School

NORTH RICHLAND MIDDLE SCHOOL

4800 Rufe Snow Drive
Principals: Johnny Nobles, E. L. Lowe, Ray Thompson.

HOLIDAY HEIGHTS ELEMENTARY

5221 Susan Lee Lane
Principals: B. J. Stigler, John Rice, Ray Williams, Marjorie Isbell, Henry Burgoon, Donna Solley. The school was constructed on land formerly owned by J. Fred Davis Sr. and his son J. Fred Davis Jr., whose house was moved to a farm near Haslet. The dairy barn was torn down.

Holiday Heights Elementary

Smithfield Middle School

SMITHFIELD MIDDLE SCHOOL

8400 Main Street
Principals: James Niendorff, Ed Logan, Doris Tipps, Susan Fisher.

CARRIE FRANCES THOMAS ELEMENTARY

8200 O'Brian Way

Principals: Cecil Hill, Joe Hallford, and Martha Oldenburg.

Carrie Frances Taylor Thomas grew up in Vernon, Texas and attended Texas Wesleyan College in Fort Worth. It was there she met Wiley G. Thomas.

Mrs. Thomas, a graduate of TWC, began teaching at Birdville in 1938 at the junior high school when the only campus was located on the corner of Belknap, Carson, and Broadway streets. She then taught third

Carrie Frances Thomas Elementary

grade at Browning Heights and then Birdville Elementary. Because of ill health, she retired in 1969 and died in 1977.

Mrs. Thomas was known for her keen sense of humor, love for children, and excellent reputation as a teacher. In May 1978 the Birdville Classroom Teachers Association requested that the School Board name the new elementary school in her honor. This is the only school in Birdville named for a classroom teacher.

FOSTER VILLAGE ELEMENTARY

6800 Springdale Lane

Principals: Howard Nix, Ann Croxdale.

Foster Village Elementary

NORTH RIDGE ELEMENTARY

7331 Holiday Lane

Principals: Don Williams, Jerry Plemmons, Nancy Mull.

North Ridge Elementary

North Ridge Middle School

NORTH RIDGE MIDDLE SCHOOL
7332 Douglas Lane
Principals: Tom Murray, Charlotte Fritz.

GREEN VALLEY ELEMENTARY
7900 Smithfield Road
Principal: Brenda Allen.

Green Valley Elementary

Renderings courtesy of Kyle Bacon

Architect's drawing of New Birdville High School. Proposed opening 1999 school year

NEW BIRDVILLE HIGH SCHOOL
Principal: Debbie Tribble, Ed.D. Mascot: Hawk (the site is located on the natural breeding ground of the native Red-tailed Hawk). School Colors: Forest Green with White and Gold.

Renderings courtesy of Kyle Bacon

Architect's drawing of Athletic and Fine Arts Complex.

NORTH RICHLAND HILLS PRIVATE SCHOOLS

TARRANT COUNTY JUNIOR COLLEGE

Tarrant County Junior College is a comprehensive community college with four campuses, one of which, Tarrant County Junior College Northeast, is located in North Richland Hills. TCJC offers two-year associate degree programs and one-year certificate of completion programs in 208 fields of study. It is an "open door" college with enrollment generally open to anyone. It is a student-centered school that provides a wide variety of services to students, including counseling, testing, job placement, and financial aid.

The Northeast Campus opened in 1969. Sitting on the boundary of NRH and Hurst, the Northeast Campus is located on 187 acres of land.

The movement to establish a county-wide junior college system originated in the early 1960s when a group of citizens decided that there were educational needs not being met by the public schools or by existing area colleges—needs such as advanced technical-vocational training and a program of community service courses. Because it is controlled locally, the junior college has flexibility in structuring programs and is able to provide specialized training to suit the needs of local businesses and industry.

The average age of students at TCJC is between 29 and 30. Nearly half the students are married. More than 80 percent work. About half attend class only after 5 P.M. Classes are kept small and teaching is student-centered. New programs are constantly introduced to serve students more effectively.

The story of TCJC is one of steady growth. Growth, whether from increased population or more widespread educational opportunities, has always been the college's most serious challenge. Knowing, however, that the process of education is continual, board members and administrators through the years have taken care to ensure that TCJC is a constantly evolving entity, prepared to meet new challenges as they arise. During its 35-year history, TCJC's leaders have made decisions based on the premise that "We learn from the past, we work for the present, and we build for the future."

St. John School opened for 1966 school year.

ST. JOHN THE APOSTLE CATHOLIC SCHOOL
7421 Glenview Drive

St. John the Apostle Catholic Church was founded in 1964. Msgr. William J. McCoey was assigned by the Bishop to serve as first pastor. In June 1965, two small buildings were purchased to be used as school buildings. Religious Education classes were held in a building on Grapevine Highway directly behind the parish property. Volunteer teachers taught 348 children in the Religious Education classes, a practice still followed in St. John's Parish.

Construction on the permanent school building, for grades one through eight, was completed for the school year 1966. It was the first Catholic school in the United States to begin teaching without nuns.

The parish day school currently has an enrollment of over 600 children from preschool through eighth grade. Four classrooms have been added to accommodate growth. The school is fully accredited and its student body includes students whose parents received their education at St. John's. Graduates of the school have gone on to a wide variety of careers and serve their communities in many diverse ways.

FORT WORTH CHRISTIAN SCHOOL AND FORT WORTH CHRISTIAN COLLEGE

7517 Bogart

The first Fort Worth Christian School Board of Trustees was established on January 21, 1957 and received a charter for the school on May 31, 1957.

Roy Deaver was elected the first president on May 3, 1957. A seven-room administration building was erected to house

FWC School first football team, 1958

the office. As enrollment grew, an 11-room classroom building was built, and four temporary buildings provided eight additional classrooms.

Classes for first through eighth grades began in the fall of 1958 with several hundred students enrolled. Twenty-seven eighth graders were graduated into high school that year and the football team completed its first year of existence without a loss.

College classes were begun in 1959. Thomas B. Warren was appointed president. During his administration the

FWC School first year 1958-59. Cardinal cheerleaders Front, L/R-Johnne Fisher, Jeanie McCullough, Elaine McHam, Suzy McDaniel, Sue Vincent. Back, Marva Miller, Marie Nutt, Anne Morris, Karen Warren, Sylvia Barnett, Marilyn French, Bonny Stalnaker

FWC School first basketball team 1958–59— Front, L/R-M. Robinson, J. Griffin, B. Goin, D. Smithwich, B. Warren, M. Stroud. Back, Myers, J. Breckenridge, B. French, J. Paul, L. Cannon, Ray Deaver, K. Moore, L. Savage

ninth grade was added. By 1961, when Claude Guild was appointed president, students from kindergarten through junior college were enrolled. Two dormitories, a president's home and two temporary classroom buildings were erected, and in 1984 a gymnasium-auditorium was completed.

The Texas Education Agency granted full accreditation to the school in 1966. The school was heavily damaged by a tornado that year, making it necessary to rebuild the high school and administration buildings.

Fort Worth Star-Telegram

Tornado-like winds ripped away the roof and slammed it against another building in April 1966.

Curtis Ramey was appointed president in 1965 and A. V. Isbell in 1969. Bert Lana became superintendent in 1974. Dean Bingham was named principal of the high school, Sondra Nash as director of the elementary school, and Helen Gleghorn, director of Day Care Center. The school was nearing 500 in enrollment.

Mrs. Laura Bynum was named head administrator in 1993. Two years later, a severe storm caused major damage to campus buildings. The end result was an opportunity to update and refurbish, making what appeared to be a crisis a chance to rebuild even better than before.

The Olen N. Mitchell Activity Center was dedicated and opened in 1995.

The "Securing the Future" campaign began in 1996–97 to secure funds for the future of Fort Worth Christian School. The spirit of the school is found in the statement "We have overcome problems and obstacles through the years with God's help, prayer, and a unified spirit of family. We have moved forward with sacrifice and joy toward a common goal that binds us together."

IMMANUEL LUTHERAN SCHOOL
7321 Lola Drive

Immanuel Lutheran School, established 1974.

When Immanuel Evangelical Lutheran Church was organized in 1970 in North Richland Hills, it purchased more than five acres of land at 7321 Lola Drive with the intent of beginning a school. The plan for a school was driven by the conviction that all Christian parents are to bring up their children in the training and discipline of the Lord.

In September 1974, classes began for nine students in six grades in a doublewide mobile home that served for a year as Immanuel's worship facility. Mrs. Annette Wulff, helped Immanuel get its school started.

Myrl Wagenknecht served as principal for the first eight years. Mr. Warren Backer succeeded him in 1982. John Melso became principal in 1986. During his eight years as principal, a kindergarten program was begun, and a four-room building was constructed. When the school building was built in 1988, it was valued at $276,000.

In 1991, Mrs. Terry (Ledermann) Immel returned to teach kindergarten for seven years. A pre-kindergarten program was added in 1993. Pastor Wagenknecht served again as principal from 1994–98. The 1998–99 school year began with 68 students enrolled in pre-kindergarten through eighth grade.

Academically, the school as a whole is 1.2 years ahead of the national average. Team sports include soccer, field hockey, basketball, softball, and a Fun Day.

Immanuel is a Lutheran school, which is both conservative and progressive, keeping up with latest technology and encouraging all staff members to engage in continuing education. It is a caring school that strives to lead each student to his or her highest potential. It is a Christian school with the prime purpose of sharing Christ Jesus as Lord and Savior.

5 Organizations

NORTHEAST TARRANT CHAMBER

EXERPTS FROM FORT WORTH STAR-TELEGRAM
Article written by Bill W. Hornaday 12-10-97

Gertrude Tarpley sat at the kitchen table of Jack Bean's Richland Hills home 40 Novembers ago, putting together a list of 75 civic leaders.

The Greater Richland Area Chamber of Commerce was chartered on December 23, 1957. Jack Bean was the first president and with the help of Gertrude initiated the organizational meeting for the Greater Richland Chamber of Commerce.

"Richland Industrial Park was just getting started. People were concerned about how it would affect their homes. Airport Freeway did not yet exist. Large housing additions were opening, and somebody needed to coordinate which school district their children would attend," says Bean, the chamber's first president and current board chairman of Surety Bank in Hurst.

But even after drawing up the list, Tarpley, a local journalist who would eventually serve as the chamber's executive director for 23 years, was not sold on the organization.

"It wasn't until after things were put together that she saw the future," Bean says of the late Tarpley, who is remembered by many as Northeast Tarrant County's unofficial matriarch. "We had to generate enough support to gain hers."

Bean's kitchen table vanished long ago, but the November 1957 meeting started what has become the 725-member Northeast Tarrant Chamber, supporting business in Haltom City, North Richland Hills, Richland Hills, and Watauga.

The fledgling organization got off to a shaky start. "I forgot to recognize a group from Colleyville and said, 'If there's anyone here who isn't for improving Richland Hills, they can hit the door," Bean recalls. "The Colleyville bunch walked out. And it took a decade to get them back."

Within weeks, the name was changed to the Haltom-Richland Chamber of Commerce. About 75 charter members joined from as far away as Grapevine. Annual fees were $25, compared with today's minimum of $200.

In the 1960s, the chamber worked to balance commercial, industrial, and residential zoning. It helped expedite Airport Freeway's construction, established beautification programs, and aided in forming the Tarrant County Junior College District.

"We gained momentum like a truck going downhill," says Charles Brinkley, the chamber's 1964 president and retired president and chairman of the board of Liberty Bank in North Richland Hills. "We had our first chamber banquet in 1962 and pulled some major strings to get Gov. [John] Connally to speak. After that, it was not unusual to have 500 or 600 people at a membership lunch or dinner."

By the 1970s the chamber's projects expanded to developing industry in North Richland Hills and to promoting new or expanding existing roads that linked several member cities, such as Rufe Snow Drive.

After using Tarpley's Richland Hills home and the old Ramada Inn Northeast in Haltom City, the chamber got its own building in 1974 at 6555 Grapevine Highway in Richland Hills, the geographic center of the cities it served.

Log cabin that occupied current chamber site, courtesy TCJC

Chamber of Commerce-Northeast Tarrant County, 1998

But by 1981, the chamber outgrew its 1,000-square-foot building and fund-raising began toward its current 2,250-square-foot building at 5001 Denton Highway in Haltom City. During the next 10 years the chamber adopted its current name, took on a new logo featuring four stars and four oak trees—the stars and the trees representing each member city. But questions arose about the chamber's effectiveness, and Watauga dropped its membership in 1993. One of the area's major employers, Tecnol Medical Products in North Richland Hills, was not a member.

"For lack of a better word, we were floundering," says Doug Terry, who was approached to become chamber chairman in 1992. "We were constantly in debt and trying to stay afloat, and there was not a strong sense of leadership."

Terry agreed to take office but only if changes were made to promote economic development, retain members, and offer programs to help member businesses. "Before, economic development support was lip service. There was never a serious push." says Terry, president of Frost National Bank in Hurst. "We became more visible in front of city councils. Cities were starting to bicker, so it was important for them to buy into each other's ideas. And we had to give members maximum service for their money."

Tecnol joined the chamber in 1993. And by 1995, Watauga returned to the fold. Membership began to grow from 585 in 1992 to 725 today. The resurgence was characteristic of the tenacity that one of its founders, Tarpley, demonstrated as a leader of the chamber for 23 years.

When Gertrude Tarpley died in 1994 at age 90, the chamber lost a tireless community leader who was lauded as a forceful mover and shaker who always made time for others. At the time of her death, Tarpley was on the boards of Liberty Bank, North Hills Medical Center in North Richland Hills, and the Tarrant County Medical Society.

That spirit remains active today. With a new influx of industry, notably technology firms, Nancy Watkins sees work-force education as an area to which the chamber should direct its efforts. But if the years—and Tarpley's example—have taught anything, Watkins says, it is that the chamber's priorities start with its members. "The economy is doing well now. But when things get hard, a lot of small businesses look at chambers as more of a luxury than a necessity, and that's a mistake," she says. "I don't know of a less expensive way to market goods or services than being part of a chamber. One of the biggest reasons a small business survives is networking. From what I know, this group got together to form a stronger voice as a group and that still stands true today."

In 1997 the City Council of North Richland Hills voted to leave the chamber. Each council member had a different reason and point of view for voting to pull out, but after the chamber hired a new CEO, Bill Ridgway, the council voted to return to the chamber in mid-1998, and pledged its continued support to the chamber and its business members.

THE KIWANIS CLUB OF NORTHEAST TARRANT COUNTY

The Kiwanis Club of Northeast Fort Worth was organized in 1957 and was sponsored by the Kiwanis Club of North Fort Worth. In 1995, the name was changed to the Kiwanis Club of Northeast Tarrant County. The first meeting place was St. Luke Methodist Church. Later, the club was moved to Underwood's Barbecue, then to the Old South Pancake House, then to Diamond Oaks Country Club. Presently, the club meets at Ryan's Steak House.

Fund-raising activities began with pancake suppers. Then, for a number of years, antique shows and sales were held at Birdville school facilities. The shows were later moved to Tarrant County Convention Center under the leadership of Zane Field. In 1964, a talent show, Our Best To You, was initiated and directed by John Lamond through 1983. He was succeeded by Dr. Dennis Arnold through 1988. Sales of advertising in show programs provided funds for prizes of $1,000, $500, and $250 awarded to the first, second, and third-place winners in the form of certificates of deposits available to the college or university of the winner's choice.

For some 25 years, through 1995, the club sponsored a senior citizens arts and crafts show and sale, run solely for the benefit of those participating. Much credit goes to Mrs. Ward Anderson and Mrs. Russ Miller who supervised the operation for more than 20 years. They were succeeded by Mrs. Kay Pryor.

Over the years, funds were disbursed to organizations such as the Texas Girl's Choir, Boy and Girl Scout Troops, Cook Children's Hospital, Salvation Army, and the YMCA. Heart and cancer research, student sponsorships, and a revolving small loan fund available to students on the Northeast Campus of Tarrant County Junior College were also supported with club funds.

The year of 1997 was an active year for the short-term loan program. As financial aid guidelines for students became more stringent, this program became an avenue that provided a way for students to enroll for their classes, purchase books, and begin their classes with a short-term payment plan to relieve the financial pressure. It has become a valuable tool for many TCJC students seeking to continue their education.

NORTHEAST-RICHLAND LIONS CLUB
The North Richland Hills Lions Club was chartered March 7, 1963, with 24 members. It was originally named the Northeast Lions Club. The first meeting was in a cafeteria in Richland Plaza mall. The original charter members were Raymond L. Anderson, H. L. Arnold, Charles C. Brinkley, Rev. Hal Brooks, A. E. Brown, Harry J. Bryant, Hiram J. Davis, Alvis Dowell, Rev. Guss Eoff, J. D. Foster, William E. French, Brian H. Haenish, Alan Hamm, John P. Hunter, W. B. Leffingwell, Chester Lewis, Charles M. Morrison, Clyde Mynatt, R. R. McKinney, A. C. Nichols, J. B. Sandlin, Hoyte L. Teague, D. Wayne Tidwell, and Woodie C. Vardeman.

The Fort Worth Founders Lions Club was the sponsor, and Verne Carrington was the district governor. Eleven members transferred from other clubs and 13 new members joined to allow us to start with 24 charter members. Charles C. Brinkley was elected president and J. B. Sandlin served as charter secretary.

Northeast Lions and the Greater Richland Lions Clubs merged into the Northeast-Richland Lions Club just a few years past charter in 1963. The Northeast-Richland Lions Club has now grown to more than 120 members and is the largest Lions Club in District 2E2 of Texas.

Lions Club projects have been a chili supper in February each year with an auction. Proceeds are used to buy eyeglasses for students and for sending crippled children to summer camp in Kerrville, Texas. Another project is the annual basketball tournament in the Wiley G. Thomas Coliseum each December. An additional project, a Cheer Fest, was held in the Wiley G. Thomas Coliseum in the fall of 1997. All funds raised are used for eyeglasses for children and Christmas food, clothing, and toys for needy families with children.

Local Lions remember a chili supper and auction which was held at the Richland Hills Methodist Church several years ago. John Parish, auctioneer, assistant Charles Brinkley, and the other Lions were selling everything in sight. Charles received a call from the church secretary the next morning inquiring about some gallon buckets of paint that the church had purchased to paint their Fellowship Hall. It had been stacked on the side of the stage. Too bad—it had been sold during the auction! Parish and Brinkley inquired about the color, brand, etc. and quickly bought some more paint as a replacement for the paint that had been sold.

Meetings were moved from Richland Plaza to the Greater Richland Cafeteria and then to the Fish Net on Rufe Snow and Grapevine Highway. From there we moved to the Chicken Shack on the Denton Highway. Our next meeting place was the Ramada Inn on Denton Highway and from there to the Sir Loin Steak House on the Grapevine Highway. This was one of Cullen Turner's favorite places to meet. From there we moved to the Holiday Inn on Loop 820 and Highway 183, then across the street to El Chico. Our last move was to Diamond Oaks Country Club. The Lions Club has been a real asset to North Richland Hills and all of Northeast Tarrant County.

Auction - Charles Brinkley at podium, John Parish points to bidder.

History compiled by Charles Brinkley

NORTHEAST YMCA

The Northeast YMCA began in 1941 in the Riverside section of Fort Worth. In 1953 it was relocated to Bonnie Brae and Bird, where there was a small house and several lots that were sold to Riverside Christian Church. In 1956 and 1957 the YMCA office was in the Riverside Christian Church and from 1958 until 1963 it was at 4009 Haltom Road in Mr. W. I. Browning's office until that office burned. The present site, 5408 Davis Blvd. in North Richland Hills was acquired on May 2, 1968. The original site consisted of 11.5 acres.

In June 1969 a freestanding gym, 88 by 98 feet, was built along with two unfinished handball courts. An outdoor swimming pool and bath-house, two lighted tennis courts, additional parking space, and fencing of the athletic fields were added in 1974. Three-plus acres of the 11.5-acre property were sold in 1980 and 1983, leaving the present 8.483 acres.

In 1984 the main building was built, incorporating 10,000 square feet of office space, meeting room, one new racquetball court and the completion of the two unfinished ones, fitness area, locker rooms, sauna, spa, and parking area. In 1991 a new day care building was built on the site.

Clyde Wood Award - Mrs. Evalyn Wood presents the Clyde Wood Memorial plaque to Scottie Morrison, executive director of Northeast YMCA. The award named for Clyde Wood, president of First State Bank, Bedford who was killed in a December 1980 automobile accident, will be presented annually to the top producer in the YMCA membership drive. First recipient of the award was Jim Harrison, not pictured.

222

Today, the YMCA serves 1,850 youth with services such as baseball, soccer, tennis, and flag football. The present child care facility serves 120 children daily and the summer program serves 164 daily.

During the summer over 7,000 youth participate in the swimming programs.

NORTH HILLS GARDEN CLUB

As the area of North Hills developed, and people began to move into the newly completed houses, some women of the area felt a Garden Club was needed to bring the neighborhood together. In the fall of 1956, this group of women met at Clovia Riley's home at 5605 Tourist Drive to form the North Hills Garden Club.

Four of the charter members are still living: Ester Ruth Hunter (Mrs. E. W.), Bernice Miller (Mrs. Vanis), Jessie Lawson (Mrs. Robert E.), Clovia Riley (Mrs. David).

Jessie Lawson served as president for the first year. North Hills Garden Club was affiliated with both the state and national Garden Clubs Councils. The Garden Club Council of Fort Worth's 1958–59 yearbook lists the 1958–59 president as Mrs. Clovia Riley. She is still a member today. She was also chairman of Flowers for U.S. Public Health Service Hospital, so the North Hills Club decorated that hospital for the holidays and also the Veterans Hospital in South Dallas.

The club focused on stimulating interest and encouraging citizens in all phases of gardening. Tree planting, both on public and private lands, was of particular interest to the club members due to the void of trees in the new subdivision. At the opening of Richland Plaza, the club provided and planted a redbud tree in the courtyard area. Club activities included an annual flower show and a yard of the month contest for the club members.

The Thanksgiving luncheon was always held at the home of Greta Koenig, a German-born woman who spoke with a heavy accent and who was a great hostess. The annual Christmas luncheon featured a traditional white elephant gift exchange. The club prospered for several years, but as society changed membership began to decline. Though a few years ago the club ended its affiliation with the state and national groups, the club remains active with meetings every month except during the summer.

History compiled by Jane West Dunkelberg

NORTHEAST OPTIMIST CLUB

The Northeast Optimist Club was established August 15, 1952, with Bill Blessing as its charter president. As the club was organized, Mr. Blessing envisioned guiding children by having a club whose members would sponsor baseball and softball teams for young boys and girls in Northeast Tarrant County.

Northeast Optimist started with baseball in an area east of Birdville Stadium and Fossil Creek. The practice field was then moved to the corner of Broadway and Denton Highway, present site of Kroger. The Lions Club gave the building and fields to the Optimist Club. It was decided later that another move was necessary, and 10 acres of land located at Loop 820 and Denton Highway were purchased. The Board of Directors paid their own money for a down payment and signed a note for the balance to buy this land.

Cecil Pokluda organized the first Mustang League for 9 and 10 year olds in 1969. He was president of the club during this time. Pokluda was presented an award from Pony Little League Baseball in Williamsburg, Penn. for his outstanding leadership in forming the Mustang League.

Bill Blessing

223

Play Ball!

In 1960, the Northeast Optimist team went to the Little League World Series in Williamsport, Penn. Representing the South Region, they won 13 straight games but lost the final game to finish in second place.

Lester Purkey and his wife, Raye, were constant volunteers. They were pleasantly surprised when the concession stand was named for them. The Purkey family had run the stand since it first opened.

The 1982 floodwaters came up to the edge of Denton Highway. It destroyed records, the history of the club, and the ladies' auxiliary records. The Optimist field was completely rebuilt and is located just inside Haltom City. Many members and participants live in North Richland Hills.

In 1983 the Optimist Club sponsored the Pony League Girls Softball Tournament with 110 teams participating. In 1998 there are more than 1,500 boys and girls participating in club sponsored activities. The club is involved in more than sports. Many programs involve recognizing students in the community and honoring them for their achievements, often in the form of scholarships. Many outstanding students from Haltom and Richland high schools have been awarded scholarships through the years because of the outstanding work of the Optimist Club of Northeast Tarrant County.

NORTH RICHLAND HILLS GARDEN CLUB

At the first organizational meeting of the North Richland Hills Civic League held March 6, 1953, a greeting committee was appointed to meet and welcome new residents to North Richland Hills. The committee was composed of Mrs. Bea Elliott, chairman, Mrs. S. K. Baker, Mrs. Laura Ray, Mrs. Myrtle Peavler, Mrs. Mable Norman, and Mrs. Evelyn Watson. This committee sponsored a coffee held at the Presbyterian Church on April 8, 1953, to which all ladies of NRH were invited. Groups of various interests were formed as a result, including those interested in playing bridge, gardening, making crafts, etc.

On April 10, Civic League Chairman W. H. Tripp appointed Mrs. Margaret Lambert to be chairman of the Garden Beautification Committee. An organizational meeting was held at the home of Mrs. Ruth Jones on May 20, 1953, and the group adopted the name Blossom Battalion. Formal activities began with the first official meeting. Luncheon and installation of officers was held at Amon Carter Field, later renamed Greater Southwest Regional Airport, on September 9, 1953. Mrs. Lambert was installed as the first president of the Garden Club.

The Garden Club soon changed its name to the North Richland Hills Garden Club and became affiliated with state and national councils. The members enjoyed the fellowship of the group as well as sharing the group's goals and purposes. Each woman was living in a new home with a large lot on which to get lawn and landscaping established. Establishing a yard at this time was very difficult since this area of Texas was in the middle of a seven-year drought in 1953.

Club members also took on community and civic projects. In December 1953, they sponsored the erection and lighting of the community Christmas tree and the helicopter arrival of Santa Claus on the present site of Greater Richland Center parking area. The *Fort Worth Star-Telegram* printed a corrected story on December 21, 1953, entitled "*Star-*

Telegram Lands Santa in Wrong Place." "The Star-Telegram—not Santa Claus—got its directions mixed Saturday. Santa landed by helicopter in North Richland Hills Saturday to take part in a Christmas party. The Sunday Star-Telegram by error said he landed in Richland Hills. North Richland Hills is an incorporated community distinct from Richland Hills." This may have been the first of many such identity errors to be endured in years to come by this brand new city.

Most of the club members shared a common bond, small children and growing families. In the next few years, as these children became school age and were involved in school activities, membership in the Garden Club dwindled. Some joined nearby clubs, others just resigned, and the club was eventually disbanded.

History compiled by Evalyn Wood Lochridge

RICHLAND HILLS MASONIC LODGE NO. 1348, A.F. & A.M.

In the early 1950s, when the city of North Richland Hills was much smaller and the population far less than that of today, Brothers Herbert L. Arnold, Clarence Jones, and Claud P. Griffith met one evening following church and decided a Masonic Lodge was badly needed in this area. They aroused interest in others, marshaled their forces, and on December 4, 1954, Richland Hills Lodge #1348 was chartered by the Grand Lodge of Texas at its annual communication. The new Lodge was set to work at Riverside Lodge #1194 on January 22, 1955. The Lodge subsequently met at Keller Lodge #1084 until September 1955, when a new Lodge building at 7115 Glenview Drive was completed. The Lodge was erected on a lot donated by Brother Clarence Jones, which was a part of the original Jones farm located near the present day intersection of Grapevine Highway and Glenview Drive.

The cornerstone of the new Lodge building was set on June 10, 1955, by Grand Master George Moffat. It was not until September 19, however, that the Lodge building was ready for use and the first degrees were conferred therein.

The Lodge labored at this site for the past 42 years, contributing quietly to the surrounding community. One significant contribution has been the granting of scholarships to the two seniors of Richland High who have shown the greatest improvement during that year and are going on to college.

Richland Hills Lodge, 1998, before building was demolished.

As of this writing, however, the property has been sold and a new Walgreen's drugstore constructed on the corner of Glenview Drive and Grapevine Highway. It is with much regret and fond memories that we vacate these hallowed premises. At the same time, we wish only the best for Walgreen's in their new business location. The Lodge building ceased to exist as such in April 1997. Few are those who knew, or will remember, that it once graced this spot.

The new Richland Hills Masonic Lodge #1348 A.F. & A.M. building has been constructed on Popplewell Street, north of Baker Boulevard in Richland Hills.

Darrell E. Smith, PM
Secretary

ROTARY CLUB OF NORTH HILLS

Rotary Club of North Hills started as a provisional club sponsored by the H.E.B. Rotary Club in June 1981. Doug Long was the organizer from the parent club. Upon receiving its charter from Rotary International on May 6, 1982, the Club was first called The Greater Haltom-Richland Rotary Club. In May 1986, the name was changed to be more inclusive of our service area.

The first meetings were held in the Sir Loin Steakhouse in Richland Hills. The first club project was to join with the Rotary Club of Burleson and acquire used eyeglasses for distribution in Mexico, Central, and South America. More than 10,000 pairs of glasses have been dis-

Rotary Club awards, 1987

tributed to date. In 1990–91, John E. Lutz III served as the district governor for District 579, which at that time contained 66 Rotary Clubs including our own.

Club projects include helping support local as well as international immunization projects. This club has donated and planted more than 1,000 trees within the community. The club each year provides a two-year vocational scholarship to an area high school student, presents vocational Service Awards to local citizens, and holds the annual "4-Way Speech Contest." The Club has hosted Group Study Exchange Teams from around the world and sponsored a matching grant that provides funding for a youth training facility in Sao Paulo, Brazil. More than 30 percent of this club's members are Paul Harris Fellows or sustaining members of the Rotary Foundation.

Currently, the Rotary Club of North Hills meets at noon on Friday at Ernie's Restaurant and is committed to the community by fostering the ideal of Rotary, "Service Above Self," throughout our service area.

SMITHFIELD LODGE NO. 455 A. F. & A. M.

The Smithfield Lodge No. 455 was organized on July 13, 1875. Originally named the Grand Prairie Lodge No. 455, its name was changed to Smithfield Lodge in 1947 at the request of lodge members. It was located at 8007 Main Street in the Smithfield area of North Richland Hills.

At the first meeting, John S. Collier, special deputy to the grand master, instructed the appointed officers in the proper manner of opening and closing the Lodge. This meeting was held in the Zion Church building (also the site of the public school), the forerunner of Smithfield United Methodist Church. The frame church building was located on the east side of Smithfield Road at Chapman Road.

At the second Lodge meeting, July 17, 1875, 12 members were present for the purpose of receiving membership petitions. The first-degree work by the Lodge was the conferring of three Entered Apprentice degrees on August 18, 1875, on D. H. Hightower, J. A. Garrett, and Eli Smith.

By April 1876, work had begun on the first Lodge building. Funds to build the building were secured in part by borrowing $23.37 from the Zion Church Missionary

Society. The Lodge was erected on a lot approximately one-fourth mile west of the present building. Labor on the two-story Lodge building was provided by Lodge members. In the early years, the bottom floor of the building was usually leased to a local business with Lodge meetings being held upstairs.

The Lodge was chartered on June 10, 1876. Officers were S. D. Sansom, D. H. Hightower, W. A. Whittenberg, J. R. Crane, and A. G. Walker, names still familiar in the area. Initiation fees were $10 for each of the three degrees. Meeting time was "Saturday, on or before the first full moon in each month." Meetings usually began in the early afternoon and lasted into the night. Strict adherence to Masonic principles was upheld as evidenced by records of several members being brought to trial for intoxication.

Lodge cornerstone

In 1894, with the coming of the railroad, the original Lodge building was moved from its first location to a lot west of the present building. Moving the building took several weeks of work by members and was accomplished by using horses and log rollers. The building served without interruption as the Lodge Hall until 1937 when it was damaged by high wind in a spring storm, necessitating moving meetings for a while to the Keller Lodge. Repairs were completed in October 1937. The Lodge was remodeled several times afterward.

Historical marker

In 1949, a building fund was established to raise money for a new building. Lots adjacent to the Lodge Hall were purchased and on June 10, 1981, the cornerstone for the new building was laid at 8013 Main Street. The old Lodge Hall was sold to Charles Mayberry, CPA, and moved to a location on Baker Boulevard in Richland Hills where it was used as Mr. Mayberry's office.

EASTERN STAR

When Clarence and Ruth Jones divided their farm to make a residential community and develop the Greater Richland Hills Shopping Center, they also dreamed that a Masonic Lodge would be a part of this North Richland area. The land on which the Richland Hills Lodge #1348 A. F. and A. M. was built at 7115 Glenview, North Richland Hills, in 1954 was donated by Clarence Jones.

The Masons knew there was a great deal of interest in an Eastern Star Chapter, and they graciously gave their permission for their Masonic Hall to be a meeting place for a Richland Hills Eastern Star Chapter.

This was all Ruth Jones needed to get things rolling. She invited a group to her home with the idea of forming an Eastern Star Chapter. It was a very cold winter day in January 1957, one of those days we have when most people stay home. However, this was a large, warm, friendly group. Many old friends, as well as new ones from North Richland Hills and the surrounding areas from Riverside to Hurst, who wanted to be a part of Richland Hills Eastern Star #1040 attended. There were 65 charter members desiring to transfer in just a short time.

Dispensation was granted by Worthy Grand Patron, Brother Ed Sharpe, with Worthy Grand Matron, Sister Pauline Smith, presenting the Instituting Ceremony on April 25, 1957. During the Grand Chapter Session in Dallas, October 14–17, 1957, Richland Hills Chapter #1040 received its charter.

Portrait and plaque in memory of Clarence Jones, one of the founders of the lodge and donor of the land for present building. L/R-Ruth Jones, H. L. Arnold, past lodge Master

Polly Williams, Past Matron of Ovala Chapter #111, became the first Worthy Matron and Myrtle Simmons was the Associate Matron. Judge Marvin B. Simpson Jr. was honored when asked to be Worthy Grand Patron from 1965 to 1966 by Worthy Grand Matron Mrs. Edna Earl Duke. This was an honor for the young Chapter also. Herbert L. Arnold, Associate Patron, and his wife, Maude, became an active part of the New Richland Hills O.E.S. Maude served as Worthy Matron from 1959 to 1960 with Jimmie Piester, and as Grand Adah from 1967 to 1968. They are still active and have been for these past 41 years. Herbert honored the Chapter by also becoming a Worthy Grand Patron from 1967 to 1968, with Worthy Grand Matron, Mrs. Nancy Bailey Allen.

Groundbreaking for a new banquet hall and kitchen for the Richland Hills Lodge #1348 was August 6, 1977, and in April 1981, the Masons and Eastern Stars dedicated it to Sister Ruth Jones.

In the summer of 1977, the Masonic Lodge was demolished as growth of the adjoining shopping center encroached on lodge space and a new Richland Hills Masonic Lodge building was erected at 3310 Popplewell, Richland Hills, Texas. The new lodge was dedicated August 27, 1997. The lodge has been a proud part of North Richland Hills.

Installation - 25th Anniversary L/R-Ruth Jones, Lawannah Hill, Ann Edwards, Herbert (H.L.) Arnold, Maxine Burns, Maude Arnold, Clara Cole, Polly Williams, not identified

6 Profiles and Volunteers of the Year

North Richland Hills has many success stories to tell. These profiles and volunteers of North Richland Hills share the legacy of creating a verifiable body of exceptional work or personal achievement with a local, national, or international impact. They also have roots in the North Richland Hills community.

These individuals have excelled in the arts, business, education, entertainment, medicine, military, politics, and sports.

Charles L. Owen

Charles Lee Owen, decorated U.S. Army veteran of World War II, commercial realtor, super husband, father and grandfather, and leading North Richland Hills citizen, was born March 6, 1922, in Fort Worth.

C. Owen

He married Faye Lamberth Nov. 28, 1941, and they had five children: Judy Owen Davis, Donna Owen Huber, Kathy Owen Michener, Suzan Owen Jenkins, and Charles Lee Owen II.

Charles joined the Army in World War II and was assigned to the Third Infantry Division. He served in Europe under Texan Audie Murphy, Congressional Medal of Honor winner and most decorated soldier of his time. Charles received two Purple Hearts, a Bronze Star, and other military honors.

After the war, he graduated from Texas Christian University, which he attended on the GI Bill, and in 1955, founded Gearhart-Owen Industries, a commercial and industrial firm, with his brother, Harold Owen, and Marvin Gearhart.

He and his wife Faye built a home in the Smithfield area of North Richland Hills in 1963. After Faye's death to cancer in October 1974, he married Linda Litchfield, on Dec. 26, 1978,

The Owens family shares a patriotic event

and they continued to live in the NRH home. He adopted her 12-year-old daughter, Michele (now Michele Owen Kelley), and was a stepfather to his wife's two grown children. From the blended families, Charles Owen had 21 grandchildren and seven great-grandchildren.

Charles was NRH councilman for two years in the early 1970s and was past president and life member of the Northeast Tarrant Chamber of Commerce. He was trustee at Fort Worth Christian School in NRH for 18 years, six as chairman of the board. At the time of his death in June 1997, he served on four NRH boards, including the Planning and Zoning Commission.

"You could always call on Charles, and usually the answer was 'yes,' if you needed help," said NRH City Manager C. A. Sanford at the time of Owen's death.

"He could always get things done, and he could make things happen," said Jon Jones, senior minister at the Richland Hills Church of Christ, where Charles served as a deacon. Jones said Charles worked tirelessly to build the Meadow Lakes Retirement Center in NRH.

"Just when we thought it was hopeless, he convinced all of us to make another run at it."

Charles also spearheaded the building of several other business developments in Tarrant County, said daughter Kathy Michener. "He was the most generous, patriotic, encouraging, and loving family man. Everyone wanted to sit next to him at the dinner table to hear what was his next dream, usually something he was going to build in NRH."

Charles Owen touched many hearts when he attended an auction after the war ended and gave a month's salary so the U.S. flag wouldn't be sold too cheaply. The flag was buried with him, said his widow, Linda Owen.

Ramona Nolen Kerby

Ramona Nolen Kerby is the daughter of North Richland Hills residents Raymond and Bette Nolen. She was born February 5, 1951, in Dallas, attended North Richland

Elementary (now Mullendore), North Richland Junior High, and graduated from Richland High in 1969. "Mona" was involved in student activities while at RHS. She was a member of the National Honor Society, Student Council, class officer, Dixie Belles, recipient of the Daughters of American Revolution Award, member of several clubs and organizations, and was selected for the Rebel's Top Ten in her senior year.

Mona received her bachelor's degree from Texas Wesleyan University, master's from Texas Christian University, and library science degree and doctorate in library science from Texas Woman's University.

Her professional career began at J. B. Little Elementary School in Arlington as school librarian 1978–93, adjunct professor at TWU 1989–94, assistant professor Western Maryland College 1994 to present.

Ramona Nolen Kerby

Mona began writing children's books in 1987, writing fiction, biography, and science. Her books *Asthma* and *Cockroaches* were both named to the Outstanding List of Science Trade Books. Minnesota students selected *38 Weeks Till Summer Vacation* to receive the 1994 Maud Hart Lovelace Award.

Other awards and recognitions have been:

• Siddie Joe Johnson Award for Outstanding Library Service to children in the state of Texas, 1990.
• National Endowment of the Humanities Teacher-Scholar Award, 1993–94.
• Who's Who in the South and Southwest, 1994.
• Western Maryland College Faculty Book Award, August 1995, 1996.
• Distinguished Alumna, Richland High School, 1988.

Ramona Nolen Kerby is proud of her North Richland Hills roots and of the firm foothold she got in life growing up in this community and in the Birdville school system.

Charles V. Scoma

Charles Scoma has extensive corporate management experience. He held executive management positions with Sears Roebuck and Company and Wal-Mart Stores over a period of 20 years. For twelve years, he was vice president of operations and engineering for an international management consulting firm. Before founding Trade Connection and purchasing Southwest Hydrokinetics, a manufacturing company, he was the director of special projects for the Federal Home Loan Bank of Dallas.

Mr. Scoma studied two years as an international exchange student and received his master's of business administration from the University of Rome, Italy. He earned his bachelor's degree in business and economics from the University of North Texas.

Mayor Charles Scoma

Charles is the grandson of Italian emigrants. He is an active member of his community, having served two terms as a City Council member in North Richland Hills and six years as a member and president of the Board of Trustees for the Birdville Independent School District. He was elected mayor of North Richland Hills in May 1998. He serves on the Board of Advisors for the Tarrant County Junior College School of Business. He is a member of the Lions Club, and past president of the Tarrant County Symphony Orchestra. Mr. Scoma is an active church member and has served over seventeen years in regional and local leadership positions for the Boy Scouting programs.

The Scoma family has lived in NRH since June 1979.

John Giordano

John Giordano (Jr.) was born in Dunkirk, N.Y., and moved to Tarrant County with his family at the age of 16. They settled in North Richland Hills in 1953, and John graduated from Birdville High School (now Haltom High School).

His love and talent for music were already a vital part of his life. He organized an award-winning swing band and was student conductor while still in high school.

Giordano holds bachelor's and master's degrees from Texas Christian University. He has performed professionally as a flutist, clarinetist, jazz saxophonist, and classical saxophone soloist. He and his wife, Mary Alice, have three children.

Giordano's conducting career began in 1968 when Fort Worth Symphony conductor Ezra Rachlin urged him to take on conducting responsibilities for the newly organized Youth Orchestra of Greater Fort Worth. Five years later he was

John Giordano

appointed music director for the Fort Worth Symphony and chairman of the jury of the Van Cliburn International Piano Competition. In 1976 he founded the Texas Little

Conductor of Fort Worth Symphony

Symphony as a chamber orchestra within the larger orchestra. This group performed at Carnegie Hall in 1980. In 1982 the name was changed to Fort Worth Chamber Orchestra and toured the People's Republic of China. In 1991 the Fort Worth Symphony Association inaugurated Concerts in the Garden, and in 1994 plans were announced for the construction of the Bass Performance Hall, which became the new permanent venue for the Fort Worth Symphony.

In January 1998, John Giordano announced that he would retire at the end of the 1999–2000 season.

Van Cliburn was quoted as saying, "John Giordano will forever be a cornerstone of the musical history of Fort Worth. His wise counsel, musicianship, and vision have brought Fort Worth Symphony to new heights of recognition and prestige around the world."

John Giordano Sr. died in 1974. Mildred Giordano, John's mother, continues to make her home in NRH, the third residential location since choosing NRH as their home in 1953.

Lisa Allred, Miss Texas U.S.A., 1983

Lisa Allred was born December 8, 1961, in Fort Worth to Carmi and Twila Allred. She has one sister, Shawna Allred Wheeler, and a brother, Steven Allred. Lisa attended Birdville schools for all of her 12 years, beginning in North Richland Elementary, North Richland Junior High, and graduated from Richland High School in 1980. She attended the University of North Texas 1980–1982.

Lisa Allred

While at Richland, Lisa was a cheerleader, homecoming queen, junior class favorite, elected Miss Dixie, and was on the tennis team.

While attending University of North Texas, Lisa was a member of Alpha Delta Pi sorority. It was following the visit of a Miss U.S.A. pageant representative to her sorority house that she became interested in trying out. In her first Miss Texas U.S.A. competition she placed first runner-up. In 1983, Lisa was crowned Miss Texas U.S.A. in the pageant held in San Antonio. She was first runner-up in the Miss U.S.A. pageant held in Knoxville, Tennessee. She was second runner-up in the Miss World pageant held in 1983 in London, England.

Lisa currently lives in the Diamond Oaks area of Haltom City. She works as a model and is owner of a small gift shop in historic Grapevine.

Lisa has been a member for 24 years of Living Word Community Church and works as assistant office manager there.

Mark Brooks

Mark Brooks began playing golf at age 8 at Diamond Oaks Country Club. He had more or less decided what he wanted to achieve when most boys his age were still playing "kick the can."

PGA champion, 1996

Mark, a native of NRH, was born March 25, 1961. His father, Hal, was pastor of NRH Baptist Church from 1959 to 1983. His mother, Paula, taught speech at North Richland Junior High, drama at Richland High School, then became director of communications for the Birdville school system from 1979 to 1984.

Mark graduated from RHS, and the University of Texas. He is married to Cynthia Spencer, also a Richland graduate. In 1996 Mark was elected to the University of Texas Hall of Honor. He was four-time most valuable player of the UT golf team, three-time All-American, 1979 and 1981 Texas State amateur champion, 1979 southern amateur champion, 1979 Trans-Mississippi amateur champion.

After turning professional in 1983, Mark won the Greater Hartford Open in 1988, Greater Milwaukee and Greensboro Open in 1991, Kemper Open 1994, and in 1996 won the Bob Hope Classic and the Houston Open and PGA Championship. In 1996 he ranked third on the money list, had 10 top 10 finishes and was a member of the victorious U.S. President's Cup Team.

Mark is president and chairman of the board for Mark Brooks Golf, Inc., a golf course design and development company. He established the W. Hal Brooks Memorial Golf Tournament and Gala in honor of his father, who dedicated his life to helping youth. The gala continued more than 10 years and raised funds for the Mark Brooks Foundation, the primary source of funding for the Brooks House Teen Crisis Center in NRH. Many well-known gala performers were featured entertainers at the event, held annually at Colonial Country Club.

Brooks House, which began in 1991, collaborated with two agency programs in the northeast Tarrant County area before joining with the Lena Pope Home in 1995, and opening Brooks House on Rufe Snow Drive in NRH. In July 1998 the decision was made to close the local facility and establish an endowment fund to serve youth of the entire county.

North Richland Hills is proud to claim Mark Brooks as one of its own; he is a remarkable person and an inspiration to young people. He was fortunate to have his father as a strong role model and desires to be that for others.

Applebees Restaurant in NRH has put Brooks in the spotlight by dedicating a wall of the restaurant to his accomplishments, claiming Brooks as their very own hometown hero.

Mark and Cynthia Brooks were honored by Richland High School in 1993 as co-recipients of the distinguished alumni award.

L/R: Lyndsay, Mark, Cynthia (Spencer), and Hallie Brooks

Mark is committed to his career and to his family, desiring to spend more time with them, especially his two daughters Lyndsay and Hallie.

Pat Nimmo Riddle

Pat Riddle is a journalist but perhaps not the usual kind. She writes good stories about good deeds and events that happen in the lives of good people. She is a popular columnist with the *Fort Worth Star-Telegram* who began her career at age 56.

Patsy Nimmo attended schools in the Riverside area of Fort Worth, graduating from Carter-Riverside in 1944. She coedited her school newspaper, the Eagle Record. As a senior, she won a first place in editorial writing in the state University Interscholastic League competition. In her 1942 school annual, the caption beside her picture notes that she

Pat Riddle

"is inclined the journalistic way and would like someday to be a reporter on a large newspaper." Her career dream did come true, just a little later than for most people.

After graduation she took a Civil Service typist job at Fort Worth Army Air Field, which later became Carswell Air Force Base.

There she met George Riddle, a 21-year-old Pennsylvania sergeant. They met at a movie theater and now, more than 50 years later, they still have Friday-night movie dates.

The Riddles have four children, and Pat's number-one job was always the mom. She did the bookkeeping for her husband's auto repair business, enjoyed oil painting in her spare time, and kept up with her writing. At 49, she entered college, graduating with honors from TCJC, Northeast campus in 1980. Then she majored in journalism at UTA, graduating with honors in 1983.

Pat receives a proclamation from Mayor Tommy Brown.

Fellow Star-Telegram columnist and an editor in the newsroom, O. K. Carter, said Pat kept coming in with various interesting stories. She already had most of the information and rarely made an error of any type. She has deep roots in the community. Her aunt, Vera Nimmo Snow, was married to Will Snow, son of Rufe Snow.

Her first column was called "Prime Timers." "Northeast People" began in 1989 with three columns a week.

Pat retired in 1995, but not really. She still has that pad and pen poised for a good story, and her column is now featured in the Sunday Hometown Star section of the Star-Telegram.

George and Pat are charter members of the Richland Hills Church of Christ and much of their lives is centered there. Pat has received many awards but feels most honored at having a Star-Telegram volunteer award named in her honor.

Perhaps one of the best salutes to Pat Riddle's professionalism was given by reporter Karen Auge who said, "We are so accustomed to Pat's role as unofficial grandmother that we risk forgetting she is also a no-nonsense journalist."

Pat Riddle has also been an invaluable member of the North Richland Hills Historical Committee.

Tommy Brown

Tommy Brown discovered North Richland Hills when he went to see a friend's new house in 1958. He liked it so well that he put a $10 deposit down on a three-bedroom brick house on Marilyn Lane. The total cost was an additional $250 down and a balance of $10,000.

Tommy started his own business in 1959, B & B Pest Control, which he operated until 1985.

He was born and reared in Fort Worth, attended Northside High School, and graduated from Texas Wesleyan College. Tommy Brown was elected mayor of NRH in 1988 and served five terms. But after 10 years he decided it was time to retire once again.

Former Mayor Tommy Brown

He is past president of the Tarrant County Mayors-Council, served on the Texas Municipal League Board of Directors, and the TML Policy Committee on Public Safety. He served as chairman of the North Richland Hills Park and Recreation Facilities Development Corporation, the NRH Crime Control and Prevention District, and served on the Regional Transportation Council.

There could never have been a more ardent supporter for "His Honor" than "Mrs. Mayor," Tommy's lovely wife, Sue. They plan to enjoy traveling now.

Tommy continues to be very active in the Northeast Lion's Club, and he and Sue have been active members of North Richland Hills Baptist Church for many years.

Lt. Gen. Phillip J. Ford

Gen. Phil Ford grew up on Reeves Street in the North Hills Addition of North Richland Hills. His dad, Jack Ford, was in the car business, and his mother, Lucile Ford, taught school for more than 35 years at Diamond Hill Elementary in Fort Worth. His sister, Diana Ford Starnes, graduated from Richland High School and now lives in Plano.

Gen. Ford said, "My only claim to fame in my school days was my physical growth pattern. In the ninth grade at Haltom Junior High, I weighed 90 pounds—when I graduated from Birdville High School in 1961, I weighed 150 pounds. Then upon my graduation from University of Texas-Arlington I weighed 195 pounds. I loved to play football; however, I was encouraged to stop after the ninth grade because one of my coaches told me, "Young man, I admire your desire, but you are so small I'm afraid you will get hurt.' So I became team equipment manager and trainer. I started back for my senior year gaining nearly 60 pounds in a little over 18 months. While I still was not big, I was bigger. One of my high school coaches, Jim Hardin, called and got me a try-out at Arlington—after my freshman year I received a full football scholarship."

Lt. Gen. Phillip J. Ford

He received his bachelor's degree from UTA in 1965, completed Squadron Officer School 1973, master's degree 1978 at Troy State University in Alabama, Air Command and Staff College 1978 at Maxwell AFB in Alabama, National War College 1984 at Fort Lesley J. McNair in Washington, D.C., Program for Senior Executives in National and International Security 1993 at Harvard University.

Gen. Ford with Russian crew

He received promotion to the rank of lieutenant general March 9, 1996. Recently he became the first American to fly a Russian bomber. He was in Russia as part of a "tension reducing" measure between our two countries. After all those years of the Cold War, he was thrilled to have his name painted on one of their airplanes.

General Ford, a three-star general, has been commander of the United States Eighth Air Force since March 23, 1996, and is stationed at Barksdale Air Force Base in Louisiana.

Charles And Polly Brinkley

Charles and Polly Brinkley arrived in North Richland Hills in 1961, accepting the challenge to help build the first bank in town, Northeast National Bank. Their son, Michael, was 11 years old. The bank officially opened in 1962 and grew rapidly, more than doubling in size by 1967. A six-story addition was constructed in 1978.

Charles was born in Weatherford and Polly in nearby Perrin. They met at Weatherford College and were married September 2, 1945. They continued their education at Texas Christian University in Fort Worth, Charles majoring in banking and finance, Polly in elementary education.

Charles began his banking career in 1945 in Weatherford where he remained until his move to NRH in 1961.

Polly and Charles Brinkley

Polly taught school until Michael was born and was a substitute teacher after he started school.

Charles and a favorite golf partner, Byron Nelson

Northeast National Bank was sold in the early 1980s to Allied Bank of Texas, then First Interstate, and presently Wells-Fargo. But the bank at the corner of Grapevine Highway and Vance Road will always be "Northeast."

Charles moved to Liberty Bank in 1987 as chairman of the board. He served as state vice president of the American Bankers, and is a member of the Federal Government Relations Network of TBA.

The Brinkleys worked on many projects to help NRH grow. Both were charter members of the NRH Library Board, helping start the first library at Richland Plaza in 1970. Polly continues on the NRH Library Board. She has served for two years on the NRH Historical Committee that is responsible for this book.

Polly held numerous offices in PTA and received a life membership in 1967. She is past president of the Birdville Unit of the American Cancer Society, volunteered for the March of Dimes, past president and 35-year member of the Fort Worth Bankers Wives Club.

Charles has served on the NRH Industrial Development Committee since 1980, and the Health Facilities Development Corporation since 1984. He has been an active member of the Lions Club since 1951 with perfect attendance. He is a charter member of the Northeast-Richland Lions Club and served as its first president, also lieutenant governor and district governor in District 2E2. He is past president of the Chamber of Commerce, worked with Boy Scouts of America, YMCA, United Way, and was town hall chairman for the committee to organize Tarrant County Junior College District in 1963. Charles, Polly, and Michael worked many nights at Tarrant County Courthouse checking signatures on the petitions that called for the election.

Their church always has been the focal point of the Brinkley family. Both have served many years as Sunday school teachers, members of the Adult Choir, and on various committees. Charles serves as a deacon. They were members of North Richland Hills Baptist Church from 1961–1985 where Charles organized a men's singing group known as "The Kingsmen." They now are members of North Fort Worth Baptist Church where they continue to be active in all these areas.

They enjoy playing 42, golf for Charles, and traveling and "semi-retirement."

Michael Skipper

Michael Skipper, better known to family and lifelong friends as Mike, considers his past to be such an important part of his life. Mike, his brother Joe and sister Pat, talked fondly of their growing-up years in one of the greatest little towns in Texas, North Richland Hills. Joe and his family live in Fort Worth, while Pat lives in Canyon, Texas. Mike's parents are Oban and Helen Skipper.

After graduating from Richland High School in 1973, Mike attended Texas Wesleyan University. He received his bachelor's degree in theatre in 1978. He spent the first two years out of college touring the country with such shows as *Fiddler on the Roof* and *South Pacific* as well as other drama and musical reviews. He later did musical comedy work.

Michael Skipper

Mike began doing commercial and television work in Dallas. After marrying his college sweetheart, Anne Street, they moved to Los Angeles where he landed several television roles on such shows as *Days of our Lives* and *General Hospital*, as well as some primetime shows like *Trapper John, M.D.*, *Dallas*, and *Falcon Crest*. He began to direct and produce some things in Los Angeles and formed a partnership with two good friends who had recently produced the critically acclaimed Meryl Streep picture, *Silkwood*.

Mike and Anne's son, Graham was born in Los Angeles in 1983. Mike realized that he really wanted to focus on producing and directing, so they moved back to the Lone Star state in 1984. Daughter Emily was born in 1987, and Mike named his entertainment company after the two of them, Gramily Entertainment.

Mike has spent much time in New York City. Since 1994 he has produced the Broadway shows, *Damn Yankees*, starring Jerry Lewis, *On the Waterfront*, with Penelope Ann Miller, and the highly regarded Duke Ellington musical *Play On!* He has produced several Off-Broadway shows and independent motion pictures. He also had a part in the production of one of America's biggest Broadway hits, Rent, a Pulitzer Prize-winning show.

When people ask Mike how he got involved in show business, he tells them the impact Paula Brooks, his drama teacher at Richland High School had on his life. He played sports, but "she made it OK to do plays and sing when these things weren't the 'in' things to do. She nurtured those talents in me and others, and gave me confidence," Mike said. He also credits Snow Heights Elementary, North Richland Junior, and Richland High School.

He continued, "A week doesn't pass that I don't think about learning to play golf on the Junior High football field, riding my bike from our house on Redondo to North Richland Drug, or playing with my buddies, Kenneth Hampton, Rod Hazlewood, and Robert Garrison. I am still really close with these guys and hope we will always be 'best buddies.'"

Mike, Anne, and their two children live in Fort Worth.

Jo Shannon Baldwin, Miss Texas, 1979

Jo Shannon, daughter of Oris and Ann Baldwin, was born November 17, 1959, two months after her parents moved to their new home on Mackey Drive in North Richland Hills. She is proud to be a native of this growing city, living in the same house all her life. She attended Snow Heights, North Richland Junior and Richland High Schools, graduating in 1978. While at Richland she was a member of the Dixie Belles drill team, cheerleader, and student council in both junior high and at Richland, Rebellaires singing group, class officer, elected Miss Dixie, class favorite, voted Most Friendly and Who's Who in American High Schools.

Jo Shannon Baldwin, Miss Texas 1979

Jo Shannon attended Texas Wesleyan College (now University) on drama and academic scholarships. She graduated magna cum laude and was the first student to graduate with a bachelor's degree in mass communications.

In 1979, Jo Shannon was awarded the title "Miss Fort Worth." She wore the title "Miss White Settlement" in 1980 and was runner-up to "Miss Texas." In 1981 her title was "Miss Abilene," and she was voted Most Talented Vocalist.

Governor Mark White proclaimed her "Yellow Rose of Texas" for her community service.

She has done numerous TV commercials for various national companies and from 1982–1993 she hosted a TV talk show on Dallas Channel 35 called *About Town* where she interviewed professionals and personalities from all over the United States and abroad.

She moved to politics in 1993–96 where she daily interviewed heads of businesses on their political opinions and transmitted those opinions back to Washington.

Jo Shannon and her father, Oris, have entertained together for many years. Oris is a talented pianist and vocalist. She said, "In 1994 I finally met a man as talented and funny as Dad and married him." Her husband is Troy Hopson, owner of a building company. They live in NRH about a mile from her parents' home.

Currently she writes original music and lyrics for Kids Who Care, a local theater performing arts group of about 150 children.

Mark Wood

Mark Wood

Mark Stephen Wood is a native of North Richland Hills, born September 5, 1955, to Clyde "Corky" and Evalyn Wood. They moved to the northwest corner of the new town in May, 1953, one month after incorporation.

Mark attended North Richland (now Mullendore) and Snow Heights Elementary schools, North Richland Junior High, and Richland High School, where he graduated in 1973. He was a member of the varsity football team. He was recognized as RHS Distinguished Alumnus of the year in 1985.

Stephen F. Austin University in Nacogdoches was the college of choice for Mark for two and one half years. He served as Supreme Court justice the entire time, was a member of Theta Chi fraternity and was chosen class favorite his freshman and sophomore years. He transferred to the University of Texas in Arlington and received his bachelor's degree in banking and finance in 1977.

Mark began a career in banking in 1976 by becoming a drive-in teller at Texas Commerce Bank-Arlington. In 1982, after having advanced to commercial loan officer, he was transferred to TCB-Hurst to head the real estate department, then he was named president and CEO of the bank in 1984. In 1985 he was promoted to chairman of the board. He completed Intermediate School of Banking at Southern Methodist University and the University of Oklahoma Commercial Lending School. He is currently on the advisory board of Security Bank.

In 1987 he and his life-long friend and classmate, Mark Howe, started the commercial real estate brokerage and development firm of Howe/Wood & Company. Their firm specializes in Tarrant County properties primarily in the northeast area.

Mark served the City of NRH for nine years on the Planning and Zoning Commission and he was a councilman from 1991–1997. Choosing not to run for reelection, he was reappointed to the Planning and Zoning Commission where he continues to serve.

He has attended North Richland Hills Baptist Church all his life and has served in numerous positions, including deacon, finance committee chairman, and building committee chairman through two major building programs.

Mark is currently chairman-elect of the Society of Commercial Realtors, Commercial Division of the Fort Worth Association of Realtors. He is also a member of the Northeast Lions Club and the Northeast Chamber of Commerce.

Debbie Tribble, Ed.D.

Debbie Tribble, daughter of Hollis and Wanda Helton, was born in Fort Worth December 31, 1952. While a student at Richland High School, she was a member of the National Honor Society, Latin Club, Future Business Leaders and editor of a literary magazine. After graduating in 1971, she began studies at Texas Wesleyan College, where she received her bachelor's degree in English and speech.

Debbie Tribble, Ed.D.

While at TWC, Debbie met Arthur Tribble, and they were married June 1, 1973 at Riverside Baptist Church in Fort Worth. She began her career in education teaching English at North Richland Junior High for nine years. After completing her master's degree in counseling and psychology at the University of North Texas, she became counselor at Watauga and Smithfield junior highs, then Richland High School. She received her mid-management certification at Texas Woman's University.

In 1990, Debbie served for two years as assistant principal at North Oaks Middle School, in 1992 became principal of Watauga Middle School, then she was named principal of Shannon Learning Center, the alternative education program in Birdville School District.

Debbie received a Delta Kappa Gamma International Scholarship in 1996, which aided in the completion of her doctoral degree in educational administration from the University of North Texas in August 1997. Under her leadership two new programs were created at Shannon. They were REACH, a program that offered continuing education for expelled students, and APOLLO, a program for at-risk ninth graders. These programs joined The Learning Center, a program for drop-out recovery, a GED program, a program for school-aged parents, and many career technology programs.

In 1997 Debbie Tribble was named principal of Birdville's third high school. In the June 1997 board meeting, the new school was officially named Birdville High School. Debbie was privileged to be a part of the entire process. Teachers, directors, consultants, parents, and students all had input in the school name, design of campus, mascot, and colors. The mascot chosen was the Hawks, and the school colors are forest green, gold, and white. The school is scheduled to open in August 1999.

Debbie Tribble has been recipient of the:
- Delta Kappa Gamma International Scholarship 1996.
- Member of Leadership Northeast.
- 1995 Chamber of Commerce Chairman's Award for initiating Vital Link in northeast Tarrant County.
- 1997 Distinguished Alumni Award-Richland High School.
- 1998 Recognized as Outstanding Principal by the Fort Worth Chapter of Texas Society of Certified Public Accountants.

Gary Morris

Gary Morris, son of Stanley and Margaret Morris, moved to North Richland Hills in 1956 along with his twin sister, Carey, and younger brother, Mark. He graduated from Richland High School in 1967, where he was involved in sports, drama, and music, including the Rebellaires, Richland High's vocal group formed that year of the best voices in the school.

After completing college, he settled in Denver, Colorado, where he sang at a supper club, developed a band, and was soon touring the country, including making the whistle

Gary Morris

stop tour with Jimmy Carter. Later he sang at the White House in the Christmas television specials for Presidents Reagan and Bush.

In 1986 Gary was honored at the RHS 25th anniversary by receiving the Distinguished Alumnus Award. Already a nationally known country and western singing star and television actor, he sang at both the Homecoming pep rally held at W. G. Thomas Coliseum and later at the football game. Remembering his school days, he said, "I was then and always will be a Rebel."

In 1991, Gary was selected to represent Texas at a command performance for the Queen of England. It has been said that "he brought the palace down." The queen wanted to meet Gary, and when they met, Her Royal Highness said, "I just wanted to put the face and the voice together."

In the midst of his Nashville-based recording career, Morris found time to appear on the Broadway stage in *LaBoheme* with Linda Ronstadt and again as Jean Valjean in *Les Miserables*, the latter of which earned him a nomination for "Outstanding Actor in a Musical" from the Drama Desk Awards.

Gary Morris is a performer, songwriter, music publisher, and former producer and host of the top-rated *North American Sportsman* television series on the Nashville Network. He recorded 12 albums that sold worldwide, and had eleven Top 10 country chart hits to his credit and five number-one singles. He won song of the year in 1983 for "Wind Beneath My Wings."

His acting credits include *Designing Women*, *The Colbys*, *Mike Hammer* and a feature film titled, *A Place to Grow*. His five years as host of his top-rated outdoor adventure series on TNN kept him busy taking celebrities and friends all over the continent to find the best of adventures. His current CD project, "Gary Morris 'Live'" is his first live acoustic offering. He produced the album, which is the first release on his record label, In House Records.

Dr. David J. Pillow, M.D.

Dr. David Pillow could easily be called North Richland Hills' hometown doctor, for he's been here longer than any other. Dr. Pillow, along with Dr. Charles Rush, opened the doors to the Pillow-Rush Medical and Surgical Clinic in 1955. The clinic was next door to North Richland Drug in the North Richland Hills Shopping Center. Clientele for the clinic and doctors grew rapidly for these two who had chosen general practice as their specialty. This field is now called family practice. Office calls were $3, house calls were $5.

Dr. Pillow did indeed take care of the needs of the entire family. He has always taken time with patients on each visit, never too busy to ask about other family members.

David J. Pillow, M.D.

Dr. Bruce Jacobson and J. Ardis Bell had joined the clinic by 1960 and 1961. They outgrew the small office space in the neighborhood shopping center and later built a new facility on Glenview Drive, changing the name to Northeast Medical and Surgical Clinic.

Dr. Pillow served as president of the hospital operating company, comprised of five other northeast area doctors. Ground was broken in 1960 and dedication ceremonies held in May 1961 for the new Glenview Hospital. As chairman of the hospital board, Dr. Pillow again broke ground for a hospital addition in 1965, which doubled the size.

Dr. Pillow was chairman of the Board of Trustees when the new North Hills Hospital on Booth-Calloway Road had its dedication ceremonies in December 1983.

Dr. Pillow always has maintained a teaching practice, and many young doctors have benefited from this. His practice is currently aimed at senior adults.

Dr. David and Annabel Pillow reared five children, each now a professional. Four of these, Kathy, David Jr., Carolyn, and Charles graduated from Richland High School. The family moved from their NRH home before John was born in 1963. They bought a larger home in Richland Hills then moved to Colleyville where John graduated from Grapevine-Colleyville High School. Kathy Pillow Hudson, Ph.D., teaches at Schreiner College in Kerrville; David Jr., M.D. lives in Plano and works in Emergency Medical Services; Charles is a CPA and lives in Grapevine; Carolyn Riggs is a certified registered nurse anesthetist and lives in Bedford; John is an emergency medical doctor and lives in Brownwood.

Lori Smith, Miss Texas, 1977

Lori Smith, Miss Texas 1977

Lori Smith, Miss Texas 1977, is a star in the crown of North Richland Hills. Daughter of R. L. and Shirley Smith, Lori was born in Fort Worth February 7, 1957. Her parents and brother, Mike, lived on Corona Street until 1970 when they moved to a new home in the Diamond Loch addition.

Throughout her school years Lori studied voice and dance. She started to school at Snow Heights Elementary where she had the lead part in *Mary Poppins* in the fifth grade and *The Wizard of Oz* in the sixth grade. She won the title of Little Miss World in the Dallas pageant when she was in the sixth grade.

Lori graduated from Richland High School in 1975. While at Richland she was in the Dixie Belles drill team and was active in the Drama Department. She was named Distinguished Alumni in 1977, the first in a newly established RHS honors event.

Lori vied for the title of Miss Haltom-Richland in the 1977 pageant and won the coveted crown. She went on to the Miss Texas state pageant held in July 1977 in Fort Worth and won the top honor to represent the state in the Miss America pageant, placing in the top 10.

She was chosen for the Miss America USO Troupe that toured the Mediterranean area in the summer of 1978. This was a great honor since there were only five young women chosen plus Miss America. She was chosen again in 1979 to tour with the Miss America troupe in the Orient.

Lori has been a guest vocalist on the Miss America pageant program several times. She has two children, Colin Madsen, age 17, and Alex Madsen, age 14.

Horst Krause

"I like to work with young people—seeing their eyes light up when they finally understand something is fun—getting phone calls, cards, or letters about five or six years later that say, 'Thanks, Coach,' is the reward you get," said Horst Krause. He probably is as well known by the title "Coach" as by his name.

Krause began his teaching-coaching career of 34 years at North Richland Junior High when the new school opened its doors in September 1963. He taught history, geography,

Horst Krause

and coached football, basketball, and track. In 1967 Krause was promoted to junior varsity coach at Richland High School when Theo Rigsby became head coach. When he retired from coaching in 1992, he had worked with every football coach in Richland's history.

Krause received his bachelor's degree from North Texas State University in 1963 and a master's degree with a German major in 1967. He started the German program at RHS from scratch, and in 1976 the German Department was a nominee for one of the best five foreign language departments in the state of Texas.

Horst Krause was born in Berlin, Germany, and came to the United States with his family in 1952. After attending Birdville junior and senior high schools, he attended Ranger Junior College on a football scholarship. It was in Ranger that he met his future wife, Nancy. They have two sons, Philip and Jeffrey.

Krause didn't go into the teaching profession for money. His teaching didn't just stop at school. Teaching has been his life, not just his occupation. He proved to be a friend who encouraged and challenged his students to do their best. The words "no" or "can't" were not in his vocabulary, and he wouldn't let a student say them.

He retired in 1997 after 34 years of teaching in the Birdville Independent School District and has been right back in the classroom ever since in the role of a very qualified substitute teacher.

Wiley G. Thomas

Wiley G. Thomas

As a child, Wiley Thomas worked on his father's truck farm in the area of South Birdville known as the "Garden of Eden." The area had abundant water from shallow wells that could be used to irrigate the vegetables.

Among his neighbors were the families of Mr. Julius Bussey and Dr. Ray Williams. Both men have spent many years as educators in the Birdville Independent School District.

Mr. Thomas began attending the first grade at Birdville in the 1921–22 school year and graduated from Birdville High School in 1933 with the first class to complete all eleven grades there. Before his time, Birdville students had to attend Fort Worth schools for the last two years to graduate from the city schools.

Wiley G. Thomas attended Texas Wesleyan College, where he met Carrie Frances Taylor from Vernon. They were later married. He began his career in Birdville for the 1937–38 school year as a sixth-grade teacher when the total staff was 17 members. In 1940 Thomas was appointed to the position of high school principal. The promotion increased his salary from $900 to $1,260 per year. He said in addition to the increase in salary, he gained the privilege of teaching those subjects remaining after qualified teachers had their full assignment.

Although his salary was increased to $1,320 per year in August 1942 he found it impossible to remain with the school since a second child was on the way for him and his wife, Carrie Frances. Nine days after his resignation was accepted, Superintendent W. T. Francisco insisted that Mr. Thomas meet with the School Board in session. The board offered him a raise in salary to return as principal and coach. Mr. Thomas said, "I agreed with minor emphasis on 'Coach,' since I did not wish to cast a reflection on the coaching profession."

Following the death of Superintendent W. T. Francisco, the Board of Trustees named W. G. Thomas Jr. superintendent of the Birdville School District effective February 1, 1944. At that time, all grades were on one campus with a total enrollment of about 700 students.

Mr. Thomas often said that his first appointment, Mrs. Alliene Mullendore, was as good, if not better, than any made during his 35-year career as superintendent. She, too, held many positions in the school district and was the first woman elected to the School Board, and Mullendore Elementary is named for her.

Carrie F. Thomas Elementary opened its doors in 1978. The Birdville Classroom Teachers Association had requested that the School Board name the new elementary school in her honor. She had retired, because of health problems after 38 years of teaching in the district and later died in 1977.

Mr. Thomas received many awards for his leadership qualities and knowledge of school finance. From a one-school to a 30-school district is quite a remarkable growth record.

He served one term on the City Council of NRH from 1980–82. He later married Claudine Williams, who had taught in the district since 1957.

Following his retirement as superintendent of the Birdville School District effective February 1, 1979, the name of the coliseum was changed to W. G. Thomas Jr. Coliseum.

"Mr. T," as he has been affectionately known, for many years and to countless numbers of people, has left a lasting impression on fellow educators, students, and the community through his dry wit, love for the schools and those he served.

Mark A. Howe

Mark Howe lives the motto of giving back to the school and community that he has received so much from his entire life.

After having three daughters born into their family, H. M. "Mc" and Inez Howe finally had a son. Mark was born September 24, 1954, in Fort Worth. His family lived in Roanoke at the time but soon moved to North Richland Hills. Mc was a pilot for American Airlines, and Inez taught at Holiday Heights and Browning Heights elementary schools before they retired to a home in East Texas.

The family's NRH home and acreage were located on Bursey Road and later became the Bursey Road Senior Center.

Mark attended Smithfield Elementary, North Richland Junior High, and Richland High School where he graduated in 1973. While at Richland, he was a member of the Rebellaires for three years, National Honor Society of which he was president his senior year, an outstanding running back on the Rebel football team, lettering three years, and on the Rebel baseball and track teams.

Mark Howe

Mark attended Southern Methodist University on a football scholarship, lettering on the team 1974 through 1976. He graduated in 1977 with a bachelor's degree in business with a special certificate in real estate.

His career began in Fort Worth with Foster Mortgage Company, then North American Mortgage Company as a commercial lender. In 1982 he moved into a Dallas real estate brokerage company. In 1988 Mark Howe and Mark Wood, a schoolmate since junior high days, joined to form Howe-Wood Company, a commercial real estate firm dealing primarily with properties in Northeast Tarrant County.

In 1983, Mark Howe established a scholarship program at Richland High School that, according to RHS Counselor Lynda Hamilton, has become one of the most sought after by seniors. The scholarship recognizes a senior for Outstanding Excellence and Versatility. The recipient is chosen by a committee comprised of faculty members of various departments following applications and interviews. The committee looks for someone who has participated and contributed to Richland student life and is well-rounded in extra curricular activities, community, and church. This annual scholarship is an example of giving back to the community and school district that has meant so much to Mark and his three sisters, Mary, Linda, and Helen, all very active RHS graduates.

Mark Howe is married to fellow RHS graduate Carol Joyner. They have three children, Lindsay, Bart, and Matt. He has been a coach of his two sons' baseball and football teams, active in the Chamber of Commerce, Women's Haven, and the family's church, First United Methodist Church of Fort Worth.

Mark was named Distinguished Alumnus of the 1994–95 year at Richland High School.

Sandra Brown

Sandra Brown

Sandra Cox was five years old when her family moved to North Richland Hills in 1953. She was born in Waco March 12, 1948. Sandra attended North Richland (now Mullendore) Elementary, Richland Junior High, and graduated from Richland High in 1966.

At RHS Sandra was active in many organizations, including the National Honor Society, Dixie Belles, and was a class officer. She was voted Most Talented in her senior year and had credits in several drama productions including a starring role in *Bye-Bye Birdie*.

Sandra Cox attended Texas Christian University and spent her summers working at Six Flags Over Texas in Arlington. It was there that she met future husband Michael Brown in 1967. They were both performing in a live stage show at the theme park. By the end of the season she had convinced him this was one summer romance that should last! They were married in 1968 and have two children, Rachel and Ryan.

Sandra is the oldest of five daughters. From the time she can remember she was read to or encouraged to read by her mother, Martha Jean "Mop" Cox, a teacher and counselor in the Birdville school system for many years.

Sandra Brown has many talents, including model, actress, businesswoman, TV personality, and since 1981, an author. After selling her first book, she was soon producing a succession of romance novels under her own name as well as under several pseudonyms. She culled her ideas from newspapers, television talk shows, and her own imagination.

In 1985, Brown decided to move from romance writing into the mainstream fiction market. Brown's crossover books, *Slow Heat in Heaven* and *Best Kept Secrets*, published by Warner Books, swiftly set her on her new course. Her next book, *Mirror Image* (1990) was her first to hit

BACK L/R: Jo Cox Carter, Laurie Cox Macons; FRONT L/R: Melanie Cox Whitson, Sandra Cox Brown, Mother Martha Jean "Mop" Cox, Jennifer Cox Smith

North Richland Hills the City and its People

Linda Spurlock Park, August 1998

Iron Horse Golf Course

NRH Fire Department

Fire in NRH

Officer Tim Samsill with friend

NRH motorcycle officers

NRH City Hall

Adventure World, August 1998

Fossil Creek Park, August 1998

The Tarantula

The special days of our lives

New life-Wendy and Samuel Janvier

Graduation Day - Stephen Clough ,1999 Richland Senior

The beautiful reward of the avid gardener

Wedding Day

BOO BASH! - Costume Contest North Hills Mall

Christmas at North Hills Mall

Easter Day - Emily Gregory

"Oscar Ray Leonard" NRH Animal Shelter Mascot until 1998

Getting ready for the play-offs [Branden Lyman]

Retired teachers raise their voices in song

Yard of the month, Crepe Myrtle

Trying out the new fire truck-Mayor Tommy Brown and
Councilman Lyle Welch

Special D.A.R.E. celebration-Gov. George W. Bush, Officer Grady Whitener

North Richland Hills Heritage Day Celebration 1997

Sean Hughes

Front - Norman Ellis, Sid Cavanaugh, Dick Faram, Deloris Wood, Widow of Councilman James T. Wood: Back - George Conant, Buck Hubbard, Gene Riddle, JoAnn Goodnight Earl, Marion Massey — All are Elected Officials of the '70s attending

Sean Hughes

Front to Back - Former Mayors Tommy Brown, Dick Faram, Marion Massey, Clyde Zellers and "Ace" Nace

Sean Hughes

Elected Officials of the '80s: Starting from left front - Marie Hinkle, Linda Spurlock, Dick Faram, Byron Sibbett, Jim Kenna, Harold Newman, Mack Garvin, Lyle Welch, Charles Scoma

Elected Officials of the '90s: Front Row - Linda Spurlock, Cheryl Lyman, Lyle Welch • Row Two - Charles Scoma, Don Phifer • Row Three - Byron Sibbet, JoAnn Johnson, Ray Oujesky • Back Row - Mack Garvin, Mark Wood

Former Councilwoman JoAnn Goodnight Earl visiting with Heritage Day Committee members Mary Ruth Ellis and Cheryl Lyman

Maude and Herb Arnold visiting with friend and Heritage Day Committee member Naomi "Sis" Jones Cummings on the right

Heritage Day '97 Former City Councilman Denver Mills, sharing stories with Mayor Tommy Brown, and former City Manager Rodger Line

Elected Officials of the '60s: from Left to right Gene Riddle, Buck Hubbard, Marion Massey, Dick Faram, Alvis Dowell

NRH Periwinkles

Herb Arnold, welcomed to Heritage Day '97 by Pat Riddle, Mary Ruth Ellis, and Jane Dunkleberg

Sean Hughes

Sean Hughes

Sean Hughes

Top and Bottom - Greater Fort Worth Christmas Pageant

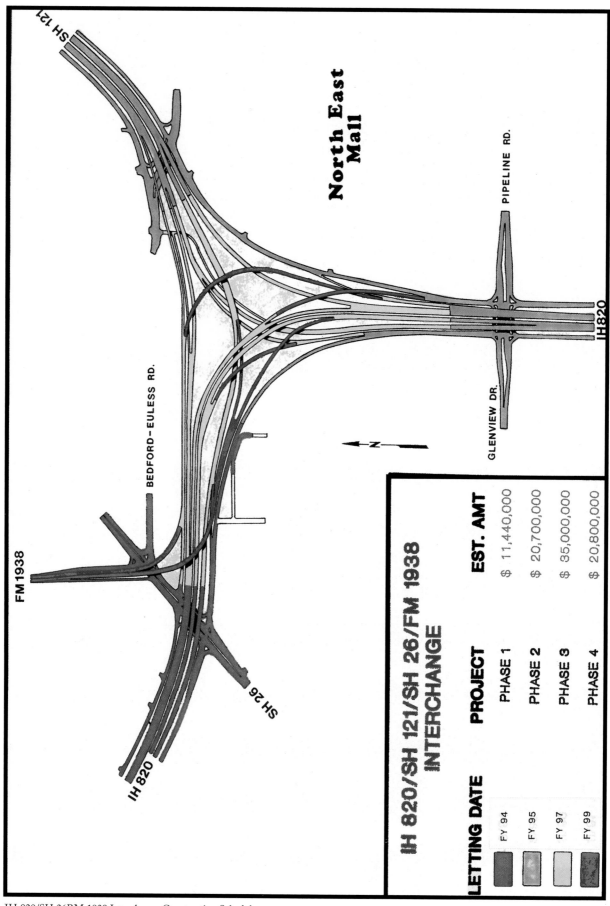

North East Mall

PIPELINE RD.

GLENVIEW DR.

IH 820

BEDFORD–EULESS RD.

FM 1938

SH 121

SH 26

IH 820

N

IH 820/SH 121/SH 26/FM 1938 INTERCHANGE

LETTING DATE	PROJECT	EST. AMT
FY 94	PHASE 1	$ 11,440,000
FY 95	PHASE 2	$ 20,700,000
FY 97	PHASE 3	$ 35,000,000
FY 99	PHASE 4	$ 20,800,000

IH 820/SH 26RM 1938 Interchange Construction Schedule

The New York Times bestseller lists. Since then, every one of her subsequent novels has achieved that same success, including reprints of earlier titles. Successive best-sellers were: *Where There's Smoke*, 1993; *Charade*, 1994; *The Witness*, 1995; *Exclusive*, 1996; *Fat Tuesday*, 1997; Unspeakable, 1998: Her 1992 bestseller, French Silk, was made into an ABC-TV movie.

Brown has had 33 New York Times bestsellers in the past eight years. There are over fifty million copies of her books in print, and her work has been translated into 29 languages.

Pursuing her career as an author while rearing two children, Sandra Brown has successfully learned to balance work and family life. She and her family divide their time between homes in Fort Worth and Hilton Head, S.C.

Bruce Wood, Artistic Director/Choreographer

Bruce Wood

Bruce Wood began his career at the age of 16 when he left his native Fort Worth on a full scholarship to New York's School of American Ballet under the tutelage of the legendary George Balanchine. After a brief engagement with the New York City Ballet, Wood refined his Balanchine training, dancing for four years as a soloist with the San Francisco Ballet. At the age of 21, Bruce joined Les Ballets Jazz de Montreal as a principal dancer, and for the next four years performed and taught all over the world. Returning to New York, he danced with the Lar Lubovitch Dance Company and the Twyla Tharp Dance Company.

Bruce has been a great artist for many dance companies, including the Margie Gillis Dance Foundation in Montreal, Stephanie Ballard and Dancers and Contemporary Dance Canada in Winnipeg, Charles Moulton Dance in New York, Banff Arts Festival in Alberta, and DV8 Physical Dance in London. He assisted in setting the movement of the Broadway hit *Into the Woods* for Stephen Sondheim. He has appeared on PBS and BBC plus numerous commercials and music videos. During recent years, Bruce has choreographed works for a variety of dance companies and has been prolific in developing works for his own dance company. He frequently serves as a master teacher for colleges and universities.

Bruce Wood was born August 3, 1960, in Hobart, Oklahoma. He moved to NRH with his parents, Toby and Colleen Wood, in 1975 and graduated from Richland High School in 1978. Colleen Wood retired from the Birdville School District as vice-principal of Haltom High School. Toby Wood was head coach of Richland High School and athletic director of the Birdville District until his retirement.

Bruce has moved his Bruce Wood Dance Company to Fort Worth. It is an educational and performance company that spotlights his creative vision in choreography while demanding the highest quality production. With performances at the William Edrington Scott Theatre, Tarrant County Convention Center's JFK Theater and Bass Performance Hall, the exposure in the Fort Worth-Dallas region is tremendous.

Pat and Darrell Robinson receiving BISD award from BISD trustee, Fred Wilson.

Darrell and Pat Robinson

Darrell and Pat Robinson have a common middle name. It is Volunteer. After being foster parents to two mildly retarded girls for five years, Pat was responsible for getting the Rainbow Club started with the ARC of Northeast Tarrant County. Pat had worked at the Fort Worth State School for five years. Personnel there and other ARC members were helpful in this effort. Pat served on the ARC board for two years. She and Darrell are supportive members of the organization.

After retiring from a career in the Air Force, Darrell established Robinson Plumbing and Repair. He became a Business Partner with the Birdville School District through the Chamber of Commerce. He mentors at North Ridge Elementary. Darrell and Pat were recognized by the BISD Board of Directors in July 1997. Darrell also has mentored at Women's Haven, a Tarrant County home for battered women and their children. He has contributed countless hours and dollars to the Women's Haven since beginning his business in 1978. He has advocated for Women's Haven in many ways to help promote and support their purpose to provide care and shelter for battered women and children.

Darrell was able to acquire support from the members of the Plumbing, Heating and Cooling Contractors and Manufacturers of plumbing equipment, etc. for more than $65,000 when Women's Haven added its first addition to the building. He was named Volunteer of the Year for Women's Haven and later the award was named in his honor and is now presented to other outstanding volunteers each year. He has also been recognized for his contributions to Open Arms Home program in NRH. He was nominated for the J. C. Penney Golden Rule Award and continues to support Women's Haven by collecting clothes for their second-hand store, "Berry Good Buys" located on Berry Street in Fort Worth.

Darrell has also supported the Northeast Business and Professional Women's local organization since 1988. Pat became a member at that time and has served in most offices including president. She currently serves as the legislative chair of the Northeast BPW as well as BPW/Texas District 11 chair. She served as editor for the NEBPW newsletter in the 1996–97 year.

Pat and Darrell have been residents of NRH since 1969. With four daughters who graduated from RHS, plus hosting three students, two from Brazil and one from Chile and through the Youth for Understanding Program, they are strong supporters of BISD, Northeast Tarrant Chamber of Commerce, and the city of North Richland Hills.

C. A. Sanford

Before C. A. Sanford got into city government in North Richland Hills, he had a 25-year career in the restaurant business. "C. A.'s" was a well-loved establishment in Hurst. He was president of the Texas Restaurant Association, has been emcee of countless gatherings, and is a sought after public speaker.

C. A. served the City of Hurst as councilman and later as mayor. C. A. kept a list of jobs he would never want. One of the positions listed was city manager. He would later comment that serving as city manager of North Richland Hills was the best job of his life.

C. A. joined the city staff of NRH in 1987, establishing the Economic Development Department. He had a real commitment and vision for community involvement, spearheading the development of Iron Horse Golf Course when others said it couldn't be done. Ground for the municipally owned course was broken in the fall of 1988. In 1989, he was promoted to assistant city manager, deputy city manager in 1993, and, in 1994, C. A. Sanford was named city manager of NRH following the retirement of Rodger Line.

C. A. also saw the building of the Richland Tennis Center in partnership with Birdville School District, NRH2O water park, the establishment of the Crime Control District and the building of the new City Hall.

C. A. loves to play golf, and he experienced the thrill of a lifetime on June 12, 1998 when he hit a hole in one. The ball hit on the green and rolled into the cup.

C. A. Sanford

A lifetime achievement award was presented to C. A. by the Home Builders Association of Fort Worth in the spring of 1998. The award, one of three to city officials, recognized his decade of support as city manager to consumers.

C. A. loves to tell and play jokes on his friends, and as a result, his friends always keep a backlog of ideas to reciprocate—and he enjoys it immensely.

At C. A.'s retirement party on April 3, 1998, it was declared C. A. Sanford Day in Tarrant County by County Commissioner Glen Whitfield and in North Richland Hills by Mayor Tommy Brown. The party was a "roast," with many friends and colleagues "getting back" at the honoree.

C. A. graduated from Southern Methodist University with a bachelor's degree in business administration in 1953. He has lived in Tarrant County since 1954, and has represented NRH on the Charity Golf Circuit since 1987. He and his wife, Gwen, have five children: Gary, Paul, Ben, Julie, and Tommy.

Randy Shiflet

Randy Shiflet was born and raised in Mineral Wells. After graduating from Mineral Wells High School he moved to the North Richland Hills area in 1972 to attend TCJC. In January of 1973, he was hired by the North Richland Hills Police Department as a police cadet and worked part-time while attending classes. In July of 1973 he was hired full time as a police officer and served in that capacity until he was promoted to police sergeant in 1978. As a sergeant, he worked in the Patrol Division then transferred to the Administrative Services Division, serving as the supervisor of Police Records, Communications, and as the department's Public Information Officer for more than 12 years.

Randy Shiflet

In 1980 he was promoted to captain, and in 1992 he was appointed assistant chief of police.

In 1993 City Manager Rodger N. Line selected Randy as an assistant city manager for the city, and in 1997 City Manager Larry J. Cunningham promoted him to the position of deputy city manager. While in the police service, Randy attended and graduated from the FBI Academy in Quantico, Virginia and received a bachelor's degree from North Texas State University. He is a member of the International City Managers Association and serves on the board of Clayton Child Care, a nonprofit organization that provides after school care at a number of Birdville ISD elementary campuses.

Randy has been married to his wife, Susan, since 1981, and they have two children, Ryan and Russell, who attend Birdville schools. Susan is a certified public accountant employed by Arthur Andersen LLP. Randy and Susan reside in North Richland Hills.

North Richland Hills Volunteers of the Year

A volunteer of the year is nominated and chosen each year as a joint effort with United Way of Tarrant County and the city to reward outstanding volunteerism in the community.

A community's volunteers are the heart and soul of that community. Springing from a desire to give of themselves for the betterment of the place they live in, the work of volunteers has long been recognized as a major factor in adding to the quality of life enjoyed by a community. The collective efforts of many individuals, engaged in a great number of disparate endeavors, and in support of a wide variety of causes, enhance their neighborhoods and help their neighbors in a myriad of ways. Proof of this is illustrated by examining the work of individuals chosen as volunteer of the year for the City of North Richland Hills. Each year since 1987, one person, judged to best exemplify the spirit of volunteerism, has been selected to receive the award and to represent all volunteers at work in our community. The great diversity of the good deeds these caring people have been rewarded for doing is exceeded only by the generous spirit of their hearts.

Eileen H. Grubbs

Eileen H. Grubbs was the first person honored by North Richland Hills as volunteer of the year. In 1987, she was recognized for her work with the Multiple Sclerosis Association. For more than 10 years Mrs. Grubbs drove multiple sclerosis patients to therapy, doctor appointments, or to any activity that helped reduce the isolation often experienced by people with this disease. She also served as a peer volunteer, visiting and counseling hospitalized or homebound patients. At the office of the MS Association, Mrs. Grubbs did routine office work, providing an extra pair of hands to relieve paid personnel. She also recruited others to volunteer their time and talents and join with her in assisting this worthy cause.

Francis Dusenbury

Francis Dusenbury was recognizied for his work as chairman of the Northeast YMCA Board of Directors in 1988. Prior to his selection as board chairman, Mr. Dusenbury led fund-raising campaigns, participated in work days, and chaired the program and coaches committees, as well as coaching several teams each year. He was instrumental in developing the YMCA's youth sports philosophy and mission. As chairman, Mr. Dusenbury and the board were credited with expanding the Y's programs and membership, improving facilities, and increasing by over 50 percent the number of children involved in youth sports.

Sandra Durbin

Sandra Durbin was selected volunteer of the year in 1989 for her work at Harris Methodist HEB Hospital. Beginning in 1986, Mrs. Durbin was the volunteer in charge of the maternity waiting room, contributing many hours to preparing pots of coffee, soothing anxieties, and coordinating visits into labor rooms by family members. She also worked as a nurse assistant in the OB/GYN unit, relieving the nurses' workload in that busy place.

Betty and Ed Jones

Betty and Ed Jones were honored in 1990 for their joint work with Big Brothers and Big Sisters of Tarrant County. Betty and Ed Jones worked with this organization for many years and each have been matched with little sisters and little brothers as well as couple matches. They also have been involved in fund-raisers like "Bowl for Kids' Sake" and craft sales in their front yard. They also have a bowling league and the proceeds from the league go to the volunteer association, which plans monthly events for unmatched children. In addition to their work with Big Brothers and Sisters, the Joneses have been foster parents, have organized FOLKS, Friends of Lonely Kicking Seniors, a group that visits, several times a year, senior citizens

who live alone, and they support the Salvation Army's Angel Tree at Christmas.

Rae Prang

Rae Prang was the 1991 recipient of the volunteer of the year award. As volunteer coordinator for the North Richland Hills Animal Care and Control Center for three years, she was responsible for the award winning Pet Facilitated Therapy Program which takes small pets on twice weekly visits to area convalescent and health care centers where the lives of the elderly and the sick are brightened by contact with the visiting animals. Mrs. Prang also helped to coordinate the Adoption Counselor program at the Animal Care and Control Center and the Warm Hugs program that provides toy bears, complete with adoption certificates, to children who have been victims of violence or trauma or who are terminally ill.

Anne Dews

Helping to feed the hungry earned Anne Dews the 1992 award as volunteer of the year for North Richland Hills. In 1991, as chairman of the board, Mrs. Dews joined with others to form Tarrant County Harvest, Inc., an all-volunteer organization to provide food for residents of Tarrant County. In the span of one year, Mrs. Dews established partnerships with 138 donors who contributed 600,000 pounds of food to be distributed to needy people.

Glenn Nerwin

Glenn Nerwin was selected in 1993 as volunteer of the year. His award was based on his service to the city with the parks department where he led efforts to establish, maintain, and protect natural environments within city parks where native plants and wildlife can survive and be available for study. Wetland areas have also been preserved. Over a hundred professional volunteers were recruited by Mr. Nerwin to help with this preservation effort. Mr. Nerwin was also instrumental in the adoption of a city-wide hike and bike trail system plan to provide additional facilities for recreation.

Presenting her award is Mayor Pro-Tem Mark Wood.

Cheryl Lyman

Spearheading a successful effort to build a handicapped accessible playground called Adventure World won the volunteer of the year award for Cheryl Lyman in 1994. Mrs. Lyman coordinated the efforts of businesses, private citizens, and city employees to build the playground over the space of a few days. She also led in efforts to raise money for the facility. Other volunteer services provided by Mrs. Lyman included chairing the Town Hall Commission which held town hall meetings, and hosting a Citicable show aimed at preventing teenage drinking and driving.

Ben Shilcutt

The 1995 volunteer of the year was Ben Shilcutt. Mr. Shilcutt, as president of the local chapter of Mended Hearts, Inc., made weekly visits to support heart disease patients at North Hills Hospital, offering them the opportunity to talk with a knowledgeable person about their illness. He also volunteered in the cardiac rehabilitation department at the hospital where, by sharing his own experience with cardiac surgery, he encouraged others to improve their health.

Henry Grimsley

Henry Grimsley, volunteer of the year for 1996, donated many hours every week for many of his 90-plus years working in the food pantry of the Community Enrichment Center in North Richland Hills. Mr. Grimsley was the first administrator of the food pantry, which was established in 1958 by the North Richland Hills Church of Christ. In the two years prior to his volunteer award, Mr. Grimsley gave 3,000 hours of volunteer service at the food pantry.

Judge Tommy Vandergriff presents her award.

Evalyn Lochridge

Evalyn Lochridge believes that our community loses part of its history each time it loses one of its citizens. Acting on that belief, Mrs. Lochridge spent two years working to record the stories of the people of North Richland Hills so their history will not be lost, and the community rewarded her efforts by naming her volunteer of the year for 1997. In 1996 North Richland Hills' City Council named Mrs. Lochridge chairman of a new historical committee. The committee was charged with producing a written history of North Richland Hills, and Mrs. Lochridge's life became consumed by the task. She spent hundreds of hours interviewing, telephoning, consulting, researching, writing, editing, and keeping track of hundreds of documents and pictures. The culmination of all her efforts was the publication of *The History of North Richland Hills, 1953–1998*—the book you are holding in your hands.

The Children

Smithfield Elementary, first grade, 1955

Dallas Morning News

Kid Fest

Blue Birds at the Orr's, 1961

Teen Dance - at the Park and Recreation Center

Dallas Morning News

Dallas Morning News

The best time of school is lunch with friends

Dallas Morning News

Band Practice at Richland High School

The Adventure World Kids

Halloween at the Graves

"Merry Christmas"

"Kasey" NRH animal shelter mascot

The Sesquicentennial Wagon Train as it moved down Rufe Snow, 1986

Ride-em Cowboy

People and Places We Recognize

Campaign time in North Richland Hills

North Richland Hills Post Office

The Arnold Building on Grapevine Highway

Town and Country Drug, originally North Richland Drug.

Courtesy of Alan Harmon

The "Mustard Jar" in the Town and Country Drug

Courtesy of Lacy Stewart Family

The Annual Smithfield Reunion at the Lacy Stewart home, 1992

Courtesy of Lacy Stewart Family

Lacy Stewart wearing straw hat visiting with Mrs. Ray Clendening, Vera Abbott Redding, and Foy Abbott at Smithfield Reunion, 1995

Dallas Morning News

Marvin Miller-The best dance man in town

Hardy Sanders, a friend of the school

Jon Jones, pastor of Richland Church of Christ for more than 20 years

Paul Paschall, director of Greater Fort Worth Christmas Pageant for 25 years

Marion and Hattie West

Reunion of Smithfield fire volunteers L/R, O. S. Autrey, Eddie Fuchs, Melton Rhine, Vera Redding, Leon Collins, H. T. Worthington, unknown, A. J. Knight, W. G. Gregory

Nurse "Granny," Richland High School, 1988

NRH 45th Birthday Celebration - Evalyn Lochridge and "Sis" Cummings daughter of Clarence Jones

Mayor Tommy Brown with wife Sue at reception celebrating Mayor Brown's 10 years of service, 1998

Fort Worth Star-Telegram

Courtesy Sean Hughes

Coucilman Mack Garvin, with 10 years of service, talking to Judge Ray and Rita Oujesky at Heritage Day Celebration, 1997

Mayor Tommy Brown and the council, saying thank-you to Linda Spurlock and Mark Wood for more than 10 years of service

Mayor Charles Scoma and wife Alice at Heritage Day celebration, 1997

Larry Antwiler, manager Winn-Dixie Grapevine Hwy

Life in North Richland Hills

Dallas Morning News

Ernest Eugene Eckhardt's 100th birthday with Sherry Eckhardt and baby Lauren

James Ray Photography

Beginning a new life and home in NRH

271

Enjoying Easter Sunday

Freddie the fire plug

Sean Hughes

7 Memories

Memories

Dream with me of days gone by, with pleasant memories
Of stardust sprinkled in the sky and of a balmy breeze.

Then once again we will recall the things we loved so well . . .
The shady lanes where we would stroll as evening shadows fell.

The park, the church, the school, the store, the friendly folks back home,
The sunny brooks, the meadows, and the hills we used to roam.

These memories are something which my heart will always store. . .
And joys and happiness they bring are mine forevermore.

Patricia Mongeau

WALTER AND MARILYN ACUFF

I remember a nice policeman who did not give me a ticket the week after we moved here. Of course, I had four frightened children crying in the backseat of the car at the time.

The owner of the drugstore on Highway 10, Ralph Hill, extended me needed credit before the days of health insurance.

I remember every day how very nice it is to live in a caring community like North Richland Hills. How very lucky we are to be in America.

GENE ANDERSON

The twins, Terry and Jerry, were each other's bodyguards. One day at school, the playground bully began to bother Jerry. Terry came over and shoved him aside with these words, "Leave my brother alone, or we'll get you."

Mer (Mother) was famous for her pies and candy. She made at least 10–12 pies a week and thought nothing of making 60 or more for family gatherings. She left the candy simmering on the stove when she went out to do the chores. She never used a candy thermometer or timed it, and it was always perfect. Her recipe book was in her head—a pinch, a taste, add another pinch. She would say, "I hear it—the candy's ready."

IDA BLACK

Time changes everything.

We moved into our home in 1963. Loop 820 was not in existence! Rufe Snow Drive was just a little two-lane thoroughfare and was not congested because North Richland Hills was just starting to become a spot on the map.

We had 12 finished houses to select from in our immediate neighborhood. Most of the land was cow pastures.

The main way to get from NRH to downtown Fort Worth was to go by the way of 28th Street or Belknap. DFW was nonexistent—Love Field in Dallas was the airport!

We are proud of the city of North Richland Hills!

JAJUANA KINNAIRD BLEVINS

My memories as a child growing up in NRH are of the horse riding stables on Glenview Drive, now a large apartment complex. My brother, Van, and I had fun at the stables and riding paths.

I remember the bicycle paths across from the Food Lion Grocery site. We rode those paths every day and sometimes found rocks that we just knew were "fool's gold."

My memories include John Parish, the principal of North Richland Elementary School (now Mullendore) and Mrs. Reed, my first grade teacher.

I can never forget my teen years with Greg Bogard and the Hardisty boys and the Burger King on Grapevine Highway, now a Beefers restaurant.

PAULA BROOKS-GOOD

Paula Brooks-Good remembers when:

She sang The Star Spangled Banner at a political rally organized by Pat Jacobson for Ronald Reagan.

Glenview Hospital was built by our family doctors, and we no longer had to go to "downtown" Fort Worth to the hospital.

She learned to sew by taking the children, the playpen, the ironing, the baking, and sewing projects one day a week to the alternating homes of Billie Whitbeck, Fay Yates, Evalyn Wood-Lochridge, and Lou Hubbard-Yates.

She and Adeline Slaughter took their children to eat at Wyatt's Cafeteria for the 39-cent special (fried chicken, two vegetables, and a roll), when Hal and Herb were gone in the evenings.

She and Lena Mae Reeder directed the Bicentennial Pageant that starred everyone in town and was presented at Birdville Stadium.

Don Dodson gave Mark his first "real" set of golf clubs.

The Dixie Belles drill team had slumber parties at the Brooks house after football games, and the boys trampled the shrubbery looking in the windows.

The glorious days of youth camp at Falls Creek, Oklahoma.

When Kriss and Mark took swimming lessons at Barrbrook Park, and Hal would join us for a picnic lunch.

CHARLES AND CARLYNE BROWN

When we moved to our new home at Holiday Lane East and Riviera in 1958 there was a barbed-wire fence across our backyard and an open field as far as you could see. Cattle with cowbells would come down to the fence in the early morning hours. Our children thought we had moved on a "ranch." One day shortly after we got settled a red helicopter landed in the field close to our house. Our neighbor was a test pilot and wanted to give our two boys, Larry, 5, and Garry, 4, a ride. Carlyne accepted and they took off out of the field for a 30-minute flight all around the area. Both boys were in the front yard when their dad arrived from work that afternoon. Their mouths did not stop until bedtime. Our boys called the field behind us "Mesquite Hill." They spent a lot of time playing on that hill. There is no more field, no more barbed-wire fence, no more freedom that we so much enjoyed in those days, but time goes on and you just have to forge ahead. Our memories are very pleasant.

TOSCA CAMPBELL

The family fondly remembers Archie's Doughnut Shop on Grapevine Highway, which is still in operation.

In November 1963, Tosca Campbell successfully organized Birdville's first art show for children at Richland Plaza, and the event was called "The Green Tea."

The event was scheduled to be covered by the local TV station; however—Lee Harvey Oswald was shot that day in Dallas, and all the TV crews moved instead to Dallas.

In 1960, Tosca Campbell was instrumental in introducing members of the Brownies Girl Scouts to the Fort Worth Ballet and Opera. Also, in 1964, Tosca Campbell promoted the initiation of a semester each of music, art, and foreign language in the seventh grade at North Richland Junior High School.

SHERRY [JOHNSON] CHRISTENSEN

"Things that I miss . . ."

- The snowcone stand on Blaney behind Buddies.
- The "Mustard Jar" at North Richland Drugstore.
- The "circle" Dairy Queen (now the U-Haul on Grapevine Highway).
- The "huge" penny candy aisles at Mott's (now Dollar General Store).
- The old Post Office on Blaney.
- Hearing the church chimes from the North Richland Hills Baptist Church.
- Ma and Pa's Chicken Shack on Grapevine Highway.
- The Cinema and Carnation Ice Cream Parlor in the Richland Plaza.
- When the only reason to travel north on the barely two lane Rufe Snow was to visit friends who lived in the "boonies."

DONNA ELLENBURG COLLINS

Some of Donna Ellenburg Collins' fondest memories of growing up in North Richland Hills were the long walks she took with her father while exercising and running his bird dogs in the fields north of Richland High School. There was nothing out there for miles except fields, mesquite trees, and occasionally a barbed-wire fence.

WILMA CRAWFORD

"Oh! How things have changed."

When we moved into our home on Cummings Drive at the corner of Marilyn Lane (site of the new City Hall parking lot) in 1959, there was no City Hall there, no Maplewood Drive, and no Loop 820. We were at the end of civilization. When there was a heavy rain, the creek would flood and Cummings Drive was cut off, with no access out. The children in the neighborhood loved it—they missed a half day of school.

KATHRYN PRYOR CREAMER

After moving to North Richland Hills in 1957, my sons had a black cocker spaniel dog that disappeared. I began trying to call the police and dog pound. I was told that all the police we had was the county sheriff.

We had a field behind our house in the North Hills addition. A strange sight in that field was a KFJZ radio tower. There were very few houses in this area between Denton Highway and Fossil Creek. Even though my house is in the NRH city limits, I got my mail from the Haltom City post office, and my boys went to the schools in Haltom City.

HATTIE CRIBBS

Hattie Cribbs looked at the "silk flower" on their magnolia tree at their new home in the Meadow Lakes area. She could not understand why a bloom stayed pretty all winter. A neighbor had placed the blossom on the branch. Then the neighbors watched the excitement as the joke was discovered.

"SIS" CUMMINGS

Lunch was always enjoyable at North Richland Drug. The conversation was so good that you could just stop talking and hear all kinds of news from the tables around you. Alan and Nancy Hamm were special people, as were those longtime employees, Eva and Marie.

In 1956, we lived on Vance Road, and at that time, there were a number of vacant lots around us. Ruth Jones, my mother, was spending nights with us because my dad, Clarence Jones, was in the hospital. In the middle of the night, our English bulldog, Pug, started barking and growling from the kennel in the back yard. Guy jumped up and went to the window to tell him to "shut up." Pug did, but the next morning my cousin, Harold Daley, the insurance man, knocked at the front door. Guy had left early to go to work and stopped to tell Harold to come tell us later that all four tires had been stolen off mom's car. There it sat on four stacks of bricks in the driveway. I had a mad mom.

Not long after we moved to Vance Road in North Richland Hills in 1955, I had my first encounter with a snake. I was stepping up to enter the house from the carport when out of the corner of my eye I saw this BIG gray snake. I think it scared me so bad that I ran in, slammed, and locked the door. Then I called my mother and told her. She said "I'll be right there." In about two minutes, she was there getting out of her car with hoe in hand. She hit the snake and it started at her. I was a big help. I was hollering, "Run, Mother, run." She did and then stopped and hit it again. I hollered, "Run to Gay's (our neighbor)." Finally, in the middle of Vance Road, she wiped out the snake. Every time she hit that snake she had a special name for him.

Then she said, "Now we'll hang it on your fence, and it's supposed to make it rain." That night or the next morning it started raining, and it poured, green skies and everything. It was before the Richland Hills floods, or I would have thought this had caused it.

JERRY DEWS

When the Jerry Dews family first looked for a home in the Mid-Cities in the 1970s, it just seemed to be too far out from the city. By the early 1980s it suddenly did not seem so far from Fort Worth, although it was still thought of as somewhat a country location. Even Rufe Snow Drive was beginning to have much traffic. Within just a few years, it seemed to all run together with Fort Worth, and Rufe Snow became a major thoroughfare.

JAMES DILL

Upon moving to NRH, we were overwhelmed with the wonderful and quaint neighborhood as well as the tremendous pride everyone takes in maintaining their homes, some of which are more than 20 years old. This feeling extends throughout the city as the BISD and NRH City Council reflect the city's strong family values. We have lived the American dream by purchasing our first home and starting our family with the birth of our precious daughter, Avery. In addition, four of our closest friends have moved to NRH within the past few months. We give God all the glory and praise for these many blessings and look to the future with great eagerness as He continues to move in our lives.

NANCY DOWLER

"SMITHFIELD"

From a tap root the family tree began—
good, strong women and fighting men.
A covered wagon in 1857 made its way
from Tennessee to Texas—took many a day.

They settled beneath a large oak tree
on a hill; in a distance they could see
the Indians camped down by a stream
The entire picture—it was their dream.

They plowed their fields and tended the stock,
built a home; had babies to rock.
As the tap root sprouted and grew
the branches multiplied; were ever renewed.

Homesteads were settled, their little town grew
Meacham, Brown, Smyth—to name a few
gave Smithfield its start, and it became
the Tarrant County seat—it was a prideful name.

To town by horse and buggy they would drive.
Luther, Alf, Guy, Carl, and Allie made five
along with their parents, Catherine and Will
to a place (and now a stadium) known as Birdville.

The old homestead stands vacant today
and for me, it's a stone's throw away.
Trees, brambles and bushes cover the site
at Watauga and Smithfield Roads traffic light.

I find it strange after all these years
to return to my roots, and it's very clear
the Meacham name may not endure
—but the tap root grows deeper year after year.

7/96

BILL AND DEANA HOFFMAN

The most memorable thing that has happened to us is the birth of our little girl, Haley Lynn Hoffman. It seems only yesterday that she was an infant coming home from the hospital. It took us 20 minutes to get her into the car, strapped into her car seat and as we drove off, we wondered what we left at the hospital. Whew! As long as we have Haley and each other, nothing else matters! Oh, what God brings into our lives in the bundle of joy called a child!

DENNIS HORVATH

The Computerization of North Richland Hills

In the summer of 1980 I returned from a vacation, and I found out that while I was gone our finance director had been dismissed. Then City Manager Chuck Williams, facing other problems at the time, said to me "I think (the departed finance director) bought a computer. Your job is to figure out what we bought and get it running."

When the computer was delivered (an IBM System 34, which is now an "antique") it was a state-of-the-art system, and I believe we were the second city in the Metroplex to get so high-tech. I can honestly say not one person in City Hall knew how to turn it on.

Within 30 days from the date of delivery, all 13,000 water customers were on our computer; utility bills were computed, printed, and mailed out. All of the credit for this accomplishment must go to Chester Smyth, Paula Gifford, Jeanette Carnet, and to a wonderful volunteer, Barbara Horvath. Those dedicated employees worked literally day and night to get the job done. What a wonderful experience.

The very funny part of it all was when I was getting educated on computers by the IBM folks they told me this thing was so high-tech that the city would probably never need another computer. We also got a pretty good price. We got five "dumb" terminals, one computer, and one slow printer—$100,000. I'm sure that any one of our current $3,000 PCs has probably 20 times the capacity of our 1980 System 34.

JAMES AND BETTY KEDING

We moved to Rufe Snow Drive in 1957. This was out in the "country." We had just gone to bed one night when I noticed the neighbor's back porch light flickering. I saw flames leaping up the back wall of the Starks' home coming from a doghouse. The dog had pups, and the neighbors had put a lightbulb and extension cord in it to keep them warm. I grabbed my flashlight and ran outside, hooked up a hose and started pouring water on the house. Betty called the Fire Department. (No 911 yet.)

When the Fire Department arrived the fire was out, and one of the firemen said I needed to put on some more clothes (I was wearing underwear only and had mud up to my knees.) At that time, we only had a volunteer fire department.

When we moved to NRH our children were 6 and 3. They played across the street by a little pond where they caught crawdads.

We were proud of Richland Plaza when it was built. We thought it was pretty special, and it beat going to downtown Fort Worth. My kids and I used to ride the bus from Buddies to town. It took the good part of the day.

When Rufe Snow Drive was widened, it took 10 feet off our front yard, and we weren't happy about that. Then the traffic started, and NRH began growing.

HORST KRAUSE

My memories of North Richland Hills are so diverse, of city growth, good friends, many fellow teachers in the Birdville school system, but mainly strong memories of 30 years of coaching many outstanding athletes. Here are a few of those:

- Jimmy Grant—First Richland football All-American in 1974
- Steve Stewart—Winner in discus throw, Texas state track meet, 1975—Steve was Southwest Conference Champion the next year at Texas A&M.
- Tim Scott—High school All-American in track, 1976
- Bill Wimberly—Winner high jump state track meet
- Lanny Basham—Won a gold medal in the 1976 Olympics in small bore rifle shooting.
- Theo Rigsby—outstanding coach and friend who served several years as president of the Texas High School Coaches Association. The Richland Relays were renamed in his honor in 1980. He was inducted into the Hall of Honor, along with four others, at the Balfour luncheon in Houston July 26, 1980.
- Hugh Hamm—Track coach at Richland whose teams won team district championships 1973 through 1976 and 1978 through 1980. I remember the retirement party that Mark Howe planned and held at Bedford Holiday Inn, May 6, 1989. It was a surprise and well attended by over 300 former track and football players and coaches.

DERETTA LICHTENSTEIN

The memories I have of North Richland Hills have to be the farms that lined Davis Blvd. I remember in 1964 we went to visit friends who lived on Rumfield Road. We crossed Grapevine Highway and were in the country. It was special to us kids to see the horses and cattle. One of the things I now miss is all the open fields we used to have. Every spring the wildflowers came into bloom and no site was ever prettier.

EVALYN WOOD LOCHRIDGE

I remember:

- Trying to put in a yard in the middle of a seven-year drought. We had a very inadequate water system, almost no water pressure in the evening. After staying up quite late to hand sprinkle newly sown grass seedlings, several cows, led by a goat, from Bill Mackey's dairy farm to the west of us, walked over a mound of gravel that had been dumped at the dead-end of Briley Street. The gravel covered the barbed-wire fence, so they had no obstacle. They proceeded through our yard leaving deep ruts and made their way through the entire community doing the same thing. The goat skinned all the bark off our young trees and I thought we would never get the ruts filled in.
- Hot summer days spent with friends and all our children at Barrbrook Park and pool. The huge shade trees, picnic lunches, and cool water made it a great place.
- Rushing daughter Donna to the Pillow-Rush Clinic when she was having a severe asthma attack. How grateful we were for the excellent nearby doctors. Boxes of medical books, etc., were everywhere. The doctors were just moving in, and the Wood family became file #18.
- An office call to the clinic was $3, house calls, a very common thing at night, were $5.
- Watching Kathy Pillow ride her bicycle around our corner every Saturday, the bicycle basket full of books on her way to the bookmobile at the shopping center.
- Keeping Kriss Brooks the night Mark Brooks was born. Hal was out of town preaching in a revival, and we had worked out a plan with another friend, Billie Whitbeck, who would drive Paula to the hospital.

ETHEL LOFLAND

One time word got out that a gang of boys was going to meet on the Richland Bowl parking lot and have a fight. Ray immediately called in a few youth that he knew would spread the word and told them there would be no fights on his property, and that if they even showed up in a group, he would call the police and have them all arrested. They did not show up. At a later time, some of them went to the "gravel pits" to have a fight, and the police showed up and called their parents to come pick them up. We did not hear of any more gangs after that.

We had a few gangsters move to our area before we incorporated as North Richland Hills. In fact, some set up a "red light" district on Rufe Snow, and they spent some time at the Bowl until Ray asked the police chief to tell them their business was not wanted. They never showed up again and moved out of the city not long after.

Between the years 1957 and 1980, when we retired (and those years passed so fast), we had thousands of people who passed through the doors of Richland Bowl either to bowl, play pool, eat our flame-kissed hamburgers or chicken fried steak, attend meetings, attend birthday parties, take lessons on bowling, etc. We had good times and lean times, and when Gerald and Richard sold the Bowl, they put this notice in the Star-Telegram:

RICHLAND BOWL
1957–1993
The Lofland family

would like to thank
you for your patronage,
your friendship and
the memories.

MARION MASSEY

When I returned to Fort Worth after serving two years in the U.S. Marine Corps in 1959, I had an opportunity to be North Richland Hills' first traffic court judge. I moved to NRH in 1960 and started holding court in an office on the Grapevine Highway provided to the city by Herb Arnold.

NRH was truly a bedroom community, having very few businesses other than service stations, drycleaners, and real estate offices.

About 1966, I was selected as city attorney for NRH and served in that capacity until 1969, when I ran for mayor and was elected at the age of 38. I served as mayor for two terms, 1970 through 1974.

I ran for mayor because I definitely wanted to be a part of a growing community. I was convinced that this was where I wanted to live and my children to grow up. I felt like I had something to offer and that serving as mayor would certainly complement the building of my law practice.

As to accomplishments during my terms as mayor, I take the most pride in the city obtaining control and ownership of the water system, which had previously been owned by a privately owned corporation. This was the beginning of NRH's emergence as truly a dynamic city. As a traffic court judge, I believe we established a court that had a reputation for being fair but firm in the enforcement of the traffic laws within our city.

DENVER L. MILLS

We moved to North Richland Hills in 1959 because of the good reputation of the Birdville school system. There was scattered housing in the area, but the bulk of development was concentrated around Blaney Drive and Grapevine Highway. This is a guess, but there couldn't have been more than 2,000 or 3,000 people living in NRH at that time. North Richland Hills was considered "growth that spilled over Grapevine Highway from Richland Hills" by our neighboring cities.

We loved our time in NRH, thought living there was great, enjoyed the people, and were proud to raise our daughters there. It was safe, friendly, and had good schools.

We often visit old friends and neighbors who still live there. When we say "We're going home for a few days," people know we are heading for NRH.

BARBARA MUSGROVE

(Resident 1960–1995)

When driving around looking for a new home in 1960, I saw a sign, "Homes For Sale" (one of very few) down a two-lane country road now known as Davis Boulevard, but at the time it was Smithfield Road. The addition was called Clearview. Looking around, I saw a big feed store at the present intersection of Bedford-Euless Road, Grapevine Highway, and Davis Boulevard, and down Davis a smaller feed store and across from it, a street called Standley. This was where the new homes were located.

At the end of Standley (which was a dirt road), and Colorado, there was a pond. A farmhouse and barn were in the middle of the present Birchwood Street. There was another farmhouse in the back playground of Holiday Heights Elementary and one by the North Richland Hills post office. In our neighborhood, a red brick home stood on Clark and another on Colorado. With the cool country breezes, windows were open at night, and all the country sounds came in. At the back of our yard, was a barbed-wire fence; in the field beyond were horses and cows. The closest grocery store was Buddies (now Winn Dixie) way down on Grapevine Highway. Eventually, the 7-Eleven and Dairy Queen were built as well as a few other small stores. The nearest department stores were at the Richland Plaza Shopping Center on Grapevine Highway, almost in Haltom City. We lived in NRH for 35 years, and no matter where we live today, NRH will always be our home.

JEAN NEWMAN

When we first arrived in town, the Richland Athletic Association needed a couple of baseball fields but did not have much money, so through the hard work of many volunteers, parks were built on property over in the Richland warehouse district. The Little League fields were manicured grass infields and outfields with dugouts that the pros would have envied. The dirt infield was made with a special mix of material that helped the dirt repel water so you could just squeegee the water off the top of the dirt. Rumor had it that the stuff was from a slaughterhouse!

The announcer's booth had excellent loudspeakers, so the primo announcer/parent, Mr. George Phillips, father of five boys, could make the games more exciting than those announced by Dizzy Dean. The umpire was addressed as "sir," and if the parents yelled anything critical, Roy Taylor would kick them off the premises. One of the many highlights of those years was hitting a homer over the Chicken Shack sign in left field. If you did, you got a free chicken dinner at Chuck Schaeffer's father's restaurant over in Haltom City. It seemed that any ball hit over the fence was always over that sign!

Tommy Newman served as councilman from 1970 to 1976. From 1976 through 1978, he was mayor of NRH.

After the construction of Loop 820 through NRH, mall development began, and the DFW Airport was planned and built during that time. My mother and brothers still live in the NRH area, but I don't get back to the area much anymore. When I do, I get lost!

Submitted by James J. (Jimmy) Newman, Ph.D., M.D.

BETTE NOLEN

Our move to North Richland Hills on September 25, 1957, from our house in the Riverside area, was certainly

NOT an impressive event. We could not afford to rent a moving van, so we and our friends made several trips in a small rented trailer to move the furniture. On the last load, our daughters and their friend, Larry Adams, begged to ride in the trailer. Since there was very little traffic, they rode to their new house sitting on the floorboard. We realize now how dangerous this was; however, they still remember how much fun they had. Husband Raymond drove very slowly and carefully, but it was impossible to miss all the "chugholes" on Rufe Snow Drive. One of the girls said on arrival: "We like our new home, but couldn't we have a new road, too?"

It wasn't too many years until the girls could ride their bicycles down to Mott's variety store and then stop by the snow-cone stand next to the post office.

When we moved, North Richland Elementary, which had been constructed in 1955, was the only public school in our neighborhood.

Richland High School opened its doors in September 1961, and I transferred from Haltom Junior High to become a biology/anatomy/physiology teacher at this brand-new school. We continued to commute to Riverside to church until Ted Spencer was appointed as the minister to organize the new Davis Memorial Methodist Church. Ted asked Raymond to go with him to visit families in the area and ask if they were interested in becoming charter members.

J. Fred and Maude Davis, who donated the land on which the church was finally built, owned the farm surrounding the church and their son had a home and dairy farm where the Holiday Heights Elementary School is now located.

Stores in downtown Fort Worth built branch shops in our area, and our friends realized that we were not in the "middle of nowhere." We considered ourselves "pioneer suburbanites."

STANLEY PARCHMAN

I remember the many dairies that stretched along the country roads in this area. Most people nowadays would never know how big the dairy industry was here. Mr. Brooks' dairy was north toward the Watauga area. Guy Reeves' dairy was at Four Points. Stretched northward along the old Watauga Road (now Rufe Snow) were dairy farms that belonged to Bill Mackey, Will Snow, Rufe Snow, the Sturcks, Parkers, and Mr. Vollintine, who milked 24 hours a day during World War II. They all contributed so much to the area. Mrs. Bill Mackey (Edith) was a Hardisty. Ruby Snow, Rufe's daughter, did most of the milking on their place and took care of Rufe. They had about 30 cows. She later married Lee Reynolds and was head of the school cafeterias in the early 1950s.

I've had a speech impediment since I was in the first grade. School board members were having a big fight inside the school. There was a demand that the School Board president be fired. I've always blamed that scene that I witnessed for my problem.

I built the Rapid Mart grocery in the early 1950s. Sully Montgomery was sheriff of Tarrant County at that time. There were several robberies, but one really stands out in my memory. On a Wednesday night, about 9:30 P.M., an armed robbery took place. There were three people involved. One stayed with the car on Pipeline Road, one stayed outside, and one came into the store. The robber thrust a gun into my stomach and told Estes to sack up the money. He said, "Do you want to give it to them?" Needless to say, I didn't hesitate. The two made their getaway through a corn patch to the waiting car on Pipeline Road. The Sheriff's Department caught them in Richland Hills and they signed a confession.

A 7-Eleven convenience store was built and opened for business on the Grapevine Highway less than one-half block from the Rapid Mart. (This is next to the present Wells Fargo bank, site of Enterprise Car Rentals.) Rev. Robert Young, minister of the Richland Hills Methodist Church, began a community-wide campaign to support local businesses. Since 7-Eleven prided itself with never having selected a bad location, I credited Robert Young with saving my business, which continued for many years. The convenience store soon closed and posted a sign on the door that said, "Oops, opened by mistake."

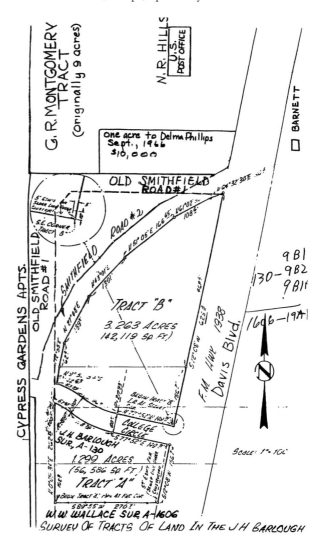

ANN PHILLIPS

John Autry, now deceased, a member of one of the earliest Smithfield families, showed this writer on one occasion where the original Old Smithfield Road went in a westerly direction along the Phillip south fenceline down to the east fenceline of Cypress Apartments where it made a 90-degree turn to the left and went southward. Mr. Autry dug down to expose the original gravel roadbed and bar ditch as he related how his family took many mule-drawn wagonloads of firewood over this road for sale at Birdville.

As automobiles came into use, right angles in the old road were a hindrance, and a wide curving arch was surveyed out in order to bypass this sharp turn. Still later a new Smithfield Highway took on a more streamlined approach, intersecting the older road in two places, and leaving a wide sweeping curve isolated on the west side of the new highway. This isolated curve came to be known as Ross Road, named for Fred Ross, who lived at the top of the hill to the east. After a few years the Smithfield Highway also became inadequate for handling the crushing traffic of a rapidly expanding Metroplex, and it would only be a drastically improved Davis Boulevard that could take on the task of moving the thousands of autos that pass over it daily.

LLOYD D. AND PAT ROBINSON

My first unforgettable memory of North Richland Hills was the day we moved on Vance Road next door to George and Pat Riddle in August 1969. The temperature was more than 100 degrees, and we did not have electricity or water. Pat Riddle was the first neighbor we saw, and she came over with a large pitcher of ice water, glasses, and an extra warm smile. This began a friendship that still exists today. Pat Riddle was our "angel of mercy" and has been a dear angel ever since.

When we moved to NRH, Darrell was stationed at Carswell Air Force Base. Loop 820 was not completed. We had to take Main Street to Long Ave. to get to the base. Rufe Snow was a narrow road north of Loop 820. There was one house on the east side of the road and fields with "cows and country" much of the way north.

We will long remember the Birdville Independent School District and how it provided all four of our girls with an opportunity to grow and learn and establish good morals as well as developing their music abilities.

The Richland Youth Association provided activities, and we were part of the original group that established soccer for our kids in RYA. Pat served as the first soccer commissioner in RYA, as well as the first woman soccer commissioner and the first soccer coach who knew nothing about soccer!

Pat was asked to help with calling on and talking to sponsors to help build the Adventure World Playground on Starnes. We held an auction and fair and raised funds, which helped pay for the equipment for the playground.

We have been privileged to attend and graduate from the Leadership Northeast program where friends were made for a lifetime and we have been a part of our community, as it grew over the last 28 years. We have met and learned to love many wonderful people who make up the wonderful city of NRH . . . TEXAS!

EDWARD L. ROGERS

Memories of Another Day in the Life and Times of North Richland Hills

When my family moved to Conn Drive in 1957, the Calloway Branch Creek which flowed beneath Glenview Drive held the attention of many of the neighborhood boys who would chase the dreams of Huck Finn in the summer with rafts of all sorts, and the dreams of Hans Brinker in the winter when occasional freezes made for ice skating and hockey games

Many a flash flood occurred on the Calloway Branch, and many memorable experiences resulted. This included the dramatic helicopter rescue of a stranded motorist who was swept away in his car from the crossing at Booth-Calloway Road. We heard the screams for help in our kitchen, ran out to find a man hanging in a tree, and called the police for help . . . long before EMS and 911 were part of our culture.

He was lucky that we lived so close to Bell Helicopter, because in those days there were no police or Fire Department helicopters either.

Farther up the Calloway Branch, on the land that is now the North Hills Mall, was the site of Happy Hollow Golf Course where we learned to play golf.

The area immediately east of this intersection was the Anderson family farm. They lived in one of those classic two-story wood frame farmhouses. They had the typical farm storm cellar outside to protect against tornadoes and also as a place for the storage of jams and jellies, which Mrs. Anderson canned in those days.

Since we Texans didn't have (and still don't have) basements in our homes, I'd never been underground, and it was a real treat to walk down the stairs underground to see the jellies on the shelves (and then to eat them later, just to see how they tasted).

One of my favorite memories was going to the Richland Hills Riding Club (on the site of what is now the Garden Ridge shopping center at Bedford Road and Highway 183) with my family to see the beautiful horses and the talented riders/owners who owned the stables in the area.

LOIS AND PATRICIA STEWART

- Marion West, "the butane man," who delivered butane to everyone in the community.
- John and Aline Shivers for whom Lois did ironing.
- The boys climbing the water tower and skinny-dipping in Aunt Lydia's pond.
- Seining in the open ponds before we built ours.
- Lois shopping at the Safeway at Rufe Snow and Grapevine Highway on a $10-a-week grocery allowance.
- The NRH annexation of Smithfield. "We didn't like

it, but that's progress. Smithfield was a small community where everybody knew everybody."

DAVID STOUT

I guess my fondest memories of North Richland Hills are of the officers with the NRH Police Department. They showed special kindness to our family when my husband's reserve unit was activated and he was sent to Fort Hood, Texas, for nine months during Desert Storm. Christmas 1990, was going to be very rough on our family, emotionally and financially, and there were not going to be very many gifts under the Christmas tree for our three children. The NRHPD surprised us with presents for the family and made our Christmas of 1990 one that we will cherish for years to come.

KITTI KELLEY THARP

- Walking to Henry's store on Rufe Snow for candy.
- Chinaberry fights in our front yard.
- Selling pears from our four pear trees.
- Momma bowling at Richland Bowl.
- Going swimming in the huge bar ditches after rains.
- Having birthday parties in the cellar.
- Going to North Richland Private School for first grade.

JAMES AND LOUISE WALKER

North Richland Hills had only a few people when we moved here in 1955, but our neighbors became like a part of our family. The children played on Snow Hill, near Rufe Snow's orchard off Holiday Lane and north of Riveria Drive. We have watched as the area has grown with improved roads, utilities, police protection, and schools. Shopping centers were constructed nearby so we no longer had to travel into Fort Worth. Good hospitals and fine doctors also became a part of our lives as the children grew.

We have been blessed with our family, two grandchildren, and many very special memories of our lives in North Richland Hills.

DOUG WILLIAMSON

When we first moved here, Rufe Snow Drive was just a rural road. A dairy was between the high school and Rufe Snow Drive. A large farmhouse was where the apartments are located above the outlet mall, and cows grazed the fields where the mall is now. We liked it because we were in the country and still in town. You could walk in pastureland from Rufe Snow Drive all the way to the Haltom mansion on the Denton Highway. The field behind our house was planted in Johnson grass hay. Where did all these people come from?

IRIS SOUSAE WOODALL

I remember how we always looked forward to going to the Fourth of July fireworks at the Birdville football stadium.

We always enjoyed going to the fiddling contests every year that were held in Richland Plaza.

We used to shop at the North Richland Drug, Buddies (which is now Winn Dixie), Penney's, and Montgomery Ward.

LOU HUBBARD YATES

In the spring of 1956, when we were new residents in NRH, Kathi was an infant. While I was bathing her one morning, Chip, 5, and Tim, not quite 2, were playing just outside the kitchen. As soon as I finished her bath, I went to the door to check on the boys to find Tim, and I couldn't see him anywhere. As I began to call, I drew several neighbors' attention, including the workmen building a house next door. By this time I was in a panic! I saw one of the workmen get into his truck and leave. In just another minute or two the workman in the truck drove up again. He had found Tim. He said that as he looked around from the roof he was building, he saw two tiny specks way up the hill—now known as Rufe Snow Drive. Tim and our cocker spaniel, Rags, had gone exploring.

Vacation Bible School at North Richland Hills Baptist Church was always a highlight in our lives when the children were young. After classes one morning, I needed to go back to the church to make preparations in my classroom for the next day. I had all three children with me to "help." This was in an upstairs room with no screens on the windows. Suddenly I heard Chip calling Kathi with a very unusual sound to his voice. As I turned to look, I saw my two and a half year old, out on the roof outside the window of the room. Before I could react, Chip had reached her and was pulling her inside. Only God kept my baby from tumbling to the concrete below!

THE FIRST MEDICAL COMMUNITY OF NORTH RICHLAND HILLS PILLOW-RUSH MEDICAL AND SURGICAL CLINIC

The North Richland Hills Shopping Center was being built in 1954–1955 and was running advertisements for tenants. In 1955 the Pillow-Rush Medical and Surgical Clinic leased space from Clarence Jones and moved in this space in July of that year. The two principals in this clinic were Dr. David J. Pillow and Dr. Charles A. Rush.

At the time of the establishment of this clinic there was only one other doctor in this area, Dr. John Jermyn. Dr. Bruce K. Jacobson joined them in 1957, and Dr. J. Ardis Bell in 1960. All four of the doctors took care of families, delivered babies, set broken bones, operated, and made house calls as necessary. Their patients went to Fort Worth hospitals, as no medical facilities were available in the area.

The Pillow-Rush-Jacobson-Bell Clinic continued to add more doctors and became the Northeast Medical Family Clinic, moving to Glenview Drive. Drs. Pillow, Rush, Jacobson, Jermyn, and Drs. Martha and Robert Chapman had Glenview Hospital built and opened in

May 1961 on Glenview Drive in NRH. In 1983 a replacement hospital for it was opened on Booth Calloway Drive. This hospital was called North Hills Hospital and it is now known as Columbia North Hills Hospital.

The doctors remained active in the community, serving as game sports doctors, bank directors, in places of leadership in clubs, churches, colleges, etc.

DR. DAVID J. PILLOW

David J. Pillow, M.D., was a graduate of Paschal High School, Texas Christian University, and George Washington University Medical School, Washington, D. C., where he received his medical degree in 1953. He came to Fort Worth after an internship at District of Columbia Hospital in Washington, D. C., and entered a rotating residency at John Peter Smith Hospital. Following the completion of his residency, he and Dr. Charles A. Rush chose the North Richland Hills area to serve the needs of the growing community in family practice.

In 1973 Dr. Pillow left the Northeast Clinic to become an assistant professor at the University of Texas-Southwestern Medical School. This involved setting up the Family Practice Residency program at John Peter Smith Hospital and serving as its director until 1977. He then returned to private practice, opening the Glenview Family Practice Clinic on Glenview Drive, moving to the North Hills Professional Building.

In 1989 Dr. Pillow retired and worked in locum tenems—covering various Texas clinics as needed for short intervals. Then in 1996, when the Senior Health Center, North Hills Professional Building opened, he was asked to help with the care of Medicare patients. He is involved in this endeavor for three days each week at the present time.

DR. CHARLES A. RUSH

Dr. Rush had also attended TCU. He was a graduate of Baylor Medical School and was a resident of John Peter Smith Hospital the same year that Dr. Pillow was there. His involvement paralleled that of Dr. Pillow for many years with Glenview Hospital, then North Hills Hospital.

His memories of the years of practice in the NRH area include the fact that office calls were $3, and house calls were from $5 to $7 each. On May 7, 1960, Dr. May Owen dedicated the 50-bed Glenview Hospital. They were scheduled to open on May 10, 1960. However, on May 9, Dr. Bob Chapman had a patient with acute appendicitis needing immediate surgery. Mrs. Pat Jermyn was the operating room supervisor. Enough equipment was sterilized for the emergency. The appendectomy was done one day prior to the official opening of the hospital.

Dr. Rush's interest in allergy expanded in the 10 years of his practice from 1955 to 1965. He took the Allergy Immunology Board's examination in New York in 1974, passed it and was officially Board Certified in Allergy and Immunology. Dr. Rush is now in practice for allergy patients and has his offices in Hurst, Texas.

DR. BRUCE K. JACOBSON

While in the Navy, Bruce Jacobson met a fellow shipmate from Fort Worth, who encouraged him to come to Texas and attend TCU. While a student there he came to know Dr. May Owen, who trained premed students in laboratory techniques. While working nights and weekends at All Saints Hospital, he met Charles Rush and David Pillow and they became friends.

In 1950 he was accepted to Baylor College of Medicine. Following his graduation in 1954, Dr. Jacobson completed two years of postgraduate medical education at City-County Hospital in Fort Worth. Subsequently he joined Drs. Pillow and Rush in the establishment of Glenview Hospital. Following 18 years of private practice in North Richland Hills, Dr. Jacobson accepted an appointment to the staff of Southwestern Medical School, and in this position became the residency director for family practice at John Peter Smith Hospital in Fort Worth.

Dr. Jacobson is now retired and spends much of his time at the family's Hillcrest Ranch near Mexia.

DR. J. ARDIS BELL

Dr. Ardis Bell joined the Pillow-Rush-Jacobson Medical and Surgical Clinic in 1960 and his family has been residents of Richland Hills since 1963. He was born in south Fort Worth, graduated from Arlington Heights High School and from the University of Texas in Austin. He attended the University of Texas Medical School in Galveston, where he graduated in 1955. He served an internship and residency at John Peter Smith Hospital in Fort Worth from 1955 to 1957 in family practice.

It didn't take long, with four doctors, their staff, and numerous patients, to outgrow the space in the Greater Richland Center. A new building on Glenview Drive was completed and renamed Family Health Care Clinic. This clinic experienced tremendous growth through the years both in doctors and patients, and Dr. Bell continued to practice here until his retirement in January 1998.

Bell not only served the medical needs of the northeast area but the community in other capacities. He was president of the Haltom-Richland Chamber of Commerce (now Northeast Tarrant Chamber), charter president of the H.E.B. Rotary Club, chief of staff of the Glenview Hospital in 1970, past president of his clinic, city health officer of Richland Hills. He also served on the original steering committee of Tarrant County Junior College, which opened in 1967 at its South Campus in Fort Worth. It was followed a year later by the Northeast Campus in Hurst, and now TCJC has two other campuses. Dr. Bell was elected to the TCJC Board of Trustees in 1965 and has been its president since 1976, an endeavor he plans to continue.

He and his wife of 51 years, Doris, reared six children and have seven grandchildren. They have been members of North Richland Hills Baptist Church for many years.

J. W. COBB, D.D.S.

North Richland Hills' first dentist was Dr. J. W. "Jim" Cobb. He worked as an electrician and a mail carrier while attending Texas Wesleyan College from 1949 to 1951, then he entered Baylor College of Dentistry. He graduated with a degree in dental surgery in 1955, working part-time at Wadley Blood Research Center and as a mail carrier.

A dental supply salesman told Dr. Cobb of a shopping center under construction in NRH. He talked to Clarence Jones about leasing a space for a dental office. The office was opened without any fanfare in Oct. 1955. It was located near the Blaney Avenue corner of the center, next to North Richland Drug and Pillow-Rush Clinic. Dr. Cobb said, "I had to subsidize my dental office by teaching at the dental school."

Years later Dr. Cobb and Dr. Lyndall Webb built a new office building on the Richland Hills side of Glenview Drive across the street from the Family Health Care Clinic. Friends teased them with the proposed idea to name it the Cobb-Webb Building. Dr. Cobb still practices at the Glenview office.

DR. JOHN W. JERMYN

Dr. John Jermyn opened his medical office at 6717 Grapevine Highway in July 1955. He and his wife, Pat, moved from Dumas, Texas, and settled in Richland Hills.

Dr. Jermyn completed Southwestern Medical School and did his residency in Baltimore. After serving in the U. S. Army in Korea, he established his first practice in Dumas. In 1962 he built a new building on the corner of Grapevine Highway and Willman Avenue and moved his medical offices there where he practiced until his death Jan. 13, 1964. The building was sold to Dr. Norman Ingebrigtsen, who continues to practice there.

Dr. Jermyn and five other local doctors served as the operating company that built Glenview Hospital which opened in 1961.

DR. TOMMY ABBOTT
DR. DON ABBOTT

After completing high school at Birdville, Tommy and Don both wanted to be doctors. Tommy enrolled at Texas A&M to study veterinary medicine. He loved animals, and after six years of preparation, he accepted his new animal clinic from his dad, Foy Abbott. The building was located at the corner of Rufe Snow Drive and Grapevine Highway on land purchased from the W. A. McGee family. It became officially known as Richland Animal Hospital and had its grand opening in August 1956.

Don Abbott attended Texas Christian University where he completed his premedical work. After four years, he enrolled in Southwestern School of Medicine in Dallas. Tommy decided to join Don at Southwestern and apply his skills to healing the human race rather than animals. Education was a long and expensive process, so Tommy continued with his veterinary work during this time. All told, Tommy did 14 years of postgraduate work after high school.

Don's last year of residency was interrupted by the Vietnam War. He enlisted in the Air Force and was based at Fort Walton Air Base in Florida. During his two-year stint, he delivered more than 200 babies. Afterward, he returned to St. Paul's Hospital in Dallas to finish his residency. Both Don and Tommy specialized in internal medicine, surgery, gynecology, and obstetrics.

Medical offices for the two Abbott brothers were set up in the clinic Foy Abbott had built for them. Dr. Tommy is still practicing in the original building, Dr. Don later built a clinic just north of the old building on Rufe Snow Drive known as Richland Medical Clinic, which provides facilities for several doctors.

FATE AND THE LIBERATORS IN THE CROSS TIMBERS
BY GENE OWENS

The site of North Richland Hills lays astride the eastern Cross Timbers and the Grand Prairie. The Cross Timbers had friends in high places in 1941. President Franklin Roosevelt and Eleanor were familiar with our area. One of their sons lived somewhere around Benbrook. Roosevelt was politically astute and knew that Texas was a keystone to any national election. As war had already commenced in Europe, he seemed to know that destiny would have us involved soon. So he had been covertly sending war material to England. The Liberators, which were built probably in San Diego, were being flown to the Canadian border where they were clandestinely pushed across the border where Canadian pilots flew them across the Atlantic. In March 1941, a few months before Pearl Harbor, the president signed the Lend Lease Act, and we more openly supplied materials of war to England and Russia. Our entrance into the fray quickened the need for production. Factories were retooled for this new purpose. Also many new factories were started.

Amon Carter, who was very active in politics, had the ear of Roosevelt and was very instrumental in having one of these new plants to manufacture the B-24s located in the Cross Timbers. Convair was the name of the plant, but we nicknamed it "the Bomber Plant." The bomber was nicknamed the "Liberator" and lived up to its designation.

The "Bomber Plant" was to change forever the demography of the Cross Timbers. The area of North Richland Hills alludes to the plant for all those changes on the prairie we see today. No longer, after the plant appeared, would our parents and their children have to rely on the products of our agrarian-oriented society for subsistence. In just a few years all those farms and dairies that the early Cross Timbers children lived and labored on would be transposed into huge communities with shopping malls, warehouses, and small businesses. Freeways would crisscross and divide the land where once small country lanes snaked athwart the Cross Timbers and prairies. But life is full of change.

Adjacent to and sharing a symbiotic relationship with the "Bomber Plant" was the Fort Worth Army Airfield, later called Carswell. During World War II, bombers were made ready to ferry to the various theaters of war. Planes were checked out and crews were trained in the techniques being used over Europe and Asia. Just northwest of NRH was Hicks Airfield that was used to train fighter pilots.

Flying in close formation was a technique developed to help protect bombers and their crews from enemy fighters as they made their bombing runs. The airspace over then unpopulated open country above the Cross Timbers, now NRH, became an area to practice close formation flying. The bombers became a familiar sight to us children, and we could recognize them and other planes flying over the prairie. One Cross Timbers girl was dating one of the Army Air Field pilots and she would wave to his plane as it flew over. The plane, as if by design, signaled his presence between heaven and the prairie with revving engines and tipping wings.

At the same time on the ground, troops and materials of war were being transported on the several rail lines that ranged across the prairie. We would watch these convoys of long trains as they hauled tanks, trucks, cannons, Jeeps, and smiling, waving uniformed troops overland. At night we had numerous blackouts when we would listen on the radio that broadcast as planes flew overhead and relayed to the radio station the sighting of any crack of illicit light which was quickly corrected as everyone assumed they were the culprit.

Big changes took place in the lives of the Cross Timbers women with the advent of the Liberator: It also "liberated" them from the traditional roles they had been born into as they became "Rosy the Riveter" or filled one of the many formerly male-type jobs as their brothers, sweethearts, and husbands marched, floated, and flew off to war. And how were they ever to be kept "down on the farm" after that?

Planes, made by former bootleggers, farmers, milkmaids, cowboys, mechanics, and other residents of the Cross Timbers like housewives and older people beyond the draft, saw engagement over Africa, Europe, and Asia. The Cross Timbers saw migrations of peoples to its prairies and bottoms that changed it forever. NRH soon became an area squeezed by the changeful times.

On the first day of school in September of 1943, a calamitous, dreadful event befell the Cross Timbers. A low, thin patchy ground fog hung in the lowlands. We children were saying goodbye to the summer and resigned ourselves to the constrictions of another school year. The fog was already dissipating when several of us saw or heard the crash on that Friday morning.

A formation of Liberators from the Army Air Base was practicing close formation maneuvers. One of the pilots knew the girl who had waved to him many times from the prairie must be down there, but he didn't give his usual signal because of the paltry, cursory ground fog and character of their training mission.

Accounts at the time said they were flying blind when one plane began to defy the laws of physics and tried to occupy the same airspace of another as its propellers chewed into the body of its companion, cutting it in twain as explosions of angry pieces of the planes filled the September sky.

Roger Brooks saw it from his father's dairy barn about three miles away near Watauga. Henry Lane watched on Broadway as one of the twin tails disappeared downward. Ronnie and Bud Stevenson were much closer witnesses. They saw the ancestral pastures become the bomber's loathsome aerodrome that day. They watched the falling, fluttering, twining pieces like black, bright, lifeless angels subside into the mesquites. Eddie Rogers in Harmonson Addition, at early morning chores, heard pieces whir as they passed overhead.

My father and I jumped in our car and drove the short distance to the crash. A column of black smoke directed us quickly to the site not too far from the banks of Big Fossil. Bodies and ground hollows from their impact were scattered around the pasture and mesquite groves. Heads had been terribly compelled into their bodies. They were attired in military coveralls that had been blown to tatters revealing clean white underwear. The skin looked peculiar and strange. Though no blood was evident, it had the singular effect of a balloon that had been painted and then blown up causing its paint to crack, split, and separate as the balloon expanded. One body had an arm outstretched as though to display his wrist watch which had exploded on impact causing the mainspring to look like some queer mechanical flower.

Opened and unopened but unoccupied parachutes were scattered around in trees. One was draped like a winding sheet over a barbed-wire fence—a white gossamer shroud. Parts of two fuselages burned and served as pyres for some of the airmen who had not been blown out of the two bombers as they exploded over Fossil Creek.

Some of the bomber engines had been contumaciously torn from their wonted place and lay despairingly among the mesquite and grass. One reposed quietly near the Belknap Highway, another in Ervin Wilson's cow lot.

A small Piper Cub-like reconnaissance military plane with two officers landed deftly in a small clearing and woefully, helplessly, bore testimony to the dreadful event and, to save others from dismay, secured the area. Then we walked up the hill a short distance to start a new school year. But for months we collected melted bits and pieces of the planes that were left behind by the accident investigators. Billy McCurry discovered one of the huge propellers buried almost from sight while hunting on Big Fossil.

Tribulations of war were not in far-away London, Europe, or the Pacific that ineffable, imprinted September morning. As we drove around the North Richland Hills area we saw those little red, white, and blue flags with blue stars to indicate the number of children that a family had in the service. We saw the blue stars turn to gold when some warrior had died and with silent lament sighed for we usually knew the giver of the great gift.

When all those enduring yet protean warriors came back to the Cross Timbers they found they weren't the only ones to have changed. They had left as prairie boys and returned transmuted into antediluvian warriors—strangers to us as we were strangers to them. We looked at each other and wondered if we had ever been concomitant brothers, uncles, and companions. Mothers were solicitous to Mars' warriors as they wondered who had supplanted their child with an outlander. A cleavage had occurred between people and the land. Time's clock had skipped a cog and we were out of sync, but not for long as we all once again faced the changes that the Fates had planned for the prairies. Lives were restarted as war's wanderers claimed by right of appanage suspended jobs, wives, and families as they pushed their dwellings out onto the prairies and called their promised land NRH.

The Liberators are gone now but when we stop to notice the countless giant passenger planes that fill the skies over Cross Timbers, we reminisce a bit.

FAMILY FARM IN THE FORTIES IN RURAL NORTHEAST TARRANT COUNTY AS RECALLED BY MARY RUTH REEVES ELLIS

My folks, Guy and Willie Anderson Reeves, realized a dream when they moved to their brand new rock home on Grapevine Highway—Four Points, as the site was known. At this writing in the 1990s it is the current site of Hudiburg Chevrolet, and Four Points has become a major traffic intersection for the city of North Richland Hills.

This was a major move from the Trinity River bottom south of Hurst, where the family had been involved in sharecrop farming and running a dairy farm.

The Hudiburg corner, as it will be referred at this writing, had a dairy barn with the dairyman's house being located facing Davis Boulevard. "Short" and Mrs. Casey, with their daughter, Delores, lived in this house. "Short" Casey was a very dependable dairyman. He always was ready in the early morning at 4:00 A.M. and late afternoon to see that the cows were milked. This was a Grade-A dairy with the milk picked up daily to be carried to a processing plant in Fort Worth or Dallas. This section of Tarrant County had many Grade-A dairy farms, which were a primary source of income for many families.

The service station at Four Points was operated for many years by Bert Starnes. Other longtime operators were Ralph Wade and Tiny Anderson. All were friendly men, as were their families, who were there to assist the public. Bert Starnes was well known in the Smithfield area (Starnes Road in NRH is named for this family.) Bert Starnes ran a feed store as well as the service station. This was the first step in things to come for one-stop shopping! Milk, bread, other food items, and gasoline could all be secured at the service station, then you could step across the parking area and buy a sack of feed for the horses or whatever pet supplies you might need.

On another "point" of Four Points stood Cunningham's grocery store, where Mr. Andrew Cunningham had a refrigerated meat case. You could buy fresh meats or wonderful bologna and cheese that he would slice for you on a big wood chopping table. There were also penny candy jars for you to select from. So many times he would give me a piece. He was a kind man with such a gentle smile.

The other two "points" were pasture land. The Four Points made up the intersection of Davis Boulevard, Grapevine Highway, and Bedford-Euless Road. At this writing the Four Points are still identifiable.

Family farm life was a busy life. The present Hudiburg corner was also the site of a huge vegetable garden and orchard, with many beautiful flowers planted in rows in the garden. At the back of the house was the chicken yard where baby chicks were raised every spring, and when ready, were dressed for the freezer for the family's food supply. Fresh eggs were available year round as well as fresh vegetables, fruits, jellies, beef, and pork. It was a good life, but a busy one.

Social activities included visiting other family members who lived nearby. Dad's sister, Maude Reeves Davis, husband Fred, and son J. Fred, moved from the Poly area in the 1940s and lived nearby on the present Davis Boulevard. Living nearby on Bedford-Euless Road was mother's brother, Gene Anderson, with wife Martine, and sons Gene, Bryan, Alvin, Wendell, Monty, Terry, and Jerry. My grandmother, Hattie Arwine Anderson, made her home with the Gene Anderson family. The site of this beautiful colonial home is now the major traffic interchange of Loop 820 and Highway 121 near North East Mall.

My mother's family moved to this site in 1903 from the Hurst area, where the pioneer family had settled in 1865.* Yes, this family member, as well as my sister Georgia Reeves Duncan, who resides in Richland Hills, has seen many changes in the northeast part of Tarrant County.

Willie and Guy Reeves believed in progress and knew the barbed-wire fences must go to make way for the thundering freeways. Yes, rural Americans were a people of vision. We are grateful to share our memories as we have shared our land.

*For complete Family History: Anderson-Arwine Family, Genealogy Reference Section, North Richland Hills Library, Tarrant County Junior College, NE Campus.

8 Families of
North Richland Hills

THE ABBOTT FAMILY

In 1958, Smithfield, with its romantic lure and historical culture, was annexed into the booming, industrial city of North Richland Hills. E. Foy Abbott and his family have lived in both cities.

Most everyone was happy when, by petition, Smithfield became a part of North Richland Hills. The two beautiful little cities needed each other. Smithfield needed the water system and the police protection NRH could provide. The city of North Richland Hills wanted Smithfield's well-organized and efficient volunteer Fire Department. Also, the sprawling rural countryside surrounding Smithfield provided North Richland Hills with room for expansion.

Eula and Foy Abbott

Foy Abbott and his family were living on his grandfather's farm where he went to live when his father died. It was here that Foy learned the value of hard work. Foy always said: "Young impressions forge good morals." As an example, he often told of the time that he, as a 5-year-old boy, cursed his granddad. His mother applied the hairbrush—but not on his head. Foy brought those values with him when he and his wife Eula, son Tommy, and mother, Lillie Thompkins Abbott, moved from Princeton to Fort Worth in 1932. They settled in Smithfield, where an aunt and uncle lived, Clara and Bud Robbirds.

The Robbirds and the Abbotts milked cows and sold cream to a company in Fort Worth. The rest of the milk they fed to the pigs. They put in a garden of black-eyed peas, which became the main item in their diet as there wasn't much money in selling cream.

It was not only hard to make a living, but also sometimes life was dangerous, too. No one except the pigs and cows could go into the wooded areas, as there were too many whiskey stills. The pigs often came up drunk.

With the election of Franklin D. Roosevelt as President of the United States, the economy improved, and more jobs were created. The family was able to buy some land east of the railroad with two houses on it. Foy moved into one house, and Bud moved into the other. They were still able to stay off the soup line.

In 1936, the family built a new home where the old house had stood. It was beautiful, roomy, and comfortable. With the addition of a layer of siding, and later a layer of brick, it stands today very much as it did when it was built. It is now referred to as the "old home place." The new house provided a happy landing. The old one was cold, drafty, and very uncomfortable.

It was in the depths of the Depression that a new member was born into the Abbott family, a baby boy, Don. He was welcomed by the family, but they wondered how they were going to feed him. Roosevelt's New Deal was working by the time the war broke out in 1941. The big family problem was no longer how to make a living; it changed to how to educate the boys. This problem was at least partly solved by their Aunt Vera, a teacher at Birdville, who took them to school with her so she could watch over them.

During the late 1930s, money began to flow more freely, and the Lord was good to the Abbott family. A farmer, Jess Hall, had given Foy a truck early in the Depression. Another friend, Ray Thomas, helped Foy to buy a dump truck and gave him a job hauling gravel. Later, Foy and his partner, Earl Newman, built a concrete, gravel, and "petunia sand" business.

Foy and Earl operated this business until Foy had a heart attack. They sold the business in 1953. Soon after selling, Foy created an investment and finance business for himself. He operated this business the rest of his life. It was during these years that Foy acquired the corner lot on Rufe Snow Drive and Grapevine Highway in NRH where he built a place of business for the boys when they finished their formal training. He also built himself an office, which he kept until his death.

Back - Tommy Jr., Melody, Front - Dr. Tommy Abbott Sr., Pearl

Foy was active in civic affairs. He was most proud of the Fort Worth Christian School, which he cofounded. The school had a direct effect on some lawless activities that were taking root in the Smithfield area.

After finishing high school at Birdville, Tommy and Don both wanted to be doctors. Tommy enrolled in Texas A&M to study veterinary medicine. After six years of preparation, he accepted his new animal clinic in NRH from his dad.

Don chose to do premedical work at Texas Christian University. Tommy decided to join Don at Southwestern and apply his skills to healing the human race rather than animals.

The Vietnam War interrupted Don's last year of residency, so he enlisted in the Air Force. After his military service, he returned to St. Paul's Hospital in Dallas. Both boys specialized in internal medicine, surgery, gynecology, and obstetrics. They set up their office in the clinic Foy had built for them. Tommy is still doctoring out of the original building. Don built a clinic just north of the old building on Rufe Snow Drive.

Back - Ann, Philip, Front - Dr. Don Abbott, Arvetta

Beginning in 1932, the Abbott family attended the Smithfield Church of Christ for 50 years. Foy was an elder there for 41 years. His sister, Vera, taught the young people. Foy taught the boys music and singing.

The city of North Richland Hills and the Abbott family practically grew up together. The family hopes it has contributed to the colorful life of the growing young city.

Submitted by Vera Abbott Redding

WALTER AND MARILYN ACUFF

Walter and Marilyn Acuff were married November 4, 1951, in Fort Smith, Arkansas. They currently reside in the Meadow Lakes area of North Richland Hills.

Walter, a true Texan, was born in Mineral Wells, educated at their schools and went to Weatherford College after a tour in the U.S. Army during the Korean War.

Marilyn met Walter while he was stationed at Fort Chaffee, Fort Smith, Arkansas, and they moved back to Texas to settle down to married life. They have four wonderful girls, all living in the Mid-Cities area, and nine grandchildren.

Walter and Marilyn Acuff

Submitted by Marilyn Acuff

DAVID ALLEN

David Gibson Allen, son of O. D. and Joyce Simmons Allen, was born March 8, 1954, in Alameda, Calif. He grew up in North Richland Hills on Briley Drive. He graduated from Richland High School in 1972, and the University of Texas at Austin in 1976 with a bachelor's in business administration. He has two sisters, Vickie Lynn Allen and Marsha Weast Gibson, who is married to Danny Gibson. The Gibsons have two children, Brendon and Brittany, ages 7 and 2.

David's family moved to North Richland Hills because the area offered new homes, and several American Airline employees lived in the area. The Allens are members of North Richland Hills Baptist Church.

David has been employed for 20 years at R. E. and Securities Investments. He has a Texas broker's real estate license and belongs to the Texas Association of Realtors and the National Association of Realtors. He has been a member of the board of directors of Tarrant County Harvest, an organization that distributes food to those in need. He also served two years on the NRH Parks and Recreation Board. During this time, the board was instrumental in the co-op agreement between NRH and the Birdville Independent School District in developing the tennis center at Richland High School. David is also a member of the U.S. Professional Tennis Association.

David remembers growing up in NRH where he spent the long, hot summer days hunting in the area where the Diamond Loch Addition is located, and swimming at Barrbrook pool. He particularly remembers Jane and Burt Burleson on Dawn Dr. Their son, Rick, called and invited David over on the Fourth of July for homemade ice cream. This was at a time in David's life when he could have chosen the wrong path. Instead, the invitation led to a great lifetime friendship, plus the confidence and self-worth needed to travel the good path of life.

AUBREY AND DOROTHY ALLRED

Aubrey and Dorothy Allred, along with their two sons, Aubrey Jr. and Ronnie, moved to Oakland Lane in North Richland Hills in July 1958. Dorothy was expecting their third son, David. New homes were being built on Winnell Way and Oakland Lane with vacant fields to the north. The homes of the field rats and skunks, as well as squirrels, were being invaded by the building of new homes. Most of the families were in their 20s, with a scattering of older couples in the neighborhood.

Front-Lance, Aubrey, Dorothy, Alexis (in lap), Sandy, Michelle (in lap), Ashlea back-Ronnie, Lisa, Aubrey Jr., David

There was only one elementary school in the area, North Richland Elementary, later named Alliene Mullendore Elementary, located not too close to their home. The Allred family was pleased when Snow Heights Elementary was built and completed before Aubrey Jr. started first grade.

The Allred family placed their church membership with the Richland Hills Church of Christ in March 1959. Their sons and their families also are members and attend the church.

Aubrey M. Allred was born in Fort Worth in 1931. He loved to fly and at the age of 15 took flying lessons at Meacham Field. He first soloed and received his wings at the age of 16. He married Dorothy Lindsay in August 1948 in Weatherford, Texas. Their first child, Aubrey Jr., was born in September 1953. Their second son, Ronnie, was born in January 1956, and third son, David, was born in October 1958.

Aubrey served in the U.S. Air Force during the Korean War and was stationed at Carswell Air Force Base in Fort Worth. He worked for Swift and Company Packing Plant for eight years before going into business for himself operating a printing plant. Aubrey ran for City Council in NRH, along with Ray Whaley, who was running for mayor in 1961. Aubrey belonged to the Kiwanis and Optimist Clubs in Fort Worth. He coached a Little League Baseball Team in the Richland Youth Association and was involved with his sons' baseball activities. He, along with three other friends, owned and enjoyed flying a 1965 Cessna 172 airplane, which was kept at Mangham Field in North Richland Hills. He has invented a baseball batting machine and a dampening system for the Hamada printing press. Aubrey now loves being a granddaddy to four grandchildren.

Dorothy Lindsay Allred graduated from Paschal High School in Fort Worth. She worked for Texas Refinery Corporation, then called Panther Oil & Grease, prior to becoming a mother in 1953. After the birth of her children, she became a member of the Snow Heights Pre-School Association and the PTA.

Aubrey Jr. graduated from Texas Wesleyan College and currently lives in Bedford with his wife, Sandy, and two daughters, Ashlea and Michelle. He works in insurance sales. Ronnie also attended Texas Wesleyan and works for Ozarka Water Company in Dallas. He and his wife, Lisa, live in NRH with their son, Lance, and daughter, Alexis. David graduated from the University of Texas in Austin and is a Certified Public Accountant with his own business in Fort Worth. He is single and lives in NRH.

Submitted by Dorothy Allred.

JAMES EDWARD AND LINDA KAY ALREAD

James Edward Alread was born November 12, 1943, in Los Angeles, California, and moved to Fort Worth at the age of 2. His parents are Helen Pemberton Alread and the late Luther Cameron Alread Sr. He has one brother, Luther Cameron Alread Jr.

James Edward went to Oakhurst Elementary, Riverside Junior High, Carter-Riverside High School, and the University of North Texas. He played on the baseball, football, basketball, and tennis teams in high school. In junior high, he played in the city tennis finals. He began to play softball with Smithfield United Methodist

Eddie, Scott, Kay, Stephanie, and Garrett Alread

Church's first softball team in 1963–64 and continued to play every year until 1993. He thoroughly enjoyed his 30 years of involvement with this sport. The team played in Hurst before North Richland Hills had a softball program.

Linda Kay Brown was born July 12, 1944, in Fort Worth and lived in Smithfield most of her life. Her parents were Burney Calloway Brown and Louise Quayle Brown. She has one sister, Shirley Brown Newman. She attended Smithfield Elementary and was in the first graduating class of Richland High School in 1962. She met Eddie Alread in 1947 in Sunday school at Smithfield United Methodist at the age of 3. The class was taught by Helen Alread, Eddie's mother, and future mother-in-law of Linda Kay. Eddie and Linda Kay dated in high school and throughout Eddie's college years at North Texas State. They married in 1966, and two years later made their home in the Riverside area of Fort Worth. In 1968, they built their home on Newman Drive, in NRH. Their son, Scott Edward Alread, was born August 29, 1969. In 1979, Kay went to work as the school secretary at Smithfield Elementary. That was an especially interesting job for her since she, her sister, both her parents, and her son attended this school. She has been a school secretary for 19 years. Eddie has enjoyed a 32-year career with Mrs. Baird's Bakery in sales supervision and transportation.

Eddie and Kay are lifetime members of Smithfield United Methodist Church. They have served on numerous committees and held positions on the church board.

The Alreads enjoy traveling when time permits and being with their family. Their special interest, as of this writing, is being first-time grandparents to Garrett. He is such a wonderful addition to their family.

When the Alreads built their home in Smithfield, now North Richland Hills, in 1968, the land around them was mostly pasture. So many changes have taken place over the last 31 years, but it still remains a great place for their family to live.

Submitted by Kay Alread

EUGENE AND MARTINE ANDERSON

Eugene Rayford Anderson and Martine "Mer" King were married January 14, 1933, and had seven sons. Their lives were filled with many family activities. After the death of Gene's dad, Jim Anderson, in 1936, Gene's mother, Hattie Arwine Anderson made her home with Gene and Martine. She felt a strong commitment to the family and helped with the rearing of seven grandsons.

The Anderson and Arwine families had a long history on the land in Hurst and surrounding areas. Land for the Arwine Cemetery, located south of Pipeline Road and adjacent to Morrisdale Estates, was donated by Hattie's father for a cemetery, church, and school. The buildings are long gone, but the cemetery is one of the historical areas in northeast Tarrant County.

The seven Anderson boys, Gene, Bryan, Wendell, Alvin, Monty, and twins, Terry and Jerry, were raised on the 100-acre dairy farm located just west of the present Northeast Mall, bounded by the Bedford-Euless Road on the north and Pipeline Road on the south. The residence, dairy barn and other buildings were located about 500 yards south of the present Chili's Restaurant. The big two-story white house was torn down in the mid-1960s. Its center section was a log cabin. Dairy operations ceased when Loop 820 bisected the property.

In the late 1940s, Gene and Bryan herded cattle from their family farm to the farm of their grandparents in Hurst, now Highway 10. The route was east on Pipeline, south on Precinct Line, and east on Highway 183 to the original James and Hattie Arwine Anderson farm directly in front of the Kelley Moore Paint Company in Hurst. They would encounter only one or two cars on these trips.

A big event occurred on most Sunday afternoons after church. The Anderson boys constructed a ball field near the present Chili's site. Chicken wire was used for the backstop, and old plow disks were

Five of the seven Eugene Anderson sons: Alvin, Monty, Gene, Terry, Jerry; Front-Aunt Eva Portwood, Martine "Mer"(mother) Anderson, Aunt Georgia Ward

the bases. Gene learned to pitch both baseball and softball at this site. He later played for the Bryan Pelicans, but there were no big contracts then. Eugene (Big Gene) donated the site where Chili's is now located to Tarrant County for use as the Northeast Tarrant County Sub-Courthouse. The courthouse was subsequently moved to Hurst in about 1985.

Eugene, in addition to dairy farming, was involved in the early grading of roads on Strummer Drive as well as other streets in the area of North Richland Hills in the 1960s. After the farm was sold Eugene and Martine Anderson moved to 1,000 acres near Maypearl, Texas. A home was built on Lynn Terrace in NRH, on what was the southwest corner of the farm property. Martine now enjoys retirement living in a nearby assisted care facility where she can enjoy frequent trips to Lynn Terrace to view the beautiful home and garden setting where Terry and Jerry Anderson live. The garden has been featured on the cover of the Dallas-Fort Worth *Home and Garden* magazine and in the *Fort Worth Star-Telegram*. Gene and Bryan Anderson are engaged in farming activities west of Fort Worth. Alvin resides in Richland Hills, Monty resides in Hurst, and Wendell died in the early 1960s. The family always had the welcome mat out for the entire family. Looking back over the years, the family recognizes it was always a very positive family that accepted progress.

Submitted by Gene Anderson

GENE RUFUS ANDERSON

Gene Rufus is the oldest of seven sons born to Eugene Rayphord and Mary Martine King Anderson. The name

Rufus comes from a family member on Martine's side of the family. Father Eugene was called "Gene" or "Big Gene," so the new baby was nicknamed "Little Gene" at birth. Little Gene's first word was "Mer" for mother. The name stuck. Martine even signs her original china and art painting with "Mer." Gene's second word was "Day" for daddy.

Gene and Becky Anderson at Texas A&M

Gene attended Birdville School, now Haltom, for 12 years from 1940 to 1952. He enjoyed playing high school sports but could not participate fully due to the chores associated with the family dairy farm.

Gene attended Texas A&M and received a degree in electrical engineering. Gene played snare drums in the band. A big thrill came in 1956 when, for the first time, while wearing Aggie senior boots, Gene stepped onto the Rose Bowl field in the band for the Aggies' initial football game of the year.

Gene met Rebecca Ann "Becky" Pack while attending Calvary Baptist Church in Bryan, Texas. He spotted her, a new girl in church, from his place in the choir and could hardly wait to meet her. They were married July 20, 1957.

Upon graduation from A&M., Gene was commissioned a second lieutenant in the Army. He went to flight school and became a helicopter pilot. He retired from the National Guard as a colonel after 35 years service.

Larry and Sherri (daughter) with Brandon and Baby Courtney

Gene has worked for Bell Helicopter for almost 39 years. In 1965, Gene was transferred, with his wife Becky, and 4 year-old daughter Sherri, to the Agusta Helicopter Company at Cascina Costa near Milan, Italy, to support electronic systems installed in Bell Helicopters. Sherri learned the Italian language while playing with the neighbor's children. She began her education in Italy's public schools, where she learned to write Italian before English.

Sherri is a cardiac care RN at Harris Hospital in Fort Worth. Her husband, Larry has a degree in law. They presently live near Weatherford. At the time of this writing, Kimmy Gene teaches in Bryan, and Tim is a senior at Texas Tech University and is chaplain of the Texas Tech Saddle Tramps, a prestigious spirit organization in Lubbock.

Tim and Kim Anderson

Gene and Becky enjoy raising Santa Gertrudis cattle and Peruvian Paso horses at the Anderson Arrowhead Ranch, located seven miles north of Weatherford. The Arrowhead Ranch borders a portion of Bryan and Jeanelle's Pecan Valley Ranch, also breeders of Peruvian Paso horses.

RAYMOND AND HAZEL ANDERSON

Raymond and Hazel Anderson and their two daughters, Avalon and Norma, moved to Haltom City from Louisiana in 1946. They had owned an automobile parts business in

Boyce, Louisiana, selling the business and moving to Texas because of their daughter's asthma. Raymond got a job as a salesman in the appliance department of Leonard's Department Store where he worked for six years. Utilizing the experience gained from his job at Leonard's, he opened a furniture business on Belknap Street in the early 1950s.

Hazel, Raymond, Avalon, and Norma Anderson

In 1952, Hazel read a newspaper real estate ad describing a two-and-one-half acre plot of land for sale in the country in northeast Tarrant County. The lot was located off Rufe Snow Drive on Harmonson Road, next door to the old Harmonson home place in North Richland Hills. The Andersons bought the land and moved there from Haltom City.

Avalon and younger sister, Norma, attended Birdville Junior and Senior high schools. Norma married Don Hunt, who is now retired from Arco Oil Company. Norma, who operated a beauty shop and sold cosmetics from a location within the family business complex, is also retired. Norma and Don Hunt have five children, all of whom attended Birdville schools. They are Shannon, Raeanne, Gary, Don, Callie, and Brandon. Shannon and Gary Don graduated from Haltom High; Raeanne, Callie, and Brandon from Richland High. Raeanne and her family live in Phoenix, but the other children still live nearby. Two grandchildren are being raised by the family. Daniel lives with Norma and Don, and Michael lives

Anderson Family Wedding-Ray, Hazel, Norma, Callie, Rae (bride), Grandma Hunt, Papa Hunt, (front) Brandon, Michael, Daniel (back), Don, Chris (groom), Gary

with Hazel Anderson. Daughter Avalon is also retired.

Raymond Anderson operated North Richland Furniture from 1954 until a few weeks before his death in June 1994, and Hazel has continued to run the store. Grandson Brandon Hunt helped her in the store for a year before he left to attend college. Now daughter, Norma, and son-in-law, Don Hunt, help out when needed. The Anderson family, operating one of the oldest businesses in NRH, has sold furniture to three generations of some families, and NRH has been their home for 45 years.

BENJAMIN F. ANDREWS FAMILY

Benjamin and Mary Andrews came to Texas in 1847 and lived at first close to Fort Worth, then settled on a farm near Birdville. They arrived and settled on the west side of Watauga Road, now Rufe Snow Drive, across from the Snow property. All the children were born in Texas except William P., who made the trip from Illinois with his parents. Mary Ray died in 1868.

On July 11, 1869, Benjamin was married for the second time to Miss Caroline Burgoon. She was born November 12, 1836, in Morgan County, Ohio, and was the daughter of Charles and Mary Giger Burgoon, who were both born in Baltimore. The Burgoon family came to Texas in a covered wagon, when Caroline was 15 and settled in the Grapevine area.

Benjamin Andrews, a brick mason, was also called Uncle Benny and constructed chimneys for the neighbors. After his death, Granny Andrews delighted in pointing these chimneys out to people, especially at the yearly birthday parties she had.

While Benjamin was away during the War Between the States, Caroline worked in the fields and kept the home together. The couple's only child, Charlie H., born April 3, 1874, married Lucy E. Merrell. Unfortunately, Caroline outlived her only son, Charlie, who died October. 3, 1911 and was buried in Birdville Cemetery. Caroline belonged to the Baptist Church in Birdville.

Benjamin served as a justice of the peace for his precinct. He belonged to the Smithfield Masonic Lodge and was a Democrat. Benjamin and Caroline are both buried in the Birdville Cemetery. He died July 2, 1894, and she died January 18, 1929.

Charlie H. and Lucy had six children: Charles H., Eli Merrill, Earl J., B. C., Lucille, and Carl Harry. Like his father, Charles belonged to the Smithfield Masonic Lodge, was a farmer and a Democrat. Charles belonged to the Woodmen of the World of Fort Worth.

In 1909 the Andrews Gardens well was dug and good water flowed from the 600-foot level. Earl Andrews' son, W. Don Andrews, stated, as children, they often visited with Rufe Snow. "He used to scold me for chasing his turkeys and told me they could be mean and to stay away from them."

The Andrews' land extended, for the most part, from Grapevine Pike to the present Loop 820, west of Rufe Snow Drive. Rufe Snow owned most of the land east of the present Rufe Snow Drive. Andrews Gardens became the present Harmonson Addition area.

Submitted by Don Anderson

W. DON ANDREWS

In March 1955, my brother Charlie and I opened the first modern service station in North Richland Hills. We sold Gulf products, and gas was 23.9 cents per gallon, going as low as 14.9 cents per gallon during a gas price war. It was a full service station where 5 gallons was an average sale and we had to clean the windshield. If the driver got out of the car we even swept the floorboard. $1.25 would get you a full detail wash inside and out and for an additional $1.25 we would grease the car. Oil sold for 40 cents a quart.

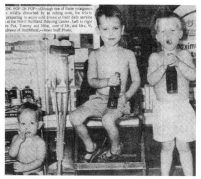
Enjoying cold drinks at Andrew's Gulf Station about 1955, Pat, Tommy, and Mike

Some of our best customers were Mr. and Mrs. H. L. Arnold, of the H. L. Arnold Construction Company, who had been contracted to build our gas station. Then there was, of course, Ruth and Clarence Jones, who came in real often. Once Clarence pointed to the shopping center and made the statement that it was his, and that up to that time he had not had to borrow money to build it.

My great-grandfather, Benjamin F. Andrews, was among the first settlers in what is now northeast Tarrant County. He arrived and settled on the west side of Rufe Snow Drive, across from the Snow property. As children, we often visited Rufe Snow. He used to scold me for chasing his turkeys and told me they could be mean, and to stay away from them.

The Andrews' garden well, in what later became the Harmonson Addition, was dug in 1909. At 600 feet it flowed with good water, according to my father, Earl J. Andrews. This well and the house were located just about where the Rufe Snow Drive NRH water tower is located. Both my father and his father, Charles H. Andrews, were born there. Dad had four brothers and a sister, Mrs. Lucille Eaton. The Andrews family plot is in the old Birdville Cemetery. The oldest grave there, bearing the Andrews name, is dated in the year 1851.

Submitted by W. Don Andrews

LARRY DON AND BARBARA ANN BRIGHT ARNHART

The family of Larry Don and Barbara Ann Bright Arnhart moved to North Richland Hills from the southwest side of Fort Worth on May 30, 1969. Their new home was locat-

ed on Susan Court. Larry was born July 12, 1940, in Oilton, Creek County, Oklahoma. Barbara Ann Bright Arnhart was born July 13, 1937, in Hobbs, Lea County, New Mexico. They met in Abilene and were married May 27, 1961, in Eunice, New Mexico. Larry's son, Michael Don Arnhart, was born September 23, 1957, in Hobart, Oklahoma. He came to live with the family in 1970.

Larry Arnhart

Thomas Randall Arnhart was born June 11, 1962, in Salina, Kansas, and his sister, Laura Jane Arnhart was born June 18, 1963, also in Salina.

Ann Arnhart

Larry graduated with a business administration degree in marketing in May 1967 from Texas Tech University in Lubbock. He received a master's degree in 1974 from Southern Methodist University. Ann received a business administration degree in economics in June 1959 from Hardin-Simmons University in Abilene.

Their son, Mike, was a 1975 graduate of Richland High School and a member of the Rebellaires singing group. Son Randall, was a 1980 graduate of Richland High School where he was student body president. He received a degree in accounting in December 1985 from Baylor University in Waco, and received his CPA certificate soon after. Daughter Laura, was a 1981 graduate of Richland High School where she was captain of the girls' tennis team. She attended two years at Stephen F. Austin State University at Nacogdoches.

Mike Arnhart

Larry was an administrative manager for IBM and is now a self-employed painting contractor. Ann is a personnel program manager for the Federal Aviation Administration, Southwest Regional Headquarters in Fort Worth. She has been with the federal government for 33 years—the last 27 years with the FAA.

Randall Arnhart

Larry played football for Texas Tech and was in the U.S. Air Force from 1960 to 1964. All of the family were members of North Richland Hills Baptist Church where Ann has been a member of the choir since 1973. Larry and Ann were divorced on May 28, 1976. Ann resides in NRH.

Mike lives in Arlington and is a

Laura Arnhart

foreman for Austin Road Construction. He is married and has one son. Randall is comptroller for Martex-Gibson Oil Company in Marshall. He is married and has four sons. Laura is a dispatcher in the National Service Center for IBM in Dallas. She is married and lives in Arlington.

Submitted by Ann Arnhart

HOLLIS AND CLYDIA ASKEW

In May, 1955, my husband, Hollis (deceased 1980), my children, Mike, 6 years old, and Vicki Lynne (deceased 1976), 1 year old, and I moved to North Richland Hills. Our third child, Michele, was born there in 1966.

Mike and Vicki (Watt) Askew

In the 17 years we lived in NRH before moving to Bedford in 1972, many changes were made as the city grew rapidly. We still attend church in North Richland Hills and have many happy memories associated with it.

I felt as if I had really come home when we moved from the Riverside area to NRH as I had grown up in Haltom City and graduated from the original Birdville High School. My children had several of the same teachers I had in school, and I renewed friendships from my school years.

We were fortunate to help organize a new Methodist Church, Davis Memorial, and were a part of two new schools. Mike started first grade at North Richland Elementary the year it opened. NRH students attended Glenview six or eight weeks until North Richland Elementary was completed. Mike also attended North Richland Junior High the first year it opened.

Clydia Askew and grandchildren back, L/R-Amy, Clydia, Jason Askew; front-Morgan and Austin PettyJohn

It was exciting to be a part of the first library in the city. I served on the Library Board, was a "story lady" and weekly volunteer. Vicki Lynne and I, with the youth from our church, worked on book drives, sorted, cataloged, and shelved books before the library opened in Richland Plaza. I was also privileged to serve on a panel for Town Hall meetings where changes taking place in the city were discussed.

Many special and important things happened in our lives in our time in NRH, the most important being the lifelong friends we made through our involvement in

Michele (Askew) and Stayton PettyJohn

church, school and community activities; friends who were, and still are, there for us in the good times and bad times.

Mike and Vicki Lynne graduated from Richland High School. Michele graduated from L. D. Bell High School.

Mike is married to Vicki Watt Askew, who also grew up in NRH. They have two children, Amy, 25, and Jason, 22. Michele is married to Stayton PettyJohn and has two children, Morgan, 6, and Austin, 3.

Submitted by Clydia Askew

STARLINE SR. AND MARY AUTREY

In 1974 my husband and I moved our little family to the city of North Richland Hills. As former residents of Fort Worth, we were anxious to make our home in a smaller town where we had the right and the privilege to choose the schools which our children, then 3, 5, and 7 years of

Melissa, Starline, Kevin, Mary, and Starline Jr. Autrey

age, were to attend.

We enrolled our oldest boy, Starline Jr., and our youngest son, Kevin, in Holiday Heights Elementary. In a few years our daughter Melissa would follow. All our children attended North Richland Junior High School and graduated from Richland High School in the classes of 1986, 1987, and 1990.

In 1977, my husband, Starline Sr., began to work for the Birdville Independent School District as their only electrician. Later, he became maintenance supervisor over all the trades. He presently holds the position of maintenance supervisor over the technical trades and is the master electrician for the district.

Our oldest son, Starline Jr., is now married to the former Janie Weatherby. They have a daughter, Rachael Elizabeth, and reside in the neighboring town of Euless. Our youngest son, Kevin Lee, is married to the former Sharon Gerhardt, also a Richland graduate of the class of 1990. Our daughter, Melissa Lynn, is single and works for a security and brokerage firm in Dallas.

My husband and I are members of Glenview Baptist Church. We enjoy our home in NRH and spend our free time fishing, gardening, and traveling.

Submitted by Mary Autrey

KYLE AND KIM BACON

Kyle and Kim Bacon moved to North Richland Hills in 1983 with their two sons, Jeffrey and Eric. Their first home here was located on Newcastle Place. At this time, Kyle was employed as an architect with SHWC, Inc. in Las Colinas. Kim was a homemaker, caring for Jeff, age 4, and Eric, 1.

Jeffrey entered kindergarten at Foster Village Elementary the following fall. Kim became active in the PTA and served in several offices, including PTA president for two years. Kyle was an active father, serving as Jeff's Cub Scout den leader for two years, and coaching Eric's soccer team for several years.

In 1990, Kim went to work for the Birdville Independent School District, first as the receptionist at the administration building, then as an elementary school secretary at Snow Heights in 1991. She continues in this position today.

In 1992, the Bacon family moved to their second home in NRH, located on Parkwood Drive. They continue to reside there today.

SHWC Inc. reorganized, moved to Dallas and became SHW Group. Kyle became a vice president and in 1997 opened the Tarrant County office of SHW Group on Rufe Snow Drive in NRH. He is currently working as project architect on many of the BISD school additions and renovations, including the third Birdville high school.

Jeffrey attended Foster Village Elementary, North Ridge Middle School, and graduated from Haltom High School in 1997 with a 3.9 grade point average. He had been active in the Pride of Haltom High Marching Band, serving as a drill leader for two years and playing the mellophone and French horn. Jeffrey was awarded a scholarship to Austin College in Sherman, where he is presently enrolled. Eric attended Foster Village Elementary, North Ridge Elementary, North Ridge Middle School, and is now a freshman at Haltom High School. He is active in the Haltom High soccer program and also plays select soccer for the NRH Area Soccer League. Kyle is currently serving on the Site-Based Team of Haltom High School.

Kyle and Kim met while working at Six Flags Over Texas. They are both graduates of Trinity High School. Kyle is a graduate of Texas A&M. They were married September 27, 1975. Their first child, Jeffrey Kyle, was born July 22, 1979, in Bryan, Texas, and Eric Scott joined the family August 8, 1982, in Plano, Texas.

MARION H. AND HELEN BAKER

It all began in 1958 when fate led us to the suburban area of North Richland Hills. We found a house that provided a large play yard with a school within walking distance. There were families living close around that had children so Phillip (then age 11) and Beverly (then age 4) could have playmates. We were so fortunate to find and settle in a house on Blaney next door to the Ray Davis family. They had three children, Mary Grace (Gracie), Ray Jr. (Bubba), and in 1959 came Donna. SuAnn Marie came to the Baker family in 1959. Also on the block, across the street, were two young boys at the Edwards (Larry and Ronald). On the corner of Blaney and Riviera lived the Kaisers with son Charles and Beverly, a daughter. These children were

older than ours. Up the street toward the south lived the Haglers who had Darla and Clifford. Darla was close to Beverly's age. They became close school friends. Yes, indeed, we had chosen well. The street had lovely children and great and congenial parents.

Donna Davis and SuAnn Baker became very close friends and regularly walked to and from Snow Heights Elementary together. Bubba and Phil bonded well from their very beginning, sharing rides, scouting experiences, school activities. The young boys on the block had a Boy Scout troop. Clinton Edwards was their scoutmaster, and Marion Baker took his turn also. Projects in our kitchen included candle making for Christmas presents. We used milk cartons, mixing bowls, and many other interesting shaped containers to mold them. By the time we had embarked on these projects Phil was about 13 years old.

The above has revealed why we are here—the tale of many years ago. Not too long into the time here, Blaney ended at Riviera. There was a barbed-wire fence across where Blaney would later continue. Our little black cocker, who ran wild in the neighborhood, would go through the fence at the end of the street, and as she would run through the grass her hair would fill with cockle burrs. The streets were rough. Houses began to be built around us and up the hill. The community was busy and buzzing. Most of the mothers on our block had gone to work during the days. The house across the street from us had been built and was occupied by Barbara and Jack Carr. Jack's work attracted Phil because he worked in radio electronics, an interest Phil continued on into his Navy career.

After 40-plus years we are still proud to be part of the Blaney Street area. The majority of the residents are old-timers. SuAnn played with the little girl that the Carrs adopted and fell in love with the house where they lived. She had always thought of living there. When she got older she bought the house. Phil lost his life in the Navy while stationed in Okinawa in 1972. Beverly is married, and she and her husband are living in Fort Worth. The street is still home to everyone, it is still a super group of people, so quiet and dignified. We are so thankful to our neighbors for making our 40 years here so pleasant.

Submitted by Helen Baker

ORIS AND ANN BALDWIN

After three years of marriage living in rent houses, we built our present home on Mackey Drive—one of the first houses on the block—and moved in September 1959. Our daughter Tracye was only 2 years old. Jo Shannon and Bart were born during the next four years so they have known no other home. How fortunate we were that they could walk to Snow Heights and North Richland Junior High with their friends.

The Snow Heights Preschool organization was one of the greatest groups going for this area. We met the parents of our children's friends and formed life-long friendships. People today snicker when I mention my "preschool" bridge club!

Tracye remembers when, at 13, we took her to apply for a job at the very popular snow-cone stand on Blaney by the old post office and they didn't hire her because she was left-handed. They didn't have left-handed equipment! She now is an RN at Harris Hospital and works with cancer patients. She and her husband, Brad McNulty, have a 13-year-old daughter, Erin, who attends Richland Hills Middle School, and son Sloan, 8, who is at Richland Elementary.

When in the first or second grade, Jo Shannon (along with Dad Oris) helped me install the Snow Heights PTA officers by singing "Harper Valley PTA." I had to call the incoming president to assure her we were not talking about her in "miniskirts" (which she wore very nicely!). Jo Shannon and her husband, Troy Hopson, live nearby in NRH, and she still entertains with Dad Oris and enjoys helping plan Richland High reunions with her school friends.

Bart stays busy being creative in construction and playing with daughters Kendall, 12, a student at North Richland Middle School, and Kelsey, 9, who attends Holiday Heights.

Along with his entertaining and being choir director in six large churches in Fort Worth and Hurst these 43 years, Oris has taught piano and voice to many of our youth. It is rather embarrassing when people come up and say, "You taught my mom or dad," or "You taught me, and I want you to teach my child," and I have to immediately tell them how young I was back then!

Choosing NRH as our home was one of the smartest and luckiest decisions we ever made, and we are grateful for the good life it has given us. We do often wonder, though, when we look across at the Meadow Lakes Addition west of Rufe Snow, why we didn't buy some of those acres of field at $350 "back then"!

Submitted by Ann Baldwin

VANCE C. AND SUE BALDWIN

Vance Clifton Baldwin was born in 1922 in south Fort Worth. The Baldwins had originally settled in the Glenwood area of Fort Worth in 1896. One sister, Katheryn, preceded Vance by two years. The happy family later moved to the Polytechnic area of Fort Worth where more children joined the ranks. Bill B. Baldwin was born in 1924, H. E. Baldwin in 1928, and Robert N. Baldwin in 1935.

Vance was drafted into the armed services in 1942 where he became a medical technician. He was later assigned to the naval ship, USS Comfort, on which he served in the South Pacific. His ship took a kamikaze attack in 1945. After the war, Vance returned to Fort Worth where he worked in

Michael, Sue, and Vance Baldwin

the floor covering and drapery business for several years.

In 1947 Vance attended North Texas State University where he majored in pre-med. He graduated in 1950 and placed an application at Southwestern Medical School in Dallas. He was given serious consideration but was not chosen, as the competition was fierce. As luck would have it, he was directed to the public school system to become a science teacher. He was hired to teach science for the Birdville Independent School District by Superintendent Wylie G. Thomas. After several years of teaching science, Vance took over the duties of principal at Birdville High School. He later became a general administrator for the school district. Vance retired in 1985.

In 1959 Vance married Alice Sue Lindsey, who was a homemaking teacher at Haltom Junior High School. Sue is a native of West Texas, having been born in Eliasville. She started her teaching career in Delwin, Texas, where she experienced fall cotton picking with her students. She later taught junior high school in Breckenridge. She moved to Haltom City in 1951, where her sister, Ruth Allen, was teaching.

In 1961 Sue and Vance built their current home on Tourist Drive in NRH. Another change was on the horizon when Sue became a full-time mother. Michael C. Baldwin was born in the fall of that year. Michael graduated from Haltom High School in 1980. He received his degree in business administration, specializing in finance, from the University of North Texas.

The family enjoyed outdoor activities together, as they traveled over the United States and Canada in a travel trailer. Several trips were also made abroad, including a trip to Europe when Michael was only 18 months old. Sue's relatives, who resided in Bordeaux, France, at the time, took care of him while Sue and Vance frolicked around Europe. The family has had their membership in St. Luke United Methodist Church of Haltom City since 1972.

Submitted by Vance Baldwin

K. D. AND RUBY BELL
CHILDREN: KING AND BOBBY

My family moved to Smithfield in 1934, from Handley. I was almost 7 years old. My father, K. D. Bell Sr., was raised near Smiley, Texas, just south of Gonzales. My mother, Ruby Machechney, was born and raised in San Augustine, Texas. My brother, Bobby, is two years younger than I am.

Smithfield had no electricity, no gas, no city water system or sewer. The school did have its own water source, a deep well of good, soft water. Some of the area residences were connected to that system. We were one of those fortunate few.

My dad had a pretty good job with Armour and Co., but he also wanted to raise some chickens just as his parents and brothers did back in Smiley. We had moved onto a small farm of seven or eight acres just north of the railroad tracks on Smithfield Road. Currently, Smithfield Station sits on that property. My mother, my brother, and

I took care of the farming chores while Dad was at work.

As we became friends with our closest neighbors, we also came to know most of the people within a two-mile radius of the town. Our closest neighbors were the Scott, Autry, and Gilbert families. Other town family names included Snider, Parkman, Hay, and Palmer. Still others were the Berry, Cobb, Zartman, Abbott, and Tarwater families.

The school at that time had one main building for all grades except the first grade, which met in a separate little house. There was also a separate gymnasium building. A lot of basketball was played in that gym. I remember at least one donkey basketball game there. The Halloween carnival was one of the many community activities held in the gym. At the Halloween carnival some of us mean boys always had a little fun by blocking up one wheel on someone's car so that when they tried to leave the car wouldn't move because the wheel would spin.

In summer, on a Sunday afternoon, there was usually something going on downtown; either a baseball game across from Snider's store or a bicycle race down Main Street. Sam Snider gave away a soda pop or candy bar to the winner of the bike race. I usually could win if Dee Miller wasn't there. If he was there, no one else had a chance of winning. He was the fastest.

In the late '30s and for the next two decades, utilities gradually became available and Smithfield began to grow. Some time in the '50s, North Richland Hills became an incorporated city. Several people in Smithfield, old-timers, foresaw that Smithfield needed to incorporate to prevent being taken in by NRH. We did that, but it didn't last very long. There were some people who wanted to be part of NRH, because they had some property to develop and believed it would be more valuable if it were part of NRH. After some trying times and some hard feelings an election dissolved Smithfield as a town. Not long after, in the late '50s, most of the Smithfield area was incorporated into North Richland Hills.

In 1950, Patsy Daniel and I were married. Her father, Merrill Daniel, was originally from Collin County. Her mother was Allie Runyon. She was the next youngest of five children, two boys and three girls. Patsy and I have two children, Debra and Randy.

Submitted by King Bell

KENNETH AND DELORES BELL

We lived with our two young children, Mike and Debra, in the 1700 block of Mike Drive, a home we purchased in North Richland Hills in the middle 1950s. The population, as I recall, was something like 8,000 to 9,000. In the early 1960s, I was elected to the first of two terms as city councilman. The City Council I served on created the first Police Department for the city. Until then, the city had only one policeman, semi-official, whom the residents paid $1 a month for such protection as he could provide.

Our council also arranged the purchase of a new fire truck and otherwise encouraged the all-volunteer fire department. This council arranged the annexation of Smithfield as a part of NRH. Then, we renamed Smithfield Road to Davis Boulevard. City Hall and all city departments were located on Glenview Drive, which now is a senior citizen facility. Our council twice tried for approval of street drainage bonds, but could not obtain voter permission. The city, I believe, thought itself too rural for planning and taxes.

Rufe Snow Drive, in those days, was a lonely country road—hard to imagine now.

Submitted By Kenneth Bell

KERRY AND CAROL BENOIT

Kerry and Carol Benoit have lived in North Richland Hills for 20 years. They met and were married in Fort Worth. They have three children, Stephen, born in 1970, Michael, born in 1972, and Julie, born in 1977. Shortly after Julie's birth, they moved "out in the country"—north of Loop 820 on Hightower Street. They came home at that time down a pretty little winding country road named Rufe Snow. It was so quiet on their street that on many days not even one car would pass the house. It was a wonderful place to raise children and make a home. The area was still called "Smithfield" and had its own little post office.

Carol and Kerry Benoit

Several years after their move, NRH began growing, and its prosperity took its toll on the family's country living. They lost the beauty and peaceful existence but gained the advantages of nearby stores and businesses and wonderful new schools.

Stephen, Michael, and Julie all graduated from Richland High School. Stephen married Melissa Clark in 1992. He graduated from Texas Christian University with a degree in psychology, and they moved to Lafayette, Indiana, where he continued his education at Purdue. He earned his master's degree in behavioral sciences in 1994, and will receive his doctorate in learning and memory research in 1998. His desire is to teach in a university, and to conduct research. Melissa's degree, also from TCU, is in radio and television communications, and she currently works for the CBS affiliate station in Lafayette.

Michael graduated from Oklahoma Baptist University in 1994 with a degree in music, and married Victoria Secrist in 1995. Victoria also graduated from OBU with a degree in radio/television communications. Both are currently working on their masters' degrees at Southwestern Baptist Theological Seminary. Victoria hopes to work in the administration area of a church, while Michael plans to get his doctorate in music composition and is writing and arranging music. Julie Benoit is currently in her sophomore year at OBU, majoring in music and minoring in public relations.

The Benoits have no grandchildren as yet. Kerry has worked at W. W. Grainger for 30 years as an account manager. Carol recently retired after working as preschool minister at North Richland Hills Baptist Church, where they have been members for 20 years.

BILL J. AND JOANNE M. BETTS

Bill J. Betts grew up on a farm outside of Naples, Texas, with his six brothers and six sisters. He graduated from Naples High School and also from Texas A&M, Commerce. Joanne Monds Betts was born in 1931, in Bonham. She graduated from Bonham High School, and later attended Texas A&M, Commerce.

Bill and Joanne were married in 1951, and moved to Ken Michael Court in North Richland Hills in 1956. The first of their three children was Tracy Clyde Betts, born in 1953. He graduated from Richland High School and North Texas State University. Tracy married Carole Nink, and they are presently living in Garland with their three children, Weston Reed, Tanner Scott, and Samuel Cole Betts.

Nancy Jan Betts, born January 15, 1957, is now deceased.

Kay Lynn Betts, born in 1960, graduated from Richland High School. When Kay was in the sixth grade, she won first place in a contest for the naming of Richfield Park. Kay used the $500 prize for her freshman year at Texas Tech University, where she later graduated. In 1996, she married Les Jackson, and they presently live in Arlington.

Bill and Joanne were members of the Methodist Church "forever." They served their church in many positions: board of trustees, administrative board, and pastor-parish board. Joanne is a member of the Methodist Womens' Club, Oakcrest Womens' Club, and Hospital Auxiliary, while Bill was a member of the Home Builders' Association, Plasters' Association, and Diamond Oaks Country Club. He also served as chairman of the North Richland Hills Civil Service Commission. Bill was part owner of Leito Supply Company for 20 years before retiring in June 1992. Bill died February 10, 1995.

Joanne adds: "I have buried a child and a husband here, but I also have wonderful memories of a community of lovely people, good friends and neighbors . . . and a great place to raise children."

Submitted By Joanne Betts

W. A. "BILL" AND RUTH HODGES BLESSING

Ruth Hodges was born in Britton, Texas, March 20, 1911. Her father, Tom W. Hodges, was with the Fort Worth Police Department from 1920 until his retirement in the 1950s. Ruth graduated from North Side High School.

W. A. "Bill" Blessing was born in Shelbyville, Tennessee. Bill met Ruth Hodges at Trinity Methodist Church after he moved to Fort Worth. They were married March 15, 1933, and had two children, Walter Allen and Ruth Ann.

The Blessings moved to Haltom City in 1945 where

Mrs. Ruth Blessing's career in child-care spanned 42 years.

Mr. Blessing had a successful plumbing business. In 1953 they purchased land, with a house reported to be more than 100 years old, from Evanda P. Haltom. Their address was on Pipeline Road, Haltom City. Later, boundary lines were changed, and they were in North Richland Hills and their street became Glenview Drive.

Mr. Blessing was well known for his work with young people. He was a Boy Scout leader and Sunday school teacher at Trinity Methodist, St. Luke, and Davis Memorial United Methodist Churches. He was a member of the DeMolay, which awarded him the Legion of Honor and Chevalier Degree. The Northeast Optimist Club, which Mr. Blessing helped start, honored him for his services to youth by naming their facility on the Denton Highway the W. A. "Bill" Blessing Sport Complex after his death in 1981.

Ruth Blessing, with the help of her daughter Ruth Ann Kemp, opened the Blessing Nursery in their home, one of the first child care centers in the area. In June 1955 the nursery became The Hobby Horse Corral Inc. The school was first licensed for 26 children and had grown to the licensed capacity for 106 children by the time it closed.

The Blessings did not confine their interest to children enrolled at the Hobby Horse Corral. Mr. Blessing would arrange his work schedule so he could go to a school if a child needed a grandparent on the annual "Grandparent's Day." Ruth Blessing provided a free nursery for Davis Memorial United Methodist Church at the Hobby Horse Corral during the building of the church from 1959 to 1961, and continued to do so for a number of years after the building was completed.

Daughter Ruth Ann Kemp, grandson Kevin Kemp, Ruth Blessing at dedication of W. A. "Bill" Blessing Sports Complex

Mrs. Blessing was a pioneer in licensed child-care in Texas. In 1977 she received the Brous Award, a prestigious childcare award named after the late Mrs. H. B. Brous. She and her daughter were both active in the Texas Licensed Child Care Association. They both served as president of the association as well as most of the other offices. In appreciation for Mrs. Blessing's work the board of TLCCA in 1991 established an award to be presented to a member who demonstrated leadership, commitment, and support for the mission of TLCCA. The award was named the Ruth Blessing Award, and Mrs. Blessing was the first recipient. Ruth Ann received the award in 1993. Mrs. Blessing and Mrs. Kemp both served on many state level committees charged with the task of upgrading childcare in the state of Texas.

In June of 1995 Ruth Ann unexpectedly passed away. Her commitment to the children and desire to carry on the traditions of the school became even stronger. Mrs. Blessing, with the help of Ruth Ann's son, Kevin Kemp, carried on the family business.

The family had decided to close the school in October 1997 before learning of Mrs. Blessing's illness. Ruth Blessing died September 7, 1997. She had been working, as usual, only one week before her death.

The comfortable, rambling old house stands empty now, but the walls hold memories of three generations of happy children who will always remember the Hobby Horse Corral.

Story by Aline Parker

ROBERT H. AND MARIE BOCKMAN

Robert (Bob) Henry and Marie Bockman moved from Haltom City to North Richland Hills in 1964 with their children Linda Marie, 12, Debra Caroline, 10, Robert H. (Bobby), 7, and Teresa Ann (Terri), 3. The children attended North Richland Elementary (now Mullendore), North Richland Junior High, and Richland High School.

The intersection of Rufe Snow and Glenview was a four-way stop. There was a vacant lot where there is now a Domino's Pizza. The children used to play on the vacant lot. They frequented Richland Plaza Cinema, later a bingo game facility, played miniature golf at a course on the Grapevine Highway, and went swimming at Parchman's pool. Richland Plaza was the place to shop with Lerner's, Kresge's, Montgomery Ward, Penney's, Pancho's, and Carnation Ice Cream stores.

During her senior year at Richland High School, their oldest daughter, Linda, was killed while on a church hayride in October 1969. Robert (Bob) Bockman passed away in April 1973. Marie is a homemaker and continues to reside in the family home on Carma.

Debra resides in Hurst and has worked at the NRH Wal-Mart for 11 years. Bobby has been employed at Lockheed 19 years, and his wife Donna Dowty Bockman is employed by the Birdville Independent School

Back-Bob, Linda, Debra, Marie; Front-Terri and Bobby Bockman

District. Bobby and Donna reside in NRH with their two sons, Robert William, 10, and Thomas Mitchell, 8. Terri married Jamie Pipes in 1995, and has been employed by NCH Corporation for 14 years. Jamie is employed by Carswell Golf Course. They reside in NRH with their son, Bradley James, 2.

Submitted By Marie Bockman

DAVID AND DARLA BOSWELL

I was born at the Glenview Hospital in North Richland Hills in 1965. When I was growing up, we lived in the area called Smithfield. I remember the feed store, the barbershop, and the little store on the corner of Main Street and Smithfield Road.

I was fortunate enough to grow up with my grandparents living on one side of us and my aunt and uncle on the other side. I was able to grow up doing things that most of us would give anything for their kids to be able to do.

We could ride our horses from Eden Road all the way to Grapevine Highway to the old Circle H arena across from TCJC for their play days and rodeos. We could ride our bikes on all the trails and hills, or go "crawdad" fishing in the big pond, which is now North Park. Instead of selling just lemonade or Kool-Aid, we could sell jars and jars of wildflowers. They were the most beautiful flowers ever, and they were everywhere. If we really felt daring, we could play "chicken" with the bulls in the pasture behind our property.

I was lucky enough to be able to buy my grandparents' place and a few acres. My husband, David, and our children,

Back, L/R-Christopher, David, Tyler; Front, L/R-Darla, Taylor Boswell, and (nephew), Scott Harmon

Christopher, 14, Tyler, 10, and Taylor, 4, have lived here for six and a half years, and every spring I can still go down the street to the corner of Rumfield Road and Kirk Lane and see the prettiest bluebonnets God ever made.

Submitted by Darla Jean Boswell

EDWIN AND HAZEL BOWEN

In June 1957, my husband, Edwin Bowen, and I, with our two teenage sons, Edwin Don, 17, and Ted Wren, 15, moved from Boyd, Texas, to Winnell Way in North Richland Hills. Winnell Way was then the last street in NRH—nothing farther north.

In the fall, I began to teach at North Richland Elementary, which is now Mullendore. Ed was elementary principal at Pleasant Run, which is now Colleyville. Ted went to Richland Junior High and then finished in 1961 with the last class in Birdville High School. Ed retired from teaching, and we moved to Florida to teach for a year. I had a year's leave of absence from Snow Heights Elementary. We decided to stay in Florida to teach for a few years, but NRH would always be home. Our plans were suddenly changed when Ed died of a heart attack. We brought him home to Bluebonnet Hills Memorial Park, and I returned to Florida to finish my 10 years to qualify for Florida retirement.

Ed Bowen was born in Enloe, Texas in 1905, and died in 1976. He received his master's degree from Southern Methodist University in August 1940.

Edwin Don was born in 1940. He received both bachelor's and master's degrees from North Texas State University, served in the Air Force for 20 years and retired as a captain. He now works for the Defense Logistics Agency in Grand Prairie as a program analyst.

Ted Wren Bowen was born in Fort Worth in 1942. He received his bachelor's degree from Northern Illinois University. He did graduate work at the University of Ontario, Canada, and is speechwriter for the premier of Saskatchewan. He lives in Regina, Saskatchewan.

I, Hazel Wren Bowen, was born in Springtown in 1914. I taught at Snow Heights Elementary from 1958 until 1968. I thought all classes were outstanding. One school year I considered special was 1963–64. That was when President Kennedy was assassinated. A student (I wish I could remember who), left the room and returned to whisper to me that she had heard two teachers talking and the president had just been shot. I think that was so thoughtful that she didn't just announce it to all the children. Many good students were in that class, including two leaders in our city today. Mark Wood, who served three terms on the NRH City Council, and Michael Brinkley, who is a popular lawyer. Also in the class was Grant Lochridge, who was later to become Mark Wood's stepbrother. I wish I could name them all. We produced a patriotic program, and we had a lot of musical talent we used in that program. There was not a problem child in the group.

Submitted by Hazel Bowen, 1997

Hazel Bowen died February 26, 1998

HARRY AND DEBI BOWMAN

Harry L. Bowman was born July 13, 1942, to Harry and Callie O. Bowman in Washington, D.C. He had two brothers and two sisters Carl, Ernest, Carol, and Vivian. Harry grew up in Washington, D.C., North Carolina, and New Jersey. He graduated from high school in North Carolina and from Atlantic Business College in Washington, D.C.

Deborah N. Clark Bowman was born June 20, 1944, in Keokuk, Iowa, to Elbert and Opal L. Wright Clark. Debi grew up and went to school in Iowa and Minnesota. She had five brothers and four sisters.

Harry and Debi married June 25, 1966. They have two children. David A. Bowman, was born December 11, 1967, in Rochester, Minnesota. David went to Mayo High School in Rochester and the University of Iowa. He was drum major for two years in the marching band. Currently he teaches algebra at Richland High School. Their daughter, Michelle A. Bowman, was born July 2, 1969, in Rochester. She also attended Mayo High School and the University of Iowa. Michelle taught math for five years in the Birdville school system and is currently teaching math at J. Erick Jonsson Community School in North Oak Cliff in Dallas. Both David and Michelle have

Back-Harry; Center-David and Debi; Front-Michelle

been involved in writing curriculum for the Birdville Independent School District.

Harry and Deborah moved to the Eden Estates in North Richland Hills in April 1989 from Carrollton. After moving to NRH they joined the North Richland Hills Baptist Church where they both serve as Sunday school teachers. Harry is a church usher, and Debi is a member of the adult choir as well as a church soloist. She has traveled over the world, sharing the Gospel in song, and both have been involved in the Greater Fort Worth Christmas Pageant ever since they have been members of the NRHBC. Deborah has served on the NRH Teen Court and as a member of the Cable Board. She said "I believe I'm the first African-American woman to serve on NRH boards and commissions. The great things about living in NRH are the wonderful neighbors and friends we have come to know."

She and Harry both enjoy golf, many areas of their church work, and he is an avid photographer. David and Michelle both enjoy many sports, activities with their friends, and church work.

Submitted by Deborah N. Bowman

CHARLES AND POLLY BRINKLEY

Charles Clarence Brinkley was born in Weatherford in 1926, to Clarence E. and Helen M. Wilson Brinkley. Mary Pauline Cranford Brinkley was the youngest child of Lee A. and Pearl M. Gragson Cranford of Perrin, Texas, born in 1926.

Charles and Polly graduated from Weatherford College where they met and married September 12, 1945. Charles began his banking career in 1945 at the Merchants and Farmers State Bank in Weatherford. They continued their education at Texas Christian University in Fort Worth with Charles majoring in banking and finance, while Polly majored in elementary education with a minor in English.

Polly taught school at Aledo and Weatherford until their son, Charles Michael, was born December 2, 1952. She then became a full-time mother, substituting at elementary schools after Michael started to school. In 1951 Charles moved to the First National Bank in Weatherford as first vice president, and worked there until 1961. He then accepted the challenge to move to Fort Worth and help build Northeast National Bank, the first bank in North Richland Hills. The bank officially opened for business in 1962. It grew rapidly, and the building more than doubled in size by 1967, with a six-story addition constructed in 1978. Charles moved to Liberty Bank as chairman of the board in 1987. He continues to be involved in a growing community bank in NRH. Charles served as state vice president of the American Bankers Association from Texas for two years and membership chairman for two years. He is presently serving Texas Bankers Association as a member of the Federal Government Relations Network.

Michael, Polly, and Charles Brinkley

The Brinkleys are very active in their community. Charles has been active in Lions Clubs since 1951, with perfect attendance since joining. He is active in the local Northeast Richland Lions Club. Charles has served as president of the Chamber of Commerce and has worked with the Boy Scouts of America, YMCA, United Way, and many other civic organizations. He was town hall chairman for the committee to organize Tarrant County Junior College in 1963. Polly and Charles are two of the organizers of the NRH Library. Charles also serves as chairman of both the Industrial Development Board and the newly chartered Health Facilities Corporation of NRH. Polly has held numerous offices in the PTA and was presented a life membership in 1967. She has been

past president of the Birdville Unit of the American Cancer Society, volunteered for the March of Dimes, was past president of Fort Worth Bankers Wives Club, where she is an active 35-year member, and she continues to serve on the NRH Library Board.

Charles was asked by Mark Brooks and his mother, Paula Good, to chair the Brooks House Advisory Board. The Mark Brooks Foundation helps fund the Brooks House, an organization where troubled teens and their families go for help and counseling. The board is made up of 20 civic leaders in Northeast Tarrant County.

Charles and Polly were active members of North Richland Hills Baptist Church, with Charles serving as a deacon, Sunday school director-teacher and music director, and singing with a group of church members known as "The Kingsmen." Polly also worked with young people as department director, teacher, and choir member. They joined the North Fort Worth Baptist Church in 1985, and continue to serve by teaching, department directing, singing in the choir, serving on committees, and supporting children's work within the church.

Son, Charles Michael Brinkley entered Snow Heights Elementary School in 1961. He attended North Richland Junior High School and graduated from Richland High School in 1970. Michael graduated from law school at the University of Texas at Austin in 1977, and married Jane Ellen Wilson of Corsicana, Texas, on April 9, 1988. His law practice is located in NRH.

ALLEN BRONSTAD

I was born on March 23, 1923, at Cranfills Gap, Texas, to Otis and Selma Bronstad. I attended Cranfills Gap High School and graduated in 1941. I then attended Clifton Junior College and graduated in 1943 with an associate's degree. Clifton Junior College merged with Texas Lutheran University, and I am an alumnus from there.

I worked at the War Production Board in Meridian, Texas, for a short time. I was called to serve in the U.S. armed forces during World War II, but after reaching the induction center, I was rejected for medical reasons. I then worked for Cameron Lumber Company in Meridian for sev-

Allen and Willie Mae Bronstad, 1996

eral years. My next employment was with Arlington Heights West Construction Company in Fort Worth. After this, I worked for Tarrant County Water Supply Corporation from 1960 to 1967 as assistant manager. From 1967 to 1971 I was general manager, until the corporation dissolved and the four participating cities took over operation of the system within their own cities. In 1972 I transferred to the city of North Richland Hills, and while employed at the city, I held several positions.

While working at the War Production Board, I married my high school sweetheart, Willie Mae Murphree, on November 25, 1944. We have two grown children. Donna M. Boelter is the Science Department head at Seguin High School. Thomas L. Bronstad is vice president at Nations Bank in Dallas. We have four grandsons. Shannon Boelter is a student at the University of Texas at Austin; Grant Boelter attends the University of Southern California (USC football program); Jeff Bronstad is a student at UT-Austin; and Jason Bronstad is a senior at Bowie High in Arlington.

When I first started working in this area in 1960, it was mostly rural. I saw a great change from a small town to a rather large city. My, what a book I could write on my 25-plus years' tenure at this now thriving city from which I retired in April 1986.

Submitted by W. Allen Bronstad

BROOKS AND BOOTH FAMILIES

Roger Brooks was born and raised on a 200-acre farm located at the southwest corner of Rufe Snow Drive and Watauga Road. The farm was located in Watauga just across Rufe Snow Drive from the city of North Richland Hills. His father, Nat Brooks, purchased the farm, in 1918. Nat built a house on the farm in 1920 and married Effie Booth in 1922.

Effie Booth Brooks was born and reared in a house on a farm located on what is now the north side of the 6400 block of Glenview Drive. The house, as of 1997, is still standing and has been used for many years as a children's daycare center. Her father, Landon Booth, and mother, Minerva, owned about 200 acres of land, part of which is now the Diamond Oaks subdivision. Landon died at age 36 from pneumonia after participating in a cattle drive in the early 1900s. He was a cattleman, merchant, and early postmaster of the area, and his father, Madison Booth, was a pioneer of the Birdville area. These three generations of Booths are buried in Birdville Cemetery. Nat Brooks, who died in 1978 at age 90, is also buried in Birdville Cemetery along with his mother, Sue Johnson Brooks, and father, Jeff Brooks, and a brother and sister.

Booth-Calloway Road was named after Effie Booth Brooks' family and the Calloway family who were good friends of the Booths. Brooks Street in Richland Hills was named after Nat Brooks' family and close relatives.

Nat Brooks at various times worked for Rufe Snow on Rufe's farm on Rufe Snow Drive. Later, Nat bought and operated a threshing machine and harvested grain for many of the early farmers in the NRH area. In the late 1940s, Roger Brooks rode a motorbike along Rufe Snow Road from Watauga to Birdville High School. Roger remembers seeing Rufe Snow almost every morning, standing or sitting on the front porch of his home, which was located at what is now the southeast corner of Rufe

Snow and Shauna drives.

Roger Brooks began attending the Watauga School in 1939 when Watauga had its own school district. About 1944, the district was dissolved, and parts of it went to three other independent school districts, Keller, Smithfield, and Birdville. Roger attended the Smithfield School, which was on the site of the present Smithfield Elementary School in NRH. In good weather, Roger rode a horse the three miles to and from Smithfield School. He finished the ninth grade, which was the highest available class. Students graduating from the ninth grade usually finished high school at either Birdville or Amon Carter-Riverside. Beginning in 1947, Roger attended Birdville High School, graduating in 1950.

In the 1930s and 1940s, almost every man and boy in the Smithfield area got his hair cut at Barber Cobb's (Clarence Cobb) shop on Main Street in the town of Smithfield (now a part of NRH). It was always cut the same way, straight up the sides, rather short and nothing fancy. Barber Cobb also was a pretty good cow trader. People would drive up in front of his shop with an animal or two for sale in a trailer. Sometimes barber Cobb would leave you sitting in the barber chair, about half finished, and go out and dicker with the seller for several minutes. If a deal was struck, he would pull out a wad of cash from his pocket, pay the seller, and tell him to deliver the animal(s) to a small-acreage lot where he lived in town.

An "ice dock" was located across the street from Barber Cobb's shop. It furnished ice for area citizens who did not have a refrigerator and who needed ice for their home "ice boxes," which, like refrigerators, kept food from spoiling.

Roger Brooks' immediate family is his wife of 35 years, Dorothy Avera Brooks, a native of Lawton, Oklahoma, and their son Douglas Alan Brooks, 28, and his wife, Jana Dunkerley Brooks, both graduates of Texas Christian University. They currently reside in the TCU area of Fort Worth. Roger and Dorothy have lived in Keller since 1981 but have kept close ties and business relations in the city of NRH. Roger is a founding director of the Liberty Bank on Davis Boulevard in NRH, a member of the Smithfield United Methodist Church in NRH, and a member of the Northeast-Richland Lions Club.

Being a native and resident of the area since 1933, except for four years at college and four years in the Navy has been very interesting to Roger. He remembers visiting some of the "old-timers" here and like them has been amazed at what has happened to the area during these last 60 years. One of the old fellows was asked one time if he "had seen a lot of changes," and he said, "Yep, and I have been against almost every one of 'em."

Submitted by Roger D. Brooks

HAL AND PAULA BROOKS

Hal and Paula Brooks moved to North Richland Hills in 1959 where Hal became pastor of the North Richland Hills Baptist Church. He served the church as minister for 24 years. They moved from NRH in 1983.

Today, the W. Hal Brooks family, Paula, Kriss, and Mark, feel fortunate to have lived in a vibrant, progressive, optimistic community, surrounded by good friends and a loving, supportive church. They would learn just how special those days were in 1987, when their lives were changed with the death of Hal.

Paula still lives in the area with her husband, Glen Good. They built Good Place assisted living residences in NRH and are building an Alzheimer's facility to be located adjacent to Good Place. Paula was campaign manager for Kay Granger's successful bid for the U.S. Congress in 1996 and is currently serving as the U.S. Congressional District 12 chief of staff.

Kriss lives in Lipan, Texas, with her husband, J. D. Meeker, and their three children. J. D. is a coach and teacher in the Lipan School District. Mark and Cynthia and their two girls live in Fort Worth. Mark is a Professional Golf Association touring professional.

Hal and Paula were married in 1957 and moved to Fort Worth so Hal could study at Southwestern Baptist Theological Seminary. He had been a pastor in Irving when North Richland Hills Baptist Church called him to be their pastor, and the family moved into the church parsonage on Vance Road. Hal's hobby was building, so he immediately converted the parsonage garage into a family room.

During those early years, both the community and the church grew. When the Brooks family came to the church, all the young people could ride in one car. In just a few short years, the church had to charter several buses to transport the youth to camp. Throughout Hal's 24-year ministry, the church was always engaged in a building project.

When the time came to build a new sanctuary, the church decided to finance the construction by selling bonds. On the Saturday night before launching into the campaign in the Sunday morning worship service, Hal spent a sleepless night. During that night, he made a decision. He believed that the auditorium should and could be built by faith—as the people gave, appropriate construction would be completed. He notified the bond company not to come, and he shared his vision with the church. The membership agreed with his plan and committed to the task. Word quickly spread in the community, and the next day Hal received a call from Herman Smith, who was a member of a neighboring church. He was a builder and developer and advised Hal that the church would never be built this way. When Hal adamantly refused to move from his decision, Herman said, "When that auditorium is built without borrowing money, I'm taking you out to Grapevine Lake and watch you walk on water." Herman never forgot that statement and when the sanctuary was indeed completed, he invited some friends and arranged a trip to the lake.

Church members watched in eager anticipation as each phase of the project unfolded. Throughout various stages of construction, worship services were conducted on the concrete foundation. Hal designed the beautiful stained-glass windows while he was on one of his trips to the Holy Land. He visited a stained-glass window company and observed the scraps being discarded. He asked Bob Votaw, a church member and architect, to translate the pictures into mosaics. The windows were then made by church members using stained glass scraps. The center double-window of the church was created by college students under the direction of Mark Wood.

To celebrate Hal's and Paula's 10th anniversary in 1969, the church sent the family on a trip to Europe. Mark was 8 years old at the time and chose to stay with Paula's parents, Paul and Wilma Griffin, instead of going on the trip. That decision became the pivotal force in his young life, as this was the first time he picked up a golf club. Paula's dad cut off a club and took Mark to play on a three-par sand course a few miles outside of the small town of Cyril, Oklahoma. Mark later announced that he was going to be a professional golfer when he grew up. In the following years, a standing

Front-Kriss, Paula, Mark; Back-Hal

account was opened with a glass company, since so many windows in the neighborhood had to be replaced which were broken by Mark's stray golf balls.

In 1968, Paula began teaching speech at North Richland Junior High School. Mark and Kriss were students at the adjacent Snow Heights Elementary. When Paula moved to Richland High School in 1971 to teach drama, she did not know that one of her students, Cindy Spencer, would become her daughter-in-law. She had the lead in one of the musicals, *South Pacific*. After college, Cindy worked for RCA Records in Nashville as a publicist, and when Kriss graduated from college she found a job in Nashville and lived with Cynthia. When Mark went on the professional golf tour, he would stop by and visit, and subsequently married the girl next door. Kriss met her husband, J. D. Meeker, at Mark and Cynthia's wedding where J. D. played the piano.

Hal completed his doctor of ministry degree from Southwestern Baptist Theological Seminary, and Paula received a master's degree in communications from Texas Christian University. Paula taught communications at the seminary for a few years and in 1979 became the director of communications for the Birdville School District. Their lives revolved around the church, the school district, and their children's activities. Upon reflection, it seems that northeast Tarrant County was the perfect place for Hal to spend the years of his ministry.

Submitted By Paula Brooks-Good

BURNEY CALLOWAY AND LOUISE QUAYLE BROWN

Burney Calloway Brown and daughter Shirley Brown (Newman), 1943

Burney Calloway Brown was born September 9, 1902, in Smithfield, Texas. He was the son of Louia B. Brown and Halcie Calloway Hightower Brown. Burney helped his father and four brothers in the cattle business. They bred and raised purebred livestock and exhibited their short-horn cattle at Fort Worth's Southwestern Exposition and Fat Stock Show.

In 1925, Burney married Louise Quayle, born January 21, 1907, the daughter of Macon F. Quayle and Mittie Belle Mitchell Quayle of Smithfield, Texas. Both Burney and Louise attended Smithfield School. Burney and Louise married under a tree in Weatherford, Texas, rather than at home, as was the custom of the time. They made their home in the Riverside section of Fort Worth when first married, but later moved back to Smithfield where they lived with Burney's parents. Three daughters were born to this union. Joanne, an infant, died December 10, 1932. Shirley Louise was born August 14, 1935, and Linda Kay was born July 12, 1944. The Browns were members of Smithfield Methodist Church, and both were active in the Smithfield community.

Burney raised cattle and farmed the home place until 1946 when he bought 60 acres on a hill east of Davis Boulevard on Shirley Drive, south of Newman Drive. They built a new home, and Burney went into the dairy business there. At this time, Shirley was 11 years old and Linda Kay was 18 months. After several years, Burney developed a serious and disabling illness, and the Browns traded their farm for a home in Haltom City owned by Earl and Ada Newman.

Brown Family Picnic—L/R-Halcie, Burney, Beulah, Louise, Walter, Bob, Maurice Brown Jackson, Dr. A. F. Jackson, and Shirley Brown (Newman) in front

The Newmans would one day become Shirley's in-laws. At this time, Shirley was in high school (ninth grade) at Amon Carter Riverside, and Linda Kay was in first grade at Smithfield Elementary. To prevent Linda Kay being moved from familiar surroundings, her mother drove her to Smithfield from Haltom City each day to attend school. After two years in Haltom City, however, the Browns realized they belonged in Smithfield and moved back. They built a home at the corner of Lewis Lane and Newman Drive. By this time, Burney was working for Tarrant County's Precinct 3 County Commissioner Jess Holder and later for Commissioner Dick Lewis.

Louise was a homemaker and a salesperson for Jackson's and for R. E. Cox Department Store in Fort Worth. She was an accomplished seamstress. Louise was also a Tarrant County election judge in Smithfield, following in the steps of her father, M. F. Quayle. She was very active in the school, serving as PTA President, and in the church as president of United Methodist Women.

Burney died April 23, 1973. Louise died August 17, 1979. Both are buried in the family plot in Smithfield Cemetery.

Submitted by Shirley Newman and Kay Alread

CHARLES AND CARLYNE BROWN

Charles and Carlyne Brown were both born in Fort Worth and married in 1948 in Azle Avenue Baptist Church, the church where they met and their families were members. They lived in the TCU area for 10 years and started their family. They moved to North Richland Hills with their children in 1958. They had four children, Larry, 5, Garry, 4, Linda, 3, and Barry (now deceased).

Charles and Carlyne Brown, 1986

They wanted a good school system for their children and decided on the Birdville District. The family moved into their new and present home on Holiday Lane East. After checking out their school-planning program, they knew it was perfect for their children. Charles and Carlyne felt blessed by the Lord in this decision. The children attended Snow Heights Elementary, North Richland Junior High, and Richland High School—all within walking distance of their home.

Charles graduated from Northside High School in May 1946, and joined the U.S. Marine Corps for a two-year program with Marine aviation units and was honorably discharged after his duty was completed. Soon after his discharge, he went to work for General Dynamics Corporation (then Consolidated-Vultee) where he had a very successful career and retired in 1991 after 43 years of continuous employment. Charles also attended TCU, U.S. Marine Corps Institute, Arlington State College, and

Back-Larry; Middle-Barry and Garry; Front-Linda, 1983

the University of Michigan. He received several achievement awards from both General Dynamics and the military. He is also a retired senior member of the American Society of Quality Control, Air Force Association, and National Management Association. He also retired as a state certified and registered professional engineer in Quality Engineering. Charles is a Master Mason and member of Tarrant Lodge, Tarrant Chapter and Council, Scottish Rite of Fort Worth, and Moslah Temple Shrine.

Charles and Carlyne are members of the North Richland Hills Baptist Church where all of their children accepted the Lord and were baptized by Brother Hal Brooks. Larry is now a deacon at Richland Hills Baptist Church.

During their children's school years, Charles and Carlyne participated in the PTA, were Boy Scout leaders, and coached Little League baseball. All of their children were very active in their schools in football, baseball, softball, ROTC Drill and Rifle teams, and Dixie Belles drill team, plus other activities. After the children finished their school years, Carlyne went to work for Mr. Alan Hamm in the North Richland Hills Drugstore in the store's pharmacy where she spent a happy 10 years. She gained many friends and retired with a gift of an authentic string of pearls from Mr. Hamm.

Since their retirement, Charles and Carlyne have been traveling throughout the United States, Germany, Austria, the Czech Republic, etc. They are both life members in the Good Sam Travel Club and Coast to Coast Camping Club. They enjoy camping, bicycling, and traveling during their retirement.

LOUIA BERRY AND HALCIE CALLOWAY BROWN

Louia Brown was born in Liberty, Missouri, on July 31, 1857. Mr. Brown came to Smithfield, Texas, with his mother, Louisa V. Bailey Brown, at the outbreak of the Civil War in 1861, when he was 4 years old. His father, Louis E. Brown, owner of a large number of slaves, traveled at night to escape troopers who had captured his two brothers.

Louia Brown married Belle Brown on November 12, 1882. She died November 23, 1884,

Louia and Halcie Brown on their golden wedding anniversary, 1936

after giving birth to their son, Louis B. Brown Jr. Louia then married Halcie Calloway Hightower, daughter of Jim H. and Elizabeth Calloway Hightower, on September 3, 1886. To this union was born five sons. Morris Thomas Brown was born November 6, 1888, and died September 21, 1916. He married Gertrude Willis and they had one daughter, Maurice Brown. Roy R. Brown was born January 15, 1891, and died as an infant. Walter Hugh Brown was born August 20, 1892, and died May 14, 1955. He married Beulah Bailes, and they had two sons, Herman Brown and Robert Louia Brown. Raymond Berry Brown was born June 17, 1899, and died Sept. 21, 1945. He married Marie Morton and they had one son, Jerry Morton Brown. Burney Calloway Brown was born September 9, 1902, and died April 23, 1973. He married Louise Quayle, and they had three daughters, Joanne Brown, who died as an infant, Shirley Louise, and Linda Kay Brown.

L/R-Walter Brown, Cecila Brown, Louise Quayle Brown, Burney Brown, Marie Morton Brown, Louise Brown, Raymond Brown, Bob Brown, friend

Mr. Brown began his business career as operator of a drugstore in Smithfield. With the arrival of the Cotton Belt Railroad in 1886, Mr. Brown established a general mercantile store. The community then moved about a half mile to be closer to the railroad. Mr. Brown, along with two other men, contributed to the construction of the first school building in the community of Smithfield.

In 1898, Louia retired from the mercantile business and moved to his 350-acre farm. The farm was bordered, approximately, by what would today be the present Mid-Cities Boulevard on the south, Rufe Snow Drive on the west, Chapman Street on the north, and somewhere in the vicinity of Smithfield Road on the east. He then became interested in the breeding of purebred livestock. For many years, his shorthorn cattle were exhibited at the Southwestern Exposition and Fat Stock Show in Fort Worth. He helped organize the first Fat Stock Show. It has been recorded that Mr. Brown bought a registered shorthorn bull, by the name of Royal Cup, for $1,000, a record price for the time. Brown wrote his personal check to pay for the bull, and a friend, Mr. Hovenkamp, took it to Maj. K. M. Van Zandt at the Fort Worth National Bank. The major remarked that, "Poor Louia is losing his mind." Later, Brown said, both he and the major laughed over the incident when many of Royal Cup's offspring sold for $1,000. Brown was said to have been the first cattleman in the state to pay $1,000 for one bull.

Mr. Brown was one of the 14 charter members of the Texas Shorthorn Breeders Association and the last survivor of the group. Mr. Brown gave up his cattle interests when he lost his stock pedigree records in a fire in 1928 that destroyed his large home on his farm in Smithfield. Also lost in that fire were numerous loving cups and other awards.

Louia and Halcie moved to the Riverside area after the fire and lived there until 1935 when they moved back to the farm in Smithfield. Moving with them was their youngest son Burney, his wife, Louise, and their 13-month-old daughter, Shirley Louise. Louia and Burney continued to raise cattle and farm the land. In 1936, Louia and Halcie celebrated their golden wedding anniversary.

Louia died of a heart attack May 1, 1939, while hoeing in his garden. He had been a member of the Smithfield Methodist Church and The Woodmen of the World. He is buried in the family plot in the Smithfield Cemetery.

Halcie continued to live with her son and daughter-in-law, Burney and Louise, after her husband's death. Another daughter, Linda Kay Brown, joined the family on July 12, 1944. Halcie died Feb. 22, 1957. She was a charter member of the Smithfield Methodist Church and is buried in the Smithfield Cemetery. She lived most of her 89 years in the Smithfield community, now a part of North Richland Hills.

Submitted by Shirley Newman and Kay Alread

TOMMY AND SUE BROWN

Tommy was working at the *Fort Worth Star-Telegram* and attending Texas Wesleyan College when he discovered this area.

North Richland Hills was not a well-recognized name when Tommy came to see a friend's new house in 1958. He was so impressed that on that very afternoon, he put a $10 deposit on a new three-bedroom brick house. The total cost was $250 down and a balance of $10,000. His friend moved, but he stayed in the same house on Marilyn Lane for 10 years.

The area was so primitive that cattle grazed in the front yard. The NRH City Hall was in a rented space at 7109 Grapevine Highway, but there wasn't need of a city office when there were no city services, city taxes, or employees. The population, including the town of Smithfield, which had been annexed, was less than 8,000. Davis Blvd. was known as FM 1938, and the speed limit there was 60 miles per hour.

Tommy and Sue Brown

In 1959, Tommy started his own business, B&B Pest Control, which he and Sue operated until 1985. Retirement was not in their immediate future as Tommy had the honor of being elected mayor of NRH in 1988. The job of mayor was a family affair, as the entire family took part in various events and campaigns. Tommy's fifth term ended in May 1998, and after serving 10 years, he retired once again. He and Sue plan to travel and enjoy their grandchildren.

Tommy's daughters, Julie and Sharon, and Tommy's and Sue's son, Randy, were all educated in the Birdville school system. Julie is married with three sons and lives in Grapevine. Sharon is single and has recently moved to Fort Lauderdale, Florida. Randy is also single, lives in Arlington, and works in Grapevine.

LLOYD AND FRANCES BROWNING

Charlie and Mae Browning purchased an acre of land in 1947 from W. E. Odell for $800. They paid for this land by paying $10 down and $10 per month on a no-interest loan. They resided on the land in a modest four-room home until Charlie's death in 1971. Mae lived in the house alone for years. When she could no longer take care of the home, she requested her son, Lloyd, take over the land and house. Lloyd and his wife, Frances, loved the North Richland Hills area so much they decided to remodel and add onto the family home to make room for their family. This was the beginning of their life in NRH. Lloyd and Frances and their three children, Daniel, Karen, and Gary, did everything in the remodeling and addition to the house, with the exception of hiring an electrical contractor.

Gary, Karen, Lloyd, Frances, and Dan Browning

Lloyd and Frances are both avid bowlers, love to work in the yard, travel, and stay involved in all activities of their six grandchildren. Lloyd was born in Tyler, graduated from Polytechnic High School in Fort Worth, and worked as a grain inspector, retiring after 40 years. Frances was born in Brownwood, graduated from Brownwood High School and Brownwood Business College, attended TCJC Northeast Campus, and worked for Lockheed, retiring after 20 years.

Daniel Tyson was born in Fort Worth, and is employed by Sygma. He married Tracy Ann Lewis, and they have one son and two daughters. He is an avid bowler.

Karen was born in Fort Worth, and graduated from Richland High School in 1983 where she lettered in basketball, volleyball, and track. She participated in Richland Youth Athletics girls' fast-pitch softball four years. Karen is also an avid bowler and has three daughters.

Gary Van was born in Fort Worth and graduated from Richland High School. He is employed by Gillis Construction Company. He joined the Army in 1987, served in Germany and in Operation Desert Shield—Operation Desert Storm. He was attached to the 24th Infantry that moved into Iraq and came within 50 miles of Baghdad. He was discharged from the Army in 1992. Gary loves to work on all types of cars and trucks, bringing to full circle his involvement in distributive education and part-time work while in high school.

OREIN AND SHIRLEY BROWNING

Orein Edwin Browning is a second-generation home builder and land developer. His father, W. I. Browning, started building in 1935, and Orein began his own company in 1954 and has built more than 5,000 houses in four counties.

Orein was born in Fort Worth, March 25, 1928, went to school at Amon Carter-Riverside High School, and later graduated from Texas Christian University. Shirley Ann went to Arlington Heights High School and later attended John Tarleton College.

Orein and Shirley Browning

Orein and Shirley met and married in 1959 and moved to North Richland Hills in 1983. They have four children. Michael Orein lives in Colleyville with his wife, Sharla, and their children, Michael, Kailea, and Carley. Martha Lee married George Dent, now deceased. She and their children, Brandy and Misty, live in Arlington. Melissa Ann Schmidt and her husband, Darrell, and their daughter, Casey, live in Woodsboro, Texas. Mallory Kay married Steve Simpson, now deceased. She and Kathy and Shea live in Portland, Texas.

Orein is a past board of directors member of the Fort Worth Home Builders Association and past vice president of the Fort Worth Junior Chamber of Commerce. He is a member and past-president of the Diamond Oaks Country Club and enjoys golf and swimming. Shirley enjoys playing gin rummy and spending time with their grandchildren. Orein and Shirley are members of North Richland Hills Baptist Church.

Their son, Michael, has formed his own building corporation and is now the third generation in this family of homebuilders.

MILDRED E. BRYAN

Mildred Bryan is relatively a newcomer to North Richland Hills, having moved to the city in 1989. She bought a duplex with her sister, Doris Hall. Mildred is a member of Smithfield Baptist Church, and participates in "Keen Agers," a senior adult group. She enjoys exercise classes at Bursey Senior Center, watching television, and doing needlework, mainly crocheting and knitting, and she enjoys gardening.

Mildred was born in Heath, Rockwall County, Texas, February 25, 1910, to Mamie and David S. Bryan. Her father was in the drugstore and grocery business. Mamie Bryan died in 1930, and David Bryan died in 1937. Following their deaths, Mildred moved to Dallas to live with her grandmother, Florence Piper Sawyer. She lived in Dallas for the next 60 years.

Mildred attended school in Heath and Forrest Avenue High School in Dallas. She worked at various nursing homes and in a dry cleaning business. Mildred said, "There are two things I never did in my life: get married and learn to drive."

Submitted by Evalyn Lochridge from an interview with Mildred Bryan

DON AND CHARLENE BRYANT

Marian Charlene Clark Bryant was born in 1927 to George Hubbard Clark and Bessie Estelle Self Clark. Charlene grew up in Johnson County, Texas, and attended school in Joshua and Burleson.

Warren Donald (Don) Bryant was born in 1928 in Georgia to William Cullen Bryant and Ardelia Joyce Bryant. Don grew up in Coffey County, Georgia, where he attended Pearson and West Green schools. He served in the Air Force from 1947 to 1950. Don was one of 14 children. All of his brothers served in the military; 68 years of service is totaled among them.

Charlene married a Fort Worth policeman, John William Arterbury, in 1952. John passed away in July 1962. Charlene and John had two sons, Brent Alan, born in 1953, and Craig William, born in 1958. Both sons attended Richland High School. Brent married Rebecca McKinley of North Richland Hills, and their children are Amy, Jamie, and Amber. Craig married Yvonne Stewart, and they had three children, Jeff, Jordan, and Ashley.

Back-Brent, Becky, Craig, and Jeff Arterbury; Middle-Amber Sanders, Jordan Arterbury, Jamie Johnson, and Ashley Arterbury; Front-Don and Charlene Bryant, Yvonne, and Amy Arterbury

Charlene and Don Bryant met and were married in 1963 in Durant, Oklahoma. The Bryants bought the Holiday Roller Rink on Carson Street in Haltom City in 1964 and remained there for 28 years, until their retirement in 1992. They moved from Fort Worth to the Snow Heights Addition of North Richland Hills in 1965. They loved meeting the children and parents that came to the rink and enjoyed going to the skating conventions. They have attended North Richland Hills Baptist Church for more than 32 years.

They have enjoyed this area greatly and had this to say: "When we moved to North Richland Hills the population was much smaller. From Loop 820 north, was farmland (roads were not good). About the only shopping centers were Richland Plaza and downtown Fort Worth. The children swam at Barrbrook Park. There were no parks like there are today. We lived across from Snow Heights Elementary School, and our children played on the playground there. The Dairy Queen was the only drive-in then."

"Some of the good things that have happened since we moved to NRH are the friends we enjoy at North Richland Hills Baptist Church, retirement, and having all the malls and grocery markets. Through the years, we have loved watching our children grow up, marry, have children of their own, and make their home in the NRH area. We've enjoyed traveling to Israel, Switzerland, Australia, and China with church friends and to Hawaii with our family. We enjoy fishing, sporting events, and golf games with friends. It has been a good life."

Don Bryant died Dec. 11, 1998.

BERLENE THROOP BUCKINGHAM

Lonnie Bearl "Jack" Throop was the third son of Minnie Ragsdale Throop and William Hardy Throop. He was born in Bransford (Colleyville), and at a very young age, began to work a team of mules along with his daddy and two older brothers, David Earl and Carl Allen.

Jack married Lorene Holder, and they had one daughter, Berlene. In 1946, Jack built the first of three rock houses on the corner of Harmonson Road and Scruggs Drive. These rocks were dug and hauled by Jack, Tiny Anderson, Herbert Walker, Finas Buckingham, and Jackson Himes from near Thurber, Texas.

Berlene Throop married Finas Buckingham, and they built a house next door to her daddy on Scruggs Drive in what later became North Richland Hills. They had three children, Rex Allen, who died in 1975, Rhonda, and Randy Bearl. All three graduated from Richland High School.

Rhonda married David Barbrick and has two daughters, Cari and Christi. Both girls are students at Tarleton State University in Stephenville. Rhonda and David live in Weatherford, where she works at Campbell Medical Center.

Randy married Sheri Middleton, and they have two children, Rex Allen and Nicole Jack. They live in Saginaw, and he works at Harris Hospital.

Jack Throop worked for Tarrant County for many years in Precinct 3 until his retirement. Jess Holder was county commissioner at that time. After Jack's retirement, he and his second wife, Lou Ella, operated a café called Lou and Jack's B-B-Que on Harmonson Road until their deaths in 1974.

Berlene graduated from Birdville High School in 1950. In 1997, seven classes combined for a wonderful class reunion. Berlene still lives in one of the rock houses that have been landmarks in the area since 1946. Two aunts, Myrtle Throop Anderson, age 93, and Lovie Throop Emery, age 83, live in the other two houses.

Submitted by Berlene Throop Buckingham

BURKHART AND KILLION FAMILIES

The family of Bob and Peggy Burkhart moved to North Richland Hills in the summer of 1965. Richland Plaza was the place to shop and hang out at on the weekends. This was back in the times of a single-screen theater, Richland Cinema.

Bob Burkhart

My parents always took an interest in the activities of their children. My dad, Bob W. Burkhart, coached my brothers, Jeff and Kevin, in Richland Youth Association baseball and football—back when only boys played. Our house on Venice Street was the "home" where all the kids came. Mom and Dad let us have parties, and they treated all the kids as if they were a part of our family. Some even called my parents "mom" and "dad." My mom, Peggy Burkhart Taylor, was a seamstress. She made drill-team uniforms for the Dixie Belles and a lot of formals for the proms. (She even made the bridal gowns and attendants' dresses for several girls after they graduated.) Mom now works for the city as the switchboard operator.

Standing-Kim, Jeff; Seated-Kevin and Peggy Burkhart (Taylor)

Blackie Frazier had horse stables on Grapevine Highway across from Tarrant County Junior College. We spent a lot of time riding our horses all over Mangham Airport. Then there were the playdays on Saturdays that all the "goat ropers" attended. I, Kim Burkhart Killion, graduated from Richland High School in 1976. Rufe Snow was a two-lane street and there was nothing on it until you got to Watauga Road where there was a Stop 'N Go grocery. Richland Plaza was pretty much obsolete and North East Mall had become the hangout.

On October 17, 1977, I went to work for the NRH Police Department as a dispatcher. My job consisted of dispatching for the Police and Fire Departments. We had two fire stations (which meant two engines and one tanker). Everyone who worked for the city knew everybody. Since that time, I have watched the city grow to one having four stations, two ambulances, animal control, HAZ-MAT response team, a bomb team, a crime scene search unit, and

L/R, Jerry, Kim holding Jesse, and William Killion

more than two officers on the street at a time.

No longer is Ma and Pa's Chicken Shack the family restaurant to go to. It doesn't even exist. We do have a restaurant row where you can get just about any food or drink that you could want.

I met my husband, Jerry, at the NRH Fire Department in 1981. It only took me seven years to convince him that he loved me. We were married in 1988 at the Smithfield Baptist Church on Main Street. We now have two sons, William and Jesse. Jerry is still working for the NRH Fire Department as a lieutenant.

To this day, many of my former classmates and friends from the area can call NRH Police Department and ask for Kim Burkhart. I have spend half my life there and some still call me "K. B." or "Burkhart." I am proud to tell people where I was reared, and that I can still be found in NRH.

Submitted by Kim Burkhart Killion

ERNEST AND DELORIES BURLESON

It was a change of pace somewhat when we moved to North Richland Hills. Some of the schools didn't seem quite ready for some of our foster sons. We were "well tenured" and had to bite our tongues at times. But we realized there was a reason not everyone understood some of the behaviors due to lack of exposure to them. This was the chief reason for moving here.

Our neighbors are the greatest anyone could ever expect. I wouldn't trade a single one of them for anything. We feel as if we have always been a part of NRH.

We both work in Dallas. Ernest has been with Dallas Nameplate Company for 41 years. Delories has been with UT Southwest Medical School for better than 30 years. At first the drive was less than enjoyable, but now it's not so bad since we are coming home to a place we love and enjoy.

We became acquainted with NRH after our daughter, Kayla, married a man who lived on Cummings Drive. They are both postal workers. We were trying to sell our house in Duncanville and move to a place with a larger yard.

We were foster parents of six boys and one girl at the time, so we needed more elbow room for them. When we saw this house at Holiday and Blaney we realized it would take a lot of improvements, but we loved the yard. It took much more than I first thought to make it what we needed, but it has paid enormous dividends in the pleasure we've received.

We are a blended family of Ernest's birth daughter Cindy, and Delories' birth children Kayla, Tommie, and Bradley. Our youngest, Bradley is 25 years old, but we've been foster parenting for more than 11 years. We were named adolescent Foster Family of the Year at the Texas State Foster Parent Conference in 1995.

LUTHER "BURT" AND JANE BURLESON

Burt and Jane Burleson, with their two sons, Richard and John, moved into their home on Dawn Drive in 1963. They are the only people who have lived in this home. Their third son, Mark, was born after they moved here.

Burt was the first vocational director of the Birdville School District, and Jane taught in Browning Heights, Glenview, and Haltom Junior High. After Jane retired, she became the director of the Bursey Road Senior Center. Burt owns his own insurance agency.

John was active in the 4-H Club and received honors with his Hereford cow. Later, he married Gwen Callicott, a local girl, and bought a home in Haltom City. John graduated from Connelly Tech and became a meatcutter. He was injured in a work-related accident and passed away in 1996.

Richard ("Rick") graduated from

Mark, Burt, Rick, John, and Jane Burleson

Richland High School where he was one of the top 21 football players in the United States. He played football for the University of Texas at Austin, and graduated from the University of Houston Law School. He lives in Houston with his wife, Cecily, and their two sons, J. R. and Jeb.

Mark also graduated from Richland High School. He was a quarterback on the football team and president of the student body. He graduated from the University of Texas. Mark presently lives in Houston with his wife, Kimberly, and son, John Samuel. He is in the insurance business.

Burt is active in Travelers Protective Association, Toastmasters, Kiwanis, Chamber of Commerce, various insurance groups, and North Fort Worth Baptist Church. Jane is a past-president of Oak Crest Woman's Club, a member of several bridge clubs, North Fort Worth Baptist Church, and the Bursey Road Gad-A-Bouts. Burt and Jane love to travel and take an interest in their community.

Jane was born in Childress and graduated from Texas Wesleyan University with a master's degree in education and administration. Burt is a native of Fort Worth and received a master's degree in administration from Texas Wesleyan.

Submitted By Jane Burleson

BURNETT
THE 127-YEAR HISTORY OF THE BURNETT FAMILY IN NORTH RICHLAND HILLS

The history of the Burnetts in this community extends back 127 years. From the Rev. John Quarles Burnett in 1870, to Jacob and Joshua Burnett six generations later, we have called this area home.

The Rev. John Quarles Burnett was born in Edgefield District, South Carolina, and moved to this area in 1870. This part of Texas was sparsely settled at that time and churches were far apart. He saw this as a challenge and an opportunity. He served as a pastor at the Mt. Gilead church, presently located in Keller, in the 1870s and is credited with raising its membership from 17 to 200. He also helped organize churches in Grapevine and Johnson Station. The church in Johnson Station would later become the First Baptist Church of Arlington.

Front view of Burnett residence in the late 1940s. Left-Precinct Line Road near intersection of Grapevine Hwy.

Sixty-three years later, in 1945, Burnett's great-grandson, Clarence L. Burnett, returned to raise his family in a white stucco home located on Precinct Line Road in Smithfield. He bought 58 acres for $7,000. This acreage is now home to Mid-Cities Boulevard, and a new Birdville Independent School District high school under construction. Clarence cared about the community and served on the town council of Smithfield. He worked as a police officer in Fort Worth, and at the Armour plant on Fort Worth's Northside. He was affectionately known as "Pop" and his wife, Wahneta, as "Bill." They were both longtime members of Smithfield Baptist Church.

Pop and Bill had three children, Curtis, Lynda, and Gerry. All three attended school at Smithfield Elementary in the 1940s and 1950s. Both Lynda and Curtis were married at the original Smithfield Methodist Church on Smithfield Road before North Richland Hills annexed the town. Curtis remained in NRH and raised two children, Kevin and Tony.

John Quarles, Clarence, Wahneta, and Curtis have all passed away but the family continues to grow in NRH. Kevin and Tony both reside in NRH, just minutes away from where their ancestors settled 127 years ago. Kevin and Pam recently welcomed little Joshua to their home one month after Tony and Melissa were blessed with Jacob. "We are very proud of our families' past involvement in this community, and look forward to the impact our kids can make."

Tony Burnett, 1997

KEVIN AND PAM BURNETT

The Kevin L. Burnett family established their home on Timberline Court in North Richland Hills in June of 1994. Both Kevin and wife, Pam Musgrove-Burnett, have deep roots in NRH. Kevin's great-great-great-grandfather, Reverend John Q. Burnett, arrived here in 1870, and Pam's family dates to 1960. Their newest addition is son Joshua Lee, born April 10, 1996, two months premature. He just could not wait to make NRH his home and playground.

Kevin and Pam both attended school in NRH throughout their lives. Kevin attended Smithfield Junior High and graduated from Richland High in 1985. He attended Tarrant County Junior

Pam, Josh, and Kevin Burnett, 1996

College before completing his bachelor's degree in arts and applied sciences at the University of North Texas in 1996. He held several jobs while working his way through college, all of them within the NRH community. He worked as a security guard at North Hills Mall, then worked as a jailer for the North Richland Hills Police Department. Kevin was also a North Richland Hills reserve police officer for several years. For the past year and a half he has been working with Harris Hospital Specialized Medical Management, Inc.

Pam attended Holiday Heights Elementary, North Richland Junior High, and graduated from Richland High School in 1985. Pam received her bachelor's degree in science from Abilene Christian University in 1989, spending her summers studying at TCJC. Pam is now a domestic engineer of one-and-one-half years.

The Burnetts have been members of the Southlake Church of Christ since 1996. Their family enjoys camping, jet-skiing, and landscaping, but most of all we enjoy watching our son, Josh, grow up in the same city where we played and grew as children.

JOHN AND SUSAN BUSH

I was born in Bridgeport, about 50 miles northwest of North Richland Hills, in Wise County on July 23, 1952. I was the second child of Cecil Melvin Bush and Jean Kelley Bush. My older brother, Charles William, who lives in St. Louis, was born July 3, 1949; my younger sister, Melva Jean Bush, still living in Bridgeport, was born December 30, 1959. I graduated from Bridgeport High School in 1970 where I won band and stage band awards and several track awards.

In 1971, while working at Tandy Leather Company's warehouse on Foch Street in Fort Worth, I met DiAnn Aschner, daughter of Irvin and Dorothy Aschner, who lived on Catchin Drive in North Richland Hills.

John and Susan Bush

In 1973, DiAnn and I joined North Richland Hills Baptist Church and were married there on June 22, 1974. We were the first church members, but the second couple, to be married in the almost completed auditorium. In 1975 we bought our first house, in Watauga, and lived there until we divorced in 1981.

I moved into the Raintree Apartments on Booth Calloway Road in North Richland Hills and lived there until September 23, 1987, when I bought the house I still live in on Lariat Trail in North Richland Hills.

On October 21, 1989, I married Susan Carol Evans Ramsey, daughter of Jim and Dorothy Evans. Susan is the best gift God has blessed me with. Susan was born in San Antonio on May 2, 1948. Her brother, Richard Wayne Evans, was born April 3, 1945 and now lives in Harrison, Ark. When she was in grade school (second grade), her family moved to Oakland Lane in North Richland Hills, where she lived until she married Jesse R. Ramsey in 1969. Susan's mother continued to live on Oakland Lane until 1983.

Susan attended North Richland Elementary, Richland Junior High, and Richland High schools. Susan had two children; Jessica Sue Ramsey who currently lives in Cape Girardeau, Missouri, born May 3, 1972, and Sheila Rae Ramsey, born August 7, 1974, who lives in Jackson, Missouri. Both daughters attended Holiday Heights Elementary, North Richland Junior High, and Southeast Missouri University. After Jesse Ramsey's graduation, the family lived in El Paso for three years and Augsburg, West Germany for three years while Jesse served as an officer in the U.S. Army to finish his internship and residency. Susan returned to North Richland Hills in 1983 from Cape Girardeau, and began working for Bedford Internal Medicine Clinic, allowing her to stay current in the new world of managed medical care.

In May 1982, I began my own swimming pool company, which I still operate today. John Bush Pool Company has been successful over the last 15 years due to referrals by satisfied customers.

Susan and I have many interests, including a grandchild, Logan Rae Clippard, born October 12, 1991. We both like to travel, especially the back roads. We have also been active in North Richland Hills Baptist Church, serving in positions as deacon, Sunday school teacher, choir member, choir president, and Christmas Pageant production staff members. Susan enjoys the piano and gardening, and I enjoy photography and singing in a quartet, The Gospel Sound. I should mention that I stutter, not severely, and like Mel Tillis, never when I sing.

Submitted by John Bush

MANUEL AND CONSTANCE ANN BUSTILLO

Our family became North Richland Hills residents in June of 1990, when our house on Red Oak Drive was completed. Since then, our family has grown to include two sons, Marshall Grant, born September 15, 1992, and Mitchell Ellis, born April 1, 1995. On October 22, 1997, our family grew again when Carlton, a Jack Russell Terrier, came to live with us.

I was born in Houston in 1965 and graduated with a computer science engineering degree from Texas A&M in 1987. My husband, Manuel, was born in Havana, Cuba, in 1960. His family immigrated to the United States in 1962 and settled in Lake Charles, Louisiana. Manuel graduated with an electrical engineering degree from the University of Houston in 1984.

Back-Manuel and Constance; Front-Marshall Grant and Mitchell Ellis

Manuel and I met at Lockheed Martin Corporation, where we both have worked as engineers since 1985 and 1987, respectively. We were married on September 9, 1989, in Spring, Texas, and started looking for a house soon after. We both were attracted to NRH because of its beautiful landscape and "mid-cities" location. Even though our street is quiet and serene, we can easily reach a number of events in minutes, making NRH an ideal place for our family to live.

Submitted By Constance Ann Bustillo

ERIC AND BONNIE BUTCHER

Eric and Bonnie Butcher moved to North Richland Hills in April 1977 from Oxon Hill, Maryland. Eric's job transfer prompted the move. He has been an employee of Southwestern Bell Telephone for 30 years. Bonnie has been a receptionist for a dental office for many years.

Eric James Butcher was born in Sussex, England, to Reginald and Frances Butcher. Bonnie Gaye Hardin Butcher was born to Lawrence Scott and Natalie Hardin in Baltimore, Maryland. Eric and Bonnie married in Maryland in 1966.

Laurie Butcher was born in 1967 in Washington, D.C. After the family moved to their new home in the Green Valley area of NRH, she graduated from Richland High School in 1985. She married James Whitt

Eric and Bonnie Butcher with grandchildren, L/R, Hayli Whitt, Eric, Hayden Whitt, and Bonnie

December 16, 1982. James graduated from Richland High School in 1989. James and Laurie, with son Hayden, born in 1994, and daughter, Hayli, born in 1991, continue to make their home in NRH.

In 1985, Eric and Bonnie Butcher moved to Hurst, Texas, where they continue to live.

WILLIAM J. (BILL) AND JUANITA BUTLER

Bill and Juanita Butler moved to North Richland Hills in 1977. Bill was born in Fort Worth, and Juanita was born in Halfway, Kentucky. Bill and Juanita graduated from North

Side High School in Fort Worth, Bill in 1929 and Juanita in 1931.

Bill started his career with Armour and Company in 1929 as an office boy. He retired as district credit manager after 47 years. He also worked for the stock show for

Bill and Juanita Butler

42 years as superintendent of livestock accounting and as livestock show auditor. Bill was an active Mason and member of Moslah Shrine Temple. He was past president of the Fort Worth Wholesale Credit Association and past president of Armour Retiree Club. Bill was a member of North Fort Worth Baptist Church for more than 60 years. He passed away July 16, 1985.

Juanita has been a member of North Fort Worth Baptist Church for 67 years. She studied oil painting and is a doll collector. She has around 200 dolls in her collection.

Their children never lived in NRH. They were all married when Bill and Juanita moved to the area. Betty Cleveland lives in San Antonio, William James Butler Jr., in San Antonio, and Robert Joe Butler lives in Colorado Springs.

FRED AND MARY YEAMAN BUZAN

Fred and Mary Yeaman Buzan were married in Waco. Fred was born in Taylor, Texas, September 16, 1929, and Mary was born in Lorena, Texas (19 miles south of Waco), August 19, 1934. They met in Waco in 1954 and were married that same year. They moved to North Richland Hills in 1957. Fred was the manager of Copeland's shoes in the North Richland Shopping Center. They are charter members of St. John Apostle Church on Glenview Drive where they helped pioneer and build the church.

They have one son, Dan R. Buzan, married to Sarah Baker Buzan. Dan and Sarah live in the Smithfield area of NRH. Dan went to Snow Heights Elementary and North Richland Junior High. He graduated from Richland High in 1973. Dan played Peewee football and baseball for the Richland Youth

Standing, Dan; Seated, Mary and Fred

Association. He played football through junior and senior high school. He was also active in the Rodeo Club at Richland High. They have one son, Dustin Buzan.

Fred and Mary were very active in the Richland Youth Association. Fred served as president and Mary served as treasurer. Fred was also a football coach for the association from 1966 until 1972. He really enjoyed working with the young people. These young men still remember the impact he had on their lives as children and still remember him today when they meet.

Fred was merchandiser and buyer for J. C. Penney Company shoe department for 30 years. He was located in the downtown Fort Worth, Richland Plaza, and North East Mall stores. It is easy to imagine that he put shoes on every child in NRH and surrounding areas from 1962 through 1981. In 1981 he had to take medical retirement due to a heart condition. People came from New York, Oklahoma, New Mexico, and all parts of Texas for Fred's retirement party. Mary says no matter where they go on vacation, he always runs into someone he knows. Fred has never met a stranger.

His first heart attack was in 1974, and he underwent triple bypass surgery in 1977 as a result of several heart attacks. If you were ever up early in the morning, Fred was the little man walking on Vance Road and surrounding streets in his red jogging suit and blue cowboy cap. He never missed a day walking until several years ago. He still tries to walk on his treadmill, and he swims. Mary worked at Zale's Jewelry in Richland Plaza and North East Mall for 35 years. She retired in 1996. Mary has sold most of the young people in NRH their wedding or engagement rings. She misses seeing and talking with all the young people.

Fred and Mary enjoy having fun camping, swimming, and seeing their grandchildren grow up.

MARSH AND KATE CALLOWAY

Marsh Calloway (1869–1945) and Kate Melbourne Calloway (1876–1951) owned hundreds of acres of farmland in both Richland Hills and North Richland Hills. Kate Calloway was Lonnie Snow's great-aunt and Marsh Calloway his great-uncle by marriage.

"Uncle Marsh accumulated 2,100 acres of land in his lifetime," Melbourne James Snow said. "Their first son died, and they had another son, Orion Calloway," Faye Belle said. "Orion married Sarah Bewley, and they had a daughter, Helen Catherine Calloway. She never married."

Memories Plentiful Near Family's Old Home

Catherine Calloway, her parents, O. H. Calloway in front of the 2-story, 14-room home just south of Texas 183 now Highway 10

"The Marsh Calloway' land stretched from the railroad south of Texas 183 and north to the intersection at Glenview Drive where Hudiburg Chevrolet now is located and west two or three miles," Snow said. It covered the present locations of North Hills Mall and North Hills Hospital.

Marsh and Kate Calloway are leaning against the posts, he on the left front and she on the right—in front of their beautiful two-story home place, south of Texas 183 in what is now Richland Hills. The American Tile Company is now located about two or three blocks north of the location of the old home place. Seated (second) to the left are: Bill Melbourne (Kate's brother); George Calloway (Marsh's cousin); Dick Melbourne (nephew to Kate Calloway).

Land was $5 per acre at the time, thus the Calloways bought only 40 acres at this location. This original 40 acres was partly in what is now Richland Hills and partly in NRH.

The home of Marsh and Kate Calloway was handed down a couple of generations and eventually belonged to O. H. Calloway. The home was demolished in September 1960. The home at that time was two stories and had 14 rooms.

Submitted by Pat Riddle

Marsh and Kate Calloway Home Place
Pictures circa 1919

Marsh and Kate are standing to the right side of the post. L/R–Ruby Snow Reynolds (Rufe Snow's daughter and niece of the Calloways); C. G. "Bum" Melbourne(brother to Kate Calloway); Mary Boaz Melbourne (C. G.'s wife); possibly Maude Booth; The Calloways; Bill Melbourne(brother to Kate and Jesse Snow); Faye Belle Melbourne James; child in front-unknown; Kate Snow Harrell(Rufe Snow's daughter).

Mary Boaz Melbourne and her husband, "Bum" Melbourne; Marsh Calloway; unknown next; Kate Melbourne Calloway; Ruby Snow Reynolds; Dick Melbourne (with cap); in front of Dick-unknown; Children-Kate Snow Harrell; Faye Belle Melbourne James; Wiley Calloway (Kate and Marsh's son who played the violin); unknown next.

T. K. AND TOSCA CAMPBELL

T. K. Campbell accepted a position with F. Kirk Johnson Oil Company in Fort Worth and moved with his wife, Tosca, and 2-year-old daughter, Angela, to North Richland Hills from Dallas in 1954, buying a house on Vance Road. There were few houses on their block when they moved into the neighborhood. The McMurreys, Schadels, Joyners, and later, Dr. David Pillow and Dr. Charles Rush and their families were among their neighbors.

At that time, it was mostly open land around the house, with grazing cows and a frog pond across the street. The nearest grocery store was the Rapid Mart located at Vance Road and Grapevine Highway. Also at that time there was a small swimming pool in back of the Rapid Mart. There was very little traffic on Vance Road, and the children could safely walk to the store. We remember we bought all our eggs "fresh" from Newton Egg Farm on old Denton Highway where our daughter loved to visit the chickens.

Angela attended Snow Heights Elementary School in 1959 after watching the school being built. Billy H. Smith was the first school principal, and Mrs. Mary A. Clark was Angela's first grade teacher. They recall that Mrs. Clark was an exceptional teacher and was loved by all her students. Tosca Campbell was room mother for Angela's class.

Angela was a member of Girl Scout Troop No. 361, and her mother, along with Rose Marie Sred, were troop leaders. Angela was a volunteer member of the American Red Cross and did community service during her junior high school years. She received a Certificate of Recognition and Grateful Appreciation from the Red Cross for her work. At age 15, she was selected to compete in the Miss Teenage Fort Worth pageant and in 1971 was a finalist in Miss Richland Area beauty contest.

Angela graduated from Richland High School with honors in 1971. She graduated from Texas Wesleyan College in Fort Worth in 1976. Angela is married and has three sons, twins Thomas and Alexander, age 7, and Johnathan, age 5.

In 1972, T. K. and Tosca purchased a building and one acre of land at 7255 Glenview Drive and opened The Clothes Rack, which later became The Bridal Gallery and was operated by Tosca for 16 years.

T. K. worked with F. Kirk Johnson's Ambassador Oil Corporation for 10 years until the company was sold in 1966, at which time he accepted the position of land manager with Shenandoah Oil Corporation of Fort Worth. He remained with that company for 10 years. T. K. is a member of the Fort Worth Petroleum Landmen's Association and served as its president in 1970–1971. He is also a member of the Fort Worth Geological Society. Tosca was a member of the Petroleum Landmen's Wives Club and served as its president in 1966.

Submitted By Tosca Campbell

JOHN B. AND MARGIE BROWN CARTER

John Bruner and Margie Brown Carter have lived on Shady Lake Drive in North Richland Hills since April 1984. John was born in Rockford, Illinois, May 16, 1935. He graduated from high school in 1954. He was in the U. S. Army in 1956–57. John was transferred to Fort Worth with Household Finance Corporation in 1960. He met Margie Brown in Tyler, and they were married there December 29, 1962. They moved to Fort Worth and settled in Richland Hills in 1964.

Margie graduated from Tyler High School in 1955 and attended Tyler Junior College in the fall of 1955. She went to work for Dr. Robert L. Duff in Tyler in 1956, and worked for him until they were transferred to Fort Worth in 1964. Margie worked for the Birdville School District from 1978 as an administrative clerk in the Textbook/Special Services unit. She has also worked part-time for Zale's Jewelers.

John and Margie have been members of the North Richland Hills Baptist Church since 1975. John is a member of the Deacon Council of the church, and both John and Margie are members of the adult choir.

John and Margie have two children, both adopted. Sheri Renee Carter Biggs came to them in March 1967, and John Bradley Carter came to them in November 1971. Sheri has two children, Cody Brent Biggs, born April 11, 1989, and Jonathon Ryan Biggs, born July 25, 1990.

WOODY AND CINDY CARTER

Woody Carter and Cindy Woodall were married May 24, 1974 in Fort Worth. Cindy's parents were Geneva and Monroe Woodall (deceased).

Woody's parents are Willie Dalton Carter and Lula Ann Woodson. Woody and Cindy both grew up in Fort Worth and lived there after their marriage.

In January 1977, Clint Travis Carter became their first-born son, followed by twins, Craig Matthew and Mindy Dawn in February 1979 and a baby sister, April Colleen, born April 1981. The family's transition to become North Richland Hills residents began in the spring of 1980 when they began to attend and joined the North Richland Hills Baptist Church. By 1984, the Carter family became one of the pioneers in the current trend to home school their children. It was a special factor that would create a family harmony and bond that has continued for fourteen years.

In 1988, the family moved to North Richland Hills, in fact, right across the street from North Richland Hills Baptist Church where their family had planted their lives for so long. In 1994, Woody started his own mobile small engine repair business in NRH.

Back-Clint, April, Woody, son-in-law David Hunt, Craig; Front-Clint's fiancée Carey Brewer, Cindy, Mindy Carter Hunt, and friend

In 1995, they "graduated" their first home school child, Clint, and he received three scholarships to Oklahoma Baptist University, in academics, music, and ministry. He is currently a junior at OBU with a 3.5 grade point average. In 1997, their twins, Mindy and Craig, "graduated" from home school. Craig is currently working with a character development program that has been approved for Birdville Independent School District and Mindy is working full time. Mindy married David Robert Hunt II of Haltom City on January 3, 1998.

Clint is engaged to Carey Brewer of Oklahoma with plans for a June 1999 wedding. April is finishing up her home schooling with plans to attend OBU and major in music in 1999. The Carter family has been blessed with their "home" (not just a house) in many ways and have enjoyed their community for the last ten years.

WILLIAM E. AND MELBA CATE

William E. "Bill" Cate was born September 8, 1927, in a house on Carson Street in "Old Birdville," across the street from the Birdville Church of Christ. His parents were Robert L. Cate, who died in 1939, and Mary Greener Cate, who still lives in the family home on Broadway in Haltom City. This property was a part of the Popplewell farm bought by G. W. Haltom in 1936. Robert Cate bought two acres from Mr. Haltom that year.

Bill Cate has a great heritage in the northeast Tarrant County area. His great-grandfather, James Cate, born in Tennessee in 1818, homesteaded on the Grapevine prairie in the 1800s with his wife, Elvira, and their 12 children.

During his early years in Tarrant County, hostile Indians were a problem, stealing stock and occasionally attacking the settlers. Cate took part in several punitive expeditions, returning from one of them with three Indian scalps. Cate opposed seces-

Ed and Saretta Cate on porch of rented house, originally home of Clarence "Barber" Cobb on Davis Blvd.

sion before the Civil War began, believing the difficulty could be settled by some means other than war. His oldest son, David, served throughout the conflict.

Grandfather Anderson B. Cate homesteaded just north of the Lonesome Dove Community. Bill Cate's father was born there Jan. 1, 1901, and grew up on that land. His mother was born near Euless in the community of Tarrant. She worked for the Birdville High School cafeteria from 1947 until she retired.

The family moved to the Portwood Farm on Highway 121 (now Texas 26) and Harwood Road. Bill went to the second grade in Smithfield in 1935. They moved back to Birdville in the fall of 1936. With the exception of the second grade, Bill attended his other eleven grades in Birdville, graduating from Birdville High School in 1945.

Bill loved sports and played quarterback on the Birdville football team. He also played basketball and helped May Della Everett get the first girls' basketball team started.

In the summer of 1941, Bill worked on a hay baler for R. M. Reeves. Mr. Reeves was a county commissioner. They baled hay all around Birdville, Smithfield, and Watauga. At one time, they baled prairie grass on the Bursey Ranch north of Watauga. This job lasted about two to three weeks and covered 1,000 acres. Bill spent several summers baling hay.

He worked one summer for Clarence Jones at his lumber yard on Belknap Street. During the school year, he worked evenings and weekends for O. B. Guynn, whose store was on Carson and Highway 121, across from Birdville school. He helped slaughter cattle, hogs, and sheep. Guynn's business advertised "Home killed meats our specialty," but the one-stop store also handled groceries, feeds, hardware, and drygoods.

Bill remembers a large gravel pit where the derelict Richland Plaza now stands—just east of Fossil Creek and Birdville School. Gravel was hauled out with teams and wagons.

Bill Cate and Melba Fay Stowe were married at the Birdville Church of Christ in 1946, by Minister Fred McClung. Melba was born in 1929, in Everman. Her family moved to lower Birdville in 1941. Bill served in the U.S. Air Force from 1945 to 1947.

In the spring of 1948, the Cates bought a home on Woods Lane in Smithfield and lived there until the fall of 1950. In 1951, they bought property at Davis Boulevard and Cardinal Lane. It was here they watched the straightening and widening of Smithfield Road, which was to become Davis from Grapevine Highway to FM 1709. They sold the Davis property in 1971 to J. C. Harston.

Bill was a fireman for the city of Fort Worth for 36 years, retiring in January 1988. Melba worked for Northeast National Bank for seven years. They have retired to their 10-acre spread in Newark, Texas, where Bill describes himself as a "country gentleman," while he raises a few head of cattle.

The Cate family includes three children and eight grandchildren: Edward L., born in 1947; Saretta, born in 1950; Garry L., born in 1954, all in Fort Worth. Each graduated from Richland High School, Edward in 1966, Saretta in 1968, and Garry in 1972. Saretta has two children and lives in Haltom City. Edward has three children and lives in Boyd, Texas. He is currently attending Texas Wesleyan University, studying to become a coach and biology teacher. Garry has three children, and the family lives on eight acres adjoining Bill's property in Newark.

Interview with Bill Cate
Submitted By Evalyn Lochridge

JAMES C. AND LENA COBB CAVENDER

James C. Cavender farmed, lived for many years, and died near the present-day Birdville Church of Christ on

Birdville Hill. Throughout most of his life he was known as "Uncle Jim." He was my great-grandfather's brother.

Uncle Jim was born in 1869 in Walker County, in north Georgia, not far south of Chattanooga, Tennessee. He was the oldest of seven children born to Joseph M. Cavender (1835–1902) and his wife, Mary Ann Bryan Cavender (1841–1918). Joe Cavender had joined the Confederate Army with a Tarrant County Regiment and had returned to Georgia after the war. He and Jim's mother were married in 1868.

While Jim was still a small child, his father moved the family to Bellefonte, Arkansas, where they lived until about 1879. In that year, Joe Cavender and his brother-in-law, W. A. Clements, moved to Corpus Christi, Texas, for a few months but moved again in 1880 and settled on Big Bear Creek south of Grapevine. There, Jim's father died in 1902.

Jim and Lena Cavender, about 1890

Jim was married to Lena Cobb, a girl who lived near him in the Bear Creek/Pleasant Glade neighborhood. They had one child, May Cavender, who lived in Tyler, Texas in later life.

Jim was murdered at his home on Birdville Hill in 1930. He had recently sold a large amount of farm produce, and his family suspected robbery was the motive. His body was hidden under a pile of oats. Jim was living alone at that time. His neighbors heard his milk cows bawling the morning after his death, and when they went to see why Uncle Jim hadn't done his morning milking, they found his body.

May Cavender

Since only one person outside the family knew he had the money, family members have always suspected they knew the murderer's identity. No one was ever arrested or brought to trial, however, Uncle Jim lies buried in an unmarked grave in Birdville Cemetery.

Submitted by Michael E. Patterson

JERRY AND LIZ CHISM

I, Jerry Chism, was born in 1953 and spent the first 10 years of my life on Vance Road. Being an only child, I loved living in a neighborhood so heavily populated with

L/R-Jerry, Liz, and Danny Chism

children. In fact, the entire neighborhood was much like one big family. All of the parents knew one another and loved sitting out in the front yards on their lawn chairs in the summer evenings. If you got out of line, any of your friend's parents would step in and discipline you just like your own mom and dad would do.

My wife, Liz Krueger, grew up around the corner on Turner Terrace. While living there she went to St. George Catholic School, North Richland Junior High, and Richland High. After we married, she returned to the neighborhood and taught kindergarten at Snow Heights Elementary School in the same room where I attended first grade. We have one son, Danny, age 15.

Liz's parents, Bud and Edna Krueger, moved to North Richland Hills and bought their home on Turner Terrace in 1958. Edna died in 1983, and Bud continues to live in the home. Liz has three sisters, Mary Ann, Pat, and Nancy.

Three houses down the street from my childhood home, the power lines crossed over Vance Road and followed a path which created a field on which to play. It was there, under the power lines, that we played football and baseball almost every afternoon after school and during the summer. After several big fights during baseball games, some of the parents decided our sandlot baseball days were over . . . until Mrs. Liscomb, who lived on the corner, volunteered to umpire our games. She was a wonderful lady and knew just how to deal with us when we were angry.

I remember the time Fossil Creek flooded down the street and around the corner from my home. All the neighbors rushed down and helped carry furniture and valuables out of homes, and comforted the owners as we all stood by and felt helpless.

Since I am now a United Methodist minister at St. Luke United Methodist Church on the Denton Highway, I realize how fortunate I was to grow up in my North Richland Hills neighborhood. Most of the children on my street were Catholic or belonged to another religious group, and it gave a Methodist kid like me the opportunity to learn about the greatness of diversity. It was a wonderful time and great place to grow up on Vance Road.

Now that we have returned to NRH, we live about six blocks from our old houses, and we have had the delight of reacquainting ourselves with former teachers, students, friends, etc. When I received the call from my bishop offering St. Luke United Methodist Church to me, I was happy to take it. It has been nice to return and give back to a community that gave us so very much.

Submitted By Jerry Chism

PERRY AND SHERRY CHRISTENSEN

Perry Dean Christensen and Sherry Elaine Johnson were married April 19, 1986, at North Richland Hills Baptist Church and moved to their current home on Victoria Avenue in North Richland Hills July 1, 1990.

Perry's History: Since three of my grandparents were born in Denmark and moved to the United States as children, I was raised in a Danish Settlement in Racine, Wisconsin. I was born November 11, 1957, to Gilbert Raymond and Lois Irene Nielsen Christensen, the first of three children. My upbringing was typical of a small-town lifestyle. We were active members of a local church, and I attended public schools in Racine. I graduated from the University of Wisconsin in Whitewater in 1980.

Perry and Sherry Christensen

As the result of a job relocation, I moved to the Fort Worth/Dallas Metroplex in 1984. After several years in the floor-covering industry with Congoleum Corporation and L. D. Brinkman Co., I transferred to the pharmaceutical industry in 1987. I currently manage a sales region for Dey Laboratories in the allergy and asthma field.

One of my favorite past-times is gardening and yard work. The NRH Beautification Committee has honored our home twice with "NRH Yard of the Month." Church and community services are a priority as well. I have enjoyed a seat on the NRH Zoning Board of Adjustments since 1992. I have also had the privilege of serving on the Finance and Missions committees at NorthWood Church, where we attend. Other community involvement has been helping to build the NRH Adventure World Playground and working with local political campaigns.

Sherry's History: I was born December 6, 1963, in Fort Worth, to James Edward and Jessie JoAnn King Johnson. I have one sister, Patricia Carol Johnson Duckett. Our family moved to Blaney Avenue in NRH in April 1965. We were privileged to live on a block where "for sale" signs did not exist. Neighbors that waved to me as I walked to school are the same neighbors that wave, as I drive into my parents' driveway today.

We attended NRH Baptist Church where I was a part of children's programs, youth ministry, and met my husband, Perry, through church singles activities. Music has

always been an important part of my life. I was privileged to participate in a church music program that allowed me, from a child, to develop and enjoy the gift of music and singing. Every Christmas season was spent with the Greater Fort Worth Christmas Pageant, where I had the opportunity to have many special parts and solos.

I attended Snow Heights Elementary, North Richland Junior High, and graduated from Richland High School in 1982. I have many special memories from school years, but the most significant part was music. Band and choir were favorites in junior high, choir and Rebellaires in high school.

My first job was after school at Whitten Pharmacy, which was located on Grapevine Highway across from Winn Dixie. Later, I worked after school at Haltom City State Bank and Northeast National Bank. In 1985, I became the music secretary at NRH Baptist Church. In 1993, Perry and I moved our church membership to NorthWood Church in Keller. I currently work part-time there as secretary.

Outside of time at church and work, my priority is spending time with my husband. Decorating (and redecorating) is one of our favorite hobbies. I am also an avid angel collector. Perry and I have had the pleasure of traveling quite a lot since we've been married. One of our favorite vacation spots is Bermuda.

Community activities include: NRH Parks and Recreation Board; 1992 NRH City Charter Revision Committee; assisting in the creation of NRH Adventure World Park; assisting in various NRH City Council campaigns; and driving for the Meals on Wheels Program.

I believe there is much to say for the security and confidence instilled in a child by being raised in one consistent place. My sister and I grew up, married, and both still live in North Richland Hills and consider it a blessing to know where "home" is.

VARNAL AND PAT CHRISTOPHER

Varnal Adell Christopher and Patricia Muriel Jane Brown Christopher have been residents of North Richland Hills since 1965. Varnal and Pat were married in 1948, in Vancouver, British Columbia.

Varnal was born in 1920, in Alazan, Texas, a small community nine miles from Nacogdoches. Varnal's parents were John Warden Christopher and Ida Mahaley Collins Christopher. Varnal graduated from San Augustine High School and attended college in Dallas. He then entered the Army Air Corps in June 1942. Varnal served in the Pacific during World War II and was a pilot. He retired from the Air Force in 1964 with the rank of major, and went to work for the Federal Aviation Agency in Euless. After 20 years of service, Varnal retired with a combined total of 43 years federal service.

Patricia (Pat) is the daughter of Thomas William Bradburn Brown and Olive I. Hardy Brown. Pat was born in Edmonton, Alberta, in 1931. She has been active in Birdville PTA, both local and council, for 31 years and is a Texas State PTA Life Member. In 1990, Pat and a few other PTA Council members founded the Clothes Connection, an organization that provides donated clothing to disadvantaged school-aged children. Pat is still active in this organization. She is also a member of North Richland Baptist Church and a volunteer at Richland High School.

Varnal and Pat have four sons: Varnal Adell Jr. (Chris), Curtis Dean, Chester Glenn, and Paul Warren. Varnal Jr. was born in 1949, in Aurora, Colorado, graduated from Richland High School in 1967, and attended the University of Texas Arlington. He served six years in the Army Reserve and works for Kroger Foods Distribution Center in Keller. Varnal Jr. still lives in NRH. He married Janetta Pullium in 1972, and they have one son, Michael Lynn. Michael graduated from Richland High School with honors in 1993, and attends the University of Texas-Dallas where he is studying medicine.

Back-Curtis, Paul, Varnal, Pat, Varnal Jr.; Front-Chester

Curtis Dean Christopher was born in 1951, in Bossier City, Louisiana. He graduated from Richland High School in 1970, and attended Tarrant County Junior College and Texas Christian University. Curtis served six years in the Air Force Reserve and one year in the Texas Air National Guard. He is presently employed by the U.S. Postal Service. Curtis married Kathy Kitterman, and they have two children: Amanda Renee, and Brandon Adell. Curtis married Suzette Fulesday in 1996. Suzette has two children: Charli Dana and Jessica Havens. Curtis and Suzette reside in NRH along with their four children. The family belongs to North Richland Baptist Church.

Chester Glenn was born in 1956 in Biloxi, Mississippi. He graduated from Richland High School in 1974, attended TCJC, and attained his private pilot's license and is employed with the FAA. Chester married Susan Sones, and they have one son, Jonathan Thomas. In 1984, he married Marcia Norton, and they have two sons, Joseph Balmat (Joey) and Bradley Andrew (Brad). The family resides in NRH.

Paul Warren was born in 1957 in Biloxi, Mississippi, graduated from Richland High School in 1976, and also graduated from the University of Texas Arlington with a certified public accounting degree. He had his own accounting practice in Mansfield for 12 years, and is

presently employed by Howard's Masonry Supply in Arlington. Paul married Denise Stalcup of Keller. They have two children: Bryan Paul and Laura Elizabeth. The family has made their home in Mansfield and are very active in their church.

Our entire family enjoys camping, traveling, fishing, golfing, and especially our family get-togethers.

Submitted By V. A. Christopher

JIMMY AND PAT CLARK

Jimmy Neal Clark and Patricia Pittman were married in 1971, in Durant, Oklahoma. Both were born in Fort Worth and are graduates of Carter Riverside High School. They moved to the Snow Heights area of North Richland Hills in 1974, and resided for 12 years on Oakland Lane. In 1986, they moved three blocks west to Corona Drive. The family liked the Birdville school system so much, especially Snow Heights Elementary, that they did not move far.

Their son, William Frank (Chip) Mundy, graduated from Richland High School in 1987, and from the University of Texas at Arlington in 1990. He and his wife, Julia, and son, Clark, reside in Hurst.

Son, Josh Pittman Clark, graduated from Richland High School in 1993, and graduated from Texas A&M in May 1998.

Jimmy, a design engineer, has been with Southwestern Bell Telephone Company for 29 years. Pat has worked part-time for five years at Cornerstone Counseling Center.

Back-Chip, Josh; Front-Pat and Jim, 1986

The family joined North Richland Baptist Church shortly after moving to the area. Church has been their main focus for fun, friends, and fellowship. Jimmy and Pat taught a young married Sunday school class for 10 years and recently began a new class, "Christianity 101."

In the 23 years the family has lived in NRH, they have seen many changes, but one thing has not changed. It is still a good place to raise a family.

BILL AND MILDRED CLINGER

The Clinger family moved to Victoria Ave. in North Richland Hills in 1958 from Haltom City. Having realized the excellence of the Birdville Independent School District, they felt their children would receive a good foundation for life in that community. Both Bill and Mildred were involved in PTA and Band Boosters. They also taught Bible classes at the Richland Hills Church of Christ.

Being interested in the political situation in NRH, the Clingers attended council meetings and worked for various candidates both in City Council and School Board elections.

In 1966, Mary Shilcutt, librarian at Richland High

School and president of the Snow Heights Elementary PTA, taught Mildred how to catalogue and process books, so that Snow Heights could have a school library. Many fellow PTA parents helped in starting and maintaining the library throughout the time the Clinger children were students there.

Back-Doug, Craig, Kent; Front-Bill, Mildred, and Lynn Clinger, 1975.

Because of that library experience Mildred was asked to help start a public library for the city. Several worked many hours to sort donated books in the old fire station in Smithfield. These books were pitched back in a big "mountain" on the floor by some unknown persons. When donated space for a library was offered in the Richland Plaza Shopping Center, shelving was ordered, and some government surplus desks were given. The City Council provided some budgeted funds to buy some new books and supplies. Bill Clinger loaned some reference books from his personal library, so that the library would be of more use to the public. Many PTA members and others interested in the community, including students, helped build the library. An NRH Friends of the Library organization was begun, and not long afterward, the first professional librarian was hired.

Bill Clinger was transferred to Kansas in 1975. Mildred, Craig, and Lynn stayed in NRH for that school year. (Doug and Kent were in college.) Craig was editor in chief of the high school paper, the Reveille, and he and his staff had already started plans for the year. The Clingers moved to Olathe, Kansas, at the end of the school year in 1976. They will always remember the good times in NRH and be grateful for the church, the teachers and school system who had such a large part in shaping the lives of Doug, Kent, Craig, and Lynn.

Nelson Wesley "Bill" Clinger was born in 1920, in Fort Worth. Bill has a bachelor's degree in history from the University of Texas at Arlington. He was general claim agent for the Rock Island Railroad in Fort Worth from 1944–1975, transferred to Kansas City 1975–1978, moved to Houston and worked as general claim agent for the Houston Belt & Terminal from 1978–1985. After retirement, he took up computers and started a typesetting business in The Woodlands near Houston.

Mildred Fay Mayes Clinger was born in 1923, in Chickasha, Oklahoma. She married Bill October 19, 1952, in Chickasha. She has a bachelor's degree in business education from Oklahoma College for Women. She worked as a dental assistant from 1941–1948, accountant from 1948–1952, and now has her own accounting business, MMC Accounting, in Spring and The Woodlands, Texas.

Mildred and Bill have four children and nine grandchildren. All four children attended Snow Heights Elementary and North Richland Junior High. The three oldest attended Richland High School. Lynn attended Olathe, Kansas, schools in the ninth and tenth grades and graduated from Spring High School in 1981. Further all four children were outstanding in their scholastic honors and accomplishments in their professional lives.

DR. J. W. "JIM" AND PEGGY COBB

Jim Cobb opened his dental office in the North Richland Hills Shopping Center in October 1955, and the family moved to a new home on Vance Road in June 1956.

Jim graduated from high school in Byington, Tennessee, in 1941. He worked for the Southern Railway as a brakeman for two years before entering the U.S. Marine Corps in 1943. He served his country for three years, being discharged in 1946. He returned to the Southern Railway for two years then entered Texas Wesleyan College in Fort Worth in 1949, then Baylor College of Dentistry in 1951. He graduated with a degree in dental surgery in 1955.

The Cobbs were charter members of the Richland Hills Church of Christ and have continued their membership there for these many years.

The Vance Road house was home to the Cobb family for eight years, but with three small children, they began feeling the need for more space. They built a home in Richland Hills where they continue to live.

Jim and Peggy met at a USO club at Eagle Mountain Lake and were later married June 14, 1947. They recently celebrated their 50th anniversary.

Their three children all graduated from Richland High School. Stan, born in October 1955, completed dental school and practiced for several years in Spearman, Texas. He currently lives in Royse City with his wife Pam and two daughters, Katie and Grace. Stan is currently attending Dallas Theological Seminary and serves as chaplain at Baylor Dental School. He always told his parents that he wanted to raise his children in a small town like the one where he grew up. He enjoys painting, writing poetry, and was an after-dinner speaker throughout West Texas for many years.

Elise is married to Randall Ford, a research chemist for Texas Eastman in Longview. She enjoys being a stay-at-home mom with children Collin and Jacob.

Hugh Cobb was born in January 1960 and lives in Euless with his wife, Susan Naughton Cobb and their six children, Christopher, Caleb, Courtney, Casey, Catherine, and Caroline. Susan grew up in NRH and is also a Richland High graduate.

The family enjoyed many activities at the Richland Riding Club when the children were young. They participated in Play Days, timed events, and Elise loved to show her paint horse.

Dr. Cobb was mayor of Richland Hills 1996–1997, past president of Richland Hills Riding Club, past president of Fort Worth District Dental Society, past vice president of State Dental Society, past board member of the Northeast Chamber of Commerce, and a delegate to the American Dental Society. He continues to practice dentistry on Glenview Drive, and Peggy manages his office.

CLEATOR AND MOLLIE COLLINS

Cleator Collins and his wife, Mollie, moved to the little town of Smithfield in February 1949. He transferred to the Quartermaster Depot in Fort Worth, bringing five of his 10 children with him. The older children were all married by the time their parents moved to this area. The younger children were twins Audrey and Aubrey, Ottis, Pearl, and the youngest, Jackie Wayne. They lived at 6901 Smithfield Road. Both house and garage were soon remodeled into living quarters for the close-knit family. Later the large piece of land was divided down the middle and a portion was deeded to North Richland Hills so that Odell Street could be extended west of Smithfield Road.

Mollie Collins

Cleator put his East Texas gardening knowledge to good use as he cultivated a large garden and orchard. Although it took lots of vegetables and fruit to feed his family, Mr. Collins always shared his "Truck Patch" garden with his neighbors. Wife Mollie never let anything go to waste. There were always delectable meals at the Collins home, and Mollie carefully canned and froze any surplus as a hedge against the long winter months. By 1952, the Collinses were divorced, and during the 1960s and 1970s Mollie worked at the Smithfield Elementary School lunchroom. She really enjoyed the school children, because by this time all her sons and daughters were grown and married.

Sons Aubrey and Leon were two of the first volunteer firemen for the Smithfield Fire Department. Aubrey currently lives with his wife Eulene in California, where he is a businessman and educator. Daughter Audrey met her husband, Roy Carter, while she worked at the old Smithfield Ice Dock. Roy retired from long-haul trucking after winning numerous awards for safe driving. Audrey worked at B. C. Redding's store for a while before starting a career in banking. They were instrumental in the formation and continuance of the annual Smithfield reunion. Roy died early in 1998, and was mourned by many old-time friends.

Two sons, Ottis and Jackie, entered the upholstery business. Ottis' business for 15 years has been in Southlake,

Collins "Kids" Minnie, Alton, Leon, Syble, Aubrey, Mollie, Audrey, Dorothy, Pearl, Ottis, Jackie

where he lives with his wife, Lorena. Jackie has passed his Colleyville business to his son. He and wife Wanda retired to Weatherford where he pursues his fascinating hobby of vintage car restoration.

An older daughter, Dorothy, was a resource teacher for the Birdville Independent School District for 30 years. Youngest daughter Pearl retired from ownership of a day-care center and lives with her husband, Roy Turnen, in Irving.

Mother Collins was a familiar sight to the neighbors as she drove along Smithfield Road. Her slight, white-haired figure could be seen pushing her mower, cutting her own lawn, well into her seventies. She died at age 92 in 1993. The children's father died at age 89 in 1990.

Each Christmas, the children take turns hosting a weekend get-together for their siblings and spouses. They are grateful for their collective good fortune. They have been gainfully employed, have been good citizens, and for the most part continue to enjoy good health.

Submitted by Audrey Collins Carter

DALE AND DONNA COLLINS

Johnny Dale Collins and Donna Sue Ellenburg were married July 25, 1981, at North Richland Hills Baptist Church by Rev. Hal Brooks. Donna is the daughter of N. A. (Shorty) and Lindell Ellenburg of NRH.

Donna was born in NRH at Glenview Hospital on March 15, 1962. In 1968, she started school at North Richland Elementary and graduated from Richland High School in 1980. Donna was active in RYA girls softball, junior bowling leagues at Richland Bowl, and various other school activities. Following graduation, she went to the University of Texas-Arlington for one year, later attending Tarrant County Junior College, graduating in 1987 with an associate degree in nursing. Since then, she has been employed by Cook Children's Medical

Back—L/R-Jason, Dale, Donna; Front-Kailey

Center, first as an RN in the emergency department, transferring in 1996 to the orthopedic clinic.

Dale was born in Fort Worth on September 15, 1957, graduated from O. D. Wyatt in 1976, and attended Weatherford Junior College where he received his paramedic certificate. He is now employed by Med Star Ambulance in Fort Worth.

Dale and Donna returned to NRH in September 1994 with two children, Jason and Kailey. Jason was born April 22, 1983, in Nacogdoches. In NRH, he attended Mullendore Elementary, and presently attends North Richland Middle School. Jason is active in athletics at school and the Civil Air Patrol.

Kailey was born October 12, 1988, in Fort Worth. She attends Mullendore Elementary School. Kailey is active in North Richland girls softball, church choir, and the church's Girl's Auxiliary (GA).

Dale, Donna, and family are active members of North Richland Hills Baptist Church. They enjoy camping and fishing.

GEORGE AND LIBBY CONANT

George and Libby Conant

The year 1960 is important to the Conant family. This is the year they built and moved into their North Richland Hills home on Dawn Drive. This is approximately 200 yards east of the picnic spot of George's boyhood on Big Fossil Creek. There are memory-building events during the next 37 years. Some large, but most are small. Let's reminisce:

- Cheryl and Ann building broom-weed houses in the field between their house and Big Fossil Creek. There are now three streets of houses in place of broom-weed houses.
- George taking Cheryl and Ann pole fishing on Big Fossil Creek, completing a 30-year reunion with a boyhood memory.
- Walking to Richland Plaza Shopping Center to shop at Montgomery Ward, J. C. Penney, Kresge, and eating ice cream at Carnation Ice Cream Shop.
- Watching floodwaters from Big Fossil Creek creep into Richland Plaza Shopping Center.
- Libby teaching and counseling at Richland Junior High School, Haltom High School, and North Oaks Middle School until 1993.
- Cheryl and Ann attending Browning Heights Elementary School, Birdville Elementary School, North Richland Junior High School, and Richland High School.
- George proudly serving as city councilman in gratitude to NRH from 1974 through 1978; and, council meetings in the old City Hall on Glenview Drive. It is now the Dan Echols Senior Citizen Center.

- Planning and participating in the building of the present City Hall.
- Planning and assisting in bringing North Hills Mall to NRH.
- Taking part in hiring Jeanette Rewis as city secretary.
- George and Libby proudly watching Cheryl and Ann performing in the Richland High School Dixie Belle Drill Team.
- George flying his little orange and white airplane from Mangham Airport (north of Tarrant County Junior College). This is now a vacant field.

Where do we stand now? George and Libby are retired, doing craft work, volunteering, and playing golf. They continue to live on Dawn Drive. Cheryl is now Cheryl Hopmann of Fayetteville, Arkansas, with two teenage boys. Ann is now Ann Bailey of Mustang, Okla., with a daughter and a son.

As they reflect on 37 years of NRH citizenship, they do so with pride in being part of a city that has chosen to grow with dignity, quality, and progressive foresight. It has been a wonderful time. There are so many pleasant memories. Thank you, NRH!

THOMAS H. "TOMMY" AND BEULAH CONN

Thomas H. "Tommy" Conn was born in Des Moines, Iowa, in 1909. Beulah DeLosh Conn was born in Omaha, Nebraska, in 1911. These two Midwesterners were married May 13, 1938, in New Braunfels, Texas. The couple never had any children, which was the way they wanted it. They were each other's best friend and loved doing things together.

Tommy returned home from the service in 1945, having served in the 9th Air Force as an electrician and radio technician in the European Theatre. At various times he was based in France, England, and Belgium.

The Conns moved to Fort Worth and lived in the Ridglea area. Tommy loved music and had played with various bands before his stint in the Air Force. This field

Thomas Conn and his Cessna plane, hangar, and landing strip located behind house on Glenview Drive, early 1950s

of work was a natural for him, and he owned and operated the Thomas H. Conn Music Company for 32 years until his retirement. For most of the time, the store was located at 310 Main Street in the shadow of the Tarrant County Courthouse. In later years, Tommy moved the store to Rosedale Street near the hospital district.

At one time, Beulah thought she needed more to keep her busy, so she opened a hamburger stand on Magnolia Street, where she sold hamburgers for 5 cents each, or six for 25 cents. She quickly admitted this was no way to get ahead financially.

Since both had their private pilot's license, and he had his commercial license, what the Conns wanted most of all was enough property to build a house, airplane hangar, and landing strip. Their hunt for the ideal

Beulah Conn walking to their plane.

site led them to the rural area northeast of Fort Worth. They bought 17 acres fronting on Pipeline Road (later Glenview Dr.) from John Hunter. They had no way of knowing their property would one day be just west of busy Loop 820 in North Richland Hills, and John Hunter would be the city's mayor in the 1960s.

The hangar and landing strip were built first for their Cessna planes, models 140 and 170. The house was begun in 1950 and completed in 1951. There was no water on the property, so the Conns bought pipe from Red Morgan, owner of Red Rooster Lumber Company on Grapevine Highway, and paid to have the pipe laid to a nearby well. They had to cover the ditch themselves.

The Conns spent many hours driving on Belknap Street to their work at the music store, but that was the only route into Fort Worth at that time.

Thomas H. Conn died in 1986. Beulah still lives in the Glenview Drive home they built 46 years ago and sells Mary Kay cosmetics. She finds the busy Loop 820, the traffic on her street, nearby Denny's Restaurant, an apartment complex, and all the other congestion almost impossible to believe when compared with the isolation and rural space they enjoyed so long ago.

Interview with Mrs. Beulah Conn

Submitted by Evalyn Wood Lochridge

THOMAS L. (TOM) AND TRISH WEIR COOKE

Tom, born in Hickory, North Carolina, and Trish, born in McRae, Arkansas, relocated from Fort Worth to Wyoming Trail in North Richland Hills in 1962 after Tom earned his bachelor's degree from North Texas State University. Previously, he had completed four years of military service at Webb Air Force Base in Big Spring, where Trish had begun

her career. In 1976, they purchased a home on Diamond Loch Drive West.

Two sons were born to Tom and Trish: Michael Thomas in 1963, and Mark Steven in 1965. They attended and graduated from Richland High School. Both Mike and Mark were elected student body presidents at the junior high in 1977-78, and 1980-81 and at high school in 1980-81 and 1983-84. They were active in football, basketball, and track at both schools. Mike was a linebacker on Richland's first Bi-district Championship Team in 1980, and Mark earned outstanding athletic award at NRJH. Both were elected to Who's Who their senior years at RHS.

In 1985 Mike earned a degree from Baylor University and in 1987 graduated from Baylor Law School. He became an associate with Law, Snakard and Gambill, and has been a partner with Friedman, Young and Suder since 1993. He is married to the former Pamela Brossart of Albany, Oregon, a graduate of Baylor Nursing School. They have two daughters, Lauren and Annie. They are members of Travis Avenue Baptist Church where Mike teaches a young adult Sunday school class and serves on several committees.

Mark obtained his degree in business from Baylor University in 1989 and has been employed with Acme Brick Company in sales since that time, winning sales awards in 1994 and 1996. Mark married the former Christie Callum in 1993, and they reside in Arlington. Christie attended Texas Tech University and is associated with the home-building industry. They attend Pantego Bible Church, and their first child, Conner Steven Cooke, was born in March 1998.

In 1970, the Cookes became members of the North Richland Hills Baptist Church. They were active in Cub/Boy Scouts, school activities and neighborhood associations, local politics,

L/R, Tom, Mark, and Trish; Standing, Mike, 1969

Jaycees, and Richland Youth Association (RYA). Tom served on the RYA Board as secretary, commissioner in football, and basketball coach. Trish was also active in the Richland Rebels Touchdown Club, 1979-84, serving as vice president, banquet chairman, and on other committees. At NRHBC, she taught in the children's Sunday School Department, served on the Personnel, Prayer, and Pastor's advisory committees, and is currently serving on women's ministry committees.

In 1979, Tom's 17-year marketing career with Gulf Oil Corporation ended with his death from cancer. Trish retired from the Federal Aviation Administration in 1993, after a 39-year career as an administrative program manager. In 1996, Trish married C. Jack Bean and relocated to Fort Worth.

Submitted by Trish Cooke Bean

ROBERT AND MARY ALICE COWNE

Robert H. Cowne and wife, Mary Alice, moved to North Richland Hills with their two daughters, Emily Ann and Judy Lynn, in the fall of 1953. Carol Jean was born in 1955, and Bob was transferred to Little Rock, Arkansas, and then to Des Moines, Iowa. The Cowne clan moved back to NRH in 1957. Subsequently, two more children were born, Robin Mary and John Ted.

When we moved into our present residence in 1957, I often said there was nothing north of us except the Schwartz family. It is so amazing to see how our area has grown today.

L/R–John, Carol, Emily, Judy, Mary Alice, and Robin Cowne, 1960

All five children attended Birdville schools. The first one went to Glenview Elementary, the second one to Richland Elementary, and the last three started at Snow Heights Elementary. Emily went to Richland Junior High, and all the others went to North Richland Junior High. All five graduated from Richland High School.

In 1955, we were without a phone for six months. Bob traveled and asked me to call him every Wednesday night. I used the telephone booth on the street, next to the Little Red Shack, which was the closest phone. After six months, we received a phone for our house, but it was a six-party line.

During the time when we had no phone, I had gone to call my husband, leaving the two girls alone. My pastor came calling and told me later how well I had trained the girls. Emily jumped up until she could see Rev. Bob Young through the glass, but she still wouldn't open the door.

We joined Richland Hills Methodist Church and remember that at least three of NRH's mayors also were members. We were all interested in politics in those days. After all, we were helping to build a city. Bob's job meant his traveling nearly all of our lives. He was an excellent father and husband and loved his family very much. Bob suffered a heart attack and died in 1964.

I have been active in PTAs (as many as four PTAs in one year), in my church, and in several other organizations. When John was in the sixth grade, I began teaching. After three years as a substitute teacher, I found my permanent position at Haltom Junior High where I taught eighth-grade history and ninth-grade general business for 17 years.

I remember the children playing on what was called "Mesquite Hill." This area was located north of what is now Riviera Drive between Holiday Lane and Blaney Avenue. There were no houses there at that time. NRH was a good place for us to raise our family. When my husband died, I had an opportunity to move, but elected to remain here. I am glad that I did.

Submitted By Mary Alice Cowne

JOHN COWSAR

I am an architect. I moved to North Richland Hills on Weyland Drive in 1984 from Hurst. I designed many buildings in the Mid-Cities area, the Town and Country Car Wash in NRH in the mid-1980s and the utility building for the North Richland Hills Baptist Church in 1993, the Northeast Tarrant Chamber of Commerce building in Haltom City, and the Richland Hills community building. I was commissioned by Charles Mayberry Jr., certified public accountant, to help find out what the original Masonic Lodge building (orig. est. 1876) looked like in the late 1800s. The Lodge was located in the old downtown Smithfield area and had been unused for many years. I redrew it as best I knew, and Mr. Mayberry had it moved overland intact to a new site in the 6600 block of Baker Blvd. in Richland Hills. The building was remodeled in 1983. I have a photo of the building being towed (moved) by the Snow Company movers. It is my understanding he sold the building later.

I bought a house on Laurel Lane in December 1987, and still live there, having my architectural practice in my home.

John Cowsar died December 8, 1998.

JOHN RILEY AND MARY ANN DARBY CRANE

Extracted from a booklet "Our Family Tree" by Luther A. Crane, the following are ancestors of Smithfield's John R. Crane.

Jasper Crane (1605–1681) was the first of the forebearers to be identified. He was one of four brothers who came from England to become original settlers of the New Haven Colony in 1639. Wife: Alice.

Deacon Azariah Crane (1649–1730), son of Jasper, married Mary Trent, daughter of Capt. Robert Trent, who became governor of Connecticut.

John Crane (1695–1770), son of Deacon Azariah. Wife: Abigail.

Benjamin Crane, son of John, buried near Craneville, Montgomery County, New York. Married Phebe Meeker, who died on the Ohio River while making the journey west with her son Jonas and family.

The family of John Riley and Mary Ann Crane, seated, standing L/R-William Franklin, Minnie Annette, Mary Lou Ellie, John David, Fannie May, Mayme Cordelia, Walter Leslie. James Lee had married and moved away.

Jonas Crane (1766–1840), son of Benjamin; married Abigail Kitchell, January 22, 1795. Moved west to Harrison, Ohio, then Seymour, Indiana.

Jonas Crane (1810–1868), son of Jonas. Married Sedarey Ann Salmon. Moved to Texas before February 8, 1859. On that date he purchased a 640-acre farm in Smith County, three tracts in Dallas County on September 3, 1859.

John Riley Crane (1848–1914), third son of Jonas and Sedarey Ann Crane, probably born in Seymour, Indiana. He moved to Texas with his parents some time before 1859. He was married in Smith County December 3, 1868, to Mary Ann Darby. She was the daughter of J. G. Darby. He was a farmer and a Methodist preacher in Missouri who moved to Smith County.

The family was living on a farm south of Grapevine when the beloved daughter, Laura Elizabeth, died at the age of 3. John Riley was forced to sell the place in 1875 for $1,000. In 1875, he purchased another place northeast of Smithfield of 120 acres out of the James Harrell Survey from J. E. Trader for $480. He built a house of logs on this place and moved his family. This place was located "near the waters of Big Bear Creek in the lower cross timbers." He sold this place in 1881 and purchased 40 acres from John W. Tyner in 1885, for $200, which was out of the Thos. Peck Survey in the "lower cross timbers," located near the settlement of Shady Grove. He sold the Shady Grove place in 1885 (sic), to Calla Wall.

In his later years, J. R. was appointed postmaster at Smithfield and held that position until his death, at which time his daughter, Mayme, was appointed in his place.

On October 16, 1900, he bought two

John Riley (1848–1914) and Mary Ann Crane (1847–1914)

more acres known as "D. E. Lebow blackberry patch" from G. H. Hollis and others for $65. A tract was sold to his son, J. D. Crane and L. A. Hightower for a "gin lot." A cotton gin was built on this lot and later sold to Winfield Scott. A large water well was dug to provide water for the boiler to operate the gin but it proved insufficient. West of the house was a well of inexhaustible supply so a hand pump was installed in this well and Aunt Ellie manned the pump and produced enough water to operate the gin. A two-acre tract was sold to J. D. Crane Oct. 25, 1905, near the "gin" lot. J. D. Crane built a house on this location and operated the gin for a while. J. R. Crane bought and sold other tracts of land in Smithfield but owned only 38 acres at his death.

J. R. Crane died October 10, 1914. He is buried in the cemetery in Smithfield. Inscription on the grave marker: "In our Father's house are many mansions." Mary Ann Darby Crane died June 4, 1914, and is buried at Smithfield. Her grave marker is inscribed as follows: "In our Father's house are many mansions." Also the following: "Darling Mother she has left us, Left us yes for evermore; but we hope to meet our loved one on that bright and happy shore."

From: "Our Family Tree-A Genealogy" by Luther A. Crane

JOHN AND MARION CRAWFORD

John Crawford and Marion Chudoba were married in 1953 in Leonard, Texas. They met in 1949 while John was working for United Geophysical Company in Peace River, Alberta, Canada. Marion was born and raised in Reno, Alberta, Canada, and completed her high school and business college in Peace River. John was born in Detroit, Texas, and attended and graduated from the area schools (Detroit, Marvin, and Blossom, Texas).

Marion and John Crawford, 1996

John served in the U.S. Marine Corps and the U.S. Army, after which he came to Fort Worth and was employed by General Dynamics. He also worked with the Fort Worth Police Reserve for approximately 10 years.

The Crawfords purchased their first home in southeast Fort Worth. This was home to their three sons, Kerry Dale, Bradley Wayne, and Michael Scott, all born at Harris Hospital. After a massive layoff at General Dynamics, John went to work at Bell Helicopter in 1961 as a dispatcher and supervisor. Marion has worked for a number of companies as executive secretary, administrative assistant, and office manager.

In 1965, they moved to North Richland Hills because they needed a larger home to accommodate their growing family. All three of the boys attended Glenview Elementary, Richland Junior High, and graduated from Richland High School. Kerry and Bradley graduated from Tarrant County Junior College and the University of Texas-Arlington. Scott graduated from Devry Institute in Dallas as an electronics

Brad's wedding, 1992, L/R-Bonnie, Shannon, Michelle, Kerry, Jodi, Brad, Marion, John, Michael, Scott, Sandy, and Eric

technician. Kerry is employed by American Airlines as a computer programmer, Bradley is a civil engineer with the Environmental Protection Agency in Dallas, Scott was a quality control supervisor with Tandy Corporation until a layoff. Kerry and family reside in NRH, Bradley and family in Mesquite, and Scott and family in Hurst.

Kerry married Bonnie Bunch, a computer programmer, in 1987, and they have four children: Eric, Michelle, Shannon, and Kelly. Bradley married Jodi Patterson, a kindergarten teacher, in Mesquite in 1992, and they have two children, Cathleen and Rachel. Scott married Sandy Clement, a flight test technician, in 1982, and they have one son, Michael.

While the children were at home, John and Marion were active with PTA, scouting programs, Little League, etc. As a family, they enjoyed fishing, camping, and traveling to Canada to visit their grandparents farm.

John and Marion are both retired and enjoying their fifth-wheel recreational vehicle and do a lot of traveling and camping as well as enjoying their grandchildren.

JOHN M. AND WILMA CRAWFORD

In 1959, the Crawford family moved to North Richland Hills from their home in Fort Worth. The family consisted of John Sr., Wilma, and their three children: John Jr., Patricia (Patti), and James (Jimmy). Wilma's mother had recently passed away and her father, Otto Petzold, came

Back-John Sr., Wilma; Front-James, Patricia, John Jr.

along with them to NRH. Mr. Petzold was a native of Germany and passed away in 1979 at the age of 89.

The children went through their school years in the Birdville School District, and all graduated from Richland High School.

John Sr. served on the NRH Planning and Zoning Board in the late 1960s.

Family Members:
- John M. Crawford Sr. was born in Keller and served in the 11th Airborne Division in the Pacific during World War II. He retired from Western Electric (Lucent Technologies) after 42 years of service.
- Wilma P. Crawford was born in Fort Worth, and she has been married to John for 51 years. She enjoys their five grandchildren, Melissa, Jessica, Stephanie, Ryan, and Jay. She has been a homemaker all these years.
- John M. Crawford Jr. was born in Fort Worth and served in the U.S. Army in Germany during the Vietnam War. He has been an electric designer for Friberg Associates Inc., for 28 years.
- Patricia L. Crawford Salmons was born in Fort Worth and married M. O. Salmons, and they have two daughters. She is employed by the Hurst-Euless-Bedford School District.
- James T. (Jimmy) Crawford was born in Fort Worth and is the father of a daughter and two sons and lives in Arlington. He is employed by North Texas Door & Trim Company. He has been in the building trades suppliers business for 20 years.

LEWIS EARL AND HATTIE BELLE REEVES CRIBBS

In 1968, Lewis and Hattie Cribbs bought a home in North Richland Hills. It was a brick house located on a two-acre lot on Oak Ridge Terrace. There were 11 families who owned about 20 acres in what is now known as Richland Centre. The three streets, Oak Ridge Terrace, Bridle Trail, and Mesa Verde no longer exist.

The Richland Riding Club arena was located on Bridle Trail. Once a month the riding club sponsored a play day, which brought riders from far and near. What fun to watch riders run poles, barrels, compete in races, and practice grand-entry drills. Since we had a barn, a dog run, and a guest house on our lot, our daughter, Lennie Lou, brought her horse home from the farm for her to ride in the arena. One night, someone opened our yard gate, and "Ol' Buck" went out—free to roam! The neighbors across the street had the same visitors that also let their horses out. All their horses were back in their stalls soon, but not "Ol' Buck." We found him running wild in the triangle between Loop 820 South, Loop 820 North, and the Airport Freeway. Cowboys, policemen, and cattlemen stopped to help capture "Ol' Buck," but no such luck. When Hattie's brother, Pryor F. Reeves, arrived, "Ol' Buck" settled down. Pryor put a bridle on him and jumped on him bareback, and rode him into the trailer. Needless to say, "Ol' Buck" was taken back to our farm and didn't spend another night in North Richland Hills.

A homeowners association was formed by the 11 families that lived on the 20-acre tract of land. Robert Chadwell was elected president, Lou Chadwell was treasurer, and Hattie Cribbs was secretary. The association was active in civic affairs of NRH. Walker Branch Creek ran through some of the homeowners' properties. Problems of the creek and developers wanting to buy all of the property were two major concerns of the homeowners association. They thought that all problems were resolved because ten of the families sold their homes and moved. Mr. Bert Collins and Mr. Herman Smith bought the property and developed the Richland Centre. A few of the houses were sold and moved to other locations. The Cribbs' 3,000-square-foot house was bulldozed down.

Hattie and Lewis Cribbs

Lewis and Hattie bought a home in the Meadow Lakes addition of NRH. They never once dreamed of living in a two-story house, but they are now enjoying life on their little lake on Lake Side Circle. They have fish, turtles, geese, ducks, and even beavers.

Their daughter, Lennie Lou, and husband, Gary J. Suggs, and their son, Jason, live on Castle Combe Place in NRH. They spend time fishing or just sitting on the dock listening to the sounds of the night while all eat watermelon. The wonderful neighborhood with so many sounds of the morning, sounds of the night, and the train whistle that makes such a grand sound—this is what makes an "Ol' country" couple happy!

Submitted by Hattie Cribbs

DUB AND AVIS CRISP

In 1954, A. W. Crisp Jr. (Dub), Avis, and 18-month-old Sharon moved into their new home on Jerrell Street in NRH. The Crisps were looking for affordable new housing located close to their places of employment.

Conveniences were pretty sparse. The nearest supermarket was located near Belknap and Sylvania streets. Water was supplied from wells owned by a private company. Garbage pickup was provided at first by a Haltom City hog farmer who came by periodically to collect trash in his farm truck. There was no local fire or police protection. A small fee was paid monthly to a Richland Hills man who agreed to act as a sort of night watchman for the area. He would also respond to calls for help at night. Fire protection was provided by volunteers. But the major deprivation for most of North Richland Hills' new residents was the absence of a place to eat out.

But the Crisp family enjoyed their new home and were busy putting in a new lawn, planting trees, getting acquainted with new neighbors, and adding to their family. Cheryl arrived in 1956 and David in 1957.

NRH was growing too. New housing developments were springing up to the north, and the Crisps moved into a larger house in 1958 on Victoria Street. They became charter members of the new Methodist Church established in the area in 1959, and set to work to help Davis Memorial United Methodist grow and prosper. In 1972, the family moved to Edmonds-Spronce Road, now Bursey Road on the northern border of the city where Dub and Cheryl had room for a barn and their horses.

All the Crisp children attended Snow Heights, North Richland Junior High, and Richland High. Sharon graduated from Richland in 1970, Cheryl in 1974, and David in 1975.

Back, L/R-Cheryl (Crisp) Clemens, Sharon (Crisp) Wadsworth, Larry Wadsworth; Front, L/R-David, Avis, and Dub Crisp

Sharon went on to graduate from Texas Christian University. She married a coach/administrator named Larry Wadsworth and teaches in the Arlington School District. Cheryl attended Tarleton State College, married an Aggie from Euless, Dean Clemens, moved to Jasper and then Silsbee in East Texas, had two beautiful and wonderful children, Kristin (born in 1980) and Andrew (born in 1982), and now lives in Franklin, Tennessee. She works as a personal trainer for the YMCA, and Dean is a human resources executive. David attended the University of Texas and graduated from Stephen F. Austin with a degree in accounting. He worked in Houston for awhile after graduation, but returned to Dallas where he owns Alpine Movers.

Dub had an opportunity to open a heavy equipment business in April 1963 in partnership with two others. Fort Worth Equipment Co. was located on Loop 820 at Highway 183. In October 1968, he bought out his partners, renamed the business Crisp Equipment Co., and built a new shop on land bought from E. R. Newman and E. F. Abbott at Midway Road and Texas 121. In 1978 he relocated to Keller, first on Highway 377, then in 1983 to Golden Triangle Boulevard, and in 1984 to I-35W. He retired from business at that location in 1985.

Avis started work on a history degree at the University of Texas at Arlington in 1964. After a five-year, nonstop effort, she graduated in May 1969, and went to work in September of that year as a social studies teacher at L. D. Bell High School in Hurst. She retired in 1992.

Much of Dub's time after retirement has been spent on horseback. He has been a member of several riding groups, including the Tarrant County Sheriff's Posse. He has been on dozens of trail rides across the country, living the life of the old-time cowboy, except he has a motor home equipped with air-conditioning and microwave oven, to pull his horse trailer.

The decision to make North Richland Hills their home was made almost casually by the Crisps back in 1954. Their choice of North Richland Hills was guided by divine providence. It proved to be a grand place to spend their lives, raise and educate their children, make lasting friendships, and reap the benefits to be enjoyed from living in a place where growth and progress provided a good environment for their family.

Submitted by Avis Crisp

E. F. Sr. and Nola Crites
by E. F. Crites Jr.

My father, Edgar Franklin Crites, was born near Roanoke, Texas, to Elonzo Franklin Crites and Nola Lucinda Davis. They moved to a farm of approximately 250 acres located a few blocks east of the present Rufe Snow Drive and a few blocks north of what became Hightower Street. My grandparents came here from Missouri in the late 1800s. My father attended Smithfield School and graduated from high school there.

I spent a lot of time at the Crites' farm, particularly in the summer. When I was 13, I started spending a number of weeks with my grandparents, assisting them with the harvesting of the wheat and oats. After the threshing

Elonzo and Nola Crites, circa 1920

was completed, the plowing was done with a team of horses or mules. Both my parents, having been raised on farms, thought it was important that I have this experience of living and working on a farm, even though it was only for a few weeks in the summer. I felt, after doing this for three years, it was quite an imposition on me and my summer vacation. However, as time went by, I found out this was the finest working family experience I ever had. It probably should

E. F. Crites, Sr., Mobil Oil Co., 1925

Elonzo and Nola Crites with grandchildren E. F. Jr. and Mary Crites

be something that all young boys could have the opportunity to do.

Sunday was set aside for resting and going to church and very little other activity. There was a tank about a quarter of a mile from the house where I could fish with friends. It was well stocked and provided some great fishing. In later years, I was allowed to bring friends out to hunt doves and ducks around the tank and farm. I remember with a great deal of pleasure bringing several of my high school buddies out, and that this was the place that I killed my first doves and first duck.

Christmas and Thanksgiving and other holidays were special times at Grandma and Grandpa Crites' house.

Conservation was a big thing with Grandpa Crites. When you came in from the field after a hard day's work, you could draw one pan of water to wash in. You could never allow the spigot to run except to fill the pan, and you could only have the one pan-ful. There was no wasting water or anything else. A complete bath was on Saturday.

Grandpa Crites owned approximately 40 acres of timberland just east of Keller for the purpose of having wood available to burn for cooking and heating. I talked to my cousin, C. L. Turner, recently, and he told me of an interesting episode that happened at this 40-acre tract of land. Grandpa had sent him there to bring back a load of firewood, and it was a distance of seven or eight miles from the farm to this tract of land. Grandpa cautioned C. L. about the care of the horses. While he was loading wood, something happened, and the horses got away and started running, and he had to catch them. He finally got them hitched up, and the wood loaded and ran them all the way home. When he got there, Grandpa saw the condition of the horses and was more worried about them than what happened to C. L. or the load of wood.

There was a storm cellar on the Crites' farm, and when a storm blew in, we all went to the cellar. Grandpa took a coal oil lantern for light and two large axes to chop our way out if a tree or building fell on the cellar door. The axe was also used to kill snakes.

There was no electricity in the Crites' home until the early 1940s. Heat was obtained from wood-burning fireplaces and coal-oil stoves. Lighting was obtained from carbide gas, but was used very little.

E. F. Jr. and Irma Crites

My name is E. F. Crites Jr. My wife, Irma, is the former Irma Jean Bradford. We live on Skylark Circle in North Richland Hills Meadow Lakes Addition. We have lived in the

Haltom-Richland area for more than 30 years. Our daughter, Judy (now deceased), and our son, Mark, graduated from Richland High School after completing elementary and junior high school in the NRH area. I am the son of E. F. and Mattie Crites, both of whom were born and raised in the Haltom-Richland area. I was born in 1926 in Wichita Falls, Texas, and moved with my family to Fort Worth in 1933. My parents were married in 1924. My mother was Mattie Reeves, one of 13 children. Her father was William Osburn Reeves, and

E. F. Jr. and Irma Crites

her mother, Marybelle Pelley Reeves. My mother was born March 1, 1900, and died September 12, 1978. My father was born September 5, 1901, and died May 3, 1986.

Irma and I were married December 18, 1943, while I was in the Army during World War II. I served in Europe and was discharged in June 1946. Our daughter was born June 2, 1947, and died November 13, 1984. She was married to Lee Herron, and they had three children, Amanda, Daniel, and David. Our son was born March 3, 1952, and lives near Azle with his wife, Gayle Griggs Crites. They have three children, Carrie, Amy Vanderpool, and Melissa.

I went to work for my father in the gasoline distributing business in 1946 and later became a partner with him in this business under the name of Crites Oil Company. We distributed Skelly, Phillips, and Fina products. We sold this business in 1962, at which time I founded American National Mortgage Company Inc., as well as Crites Insurance Agency. Our other businesses were Crites Builders and Builders of America.

Irma and I have been members of Richland Hills United Methodist Church more than 30 years. It was my pleasure to be a member of the Richland Industrial Development Board for a number of years. I am a past trustee of Birdville Independent School District.

Submitted by E. F. Crites Jr.

GUY L. AND NAOMI "SIS" CUMMINGS

Guy Lindsay Cummings Jr. was born to Guy L. Cummings and Alma Chandler Cummings in 1923, when they were living in Boynton, Oklahoma. He graduated from Riverside High School in 1941, and from Texas Christian University in 1951. He served in the U.S. Army Air Corps during World War II as a B-17 pilot in the 5th Air Force. He was a captain in 1945 when he returned home.

I, Naomi Ruth "Sis" Jones Cummings, was born in Fort Worth to Alma Ruth and Clarence Jones in 1924. I graduated from Riverside High School in 1941 and TCU in 1944.

Guy and I married in September 1946, and lived in Riverside until we moved to North Richland Hills in the fall of 1955 on Vance Road. Our good friends, Gay and

Hubert Joyner, lived across the street. Houses were in the process of being built, but at that time there were a number of vacant lots. We lived on Vance Road until 1957. The Roy Millers bought this home, and we moved to Riviera Drive.

Our son, Mark, was born in 1960, while we were living here, and this was a very special time. He really liked being pushed in his stroller to the corner of Riviera and Cummings Drives. Here he could watch the big road equipment working on all the new roads north of us. He graduated from Haltom High School in 1979, and was a graduate of North Texas State University in 1982.

Naomi "Sis" Cummings

We lived close to my mother and dad, Ruth and Clarence Jones, and my sister, Dorothy Turner, and her family. Mark received much attention with his grandmother and Pa Pa coming by often for a hug and a visit.

I was involved with Richland Hills Eastern Star Chapter No. 1040, and was Worthy Matron from 1961 to 1962. There are so many wonderful friends that I met at that time. I wouldn't have missed having the fun and companionship. We joined North Richland Hills Baptist Church in November 1957.

Mark has a small farm in Weatherford that he shares with his cats and a dog. He restores and collects Italian motorcycles. In the summer of 1996, he traveled with the

Mark Cummings

Olympic Torch Relay as a video camera motorcycle driver as well as covering bicycle racing, marathons, and race walking at the Olympics. He also ran with the torch during the relay. He works as a video camera motorcycle driver for such events as the Tour Du Pont, the Ironman Triathlon, and the New York Marathon. The Olympics were a wonderful experience for him.

Guy was working at the Haltom City State Bank when we moved to NRH in 1955, and was president when we moved from NRH in March 1966. He was very active at Diamond Oaks Country Club for a number of years.

My memories of living on the farm with my family, and then when it became NRH, are very fond ones. This will always be a special time—a special memory.

Submitted by Naomi "Sis" Cummings

LARRY AND JULIE CUNNINGHAM

Larry and Julie Cunningham and two of their three children, Kril and Kristen, moved to North Richland Hills in

March 1993 when Larry became finance director for the city of NRH. Their third child, Kim, was enrolled at Southwest Texas State University and continues to live and work in the Austin area. Julie continued her career as a fifth-grade teacher in Grace Hardeman Elementary School.

Kril enrolled at Richland High School and graduated in May 1996. He spent his junior year in Olpe, Germany, and although he enjoyed it, he was glad to return home to NRH. Kril is currently enrolled at Abilene Christian University majoring in International Business.

Kristen completed her college degree in finance at Lubbock Christian University in May 1997, and lives and works in the North Texas area. Larry later became assistant city manager and then became city manager of NRH in July 1997.

Larry and Julie Cunningham

The entire Cunningham family continually comments about the warm welcome and friendliness shown as they adjusted to their new home! A City of Choice—for families to live, work, play, and make friends!

L/R-Kril, Larry, Kristen, Julie, and Kim Cunningham

WAYNE AND BETTY PORTER CUNNINGHAM

Wayne C. Cunningham and Betty J. Porter Cunningham grew up on the north side of Fort Worth. We started to

Wayne and Betty Cunningham

school together in the third grade and attended the same schools until we graduated from North Side High School in 1952. We married a month later in June 1952.

My parents, Jack and Opal Porter, owned and operated the Feed Trough, a popular eating spot on Northwest 25th Street on the north side of Fort Worth for many years. Opal later was an employee of North Richland Drug for 17 years.

Back - Sandy, Gale, B.J. Front - Gary, Cathy, Tommy

We moved to Richland Hills in 1952, and then to North Richland Hills in 1959. At that time we had one child, Gary Wayne, born in 1954. We were blessed with five additional children: Cathy Sue, born in 1959; Tommy Warren, born in 1960; Betty Jayne (B. J.), born in 1963; Gayle Ann, born in 1966; and Sandy Kay, born in 1968.

All the children attended Snow Heights Elementary School where each had Mrs. Mary Alice Clark for their first-grade teacher. They attended North Richland Junior High and Richland High School. I was in Snow Heights Preschool and PTA for 20 years and was awarded a lifetime membership in that organization. At one time, we had a child in kindergarten, elementary school, junior high school, high school, and college.

Our family joined North Richland Hills Baptist Church in 1968, transferring from Richland Hills Baptist. The entire family is active in church work. Wayne is an usher, and I am a greeter.

All our children were very active in sports. Gary, Cathy, and Tommy were members of the Mid-Cities Swim Team. Gayle was all-around Texas state champion in gymnastics. Tommy played Peewee football. Cathy, B. J. and Sandy participated in softball, basketball, and track. Wayne helped coach each of these teams.

We had one of the first backyard swimming pools in NRH. We often had as many as 50 friends over at one time enjoying the pool. We let each child have a class end-of-school swim party. We also taught swimming lessons for eight years during the month of June. We only accepted 100 children during that month. Each of our children helped with the lessons. The money charged for the lesson was equally distributed among old and young children alike. Enough money was earned for each child to be able to purchase his or her first "used" car at age 16.

We lived on the corner of Karen Drive and Loop 820, but there was no Loop 820 at that time. We watched it being built. The present City Hall was just a cow pasture where our children rode their bikes.

As our children grew, Tommy was elected president of the student body at Richland High School. All our girls were members of the Dixie Belles drill team and cheerleaders at Richland High School.

In 1983, our family was selected as Family of the Year in the Mid-Cities area.

Tommy opened his own boot store, Tom-Bo's Boots, at age 16 while still in high school. He was in the boot business for 10 years before becoming a home and commercial builder. He graduated from Texas Christian University and now owns three strip-shopping centers. He and wife, Shelly, live in Colleyville and have three children. Gary graduated from the University of Texas at Arlington and is now an architect living in Vienna, Austria.

Cathy attended Tarrant County Junior College and has her own business, "Mansion Managers." She and her husband, Art Romack, live in Colleyville and have four children. B. J. graduated from Baylor University, married a Boston banker, Andy Doherty. They live in Atlanta and have three children. Gayle attended Baylor University and has now started a gymnastics school. She and her husband, Butch Shank, have three children and live in Farmers Branch. Sandy graduated from cosmetology college. She worked three years for the Birdville School District. She and her husband, Tommy Riley, live in Lewisville and have one child.

Wayne sold our business, Wayne's Boots, in 1990 after 35 years in the business. At this writing, 1997, Wayne and I have been married 45 years. We have 14 grandchildren—7 boys and 7 girls. Their ages range from 1 week old to 17 years old. Wayne and I now travel, play bridge, walk, enjoy our children and grandchildren and church.

Submitted by Betty Cunningham

HARRY AND MARGARET DAGGETT

Harry Daggett was born in Fayetteville, Arkansas; Margaret Porter Daggett was born in Olney, Texas. They moved to North Richland Hills in 1960. There are two daughters, Linda Jean, born in Jacksboro, and Cherilyn Sue, born in Fort Worth.

Harry served three years in the U.S. Navy as petty officer second class from 1942–1946. He served through the Pacific battles, from San Diego to Oahu, Hawaii, on a merchant ship to Manila, aboard the repair ship, Medusa, and back to the states to Long Beach, California.

He became an accomplished industrial pattern maker and began working for a small company in Mineral Wells after the war. When the company burned, he moved to Fort Worth. He went to work for AAA Patterns, Inc., owned by Joe Scott. He retired after 40 years with the company.

Harry has always enjoyed working with his hands. His children have said there is nothing he couldn't make. He enjoyed models, making model trains and scale models of the electric power plants on Main Street and the

Handley plant. These were on display for years in the lobby of the Texas Electric building in downtown Fort Worth. He also made three Bell helicopter models for the Shah of Iran. These were about two-feet-long, cast in brass, then polished and mounted on pedestals to resemble the blowing sands.

Margaret Porter Daggett was a laboratory technologist until her retirement in 1987. She worked at St. Joseph Hospital and for Dr. James Linton.

Daughters Jeannie and Sue were both graduates of Fort Worth Christian School where they were involved in many extracurricular activities. Jeanie is married to William Dan Carter, a minister. They have two sons and live in Killeen, Texas. Sue is a pharmaceutical aide, has three children, and lives in North Richland Hills.

The family has enjoyed caring for 11 foster children through the years, each for various lengths of time. They loved each of them equally and continue family ties with each even though they are now quite scattered geographically.

The Daggetts have been active members of the Smithfield Church of Christ where Harry has served as an elder since 1963. Both have been actively involved in the Fort Worth Christian School Parent-Teacher Organization, and both Harry and Margaret sang with the Community Chorus and Concert Chorale at TCJC.

HAROLD AND DELORES DALEY

Delores Jean Spencer Daley and Harold Bernard Daley Jr. moved to North Richland Hills in 1954. High school sweethearts, the Daleys married after graduating from Amon G. Carter-Riverside High School.

Following Harold's service in the Navy, the couple decided to locate in NRH where Harold's aunt and uncle, Ruth

Delores and Harold Daley-1959

and Clarence Jones, were developing the small town by selling family farmland. Several of the streets located along the original homesteads were named after family members. The Joneses named Daley Avenue after Harold's parents, Harold Sr. and Agnes Daley, who lived in Haltom City.

Harold and Delores lived in NRH before city services were available. There were no streetlights. The Daleys, along with other homeowners, paid a security guard to serve as the police.

In November 1995, the Daleys opened Eastern Tarrant Insurance Agency in Greater Richland Center located on Grapevine Highway where other small businesses and city offices had recently located.

In 1956, Delores's sister and her husband, Betty and Walter Cooke, and their son Michael, moved down the street from the Daleys to a home on Vance Road. Tony Cooke, their second son, was born in 1961. The Cooke family still resides on Vance Road today. While living in NRH, two daughters were born to Delores and Harold, Monica DeAnn and Vickie Elaine.

Delores's parents, Alice and Claude Spencer, also moved to NRH in 1965, to a home located on Holiday Lane, down the street from the high school. Harold's sister and her husband, Audrey and Rae Womack, and their twin boys, Patrick and Michael, also moved to town. Edward "Toby" Daley, Harold's brother, his wife Dot, and their son Toby Lee later also resided in North Richland Hills.

Harold and Delores were involved in the small bustling community. Harold served on the City Council from 1965 to 1969. He was also a representative on what was then called the Tarrant County Water Supply Corporation. Delores was one of the first members initiated into the Eastern Star and was a member of the Richland Hills Garden Club. She was also active in the local Republican Party, headquartered at 7109 Grapevine Highway. Delores and Harold were members of the North Richland Hills Baptist Church. They also belonged to the Lion's Club and the Chamber of Commerce.

In 1962, the family moved down the street to 4916 Harrell Street. DeAnn and Vickie attended the neighborhood elementary and junior high schools, Snow Heights and North Richland Junior High. DeAnn also attended Richland High School. Delores later moved to California where she worked for several years as an electronics manufacturing representative in Silicon Valley. Harold continues to work in finance and investments and lives in Haltom City.

Vickie attended Southwest Texas State University in San Marcos. She later moved to Los Angeles to pursue a successful career in the electronics and telecommunications industry. She attended the University of California at Los Angeles to continue her studies in music. DeAnn graduated from Texas Tech University with a degree in journalism. She moved to Midland to work at the ABC affiliate television station as a news reporter.

In Midland, DeAnn met Harold Gregory Holcomb, and in 1982 the couple married at North Richland Hills Baptist Church with pastor Hal Brooks presiding over the ceremony. In 1991, Spencer Gregory was born, and DeAnn and Greg are expecting a second child in February 1999. They now live in Plano, Texas.

Submitted by DeAnn Daley Holcomb

BURL DANIEL

Burl Baker and Pauline Daniel moved to Holiday Lane East in 1955. Burl was born in Grapevine in 1900. Pauline was born in Winnsboro, Texas, in 1904. Burl and Pauline met in Grapevine in 1926 and were married in Dallas in 1927. They made their home in Grapevine until 1930 when they moved to the north side of Fort Worth.

Burl was a registered pharmacist and owned and operated Daniel Pharmacy and Daniel-Cunningham Drug in Fort Worth. They resided in the Arlington Heights area of Fort Worth from 1932 until their move to North Richland Hills.

Burl and Pauline joined the Richland Hills Methodist Church soon after moving to NRH. They were active in the early formation of NRH, taking part in many functions involving the early city government.

They had two sons, Jerry Seburn Daniel and Burl B. Daniel. Burl passed away in September 1969. In the early 1970s, Pauline moved back to the Arlington Heights area of Fort Worth. She died in June 1991. Both Burl and Pauline are buried in Blue Bonnet Hills Cemetery in Colleyville.

Jerry Seburn Daniel, son of Burl and Pauline Daniel, moved to NRH with his parents in 1955. At the time, he was a student at Texas Christian University. Jerry was born in Fort Worth in 1935. He married Sue Mason of Fort Worth. They had two children, Todd Mason and Courtney Sue Daniel. Jerry is in the insurance business in Fort Worth.

Burl B. Daniel, son of Burl and Pauline, moved with his wife Dorothy Ardell (Gant) to North Richland Hills in September 1958. Burl finished his degree in pharmacy at the University of Texas in Austin in August 1958 after serving as an officer in the U.S. Air Force Medical Service. Dorothy was a nurse in the U.S. Air Force when they met at Gunter AFB, Montgomery, Ala. They were married in November 1951 in Durant, Oklahoma in the First Presbyterian Church. Dorothy and Burl had three sons: Burl Brian, Mark Gant, and David Wayne. Burl Brian was born in the Canal Zone in November 1953, Mark Gant was born in Austin in October 1955, and David was born in Fort Worth in March 1960. All three reside in the Tarrant County area.

Dorothy died in May 1969. Burl married Margie Jarrell Frederick in 1970. Margie had two daughters, Martha and Melissa. As of February 1998, Burl and Margie reside in the Overton Park area of Fort Worth.

Burl became involved in city activities in North Richland Hills in the late 1950s and 1960s. He was selected to help write the charter for the city in 1960–61. He headed up the effort for the first bond election for the city (an $800,000 street improvement effort that was defeated by eight votes). In 1961, Burl opened the Daniel Drug at 3520 Denton Highway in Haltom City. At that time, Dorothy and Burl lived on Tabor, a home they occupied for nine and one half years. In 1962, Burl was appointed to the Birdville School board and served for 11 years. Dorothy and Burl moved to Holiday Lane West in 1967.

When Burl and Margie married, they moved to Diamond Loch and resided there until 1976. Burl purchased and operated several drugstores in Tarrant County, including the Daniel Pharmacy in Haltom City, Daniel Pharmacy in River Oaks, and Daniel Drug on the West Side of Fort Worth. He was a founding director in the First National Bank North East on Rufe Snow Drive.

Submitted by Burl Daniel

TRAVIS AND DORIS DANIEL

Travis and Doris Daniel moved to North Richland Hills in 1963 after having lived in west Fort Worth since their marriage in 1948. Moving with them were their children, Deb and Rob, who both attended Snow Heights Elementary, North Richland Junior High, and Richland High School.

Travis attended Tarleton State College and Texas Tech before beginning his career in the Railway Mail Service, later becoming a part of the U.S. Post Office in Fort Worth. He retired in 1983. Doris began her banking career in Ballinger, continuing with Texas American

Travis and Doris Daniel

Bank in Fort Worth until her retirement in 1987.

Deb received her business degree from Texas Wesleyan College and went into banking. She and John Levitt were married in 1975. He received his civil engineering degree from University of Texas at Arlington and operates his engineering firm in Grapevine where they have lived since 1978. They have two daughters, Lori and Katlyn. They're all active in community, school, and church activities.

After attending Texas A&M, Rob married September Barclay in 1976. They have resided in North Richland Hills since 1979. Rob owns his own business, Southern Mill Works, and September is in management with Northrup Grumman.

The entire family enjoys many activities, including outings at the family farm near Stephenville.

DAVID AND DENISE DARWIN

Denise Helton moved to North Richland Hills at the age of 13 and became a student at Richland Junior High and Richland High School. In 1974, her senior year at Richland, Denise joined the vocational office program and was placed for employment at Lewis Label Products in Riverside. Denise has worked for Lewis Label since that time, becoming the state secretary for State Representative Gib Lewis during his terms as Speaker of the House, and later office manager for Lewis Label Products.

Denise met David Darwin, a graduate of Azle High School in 1982, and they were married at Lake Arlington

Baptist Church on June 25, 1983. At that time, David was a salesman for Hillard Auto Park in Fort Worth. In September 1994, he opened the Saturn of Hurst plant as its first sales manager.

The couple lives on Shady Lake Drive, and they are members of Lake Arlington Baptist Church.

David and Denise Darwin

J. FRED DAVIS

Two landmarks in North Richland Hills are named in honor of the family of J. Fred Davis: Davis Memorial United Methodist Church and Davis Boulevard. J. Fred Davis Sr., born in 1897 in Alvarado, Texas, was one of nine children. He was the son of the Rev. George Crockett Davis, a circuit-riding Methodist preacher for over 50 years.

Mr. Davis was married to Maude Reeves, also born in 1897, when he was 21. The couple met in church at Isham Chapel. Her parents owned a farm on the Trinity River just west of present-day Newell and Newell Industrial Park. Mrs. Davis was a graduate of the forerunner of the University of North Texas. After graduation Mrs. Davis taught Latin in a Fort Worth public school in the Handley area of Fort Worth until her only child, J. Fred Davis Jr., was born in 1928.

J. Fred Davis Jr. pictured at Four Points in the forties ready to help uncle Guy Reeves ride the range

In the early 1940s the Davises bought a farm on Smithfield Road in what would one day become North Richland Hills. Their move to Northeast Tarrant County was in part due to their son's interest in making agriculture his career. Their farm was located a short distance north of Guy Reeves' farm on the Grapevine Highway. Guy Reeves was Mrs. Davis' brother. Regular family get-togethers on Sundays at his grandparents' farm and summers spent working with his Uncle Guy had convinced Fred Jr. that agriculture, specifically dairy-farming, was what he wanted to do. The Davis home was located where Holiday Heights Elementary School now stands.

Fred Jr. graduated from Texas A&M. While pursuing a postgraduate course at Purdue, Fred Jr. met Jean Cravens, who was also working toward a degree. They were married in 1951. Shortly thereafter, the young couple moved into a house across Smithfield Road from the elder Davises. Eventually, they would build a house on the family farm and begin their distinguished career in the dairy industry. Later, two children, Anne and Robert, were born into the family.

Maude (Reeves) and J. Fred Davis Sr.

Robert is still involved in the family business, and Anne's son has expressed an interest in carrying on the Davis family tradition of raising nationally acclaimed, prize-winning dairy animals.

In the late 1950s, J. Fred Sr. and Maude made a gift of five acres of land to the Methodist Church as a site for a new church, and in July 1959, Davis Memorial United Methodist Church was established as a living memorial to Mr. Davis' father. The Davises moved their church membership to the new church, and both became very involved in getting the church built and in helping it thrive through the years. Fred Sr. was also involved in civic affairs. He was on the original board of directors of Northeast National Bank and was a charter member of the Library Board.

As the area around the farm on Smithfield Road began to develop, Fred Jr. and Jean moved their dairy operation to Haslet in 1956. Fred Sr. and Maude followed in 1966.

J. Fred Davis Family pictured at a Reeves reunion held at the Davis Farm where farm life and fellowship was enjoyed for the day.

The Davises retired from their furniture business in the 1960s. Mrs. Davis died in 1978 at age 80. Mr. Davis died at 99 years of age in 1997. Mr. Davis was known as a great teller of tales. He nearly always had a funny story or joke to share with friends. In his later years, he laughingly told his daughter-in-law, Jean, that since he had outlived most of his contemporaries, he could embellish his tales or make up any story he pleased, because there was no longer anyone around who could dispute the truth of what he said.

Fred Davis Jr. died in an automobile accident on June 23, 1998. Ironically, the accident occurred at the intersection of Davis Boulevard and North Tarrant Parkway.

Submitted by Jean Davis

MILLARD AND PAULINE DEMY

Pauline Owen Demy, a native of northern Mississippi, was raised on a farm in Union County by her "sharecropper" family. She is quick to point out that the life of a sharecropper is not wealthy plantation life, but rather a hard-working life of toiling daily in the fields. This fieldwork involved planting corn, cotton, and various crops, chopping cotton and food crops, and at harvest time, picking cotton. School was always held between the planting and harvest seasons.

In later years, Pauline attended Moody Bible Institute in Chicago, where she met Millard Demy, who was pursuing his study for the ministry. Throughout his life, Millard cultivated traits and interests that were instilled in him by his family during his formative years. He had an inquisitive mind that loved science and mechanics, art and music, animals and people. His father had a construction business, a blacksmith's shop, and an ice business in which Millard worked and from which he learned the dignity of labor and job of craftsmanship. He learned his lessons well and was content in every endeavor he pursued. As the only son, he left with his father's blessing and encouragement to pursue his devotion to the Scriptures and the Savior.

After their marriage in September 1940, Millard and Pauline pastored churches in Arkansas while waiting for an appointment to the foreign mission field. They were appointed as missionaries to Haiti, then served in Louisiana and South Texas. Millard served as assistant to the president of Dallas Bible College from 1967–1985 and joined the staff of Scofield Memorial Church in Dallas until his retirement in 1989. After his retirement Millard served as a volunteer chaplain at Columbia North Hills Hospital, which was near his home.

The Demy's only child, Timothy J. Demy, attended Glenview Elementary, Richland Junior High, and graduated from Richland High School in 1973. He received his bachelor's degree from Texas Christian University and his master's degree and doctorate from Dallas Theological Seminary. Additionally, he earned a master's degree in European history from University of Texas at Arlington and a master's degree in human development from Salve Regina University. He is currently pursuing a doctorate in humanities.

Commander Tim Demy, CHC (chaplain), U.S. Navy, spent a tour of duty in the Pacific aboard the USS England and served as chaplain to the Marines, the Coast Guard, and chief of Navy chaplains in Washington, D.C. At the present time, he is teaching on the staff of the Navy Chaplain College in Newport, R. I., and teaches a course in the Navy War College.

Tim and his wife, Lyn, have been married for 18 years. Lyn is a graduate of Southwest High School and Texas Christian University. She received her master's in business from Dallas Baptist College and is a graduate of Dallas Theological Seminary. As a registered nurse, Lyn served in the Navy Reserves and was called to active duty in Desert Storm.

Both Lyn and Tim have enjoyed their ministry in the Navy and consider it an honor to serve their country.

Millard N. Demy died in March 1997. Pauline continues to live in their North Richland Hills home. They were married 56 years.

Submitted by Pauline Demy

DONALD F. AND MARIE DENNEY

Donald and Marie Denney moved into their new home on Cummings Drive in North Richland Hills in February 1953, with their two daughters, Dolores and Donna. Dolores was born February 23, 1942, in Houston. Donna was born in Halletsville, Texas, December 26, 1947, while Marie was visiting her family. Don, Marie, and Dolores lived in Galveston at the time.

Don was born in Kansas City, Missouri, May 23, 1918.

Donald and Marie Denney

He was a Navy veteran of World War II He majored in engineering at Texas A&M and was with the U.S. Army Corps of Engineers for 35 years. Among many other jobs with the corps, he taught construction management in Saudi Arabia, Korea, Japan, Germany, and other European countries. He was involved with the NASA Atlas Missile launch pad construction.

Marie Schutz was born August 2, 1921, in Halletsville. When floodwaters raged through the town from the Lavaca River in 1940, Don was sent by the Corpus Christi firm he worked for to do repair work on roads and bridges. It was at this time they met and were married December 22, 1940.

When the Denney family moved to NRH, there were no houses on either side of theirs, but they soon met nearby neighbors. Dick and Marge Lambert, Joe and Polly Williams, Paul and Doris Kutilek, and Jack and Evelyn Watson became good friends. The family became members of Calvary Lutheran Church in Richland Hills.

Don had always been interested in politics but never held an office before becoming the second mayor of NRH. He served two terms, 1954–56, terms being for only one year at that time. There was so much to be done, and he spent decades helping the small town grow into what it is today. Some of the first items of necessity for the new mayor and council were paving the streets and getting streetlights

Dolores Denney

installed in the new town, just one year old when he took the helm. The plan was set in place by the paving committee of

Donna Denney

the NRH Civic League that each homeowner would pay $1.25 per frontage foot for paving. Some residents refused, and their part of the street remained graveled, muddy when it rained and had potholes. Each house was also on a septic tank system. It was a decade later when the city began installing a sewage system.

The City Council met in the

Denneys' living room during the time Don was mayor until the civic building was completed in October 1956. Don predicted in 1956, after NRH issued 248 building permits, that this area would show the fastest growth in Tarrant County and maybe in the state.

Dolores attended Birdville and Richland elementary schools and graduated from Birdville High School in 1960. She received her bachelor's degree in business from North Texas State University in 1964. She is married to Don Gates, and they live in Keller. They have two daughters and sons-in-law, Christine and Rick Donaldson and Nicole and Adam McGilvray.

Donna attended Glenview Elementary and graduated from Richland High School in 1966. She received her bachelor's degree in special education from Texas Christian University and her master's and doctorate from Texas Woman's University. She is married to James Tynan, and they live in Crystal Lake, Illinois with daughters Tiffany, Brittany, and Courtney.

Don Denney retired in 1976, but he didn't stay retired long. He soon joined the construction and engineering staff at North Texas University, serving as project manager for the construction of the Texas College of Osteopathic Medicine in Fort Worth. He also worked on projects to rebuild many North Texas University buildings and the athletic stadium.

Don had always been in good health until he developed leukemia in March 1992. He and Marie celebrated their 54th wedding anniversary December 22, 1994, and Don died December 31 at age 76.

Submitted by Evalyn Lochridge from
Interview with Marie Denney

JERRY M. DEWS

The Dews family, Jerry Michael, Anne Maureen Wakefield, and daughter, Kathleen Anne, moved to North Richland Hills in October 1982. Jerry and Kathleen were both born in Fort Worth. Anne was born in Hinsdale, Illinois.

Jerry graduated from Handley High School and then from Texas Wesleyan College in 1963. He taught in the Fort Worth School District until 1965 when he entered the aerospace industry. Except for a brief period of pharmaceutical work, he has remained in various facets of this business and is currently employed by Bell Helicopter Textron as an associate logistic specialist.

Anne graduated from Eastern Hills High School and Texas Wesleyan College and earned a master's degree from Texas

Left-Jerry, standing-Anne, Front-Kathleen

335

Woman's University. She has been a registered dietitian since 1974, working at St. Joseph and Medical Plaza hospitals, where she became food service director in 1980. She is currently employed as a health care specialist at the C. D. Harnett Co.

Kathy graduated from Nolan High School and the University of North Texas. She has been a buyer for San Lorenzo Inc. and a community liaison for Premier BioResources, a blood plasma company. She is currently an external relation events executive for Harris Methodist Health plan.

The Dews family has been active in volunteer work, especially with Tarrant County Harvest, an organization that transports excess food from eating establishments to agencies that feed the hungry. Jerry and Anne received the Kaleidoscope Wesleyan Award from Texas Wesleyan University in 1993 for their work in making Tarrant County Harvest a reality. Anne also was named Volunteer of the Year in 1993 by the city of North Richland Hills. She received the 1993 U.S. Mayors' End Hunger Award. She received the *Fort Worth Star-Telegram* award for Tarrant County Harvest being the volunteer organization of the year in 1993. Both Anne and Kathy have done volunteer work for the American Heart Association, the March of Dimes, and the United Way.

JAMES AND BRANDEE DILL

Our family is comprised of myself, James E. Dill, my beautiful wife, Brandee M., our daughter, Avery Megan, and our 5-year old basset hound, Chelsea. My wife and I were both born at Harris Methodist Hospital in Fort Worth. I was born on June 23, 1970, and my wife was born on October 10, 1969. Our daughter was born at Columbia Plaza Medical Center in Fort Worth on April 29, 1997.

Brandee and I enjoyed brief encounters as fourth, fifth, and sixth graders at Wilshire Elementary School. We were later reunited as classmates our senior year at Trinity High School. We went on our first date October 16, 1987, and were eventually married May 16, 1992.

Brandee and I both attended the University of

James, Brandee, and Avery Megan Dill with "Chelsea" the dog

Texas at Arlington where she received a degree in accounting, and I received a degree in finance. Brandee later went on to pass the CPA examination in 1994. She was employed by TTI Inc. as a reporting accountant for two years before resigning to become a full-time mom.

I have been working for PACCAR Financial Corporation as a credit analyst for the past nine months with the previous three years spent in the commercial banking industry.

Brandee and I are members of First Baptist Church in Euless. We are active in city, county, state, and national affairs through the power of our vote. We enjoy camping, traveling, and spending time with our family and friends. We moved to North Richland Hills in November 1993 when we purchased our first house on David Drive.

ALVIS AND DARLENE DOWELL

Alvis Lee Dowell has the distinction of being the only person to lose an election in North Richland Hills by one vote. The election was a runoff between Alvis and two other candidates for the office of mayor in 1965. In the general election preceding the runoff, Alvis missed winning the mayor's post by fewer than two dozen votes. Unfortunately, dur-

Back, L/R–Darlene and Alvis Lee Dowell; Front–L/R, Deborah, Darcus, Travis, 1970

ing the runoff campaign, emotions ran high, and opponents put sugar into Alvis's gas tank and threw rotten eggs into the car of his wife, Darlene. He also had to deal with the loss of former supporters who were influenced to actively back an opponent. Alvis had already served two terms as councilman, one as mayor pro tem, so the loss, while a disappointment, was not a devastating blow as he had been able to achieve some of the goals that led him to run for councilman in the first place. Also, a move to Dallas soon after the election offered exciting new opportunities to advance his career and to serve in leadership positions in his new community.

Alvis also lays claim to another first: He was the first person to land an airplane at Dallas/Fort Worth Airport. He had a Cessna 172 that he kept at Mangham Airport. Flying from that airport to the family farm in Wood County one day, Alvis noticed that graders and bulldozers were clearing the land DFW Airport would be built on. A smooth area which looked like it would make a good landing strip had been cleared, so, on a whim, and against all Federal Aviation Authority rules, Alvis put the plane down just behind a road grader, much to the surprise of the operator, before continuing on his trip.

Alvis Lee and Darlene Dowell moved to North Richland Hills in 1961, living first on Colorado Boulevard and then later on Eden Road in the Smithfield section of town. They had chosen NRH because of the available, affordable housing. However, Alvis soon came to believe there was reason for concern as the city was allowing developers to build substandard streets in the young city.

Another concern was fire protection. Fire hydrants were served by inadequate two-inch water mains, further evidence of poor planning. Alvis had graduated from the University of Corpus Christi with a degree in petroleum engineering, but the job that brought the Dowells to Fort Worth was a position as a safety engineer, as Alvis was also a certified safety professional. As an engineer, there was no doubt in his mind that stronger codes and tighter controls on developers were necessary to ensure a good future for NRH. So he was determined to run for City Council in the hope that he could make a contribution to the city's future.

In addition to being on the City Council, Alvis served as the charter president of the Safety Council and as a captain for the Tarrant County United Fund.

Alvis Dowell has had a distinguished and successful career in the petroleum industry. He has worked in all facets of the oil business in many parts of the world, including Denmark and Saudi Arabia where the family lived for extended periods of time. And even though it lacks the exotic appeal of foreign countries, Darlene Dowell still thinks that NRH compares favorably with any city in which she has lived. NRH is still remembered fondly by the Dowells as a place where they loved to live, where they made lasting friendships, and where they were able to contribute to the improvement of their community.

Submitted by Alvis Dowell

DEBRA WOODALL DUBBERLY

I, Debra (Debbie) Lynne Woodall Dubberly moved to Briley Drive in North Richland Hills in 1958 from the Polytechnic section of Fort Worth. I was born in Fort Worth in 1957 to Iris Corinne Sousae and Billy J. Woodall, now of North Richland Hills. I attended local schools and graduated in 1975 from Richland High School where I played for the varsity basketball team. I also was a member of the German Club, the Drama Club, Young Life, and the National Honor Society. I earned a secretarial degree at Tarrant County Junior College Northeast in 1977.

I am an executive secretary for Texas Utilities where I have worked for 16 years. I am a member of Richland Hills Christian Church. I played softball for the Richland Youth Association for seven years at the girls softball-park on Onyx Drive in North Richland Hills.

I was married to Michael (Mike) James McKnight in 1976 in Richland Hills Christian Church. We lived in NRH for a year then bought a home in Watauga. We have a daughter, Malia Christine McKnight, later adopted by Tommy Dubberly, who

Malia, Debbie, and Derek Dubberly

was born in 1978 in Fort Worth.

Mike McKnight was born in Sioux City, Iowa, in 1954 to Carol Sue Jansen and Harry Eldon McKnight Jr. who live in NRH.

My second marriage was to Tommy Lee Dubberly in 1981, in my parents' home in NRH. Tommy Dubberly was born October 9, 1949 in Fort Worth to Alice Ethel Kasner and Bert Lee Dubberly. We have one son, Derek Ryan, born in 1984. Tommy and I were divorced in 1995, and I now own my home in Bedford on Vicksburg Drive.

Mike McKnight later married Cynthia Darlene Mayhan and they have a son, Eric Michael McKnight of North Richland Hills, born January 26, 1984 in Fort Worth.

Malia attended Wilshire Elementary, Harwood Junior High, and graduated from Trinity High School in 1996 and is now attending Tarrant County Junior College Northeast and working part-time at the YMCA in Bedford.

Derek attended Shadybrook Elementary and is going to Harwood Junior High where he enjoys playing baseball, football, basketball, track, and soccer.

Submitted by Debbie Dubberly

DANNY AND PATRICIA DUCKETT

Timothy Daniel "Danny" Duckett was born in 1955 in Anderson, Indiana, the third child of the Rev. William Paul Duckett and Peggy Jean Pate Duckett. The Duckett family settled in North Richland Hills in 1966 while Rev. Duckett served as pastor at Memorial Baptist Church in Haltom City.

Danny attended local schools and graduated from Richland High School in 1973. He played trumpet in the Richland Rebel Marching Band. He attended Baptist Bible College in Springfield, Missouri, graduating in 1977 as a music major.

Patricia Carol Johnson was born in 1956 to James Edward Johnson and Jessie JoAnn King Johnson. The Johnson family moved to NRH in 1965. Patricia's parents and sister, Sherry Elaine Johnson Christensen still live in NRH. Patricia attended local schools and graduated from Richland High School in 1974.

On April

The Duckett Family: Back, L/R-Alicia, Josh, Jeremy; Front, L/R-Danny and Patricia Duckett

28, 1978, Danny and Patricia married. Their first child, Joshua "Josh" Daniel Duckett was born in 1980. Alicia Marcelle Duckett was born in 1981, and Jeremiah "Jeremy" Daniel Duckett arrived in 1983.

The Danny Duckett family moved to the Noreast addition of NRH in 1983.

For 11 years, Danny was employed by TU Electric where he was chosen to represent the employees in Washington, D.C., accepting a citation from President Reagan for the "Paint the Town" project.

Danny and Patricia served on the staff at Memorial Baptist in Haltom City, Central Baptist in Sulphur Springs, and currently Danny is minister of music/youth and Patricia is church pianist at Saginaw Park Baptist Church. Danny is also presently employed by Tri-County Electric in Azle.

The family attended North Richland Hills Baptist Church from 1981 to 1997. Danny was a Sunday school teacher, Royal Ambassador Mission Director, member of the adult choir and Kingsmen. Danny, along with the children, participated in the Greater Fort Worth Christmas Pageant for many years. The children completed the Royal Ambassador and Girls Auxiliary Missions program and sang in the children and youth choirs.

At age 6, Josh ran a recycling business by pulling a wagon door-to-door to the neighbors on Greenwood Way to collect old newspapers and aluminum cans. He is currently working at A&A Media. Josh is also a worship leader for the youth in his church.

In 1993, Holiday Heights Elementary celebrated its 25th anniversary. Alicia was given the privilege of accepting a flag presented by Congressman Pete Geren during the ceremonies.

Jeremy was chosen in the summer of 1995 to go to Richland Elementary and talk to American astronauts while in space, and afterward he was interviewed by several TV and radio news reporters. Jeremy is presently the sound technician at Saginaw Park Baptist Church.

Josh and Alicia attended North Richland Hills Middle School. All three attended Holiday Heights Elementary, Temple Christian School, and home-based school.

The Ducketts participated in building "Adventure World" creative playground and other community activities. The children also played an active part in the city campaigns for the election of their grandmother, JoAnn Johnson for NRH City Council.

Submitted by Patricia Duckett

PAUL AND PEGGY DUCKETT

William Paul Duckett Sr. was born to John Arthur Duckett and Bessie Laverne Wiser Duckett, in 1929 in the family home on Race Street in the Riverside area of Fort Worth. He was raised in Fort Worth and Athens. He attended Bible Baptist Seminary in Arlington and Texas Wesleyan College.

Peggy Jean Pate Duckett was born in 1931, in Hubbard, Texas, to Ruby Beatrice Vaughan Pate and Carlos Marion Pate. She attended schools in Hubbard and Athens. Peggy worked five years as a secretary to the advertising manager of Stripling's and 10 years as recep-

tionist for Mount Olivet Funeral Home.

Rev. Paul and Peggy Duckett

Paul and Peggy were married in 1949, in Athens. In 1960, the Duckett family moved to Fort Worth where the Rev. Paul Duckett assumed the position as associate minister and choir director at First Baptist Church of Fort Worth. In 1961, he established the Memorial Baptist Church in Haltom City and moved his family to a home in North Richland Hills on Tabor Street. Paul and Peggy have lived in NRH for 31 years, except for a nine-month stay in Houston and a five-year pastorate in Bay City, Texas. Paul is currently employed by Mt. Olivet Funeral Home and serves as music minister of Southwood Baptist Church.

Paul and Peggy have five children: William Paul Jr., Brenda Jean Duckett Correll, Timothy Daniel ("Danny"), Donald Mark ("Donnie"), and Jonathan Craig ("Jon"). All attended NRH schools and were graduates of Richland High School between the years of 1970–1976.

Dr. William Paul Duckett Jr., born in 1952, is a graduate of Hardin-Simmons University. Paul married Martha Delene McGee, and they have three children, Amy evvone, Rebecca "Becky" Denise, and Matthew Paul. Currently Paul Jr. is associate pastor and minister of music at Longview Baptist Temple in Longview, Texas.

Brenda Jean Duckett Correll, born in 1953, is currently dean of women at the Baptist Bible College in Springfield, Missouri, from which she graduated. In 1973, Brenda married Ken Correll, now deceased. They have one son, Nathaniel ("Nathan") Aaron Correll.

Timothy Daniel ("Danny") Duckett, was born in 1955. Danny and Patricia Carol Johnson were married in 1978 and have three children: Joshua ("Josh") Daniel, Alicia Marcella, and Jeremiah ("Jeremy") Daniel. The Danny Duckett family currently resides in NRH. Danny is employed by Tri-County Electric and serves as music/youth minister at Saginaw Park Baptist Church.

Donald ("Donnie") Mark Duckett, born in 1957, is a graduate of Baptist Bible College in Springfield, Missouri. He was formerly married to Donna Marie Marr. They have one son, Jonathan David. Donnie currently resides in NRH.

Jonathan ("Jon") Craig Duckett, born in 1960, attended Tennessee Temple and currently resides in Pennsylvania. He is married to Dawn Sheri Aurand, and they have two children, Lauren Elizabeth and Andrew Stephen.

One of the things Peggy remembers about the early days in NRH is their boys trying to catch "wild" animals in the field in back of their house. When they finally succeeded, they caught a skunk!

TOMMY AND DEBBIE DUER

Tommy Duer grew up in Richland Hills on Landy Lane, with his sister, Patti, and brothers, Mickey and Connie, in the early 1960s. North Richland Hills seemed almost rural then. There were daily trips to Buddies, now Winn Dixie, for groceries and Rapid Mart at Vance and Grapevine Highway for ice-cold watermelons and bubble-gum baseball cards.

Dr. Tommy Duer with Clara and Jonathan

We had one of the largest *Fort Worth Star-Telegram* paper routes. At that time the paperboys had to "porch" the papers, twice a day, morning and evening. From a monkey-bar bicycle, that was a challenge. However, with enough practice and bicycle speed it could be done. The main problems were glass milk bottles left on the porches and the advent of glass storm-doors. Shattering glass, at 5 A.M. for a 12-year-old boy, was very frightening.

Debbie Fielder was a Raiderette at L. D. Bell High School and lived on Hurstview Drive. A Richland Rebel marrying a Raiderette, instead of a Dixie Belle, raised a few eyebrows. But Debbie has now, after living in the Birdville School District for 16 years, been converted. Tommy and Debbie met at Texas A&M while he was pursuing a doctorate in veterinary medicine, and she was studying to be a registered nurse. After graduating he started an animal clinic in North Richland Hills. It was named North Hills Animal Clinic and was located less than a mile from his alma mater, Richland High School. Debbie is an RN in the intensive care unit at Baylor-Grapevine Medical Center. Tommy has served NRH in many ways, being on several charter review committees, and as chairman of the Zoning Board of Adjustments.

Tommy and Debbie are the proud parents of a daughter, Clara, and a son, Jonathan. One of Tommy's favorite memories of the changing times in NRH was back in the late 1970s, while watching television one summer night. The plates on the walls started violently shaking. This went on for about 10 seconds. It seemed like a mild earthquake. They ran outside the house to find nothing unusual. They returned inside to find the walls still shaking. Suddenly it sounded as though a jet plane had taken off in their backyard. It turned out to be the vibrations of a jet-car drag race at Green Valley Raceway a quarter mile away. Those were the days.

STEPHEN B. AND JANE WEST DUNKELBERG

According to Corse family stories, Malcom Sears and Nancy Holmes Corse stopped in the Birdville area on April 24, 1875 for the birth of Chancy Henry Corse (Jane West Dunkelberg's grandfather). This is the first connection that Jane's family has with the Birdville area of which 50 percent is now North Richland Hills.

In 1929, Jane was born "right in the middle of 121" when the future state highway 121 was the bedroom of her childhood home (3901 Race Street) long before freeways were envisioned. Her parents were Cecil B. West and Mary Virginia Corse West.

Stephen Blair Dunkelberg was born in 1929 in Fort Worth. Both sets of parents were residents of the Riverside section of Fort Worth. Jane graduated from the University of Texas at Austin with a bachelor's degree in microbiology. Stephen graduated from Texas A&M with a bachelor's degree in mechanical engineering and a second lieutenant's commission in the Army Reserve. The couple was married in 1950. Within a few months, Stephen was called to active service during the Korean War. After the war Stephen stayed in the reserves for the next several years and was discharged with the rank of captain.

After several years the couple decided to settle down in Tarrant County. Stephen pursued his career in engineering at Convair. Jane fell into domestic life because children were on their way. Stephen Lee Dunkelberg was born in 1952 at Carswell Air Force Base in Fort Worth. Stephen and Jane moved to Haltom City shortly after Marc was born in 1953. Kenneth Ben Dunkelberg was born in 1954.

After eleven months in Tennessee the family came home to Texas. They found the perfect place for a home in the NRH area in 1958.

The boys all attended Birdville schools and graduated from Haltom High School. All three boys earned the Boy Scout God and Country Award at St. Luke Methodist Church where the family was very active.

At Haltom High, Lee became serious about journalism. His interest in journalism continued on to Texas A&M and University of Texas at Arlington. After winning several Texas Associated Press Awards he signed on with KSAT. He wrote and produced a documentary on the aircraft carrier Lexington for Public Broadcasting System. The

Top row, L/R-J. Lee, Stephen, Jane, Marc, Frieda, Suzanne; Bottom, L/R-Clare, Joel, Kenneth, Ian, Laurie holding Toby.

Lexington documentary won the 1998 Telly Award.

Lee married Clare Campbell, a native of San Antonio. Clare graduated from St. Mary's University in San Antonio and is a longtime employee of USM Insurance as a computer programmer.

He majored in drama at UTA and appeared in several student productions. He wrote and directed a screenplay, *La Bamba*, that starred Lou Diamond Phillips ("I gave him his start.") and was student director and set designer for a production of *Teahouse of the August Moon*, which also starred Lou Diamond Phillips, and he was the first UTA student to receive an internship from Theater Three in Dallas. He became the assistant technical director of the Summer Theater of the University of Rochester, Rochester, New York. There he met Suzanne Walker and married her. She graduated from Syracuse University with a major in voice and costume. Her singing talent is now devoted to her church, and her costume talent is used to keep Chuck Norris and the cast of *Walker, Texas Ranger* in the right clothes at the right time.

He is now on staff with the Dallas Symphony Orchestra. They have one daughter, Frieda Celeste Dunkelberg, born in 1993.

Kenneth kept up the journalism tradition by working as photographer for the Haltom Buffalo and won a first prize in the statewide Texas Interscholastic League. He attended UTA for two years, majoring in biology, then transferred to UT Austin majoring in mechanical engineering. He has had a distinguished career at Boeing in Seattle, holding responsible positions in their propulsion engineering section. He married Laurie Hammack of Seattle, and they have four sons: Joel Kenneth, Ian Blair, Toby Matthew, and Zachary Thomas.

Zachary Thomas Dunkelberg, born 1997

Jane helped open Tarrant County Junior College Northeast Campus and was associated with the Biology Department for 15 years. While there, she also earned a master's of science in biology from East Texas State University. In 1980 she began a new era of volunteering as a way of life. Always actively interested in the environment, in 1995 she won the Keep Texas Beautiful O. P. Schnabel Senior Citizen Award. She was a founder of the Tarrant County Master Gardeners Association, designed and supervised the xeriscape landscape of Tarrant County Courthouse. Jane has been active in the Tarrant League of Women Voters, Tarrant County Democratic Woman's Club, and a Democratic precinct 3289 chair for 18 years.

Jane has served on numerous NRH Committees or commissions, including the Sesquicentennial Committee, at which time she and Stephen wrote the first NRH history booklet, Beautification Commission, Keep Texas Beautiful Coordinator, the NRH History Committee, and Northeast Environmental Team (NEET).

At Convair, Stephen has been most fortunate that in his career he has helped design seven airplanes: B-36, B-58, F-111, F-16, F-22, KTX-2, JSF, the Centaur rocket, and many more that did not make it off the drawing board. The KTX-2 is a Korean plane being built by Samsung Aerospace in Taijon, Korea. All the others were built by Convair, General Dynamics, or as the "Bomber Plant" is known, Lockheed-Martin. Though caught by a quick retirement when the Bush administration canceled the A-I 2, Stephen has become a consultant thermodynamic specialist, thus being included on the KTX-2, F-22, and the JSF. Stephen has served on the NRH Citicable Board and on the Charter Revision Committee.

Submitted by Jane West Dunkelberg

DAN AND DOROTHY ECHOLS

Dan Echols, his wife Dorothy, and their 10-year-old daughter, Janlyn, moved to North Richland Hills in June 1968. Dan was born in Abilene in 1928. He received a bachelor of science degree from Abilene Christian University in 1949 and a master's degree in education from East Texas State University in 1965.

From 1950 to 1953, Dan was on active duty with the U.S. Air Force; upon his release from active duty, he became a major in the Air Force Reserve. From 1954 to 1966, Dan was a science teacher in the Andrews and Abilene school districts. In 1966, he became director of audio visual services for the McAllen School District, and in 1968 was appointed dean of learning resources for the Northeast campus of Tarrant County Junior College.

Dorothy Echols was a fourth-grade teacher at Southwest Christian School. Janlyn Echols is a television news anchor in Abilene.

Dan's interest in community affairs led him to run for mayor of NRH in 1984. He was elected and served in that capacity until 1988. He was also actively involved in a great many civic, governmental, and professional organizations.

BILL AND BOBBIE EDDINS

Originally from West Texas, Bill and Bobbie Eddins, along with 3-year old Monti Elizabeth Eddins, moved to Oakland Lane in North Richland Hills in 1960, via Wichita, Kansas and Bedford, Texas. In 1962, their first NRH native, John Robert Eddins, was born. They resided in their home for eight years. In 1967, they moved two long blocks to Oakland Lane. Bill and Bobbie still reside at this address.

Raising a family in NRH, the Eddins were very involved in many organizations and community happenings. As a family, they attended Davis Memorial Methodist Church, where Bill and Bobbie sang in the choir. Bill and Bobbie have been actively involved in the Fort Worth Elks Lodge for many years, where Bill is past exalted ruler. Bill also served as president of the Dallas-Fort Worth chapter for American Institute of Industrial Engineers. Bobbie was active in the Richland Garden Club, Fort Worth Junior Women's Club, Industrial Engineering Wives Club, and a North Richland Hills bridge club.

Monti and Rob both attended local schools and graduated from Richland High School, Monti in 1975 and Rob in 1981. Growing up, Monti spent time in Brownies, Girl Scouts, and chasing boys

L/R, standing-Robin and Rob Eddins, Stan and Monti Hackenberg; Seated-Alexandra Eddins, Bobbie, and Bill Eddins

with her best friend and schoolmate, Shawna Allred. At Richland, Monti served three years in the Dixie Belles Drill Team. Rob was involved in RYA (Richland Youth Assn.) football, basketball, and baseball for many years. Bill coached many of those teams as well. Both Monti and Rob graduated as members of the National Honor Society from Richland High.

As Texas Tech Alumni, Bill and Bobbie were delighted to see their children, Monti and Rob, go on to attend Texas Tech University, both make the dean's honor list. Monti joined the Alpha Phi sorority at Tech and graduated with a degree in home economics design. Currently, Monti is a regional manager for Barnes and Noble College Book Stores, is married to Stan Hackenberg, and they reside in Houston. Rob graduated in 1985 with a degree in mechanical engineering technology. Rob is a manufacturing engineering supervisor at Bell Helicopter Textron. Rob, his wife, Robin Rogers Eddins (also a Richland graduate) and daughter, Alexandra Elizabeth Eddins, reside in North Richland Hills.

FRANK AND GLORIA EDGE

Frank and Gloria Edge and their daughter, Donna, moved to North Richland Hills in 1974 from Burleson. Donna attended Tarrant County Junior College and University of Texas at Arlington and majored in nursing and health care. She married Ruben Rucker on November 3, 1979, and they now have two children and live in Watauga. She is a nurse at John Peter Smith Hospital and Ruben is a policeman in Saginaw.

Frank fought in five major battles during World War II, received

Frank, Donna, and Gloria Edge

several medals, one being the Bronze Star, for service beyond the call of duty. Gloria passed away September 3, 1996. They had two other children, Wade Thomas of Cartersville, Georgia, and Linda Lowe. Linda was gunned down in 1984 by a "madman."

When they moved to North Richland Hills area, there was hardly anything on Rufe Snow Drive from Loop 820 to Watauga Road. It was rural, but that has all changed. They have seen hospitals, supermarkets, freeways, restaurants, banks, malls, and now a mixmaster built all around them.

Frank spent his years of civil service with the U.S. Postal System as a city letter carrier from 1949 to 1974. He retired November 30, 1974 with more than 30 years of government service. He is involved in the NRH Crime Watch program and enjoys woodworking as a hobby.

NATHAN A. AND LINDELL ELLENBURG

Nathan A. (Shorty) Ellenburg and Lindell (Linda) M. Leach Ellenburg were married in 1937 in Los Angeles, California. They moved to Texas in 1947, then to Tarrant County (North Richland Hills) July 1951. They built one of the first homes in this area. There were no stores or businesses around. Groceries were purchased near Jacksboro Highway.

Lindell Ellenburg

Nathan was born in Dewitt, Arkansas in 1914 and went to school and college in Kansas. After moving to Fort Worth, he was employed at Convair (later General Dynamics and now Lockheed) as a foreman until laid off in 1962. Then he went to Bell Helicopter as a foreman, from 1962–1979, when he retired. Nathan was on the first City Council of NRH in 1953, then served four more terms. He was an active member of the Richland Masonic Lodge.

He enjoyed hunting and fishing, which he spent most of his free time doing. He belonged to multiple fishing and skeet organizations and will be remembered for his skills in these sports.

Lindell Ellenburg was born in Sidon, Arkansas, on April 19, 1919, and attended school in Arkansas. She was employed by Convair from 1949 until 1962, when she and Nathan adopted their daughter, Donna S. Ellenburg Collins. Linda enjoyed bowling. She attended the majority of state and national women's bowling tournaments, traveling over the United States from 1958 to 1986.

Linda was a member of Richland Hills Baptist Church until she transferred her membership to North Richland Hills Baptist Church in May 1956. She has been an active member since. She also is a member of the God Squad and Lay Witness for Christ, with whom she attended the 1996 Atlanta Olympics.

Linda Ellenburg continues to reside in NRH at her original home. N. A. (Shorty) Ellenburg passed away in June 1982.

Donna married J. Dale Collins. They now live in NRH with their two children, Jason and Kailey Collins.

NORMAN DEAN AND MARY RUTH ELLIS

Mary Ruth Reeves and Norman Dean Ellis met in 1950 at North Texas State University in Denton. Both were recent high school graduates, Mary Ruth from Birdville High School and Norman from Woodrow Wilson High

Norman and Mary Ruth Ellis

School in Dallas. St. Luke United Methodist Church in Haltom City was the site of their marriage in 1952.

After completing college with a degree in home economics, Mary Ruth returned to Birdville to teach, later becoming director of food services for the Birdville schools, serving in that capacity until retirement.

Norman received his commission in the U.S. Air Force through the ROTC program at North Texas. After completing college in 1954, Norman served in the Air Force for the next three years, including one year in North Africa at Tripoli, Libya.

During this period in North Africa, Mary Ruth returned to the area to live with her parents, whose home and dairy farm were located at the present site of Hudiburg Chevrolet. It was in 1955 that North Richland Elementary opened, now called Mullendore Elementary. Mary Ruth was the only sixth-grade teacher, and the class size was 40 before the end of the school year.

In 1957, Mary Ruth and Norman returned to the area, buying their first home on Winnell Way in North Richland Hills. Their second and present home on Holiday Lane West was purchased in 1970 from the Burl Daniel family. Lou and James Walker and John Mitchell are neighbors and original owners of their homes, which were built in the 1950s. We all think we are fortunate to live in such a great neighborhood as well as a wonderful city.

After returning to NTSU in Denton to complete his master's degree (MBA) and later completing his doctorate, Norman joined the staff at Tarrant County Junior College Northeast Campus, teaching in the management and marketing fields. Norman retired in 1992 from TCJC.

In the 1970s, Norman served as councilman in NRH and as mayor pro-tem his second term under the leadership of Mayor Dick Faram.

The early 1970s was a period of rapid growth for NRH. Many new subdivisions were built. Commercial development was on a rampage, and the City Hall facilities were far from adequate. The voters had turned down a bond issue for building new facilities a few years earlier. But the city's rapid growth continued to stretch the capacity of the former City Hall, which is now the Dan Echols Senior Center on Glenview Drive. Something had to be done! Norman, working with Alan Hamm, was able to secure the site of the current City Hall on Loop 820 for only $10,000. Once again the voters refused a bond issue to build new facilities.

The City Council began to look for other sources of funding. It was discovered that much of the city's sales tax that was due NRH was being credited to Fort Worth because NRH had no post office zip code and was serviced by Fort Worth. Norman, Dick Faram, and City Manager Gene Riddle went to Austin armed with their findings. Shortly after their return, the good news came from Austin that more than $250,000 was owed to the city of NRH. This windfall provided the impetus for pursuing other avenues of funding. A grant for the Police Department and a $75,000 grant for the library moved the council even closer to their goal. Water Department surplus funds, as well as some surplus funds from the city coffers, were used to apply to the building project. An architect was selected, and building plans were under way. The building was completed in late 1975. Interestingly enough, Norman and Dick Faram were defeated in 1976. Many of the voters didn't understand that the city complex was built with no funds borrowed.

Our first child, Deana Lynn, was born in 1960, and our son, David Wayne, was born in 1962. Deana graduated from Richland High School in 1978 and David in 1981. Each attended TCJC Northeast Campus and completed their college degrees.

Deana received her bachelor's degree in Nursing at Texas Woman's University in Denton. She and her husband, William (Bill) Hoffman, reside with their daughter, Haley Lynn, in the Meadow Lakes addition of NRH.

Back, L/R-Deana, Bill, and Haley Hoffman, David and Debra Ellis; Front-Mary Ruth, Danielle, Norman, and Duncan Ellis

Deana, a registered nurse, is at Harris Hospital in Fort Worth. Bill, a graduate of Texas A&M, is a network specialist in the computer field.

David and his wife, Debra, and children, Danielle and Duncan, reside in the Diamond Oaks addition of Haltom City. David is currently working on his doctorate at the University of North Texas. Debra has her master's degree from Texas Wesleyan University, Fort Worth. David and Debra are both employed by Birdville schools.

The Ellis family feels very fortunate they selected NRH as a place to hang their hats and raise their family. The community spirit and friendliness of the people have contributed significantly to their quality of life.

DICK AND BETH FARAM

Dick Dee Faram was born in 1926 in Gulfport, Mississippi, one of three children of Ernest Patrick and Lucille Cooke Faram. The children were reared in Fort Worth where they attended public schools.

Ernest Faram was a "cooper" who made barrels for the Fort Worth Barrel Company. He immigrated from Manchester, England, in 1901 at the age of 5. Lucille Faram was a pharmacist.

Dick served in World War II and the Korean Conflict in the U.S. Navy. After World War II, Dick enrolled in pharmacy school at Oklahoma University, the same school his mother attended. He graduated with a bachelor's degree in pharmacy.

Dick married his college sweetheart, Joe Beth Aldridge, who was born in 1926 in Maud, Oklahoma. She was the daughter of Earl and Ruby Williams Aldridge. She graduated from high school in Shawnee, Okla. and the University of Oklahoma with a bachelor's degree in social work.

Dick and Beth were married in 1949. They moved to Eldorado Drive in North Richland Hills in 1959, so their children could attend the Birdville schools. Beth was PTA president of the elementary, junior, and senior high schools where the children attended. She was also president of the District's PTA. In addition to being a homemaker, she did substitute teaching. Beth died January 29, 1985.

Dick and Beth had three children:

Dee, born in 1951, is married to Marsha Dyer and lives in Dallas. He graduated from Texas Wesleyan College and Southern Methodist University, works for a respiratory equipment company and is an ordained Methodist minister. His wife is employed as a personnel counselor. They have three children.

Dave, born in 1952, is married to April Hospers and lives in Keller. Dave graduated from Texas Wesleyan College. He is self-employed as a broker for starch products for corrugated manufacturing companies. His wife is a pharmacist. They have three children.

Cindy, born in 1957, is married to Richard Valenta and lives in Keller. Cindy graduated from North Texas State University, teaches business at Haltom High School, and her husband is the assistant personnel

director for the Birdville School District. They have three children.

Dick and Beth were both members of Richland Hills United Methodist Church where they were involved in youth activities. Dick belongs to the Hemphill Heights Masonic Lodge and the Fort Worth Scottish Rite Body. Dick coached boy's baseball for ages 8–19 and was a Peewee football coach for five years.

Dick was a medical service representative for Parke Davis Pharmaceutical Company for 37 years, retiring August 1, 1992.

Dick realized that NRH was not offering any services for the youth after making a presentation at the Richland Athletic Association. This led to many people asking him to run for the City Council.

Dick served on the NRH City Council from January 1965 to April 1972, being mayor pro tem the last four years. He was elected mayor of NRH and served from April 1974 to 1976; again as mayor from 1978 to 1984—a total of eight years as mayor. Much progress was made during this time.

Dick was the author of the highway interchange of Loop 820 and Grapevine Highway that is now under construction in the 1990s. He spearheaded the development of Rufe Snow Drive and was involved in the negotiations that led to North Richland Hills getting water from the Trinity Water Authority.

Dick's professional and family life have made a complete circle. His mother was a pharmacist, Dick was a pharmacist, his son married a pharmacist, and his sister's son, Mark Shadle, is a pharmacist. His dad loved politics and sports. Dick coached youth teams. His grandchildren are in sports, and both his sons and son-in-law are youth coaches. Dick was involved in his community and gave countless hours of service. Dick said that his hobbies were his grandchildren first, then fishing, golf, and hunting. Dick is in the process of selling his home of nearly 40 years and moving to a new home in Keller so he can be closer to his grandchildren.

Family history told to Geraldine Orr, March 1998

BILL AND JANICE FENIMORE

Bill Fenimore moved to Northeast Tarrant County with his parents, Bob and Alice Fenimore, and his brother, Bobby, in 1951, before North Richland Hills was incorporated. The brothers both graduated from Birdville High School. During this time, they also worked for their father's masonry

Bill and Janice Fenimore with grandson Luke Spicer

company, building Richland High School in North Richland Hills.

Bill attended North Texas State University, during which time he married Janice Lane Howard. They both graduated from NTSU (Bill in 1966, Janice in 1964) after doing their student teaching at Richland High School. Both remember traveling from Denton and driving on the two-lane potholed street through the outskirts of NRH, which later became the busy five-lane thoroughfare, Rufe Snow Drive. After moving to NRH in 1965, Bill taught at North Richland Junior High for one and one half years, and Janice taught at Richland Junior High and Richland High for four years.

Bill left teaching to become a builder/developer, developing more than 200 lots in North Richland Hills alone. Janice quit teaching after the births of their two daughters (Jill in 1968 and Paige in 1970), but returned to the classroom at Richland High in 1990 where she is still teaching and Bill continues to build in the area.

Bill served two terms on the Birdville School District's Board of Trustees and is a member of the Northeast Lions Club. He also has served on the Zoning Board of Adjustments and is presently on the Civil Service Commission Board. Janice served on the 1985 bond committee and the North Richland Hills Library Board.

Bill enjoys officiating basketball, golf, scuba diving, and travel. Janice's hobbies are reading, aerobics (at NRH recreation center), scuba diving, and travel. They attend North Fort Worth Baptist Church. Each of their daughters has one child: Luke Spicer—son of Jill and John Spicer of North Richland Hills and Chandler Welch—daughter of Paige and Doug Welch of Euless.

During their 34 years of marriage (November 16, 1963), the Fenimores have watched the growth of NRH, as it moved from a small town to an important city in Northeast Tarrant County. They remember burying a beloved family pet in 1968 on raw land that Bill later developed into Park Ridge Estates. They also remember the land directly behind their former home on Riviera Drive before it became Iron Horse Golf Course.

As recently as 1996, Bill saw a coyote running loose in the city. They both love the advantages of living in a smaller suburban city and being able to travel around Tarrant County with comparative ease. They feel certain that city officials will stay on top of any transportation, housing, and roadway problems because of the interest of the local citizenry.

Submitted by Bill and Janice Fenimore

JACOB AND ESTELLA FILBERT

Jacob Filbert was the son of Russian emigrants. He was born near Russell, Kansas, October 12, 1901. His father was a wheat farmer and Methodist minister in Kansas. Like his father before him, Jacob was called to the ministry.

Jacob's first wife was Esther Schenkel. They had three children before her death in 1934. Later that year he mar-

ried Estella Beal who was also a minister. She was born in Indian Territory, now Oklahoma, on May 8, 1889. They had one daughter.

In 1940, Reverend Filbert was called to the pastorate of a church in Alvord, Texas, where he served until being called to pastor the North Side Assembly of God Church in Fort Worth. Under his able ministry, this church flourished.

In 1956, the family moved to Turner Terrace in North Richland Hills. Reverend Filbert retired from a fruitful ministry in 1971 because of declining health. Before he died in 1974, the congregation he fostered at North Side Assembly of God, moved and became Bethesda Church in Haltom City, Texas.

Jacob and Estella Filbert

Submitted by Betty Leslie

LEONARD AND BOBBETTE FLORY

Leonard Edwin Flory Jr. was born in Carter, Oklahoma in 1928 to Ruby and Leonard Flory Sr. His family moved to Fort Worth in his elementary school years where he attended north side schools and graduated from North Side High in the class of 1946. He served in the Army Air Corps from 1946 to 1947. Leonard is retired after working for the Armour Meat Company for 20 years and Butler Gas Company for 33 years.

I, Kathleen Bobbette Edwards was born in Birmingham, Alabama, in 1929 to Horace and Thelma (Parker) Edwards. My father died 10 days before I was born. As I was growing up, we lived in Alabama, Mississippi, and Tennessee. In my teenage years, our family moved to Fort Worth where I attended Polytechnic High, Class of 1948. I love to paint, teach art, and deal in antiques.

Leonard and I married in 1948. We celebrated our 50th wedding anniversary August 1998. We lived in Fort Worth, Haltom City, and moved to North Richland Hills in 1964.

We have three children. Sue Ann Flory was born in 1954 in Fort Worth, was in the Richland High class of 1972, and attended Tarrant County Junior College and University of Texas at Arlington where she received her bachelor's degree in accounting and CPA. Since 1989 she has worked as internal audit senior for ENSEARCH Corporation, now Texas Utilities. She lives in Arlington, loves watching musicals, plays, and movies.

Janet Flory was born in 1959 in Fort Worth. Janet was in the Richland High class of 1977. She is married to Don Charles Golightly (Donnie) and has two children, Jennifer Dawn Golightly and Jeremy Don Golightly. Janet is the owner of the antique and decorating store, Golightly's Gallery, in NRH, and Jennifer manages the

344

store. Janet and Donnie are residents of NRH.

Trey Flory was born Leonard Edwin Flory III in 1961, also in Fort Worth. Trey attended Birdville schools and was in the Richland High class of 1980. He is married to Dena Carol (Orrick). They have two children, Derek Edwin Flory and Desiree Carol Flory. Trey is a music writer and plays the guitar, banjo, and piano.

We are members of North Richland Hills Baptist Church. For the 100th anniversary of First Baptist Church of Smithfield I was privileged to paint an oil painting of the old downtown Smithfield Main Street. To help get an idea of how the area looked in the early 1900s, Bessie Autrey gave old church record books and some photographs of Main Street before the fire destroyed the town. My painting shows the "Old Smithfield" from Smithfield Road to Sam Snider's feed store. I named the painting "Memory Love," and it hangs in the entry of the First Baptist Church Smithfield.

Submitted by Bobbette Flory

BILL AND JOYCE FOLEY

The Foley family, Bill and Joyce, and son, Ron, moved to North Richland Hills in January 1960. A close friend of ours, Alan Hamm, built our home on Ashmore and lived a few doors from us. I, Joyce Foley, remember, when we first moved here there were no close businesses, except for Buddies Grocery Store. It seemed almost as if we had moved to the country, and in a way, I guess we had. Our son, Ron, was 12 when we moved from the Polytechnic area.

After Bill retired from the insurance business, he did engraving work, making most of the signs and diagrams for such places as the NRH Public Library buildings under the business name of Classic Engravers.

We are still at the same home on Ashmore after all these years, and as I look around now at the growth and development of NRH, it amazes me.

I retired from A&A Insurance and at the time, we provided coverage for the city of NRH; in comparing the city's annual payroll then and now, it is unbelievable at how much growth is involved.

Submitted by Joyce Foley

BOBBY AND SHERRY FORD

Bobby and Sherry Ford moved into their North Richland Hills home on Finian Lane in 1974. At the time there was only one way to get to Finian Lane. There was no light at the intersection then. The large intersection where Hudiburg Chevrolet was located had a Safeway grocery store (where Office Depot now stands) and Mott's 5&10 was in the shopping center across the street, and we shopped at both. As you drove out Davis Boulevard, there were two quick-eating places, the Dairy Queen and a Whataburger (which has been torn down and rebuilt).

Most of the businesses that now exist were not there in 1974. Emerald Hills Way had a dead end just past Finian Lane. East from that point was an open field where the young boys loved to make jumps with their bicycles over the hills. There was a tank somewhere, because we saw boys walk by with fishing gear pretty often. In 1974, although we had our back yard fenced, we had a family of cottontail rabbits that we'd see grazing early in the mornings. Very late one night my husband "faced off" with a possum that the dog had found. Carrie Thomas Elementary School was completed in time for our first child to begin kindergarten there.

Dana Michelle Ford was born in 1974. Dana started school at Carrie Thomas Elementary, attended Smithfield Junior High, receiving the outstanding student award (highest scholar) when she completed ninth grade. When she graduated from Richland High School in 1992 as the valedictorian, she was awarded eight scholarships, including a National Merit scholarship. Dana went to Abilene Christian University for two years and completed her education at the University of North Texas, graduating with a degree in computer technology. She married her high school sweetheart, Glenn Harris, and they live in Lewisville.

Cary Ann Ford was born in 1976 and attended the same schools as her sister. At Richland High School she excelled academically and graduated sixth in her class, and attended TCU on scholarships.

Amy Dawne Ford was born in 1982. She attended NRH schools and is now attending Richland High School.

The Ford family has attended Baker Boulevard Church of Christ for the past 23 years.

LOYDE AND LEVADELL FOSTER

My memories of North Richland Hills begin on the day we moved into our new home on Vance Road December 12, 1952. My parents, Loyde and Levadell Foster, and little sister (Paula Don), had kept our home a secret from me after we moved from Amarillo. It was a "model" home in the area. I thought it was so beautiful because it had a huge front window in the living room where my piano would be placed. I loved everything about it.

I remember standing in our back yard and looking as far as we could see. For miles, the countryside was wide-open spaces. We could see the train on the railroad track where it crosses Rufe Snow Drive toward Watauga.

There was a big red barn on a huge grassy field behind our house, close to where North Richland Elementary was built. We could see downtown Fort Worth far in the distance from our back porch—no trees and no homes west of our house.

Paula was in the second grade, and I was a senior at Birdville High School. The best memory I have of Birdville High School is sitting in the band class by John Giordano. He played the alto saxophone, and I played the baritone sax. Of course, we had no idea then that he would become conductor of the Fort Worth Symphony, and I would teach in the Birdville school system for 30 years. We met again in 1964 while getting our passports for trips to Europe. He was going to Brussels, Belgium, to study music for two years, and I was going on a 43-day tour as a college graduation present from my parents. We were two "neighborhood kids," who saw dreams come true, careerwise!

Teaching for the Birdville Independent School District was a joy after graduating from Texas Wesleyan College (now University). I taught at several elementary schools and retired from Grace E. Hardeman Elementary January 15, 1987.

The greatest part of living on Vance Road is that it's in walking distance of our church. My mother, father, and I are charter members of North Richland Hills Baptist Church, and I was the first church pianist. I am proud to be a part of this church family. My daddy thought living that close to church was "next door to heaven." He owned car lots on Belknap Street and Riverside Drive. He was a deacon in our church, Sunday school teacher, and a gourmet cook. He loved to cook fancy desserts and surprise the church staff and Dr. Hal Brooks by delivering something special he had made. Loyde Foster died December 7, 1982.

Later on when the big hole was dug for the new church sanctuary, my mother would walk her twin grandsons, Joey and David, and granddaughter, Lori, to play in the sand. Then they would go to the Rapid Mart to buy candy and soda. This was a daily routine until after the "big church" was built.

I remember the huge rock house with the big rock fence and windmill where Wells Fargo Bank is now. This was the most beautiful landmark in 1952. I cried when it was torn down.

I remember our happy home, watching the world around me change, growing from the "country look" to the big city we know today. We've loved the neighborhood, making new friends in a lovely community. I remember the laughter, joys, sorrows, tears, and tragedies. Through it all, NORTH RICHLAND HILLS has and always will be HOME!

Submitted by Vilda Loyde Foster

A. L. (ROY) AND MILDRED FREEMAN

In 1947, Roy and Mildred Freeman moved to a two-acre place on the corner of Pipeline Road (now called Glenview Drive) and Vance Road. The two acres were bought from W. H. Parchman, who owned several acres in this area.

At this time, we thought we were moving into the country. We had no streets, just two lanes. Pipeline Road was very narrow, with room for only two cars to pass and deep ditches on both sides for water to drain. Very little traffic was on the road in those days. The mail was a rural route.

Across the road from our two acres was a large farm owned by Clarence Jones where numerous head of cattle were raised. In a few years, we saw the fences cut down and streets cut through this large farm. Vance Road was widened and extended on the north. Houses were being built, and people began to move in.

Joining Mr. Jones' farm was a large dairy farm owned by Mr. Bill Mackey. He also had a large herd of cows. We had no water at our place, so we hauled water from Mr. Mackey's deep well until our water lines were installed. Later, as the years passed by, streets were cut on the Mackey farm, and houses were built. Mackey Drive was named for him.

Joining the Mackey farm on the north was Mr. Rufe Snow's farm, which was also developed into houses and schools. The entire development was named Snow Heights Addition, for which Snow Heights Elementary School was named.

On the corner of Grapevine Highway and Vance Road was a beautiful rock house owned by Mr. Wade Cutchin. The house was torn down and the Northeast National Bank was built on that corner.

In the year 1962, after my husband passed away, our two acres was sold to North Richland Hills Baptist Church, and a beautiful new sanctuary was built.

We had only one school, Birdville, for grades one through twelve. This is the school my son, Leroy R. Freeman, attended from the first grade. He graduated in 1959. As years went by, Birdville became crowded, and several grade schools and junior high schools were built, including a new senior high in North Richland Hills.

As future years pass by, we will see more progress in the city that was once just a lot of farmland.

Submitted by Mildred Freeman

WILLIAM E. (BILL) FRENCH
1933–1992

William E. (Bill) French was the first full-time employee for the City of North Richland Hills. He and his wife, Janet, moved here in 1959 when he went to work for the city. He held many different positions with the city as it grew and added departments. This includes building inspector, Public Works director, and fire marshal. He ended his career with North Richland Hills in the late 1960s as city director. Bill passed away in 1992.

Bill and his wife, Janet, were blessed with two daughters, Felicia Coleman and Valerie Hughes, both now residents of Keller. Felicia works for an insurance company in Dallas. She has two children, Brooke and Craig. Valerie is a realtor in Keller. She and her husband, Patrick, have two children, Kevin and Katie. Patrick has been with the North Richland Hills Fire Department for 22 years. Janet currently lives in North Richland Hills.

AUSTIN LEE AND BONNIE FRITZ

The Austin Lee Fritz family moved to the 5100 block of Susan Lee Lane in North Richland Hills in 1959. The family consists of Austin Lee, Bonnie Lee, Richard Lee, Connie Marie, Kathaleen Darlene, and Judy LaVerne. Each of our family is a member of the Church of Christ, and each of the children was very involved in Boy Scouts and Girl Scouts.

There wasn't much to see in North Richland Hills nearly 38 years ago, but it certainly has grown since then. We didn't have very good roads or streets, and most of this area was vacant. On the east side of Davis Boulevard was one old house and lots of mesquite trees. On the other side of our street, there were no houses. The land where Holiday Heights School is now located was an old vacant house. Where Hudiburg is now, there was a beautiful rock house with a feed store nearby.

Back, L/R-Richard, Connie, Kathy; Front-Austin, Bonnie, and Judy

Suddenly, houses began to be built all around us, with construction on Grapevine Highway, Davis Boulevard, and Rufe Snow Drive. All of this area grew up fast, and buildings and homes are still going up. We have heard North Richland Hills is one of the fastest-growing cities in the area.

Richard was born in Fort Worth but with several family moves, he attended school in three states and graduated from Richland High School. He attended Arlington State College, served in the U.S. Army, and presently resides in Fort Worth.

Connie was born in Abilene, attended several schools, and graduated from Richland High School. She continued her education at St. Joseph School of Nursing, and that has been her life's career.

Kathy was born in Fort Worth and was fortunate to attend only schools in North Richland Hills including Richland High School. She followed Connie's footsteps into nursing, attending St. Joseph and Tarrant County Junior College schools for nursing. She is still a nurse and lives in Haltom City.

Judy was born in San Antonio, attended NRH schools including Richland High School. She attended Richland College in Dallas and now lives in Tetonia, Idaho.

MICHAEL AND CHARLOTTE FRITZ

James Michael "Mike" and Charlotte Fulkerson Fritz have devoted much of their adult life to serving the needs of the children of northeast Tarrant County. Both have been employed for 20 years with the Birdville Independent School District. Mike is currently the director of transportation for the school district, and Charlotte is the principal of Northridge Middle School.

Charlotte's parents are Charles Edmon and Ima Jean Hux Fulkerson. Mike's parents are James Oliver and Imogene Persky Henson Fritz. The Fritzes grew up in north Fort Worth where they attended the local schools and were involved in sports, the Royal Ambassadors, and

the Girl Scouts. They moved to their first home in North Richland Hills on Briley Drive in 1971. Their two children are Jennifer Michelle Fritz Miller, a teacher at The Academy at West Birdville, and Lara Leigh Fritz, a student at Baylor University. Both girls graduated from Richland High School. Jennifer is married to Randy Scott Miller, and they also live in North Richland Hills. The Millers have one daughter, Cara Michele, and are expecting another child.

Mike and Charlotte have attended North Fort Worth Baptist Church for eight years. They both teach Sunday school and sing in the church choir. Mike has served on the North Richland Hills' Teen Court and on the Library Board. Their leisure time is spent working-out, walking, and going to movies. Their special memories of life in North Richland Hills include the lunch counter at North Richland Drug and a less traveled Rufe Snow Drive with two lanes of traffic and four-way stop signs at Loop 820. Another memory is of a drive-by-shooting in their neighborhood. The Fritz family cite their enlarged circle of friends, more restaurants, and larger shopping areas as being good changes that have occurred since they arrived in North Richland Hills in 1971.

Submitted by Michael Fritz

GEORGE AND CHRISTINE FRY

George B. Fry and Christine Presley Fry were married July 19, 1945, in the North Fort Worth Baptist Church. George worked as a salesman for 30 years before his death in November 1975. Janice Christine Fry was born August 21, 1920, to Amy Daisy (Davis) and S. G. Presley in Thalia, Texas. Christine had three brothers: S. G., R. E., and J. H., and one sister, Marie. Christine grew up and went to school in Chillicothe, Texas.

George and Christine's son was born May 24, 1948, in Fort Worth. They named him George B. Fry Jr. He went to Castleberry Public Schools and received his bachelor's degree from Texas Wesleyan College. He is married to Diane Dennis. They live in Denver, Colorado.

The Fry family moved to Noreast Drive in North Richland Hills in September 1971 from River Oaks. Christine has attended the North Richland Hills Baptist Church for the last 13 years.

George, Christine, and George Fry Jr., 1971

GARRETT FAMILY

Some of the earliest settlers in Smithfield were members of the Garrett family. Five of the 10 children of Benjamin Franklin and Sarah Woods Garrett migrated to Texas, established farms in Smithfield, and raised their children in a very close-knit family atmosphere. Times were hard and, as ever, farming was unpredictable, but by staying close and supporting each other, they managed to survive and prosper.

Benjamin and Sarah Garrett's firstborn was Elizabeth Ann Garrett Childress. She never migrated to Texas.

Their second child, Rapley (Rapp), was born in 1842 and died in 1901. He married Louisa Jane Sparger in 1877. A newspaper article in the LaFayette Messenger in October 1885 said that Rapley had sold his crop and was preparing to emigrate to Texas. By 1900 he and his family were living in Tarrant County, probably in Smithfield. Louisa Jane's family, the Spargers, were prominent landowners in the Smithfield-Colleyville area. Both Rapley and Louisa are buried in the Smithfield Cemetery.

Two of Rapley and Louisa's children lived in northeast Tarrant County. Their oldest daughter was Mary Ann Garrett Pirkle Daniel. She loaded up her children, their nanny, and all the family possessions into a wagon and moved to Texas to be near her family when her first husband died in Georgia. She married Isaac Newton Daniel in 1899 in Colleyville, and they had four children.

Rapley's second child was Richard G. Garrett. He married Mattie Averella Benton in 1904. They had three daughters.

Benjamin and Sarah's third child, John A. Garrett, never came to Texas. However, John's son Gordon Garrett came to Texas by himself after his parent's death. He was shot to death in Burleson in 1917 and is buried in the Smithfield Cemetery.

James Alexander (Jim) Garrett was the fourth child born to Benjamin and Sarah. (After Benjamin's death, Sarah lived with Jim and his family in Smithfield until she died.) Jim was married four times and had 12 children. Jim was a member of the Masons and was a charter member of the Smithfield Lodge No. 455.

Benjamin and Sarah's fifth child, Manning, never lived in Texas. He was struck by lightning near Atlanta, Georgia, and killed.

Mary Elizabeth Garrett Autrey was the sixth of the Garrett's children. She wed Rayford Autrey in Georgia in 1867 at 15 years of age. They had 13 children. Mary Elizabeth and Rayford moved to Texas, finally settling in Smithfield where they lived in a tent until their house was built.

Nathaniel (Nathan) Garrett was the seventh child in the Garrett family of 10 children. Nathan never emigrated to Texas. Benjamin and Sarah's eighth child was George Washington (Wash) Garrett.

The ninth child born to Benjamin and Sarah was Sarah Jane Garrett Wallin who never lived in Texas.

The tenth and last child of Benjamin and Sarah was William Morgan (Morg or Maug) Garrett.

It is obvious that for several decades the Garrett family created quite a presence in the Smithfield community. A large number of them are buried in the Smithfield Cemetery, and many of their descendants still live nearby. Even though the homes they built are gone, the land where they lived and farmed remains, and it now supports some of the finest homes and businesses in the area.

Submitted by Lorene Garrett Wofford

RAMON AND JEANELLE GILES

North Richland Hills residents, Ramon and Jeanelle (Jan) Giles, were married November 10, 1956. Ramon retired from J. R. Clearwater Chemical Company in 1990, and Jan owns Jan's Flowers on Glenview Drive in Richland Hills. Ramon is a member of the Smithfield Masonic Lodge and is a Shriner. Jan is active in the Fort Worth Women's Club and Pan American Round Table. They attend North Richland Hills Baptist Church, where Ramon is a charter member.

Ramon and Jan have three children:

Their son Ken married Tammy Gatewood in 1982. They live in Richland Hills and have three children: Colt, Logan, and Lacey. Ken is in commercial construction and Tammy teaches in the Hurst-Euless-Bedford School District.

Nena is married to Doug Hofsteter, and they live in Possum Kingdom. Nena has two children: Chase Amyett and Jamilyn.

Their adopted daughter, Esse, is married to Dale Davis. They reside in North Richland Hills and have one daughter, Hannah.

Jan's parents were Pratt and Arminta Stevens, who moved to Smithfield in 1944.

JOHN AND MILDRED GIORDANO

John and I,(Mildred Giordano) moved to North Richland Hills in the summer of 1953 with our two children, John and Carol Ann. We moved into one of the many new areas that were being developed there. Although we relocated our residence two more times, we still remained in the North Richland Hills area from Jannie Street to Carma Street, then to Green Meadow Drive.

John, who was in the 11th grade and Carol Ann, who was in the 4th grade, both attended Birdville on the same campus located on Belknap Street. While attending Birdville, John played the saxophone and organized an award-winning swing band. Richland High School was formed during Carol's senior year. However, she chose to

Mildred Giordano with son John Giordano, 1969

remain on the older campus, which became Haltom High. While there, she played the flute and was a drum major in the band. Both John and Carol graduated from Texas Christian University. John continued his study of music, and Carol studied English, which she later taught at Richland High School.

Our children met their mates in Texas. John and Mary Alice have three children: Anne, Ellen, and John, and one grandchild, John Charles. Carol and her husband, Tom, reside in Maryland where she continues her teaching career. They have two children, Jordana and Lucas.

John has remained in Fort Worth where he is the music director and conductor of the Fort Worth Symphony Orchestra and jury chairman of the Van Cliburn Piano Competition. Throughout his musical career, John has achieved a variety of honors, including being recognized by the Birdville school system as an outstanding graduate. His most recent honor was having TCU's new piano wing named after him. He plans to retire as symphony conductor in the year 2000.

John brought his expertise as a technical illustrator here to help open the new Bell Helicopter plant in Hurst. He retired in 1973 as a supervisor in Technical Publications. He was also an artist and musician. John passed away in June 1974.

Mildred also shared her family's interest in the arts. Before marriage, she sang and danced and still continues these pursuits, including a study of painting. Her business career was that of credit manager for Haltom City State Bank. During her 25-year career in banking, Mildred was the president of her local Credit Women's Club, as well as national officer and was honored as Credit Woman of the Year by the International organization. She is a member of AARP, having served as president.

Indeed, John's dream for his family has come true by moving into this growing area of opportunity.

Submitted by Mildred Giordano

H. T. "HANK" AND GWEN GRADY

Henry T. "Hank" Grady, born in 1923, and his wife, Gwen (Coker) currently live on Morgan Circle, North Richland Hills. In 1958 they lived in a house on Rufe Snow that was torn down so the Abbott Medical Building could be built. This house was built by W. A. and Roberta McGee.

Hank served in the Air Force in World War II from 1942-1945. Following military duty, he was a carpet layer

Hank and Gwen Grady, Christmas 1986

for 35 years. Gwen was a "stay-at-home mom" for many years, raising her children and looking after her brother's offspring. Later, she became a certified nurse aide, working in private home health.

Hank is active in the Masonic Lodge, and they are both active church members. They enjoy 7 children, 16 grandchildren, and 3 great-grandchildren.

STANLEY AND ANN CARNATHAN GRANER

The Graners moved to Cummings Drive in North Richland Hills in November of 1954. Stan was born in Dallas in 1925. Ann was born in Dallas in 1928. Stan was a graduate of Highland Park High School and attended SMU on a V-12 (Navy) Officer's program. He graduated from the University of Texas in Austin with a degree in mechanical engineering and a master's in industrial management. Ann was a graduate of Henderson High School in Henderson and attended the University of Texas in Austin.

Stan's career has been in the cold storage industry, and he has been semiretired since 1990. Ann is a homemaker and community volunteer.

Stan's military service involved the V-12 program (Navy Officers) from 1943 to 1946. He received an honorable discharge in 1946 with the rank of lieutenant (j.g.).

Stan and Ann Graner

Stan holds memberships in many career and community related organizations.

He was mayor pro tem and councilman in North Richland Hills from 1958–61. During this time NRH annexed all land up to the present northern border. The Police Department was also started during his term.

Ann's involvements include membership in many civic and community organizations including NRH Garden Club, PTA, Girl Scouts, and many others. The family has been active members of Richland Hills Methodist Church for many years.

They have four children: Ann Pickel lives in Arlington and has three children, Stephanie, Matt, and Andrew. Lane Peters lives in Southlake and has three children, Tricia, Jeremy, and Erin. Stan Jr. lives in Dallas, and Jane lives in Denton.

JAMES WILLIAM AND MARY BARRINGER GRAVES

James William Graves was born December 23, 1913 in Rushville, Ohio. He was employed by Sears and Roebuck in 1955 in Palestine, Texas. He was later transferred to Vernon, then to Ardmore, Oklahoma, and then to Fort Worth Catalog Sales on Belknap Street. Later he was

James W. Graves

sent to Town & Country Store on Jacksboro Highway in Fort Worth. His last assignment with Sears was at the River Oaks store. During this period, he served as vice president of the Town & Country Business Association. James passed away in 1987.

Mary Barringer Graves was born November 30, 1923, in Stuart, Iowa. She became the credit manager, and then personnel manager of the J. C. Penney store in Richland Plaza.

Mary Graves

James and Mary had one daughter, MariLee, who graduated from Richland High School in 1968. They have two grandsons, Mike Wesley and Brian Carse.

RICK AND KATHY GRAVES

Rick and Kathy (Bowen) Graves moved from Garland to North Richland Hills in 1985, with their two children, Kelly and Laura. They followed Kathy's sister, Janie and her husband, Jimmy Shoppa, who were already NRH residents. Kelly enrolled at Smithfield Elementary School as a sixth-grader. He found it easy to make new friends in the elementary school setting. Laura who was born in Garland, was 4 when we arrived here.

We moved to the Londonderry area, a quiet, peaceful neighborhood in the middle of nowhere on the north side of town. Springtime arrived, and we went to work landscaping the yard. One evening after planting and watering the new lawn, we collapsed on the front porch to watch an approaching thunderstorm. Weather alerts were sounding, and we became quite alarmed as a roar began in the distance. The roar became louder and louder, but it was no tornado. It was the jet cars at the Green Valley Raceway! So much for our peaceful neighborhood.

It has been a great place to raise children. Kelly became captain of the tennis team at Richland High. He graduated from University of Texas in Arlington with a degree in computer science engineer-

Front, L/R-Laura, Kathy, Rick; Back-Kelly, 1985

ing. He is currently living in Dallas and has a new job at Technology Solutions Co. Laura also graduated from Richland High School.

Rick works as a consulting systems engineer at Burlington Northern Santa Fe railroad. Kathy spent several years rearing the children and volunteering at the schools. She began a home-based craft business called "The Ghost Factory." She was treasurer of the Adventure World Foundation that raised the funds and built the playground on Starnes Road. She is now serving on the advisory board for the NRH Teen Court and is the chairman of the Londonderry Homeowners Association, which she and Rick helped form in 1985. Rick is currently serving on the NRH Town Hall Committee. Both Rick and Kathy were born the same year as North Richland Hills in 1953, so I guess there will be no secret regarding their ages.

EVERETT AND WILMA GRELLE

Everett and I, Wilma Grelle, and our four children, Dixie Lee, Kent, Jimmy, and Brenda, moved to North Richland Hills in 1961. Before that we had lived in Lampasas where three of our children were born: Dixie Lee in 1939; Kent in 1943; and Jimmy in 1947. Brenda was born in 1951 in Burnett.

While at Lampasas, Everett worked at nearby Fort Hood in Killeen for the Atomic Energy Commission. We lived in Las Vegas, Nev., San Antonio, and Bossier City, La., before moving to NRH. There was no place to eat out or buy groceries when we moved here. The nearest place to eat was on Lancaster Avenue. Everett worked on weekends at the Rapid Mart, a small convenience store where we could buy soft drinks and ice.

Dixie Lee finished school in San Antonio, married Bob Ferrier, and moved to Shreveport, Louisiana. They have four children: Jonette, Robert Lee, Ronnie, and Tammy and have three grandchildren: Katy, Erin, and Caleb.

Kent graduated from Richland High in 1962, attended the University of Texas at Arlington and was in the Navy four years. He married Donna McCarthy. They live in Hurst and have two children, Ryan and Jill.

Jimmy graduated from Richland High in 1966 and attended Texas Wesleyan College. He married Jan Hancock and they live in Katy, Texas. They had two daughters, Jody and Jamie. Jamie passed away in September 1994.

Brenda graduated from Richland High in 1970 and attended Tarrant County Junior College. She married Phil Martin. They live in Keller and had two children, Amy and Chris. Chris passed away in December 1995. They have one grandchild, Andrew.

Everett passed away in March 1995.

North Richland Hills is a wonderful place to live and raise a family. We have been blessed. We loved trailering and have visited 45 states.

Submitted by Wilma Grelle

CHARLES LELAND AND LOUISE W. GRIFFIN

Charles Leland and I, Louise W. Griffin, moved to North Richland Hills in 1961 from Haltom City, into a house Leland built himself.

Our lot in NRH is on the corner of Briley Drive and Lariat Lane. The area west and north of us consisted of mesquite trees, rocks, weeds, and some of everything else that people had dumped there. Over the hill, and slightly northwest of us, was a lake. Our children and grandchildren took great delight in exploring this area as we took our regular walks.

Our two daughters, who were 14 and 11 years old when we moved to NRH, finished their school year at Haltom Junior High and Birdville Elementary. The next fall, our oldest, Dolores, entered Richland High School. The younger child, Eileen, attended Snow Heights Elementary in the sixth grade. The new Richland High School was not quite finished when the 1961 fall semester began, so there was a great deal of construction going on during classes that year. The North Richland Junior High had not yet been built, so Eileen attended Richland Junior High.

Both daughters graduated from Richland High School, Dolores in 1964 and Eileen in 1968. Dolores received both bachelor's and master's degrees from the University of North Texas. Her bachelor's degree was in English and Latin. Her master's degree was in public school administration. Eileen received her bachelor's degree with a double major in marketing and economics from the University of Texas at Arlington.

Our family grew considerably as our children married. Dolores wed Roger Craig Webb in 1966. He had been a high school classmate who lived in Richland Hills. Eileen married Richard Harry Ran from Arlington, whom she met in Houston where they both were living and working after college. They were married in 1978.

Dolores and Roger have three daughters, Amy, Alicia, and Andrea. They now have four grandchildren. Eileen and Rick have two children: a son, Ryan Griffin Ran, and a daughter, Regan Gabrielle Ran. Dolores and Roger live in North Richland Hills, and Eileen and Rick live in the West University section of Houston.

Dolores taught honors English classes at Haltom High School for 12 years. She was an assistant principal at both North Oaks Junior High School and Haltom High School for six years. She later resigned and went into the insurance business in NRH where she is still located. She has served on the Birdville Independent School District School Board for three terms. In 1995 she received a Master Trustee Status pin from the State of Texas. She served eight years on the Board of Directors of Northeast Tarrant Chamber of Commerce. She has served three years on the Board of Directors of the YMCA and is a member of the northeast area Lions Club.

Leland retired from the *Fort Worth Star-Telegram* credit department in 1981 after 34 years of employment.

HAZEL USSERY GRIMES

Hazel Ussery was born in Weatherford on May 19, 1912, to Parker and Ethel Ussery. Her daddy was a tenant farmer who enjoyed moving from place to place. Because of this, Hazel attended many schools after beginning first grade in Weatherford.

Hazel graduated from Smithfield School in 1931. There were only 10 grades in the school at that time. The two-story, red-brick school building, built in 1912, was located on the same site of the present Smithfield Elementary School. She remembers there were nine students in the graduating class.

Ethel and Parker Ussery

Hazel's memories of the Smithfield School included a long, wide hall down the middle of the building. Most rooms had two grades in them. She remembers several teachers: C. C. White, who taught seventh-grade math and tenth-grade civics; Emma Ousley, who taught English and history; and Modena Fitzhugh, who taught home economics. Home-ec classes were held in the Home Demonstration Club building, a one-room building north of the school. It was here she learned to sew on a treadle sewing machine.

Hazel joined the Smithfield Baptist Church (First Baptist Church of Smithfield) where she is still a member. She served as church clerk and also taught Sunday school for many years. She enjoyed helping the church celebrate its 100th anniversary in 1995.

Hazel worked for Mrs. W. O. Quinn at the Smithfield telephone exchange in 1935 until June 1936. The switchboard, located in the

Hazel Ussery Grimes

Quinn's home, was about three feet wide and quite tall. Two girls worked the board at one time. Mrs. Quinn rented rooms to school teachers and also prepared lunches for them. Mr. Quinn delivered them to the school.

The original telephone exchange had burned in February 1930 in a fire that practically destroyed half of the business section of Smithfield. Mrs. Lora B. Buckworth, mother of Mrs. Quinn, died in the blaze. She had moved from Kansas three months before to make her home with her daughter. Mrs. Buckworth was bedridden. Three men were burned in an unsuccessful attempt to reach her through the burst of flames that followed the explosion of a kerosene stove in her room. The telephone exchange, Walker's filling station, a blacksmith shop, and a barbershop were all destroyed. When the fire spread across the street, the V. G. Lewis grocery store, which had lodge rooms of the Odd Fellows and Woodmen on the second floor, was consumed. An adjoining building checked the flames from spreading further. A bucket line was formed carrying water from a nearby well and water holes, but the bucket brigade was unable to combat the fast-spreading fire. There was a well at the schoolhouse with a Delco generator on it. Most people hauled water from the school for their own use.

On June 28, 1936, Hazel Ussery and Lawrence Robert Grimes were married at the First Baptist Church in Euless.

Lawrence Robert Grimes was born in Keller January 28, 1911. The couple had two children. Robert Lee Grimes, who was born in 1939, married Linda Miller and they live in Arlington. Robert and Linda have three children, Vicki, Gary, and Bob. Jean Grimes, born July

Bonnie Ussery Hardin

29, 1941, in Fort Worth, married Paul Rippe and has two children, Ronald and Ginger, and lives in Bedford. Hazel enjoys her grandchildren and seven great-grandchildren.

Hazel had never worked outside the home after her marriage and considered being at home and raising her children the most important job she could have. After her husband died February 17, 1959, and her children were on their own, she found she had a lot of time on her hands. She thought she could certainly work in retail sales, so she went to work at Mott's Variety Store in Greater Richland Shopping Center. Later she worked at Kresge's Variety Store in Richland Plaza until the parent company built the K-Mart store on Pipeline Road and Loop 820, and Kresge's store was closed. She worked at K-Mart until her retirement.

Her home is the background for her artistic talents, one of which is painting. She developed this talent as an adult in her 70s. Her son, Robert Lee, is an accomplished artist and gave her lessons.

Mrs. Grimes' story as told to Evalyn Lochridge

CHARLES HAGER AND FAMILY

The Charles Hager family moved to North Richland Hills in 1962 to the Woodcrest Addition, which was being developed by Herman Smith and John Barfield.

In 1962, there was no Loop 820, nor Airport Freeway. When Smith & Barfield began developing Woodcrest, they poured two or three slabs for houses on the lower corner of the area. The County Commissioners advised them not to build in that area. They said there will be a major highway built in the area: "We don't know just where or when, but it will be built somewhere through that area. Don't build any houses that might have to be torn down."

When I inquired about the city limits, Herman told me that the backside of the lot I had purchased was the city limit between NRH and Hurst. He said the two cities had gotten together and established the city limits along the "fall line" so that both cities would not have to get into the other city's property to service their utilities.

In 1970, I was appointed to the NRH Planning and Zoning Commission. At the first meeting, I was asked to chair the commission. Being new at this sort of thing, I declined. After just a few meetings, the need for a new chairman arose, and I again was asked to be chairman. This time I accepted. Being a psychologist, I utilized my knowledge as we guided the work of the commission. It seems to be that the 1970s was the time this area really began expansion. New businesses came to the area, more people moved in, and land development picked up and has not slowed down yet.

One anecdote might be of interest: One evening one of the developers told the city secretary, "It's almost a pleasure to come out here for a P&Z meeting. You conduct the meeting with dignity and dispatch and go home." (Or something to that effect.) One thing I did as chair was to open the meeting with a comment that we wanted to hear from anyone who had anything to say on the subject before the commission. "We will listen patiently the first time you have something to say; we will listen with indulgence when you repeat what you have said, but the third time you begin to say the same thing over, we will cut you off. We want to give everyone an opportunity to be heard," I told the audience.

After four and one half years, I resigned. It seemed to me then, and it still does, that one term is as long as anyone should serve on P&Z because of the power inherent in such a commission to influence the market value of a piece of real estate.

Submitted by Charles Hager

L. B. AND VERNEY HALL

In the summer of 1977, L. B. Hall, his wife Verney, and daughter Mary Jane moved to Circleview Drive in North Richland Hills. The Halls moved from Richland Hills where they had lived since 1949.

Mr. Hall was a retired pilot for American Airlines. He died December 29, 1987. L. B. and Verney were married 44 years. Verney is a homemaker. Mary Jane works for Southwestern Bell Telephone Company.

Mary Jane married Dan Hada on July 2, 1984. Dan is with Sears. Their daughter, Suzanne, is a student at North Richland Middle School. They continue to reside at the Circleview address.

Submitted by Verney Hall

L. B. and Verney Hall with granddaughter Suzanne Hada

BILLY JACK AND ROMELL HARDIN

Billy Jack Hardin was born in 1936, in Brady, Texas, and graduated from Brady High School in 1954.

Billy Jack, Romell, Monica; Back, Darren Hardin

Romell Surber Hardin was born in Mason, Texas, and graduated from high school there in 1960. They were married October 15, 1960, and lived in Brady where Billy Jack worked for the City of Brady in the Public Works Department as an electrician. Romell worked for the telephone company as an operator. They lived in Brady until 1970 when they moved to North Richland Hills.

The Hardins have two children: Darren, born in Brady on December 17, 1968, and Monica, born in Fort Worth on September 15, 1972. Both graduated from Richland High School, Darren in 1987 and Monica in 1991.

When they moved to NRH, the Hardin family bought a house on Winnell Way from Norman and Mary Ruth Ellis and they continue living there. Billy Jack worked for Tarrant County Junior College in the maintenance department, then for Reeves Manufacturing Co. in Hurst before becoming building superintendent for North Richland Hills Baptist Church for the next 16 years. He retired in September 1998.

Romell has been employed in doctors' offices in NRH for about 20 years. She currently works for Dr. Tommy Abbott.

The Hardins joined the NRH Baptist Church in 1970. Romell was active in Snow Heights PTA, served as president one term and received a life membership award. She remembers when Richland High School was the farthest thing to the north and when Kresge's at Richland Plaza was a good place to shop.

The favorite family vacation was to Hawaii in 1997. The vacation was described as "interesting," because they flew in an Army cargo plane. The trip was free, since Billy Jack is a retired National Guardsman, but the plane was so loud they had to wear earplugs for the entire trip.

Submitted by Romell Hardin

PAUL J. HARMON AND FAMILY

Paul and Doris Harmon moved to North Richland Hills in early 1957, living first on Tabor Street, then Shauna Drive (before Loop 820 or the schools were built), then to Eden Road in early 1966. Their home and the home of their daughter, Darla Boswell and family, were built on the old J. B. Eden farmhouse site.

Paul was born in Milwaukee, Doris in Fort Worth, and they have a grandson, Scott Jared Harmon, who was born in Arlington. Paul and Doris are members of St. Paul's Methodist Church in Hurst. Paul has served over the years in various offices: president of Haltom-Richland Chamber of Commerce, Diamond Oaks Country Club, Fort Worth Jaycees, Fort Worth Executive Association, chairman of the board of the Tarrant County Heart Association, vice chairman of Tarrant County Business Bureau, trustee of Tarrant County Charitable Foundation, organizer of Greater Richland Area Jaycees, coached Peewee football and baseball in Richland Youth Association for six years; served on the first NRH Charter Commission, was active in NRH politics in the late 60s and early 70s.

Paul retired in 1982 from the First National Bank of Fort Worth as vice president-manager, national corporate and correspondent banking departments after 30 years of service.

Paul and Doris' three children were raised in NRH, and all graduated from Richland High School, Paula Harmon Capshaw in 1965, William Jary Harmon in 1971, and Darla Harmon Boswell in 1981. Paula has been teaching in the Birdville ISD for 25 years, Jary lives in Ontario, Canada, and Darla and family live on Eden Road in NRH.

Paul and Doris Harmon celebrated their golden wedding anniversary on May 19, 1998.

HOLLIS AND WANDA HELTON

Wanda Hurst and Hollis Helton were married on January 21, 1947, in east Tennessee. They moved to Fort Worth in the Polytechnic area of town almost immediately, and Hollis went to work at the *Fort Worth Star-Telegram* in 1948. Amon G. Carter Sr. was the owner of the paper when Helton first began unloading rolls of paper from boxcars on Lancaster Street using rope cables and old-fashioned forklifts and trucked them to the Seventh Street plant.

Hollis and Wanda Helton

Wanda was a homemaker and mother of two daughters born in Harris Hospital: Deborah on December 31, 1952, and Denise on September 25, 1955. In January 1968, the family moved to Keeter Drive in North Richland Hills where both girls graduated from Richland High School.

Hollis Helton worked for the Star-Telegram for 43 years, holding every position in the paper-handling department, including foreman and supervisor at both warehouses and the pressroom. He retired in January 1991 after witnessing great advances in the technology of newspapers, including installation of two new types of presses and the movement of the paper to the new state-of-the-art plant on South Loop 820.

Wanda, an accomplished seamstress and artist, has devoted her life to her husband, children, and then her grandchildren, Aaron and Elisa Tribble, as well as to her neighbors and her friends at Lake Arlington Baptist Church.

GENE AND KATHY HICKS

Helen and Joe Hicks built a house in Richland Hills in early 1953 on Grapevine Highway across the street from the Hobby Lobby. My mother lived there until her death, December 19, 1997. We had lived in River Oaks before that.

I first came to NRH when I came home from the Navy in November 1953 and lived with my parents. I lived there until 1956 when I built a house in NRH on Parchman in 1956. My dad bought land from Mr. Parchman and built a full service station on the Grapevine Highway between the Dairy Kreem and Rapid Mart. The station opened as a Premier station in 1956. About 1960, it was changed to Shell.

Top-Gene Hicks; Front, L/R-Helen, Monica, and Kathy

I became the manager of the Grapevine Highway station after I came home. I remember all the city of North Richland Hills had was a volunteer fire department on Glenview Drive and an old fellow that drove a Pontiac around the businesses on Grapevine Highway at night to make sure there were no break-ins.

My father was one of the initial directors of the Greater Richland Chamber of Commerce, established in December 1957. Dad passed away in 1993.

I have two brothers and one sister: Joe Don, Mary Helen Hicks, and Benny Michael.

I was first married to Carol Cline. We had a son, Gene Jr. I have been married to Kathy Mayberry for 16 years. Kathy's family has lived in Richland Hills since 1956. Kathy has a son, William Christopher, 24, who lives in Euless. We have two daughters, Helen Elizabeth and Monica Katherine, ages 15 and 12, living at home.

Some of my early memories about NRH were when I was a little boy. My grandparents lived in Grapevine, and we lived in the Poly area of Fort Worth. We went to Grapevine just about every weekend, and I remember dropping off the "Birdville Hill," as we called it. When you dropped off Birdville Hill, it was all country after that. Where the Sirloin Steak House is now, there was a red brick house with an "S" on the chimney. Past that was the old Will Snow house upon the hill where the Shamrock station is today. To the right, was the Scrugg's old house. Farther down and on the left, there was the Parchman's house, and the Wade Cutchin home, a big rock house, was where the Wells Fargo Bank is now. Where Hudiburg is now was Starnes Station, a two-story station with a couple of gas pumps next to a feed store. The Reeves home was also on that corner. I'll always remember that house because it had a carport that was fixed with a patio on top where they could sit out there in chairs in the evening. I thought that was so nice. After

that there were only farmhouses all the way to Colleyville. If you turn right on Glade Road off of Grapevine Highway, go all the way to Main Street in Euless, that's where my great-grandfather John McDonald Hicks had 160 acres. My great-grandmother was a Green. My great-great-grandfather Green's house was where Trinity High School is now. He owned about 500 acres there in Bedford. He came from Bedford, Tennessee. Great-great-granddad Green was a nurse in the Confederate Army. When he came home from war to Bedford, Tennessee, the Union Army had burned down everything. So they left on a wagon train and settled where Bedford, Texas, is today. They called it Bedford, Texas, after Bedford, Tennessee. He's buried in the Bear Creek Cemetery. A plaque was placed in the cemetery for him by the Daughters of the Confederacy. My grandfather, Joe H. Hicks Sr., was the first veterinarian in Grapevine. My family has been around here for a long time.

ZANE AND KAREN HILGER

Zane was born in Searcy, Arkansas. Karen Ashley was born in Wichita Falls, Texas. They celebrated their 25th anniversary in October 1997.

Zane moved with his parents, Lowell and Joyce Hilger, and sister, Zanda, to North Richland Hills in the summer of 1966. Although Zane entered his senior year at Richland High School, a motorcycle accident one night after working at the old Richland Cinema led to home schooling. He was able to graduate with his class in 1967, and he attended the newly opened Tarrant County Junior College South Campus. For a few years, he worked at what was then Ling-Temco-Vought in Grand Prairie, and then for Radio Shack in Dallas.

Karen attended Midwestern University in Wichita Falls and, following her interest in the sciences, worked in the new field of nuclear medicine as a technician in the late '60s.

Zane's daughter, Judi, was born in Arlington in 1969. In 1972, Zane and Karen, newly married, along with Judi, moved to Chicago, Illinois, where Zane was transferred to work in repair with Radio Shack.

Within three years, he was transferred from his job as a Radio Shack store manager in Illinois to Fort Worth where he managed the Radio Shack Southwest Repair Center. The family moved into one of four houses in (what was then) rural North Richland Hills just south of (what is now) North Tarrant Boulevard and Glenn Forest section of the city.

Searching for a career change, Zane found his life work: law enforcement. Having volunteered as a deputy constable and completed basic peace officer training at TCJC, NW Police Academy, he was chosen chief deputy of Precinct No. 3. In 1986 he was elected constable and holds that office today. Zane is a member of the HEB Rotary, the Lions Club, teaches at the TCJC Law Enforcement Training Center, was one of the first instructors for handgun licensing in Tarrant County, and is very active in local politics. Zane is also an animal lover, both domestic and wild.

Karen is the manager of the Civil Division of the Tarrant County Clerk's Office. Karen is also active in the community, having served as election judge and is a precinct chairwoman. Karen's family also has been her priority. She is very involved in the life of her new grandson, Anthony Jason Moreno (AJ), born to daughter Judi in June 1997. She also shares her life with her two furry, four-legged canines that she and Zane call the "girls."

DRURY GLEN AND DOROTHY HILL

Glen Hill was born in 1919 in Johnson County, Texas. His family moved to the White Settlement area of Fort Worth in 1934. Dorothy Coker, born in 1920 in Alabama, was one of 11 children. The Coker family moved to the north side of Fort Worth in 1928, and Dorothy graduated from North Side High School.

Dorothy had two brothers who worked at Crystal Springs, a swimming pool and western dance hall. Glen and Dorothy met when neighborhood boys often gathered at the Coker home. They were married in 1938 in Weatherford.

Glen and Dorothy Hill

Glen was drafted into the Army and saw action in France, Germany, Belgium, Austria, and Yugoslavia. He was discharged in February 1946 after having earned the Bronze Star.

After military service, Glen worked for General Dynamics and then Bell Helicopter. Dorothy also worked for GD and both retired in 1982. After retirement, the couple enjoyed travels in their motor home and gatherings with family and friends.

They were members of the Elks lodge and the GD Retirees Club. Glen died in 1977, and Dorothy continues to live in the home on Turner Terrace where they moved in 1957.

Jimmy Lee Hill was born in 1942 in Fort Worth. He and his wife, Wanda Joyce Auten, both graduated from Birdville High School. They moved to Whitney, Texas, in 1972. Jimmy currently drives into Hurst each day where he is manager of flight operations at Bell Helicopter. They have two daughters, both born at Glenview Hospital, and four grandchildren. The oldest daughter, Lucretia, lives with her husband, Joe Price, and two sons in Whitney. The younger, Joy Suzanne, lives with her husband, Jimmy Sessums and two children in Waco.

Jimmy and Joyce Hill

Glenda Fay Hill was born in Fort Worth in 1940. She graduated from Birdville High School in 1958 and later that same year met and married Glenn Cordts, a native of Illinois. He was an airman stationed at Carswell Air Force Base. During the 10 years they lived on Keeter Drive in North Richland Hills, they had four children, all born at Glenview Hospital. The children are Lori Lynne, Cheryl Ann, Christopher, and Joni Renee.

L/R-Christopher Cordts, Cheryl (Cordts) Shaver, Joni (Cordts) Robertson, Lori (Cordts) Little, Glenda (Hill-Cordts) Clark, Larry, David, and Kyle Clark

Glen died in 1983. Twelve years later, Glenda married Larry Woods Clark. Larry and his first wife, Ann, were neighbors of Glenda and Glenn many years before when both families lived in Hurst. After Ann's death in 1994, the two old friends started seeing each other and they were married in 1995. He has two sons, David and Kyle.

KEVIN AND LADONNA HILL

Ladonna Leslie was born November 8, 1962 in Fort Worth to Marvin Leo and JoAnn Leslie. She attended schools in Hurst, graduating from L. D. Bell High School in 1981. In 1981 she met Kevin Lee Hill, a new management trainee when both worked at Taco Bueno. They were married April 27, 1985 and make their home in North Richland Hills.

Kevin was born in Lufkin October 25, 1959, and attended Angelina Junior College on a baseball

Kevin, Ladonna (Leslie), and Ryan Hill

scholarship, finally moving to Texas Wesleyan College in Fort Worth where he graduated in 1983 with a degree in business management. They have one son, Ryan Matthew Hill, a gifted athlete, who is a member of the National Association of Youth Athletics, playing baseball and football. Ryan is an honor student at Smithfield Elementary.

After owning and managing a coffee espresso business in North Hills Mall, Kevin is currently working in sales and Ladonna is a postal clerk in Roanoke. The family is active in church and community baseball.

Submitted by Betty Leslie

LLOYD AND MARIE HINKLE

Lloyd and I (Marie Hinkle) were married March 3, 1952, at Riverside Methodist Church. I am a native of Fort Worth and a graduate of Poly High School. Lloyd is from Missouri. He joined the Air Force at age 17 and was stationed at Carswell Air Force Base in Fort Worth.

After marriage, we traveled and lived all over the United States and spent three years in Alaska at the expense of Uncle Sam.

The four Hinkle children, Vickie, Marsha, John, and Ronald, were all born during those years of travel, but all graduated from Richland High School. John was born in the territory of Alaska, and Ronald was born there after statehood.

After Lloyd's retirement from the Air Force, we moved back to Texas, and Lloyd started a second career with Gifford Hill Pipe Co.

Marie and Lloyd Hinkle

We moved to North Richland Hills in 1984. By this time, I was busy with a real estate career and owned Lightfoot Realty and later, Elan Custom Homes.

In 1982, I was elected to the North Richland Hills City Council where I served for six years in Place One. During that time I served as president of Region 8, was on the board for the Council of Government, and served on the Texas Municipal League Board of Directors. I was also vice president of the Mayors Council of Texas.

I enjoyed being a part of NRH's growth, but Lloyd's transfer to Phoenix, Arizona, in 1988 ended my political career. Living in Scottsdale did help prepare us for retirement, and we returned to Texas in 1992.

We now live on a small ranch in Lipan, Texas, and raise Black Angus cattle.

Our children are somewhat scattered but come home often. Vickie has a 17-year-old daughter at Bell High School. They live in Hurst. Marsha and her family live in

L/R-Ronald, John, Marsha (Cassie), and Vickie (Pacek) Hinkle

Lipan. She has two sons, a 19-year-old in college, and a 7-year-old. John has three boys, and the family lives in Cary, North Carolina. Ronald is married and works for the State of Texas in Austin.

Submitted by Marie Wilson Hinkle

BILLY AND LaFONNE HOBBS

The Billy W. Hobbs family moved to North Richland Hills in 1957. They were a family of four: Bill, LaFonne, Sarah (age 3), and Mark (age 1). Martha was born in July 1958.

Bill worked for Howell Instruments of Fort Worth as a tool and die maker. The spring of 1957 was a very rainy one, and flooding was rampant in the Richland Hills area, making us grateful we had bought here instead of in that area, for we had looked there also.

At the time we moved here, Riviera Drive was the most northern street in our city. The 820 Loop, the high school, and all points north came later. Our children played in the little creek that is now under the parking lot of Office Max, Wickes, the movie theatre, etc.

Top, standing-Mark, Sarah; Front, sitting-LaFonne, Martha, Billy, 1968

As our children grew up in the '50s and '60s, they had much more freedom than children today can have. Crime was a rare thing, and they were free to do many more things than we would dare allow them today.

Our children attended Snow Heights Elementary, North Richland Junior High, and Richland High schools. They took part in many school activities and did well in school. They each attended Abilene Christian University where they obtained their degrees.

LaFonne Hobbs was active in the PTA during the children's school years. She served as president of all three schools for two years in each school, and also other offices in the local units. She worked with the Birdville Council of PTA, as well as the First District.

Sarah married Dale Henry, and they have two sons, Matthew and Jonathan. Both attend Richland High School where they are honor students and excel in music. Matthew won all-state in jazz piano for two years. Dale has his own business, Dale Henry Design and Advertising.

Mark married Brenda Smith of Brownfield and Dallas. He is a money manager for a New York firm. They live in Dallas with their three young children, Grant, Allegra, and Landon.

Martha married Ronnie Lee of Abilene, whom she met in college. He is an elementary principal in Katy, Texas, and Martha is a seventh-grade English teacher at a Katy middle school. They have two sons, Andrew and Aaron. Both of their boys are honor students and excel in music.

Bill went into business for himself 31 years ago, when he built his car wash. He has had several car washes, a station, and a laundry during the growing-up time of the children. Bill has been an elder of the Handley Church of Christ of Fort Worth for 26 years, and both parents have been active in the teaching program.

Coronet Avenue has had many new faces since that day 40 years ago when the Hobbs family moved into their home. They have added extensively to the home in lieu of relocating and are one of the few "old-timers" left on this one-block-long street.

This has been a great place to raise a family and now to enjoy the grandchildren upon their visits. We have been greatly blessed.

WILLIAM E. HOFFMAN AND FAMILY

William Edward "Bill" Hoffman II and Deana Lynn Ellis were married in 1993 at St. Luke United Methodist Church in Haltom City, Texas.

Bill, Deana, and Haley Hoffman

Bill is the son of William E. and Maxine Hoffman. He was born August 29, 1963, in Wichita Falls at Sheppard Air Force Base. He grew up in Iowa Park, 11 miles west of Wichita Falls, attending public schools there and graduating from Iowa Park High School. He then attended Midwestern State University in Wichita Falls, then transferred to Texas A&M University where he graduated with a bachelor's degree in engineering technology electronics.

Bill has one brother, Royal David Hoffman, who lives in Iowa Park, and one sister, Cheryl Ann Hoffman Wood, who lives in Fort Worth. His occupation is a network consultant. For the past two years and prior to that he worked at Harris Methodist Health System for eight years in the Network Engineering Department. "The ever-changing world of electronics, computers, and technology makes our life so interesting," Bill said.

Deana was born in 1960, in Fort Worth. She is the daughter of Norman Dean Ellis and Mary Ruth Reeves Ellis. Deana grew up in North Richland Hills, attended Snow Heights Elementary, North Richland Junior High, and graduated from Haltom High School. She graduated from Texas Woman's University with a bachelor's degree in nursing. She has one brother, David Wayne Ellis, who lives in Haltom City.

Deana is currently a cardiovascular nurse at Harris Methodist Health System in Fort Worth where she has worked for the past three years. She has worked in dialysis and infant care spanning another seven years. Currently, Deana is working part-time at Harris and taking care of Haley Lynn, who was born October 17, 1996.

They have attended the St. Luke United Methodist Church for many years, Deana for all of her life. Bill has served on the Board of Trustees for the past three years, and Deana is actively involved in the handbell choir along with many other functions, including their Sunday school class.

In their spare time, they love to play recreational coed softball, attend Texas Ranger baseball games, and go swimming. Deana loves to work in the yard—always improving, planting, and relocating plants and shrubbery to make their house look beautiful. Bill loves to tinker with computers, build computer networks, and play any sport around. They enjoy their home in Meadow Lakes, the second home they've had in NRH. Their first neighborhood on Cross Timbers Drive was relatively new. Many, many houses were built a few blocks from them during their time there.

Likewise, in Meadow Lakes, they have seen many houses being built along the Iron Horse Golf Course and love the many older houses in this area. Five-Star Ford has recently moved onto the real estate along Loop 820, and this has affected the neighborhood somewhat. Across the loop, Wal-Mart, Home Depot, and other businesses were only a forethought a few years back, but they are now thriving along the busy thoroughfare that runs through the vast North Texas landscape.

Submitted by Bill Hoffman

GARLAND AND MOISE HOLT

I, Garland Edward Holt, was born in 1919, in Gatesville, Texas, one of seven sons born to Annie Powell and William Albert Holt. I grew up in West Texas and New Mexico, moving back to Gatesville where I graduated from high

Garland and Moise Holt, 1992

school in 1939. I received my bachelor's degree from the University of Omaha, master's degree from Oklahoma City University, then completed further study at North Texas State University.

My career in the U.S. Air Force from 1942 to 1969 as a pilot and electronics officer took me all over the world. I flew 137 combat missions in World War II, flying P-39s and P-40s, and was awarded the Distinguished Flying Cross, Air Medal with Oak Leaf Cluster, Joint Service Commendation Medal with Oak Leaf Cluster, plus several others. Overseas assignments included the southwest Pacific, Germany-France, Thailand, and Denmark. After my military career, I began a teaching career at Tarrant County Junior College, Northeast Campus in the business administration division for 18 years.

Moise Colvin and I were married in 1942, at her parents' home in Gatesville. She was born in 1923, near Gatesville to Ethel Brookshire and Gilbert Jesse Lee Colvin. She graduated from Gatesville High School in 1940, and Draughn's Business College in 1942. She has always enjoyed club work. While I was in the Air Force, she was president of four different officers' wives clubs in the United States and overseas. She was also president of the TCJC Women's Club, North Hills Garden Club, and the gourmet group she belonged to in northeast Tarrant County. When we married, Moise was a legal secretary. She continued to work while I was overseas during WWII and except for being a hospital Grey Lady volunteer, she has never worked outside our home since.

We have two sons, Donald Hayden Holt, born in 1946, in Sherman, and Garland Edward Holt Jr., born in Biloxi, Mississippi in 1948. Donald graduated from International High School in Bangkok, Thailand, in 1964. He received his bachelor's degree from Baylor University in public administration and a master's degree in personnel management from Troy State University, Troy, Alabama. He and Jeannine Thorn Holt have two children, Sarah Courtney and Patrick Hayden, who hopes to become an Eagle Scout like his father. The family lives in Colorado Springs, Colorado.

Garland Edward Holt Jr. graduated from high school in Midwest City, Oklahoma, and from the University of Houston with a bachelor's degree in hospital administration. He has five children, Garland E. Holt III, John Paul, Dianna Rene Holt Walker, Brittany Holt (died 1980), and Brenna Holt. He married Carolyn Hartnagle in 1992, and she has two daughters, Amanda and Amy. They live in Mineral Wells.

We have four great-grandchildren.

We moved to our home on Blaney Avenue in 1970 from Oklahoma City. We have been members of the First Baptist Church of Hurst (later changed to Hurst Baptist Church) since early 1971. I have served as a deacon and taught a men's Sunday school class. I was a member of the Mid-Cities Optimist Club and was named Optimist of the Year for 1984–85. I served as election judge for NRH for three years while Dan Echols was mayor.

It is difficult to imagine the growth and population explosion since we moved here. Loop 820 was completed to the west only to I-35, and Airport Freeway did not exist. There was not much in the residential or commercial structure north of Loop 820. There was no golf course and very few parks. The northeast campus of TCJC was new. North Hills Mall was not yet built. Prices were low, but so were wages and salaries. There was a Buddies grocery store near us, but for clothing, furniture, appliances, etc., we mostly shopped in downtown Fort Worth. NRH has changed from a relatively small town to a meaningful part of a huge Metroplex. Schools, churches, and businesses flourish. Our schools and colleges are investigating needs for an increased variety of curricula, so they may better serve the needs of our community.

Submitted by Garland E. Holt

JOHN HARRISON HOLT AND FAMILY

When the Holt Family moved to Texas from Tennessee in August of 1969, we heard there was no rental property avail-

able, and we did not want to leave Tennessee! Our family consisted of John H. Holt Jr., born in 1925, and Marie Battle Holt, born in 1928, and our three daughters: Rebecca Lynn (Becky), born in 1958; Martha Leigh, born in 1961; and Sarah Leslie, born in 1963. John and Marie met in high school. John went into the Army in World War II but came back in time to graduate with Marie in 1947.

Marie and John Holt; Front-Martha, Sarah, Rebecca, 1970

After graduation, they both went to work for the FBI in Washington, D. C., where they were married in 1949. Seven years later they returned to Tennessee where John entered the University of Tennessee at Knoxville and earned a degree in agriculture. In 1958, the Holts moved to Nashville where John worked for the Tennessee Farmers Co-op and later the Baptist Sunday School Board.

After it became clear that we would definitely be moving and representing the Baptist Sunday School Board headquartered in Nashville, we prayed for the Lord to provide a rental house that would allow us time to find something more permanent. We also prayed for the house to be near a school, grocery store, and interstate highway. Shortly thereafter, two cousins, Mrs. Ruby Evans and Mrs. Eva Lee Gibson, had some good news for us. Their mutual friend had a house for rent, and it was ours if we wanted it. We said yes, sight unseen. The address at 5220 Caroldean, in Haltom City—across the street from O. H. Stowe Elementary School, only a half-block from a grocery store, less than a mile from Loop 820, and near our friends, George and Nadean Appleton and their three children, who had also recently moved from Tennessee!

The late summer of 1969 was very hot! Our youngest daughter, Sarah, declared that she didn't like "Ol' hot Texas" and strongly suggested that we move back to Tennessee immediately! We stayed. All three daughters began school that September at O. H. Stowe. Back then, school began after Labor Day. Marie vividly remembers registration day that first year. Marie and Nadean took all the Holt and Appleton children to school, only to find they were all lacking some shots they needed to enroll.

The Holt family in their 1915 Model-T Ford

After a mad dash to Northeast Clinic and a long wait, all the shots were administered and registration completed.

In 1973, we bought a home on Deville Drive in NRH. It is here that John, now retired, is in the process of restoring a 1930 Model A Ford. All three daughters graduated from Richland High School, where Sarah was a Dixie Belle. At that time, Richland High School was out in the field with few houses nearby. Our oldest daughter, Becky, later graduated from Hardin-Simmons University in Abilene, with a degree in elementary education. She is married to Dr. Wayne Shuffield, pastor of Royal Haven Baptist Church in North Dallas, and they have one daughter, Amy. Becky teaches at Carrollton Christian Academy. Our second and third daughters, Martha and Sarah, both graduated from Texas Christian University with registered nurses' degrees. Martha is married to Mark Carr, associate pastor of Arlington Community Church in Arlington, and they have four sons, Andrew, Caleb, Luke, and Nicholas. Sarah is married to Tom Reinmiller, a computer training specialist for Tarrant County, and they have three children, Hannah, Samuel, and Joseph. Sarah works part-time at Harris Methodist H.E.B.

The Holt family has been a part of many changes in North Richland Hills since 1969. For example: Glenview Drive, between Rufe Snow and Old Denton Highway, was a rough two-lane road. Rufe Snow was only two lanes all the way from Loop 820 to Keller, and after crossing the railroad track you were out in the country. We watched Northeast National Bank (now Wells Fargo) being constructed, as well as most of North Richland Hills Baptist Church, where we have been members since 1969. We watched with great interest as North East Mall and North Hills Mall were completed, because mall shopping in 1969 was confined to Seminary South and Richland Plaza shopping centers. Marie remembers when North Richland Hills Public Library consisted of one small room in Richland Plaza Shopping Center. Pancho's was one of the few restaurants nearby, and our girls loved raising the flag for more sopaipillas (now our grandchildren do that). Airport Freeway from North Richland Hills to downtown Fort Worth was incomplete. The Lake Worth Loop 820 bridges were not finished. The Turnpike was still a toll road. We watched as the tall buildings in Fort Worth and Dallas went up. Remember the old Fort Worth Airport? John flew out of that airport on one business trip. Then came DFW International Airport.

One of the joys of our family is the 1915 Model T Ford purchased by Dad, John H. Holt Sr. in Tennessee for $100 in 1920. "Dad's First Car." It was used as a family car through the "1930 Great Depression years." After Dad purchased a 1929 model it was pushed into Dad's barn and jacked up. Our chickens roosted on it and hay fell in to it from the loft above mixing with droppings and broken eggs. In 1941 John restored the old Model T Ford and brought it with us to Texas.

Now we watch with great interest the growth presently taking place all over North Richland Hills, and especially north of our community—places like the new Alliance Airport and Texas Motor Speedway. We speculate about what life will be like in another 28 years. One thing for sure, if the people of that era are as friendly and nice as those living in the Deville Drive vicinity today, North Richland Hills will be a great community in which to live, work, and raise families for the future.

Our daughters married Texans. All of our grandchildren are Texans. Guess the Holts are here to stay.

ROSS AND JOYCE HOOD

I, Ross Damon Hood, was born in 1963, in Edmond, Oklahoma, to Warren Weslyon Hood II and Marla (Novatry) Hood. I grew up in Midwest City, Oklahoma, and went to school at Midwest City High School and later to the Central State University. I have three brothers and two sisters. I have worked in the management information services for the past 11 years. During that time I met and married Joyce Leanne Flynn. We married in 1989 at the Diamond Oaks Country Club.

Ross and Joyce Hood with pets, 1995

Joyce was born in 1960 to Jack and Nancy (Watkins) Flynn, in Orlando, Florida. Later, Joyce's family moved to Haltom City where she grew up. She went to Haltom High School and has a special interest in ballet. Joyce has two sisters. She has been a hairstylist for 13 years.

We moved to the Briar Wood Estates of North Richland Hills in Oct. 1992 from Haltom City. I am proud to be a part of the Teakwood Court Home Owners Association, serving as president; the association for Image and Information Management, Communications Official; the Adventure World Chairman, and currently serve on the NRH Town Hall Committee as Chairman.

When we have spare time we like to travel. In 1996 we went to England and Ireland. In 1997, we went to Amsterdam and Venice. I also enjoy softball and playing music in a band.

Our neighborhood was three-fourths filled when we arrived, and within six months the entire neighborhood was complete. Our neighborhood has experienced flooding problems, but the NRH City Council has been very active in helping us address those problems.

Since coming to NRH, one of the good things that has happened to both of us is we have become more actively involved in volunteer activities which has expanded our sense of civic responsibility. Also, since moving here we have adopted a greyhound and named her Cleopatra. One of our neighbors told us about Cleo's plight, so we consider her our NRH "Favorite Memory."

Submitted by Ross Hood

H. M. HOWE AND FAMILY

H. M. (Mc) Howe family moved to their Bursey Road home in North Richland Hills in 1961. Mc was born in 1924 in Roanoke, Denton County, Texas, and graduated from Roanoke High School in 1941. He attended Texas A&M, then enlisted in the Naval Air Corps and flew a Torpedo Bomber in WWII. Later he was a pilot for Central Airlines, then Frontier Airlines. He retired in 1984 from flying. He continues to farm and ranch in Bowie County, Texas.

Inez Cannon Howe was born in 1924 in Roanoke and attended school there until 1938. She moved to Fort Worth and graduated from Polytechnic High School in 1941. After having a family, she returned to college and graduated from North Texas University, then taught fifth grade in the Birdville ISD (Browning Heights and Holiday Heights). Mc and Inez now reside in Simms, Texas, where they moved in 1979. The family was active in the Smithfield Methodist Church, then the Davis Memorial and the Richland Hills United Methodist Churches. They were active in the school activities and the NRH athletic programs. They were charter members of Diamond Oaks Country Club.

Mary Lois Howe Knowles, born in 1947, attended Richland Junior High and graduated from Richland High School in 1965. She was a band member and ROTC sponsor. She graduated from Texas Tech University majoring in math and is now teaching in the BISD. Her husband, Jack Knowles, is also a graduate of Texas Tech and is with BISD. Jack began his career as a teacher/coach at North Richland Junior High. He has since been assis-

tant athletic director, director of buildings and grounds and currently is director of business. They are the parents of David and Sean and live in North Richland Hills.

Linda Jean Howe Harden, born in 1949, attended NRH schools and graduated from Richland High School in 1968 where she was a Dixie Belle in high school. She graduated from Texas Tech University with a master's degree in food and nutrition. She teaches home economics at Dekalb High School. Her children are Jessica, Jeffrey, Jeremy, and Joshua. They live in Dekalb.

Helen Howe Parker, born in 1951, attended NRH schools and graduated from Richland High School in 1969, and was in Rebellaires and Dixie Belles. She graduated from Texas Tech University with a bachelor of science degree in animal science and was on the Texas Tech Livestock Judging Team. She lives in Lubbock, works for Texas Tech, and has one daughter, Cary.

Mark Anson Howe, born in 1954, attended NRH schools and graduated from Richland High School in 1973. He was in athletics and Rebellaires and received many nice honors at RHS. He attended Southern Methodist University where he played football and graduated in 1977 with a bachelor's degree in business. He married Carol Joyner, who also went to Richland High School and graduated from North Texas University. They have three children, Lindsay, Bart, and Matt and live in Colleyville. Mark is a commercial real estate broker in the Howe/Wood & Co. located in Hurst.

Submitted by Inez Howe

KENNETH AND LOU HUBBARD

The Hubbard family, consisting of Ken, Lou, "Chip," Tim, and Kathi moved into their new home on Mackey Drive in March 1956. The Bill Mackey dairy farm had just been carved up into new streets with houses adding to the size of the very new North Richland Hills. The family joined NRH Baptist Church in July 1957 and began friendships that would last a lifetime.

Ken and Lou Hubbard

Ken and Lou both received their bachelor's degrees from Baylor University where they met in 1945. Ken, born March 6, 1928, in San Antonio, played right tackle on the Baylor Bears football team. Lou, born December 25, 1928 to Jim and Emma Cannon in Dallas, was a drum majorette with the Golden Wave Band at Baylor. Lou and Ken were married December 14, 1948.

Ken worked his entire career for Montgomery Ward Company in various positions. Lou taught fifth grade at Richland and Holiday Heights elementary schools.

Ken was transferred frequently by his company. From NRH, they moved to Salt Lake City, Albuquerque, and back to NRH and their home on Mackey Drive for three years.

L/R, Back-Jack Knowles, Linda (Howe) Harden, Helen (Howe) Parker, Carol (Joyner), and Mark Howe; Front-Inez and Mc Howe, Mary (Howe) Knowles

Then a move was made to Omaha, then to the main buying office in New York, at which time they lived in New Jersey then back to NRH where they bought a new house on Neal Street. The next move was made to Amarillo, then Kansas City, where he was made district manager, then to Beaumont, where he retired in 1982. This time the family moved to Garland to be near Lou's parents.

Lou taught school in most of these cities. Their children, Chip, Tim, and Kathy, had to be very flexible and strong to make this many moves with the many school and social challenges that teens have.

After Ken's retirement, he and

Chip, Kathi, and Tim Hubbard, 1959

Lou both worked actively in her father's business, Cannon's Uniforms, which he had owned since 1933. Mr. Cannon died in 1988. Ken Hubbard died suddenly August 29, 1992. Lou sold the business in 1993 and continued living in Garland until she and Alvin Yates were married May 29, 1993. They were longtime friends and former neighbors in NRH on Mackey Drive. Lou refers readers to Alvin's entry in this family section for the "rest of the story."

Chip Hubbard and his family live in Houston. He started first grade in NRH, continued his public education in several other states, then received his bachelor's degree from Baylor University and his master's degree from Gonzaga University in Spokane, Wash. While at Baylor, he met Paula Long from Atlanta, Texas. They were married August 16, 1976. They have two sons, Matthew, who plays trombone in the school band, is a member of the school track team, and plays Little League baseball. Nathan plays Little League soccer.

After graduating from Richland High School, Tim attended Tarrant County Junior College and now lives in Garland with his wife, Bruna, and 17-year-old daughter, Mauri. Tim and Bruna were married July 16, 1977, by the Rev. Hal Brooks.

Kathi received her bachelor's degree from Baylor University where she met Rick Long, her brother's brother-in-law. They were married September 9, 1978, and have two daughters, Heather and Nikki, 11.

Story submitted by Lou Hubbard Yates

M. M. (BUDDY) AND FAYE HUDLER
CHILDREN: DORIS, JOE, RICHARD

In August 1939, M. M. (Buddy) and Faye Hudler, along with their nine-year-old daughter, Doris Jeanette, moved to Smithfield. We moved from Joshua where my dad worked for my uncle on a farm taking care of the stock for $20.00 a month. My cousin worked for B. A. May in Smithfield, and he was going back to school in September. Mr. May paid $25.00 a month, and we thought we were

going to be rich with $5 more a month.

We lived in a three-room house on the May property. The Eastman family were our nearest neighbors. The parents, Joe and Maggie, had four children: Catherine, Venita, Sarah Jo, and Jimmy Ray. Jimmy and I were about the same age. I started going to the Smithfield Baptist Church, and in September I started fourth grade at the Smithfield School. Mrs. Turner was my teacher and I loved her.

At this time, I was the only child, but that soon changed. The Eastmans told me that I had a little brother. I thought they didn't know what they were talking about, but they did. Brother Joe was born on November 5, 1939. Then on April 15, 1941, my dad took Joe and me to the free movies held on the school grounds. Then Dad walked to the store and called the hospital, and guess what? I had another little brother. His name was Richard Wayne. I thought my brothers were mean little boys, but they grew up to be wonderful men and married wonderful women. Joe married Laura Newman from Haltom City, and Richard married Jean Womack. I was very fortunate, also. I married Bill Shipman from Honey Grove on June 12, 1947. We have five children, Billy, Janie, Buddy, Jeanna, and Joannie. Four generations of my family attended both the Smithfield School and the Smithfield Baptist Church. We love it here and don't plan to ever move.

Submitted by Doris Hudler Shipman

MARTHA HUNTSINGER

My parents lived on a farm on the present site of Bedford library when I was born in 1941. Two years later they moved into Fort Worth because my mother did not like living so far out in the country. We lived in the Polytechnic area of Fort Worth during my growing-up years but made periodic trips back into the area of Richland and North Richland Hills as my father preached occasionally in the rural country churches. During the '50s, a group that had moved to this area from Fort Worth started the church that is now the Richland Hills Church of Christ located on Grapevine Highway, and we visited there quite often.

In 1958, my brother and sister were enrolled in the first graduating class at Fort Worth Christian School. I drove them to school through what we called the "bottoms" by White Lake Dairy and Randol Mill Road up to the old Highway 183 and Booth Calloway Road out to Smithfield. This was before Loop 820 was built, and I watched them building the nice brick homes along that area and thought one day I would like to live in one of them.

In 1960 my father died, and my mother sold the property she had in Fort Worth and moved to North Richland Hills to be closer to Fort Worth Christian School. She bought a beauty shop that was in the strip shopping center at the corner of Grapevine Highway and Blaney Avenue.

Her health forced her to sell in 1966. During that time, I married, and my husband and I lived in Bedford. I was a patient of Dr. J. Ardis Bell, who had a clinic in the same shopping center where my mother's beauty shop was located. I gave birth to three children at the old Glenview

Hospital on Glenview Drive. My husband was an agent with American National Insurance Company, and his area was North Richland Hills, Smithfield, and Keller. We both spent a lot of time driving through the area as he collected the insurance premiums from his policyholders. Most of the area north of Grapevine Highway was still considered country. I remember going to a farmhouse at the corner of what is now Rufe Snow Drive and Loop 820. I would have never believed that corner would look like it does today.

In 1972, we moved from Bedford to North Richland Hills to one of those brick homes I had watched being built in the late '50s. My children all went to schools in the Birdville District and graduated from Richland High School.

It has been amazing to me to watch the area grow and change like it has. I am sure the residents who have been here longer than I have feel the same way.

Submitted by Martha Huntsinger

MARJORIE ISBELL

In 1954, the North Richland Hills area was a picturesque country setting, complete with grassy pastures and many gravel roads. Three paved narrow roads: Denton Highway, Grapevine Highway, and Highway 183 to Dallas, crossed the countryside to the east. To the west there were East Belknap and East Rosedale streets. Watauga was not a city but an area, and Smithfield was a small farming town. And North Richland Hills was the beginning dream with a progressive future.

We moved from Oklahoma into the area in the summer of 1954 when my husband, Jean Paul, was hired as a pharmacist by M. T. Acker at Haltom Drug. (There were only two drugstores in the area, Haltom Drug and Collier Drug, which was close to 28th Street.) My husband found an apartment and moved in June. I remained in Oklahoma until our daughter, Janice, was born in July, then caught the night train to Fort Worth when she was 10 days old.

In the early 1950s, there were no supermarkets or malls, and only a few restaurants. The nearest restaurant was Harold's Log Cabin at the intersection of Denton Highway and East Belknap Street. Floyd Harris operated a country grocery on the south side of East Belknap, and the Haltom Theater and Haltom Drugstore were on the north side. The closest large grocery store was Safeway on East Belknap near Six Points. Later there were two small Buddies stores, one on Grapevine Highway and the other on East Belknap Street.

In 1956–57, Truett Owens and L. B. Mayfield began building houses and developing the land in the North Hills Addition of North Richland Hills. This pasture was bordered on the west by Denton Highway, the east by Fossil Creek, and the south by Haltom City. My husband and I selected a lot in this pasture, now the corner of Webster and Bewley streets. This quiet neighborhood was perfect for a new home. It was the best of two worlds—country living with the convenience of Fort Worth shopping not far away. We moved in November 1957; our son, Darren, was born in June 1958. We claimed North Richland Hills as home—the only home we have ever known. We still live in the same house today.

Webster Street currently is the dividing line between North Richland Hills and Haltom City, but that was not the case when the North Hills Addition was developed. The first tax notices we received were from both cities. A long strip of land several feet wide on the north side of Webster was in Haltom City. The rest of the land was in the city of North Richland Hills. Our three bedrooms were all on the south side of our house and were in Haltom City. When people asked me where I lived, I replied, "I live in North Richland Hills, but I sleep in Haltom City." The city officials met and made a boundary switch. Haltom City gave North Richland Hills the land north of Webster, and North Richland Hills gave Haltom City the commercial land on Denton Highway in front of the North Hills Apartments.

In the late '70s and early '80s, North Richland Hills was attempting to provide the very best cable TV service franchise possible through the Black Hawk Cable Company. The city created a board that was active in implementing and improving services to the residents. A TV station was constructed in one room of the library in the building next to the police station. Library programs, as well as area activities, were broadcast over the city's channel.

I represented Birdville schools and served on the Cable Board for a number of years with Dan Echols. In addition to the Cable Board, I was an active member of the Library Committee for several years on a project that included surveying North Richland Hills residents to determine their needs, expectations, and desires for future library-media services. Since 1954, I have observed the building of 11 BISD schools in the city of North Richland Hills. As executive director of the BISD School Board, I was directly involved in the construction of four of them.

Over the past 43 years, many things changed, while some things remained constant. The city grew and became one of the leading cities in the Metroplex because of the wisdom and foresight of its leaders. Parks were developed, and services were improved for all age groups, including two centers for senior citizens.

Personally, change was not so dramatic. I worked for only one school district, BISD, for 29 years; my husband was a pharmacist in a two-block area on Denton Highway for more than 40 years; and we still live in North Richland Hills in the same house we built on Bewley Street in 1957. Our choices were all good choices. The city of North Richland Hills was then and is still today, "a great place to live."

Submitted by Marjorie Isbell

DR. BRUCE AND PAT JACOBSON

Dr. Jacobson was born in St. Paul, Minnesota, in 1926. His family moved to northern Wisconsin, and it was there that Jacobson graduated from Shell Lake High School in 1944. He served in the U.S. Navy as a gunner's mate on the USS Donald W. Wolf, a destroyer escort. On the ship he met a Fort Worth native named Henry G. Stephenson who persuaded Jacobson to come to Fort Worth and enroll at Texas Christian University.

In 1947 Patricia Sue Morrow and Bruce Jacobson were married. In 1956 the Jacobsons moved to North Richland Hills, where Bruce joined the Pillow-Rush Clinic staff.

Dr. Bruce and Pat have seven children. They are Lynn, Jan, Julie, Bruce Jr., Michael Malloy, Jennifer, and Eric. All of the children were delivered by a wonderful physician, Dr. M. C. McCarroll of Fort Worth. All of the children attended Glenview Elementary, Richland Junior High School, and Richland High School. Lynn became an X-ray technician, and Julie attended Tarrant County Junior College. Jan, Bruce Jr., Michael, Jennifer, and Eric all received their bachelor's degree from Baylor University.

Both Pat and Dr. Jacobson were involved in community projects and in local, state, and national politics. Pat was the first woman appointed to the board of Northeast YMCA, and she worked with Mrs. Gertrude Tarpley on chamber projects such as the 4th of July rallies. Dr. Jacobson served as a trustee of the Birdville Independent School District from 1968 to 1979. In 1982 he was appointed by the secretary of health and human services to the Advisory Board of the National Center for Child Abuse and Neglect. In 1983 he was appointed by President Ronald Reagan to serve on the President's commission for the study of ethical problems in medicine and in biomedical and behavioral research. Pat served a number of terms as a member of the Republican State Committee and was involved in a number of capacities for the election, and reelection of President Reagan, Vice President Bush, and President Bush. She was involved in the campaigns of many local and state office candidates.

Dr. Jacobson has retired from active practice, and the couple still resides in NRH on Jennings Drive and also enjoys time spent at their Hillcrest Ranch home. Four of their children live in NRH, and three others live in the nearby Metroplex.

PHILLIP AND LINDA JACOBSON

Phillip Davidson Jacobson was born in Wadena, Minnesota, in 1943. He grew up on the family farm and attended Oak Grove Lutheran High School. He enlisted in the Navy in 1961 and was promoted to a naval aviator in 1963. Upon completion of flight training, he served in the Vietnam War, flying E1B aircraft off the aircraft carrier Bon Homme Richard.

Phil has served in the community as a past president of Skylark Circle Community Improvement Association, as well as serving in the adult choir at North Richland Hills Baptist Church, the Greater Fort Worth Christmas Pageant, and has been on international mission trips with the church. He also teaches kindergarten Sunday school. Phil is presently a 747–400 captain with Northwest Airlines and is based in Detroit. He flies international

routes to mainland Asia, Japan, and Europe.

Back-Linda and Phillip Jacobson; Front-Lindsey and Trevor

Linda Lee Drozd was born in Houston on March 17, 1958. She attended Arlington High School and then moved to Iowa City, Iowa, attending the University of Iowa in August 1975. In 1979, she moved to St. Paul, Minnesota to begin a career as a flight attendant for Northwest Airlines. After the birth of her daughter, she retired to stay home. She has served in her community as PTA president and PTA fundraising chairwoman. She currently teaches kindergarten Sunday school and Bible Drill at North Richland Hills Baptist Church.

Phillip and Linda were married in 1985, on Vashon Island, Washington. Their daughter, Lindsey Lee Jacobson, was born in Seattle. Soon after the family moved to Arlington, Texas, where they settled for three years.

In 1990, their son, Trevor Judd Jacobson, was born in Arlington. Shortly thereafter, the family relocated to North Richland Hills. Both children presently attend Fort Worth Christian Elementary School.

Phillip and Linda were drawn by the proximity of the community to Dallas/Fort Worth Airport, as well as the quality of life offered here. Our family has had the distinction of being able to move twice into the North Richland Hills community. Phillip was transferred to Anchorage, Alaska, for a year in 1993. We kept our home and moved to Alaska and moved back one year later.

LISA GOSS JERNIGAN

In the spring of 1957 my parents, Lee and Fredine Goss, built our home on Cummings Dr. in North Richland Hills. At the time the Gosses had two children, Barbara Lee, who was four years old and Freddy Lee, who was one. Soon after they moved in the third child, Horace Neal, was born.

The house sits on the corner of Cummings Dr. and Blaney Ave., just across the street from what use to be the North Richland Hills Drugstore.

Lisa Goss Jernigan with daughters Lauren Leigh and Jennifer Ryan

Alan Hamm owned and operated the drugstore, and while he was getting the business started he lived with my family for a short time.

I was born in June 1961, and at this time my dad was a truck driver for Central Freight and working at night starting his own pallet manufacturing business. My mom worked for a short time at the North Richland Hills Drugstore in the Fountain (soda shop). Some of my fondest memories are eating hamburgers and drinking milkshakes at the Fountain.

In 1964 my dad opened his pallet manufacturing business, Trinity Wood Industries, in Fort Worth at 820 Beach St. At that time my brothers were just big enough to help my dad build pallets. My family owned and operated the business until it closed in 1993.

My brothers, sister, and I grew up in the house on Cummings. All of us attended NRH schools we all graduated from Richland High School.

When I was ten years old, my mother's brother, Harold Hail, bought the house across the street from us, and moved his family from San Saba, Texas, to work for my dad. It was a lot of fun to have my cousins live so close.

In 1971 I was in the fifth grade. My teacher, Mr. Teddie, was coordinating the "Presidential Physical Fitness Award" during our recess time. I was the first at North Richland Elementary to receive this award, and I even got my picture in the *Fort Worth Star-Telegram*. The award was based on a number of physical activities such as running the 50-yard dash within a certain time, doing a set number of chin ups, throwing a ball so far, etc.

I lived on Cummings Dr. from June 1961 until I married in June 1979. At that time I moved a long way from home, six miles, just north of 820, but still in NRH!

In October 1980, my first daughter was born, Lauren Leigh Jernigan. Then in March 1983, Jennifer Ryan Jernigan was born.

In May 1987, the house across the street from my parents, yes, the house my uncle lived in, came up for sale. My uncle had moved from NRH long ago. We were not looking to move, but I had to have that house. I loved that neighborhood and wanted to move back. As faith would have it, we were able to sell and buy the house.

My children attend the same school that I did. We have even had some of the same teachers. They loved their fifth grade teacher, Mr. Teddie, just as much as I did. Lauren graduated from Richland High in May 1998, and Jennifer is a sophomore this year.

I have 37 years of fond memories in North Richland Hills, and I would not change any of them. My children have walked barefoot to the same snowcone stand that I did as a child. They have even had a chance to eat a hamburger at the Fountain before the Drugstore closed several years ago. I was brokenhearted.

I remember Winn Dixie when we called it "Bubbies" located at the far end of the shopping strip. I remember walking to "Bubbies" in the summer, of playing in the ice cold water where they kept the watermelons. I miss Mott's but thank goodness the barber shop is still there. I even remember when Blaney was a quiet street!

I have seen a lot of changes in North Richland Hills and while at times I miss the past, I am proud of the progress that our wonderful city has made.

Submitted by Lisa Goss Jernigan

KENNETH JOHNS AND FAMILY

I, along with my wife, Sally Henry Johns, and our three children, moved to North Richland Hills in March 1958. Our children are Ken Jr., Judith, and Bill. We first lived on Cummings Drive but later built a home on Shauna Drive. Ken Jr. attended Birdville High and graduated in the first class to graduate from Richland High School. Judith attended Richland Elementary, and Bill attended Smithfield and later Snow Heights.

We were members of the Richland Hills Methodist Church.

I served on the NRH City Council from 1960–64. While serving, we purchased the first City Hall, started the first Police Department, and assessed the first tax rate of 35 cents. During this time, NRH became a home-rule city with the charter similar to the city of Alamo Heights in San Antonio. Smithfield was also annexed during this time.

At the time, I was a sales representative for a national company, promoted to district manager, and transferred to Memphis, Tennessee.

Tom Christopher was the first city attorney, later replaced by Glenn Goodnight. Laura Ray was the city secretary, and Bill French was the first city manager. George Coe was the first police chief.

During this time, we also contracted for a street and drainage program. NRH was one of the best places we have lived, and we still remember our friends and our time there. We now live in Hearne, Texas.

I returned several years ago when former city officials were honored. I couldn't believe how the city had grown. Frankly, I got lost.

Our best friends were the Bill Betts family and the Clyde Zellers family, who still reside on Reynolds Road.

JAMES AND JOANN JOHNSON

James Johnson and I, JoAnn, moved to North Richland Hills in 1965 with our two daughters, Patricia and Sherry. When we raised the windows that first summer, a cool breeze blew throughout the house. We thought we had moved to the country. How things have changed in the past 35 years.

James Edward Johnson was born December 21, 1933, to Hugh and Velma (Matheus) Johnson in Whitney, Texas, where he was raised and attended school. James is one of seven children. His family moved to Fort Worth in the early '50s where we met. We married in 1955. In the '60s, James began working for Trailways in Dallas. The commute to downtown Dallas was a simple one in those days, with light traffic and few signal lights. After 16 years with Trailways, he became the general manager of Overland Stage Lines

Perry and Sherry (Johnson) Christensen, Danny and Patricia (Johnson) Duckett, James and JoAnn (King) Johnson, Alicia, Jeremy, and Josh Duckett

and today is self-employed. James is a "do-it-yourselfer." He has taken on such projects as adding a second story to our home. We became acquainted with some of our neighbors as they took their morning walk and found themselves in front of our house watching this man and his teenage daughter taking the roof off of their house. He also built a 40-foot-by-25-foot swimming pool in our backyard, not to mention hundreds of other "minor" projects that sometimes turned out "major."

I was born Jessie JoAnn King on June 24, 1939, in Fort Worth to Shelby L. and Bertha A. (Butler) King, the oldest of three children. I worked in banking, owned my own dress shop, and am now retired. It is my joy to be a soloist and Sunday school teacher at the North Richland Hills Baptist Church where we have been members for more than 25 years. I have been a part of the Greater Fort Worth Christmas Pageant for 24 years and currently serve as production manager.

I was elected to the North Richland Hills City Council in 1991 and in 1995 became NRH's first woman mayor pro tem. It is my pleasure to be on the Board of Directors for the Adventure World Foundation, which oversaw the building of the NRH Adventure World Playground on Starnes Road. I have served on the board of the Northeast Chamber of Commerce, as well as

John Holt, JoAnn Johnson and Dan Kennedy on stage at Greater Fort Worth Christmas Pageant, Tarrant County Convention Center

on the Advisory Committee for CAN (Cornerstone Assistance Network).

Our daughter, Patricia Carol, was born February 15, 1956. She graduated from Richland High and married Timothy Daniel (Danny) Duckett, also from NRH, April 28, 1978. They live in NRH and have three children, Joshua D. (Josh) Duckett, Alicia M. Duckett, and Jeremiah D. (Jeremy) Duckett. Patricia home-schools all three of our grandchildren and has done a wonderful job. Josh graduated in 1997 and began attending college in the spring of 1998. They are members of the Saginaw Park Baptist Church where Danny serves as Minister of Music and Youth and Patricia as church pianist.

Our daughter Sherry Elaine was born December 3, 1963. She also graduated from Richland High where she sang in the Rebellaires. Sherry married Perry Dean Christensen April 19, 1986. They also live in NRH and are members of the North Wood Church where Perry has served as chairman of the Stewardship Committee and small group leader. Sherry is active in the church's music ministry as a soloist and is a church secretary.

In 1995 my mother came to live with us and brought much joy to our household. Mother loves to work in the yard, feed the birds, fellowship with her church friends, and keeps our kitchen smelling like fresh baked cookies. It's a pleasure to have both of our daughters, my mother, my brother, Norman King, and his family living nearby. We are also fortunate that most of the neighbors living on our block when we moved here are still here after 30 years. It has truly made this community our home.

By JoAnn Johnson

CLARENCE AND RUTH JONES

The future was always on Daddy's mind. He always said, "Development first will start east between Fort Worth and Dallas and later north toward Keller." He always believed that before long, all the area between Fort Worth and Dallas would be populated, and that has come true. He felt the value of land would soon be extremely good, and it didn't bother him how long it took.

Clarence Jones

But the story of Clarence and Ruth Jones began long before they found their 268-acre dream farm.

Ruth Daley Jones

Clarence Jones was born in 1895, in London, Laurel County, Kentucky. He was number 13 of 14 children. He had some schooling at London, but left at a very early age.

He came to Texas and took up his trade as an apprentice machinist in Fort Worth. He later went to Baltimore, Maryland, to work. Two machinist friends, Allen and Harold Daley, took him home to dinner and introduced him to their sister, Alma Ruth Daley. They soon were in love and were married. Mother, Ruth Jones, was born in Baltimore August 12, 1899.

In 1919, they moved with their daughter, Dorothy Maude "Dotty," to Fort Worth in the Riverside area. Sometime during all of this, I, Naomi Ruth "Sis" Jones, was born March 18, 1924.

Mother and Daddy sold the water system in 1928, and he started the Jones Lumber Company. In time there was a lumber company office and sheds on the south side of 4224 East Belknap and a mill building on the north side.

In 1936, Briley Jones became a welcomed part of our family when he was 6 years old. He was Dad's great-nephew from London, Kentucky, his older sister's grandchild. He was born December 6, 1929.

When I was a student at Riverside High School, my family often went driving, looking for a farm. Mother wanted a colonial-style house and Dad wanted a big barn. I know now he also wanted to choose land that would be great for a future development. They found their 268-acre farm on the Grapevine Highway, Texas 121, now Texas 26, and Pipeline Road, now Glenview Drive. It was purchased in the early 1940s, and we moved there in 1943. They built the colonial-style house for Mother and had a big white barn with a red roof for Daddy.

The soil was so black, and I couldn't believe the way it stuck to your shoes when it was wet. There were some mesquite trees scattered around, and Daddy assured us that both black soil and mesquite trees were good signs. It was level, and there was not a worry about serious flooding.

We didn't have a telephone and you had to leave a message at our lumber company. Another problem was the well. At times there wasn't enough water. We would have to call Dan McKee to come get things back on track. I graduated from Texas Christian University in 1944 and then moved to the farm.

My sister, Dotty, and Cullen Turner had married in 1936, and their son, Cullen Wayne, was born in 1940.

Mr. Rodgers and Briley rode horses into Fort Worth to ride in the Stock Show Parade, and then rode back to the farm. I don't think that either one tried the Stock Show Parade again.

I married Guy L. Cummings Jr. in 1946, and we moved to Riverside. In 1956, we moved back to North Richland Hills to Vance Road. Guy was associated with Dad in the development of NRH. We lived in the area for about 10 years, and our son, Mark Cummings, was born in 1960 while we were living on Riviera Drive. We moved to the Diamond Oaks area of Haltom City in March 1966, as Guy was then president of the Haltom City State Bank.

Briley went to Texas A&M and received an architectural degree in 1951 and an engineering degree in 1952. In 1953, he was sent to Craig Air Force Base as a first lieutenant and was discharged in 1955. He remained in the Active Reserves and attained the rank of major prior to suffering a disabling illness in 1965. Briley married Pat Southard in March 1964, and their daughter, Jennifer, was born July 27, 1965.

Dad was president of J.C.T. Corporation, Deville Development, and Daley Construction Company. He built and leased a number of post offices in Texas, including the NRH post office in 1955 on land he donated. The first post office was located on Blaney Avenue, just off of Grapevine Highway.

In 1952, Daddy subdivided the farm for a suburban development. He named it North Richland Hills. There were 12 acres that were reserved for a shopping center, built later and completed in December 1955. It was named Greater Richland Center. Since the colonial-style house sat on this property, Daddy had it moved north to Cummings Drive, just behind the center. Dad wanted good businesses and professionals located in the center, for he was going to be living there, too. Most of them were also our neighbors and friends. Dad was so close that he could always find someone there to visit with. In the afternoon, he could usually be found in the cafeteria drinking coffee and visiting.

On April 5, 1966, there was a groundbreaking for the Diamond Industrial Park, a 72-acre industrial complex in North Fort Worth Industrial Park. Dad had purchased the property many years before, and this was his last project.

Mother and Daddy were members of the Riverside Baptist Church for many years. Dad was one of the founders of Richland Lodge #1348 A.F. & A.M. and gave the land for the building on Glenview Drive just off Blaney Drive and Grapevine Highway. This building was torn down in 1997 to make room for additional parking for a Walgreen Drug. The lodge relocated to Richland Hills.

Mother was the founder and often called the "Chapter Mother" of the Richland Hills Eastern Star Chapter No. 1040.

Ruth and Clarence Jones lived in NRH until he died April 25, 1966. Ruth Jones continued living in the colonial house on Cummings Drive until 1973 when she moved to a smaller place. She passed away in 1982. Briley Jones died June 6, 1998.

North Richland Hills started as a great area and still continues to grow.

Submitted by Naomi "Sis" Jones Cummings

HAZEL JONES

Hazel Inez (Hughes) Jones was born in Coleman, Texas, March 6, 1918, the second child of Fannie and Alf Hughes. Hazel grew up in Coleman County and went to school at Loss Creek. Albert Stanley Jones was born in Brownwood to Alice (Sweat) and Albert Jones, January 12, 1918. Albert and Hazel were married October 10, 1937. They had three children.

Jackie Wayne (Jack) Jones, was born July 11, 1939, in Coleman. Jack has two children, Tammy and Allen Jones. Jack and his wife, Donna, now live in the city of Watauga since his retirement from Ling-Temco Vaught.

Bennie Mack (Ben) Jones was born August 17, 1945, in Coleman. He is married to Nelda Ruth (Meadows). They have one daughter, Shelly, and one grandson, Kevin. Ben is the manager of the McFrugal's store on Rufe Snow

Drive in NRH. He and his family live in Haltom City.

Patricia Ann Jones was born January 7, 1948, in Coleman. She married Bill Conrad, and they had a girl and a boy, Michaela and Heath Conrad. Patricia is now married to Joe Zeman. Patricia and her family now live in Bridgeport. She works as a receptionist at Harvest Baptist Church in Watauga. Heath is in the Air Force and has one son, Austin.

The Jones family moved to NRH in 1987. Mr. Jones passed away December 27, 1989. Hazel has attended the Harvest Baptist Church since 1991. She loves to visit and help shut-ins of her church.

HUBERT AND GAY JOYNER

Hubert and Gay Joyner moved to North Richland Hills on December 20, 1954, to their new home on Vance Road. They have lived there 43 years and have seen the area grow from a few houses on new unpaved streets to the thriving city it is today. They have been members of Richland Hills United Methodist Church since 1956 and attend services regularly. They have been members of Diamond Oaks Country Club since 1962 and both Hubert and Gay play golf several times a week, weather permitting.

Hubert L. Joyner Jr. was born in Corsicana, Texas, on August 25, 1924. He grew up and attended school there until his family moved to the Riverside area in Fort Worth in 1940. He graduated from Riverside High School in 1941. He attended North Texas Agricultural College in Arlington one year and then Texas Christian University, where he graduated in 1947. He was employed at W. C. Stripling in downtown Fort Worth from 1947 to 1958 as a shoe salesman and buyer for the shoe departments. In 1959 he went to work for Leonard's Department Store in Fort Worth in the personnel department as employment manager. In 1966, he returned to Stripling's as personnel director. In 1971, he was chosen to be store manager for the new W. C. Stripling store in the North East Mall. He served in many positions in the North East Mall Merchant's Association. In 1977, Stripling's Department Stores were

Back L/R: Jimmy and Jan (Joyner) Grant, Hubert and Gay Joyner, Carol (Joyner) and Mark Howe. Middle L/R: Scott Grant, Brittany Lefan, Lindsay, Bart and Matt Howe. Front L/R: Bryan Grant, Amy Grant, Amanda, Brooke and Ben Joyner. 1997

sold to Dunlap Stores, and he left to become business manager for L. D. White & Associates, an architect and engineering company in Fort Worth. He retired in 1986.

Norma Gay White was born in Fort Worth on January 13, 1925, and lived in the Oakhurst area in Fort Worth. She attended Oakhurst Elementary and Riverside High School and graduated in 1941. She attended NTAC in Arlington and TCU. She was employed at Commercial Standard Insurance Co., Panther Oil & Grease Refinery, Civil Aeronautics Administration, and as a secretary in the Walk Over Shoe Co. office until she had children. After her three children were in school, she worked for Lloyd Moore, owner of 10 Dairy Queen stores in Haltom City and Denton, as office manager for 22 years. She retired in 1987.

Hubert and Gay married May 3, 1947 and celebrated their 50th anniversary in 1997. They have three children who all grew up in North Richland Hills and attended Snow Heights Elementary, North Richland Junior High, and Richland High School.

Ben Hubert Joyner was born December 4, 1951. He was three years old when his parents moved to their home on Vance Road. He attended school close to home, so he walked to school each day. After graduating from Richland High in 1970, he attended North Texas State University in Denton and received his bachelor's degree and MBA degree in banking. He worked for banks in Dallas, Fort Worth, Hurst, Grapevine, and is now senior vice president at First State Bank of Texas in Denton. He is married to Amanda Parr, and they have two girls, Brittany and Brooke. They live in Denton.

Jan Leslie Joyner Grant was born January 19, 1956. She also attended Snow Heights Elementary, North Richland Junior High, and Richland High, graduating in 1974. She attended Texas Wesleyan College in Fort Worth and graduated in 1978. She received many honors and grants while attending TWC. She married James (Jimmy) Grant in 1980. He also attended Richland High School. They have three children, Amy, Scott, and Bryan. They live in North Richland Hills and are active in their children's sports, school, and church activities. Jan is employed at Bass Companies. Jimmy has his own business, Caprock Holdings Inc., an investment banking company.

Carol Gay Joyner Howe was born March 3, 1957. She also attended Snow Heights Elementary, North Richland Junior High, and Richland High School, graduating in 1975. She attended NTSU in Denton and graduated in 1979. She taught school in Birdville ISD for three years. She married Mark Howe, a Richland graduate also, in 1977. They live in Colleyville and have three children, Lindsay, Bart, and Matt. They are active in church, school, and their children's sports and activities. Mark has his own business, Howe/Wood & Co., a commercial real estate firm in the Northeast area.

GEORGE AND DOROTHEA KAISER

The Kaiser family, George, Dorothea (Dottie) and children, Charles and Beverly, built their home on Riviera

Drive and moved in August 20, 1954.

George was born and raised in Weatherford, Oklahoma, and Dottie was born in Cisco, Texas, and raised in Cleburne, Lubbock, and Fort Worth. Charles and Beverly were both born and raised in Fort Worth and North Richland Hills.

George worked for William Cameron Building Products until his death August 13, 1978.

Dottie attended school through seventh grade in Cleburne. Her father was transferred to Lubbock by Southwestern Bell Telephone Company, and she graduated from Lubbock High School. Her father died in February before her graduation in May. She and her mother moved to Fort Worth and lived at 1400 Hurley Avenue until Dorothea married and later moved to NRH in August 1954. The family joined the Richland Hills Christian Church where Dottie is still a member. Charles and Beverly started to school at Glenview until North Richland Elementary was finished, then they transferred. Both graduated from Richland High School.

Following the move to Fort Worth, Dottie began working for Southwestern Bell where she became a long-distance operator from 1940 to 1942, then a switchboard operator at the T&P Station from 1942–1944. She also worked for attorneys until the family moved to NRH. She went to work for Haltom Bank as a switchboard operator, was made secretary to loan officers, secretary to the president of the bank, and a loan officer. She retired after 25 years of service.

After working for Porter Insurance Company for five years, she began doing volunteer work at NRH Library. This led to employment in August 1988 to present time.

Charles now lives in Haslet with his wife and her mother. He has two sons, Michael and Judd. He is a Tarrant County deputy sheriff. Beverly lives in NRH with Dottie. Beverly has one daughter, Tammie, who is a hairstylist at DuVall Hair Design.

Submitted by Dorothea Kaiser

VAUGHN AND MARCELLA KANKEY

Vaughn Gaylon and I, Marcella Ruth Bagwell Kankey, originally from North Arkansas, were transferred from Albuquerque, New Mexico, to Fort Worth in September 1965. Vaughn worked for the Federal Aviation Agency and was reassigned to the Fort Worth Air Traffic Control Center. North Richland Hills became the choice for our new home. It seemed to be a good place to live and raise our family.

We rented a house on Eldorado Drive for a short time where we had a wonderful, friendly neighborhood. First-grader Vaughn Gregory and fourth-grader Deborah Ann were enrolled in Glenview Elementary School. It was a very rural neighborhood at the time, mostly cow pastures with cows grazing everywhere. Of course, there was no North East Mall and no "restaurant row." There was one native-rock house at Grapevine Highway and Davis Boulevard where Hudiburg Chevrolet is now.

We bought a new home on Lola Drive near Richland High School in June 1967. The family lived there until both children completed college, married, and entered the business world. Deborah is a dental hygienist, and Greg is a roofing contractor in NRH and the Dallas-Fort Worth Metroplex.

Deborah married Gary Steven Crandall on October 4, 1980. They have two sons, Steven Andrew, born October 3, 1990, and Matthew Aaron, born October 27, 1992. The Crandall family lives in Grapevine.

Deborah graduated from Richland High School in 1974. She and Gary met in 1979 when he traveled the professional golf tour as a caddy for Andy North and came to Fort Worth for the Colonial tournament. His home was in Wethersfield, Connecticut. He had been with North the previous year when North won the 1978 PGA championship at Cherry Hills Course in Denver, Colorado. Gary quit the tour after marriage but caddied for Andy North at the Master's tournament in 1984. This was the first year non-Augusta residents were allowed to caddy, and Gary was very excited when North asked him to caddy for him. Gary is now employed by MBNA credit card company.

Greg graduated from Richland High School in 1977 and married Deena Lee Castleberry of North Richland Hills February 13, 1981. They have two daughters, Rachel Marie, born June 25, 1986, and Rebecca Lee, born July 1, 1992. The family continues to make their home in North Richland Hills.

NRH offers a wide variety of good churches. We chose NRH Baptist Church and have been active members for 32 years.

The family has especially enjoyed watching the city's huge growth and improvements. The children grew up feeling safe in a strong community. They enjoyed chasing rabbits through the open wheat fields from Holiday Lane to Rufe Snow Drive. There were no businesses along Rufe Snow then and only one house.

The Kankey family is grateful to the city for a well-run government, police force, and especially the fine Fire Department that helped save Vaughn's life following a heart attack in June 1994. He is glad to be able to pursue his first love in sports, a good game of golf.

We especially appreciate the excellent school system that Birdville offers and the many dedicated, caring teachers and faculty. With two teenagers, we especially enjoyed all the sports activities, traveling near and far with Richland basketball and football teams.

We now enjoy living in the Thornbridge Addition and would not trade North Richland Hills for any other city on earth.

Submitted by Marcella Kankey

JAMES AND BETTY KEDING

Our family moved to North Richland Hills November 20, 1957. James C. Keding was born in Wisconsin Rapids, Wis., moved to Baraboo, Wis., and graduated from

Baraboo High School. He went into the service in 1945. When he got out of the service he went to Spartan School of Aeronautics in Tulsa. He married Betty Jo Embree in 1949 and started to work at Central Airlines in August 1949. He worked there for 20 years until they moved to Denver. He went to work at Texas International Airlines for 11 years, and when they moved to Houston, he changed jobs again, this time at Southwest Airlines in Dallas and where he worked until he retired in 1994.

Betty Jo Keding was born in St. Lewis, Oklahoma, moved to Tulsa when she was a small child, graduated from Will Rogers High School, and moved to Fort Worth in November 1949. We lived there until we moved to NRH. We have been members of North Richland Hills Baptist Church since 1958.

Front-Jim and Betty; Back-Linda and Chuck.

Linda Kay Keding Simpson was born in 1951 at St. Joseph Hospital. She was 6 when we moved here. She went all through school here and graduated in 1969 from Richland High School, where she was in the top 10 in her class. She starred in *The Music Man*, was Miss Richland Area in 1969, also was a Dixie Belle and was in the Rebellaires music group. She was voted the most talented in her class. She is married to Mike Simpson, who was "The Music Man." They have two children, Jodi, 21, and Ryan, 18, and live in Kerrville.

Chuck Keding was 3 when we moved here. He graduated from Richland High School in 1972. He was voted most popular in his sophomore year, was in the Rebellaires, and went to the Holy Land with them in 1969. He was in the band and was band president in his senior year. He went to Tarrant County Junior College one year and DeVry for three years, where he received a Technology Development Outstanding Achievement Award in 1988. He was salutatorian with a 3.95 grade-point average in 1986. Chuck is married to Mary Pinson of Italy, Texas. They have two daughters, Miranda and Rebecca Suzanne. They live in Argyle, Texas.

KELLEY-PAUL FAMILY

My name is Kathleen Loetta Kelley Tharp, middle child of Roy Chandler and Mary Etta Kelley. I was born September 23, 1954, when my parents lived on Harmonson Road in North Richland Hills. My older brother, Rickey Paul Kelley, was born March 15, 1948, and younger sister, Guyleen Elize Kelley Hill, whom we call "Sam," was born May 11, 1959. I have always been called "Kitti."

Momma's parents, Morris Howard Paul and Johnnie Lenora Piester Paul, moved from Weatherford to 6532 Harmonson Road about 1936. They had a three-room house for son James Howard, the oldest child, and

The Kelley-Paul Family. Back-Mary Etta (Kelley), James Paul; Front-Lois, Johnnie, and Morris Howard Paul

daughters, Mary Etta and Melma Lois. My momma was about 8 years old when our family's lives began on Harmonson Road.

Momma (Mary Etta) attended the Birdville school system, graduated and in 1947 married Roy Kelley. They lived in Smithfield for awhile, where Rickey was born. Then about 1951, they moved back to Harmonson Road and lived next door to her parents, Howard and Johnnie, in a one-room building, while Roy spent two years building a house. I was born after they moved into that house. In about 1955, we moved to 6601 Harmonson, and Howard and Johnnie moved from their original three-room house into the one that Roy had built.

In 1957, Howard Paul was on his yearly deer-hunting trip to New Mexico when he became ill and died in a hospital there. We moved in with my mammaw. Her brother and his family bought the house at 6601 Harmonson. Later, Roy moved the three-room house to the rear of the house at 6528 Harmonson and began building a new house at 6532 Harmonson. My sister, Sam, was born while our family lived here, and my brother, Rickey, still lives in this house.

This all sounds like a game of "musical houses," but our family has deep roots in this neighborhood.

Mary and Roy were divorced in 1967, and Mary later married Jesse Thomas Dennis. They moved to Richland Hills, and Momma sold the house to Rickey and his wife, Pam Williams. Their first daughter, Robbi Loetta, was born while they were living with us. Their second daughter, Shelia Lynn, was brought home from the hospital to the Harmonson Road house, too.

I married Billy Tharp in 1979. He has a son, Jim, and we have a daughter, Jessi Nicole, and a son, Cody James. We have lived in Haltom City all of our married life. His parents, Jean and James Tharp, have lived on Venice Street in NRH for about 26 years.

Sam is married to Bobby Hill. They have a daughter, Rusti Jo, and they recently moved from Harmonson Road to Reno, Texas.

Mammaw (Johnnie Paul) lived at 6528 Harmonson Road until she died in 1978. Rickey continues to live at 6532 Harmonson Road. Rickey is considering leaving Harmonson Road to buy some Piester land in Weatherford where our grandparents were from. Things seem to be going full circle—the family will continue on Harmonson Road even if Rickey moves. His daughters, Robbi and Shelia, are planning to move in with Robbi's son, Tyler Joe. Tyler Joe Estes will be the fifth generation of our family to live on Harmonson Road. All three of the family houses are still there.

Submitted by Kitti Kelley Tharp

BOBBY AND ANN KENNEDY

I, Bobby Kennedy, was born in Haltom City on March 25, 1941. My grandparents, Oscar and Eva Mae Autrey, lived in Smithfield, on Smithfield Road, across from the Methodist Church. When I was a child, my grandfather would pick me up from school on Friday and take me to Smithfield by traveling down unpaved Grapevine Highway. We would pass the Clarence Jones farm, through what is now North Richland Hills. He always stopped at Wade's Four Points Store, where Hudiburg Chevrolet is current located. I would get to fill the tank of his car from a gravity-fed gas pump and then go in the store to bag up and weigh chicken feed. He would buy me a box of .22-caliber bullets, and we would drive out unpaved Smithfield Road (now Davis Boulevard) to his house for the weekend. He let me drive from Wade's store after I became 12 years old.

My father, John Kennedy, worked for Clarence Jones at the Jones Lumber Company in Fort Worth before I was born. He hauled lumber from East Texas and used to say that Mr. Jones treated him like a son. My father bought our house in Haltom City from Mr. Jones before I was born. I have the original abstract. My mother lives there today. Mr. Jones offered to trade one of the houses he was building on Cummings Drive for our house, but my father didn't want to move that far "out in the country."

As a teenager, I used to go to the Green Valley Dragstrip (Green Valley Raceway) on the east side of Smithfield Road (Davis Boulevard) every Sunday. My father bought a new 1954 Ford, and we took it straight to the races. Although I was only 14 years old at the time, he let me enter the "grudge" races, and we did quite well. However, he gave me a stern warning not to tell my mother.

We went back to the races the next Sunday. Grapevine Highway, still unpaved, was being graded. Since the back wheels of the Ford had bounced tremendously on acceleration the week before, my father decided to weight it down with several huge rocks that were lying by the side of the road, which sounded good to me. The very first time I let the clutch out at the racetrack, the transmission broke. We still had second and third gears, so we got the car home that way. With no reverse gear, my father parked on the street and we sheepishly sat on the porch until my mother began questioning us. We admitted what we had done, and she told us she had known we were racing the car all along.

My wife, Ann, and I moved to our current home on Deville Drive in August 1972. I was a serious runner in the '70s. I would train for marathons by running from our house out Rufe Snow Drive to my aunt's house on Bear Creek Road in Keller (now an extension of Rufe Snow). Many times I ran there and back, a distance of 21 miles,

without seeing more than two or three cars the entire time. I probably can't drive it much faster now because of the traffic congestion.

Submitted by Bobby Kennedy

DICK AND BILLIE KILLINGSWORTH

My parents, Dick and Billie Killingsworth, bought six acres on what is now Rufe Snow Drive in the summer of 1933. I, Jane Killingsworth Logee, had just turned 5 and my sister, Bettie, was 6 years old. She was entered in the "high first" grade at Birdville that September, and I began school in 1934.

Our little acreage was without any near neighbors, and when somebody drove down our little gravel road, we would run to the door to see who it was. Dust would fly everywhere. This was deep in the Depression, and Daddy said if we just had a cow and some chickens and a good garden, we would do all right. We were lucky that Daddy had a job at Consolidated Chemical during that whole time. Many of my schoolmates were on relief and came to school barefoot all year. Our house had running cold water from the well (complete with windmill) next door on the north, now the location of a water tower. We had gaslights. We traded our electric radio, Frigidaire, fan, and iron for the cow—a little Jersey named "Lady."

I well remember in about 1936 when our house was wired for electricity. Daddy immediately came home with a radio so he could listen to the World Series. Unfortunately, with an electric iron, Bettie and I could be taught to do the ironing. Mom would starch everything and sprinkle it, and we would start early in the morning before it got too hot. We ironed tablecloths, pillowcases, handkerchiefs, napkins, and underwear, as well as dresses, blouses, and white shirts. I hate ironing to this day!

Since our daddy worked rotating shifts, we often walked either to or from school. It seemed a very long way down the highway and then north down our road (Rufe Snow). No one would let little children do that today. My first-grade teacher was a Mrs. Clark, and our class was in a little new white annex just north of the brick two-story structure at Birdville school. I thought the outdoor privy was especially great: It must have been a 10-holer! One side had cubicles, but the other did not. At that age, I couldn't understand why the grown-ups seemed so ashamed of it. When I was in the third grade we got indoor toilets—very ordinary, I thought—in the same space where my second-grade classroom had been. It was nice not to have to go out in the rain to "be excused."

My teachers after Mrs. Clark were: Miss Lucas (who later married Mr. Box), a red-haired lady I loved named Miss McLean, Mrs. Gray, and Mrs. Carter. The teachers must have had their hands full with a class as big as ours. We played softball during recess, or played on the "acting bars." The girls played on one side of the building and the boys on the other. There were swings and see-saws for younger kids, and jacks, jump rope, and marbles were popular games. We were free to just play—something I think society has lost.

Over the years, the Harmonson Addition built up, and we did have a few kids within walking distance, but summers were long. We had a little creek that had crawfish we could catch, and Mama took us to the library once a week. Grandma would come, and she taught us how to crochet.

World War II was in full swing during those years, and we brought quarters to school for "savings stamps," which eventually added up to a war bond. We learned Morse Code in general science. We were very much hampered by gasoline rationing and the sugar shortage (nothing to put on the Wheaties or in the iced tea). The "Service Flags" flew in the windows of those families who had sons and daughters in the service. I remember huge Army convoys passing by the school, carrying personnel, guns of various sizes, and other equipment. Sometimes it would take eight or ten hours for a convoy to pass. We would go to the highway and cheer them during the day. One boy from our church was killed in action, and we had a memorial service for him. When Bettie graduated in 1943, almost every boy in her class went directly into the armed services, as they "couldn't wait to get over there." I graduated in 1945. That year included the death of President Roosevelt (the only president I remembered), V-E Day (Victory in Europe), and two months after our graduation V-J Day (Victory in Japan). I joined the Cadet Nurse Corps.

They say you can't go home again. It's true. Hardly anything is left of the Birdville I knew. But those memories are etched on my heart.

Written by Jane Killingsworth Logee

P.S. People ask me if there really was a Rufe Snow. Yes, I remember him well. He lived in an old house up north of us and would come shuffling by our place on the way to see his son who lived on the highway. We thought he was very old.

BERTHA KING

I've often said, I was born under an oak tree, but the fact is that the branches of a huge old oak tree hovered over and covered the house where I was born. I was named Bertha Allie Butler, born May 15, 1915 in Weatherford to Alfonzo and Rebecca A. (Morgan) Butler. There were eight children, Jessie, Joel, Curtis, Ina, Dovie, George, and Lucille were my brothers and sisters. Some of my fondest memories were of my school years at Tin Top near Weatherford in Parker County.

Shelby L. and Bertha (Butler) King

I met and married Shelby L. King in 1936. We have three children: JoAnn (King) Johnson of NRH, Harman King, and Norman C. King and his wife Pat of Bedford. We have four grandchildren: Patricia Carol (Johnson) Duckett, Sherry Elaine (Johnson) Christensen both of

NRH, Cynthia Denise (King) Stanley, and Justin C. King, six great-grandchildren: Josh, Alicia Jeremy, Lonnie, David, and Amber.

It has been a blessing being a member of the Azle Avenue Baptist Church for more than 20 years.

I came to North Richland Hills in 1995 when I moved with my daughter and her husband James and JoAnn Johnson. One of the best things about living in North Richland Hills is each morning having the opportunity to feed the birds that gather around our yard. In these busy times I wonder if we all take the time to appreciate the nature that is around us. Residents of NRH are truly blessed with the beautiful red birds, blue birds, doves, sparrows, robins, blackbirds, and hummingbirds in our front yards. I also spend as much time as I can in our flower beds and vegetable garden, and every once in awhile I bake a cake and cookies for friends, city staff, and firemen.

CLARENCE AND IMOGENE KINNAIRD

Clarence and Imogene Kinnaird were two "pioneers" who braved the mesquite and barren prairie east of Fort Worth, now known as North Richland Hills. This move came in 1952, before there was even an incorporated town. Their homesite, at the corner of Blaney Avenue and Turner Terrace, remains the same, but the years of dry prairie and no town or businesses are just a memory. There were no other houses around. In fact, they furnished water to building sites, as neighboring houses were constructed.

Clarence and brothers, Jess, E. R., John, and Charlie, owned and operated Kinnaird Brothers Motor Company on Henderson Street in Fort Worth. With all the brothers deceased or retired, the business is now operated by the nephews.

Clarence and Imogene were members of Richland Hills Baptist Church, then became charter members of North Richland Hills Baptist Church in February 1956. Clarence was the first music leader of the church. He and his brothers had always sung gospel music. They were known as the Kinnaird Brothers Quartet. Imogene worked her entire career in women's fashions, retiring in 1996 from Lillie Rubin Fashions. Clarence retired in 1995.

With the move to NRH, teenagers Jean and Jimmy attended and graduated from Birdville High School, where Jean was football queen in 1955. Jimmy was an accomplished tight end on the 1952 Birdville football team. He went to the University of Texas at Arlington after graduation and is now a residential designer in the North Texas area and lives in Fort Worth.

Jean married Kenneth Dick and also resides in Fort Worth. She is a child counselor for Clayton Services in Fort Worth.

Imogene Kinnaird said their second family began with the birth of daughter, Jajuana, November 14, 1955, and son, Van J., born July 18, 1957. Both graduated from Richland High School in 1973 and 1975 respectively.

Jajuana married Michael L. Blevins, a veteran of the

Vietnam War, on May 27, 1989. They have three children, Danny Danford, Lindsay Danford, and Jason Danford. They continue her NRH roots, making their home in the northern part of our city. Jajuana was a paralegal in Fort Worth and is now enjoying the antique business. Mike works in forklift sales for Briggs Equipment Company in Dallas. The children all graduated from Richland High School, and Lindsay attends Stephen F. Austin University in Nacogdoches.

Van works in the linen sales business in Fort Worth. His wife, Karen, works for Associates Mortgage Company in Irving. They have one daughter, Bailey, and live in Watauga.

The entire family of Clarence and Imogene Kinnaird lives in the Fort Worth area, along with many other relatives. "We love NRH and will be firm supporters of any expansion for years to come."

Clarence Kinnaird died May 20, 1998.

Submitted by Jajuana Kinnaird Blevins

HORST AND NANCY KRAUSE

Horst E. Krause was born into a railroading family in Berlin, Germany, on September 11, 1939. His father, Erich Albert, and mother, Franziska, brother, Joe, and sister, Ruth Irene, completed the family that was already beginning to experience the dawning of World War II that would drastically alter their lives.

The elder Krause never had to go into the military. Adolf Hitler left railroad people alone because the country needed the railroads so much during the war.

Krause has many memories of his early childhood in Germany, and most of them are not pleasant. When he was four years old, Germany was well into war, and he remembers sitting on a haystack watching fighter planes duel over his head. He remembers many bombings, air raids, and hunger. He said "You couldn't get simple things like milk and butter. I saw people rummaging through trash cans searching for potato peels to cook and eat. The only problem was they had to fight the rats for the peelings."

In 1942, the Krause family was transferred to Poland, where the elder Krause was foreman in a shop that built

L/R-Philip, Horst, Jeffrey; Front, L/R-Denise, Hailey Marlane, Nancy

and repaired rail cars. By 1944, however, the Russians made their push into Poland, and the Krause family headed back to Berlin. Erich Krause put his family on a train for the trip to Berlin but the rail tracks were bombed out and during the process of escaping from Poland to Germany, the Krause family and many others were put into a concentration camp by the Germans. "They just didn't want to deal with us, and we were treated like a bunch of animals," Krause said. Their dad had told the family that no matter where they were that he would find them, and because the railroads were so vital, and the people associated with them were so powerful, their dad was able to find them.

Horst said, "Near the end of the war, we ended up in eastern Germany, and around 1945 we returned to Berlin, just barely escaping the Communists. If we'd stayed in eastern Germany much longer, we might still be there." His mother died when he was 9 years old.

His sister left Germany in 1947 to come to the United States. She married an American soldier, William Chester Edmonds. Ruth was one of the first war brides in the country. Krause celebrated his 13th birthday on the Atlantic Ocean on his way to America with his father and new mother, Minna Frieda Leuchten-Berger, in 1952. They spent 14 days traveling by ship to Houston where his sister and brother-in-law picked them up. Horst said, "There was never any question about our coming over here. The standard of living was so bad in Germany, and America promised so much—even though things were very difficult for us at first—that we finally decided to leave Germany."

The family moved to Haltom City, and Horst began a long association with the Birdville School District. He entered the seventh grade when school started that year. With only one year of English study behind him and much abuse to experience, he always stood up for his rights and learned to adjust.

Krause starred in athletics at Birdville High School. He went on to play football for Ranger Junior College on a scholarship, then continued his education at the University of North Texas, receiving his bachelor's degree in 1963. He got his master's from the UNT in 1967 in secondary education with a leading field in German.

Krause began his teaching-coaching career at North Richland Junior High when the school opened in 1963. He coached and taught history there until 1967 when he joined the teaching staff at Richland High. The first year at Richland, he taught history along with his coaching duties. In 1968, more than 100 students requested that German be offered as a foreign language, and Krause was pegged to start the program. In 1976, his German program, along with Minerva Kimbell's Spanish program, were judged to be in the top five foreign language programs in the state of Texas.

Horst Krause married Nancy Cantwell of Ranger, Texas, February 28, 1964. Horst met her when he was a student at Ranger Junior College. They have two sons, Philip, born September 5, 1967, and Jeffrey, born October

19, 1970. Philip graduated from Richland in 1986 and followed in his dad's footsteps, graduating from UNT. He is married to Denise Harris, and they have one daughter, Hailey Marlane. Jeffrey graduated from Richland in 1989 and also from UNT. He is a physical therapist specializing in sports medicine in Arlington. He is to be married in December 1998.

Horst Krause made his first trip back to Germany in 1993. He said the reasons it took so long for him to make the trip back were financial, not political. He never had time while he was going to school, and once he and Nancy got married, they needed the money for other things. He has many relatives in Germany and they write often. When the family did go back, and they've made several trips, it wasn't to relive the past, but to see friends and relatives.

Krause retired from coaching and teaching in May 1997, after 34 years. He taught many lessons along the way, not just about history, German, or football plays, but about life. He ended his teaching career coaching alongside three former students, Gary Pewitt, Chuck Berry, and Sandy Staples. He had a lasting impact on hundreds of people who will never forget him because he instilled qualities in them that would last a lifetime.

Ken Mizell, former student and now a coach, said, "Horst is why I wanted to become a coach. I knew from the time I met him and admired his personality and traits, that this is what I wanted to do. We've remained close friends. He was a loud, boisterous, gregarious guy. He had forearms as big as Popeye's. He'd grab you and get after you, and the next second he'd have his arms around you, loving you. He really had the respect of all the players."

Submitted by Evalyn Lochridge

BOBBIE AND JUNE LAMBERT

Bobbie and June Lambert and two children, David and Julie Ann, moved to North Richland Hills June 1, 1961, when Bobbie got a job teaching and coaching at the new Richland High School. When they arrived in June, the school was a concrete slab, and the only access was Holiday Lane, Bobbie said.

When the school opened in September with about 370 students, the cafeteria, gymnasium, band hall, and auditorium were still incomplete. The band had to practice in the school foyer. Bobbie became vice principal at Richland High and later principal at Richland Middle School where he retired in 1991. They built their first home on Marilyn Lane. At that time, Marilyn Lane backed up to open fields where Loop 820 is today. They have been

Bobbie and June Lambert

members of the North Richland Hills Baptist Church since they first came to NRH in 1961, Bobbie said.

Bobbie Lambert was born to Lonnie and Grace Lambert in Nixon, Texas, where he grew up and attended school. June Lambert was born to Marvin and Ruby Smith, also in Nixon, where she grew up and attended school. Bobbie and June were childhood sweethearts and married soon after graduation.

They have three children. David Lambert was born in 1956 when they were stationed in Germany while Bobbie was in the Army. David lives in Irving with his wife Nina and their children, Amanda and Daniel. He is a graduate of Richland High and the University of Texas at Arlington. He works in Dallas. Julie Ann Lambert Hunter was born in 1958 in Alice, Texas. Julie is a graduate of Richland High. She and her two sons, Lance, a senior at Richland High, and Trent, a sophomore at Richland High, live in NRH. Matthew Paul Lambert was born in 1971. He is a graduate of Richland High and UTA. Today Matthew lives in NRH and works at Harris Packing.

MYRENE LAW
PIONEER LIVES IN THE PRESENT!

Myrene Law, 94, can look back on almost a century of living, but she still enjoys the present, especially if it contains a good joke.

"On my 94th birthday, something was said about it in church," said Law, who has lived in the Smithfield area of North Richland Hills since 1944. "I told them, 'You know the old song about another year older and deeper in debt.' Well, I told them, 'I'm another year older and deeper in blessings,' especially when I go to church and get to do all those other

Myrene Law at her 92nd birthday party

things." Law has been a member of the First Covenant Church in Irving for 45 years.

Myrene married Nugent L. Law in 1926, and they had two children. Nugent Law, a general agent for Frisco Railway for 30 years, died in 1952. Their 2-year-old daughter died in 1935 and their son, Leroy, and his wife, Julie, live in North Richland Hills. Myrene has three grandchildren and five great-grandchildren.

When the Laws moved to their present location in 1944, "We bought 30 acres from Simmons Drive to Crane Street down to Main Street and Martin Drive," she said. "When I came out here, there wasn't anything but Snider's Store at one end and another grocery store on the other end. There was a little barber shop, the Methodist Church, the Baptist Church and the Church of Christ, the telephone exchange and the Masonic Temple."

She recalled several unusual stories from the past:

Her husband loved to come home from his "white collar job" and get out on the tractor, she said. "We raised pure-bred Angus cattle and had a beautiful black bull."

"One winter it stayed around 10 degrees all week, and our little pond froze over. My husband was shaving one day and looked out the window and saw the head of this little bull just above the water. He had tried to get water and fell in. He was standing on his hind legs, with his front legs on the ice. We didn't know how to get him out."

They called a veterinarian, a Mr. Bridges, who brought a ladder, so he could crawl out on the ice to the bull. As he broke the ice with a hammer, this bull would walk on his hind feet until he got to the edge of the pond, and he finally got him out." The vet put him in the barn "with the heifers around him for warmth," Law said. "The sun came out later and with that sun hitting the bull, you couldn't see him for the steam. but he wasn't sick, and it didn't bother him a bit."

Next she told about the time her husband put guinea eggs to hatch under a hen, and a chicken snake swallowed them. The guinea shells were very tough, so her husband killed the snake and retrieved the undamaged eggs. "He put the eggs back under the hen, and they hatched," she said.

After her husband's death, Myrene decided to build a smaller but more modern home for her and her son. She stored her furniture in the barn, but it burned down, she said. "They got a few things out but not a whole lot. Our place is on a hill, and everybody in town must have seen the fire."

Before concluding the interview, Law told a few jokes on senior citizens, one about two older people in their 90s sitting on a front porch. "If we don't die soon, all our friends will think we've gone to hell," Law said with a chuckle.

Interview by Pat Nimmo Riddle

LEACH FAMILY

B. H. Leach (1914), Syble U. Eubanks Leach (1922).

Daughter: Barbara Ann Leach Earle (1943), children: Elisabeth Ashlea Earle (1968) and Charles Jason Earle (1969).

Son: Richard Allen Leach (1949), children: McKenna Loudon Leach (1985) and Cameron Loudon Leach (1989). The B. H. Leach family moved into North Richland Hills (on Pipeline Road, now Glenview Drive) in 1948 after purchasing a home in the Harmonson Addition from my mother's brother, Charles Fred Eubanks. They have continued to live in the area since that time, moving only once.

The Leach Family, Back-Syble, Hanford; Front-Barbara, Richard

When we moved into the house I was very excited because I finally was able to have my very own "Lassie" dog. We also inherited a few chickens, turkeys, and rabbits from my uncle. I used to put the baby rabbits in my doll buggy

and push them up and down the street. Most everyone around us had horses, so I nagged my parents into finally getting me a small pony. I was never able to handle the pony because it had been used for a pony ride, so it would only turn in one direction. Since there were few fences between neighbors he would take off and then stop in someone else's pasture for me to lead him home.

Syble Leach holding Richard, Barbara Leach (Earle) on left, 1949

Our neighbors on one side were the Sullivans who sold to the Browns, and on the other side were the Ridges, then the Stovers, and Murray and Rogers on the corner. One of the Haltom ranches was across the street from our home. The land was used as pasture for cattle. The Haltoms had some prize bulls in the pasture and we were told never to go into the pasture for fear of being hurt by one of them. Every year the Haltoms would round up the cattle to sell and slaughter, and they would cut the horns off. My dog would sometimes bring some of the cut-off horns to our house. After the roundup the Haltoms would have a big barbecue and it seemed like hundreds of cars came down our road to go to the barbecue. The party would last all day and into the evening. This was the most traffic we saw all year. It was rumored that all the wealthy people in Fort Worth were invited.

When I started to school in 1949 the bus would pick me up in front of my house and take me to Birdville Elementary. Then Richland Junior High was built and I went there my eighth and ninth grade year, going back to Birdville for the rest of my high school years. I was the featured twirler for the band, football sweetheart nominee, and was in the last class to graduate from Birdville in 1961. I married Ronald Dale Earle of Haltom City. He graduated from Birdville in 1960 and we moved to Austin in 1963. My brother, Richard Allen Leach, started school at North Richland Elementary (now Mullendore), went to Richland Junior High for two years then to North Richland Junior High when it opened. He graduated from Richland High School in 1967. He attended the University of Texas at Austin and after graduation moved back to the area. He bought a home on Tabor Street about two blocks from where he was born. Tabor Street is located on the Haltom's land that we once played on as kids. He bought a building for his insurance business that has since been demolished for the construction of the intersection near Hudiburg Chevrolet on Grapevine Highway. He says he has never really left where he was born. He presently works for ARRI as a research engineer and project coordinator and is in charge of the US First program that took Richland High science students to Disney World in 1996 as part of a robotics program.

Barbara is the director of committees, sections, local bar associations, and the annual meeting for the State Bar of Texas. She has been affiliated with the Heritage Society of Austin and numerous other civic groups in Austin and presently serves as a director for the Austin-Travis County Livestock Show.

B. H. Leach worked for General Dynamics and retired after 35 years of service. He passed away in May of 1995. Syble Leach retired after 25 years from the Birdville Independent School District, still resides on Corona Drive, and is active in the Retired Teachers/School Food Association and Birdville Baptist Church.

Submitted by Barbara A. Earle

MICHAEL AND MICHELLE LEONE

As parents of two school-age children, our first priority in choosing a home in the Fort Worth, Texas, area was its location. The district had to have a good reputation, and the schools needed to be fairly close by. My husband's job with American Airlines brought us to this region of Texas, so another concern was relative proximity to the DFW airport. North Richland Hills met both of these important criteria.

After deciding on the town, we started looking for a home. Home to us meant someplace that would be warm, inviting, and easy for four of us to live comfortably. When my husband discovered the house on Lincoln, he knew right away it was the place for us.

The day he drove me up Spring Lea to see it for the first time, I was committed to making it our home. What made it so special for our family, besides the comfortable floor plan, was the pasture to the right and back, surrounded by white wooden fences. Cows grazed there among the many oak trees. As the seasons changed we watched the fields fill with colorful flowers, and then the leaves changed color.

Soon after we got settled, we met our neighbors. Our favorites were the Smiths. They live up the hill at the top of the pasture, and they immediately showed us that famous Texas hospitality we'd learned to expect. We've lived here now for almost 10 years, and we continue to love the area. We feel fortunate to have discovered this lovely spot on a hill in North Richland Hills.

Submitted by Michelle Leone

DARRELL AND JOLANA LESLIE

Darrell John Leslie and his wife, JoLana (Donahue) lived on Jerri Jo Street in North Richland Hills from 1970 until 1972. They were music directors at Christian Temple in NRH from 1970 until 1976, where they were noted for their musical duets. They have three children and three grandchildren. Their son, Gary, and his wife, Lea Ann, live in Dallas. Daughter, Laurie, lives with her husband, Mickie Woods, near Austin. Second daughter, Jana, lives

with her husband in Maryland.

Darrell's parents, John M. and Alma Daniel Leslie moved the family to Texas from Minnesota where they settled on the north side of Fort Worth. Darrell attended

Lana, Alma, and Darrell Leslie

Sam Rosen Elementary, J. P. Elder Junior High, and was an honor student at Technical High School, graduating in 1958. He attended Texas Christian University on scholarships, graduating in 1962.

Submitted by Betty Leslie

MARVIN DWAYNE AND VICKI LESLIE

Marvin Dwayne Leslie, son of Marvin and JoAnn Leslie, born August 10, 1956, graduated from L. D. Bell High School and earned his associate degree from Tarrant County Junior College in 1976. He is a purchasing agent for Lockheed Martin of Fort Worth. He is married to Vicki Renfro Leslie and they have two children. Charity Diane was born September 10, 1981 in Fort Worth, and Amanda Kay, born July 17, 1984. After being residents of North Richland Hills for seven years, then moving to Hurst, they built a new house on Ridgeway Court in North Richland Hills in 1992.

Vicki is employed by the Birdville School District as a Personal-Educational Assistant at Snow Heights Elementary. Both daughters attended North Ridge Middle School and are now students at Richland High. Charity has been on

L/R-Dwayne, Amanda, Vicki, and Charity Leslie

the varsity golf team since her freshman year, a member of the National Honor Society, and a newly appointed member of the Youth Advisory Committee for the City of North Richland Hills. In college, she plans to major in computer science.

Amanda is an honor student and is in the marching band. She hopes to major in elementary education in college. The Leslies are active members of the Harvest Baptist Church.

STANLEY AND INA LEVELL AND FAMILY

Stan Levell, born in Matador, Texas, February 1924, graduated from Matador High School. After serving in the Navy Cadets and the U.S. Army Air Force, he graduated from West Texas University with bachelor's and master's degrees. He worked at Amarillo Air Base for six years prior to moving to Fort Worth. Stan worked for General Dynamics for 12 years and retired from Ling-Tempco Vaught in 1986 after 17 years. Stan is an avid golfer who can still "shoot his age."

Ina Levell, born in Amarillo, April 1929, graduated from Stratford High School in Stratford, Texas, and West Texas University. She met Stan Levell while attending WTU, and they were married in March 1951. Ina worked for GE and Phillips Petroleum in Amarillo. After her children were grown, she began working for Vandervoort's Dairy where she worked for 10 years, retiring in 1986. She enjoys cooking, exercise, and reading.

Stan and Ina have been active members of Richland Hills United Methodist Church since 1965. They are avid recreational vehicle travelers and are active in the Good Sam Club and the Avion Travel Club. They also enjoy spending time with their friends and family. They are dedicated attendees of their four grandchildren's school and sporting events and are eagerly awaiting the arrival of their fifth grandchild.

Brad Levell, born in Amarillo in April 1952, started North Richland Junior High in seventh grade and graduated from Richland High School in 1970. He attended the University of Texas at Arlington, Tarrant County Junior College, and Texas A&M. Brad served a brief stint in the U.S. Navy. Brad married in 1997, and he and his new family, Kimile and Nathan, live in Salt Lake City and are expecting their first child.

Janet Levell Walz, born in Amarillo in January 1954, started Snow Heights Elementary in the fifth grade, attended North Richland Junior High, and graduated from Richland High in 1972. Janet attended TCJC, Texas Wesleyan, and graduated with honors from North Texas in 1978 with a degree in special education. Janet married Steve Walz in August 1978. After being diagnosed with cancer, Janet died in January 1979.

Jeanne Levell Arnold, born in Amarillo in May 1956, attended NRH schools and graduated from Richland High School in 1974. She attended TCJC and Tidewater Community College in Virginia Beach, Virginia. Jeanne married Doug Arnold in December 1975. After living in Virginia Beach for 10 years, Doug and Jeanne returned to North Richland Hills to raise their family: Stephanie and Daniel.

Gayle Levell Hale, born in Fort Worth in March 1958, attended NRH schools and graduated from Richland High School in 1976. She then attended TCJC. Gayle married Monty Hale in 1980. Gayle and Monty lived in Waco for nine years and now live in North Richland Hills where their two children, Brandon and Joseph, attend school.

LEON AND DOROTHY LEVITT AND FAMILY

We moved from Dallas to North Richland Hills on October 31, 1955.

Leon was born January 16, 1924, in Cairo, Illinois. He served three years in active duty in the U.S. Army Air Corps, including flying 17 combat missions as a P-51 pilot in the European Theatre of Operations. After the war, he attended college on the GI Bill, and received a bachelor of science degree in civil engineering from Southern Methodist University in June 1951. He remained active in the Air Force Reserve as a pilot until 1965. He was then assigned as wing engineer of the 512th Military Airlift Wing, Carswell Air Force Base until his retirement from the reserve in 1972. After various engineering assignments in Dallas, Kentucky, and Florida, he moved to North Richland Hills. He spent two years working for design-build General Contractor. Since April 1958, he has been engaged in the private practice as civil and structural consultant.

Dorothy J. Blumer was born January 12, 1929, in Fort Worth. She grew up in Dallas and attended North Texas Agriculture College in Arlington before their marriage on June 26, 1950.

Five children were born to this marriage: John E., Kathleen A., Charles A., Mary E. (deceased June 27, 1980), and Patricia J.

The four oldest children graduated from Richland High School in 1969, '71, '73 and '78, respectively. Patricia is a 1987 graduate of Nolan High School, Fort Worth.

John graduated from UT Arlington with a bachelor's degree in civil engineering, and married Debra L. Daniel of NRH, a graduate of Texas Wesleyan with a bachelor's degree. They have two daughters and live in Grapevine. John has an engineering practice in Southlake.

Kathleen graduated from UT Arlington with a bachelor's degree in teaching and was married and has a son. She is currently teaching in the Fort Worth Independent School District.

Charles graduated from UT Arlington with bachelor's and master's degrees in criminal justice from American Tech University. He married Rosie Gonzalez of Fort Stockton. She is a graduate of UT Austin, with a degree in computer science. Charles is presently employed by Lockheed Martin. They live in Fort Worth and have four children.

Patricia attended TCJC and earned an associate's degree in marketing. She is presently in retail management and is engaged to be married to Paul Lussier of NRH. Paul is a graduate of Texas Wesleyan University with a degree in business administration.

Leon and Dorothy are charter members of St. John the Apostle Catholic Church.

DICK LEWIS AND MATTIE BELLE LEWIS BORDEN

Richard Franklin Lewis was born in the Smithfield area of North Richland Hills. His parents lived just to the north of the present Smithfield Elementary. His parents were Verne and Darthula Lewis, and they owned a grocery store located on the lower floor of the Masonic Hall on Main Street in Smithfield. It was the only grocery store located in downtown Smithfield.

The store burned in the big Smithfield fire of 1929. The

fire started in the telephone exchange building. The wife of the owner of the telephone exchange had an invalid mother who accidentally set the building on fire by knocking over a kerosene heater while trying to get out of bed. The building was quickly engulfed, and the invalid mother died in the fire. There was no fire department, but the school was alerted, and all the boys able to carry water formed a bucket brigade and eventually stopped the spread of the fire. On the north side of Main Street, the Masonic Hall and grocery store, the barber shop, post office, telephone exchange and part of the service station all burned. The bank, which was brick, and the general store building at the end of the street were not burned. The general store, which had once been a drugstore and later became the Smithfield Feed Store, is still standing. Buildings on the south side of the street were also saved. Verne Lewis relocated his store to the undamaged bank building.

Mattie Belle Quayle Lewis Borden

Dick Lewis attended Smithfield School as his mother had before him. It stood where Smithfield Elementary now stands. In all, five generations of the Lewis family attended school on this site. Both Dick Lewis and his father served as presidents of the Smithfield School Board.

Dick and Mattie Belle Quayle were married in 1931. Mattie Belle was the daughter of Macon F. and Mittie Belle Quayle who had moved to the Smithfield area from Grapevine in 1906. Mr. Quayle bought 13.5 acres at the corner of what is now Davis and Mid-Cities boulevards. Mattie Belle's older sister, Louise Quayle Brown, was born in 1907, and Mattie Belle was born in 1913.

Mattie Belle also attended Smithfield schools. Memories of the Smithfield School include the fact that there was no running water at the school, which meant there was no lunch room nor any bathrooms. Students brought their lunches from home and ate them outside on the sunny side of the building. Mothers and teachers always stressed that on cold days coats, caps, and gloves be worn during lunch and recess.

After graduation, Mattie Belle moved into Fort Worth to live with her sister on Fourth Street. She worked at The Fair Department Store, riding a city bus to work. She was working at The Fair when it moved into a new building at Seventh and Throckmorton streets in downtown Fort Worth. She remembers all store employees were required to wear black in order that the store appear uniform. Her job at the store was in the hose-mending department. People would bring in real silk hose (nylon was unheard of) to be mended. Very wealthy people, not just folks who had to watch their pennies, would bring in stockings and pay $4 or $5 to have them repaired.

After they married in 1931, Dick and Mattie Belle

lived in Fort Worth for almost a year, but they just couldn't take it any longer than that. Both were Smithfieldites and had to get back to Smithfield. Dick was working for Coca-Cola, and Mattie Belle was still working for The Fair. Back in Smithfield, Mattie Belle became a housewife and mother and didn't work outside the home. Four children were born into the Lewis family: Latrelle Lewis Berry, Laverne Lewis Williams, Richard F. Lewis Jr., and Janice Lewis Edwards. Dick and Mattie Belle built a home for their family near the intersection of Davis and Mid-Cities boulevards on part of the land her parents had bought when they moved to Smithfield.

In 1947, Sully Montgomery was elected sheriff of Tarrant County, and he hired Dick as a deputy sheriff. Later, Dick became bailiff of the jury room. He became well known, and very well regarded in the area, and this gave him the confidence to run for Precinct 3's county commissioner post in 1960. Three or four others, including the incumbent, were also running for the office. Dick was interested in the job because he wanted to do something about the terrible condition of the roads in the area. His son-in-law, Wendell Williams, made the picture Dick used on campaign literature. Wendell had him wear his hat for the picture, and Dick said, "Those people see this bald head every day, and they won't know who it is running if I have my hat on." But he was elected, and daughter Latrelle Berry said he was elected by word-of-mouth. Family members and friends went door-to-door asking for support. For three months, every day and all day long, they walked until the entire precinct was contacted.

Dick Lewis was county commissioner for 15 years and was very important to the growth of this area. He became county commissioner at about the same time that North Richland Hills annexed Smithfield. The growth of NRH was largely the result of developers who wanted to build and sell houses, and many people in Smithfield were not happy to see this happening. Many felt their farm community was going to be invaded, and being added to NRH just seemed to guarantee that unwanted growth and change were inevitable. But Dick Lewis was going to be commissioner of all of Precinct 3, including North Richland Hills, and this helped ease some of the bitterness felt by Smithfield citizens.

Dick and Mattie Belle were active in all areas of the community, especially as members of Smithfield United Methodist Church. Mattie Belle, still active in the church, was baptized as a preparatory member in 1913, when she was six weeks old. Dick was the church's lay leader, and at his death in 1975, had just seen the completion of a new worship center. Dick also helped establish a system of perpetual care for Smithfield Cemetery.

Mattie Belle Lewis Borden, who married Frank Borden after the death of Dick Lewis, is very positive about the changes that have occurred in her lifetime, first in Smithfield and then in North Richland Hills. She says, "I enjoyed what you would call those 'old-fashioned' days, but you wouldn't want to go back. Dick always said 'you can't fight progress,' and I've always tried to adjust to whatever the situation."

Submitted by Mattie Belle Lewis Borden

GEORGE AND DERETTA LICHTENSTEIN

My husband, George Charles Lichtenstein, first moved to North Richland Hills in October 1971. He was born on Staten Island, New York, and spent six and one-half years in the Air Force. George has worked at Southwestern Bell Telephone Company for 24 years. He is a member of the Telephone Pioneers. I, Ginger Deretta Lichtenstein, moved here when we got married on March 17, 1979. I was born in Pittsburg, Texas, but lived in Euless where I graduated from Trinity High School in 1970. I worked for 16 years for

George and Deretta Lichtenstein

Southwestern Bell, but 11 years ago decided to stay home and become a homemaker. We love to go camping and traveling around the United States. Our home means a lot to us so we are constantly working in our yard and house.

Submitted by Deretta Lichtenstein

RODGER AND SHELBY LINE

Rodger and Shelby Line married April 22, 1983, in Fort Worth and moved to North Richland Hills in 1984.

Rodger Newton Line was born to Alta Lena Rodgers and Harvey Hugh Line on August 6, 1934, in O'Donnell, Texas. He attended the local elementary and high school, then entered Texas Tech University. His studies led him to a career as city manager of Fort Worth for seven years, then city manager of North Richland Hills where he remained 13 years. Rodger retired in 1994 and has since become an avid golfer and enjoys fishing as a second hobby. He grew up with one sister and a brother.

Shelby Jean Martin Line was born in Cresson, Texas, on September 29, 1935, the daughter of Lucille Smith and Shelby Martin. Shelby has one brother, Bob Martin, and a sister, JoAnn Parselley. She attended elementary school in Cresson, Granbury High School, St. Joseph's School of Nursing, and Our Lady of Victory parochial school. Shelby became a registered nurse, enjoyed modeling, and was a buyer/fashion consultant, finding time to also work in the investment field. Shelby was previously married to B. Don Magness, and

Rodger N. Line

they had one son, Martin Scott Magness, born May 18, 1960, in Fort Worth. Martin attended Richland High School and is married to Nancy Newman (Magness).

Rodger was previously married to Mary Jane Clarkson. They have two children, Rodger Scott and Tracie Leigh. Scott was born in Lubbock, Texas, November 12, 1955, and attended Texas Tech University. He married Shannon Campbell, and they have two children, Erin and Allyson. Daughter Tracie was born July 9, 1959, in Fort Lauderdale, Florida. She attended Texas Tech University and Baylor University, and presently lives in Dallas.

In North Richland Hills, Rodger and Shelby Line found peacefulness, good neighbors, and a special way of life to raise their family in this small, suburban town.

H. OSCAR LOCHRIDGE FAMILY

H. Oscar Lochridge, Corrie LaVerne Stewart Lochridge, and their sons, Gary Lane and Grant Allen Lochridge, moved to North Richland Hills in 1961. Corrie and Oscar had married in 1952 and lived in Montana for the first year of their marriage. They moved back to Texas just before Gary was born in 1953. Oscar had been employed in oil exploration in Canada and Montana since his 1949 graduation from Texas Tech.

Grant, Oscar, Gary Lochridge, and Gary's son James.

When they moved to NRH in July 1961, Richland High School was in the finishing stages of construction and was opened two months after they moved into a home on Laurel Lane. This home, for the first four or five years that they lived there, was the closest house to Richland High School. Gary started in the third grade in Snow Heights Elementary, while Grant entered the first grade in September 1961. They both graduated from Richland High School, Gary in 1971, and Grant in 1973.

Corrie returned to her teaching career in September 1964, teaching fifth grade at Smithfield Elementary. She taught there for several years before joining a team-teaching situation with seven other teachers at Watauga Elementary. She taught there until her illness and death in July 1982.

Gary and Grant both married class-mates from Richland High School and raised families in this area. Gary died April 30, 1987. His widow, Brenda McKinley Lochridge, still lives in

Corrie Lochridge

NRH with their two children, James and Corrie, both of whom attend Fort Worth Christian School in NRH. Grant's wife, Carol Creedon Lochridge, is a graduate of Richland High School. His eldest daughter, Karen, is a student at University of Arkansas at Fayetteville, Kathryn graduated from Dallas Baptist High School in May 1998 and entered Texas Tech University in Sept. 1998, and the youngest, Allen, attended W. A. Porter Elementary in the Birdville School system until the family's move to Albuquerque, N. M. in late 1997.

Oscar and Evalyn Lochridge

In late 1982, following Corrie's death, Oscar retired from his insurance career and in June 1983 married Evalyn Nichols Wood, a close friend of the family. Evalyn had taught home economics in the Birdville system for 20 years. As a matter of fact, her entire teaching career was accomplished in the same room at North Richland Junior High, three blocks from her home.

Evalyn retired after the 1982–83 school year just before her marriage to Oscar. They left on a trip immediately, and since their marriage, have done extensive traveling. On May 10, 1988 they completed a project begun in 1986 of visiting, photographing, and doing historical research in every county seat in Texas. They drove more than 25,000 miles visiting these courthouses. During that project, they did extensive traveling in Europe, Asia, Australia, and New Zealand. They also became interested in visiting the state capitals. In August of 1996, they completed this project by visiting the 50th one in Juneau, Alaska.

During these years, Evalyn and Oscar have become deeply interested in genealogy, and have been active in researching their families. In addition, they have enjoyed participating in the family reunions of the four families of their parents. In 1991, Oscar was elected president of the Lokrig Family History Association, which is worldwide and includes members of all spellings of the name Lochridge. He served in this capacity for four years and has edited the family chronicle, *The LOCK ON*, since 1991. This is an 80-page magazine-type publication.

The Lochridges' most important association, however, has been with their church. Evalyn and her family have been members of North Richland Hills Baptist Church since its official founding in 1956. Oscar and his family joined this church in late July 1961. It has been a meaningful part of their lives as well as the lives of their children, since that time. Evalyn has been a part of the choir and the Greater Fort Worth Christmas Pageant of this church since its beginning. Oscar served as chairman of the Deacon Council in 1966 and has been on the Deacon Council since 1961.

They have both had an interest in the city of NRH through the years. Oscar served on the Charter Committee several years ago, later serving on the Town Hall Committee and the Historical Committee. In addition to his commitments in NRH, Oscar has served on the Tarrant County Historical Commission since Jan. 1, 1993. He is currently serving as a Tarrant County Grand Jury commissioner.

Evalyn is the chairwoman of the NRH Historical Committee, which is preparing the research for the writing of the *History of North Richland Hills*. She served on the site-base team of Snow Heights Elementary School for three years, and was a yard-of-the-month judge for the NRH Beautification Commission for four years.

The association of all members of this family with the city of North Richland Hills has been a pleasant and rewarding experience. They are very proud of the accomplishments realized by the leadership since its inception. It has certainly been a pleasant home for them and their families through the years.

Submitted by H. Oscar Lochridge

RAYMOND S. AND ETHEL CAMPBELL LOFLAND

Raymond Sidney Lofland was born in 1911, at Gravelly, Arkansas. Ethel Campbell was born in 1915, at Durant, Oklahoma. They met at Texas Tech College and were married in 1936. They had three sons, all born at Lubbock, Gerald Ray Lofland, Richard Clifford Lofland, and Larry Doyle Lofland.

Ray and Ethel Lofland

Ray graduated from Rockwall High School in 1930. Frank Bridges got him a scholarship to Texas Military College at Terrell, Texas (for which Ray's dad contributed three old milk cows). Later Ray received a scholarship, which consisted of a job at Texas Tech.

Ray then got a job teaching math and physical education in grade school at White Deer, Texas. Those were the "lean years." Take-home pay was $87.50 per month. We paid $15 per month for a furnished three-room house, $200 for a used Model-A Ford, bought a refrigerator for $60 and paid it out $5 per month.

He tried farming for a few years and was exempt from service during World War II. His draft service listed farming as important to our armed services for food raised.

In 1952, Ray sold the farm at Lubbock and moved to Richland Hills. Along with the insurance company he joined, he organized Lofland Construction Co. They bought a tract of land that was then called Richland Hills West and built several homes, including his own on Rogene Street in what later became North Richland Hills.

In 1957 Richland Bowl was built, first with 16 lanes.

The following year eight more lanes were added along with a large recreational room, which was converted to eight additional lanes in 1971. The recreational room was a meeting place for nonprofit organizations such as the Junior and Senior High Acteens on Friday and Saturday nights and also for the newly organized Jaycees of Richland Hills. The Davis Memorial Methodist Church and Sunday School held services at the Bowl before their church was built.

The Loflands attended the organizational meeting of the Chamber of Commerce, and Ray was its second president. Through the chamber efforts, Rufe Snow Drive was extended as a major thoroughfare. Ray was also a director in the Diamond Oaks Country Club as well as of the Tarrant County Water Supply Corporation. Ray was active in politics and helped get Ace Nace elected as one of the early mayors of NRH in 1957. Besides offices held in the Bowling Proprietors organization, he was most proud of being inducted into the Fort Worth Bowling Association's Hall of Fame and being asked to serve as a director of the First United Bank of NRH, which opened in 1980.

Ray and Ethel retired in 1980. The bowl was leased out for a few years; however, the sons would not sell it until after Ray died July 22, 1994. Ethel now resides at Parkwood Retirement Community in Bedford. She loves to go to Shreveport and Las Vegas and spends a lot of time trying to learn to use her computer. She enjoys her grandchildren and great-grandchildren.

Gerald married Elaine Walton in 1964, and they still live in NRH. They had twin boys, Christopher Lee and Kenneth Kyle. Richard married Roberta Anne Reynolds January 25, 1964. They live in Bedford and have three children. Larry Doyle was stationed in Italy while in the service during the Vietnam War. He died October 17, 1972.

Submitted by Ethel C. Lofland

MOSES AND BEATRICE LOPEZ AND FAMILY

The Moses and Beatrice Lopez family moved to North Richland Hills on Vance Road in 1977. Moses Lopez was born in Nixon, Texas, in 1919. He had a long and distinguished career in the Army Air Corps and the United States Air Force having served in both the Second World

L/R, Back-Helen (Lopez) Weissinger, Joseph, Moses, and Ray Lopez; Front-Lucy (Lopez) Griffin, Beatrice, and Emily Lopez

War and the Korean War. Following military service, Moses worked for the General Service Administration until his retirement. His wife, Beatrice, a homemaker, was born in San Angelo.

Three of their five children have settled in the North Richland Hills area. This includes Amelia Lopez, a health care insurance manager, and her husband, Jerry Jenkins; Helen Lopez Weissinger, North Richland Hills Library employee, and her husband, Glenn Weissinger; and Lucy Griffin, a bank customer service representative and her husband, Eric Griffin. Ray Lopez, an independent businessman and Kerri Tullous live in nearby Watauga, while Joseph Lopez, a plant manager, lives in El Paso.

Amelia Lopez has three children. Her son, Jeff Porter, and his wife, Jerlette, live in North Richland Hills. Amelia's other children, Ami Allison and Chris Harrelson, live nearby in Fort Worth. Lucy Griffin has two children, Jennifer Griffin and Nicholas Griffin, who attend school in North Richland Hills.

The family is very active at St. John the Apostle Catholic Church in North Richland Hills, and Moses Lopez is a member of the Knights of Columbus. Moses and Beatrice Lopez instilled in their children the importance of education. Amelia received a nursing degree at Tarrant County Junior College. Helen, Joseph, Ray, and Lucy all graduated from Haltom High School. Helen received a master's degree in education at Texas Woman's University. Joseph went on to achieve a master's in business administration from the University of North Texas. Through the years, the Lopez families have dedicated themselves to supporting their families, church, and communities.

HOMER AND JEAN LUDIKER

I, Helen Jean (Schieman) and Homer Ludiker married in May 1947. We were high school sweethearts and still are. While we both attended TCU, we lived in Haltom City 10 years in a house built by Homer and Orien Browning.

Our children are: Lee Ann Nave, born in 1953; Lane, born in 1956; Lynn, born in 1959; and Les, born in 1964. Our children have all married and blessed us with 10 grandchildren. They range in age from 25 to 9, so we really have a wide range of Christmas gifts to buy.

Lee Ann married Jackie Nave. They live in Weatherford in a partially underground house they built themselves. They have two children: Shannon, who is a hydrologist with the Grand Prairie Water Department, and Valerie, who married Chris Piercy in 1995 and attends North Texas University working toward a teaching degree.

Lane married Anita Husbanett. They live in Burleson with their two sons, Robert and Danny. Lane is an auto mechanic, and Nita works for a doctor.

Lynn married Debbie Schnieder, and they live in Hurst. Their children are Dustin Schnieder, who works for Southwestern Bell Telephone Company; Whitney, a student at L. D. Bell High School; and Chelsea. Lynn has worked for Southwestern Bell for many years.

Les married Kim Diechert, and they live in North

Richland Hills. Their children are Emily, Eric, and Evan, who passed away in March 1997. He is sorely missed by all of us. Les works at Binswanger Glass Company.

Ludiker's 50th wedding anniversary, May 1997; L/R-Les, Lynn, Jean, Homer, Lane, Lee Ann Ludiker Nave

We moved to Oakland Lane August 1, 1959. We were the third family to move in on our street. Matt Jones' family lived on the corner, Del and Martha Browning in the third house, and we had the fifth house. When our block was fully occupied, there were 35 children plus kids from Shauna Drive and Marilyn Lane.

Snow Heights Elementary opened that September, and Lee Ann was in the first grade. She also had the first case of mumps in the school. Our 3-year-old Lane had them, too. We never knew if our 8-month-old Lynn had them or not because his face was so chubby! We eventually had four children and two grandchildren attend Snow Heights.

The Snow Heights Preschool was organized that year also. We had a booth at the carnival. A local nursery gave us plants to sell, and we got to keep all the profits. Eventually we were able to buy books for the PTA.

We had several very busy years. We were involved in Camp Fire Girls, Boy Scouts, football, baseball, Coaches Club and Coaches Wives Club, PTA, preschool, and bridge club. Homer helped organize the Jaycee Club.

We had lots of cuts, scrapes, bruises, broken bones, but only one really serious car accident. (All came out well.)

We have enjoyed living in North Richland Hills. We have made many good friends, and are still at it. The truth is, we plan to keep on living here a very long time, and making many more friends.

Submitted by Jean Ludiker

CALVIN "CAL" AND PAULINE LUPER

Calvin "Cal" Luper was born in Rowlett, Texas, and attended schools in Mesquite, then Texas A&M. Pauline Ridner, born in Mesquite, attended school in Garland, where she met Cal. They were married in Dallas, Texas.

Their first daughter, Linda, was born in Dallas, where the family lived until moving to Fort Worth in 1950. Their second daughter, Sylvia, was born in Fort Worth where the family lived until 1953 when they moved to Richland Hills. The Lupers moved to North Richland Hills in

1961. Pauline still lives in the same house on Eldorado Street that became their home.

Linda attended North Texas State University and married Robert Szot. They had one son, Wayne, who is with a computer company in New Orleans. Robert died of a heart attack, and Linda now lives in Burleson, Texas. She has been a teacher for 30 years. Her first year was with the University of Alaska in Fairbanks; the last 29 years she has taught at Arlington Heights High School in Fort Worth.

Cal Luper

Sylvia attended Tarrant County Junior College and married Randall B. Mobley, now minister of music at the First Baptist Church of Jena, Louisiana, where they live with their two children, Megan and Jonathan.

Cal was a member of the Boy Scouts of America, receiving its Silver Beaver award, the highest award given to adult leaders. He was a 17-year member of the Downtown Lions Club of Fort Worth, a deacon, and Sunday school teacher at Shady Oaks Baptist Church in Hurst. He was an area chairman for the United Fund Drive and served as president of the Fort Worth Association of Building Owners and Managers.

As mayor of North Richland Hills from 1966–1970, Cal presided over the city's first bond election of $6.85 million to purchase a water company for the city. The proposal passed; so did the city's first sales tax election, also approved under Cal's administration, which set the sales tax rate at 7.25 cents. That rate held until August 1992, when it was increased to 7.75 cents. He served as chairman of the Charter Commission and was a member of the Regional Planning Committee that formed the Regional Airport Council.

Following his two terms as mayor, Cal continued to be involved with civic affairs, serving on several city committees and as the city election judge from 1987 to 1990. He was a retired building manager and died of a heart attack December 12, 1992.

Friends and city employees with whom he had worked described him as "a fine person; a good friend who left his mark on this city."

TOM AND CHERYL LYMAN

In October 1984, Thomas James and Cheryl Renee Cowen Lyman built their first house and moved to North Richland Hills. Being from Dallas, they thought they were moving to the country. The only thing either knew about NRH was that Cheryl had once attended a race at Green Valley racetrack. Ironically, they built their house near that very same racetrack.

Tom was born in Indianapolis, and Cheryl, a native Texan, was born at a Dallas hospital and grew up in Richardson. Brandon, Tom and Cheryl's son, was born at the same hospital December 22, 1989, and came home to NRH when he was three days old.

Cheryl, Tom, and Brandon Lyman

Tom went to elementary school in Indiana and Michigan. He came to Dallas in 1970 where he attended junior and senior high school. After graduating from Hillcrest High School, he attended Richland Junior College and the University of Texas at Dallas. Currently, Tom works for Michael's Corporation. He spends his spare time coaching Brandon's baseball team. Tom's favorite hobby is golf, but he also enjoys playing baseball with Brandon.

Cheryl went to school in Richardson. After graduation from J. J. Pearce High School, she attended North Texas State University. She owns CS Publications, a creative service/digital imaging company. Cheryl is very involved in community affairs. As chairman of the Adventure World Foundation, she coordinated the building of Adventure World Park. She is a member of NE Tarrant Chamber of Commerce, Northeast-Richland Lions Club, the *Fort Worth Star-Telegram* Citizen's Advisory Committee and Green Valley Elementary PTA and is also a graduate of Citizen's Police Academy. Cheryl was elected to the City Council in May 1997. Prior to that, she served on the city's Town Hall Committee, Parks and Recreation Board, and on the historical committee. In 1994, she was named NRH volunteer of the year.

Brandon attended Angel Land preschool at North Richland Hills Baptist Church and has completed kindergarten, first, and second grades at Green Valley Elementary. He loves all sports, but golf and baseball are his favorites.

The Lymans are members of North Richland Hills Baptist Church. Brandon is active in the Greater Fort Worth Christmas Pageant, choir, and Royal Ambassadors. Cheryl is also active in the pageart and choir and Tom teaches second grade Royal Ambassadors.

Submitted by Cheryl Lyman

SCOTT AND VIRGINIA MAGRUDER

The Magruder family moved to Southhampton Drive in North Richland Hills in September 1978. At that time there were two of us; now there are five.

D. Scott Magruder was born September 17, 1956, in California. He attended L. D. Bell High School, Panola Junior College on a baseball scholarship, and Tarrant County Junior College where he earned his degree. He has been certified for eight years and a coach of youth sports for 13 years. He coached baseball and soccer for youth associations and was all-star coach several times. He has been actively involved in the PTA and volunteering at the children's schools. He has been a softball umpire for 20 years.

He is in the electrical business and is a Master Mason.

Virginia Beth Subke Magruder was born March 2, 1957, in Fort Worth. She attended L. D. Bell High School, Fort Worth Business College, and TCJC. She has been involved as a coach of youth sports for 10 years. She was awarded "Friend of Education" through Birdville Independent School District lifetime membership in PTA through Foster Village Elementary. She is now employed in Birdville ISD.

Grant Scott Magruder was born February 18, 1980, in Bedford. In 1998, he is a senior at Haltom High School. He has played baseball, soccer, indoor soccer, and was an all-star player many times. He was a Who's Who recipient for three straight years, won a perfect attendance award and is a member of the National Honor Society. He played soccer for Haltom as a midfielder.

Angel Nicole Magruder was born May 18, 1982, in Bedford. She is a sophomore student at Haltom High School in 1998. She has studied dance for 12 years. She has been on junior and senior production companies at her studio, Doubletake.

Back, L/R-Virginia, Scott; Front-Angel, Jake Thomas, Grant Scott

She was a junior Dallas Cowboy Cheerleader, involved in Student Council and is now a Haltom Highstepper Drill Team member.

Jake Thomas Magruder was born November 15, 1984, in Bedford. In 1998, he attends North Ridge Middle School. He has played baseball and soccer, indoor soccer, and was an all-star player many times. He has been involved in student council, elected to the Wall of Fame at North Ridge and elected Mr. Dream Team by the sixth grade.

MARY JANE THAYER MANDEL

David Michael Thayer, and I, Mary Jane Thayer Mandel, moved to Deville Drive in North Richland Hills in August 1977 from Norman, Oklahoma. Our daughter, Matilda Jane Thayer, was born February 7, 1985. David took a job with General Dynamics as a tech writer. We bought our house from Mary Alice Clark, a former teacher at Snow Heights Elementary.

It was a terrific house, dating from the '50s. When the workers came to put a new roof on after a hail storm, they commented on how well the house had been built, with thick timbers for great support, unlike some of recent construction.

Our son, Christopher Robert Thayer, attended Snow Heights Elementary school where he had some outstanding teachers. That neighborhood was wonderful for children growing up, although by the time we bought there, the Baby

Boomers had graduated, and the parents were aging.

The houses had big lots compared to those on the market today, and the hills of NRH were wonderful for long bike rides. The snowcone stand by the Winn Dixie on Blaney Drive and Grapevine Highway was open every summer where kids and parents lined up for delightful frosty treats. It's gone now and it is missed by the residents.

Another spot for great conversation, coffee, and grilled cheese sandwiches was the Town and Country Drug in the Greater Richland Shopping Center. The older generation congregated there for hours every day, chatting about their grandkids and the latest neighborhood news and drinking pots of coffee. It also closed some years back, and I've always wondered where those folks go now for conversation.

Our home wasn't far from the library. It was then, and still is, a wonderful library.

In 1991, I married Stephen Paul Mandel, a transplanted Australian, and sold the house on Deville. I still miss that old neighborhood, but much to my surprise I discovered a new area of NRH I had only heard about. As far north as you can go in NRH, you come to a spot off Smithfield Road called Green Valley. There used to be a raceway here, but now there are just some longhorns, green meadows, and rolling hills. The view from our house is awesome, especially on a misty morning. I've been told that the old stagecoach run from Denton to Fort Worth used to stop at Green Valley—just about where the new soccer park is located.

My daughter graduated from Green Valley Elementary in 1995 and now attends North Ridge Middle. The doctor who delivered her at North Hills was Dr. J. Ardis Bell. He was our family physician until he retired in December 1997.

I recently moved my mom, Matilda Jane Black, here from Tulsa. She is adjusting well to the Texas heat and the Mexican food, for an octogenarian, and enjoys shopping at North Hills Mall and dining at Luby's Cafeteria there. Of all the cities in the Metroplex we could have picked to live in, I am really glad we chose North Richland Hills.

Submitted by Mary Jane Mandel

G. G. AND JUANITA MARTIN

On April 27, 1964, after a long and extensive look at several properties, G. G. and Juanita Martin decided to purchase 20 acres that were part of the extensive holdings of Dr. H. C. Allison in Smithfield. G. G. designed the house that he and his kin would build.

They brought their kids out, including their oldest daughter, her husband, and their one-year-old son to have a picnic and stake out the house. The property had an abandoned house sitting on the western corner of where our house was to be built. A barbed-wire fence, complete with barbed-wire gate surrounded the old house. We kids decided to explore the structure before it was torn down. There was a musty odor everywhere, and as our eyes became accustomed to the faint light drifting through the broken windowpanes, we noticed that faded newspaper covered the walls. One room was covered in cartoons. I remember trying to get in to see the house. I was too scared to go through the fence, so I crawled under the gate, raised up too soon, and got a scratch producing a scar I have to this day.

Fiftieth wedding anniversary of G. G. and Juanita Martin; Back, L/R-Judy Martin Newman, Gwen Martin, Gary and Steve Martin, Jean Martin McKinney, Jane Martin Ratliff, and Ann Martin Tucker; Front-Juanita Brown Martin, G. G. Martin, Vera Brown

By August, the house was finished, and we moved to the country. Later, my uncle bought the property across the road from us. There he built his family a home on a little hill, surrounded by oak trees. He had 40 acres, part of which, today is Green Valley Park. There was a wooden ladder over his barbed-wire fence so we could go across to their house. There was also a pond that was straight out our front door on his property. In May 1970, my little sister, Lisa Gay, who was brain damaged from birth, drowned in that pond. We were devastated, but comforted by God, family, and friends.

Not much was out here back then. Now in 1998, there is quite a difference. In 1990, we sold all but three of the original acres. Today, we are in the Bridlewood Estates, although our house sits outside the main fence of the development. The house is on Smithfield Road, just across from Green Valley Park. Back in 1964, that road was a narrow two-lane country road that led past Green Valley Race City. We could hear the noise from the races on the weekends.

My twin sisters and I attended Smithfield Elementary. Many times we walked or rode our bicycles home. My brothers went to Richland Junior High until Watauga Junior High was completed. We all graduated from Richland High School.

Many times as I drive my mom past other properties we had considered back in 1964, she will say, " I'm so glad we didn't get that place, I'm happy right where I'm at." We have all stayed pretty close, with only two family members living outside North Richland Hills.

Submitted by Ann Martin Tucker

JOHN AND CARLA MARTIN

John Lee and Carla Denise Martin reside on Chapman Drive in North Richland Hills. John and Carla moved to NRH in August 1995.

John was born in NRH and attended Mullendore Elementary School, North Richland Junior High, and

Richland High School. John graduated cum laude from the University of North Texas with a bachelor of science degree in criminal justice in May 1992. He has been employed with the state of Texas for three and a half years and is a member of the Alpha Phi Sigma Criminal Justice Honor Fraternity. John enjoys sports and landscaping.

John and Carla Martin

Carla was born in Arlington. She attended Crow Elementary School, Carter Junior High, and Arlington High School. Carla graduated magna cum laude from the University of North Texas with a bachelor of science degree in counseling in May 1994. Carla is employed with Norwest Bank (formerly Central Bank & Trust). She was first lieutenant of the Arlington High Colt Kickers in 1988–89. She is a member of Alpha Chi and Psi Chi honor societies and enjoys traveling and marine life.

John and Carla were married at Fort Worth Botanic Gardens on June 25, 1994, and live with a cat named Bubba.

TOMMY AND SUE MARTIN

Tommy and Sue Martin moved to Susan Lee Lane in North Richland Hills in August 1965, a house they built that year.

Tommie Sue was born January 10, 1942, the third child of eight born to Doyle Thomas and Gladys Vandell Ice of Saint Jo, Texas. They farmed land that had been in the Ice family for years.

Tommy was born January 25, 1936, in Diamond, Missouri, near the Joplin area. His parents, John Lee and Laura Elizabeth Martin were originally farmers, but later his dad became a minister. The family moved to Fort Worth so his dad could attend Southwestern Baptist Theological Seminary in 1952.

Tommy and Sue met when Tommy's dad began pastoring the church in North Texas that Sue's family attended. The children of both families spent lots of time together on the Ice farm. After Tommy graduated in 1956, he entered the Army. When he completed his tour of duty, his family had moved back to Missouri where he attended college.

Tommy and Sue were married on September 8, 1961, by Tommy's dad in the rural church where they met. They lived in Denton until Sue graduated from North Texas State

Back, L/R-Eric, Sabrina; Front-Sue, Tommy, 1989

University in 1962. Sue began teaching at Browning Heights Elementary in the Birdville Independent School District. Tommy worked as assistant manager of the Ben Franklin Store in Cox's Shopping Center.

In 1965, J. B. Sandlin built a house for Tommy and Sue on Susan Lee Lane. Tommy and his brother, Montie, hunted quail and dove on the land right around their house. Later, Tommy and Sue and their children rode trail bikes on this land.

When they moved into their new home, the Martins had a 1965 Plymouth Barracuda. Soon after moving, they bought a 1966 Red Dodge Charger that they still have. Collecting Mopar cars has become a hobby of Tommy's, and it started with those two cars.

Sue began teaching at the new Holiday Heights Elementary. She continued to teach until they adopted their first child, Sabrina Renee, born in 1968. In 1969 Sue went back to teaching first grade at Holiday Heights for another year. Their second child, Eric Thomas, was born in 1970, and came to live with them in February 1971.

After teaching at Watauga, Holiday Heights, and Grace Hardeman Elementary, then working at the central BISD office as a consultant for six years, Sue became principal of Snow Heights Elementary. In 1983 she returned to the central office as an administrator.

Tommy helped to start an import company in Dallas called Tanco Imports, which specialized in flowers and home decorative items. As the company grew, he was vice president in charge of the sales force. He stayed with Tanco until December 1984, when he began teaching an auto body course at Haltom High School.

The Martins joined North Richland Hills Baptist Church in 1972. The church became the center of many of their activities over the years.

Sabrina graduated from Richland High School in 1986, attended Dallas Baptist University, then Baylor University, where she graduated in December 1990. She taught school at W. T. Francisco and Glenview Elementary until her marriage to Kevin Lindsey of Weatherford. The couple spent the first year of their married life in the West Indies, then returned to the North Richland Hills area where Sabrina taught at Carrie Thomas Elementary.

Eric graduated from Haltom High School in 1989. He married Lesa Ann Jara of Haltom City and then attended Baylor University. He returned to the North Richland Hills area to work for Allen Samuels Dodge on Loop 820 as assistant manager. In January 1997, he became manager of the parts department of Allen Samuels Chevrolet in Corpus Christi. Eric has two children, Brittani and Alex.

Sue is currently in her 36th year with the BISD, now as director of personnel, and Tommy is still sharing his love of young people and cars with the students from Richland High School, Haltom High School, and Shannon Learning Center. They have plans to retire in the near future to spend more time with their grandchildren, activities of their church, and to travel.

PAUL AND JUANITA MASON

Paul Mason was a builder, businessman, and dynamic boost-er for North Richland Hills and the surrounding areas. He was busier than most, but when asked if he was too busy to make his experience and talents available to the newly formed Richland Chamber of Commerce in 1957, his reply was, "When a man needs help in getting something impor-tant done, he'd better look for a busy man for that help." He served on the chamber's first board of directors.

Paul Mason

Mason was a big, quiet fellow with a dry wit often compared to his boyhood neighbor, Will Rogers. They both lived on the Cherokee Lease at a place called Bushyhead, near Oolagah, Oklahoma.

One of his memories of the "hard days" in the 1930s was when he operated a bowling alley in Paul's Valley, Oklahoma. Later in North Richland Hills, there was nothing that he and wife Juanita enjoyed more than an evening bowling each week.

Just before World War II, Paul Mason was in the con-struction business. In 1941 he was in Fort Worth as an assis-tant foreman over electrical, radio, and radar for Consolidated (now Lockheed), a post he held until VE Day. Then he became a builder again. He started the Meadow Oaks addition on Denton Highway.

Juanita Mason

Paul came to Richland Hills in 1951, and was building houses in North Richland Hills when there were only a dozen res-idences in what was then the entire incorporated city. He had been asked by North Richland Hills developer Clarence Jones to come here to build houses. He credited his wife as being 90 per-cent of the business. She was the designer and interior decorator. By 1957 they had built 50 houses in the $17,500 to $37,500 price range in North Richland Hills.

They built Mason's Hobby Lobby at 6905 Grapevine Highway in 1953. "Nita" Mason was able to share her love of art with the community through the business. She taught art lessons and stocked supplies for her many customers. Later, art classes were taught by Loretta Schapansky.

The Masons were members of St. Luke Methodist Church where Nita was a member of the adult choir. They had one daughter, Cherry, who married John McGuffin. He was a career Air Force master sergeant stationed at Carswell Air Force Base. Cherry died in a car accident on Loop 820 in 1967 near North East Mall. John currently resides in Bedford. The four Mason grandchildren graduated from Richland High School in 1976, 1977, 1978, and 1984. The four children were, John "Tripp," Mark, Kim, and Erik McGuffin. When the first, "Tripp," was born, Paul Mason

was no different than any other grandpa. "Grandbabies weren't worth a darn until I got mine," he said.

One scarcely known habit Paul Mason had was of quiet charity, which showed he never forgot those early "hard days" of his life, or maybe he just liked people. Every Christmas he hauled himself out of bed on Christmas Day to go to his store and load his paneled, blue station wagon full of toys. He drove to a part of town that Santa forgot. He found a kid in rags and handed him a toy, or two or three, and watched the child's face light up. Then he'd drive away to find another, and another, until all the toys in the paneled station wagon were spread around. He would then return to his own neighborhood for a quiet Christmas. If someone who knew him well asked point-blank about his giving, he'd either deny that it happened or shrug it off as "nothing."

The community lost a forceful, benevolent leader when Paul Mason died in 1977. Juanita Mason continued to oper-ate Mason's Hobby Lobby with grandson John "Tripp" McGuffin as manager until her death in September 1988.

Mason's Hobby Lobby carries a proud name and contin-ues to be the oldest business in North Richland Hills con-tinuously run in the same location.

Story by Evalyn Lochridge from interview with John "Tripp" McGuffin

The Review—December 20, 1957

NRH Profiles Channel 39—Interview of Juanita Mason by Arlita Hallam

BOB AND SUE WEST MATHIS

I was 2 years old in 1940 when we moved to Smithfield. We rented a house on Smithfield Road (now Davis Boulevard), where the YMCA is. It was across the street from Dawson's Washateria, where we went for years to wash our clothes. We lived there until Dad built our house, in the fork of Davis Boulevard and Smithfield Road. My parents were Marion and Hattie Helm West.

Bob and Sue West Mathis

Dad was one of the first volun-teer firemen. At one time, he was fire marshal. I remember the phone ringing at night (that's how they contacted the firemen) when there was a fire. Many times we would go to the fires with Dad. I remember going to one house on the Denton Highway that Mom had lived in when she was a young girl growing up.

I can remember Dad telling me about living down the hill below Birdville Stadium on the other side of the creek. Their neighbor, just up the road close to the mall, made moonshine, and Dad would go up and visit with this family. One day when Mom and Dad were gone, the revenue people came in and destroyed the still and smashed all the liquor in the bottles.

I remember the old two-story school, then Smithfield Independent School District. It had a fire escape slide from the second story to the ground. I remember sliding down it many times. It was torn down, and a more modern building was constructed. There was a stage with the old curtain that had many advertisements on it. I went to school there from first grade to the eighth grade. Two of my beloved teachers were Mrs. Isbell, and Mr. Little who later died on the steps of the school with a heart attack.

We had a girl's basketball team on which I played. Back then, the girls could only play half-court. We traveled to Hurst, John T. White, Crowley, and other schools to play.

I married Bob Mathis from Fort Worth. We lived in Riverside for one year, then moved down the street from the old Birdville High School, which became Haltom High School. Now we live in the North Hills addition. We have four sons, Tony, Mark, Michael, and Phillip. They all attended Haltom High School. Phillip was in the last graduating class from old Haltom High. Three of my sons have worked for the Birdville Independent School District at one time or another. Phillip Mathis, the youngest son, has just taken over maintenance of the football field at Birdville Stadium. Tony married Laura Turner and is an electrician. They live in Azle with their five children. Mark married Patty Burris. She is a waitress at Pancho's restaurant, and they live in Fort Worth with their three children. Michael married Laurie Foster. He is head of building and grounds at Crowley ISD and has his own pest control business. They live in Cresson with their three children. Phillip married Tina Jordan, works for Birdville ISD. They live in Cresson and have one son.

There has been so many changes over the years. The dangerous "S" curve before you got to our house was even straightened. There were so many wrecks on that curve, it was before you got to the present post office on Davis Boulevard. On the other side of Smithfield, there was a drag strip where we attended races many times.

One of my memories is of winning the Miss Flame contest for the Smithfield Fire Department. I really thought I was something until they had the one for Tarrant County. There were lots of pretty girls there. I was just a young country girl. What was once the Smithfield Fire Department became the first fire department in NRH.

A. MARWOOD AND DOROTHY MCCLELLAND

After the arrival of two young sons, Arthur Marwood Jr. and Randel Mark, both born in Oklahoma, Marwood and Dorothy McClelland headed for Texas, leaving behind a very promising career with the Tulsa Opera Company.

Marwood started to work May 1957 at Convair. The first move was to Bucko Homes, a housing area near Carswell Air Force Base, which provided temporary housing for families moving to the area.

After carefully shopping for a home, one was purchased on Winnell Way in North Richland Hills. There the family was greeted by wonderful neighbors, which resulted in lifetime friends. The two sons, Woody and Randy, had great playmates and a safe neighborhood that the entire "Winnell Way Family" enjoyed.

Mary Ruth and Norman Ellis were next door neighbors. Mary Ruth always credited "Nurse" Dorothy for the expertise in knowing what to do when there were emergencies in rearing the young children in the neighborhood.

In 1962 the family moved to the Hurst-Euless-Bedford area, where the boys graduated from Bell High School.

Art "Woody" now resides in Tyler with his wife Elizabeth (Bledsoe). Their children are Michael Scott, 24; John Cary 19; Lesley Marie, 15; and Ashley Danielle, 5. Art is with the *Tyler Courier Times* and *Tyler Morning Telegraph*.

Mark "Randy" now resides in NRH with his wife Annette (Wallace) with their children. Mary Jessica, 15, is a very active student at Richland High School, being involved in music and tennis. Micah Joseph, 11, just completed Snow Heights Elementary (also his dad attended Snow Heights) and will be attending North Richland Middle School. Micah enjoys playing baseball and football.

Marwood and Dorothy (deceased April 1998) had wonderful memories of the time spent in NRH; and were also pleased to see Mark and Annette select NRH as "home" to rear their family.

W. A. AND ROBERTA MCGEE

W. A. "Mac" and I, Roberta Hale McGee, moved to what is now known as North Richland Hills in December 1943. Mac's folks had some five acres of land located on Grapevine Highway and what is now Rufe Snow Drive. This road was named for one of the earlier settlers, Rufe Snow, who had a farm located close to where the North Richland Junior High was built. His son, Will Snow, who had property east of us on the Grapevine Highway, had a deep well from which he supplied our small addition with water for several years.

At the time we moved out here, we resided in a small house behind the McGee family home. We later built our home in 1948 on part of the property facing Rufe Snow Drive. There was no natural gas available to us for several years, so we used butane for cooking and heating.

Our home was in a small section known as the Harmonson Addition, which had a few houses on Flory, Scruggs, and Parchman, along with some scattered farms from the Grapevine Highway north to Watauga Road. Rufe Snow Drive at that time was a two-lane, asphalt road, very rough and full of chug holes.

The closest stores were Guynn's and Portwood's on Belknap and Carson Street. There was also a Fisher's Drugstore there. Later on, the Parchmans built a nice store, Rapid Mart, located at Vance Road and the Grapevine Highway. Things were beginning to build up at this time. The only bus service for awhile was the one that came by the house around 7:30 A.M. on the way to Fort Worth and returned at 5:30 P.M. to Grapevine.

We had a rural phone service with the old crank-type phone. We had to go through "central" from a switchboard located in a house on the corner of Carson and Broadway in Birdville. If some of the family tried to contact the house, and no one answered, the operator would take the message and call us later.

Numerous changes began, and in 1957 E. F. Abbott of Smithfield approached us about buying our place. He wanted to build a doctor's building for his two sons, Tommy and Don. We agreed to sell and in May 1957 moved across the highway to Hardisty Street in Richland Hills where I still live. The only visible thing left of our home place is a Chinese elm tree on the parking lot of the doctor's building. We planted it as a small twig in 1949 and are amazed each time we pass to see it is still alive.

In 1959, we purchased an automobile garage from Luke Davis, and McGee's Garage is still in operation at 3810 Rufe Snow Drive. Our sons, Bill and Bob, ran the business. The youngest, Don, was still in school.

The family joined the North Richland Hills Baptist Church in September 1956. The marriage ceremony of Bill and Dell Livingston McGee was the first performed by Pastor Hal Brooks after he came to the church.

Don McGee served in the Vietnam War. When he returned, he became a dispatcher with the NRH Police Department, then a detective. He went to work for the sheriff's department in Clear Lake, Texas, and was killed in the line of duty.

Mac McGee was a painting contractor, but in later years he ran the business end of the garage. He died October 24, 1997. I worked many years for Mrs. Ruth Blessing in her nursery school. Now I work at the garage and also manage the office for the gymnastics school owned by Mrs. Blessing's grandson.

Submitted by Roberta McGee

CLAYTON AND ANN MCGILVRAY AND FAMILY

Clayton and Ann McGilvray moved to North Richland Hills in 1958. Since they had lived in the more populated Polytechnic area of Fort Worth from 1940, this area seemed pretty much out in the country.

Clayton was born in 1925 in Hill County, east of Waco, and Ann McHone McGilvray was born in Collin County. In 1940, their families moved next door to each other. They both graduated from Poly High and were married in 1946 after Clayton returned from World War II, having served in the Navy in the South Pacific.

Clayton attended Texas Wesleyan College, graduating in 1952 as an accounting major. David, their oldest son, was born in 1947, and the family moved to Amarillo where Clay was born in 1956. Since they moved to North Richland Hills in 1958, it was the only home Clay remembers before he married.

Clayton and Ann McGilvray family, 1991

David graduated from Richland High in 1966 and Clay in 1973.

The family has attended the Richland Hills Church of Christ since 1957 when it was meeting in Glenview Elementary in Richland Hills. Clayton served as one of the church's elders from 1963 to 1980 and taught an adult Bible class for many of these years.

David McGilvray, a pilot with Southwest Airlines, married Mary McKee. They live in North Richland Hills and have four children: Adam, Mac, Daniel, and Amanda. Mary's mother and father, Dan and Ginny McKee, also have lived in North Richland Hills many years.

Clay McGilvray married Lynne Wood, and they live in Fort Worth. They have three children: Jennifer, Stephen, and Amy.

Clayton and Ann are both retired, and Clayton helps his son, Clay, in his auto repair business in Haltom City. Ann works with a group of ladies who make quilts at the Community Enrichment Center.

Clayton and Ann enjoy traveling and have camped more than 20 years with their family and friends near Creede, Colorado. They've been to Europe many times and have taken several cruises, the last two in 1997, through the Panama Canal and to Alaska.

They have enjoyed their years in North Richland Hills very much and consider it a wonderful place to live.

Submitted by Clayton McGilvray

C. E. "PAT" AND STEL MCGUIRE

In 1951, Larry Bell of Bell Aircraft, a Buffalo, New York corporation, announced that the helicopter division was being relocated to the Fort Worth area.

C. E. (Pat) McGuire was a member of the helicopter design engineering department. He, his wife, Stel, and their two sons, Mike (age 5), and Chuck (age 2), looked forward to the move in June 1952. Mike was born in Rockport, New York, March 19, 1946. Chuck was born in Rockport January 21, 1950.

Two other families from the engineering group (S. K. Baker and Warren C. Jones) had arrived in Texas in March 1952. Both had selected North Richland Hills as the ideal spot in which to reside because of its proximity to the new Bell plant and the bright outlook that was evident for the area's future. They told us there were only 23 families in

North Richland Hills at that time, but it is believed that their head count was a little short.

The more we looked at schools, churches, accessibility of main thoroughfares, shopping, medical care, banks, and other essentials, the more we were attracted and led back to North Richland Hills.

By late July, we had a contract with a builder, Clarence Taylor, and in August 1952, we moved into our new home on Vance Road.

We had few neighbors, no streetlights, fire or police departments and traveled on dirt streets. The back lot line was fenced with three-strand barbed wire, and cattle roamed the fields beyond, congregating around a large water tank that we referred to as the cow's lake.

After 10 weeks in the hotel, the boys thought that the big backyard was great and often would sneak off, over the fence, with their German shepherd acting as guide and guard.

We thought that we were really getting "uptown" when our streets were black-topped. I guess we appreciated it more because each homeowner paid for the street in front of the home. There were a few tightwads that refused, so there were still some plain dirt patches along the way.

From our house, the area began to grow to the north, and soon signs appeared announcing the new "Snow Heights area." We became very familiar with this addition, because the boys often camped there and drove their little "race" car to the high ground, which was called "Mesquite Hill."

About five years went by, and lots were laid out all over "Mesquite Hill." Shortly thereafter, with some urging by the boys and their grandfather, we selected a lot where a builder, Paul Geron, had already started construction. In August 1960, we moved into our new and present home on Marilyn Lane

Our older son, Mike, was in the first class that graduated from Richland High, and Chuck graduated there in 1967.

Stel retired after two terms as president of the Emerald Garden Club, and Pat retired as a vice president from Bell Helicopter Textron in 1983. Both have decided to keep the house on Marilyn Lane as their retirement home.

Submitted by Pat McGuire

JOHN WILBURN AND GENOVEVA "GENE" MELLADO MCINTOSH

Gene Mellado and Johnny McIntosh were married at North Richland Hills Baptist Church on June 18, 1983. Gene is the daughter of Ed and Aggie Mellado (from "wherever they hang their hats"). She has a sister and two brothers: Eddie, Jimmy, and Birdie Mellado Brazil. After living outside the United States for 18 years in seven different countries and visiting many other countries, they arrived in the Metroplex on January 2, 1980.

Johnny is the son of Doyle Jack and Mary Evelyn McIntosh, formerly from Colleyville, now residing in North Richland Hills. He has two brothers and a sister: Joe McIntosh, Janice McIntosh Callaway, and James McIntosh.

Gene was born in Lincoln, Nebraska, on September 19, 1961. She graduated from Balboa High School in 1979, in the Canal Zone. She was active in her church youth group and choir, involved in her school's extracurricular activities like choir, band, and athletics. She

Back, L/R-John Jr., Abigail, Gene, John Sr.; Front-Chloe and Lydia

attended Mississippi College and Texas Wesleyan College where she graduated in 1982 with a bachelor's degree in elementary education with a bilingual endorsement. She worked for the Birdville School District as a fourth-grade teacher until John Jr. came along.

Johnny was born in Fort Worth on December 8, 1960. He lived in Colleyville from age 2. He attended Smithfield Elementary, North Richland Junior High, and he graduated from Richland High School in 1979. He was involved in his church youth group and choir. In the summer of 1978, Johnny went to Nicaragua with his church. This is where he met Gene. He was also involved in school-related activities such as Rebellaires, student body, and German Club. He attended Texas Wesleyan College. He worked part-time at Northeast National Bank until he graduated in 1982. He graduated with a degree in business administration. Upon graduation he became a loan officer for Northeast National Bank. He later became a graduate of the Southwestern Graduate School of Banking at Southern Methodist University. In 1992, after 12 years and three mergers, Johnny decided to leave banking for travel. He is now president and part owner of North Hills Travel and Cruises located in North Richland Hills.

After 14 years of marriage, they have four children: John Wilburn McIntosh Jr., born October 25, 1985; Lydia McIntosh, born November 12, 1987; Chloe McIntosh, born January 31, 1990; and Abigail McIntosh, born September 8, 1992. John attends North Richland Middle School, Lydia and Chloe attend Snow Heights Elementary, and Abigail attends preschool at church. Except for a short time in Euless, they have lived in North Richland Hills all their married life.

"The wonderful friends and neighbors we have has made North Richland Hills a wonderful place to live."

Submitted by Genoveva (Gene) McIntosh

MEACHAM FAMILY

During the year of 1879, William Henry Harrison Meacham (1839–1893) of Chatham County, North

Carolina, and his wife, Martha Ann Brown (1839–1914) of Ripley, Tennessee, moved their family of six children by covered wagon from Tennessee to the Birdville-Zion area, later named Smithfield. Settling on a farm, their house stood where Holiday Heights

William Alvin and Catherine Texana (Hightower) Meacham

Elementary School now stands on Susan Lee Lane. The Meacham children were George, William Calvin, Oliver, Walter, Tom, and Nancy.

William Calvin (Will) Meacham (1863–1925) married a local Smithfield girl, Catherine Texana Hightower (1865–1945) in 1886. Catherine was the daughter of Alfred M. and Sarah J. Grantham Hightower. Alfred is buried in the Smithfield Cemetery with a historical marker adorning his gravesite.

In 1897, Will and Catherine sold the dairy and moved the family by covered wagon to Norman, Oklahoma. After two years of farming in Oklahoma, the family moved back to Fort Worth to the Riverside Area. It was here that Alf, 9, and Guy, 6, attended a one-room school jokingly known as "Grass Burr College."

Will and Catherine eventually built the Meacham homestead on 100 acres at the southwest corner of the intersection of Watauga (Mid-Cities Boulevard) and Smithfield roads. There was evidence that Indians had a camp on the southwest quadrant of the land. Nearby was a spring from which the Indians got their water. There is no trace of the spring today, but during the ensuing years the Meacham children found many flint chippings and arrowheads in the vicinity.

The Meacham family's principal crops were cotton, corn, fruit, and berries grown on the sandy land, and wheat, oats, corn, and cattle on the black clay. After cotton became "king," they found it would grow on black land, too. Most communities had at least one cotton gin; Smithfield had two. Before cotton was cultivated in this area, the community had a lot of fruit and vegetables grown on the farms. There was a cannery at the triangle of Main and Amundson streets. The foundation for the cannery is still visible in front of a residence on this site. North of the cannery was a railroad station. The line was the St. Louis, Arkansas, and Texas Railway Company, which came to Texas in 1887. The Meacham children were kept busy during the week with school and chores, but Sunday was considered a special day, and the boys would gather at the train station morning and evening to experience the excitement of seeing the passengers come and go.

On the north side of the Meacham home was a storm cellar, which many homes had in those days. Not only was it used to store the food, which had been canned, but the ever-present danger of tornadoes made the cellar a neces-

sity. The cellar remains today. Much later, Will and Catherine moved to the Riverside area, selling the homestead to Guy and his family. Guy, his wife Madge, and daughter Margaret continued to live in the home until the 1980s when Guy sold the home and moved to Owen Drive. The house has since been demolished.

The family tree grew as Will's and Catherine's children married and had families. Alf married Becky Stovall and spent his life in education, retiring as assistant superintendent of schools in Fort Worth. Luther married Julia Louise Lyne. He was a real estate developer and appraiser, and Julia worked for a time as clerk of the 92nd District Court in Tarrant County. Allie remained single. She and her mother, Catherine, lived together on Rand Street, along with the families of Alf and Luther, on the east side of Fort Worth. Alf and Becky had four children: Jane, John Calvin, William Ross (Bill), and Marjorie. Luther and Julia had two children, Nancy Katheryn and Thomas Lyne.

Guy was called into service with the Army during World War I. When he returned from the war, he went to work for the U.S. Postal Service delivering mail in the Smithfield area. He married his high school sweetheart, Madge Smyth. A daughter, Beth, was born, but died the same day. On November 16, 1927, Mary Margaret was born. Guy knew everyone and he, Madge, and Margaret were well loved. They belonged to Smithfield Methodist Church along with their relatives, the Smyths and Browns. Many Sundays after church they would have a picnic at one of their homes and spend the afternoon eating homemade ice cream and visiting while the children safely played on the surrounding acreage.

Later, the Meacham grandchildren, Calvin, Bill, Marjorie, Nancy, and Tom, spent many happy days during their summers on the Meacham homestead. They would swing on the old tire, which always hung from a large tree in the front yard, play in the storm cellar, ride horses, and cross the road to the woods. The woods were a magical place where one could swing on grapevines, climb trees, and fish in the stock pond.

Alf's and Becky's children, Jane and John Calvin Meacham, did not marry. Both are now deceased. William Ross (Bill) Meacham married Irene Ashenfelter, and they had three children: William Kirk, Randall Browning (Andy), and Carolyn Ross (Carrie). Bill served in the Army during World War II, surviving the Battle of the Bulge. He returned to complete his studies in biology and spent 38 years as a professor of biology at the University of Texas at Arlington. William Kirk and Andy are not married. Andy, an urologist, lives in Denver,

Newlyweds-Mary Margaret (Smyth) and Arthur Guy Meacham

The Meacham boys

Colo. He has published a scientific journal and travels extensively speaking to various medical groups. Carrie, an attorney, married George Vogt, and they reside in Portland, Oregon, with their two boys, Sam and Thomas William. Bill later married June Huff, who died in 1994. He is now married to Helen Riley.

Marjorie married Charles Bounds, and their children are Rebecca Gee (Becky) and Charles Christopher (Chris). Marjorie, a teacher, and Charles, a clinical psychologist, have retired and continue to live in their family home in Austin. Chris also resides there with his wife, Melissa Myrlik, and two children, Katheryn Melissa and Charles Benjamin. Becky is living and working in Denver, Colorado.

Tom, the son of Luther and Julia, graduated from Texas Christian University and went directly to work for Continental Oil Company. He is presently vice president of Fairmont Supply Company in Washington, Pennsylvania. After graduation, he married Peggy Wills, and they had two daughters, Susan and Cinda. Susan married Loren Schmidt, and they have two sons, Alex and Maxwell. The Schmidts reside in Hockhessin, Delaware. Cinda married Bruce Munroe, and they reside in Denver, Colorado. Later, Tom married Karen Lundgren of Minneapolis, and they have one daughter, Kiersten, who attends the University of Michigan.

Nancy Katheryn had one career in federal service and another in the Fort Worth mayor's office before retiring in 1997. She married Edward (Eddie) Pafford, and they had two boys, Michael and Mark. Michael, a computer programmer, married Tina Boyd, and they have one son, Kyle. Michael presently resides in Atlanta, Georgia. Kyle lives in Haltom City with his mother, Tina Bennett, and is a junior at Haltom High School.

Descendants of the first Meachams to arrive in Smithfield still reside in this area. Nancy later married Charles Dowler (deceased), an administrator in the Birdville School District, and she presently lives within walking distance of the site of the Meacham homestead. Her son Mark's family lives in the same general area. Mark, who owns Bass Printing Company, and Montie (Hochreiter), have two children, Amber Nicole and Nicholas Ryan (Nick), a senior at Richland High School. Amber graduated from Richland in 1997 and is now studying marketing at Wade Marketing College in Dallas.

As the generations unfold, there is truly a draw to the North Richland Hills area, and in all probability, future generations will also reside in this pleasant family-oriented city.

Submitted by Nancy Dowler

ROBERT A. (R. A.) AND ANN MEEK

We moved to North Richland Hills in February 1977 when our new home on Camelot Court was completed. Our home was located in the Diamond Loch Addition. We are proud of our home!

The Meek Family: R. A. and Ann

When we first moved to the Diamond Loch area, we had some misgivings about a traffic problem. There were so many of our fellow North Richland Hills Baptist Church members living near us, we were concerned about traffic jams and automobile accidents due to the heavy traffic at that particular time each week when we all started to church.

It was when we decided to install our own lawn sprinkler system that we realized how bad the soil in our yard really was. We said it was 85 percent rock. Of course that was not true—it only seemed to be so when the ditching machine we rented threw me all over the yard. It was amazing that the job was ever finished! Only recently we learned that the lake in the center of the addition was at one time a gravel pit.

We have watched NRH grow from a small town to a city where we are proud to live. We have seen Rufe Snow grow from two lanes to at least four. In 1977, Keller was another town. Now, it is hard to tell where NRH stops and Keller begins. In spite of the growth it is still a place where we want to be!

Although I was born in Cisco, Texas, I grew up in north Fort Worth, graduated from North Side High School in 1949. By the middle of 1950, the Korean War was heating up and being concerned about the draft, I enlisted in the Air Force. The next four years were spent in the Air Force, 18 months of that in Japan and Korea. I came back to the States and was stationed at Roswell, New Mexico. It was a short 500-mile drive from there to Fort Worth, so my 1950 Studebaker made the trip many times.

The Corngrinders; L/R-J. E. Box, Lloyd Hinkle, R. A. Meek, Frank Shiller

Ann was born and raised in Oklahoma. Shortly after her graduation from high school in Achille, Oklahoma, Ann moved to Fort Worth to find a job. Ann and I met on one of my weekend trips from Roswell at Castleberry Baptist Church. After a very short courting period, we were married on June 12, 1953. The first five months of our marriage found Ann recuperating from a lung operation and my being transferred to Limestone, Maine. By the way, on the first leg of my flight to Limestone, Maine, I flew out of Amon Carter International Airport. I was transferred back to Carswell in November, 1953, and received my discharge from the Air Force in July, 1954.

We moved to Austin where I earned my bachelor's degree from the University of Texas School of Business, and Ann earned her PHT ("Putting Hubby Through").

After 12 years in Houston, we returned home to Fort Worth in 1969.

We soon found that we were missing family and friends who lived in the NRH area, so we decided to move here.

We have both been active in the North Richland Hills Baptist Church since 1973, and have been in every Greater Fort Worth Christmas Pageant that has been presented, starting with the Richland High School presentations and continuing at the Convention Center in downtown Fort Worth. We are both active in choir and members of the gospel group, The PraiseSong Trio, with Mary and Dan Kennedy. I sing and Ann is pianist for the group. We have been harmonizing together since a mission trip to Nicaragua in 1978 while riding in a bus on bumpy roads. This group has been a great blessing in our lives.

Another group that has been a big part of our lives since 1969 is "The Corngrinders." Lloyd Hinkle plays the harmonica, Frank Shiller plays the steel guitar and the banjo, J. E. Box plays the lead guitar, and I fill in on the bass guitar. We have just completed our 29th year of playing together and entertaining all sorts of groups—church, civic, business, anniversaries, birthdays, cowboys in the Davis mountains, fundraising luncheons at Fort Davis, family and friends in Rhode Island, to name just a few. One of our favorite places to play for the past 23 years has been the Fort Worth Woman's Club Summer Buffet. We four couples have traveled many miles together and had lots of fun. In all those miles and all those times on the road, we had car trouble once because someone had failed to put the radiator cap back on properly!

Submitted by R. A. Meek

L. E. AND FRIEDA MERRELL

L. E. (Gene) Merrell made a contribution to the growth of North Richland Hills. The Eden Addition, located off of Eden Road, was developed by Gene and a partner in 1986–88. There were 101 homes built in the addition. The streets in the addition were named for the Merrell's grandchildren, Melissa, Nicole, Jeffrey, Gregg, and Bradley.

Gene and Frieda Merrell moved from Richland Hills to North Richland Hills in 1963 when they built a home on

Vance Road. They have attended North Richland Hills Baptist Church for 32 years. Gene has served as a deacon since 1955 and has been chairman of the church's Finance and Missions Committees. He also served the Dallas-Fort Worth area as chairman of the Muscular Dystrophy Association from 1975 to 1992.

Gene and Frieda Merrell

Gene was born in Greenville, moving to Fort Worth as a teenager. He graduated from North Side High School and attended the University of Oklahoma. He married Frieda Morris in 1995. She was born in Fort Worth and graduated from Polytechnic High School. Gene was Santa Fe Railway's chief clerk for 37 years. After retiring, he became a real estate broker and a developer/builder. Frieda was a school secretary for the Birdville School District for 20 years. The Merrells moved to Hurst in 1981.

The Merrells have two children: Gene Franklin Merrell, who graduated from Richland High School and the University of Texas at Arlington, and Jane Lynn Merrell, also a graduate of Richland High. Gene Franklin has three children: Melissa, Nicole, and Jeffrey. Jane Lynn has two children: Gregory and Bradley Powers. The Merrells also have two great-grandchildren, Renae Lynn Powers, born August 29, 1995, and Madison Kate Lowrie, born September 19, 1997.

One of their most vivid memories of NRH is being able to hear from their Vance Road home the very loud dynamite explosions that occurred when Loop 820 was being built.

Submitted by L. E. Merrell

MATT AND SHERRY MILANO

Matt and Sherry Milano are originally from the Washington, D.C. area. Matt grew up in Maryland and Sherry in Virginia. Most of Sherry's family still resides in Virginia, with a brother in San Francisco. Matt's mother lives in Scottsdale, Arizona, and his father in Ft. Lauderdale, Florida. The Milanos moved to North Richland Hills in the summer of 1995 from San Francisco. Their hobbies are snow skiing, scuba diving, and all types of water sports. They have no children.

Matt and Sherry Milano

Matt attended the University of Maryland and earned his Ph.D. in clinical psychology at Ohio University. He moved to San Francisco to complete his internship at the Veterans Hospital in Martinez, California. He and Sherry met in San Francisco and they remained there for six years. Matt is vice president and chief operating officer of Trial Behavior Consulting Inc., a nationwide litigation consulting company. He also serves on the Board of Directors of the American Society of Trial Consultants. He has conducted research at the National Institute of Mental Health and has published research in national journals.

Sherry has been working in Information Technology (data processing) as a project manager in the Finance and Defense Industries for the past 18 years. Most of her Finance career has been with Wells Fargo and Nations Bank. Today, she is an independent consultant to companies throughout the Metroplex.

In late 1997, Matt and Sherry became active in local planning and zoning issues. In May 1998, Matt won the election for City Council-Seat 6 and was honored to be sworn into office by retiring Mayor Tommy Brown. Sherry has also just accepted an appointment on the NRH Park and Recreation Board. They are both excited to be a part of such a progressive and growing city.

ELMER AND GENEVA MILES

We were married July 3, 1954, in Arlington, Texas, and made our home in Fort Worth. At the time of our marriage, I was in the U.S. Air Force and stationed at Carswell Air Force Base, and Geneva worked for Houston Fire and Casualty Insurance Company in Fort Worth. Our main reasons for moving to North Richland Hills were to locate closer to my job at the new Amon Carter Airport, the availability of affordable housing, and we liked the area. We moved to NRH in April 1958 when our new house was completed in the Richland Terrace Addition. Our home was located at the corner of Oakland Lane and Cummings Drive. We lived at this address until December 1993 when we moved to our current address on Tabor Drive in NRH.

Our first child, Sharon Miles, was born July 1, 1960. James (Jimmy) Miles, was born August 16, 1963. Both children attended Snow Heights Elementary, North Richland Junior High, and graduated from Richland High School, in 1978 and in 1981. Both our children now live in Arlington.

When we moved into our new home, this part of the city was a new development. Cummings Drive ended at the back of our lot, and only a small-car, dirt path continued across Calloway Creek and into

Elmer and Geneva Miles

vacant pasture land that extended to Watauga Road. We thought we really lived in the country with no neighbors to our north and only a few houses to our west along Oakland Lane toward Holiday Lane. This life was too good to last, however, as a few years later Loop 820 was built a half block from our back property line. This was bad, and it was good. It was bad that Loop 820 was located in our back yard, and our quiet country atmosphere was gone. It was good that we now have other routes available to go downtown Fort Worth or southeast Fort Worth other than having to drive Belknap Street or take Handley Ederville Road to Oakland Boulevard, Miller Street, etc.

In the early 1960s, there were only a few businesses in NRH other than the small shopping center where Buddies Grocery and Hardware, a cafeteria, Mott's 5 & 10, barber shop, and drugstore were located. Also there was a 7-Eleven convenience store and some service stations. If you wanted to eat out, go to a movie or an evening's entertainment, you had to go to Fort Worth or Dallas.

DEE OWEN AND BETTE JO MILLER

I was born November 18, 1926, in Fort Worth and started to school at W. J. Turner. In 1933, we moved to Smithfield, and they put me in the second grade. Some of my teachers and superintendents were Martha W. Meissner, C. C. White, Maxine Shaw, Roy Clendinning, Floyd E. Smith, Berte C. Ragsdale, R. N. Riddle, and A. D. Roach. At Smithfield School, we played softball, pitched washers, played marbles and wolf-over-the-river. We furnished our own stuff to play with; there was not a coach or director except the principal or sometimes a teacher.

Smithfield discontinued its high school, and I transferred to Riverside for the ninth grade. My teachers at Riverside were Ellis, Truelson, Scott, Cunningham, and Chrisman. Julius Truelson wanted me to play football, but I wanted to take shop, so he made me play volleyball with the girls, and I quit school. That was the end of my formal education. I went to Amon Carter-Riverside High School two and a half semesters, and I quit in January 1941, to get a job. The rest of my schooling was the "school of hard knocks" and self-learning.

My grandmother would walk with me to Messick's Corner, and there I would meet Alice McCamble, and we would walk down the railroad tracks to Smithfield. Grandmother would meet me there in the evening or at Amundson's. In 1935 or 1936, the school got a new Ford bus. Oscar B. Tallman was our first driver; he later went to work for Leonard Brothers, and Jim Holder drove the bus. We were supposed to live two miles from the school to ride, but they let Johnny Rumfield, his sisters, and me ride anyway.

I remember in about 1939 or 1940, we had bicycle races from Snider's Store to the Smithfield School Road and Redding Grocery Store. Barber Cobb would give the winner a free haircut (worth 15 or 25 cents), or Margaret and Sam Snider would give a pint of ice cream, whichever you wanted. I won several of those races. Leonard Brother's store would provide free picture shows on Wednesday night on the school ground. We used to have medicine shows between the ice dock and Wiseman Filling Station. The filling station, across the street from the Baptist Church, used to be Walker's before Wiseman and Redding ran it.

After I quit school, I worked at the ice dock for Lewis Fry for $1 a day, seven days a week. Lewis Fry's mother and George Fry ran the store next to the old post office operated by Jess Turner and Charlie Ed Turner. After the ice dock job, I got a job with the NYA. I dug up stumps at Carswell Air Force Base—for one day—and that was enough for me. My next job was as a mechanic's helper at the city garage. From there I transferred to the county garage, and then, later, I worked for the county jail until it closed down. After that, I worked at the Precinct 3 Garage in Birdville. There I worked with Jess Holder, John McCain, Tony Turk, Tuffy Gilbert, and Walter Autrey. We built and patched roads and built fences.

Finally, I ended up working at the American Manufacturing Co. until I went into the Army.

I married Bette Jo Gerth of Smithfield on October 8, 1943. We were married 39 years. She passed away February 24, 1984, in Smithfield. We have four daughters, six grandsons, one granddaughter, two great-granddaughters, and one great-grandson.

Daughter Deena Miller Bailey, born in 1945, married Charles Henry Bailey Jr., born 1963. They had three boys. Daughter Deborah Dene Miller Easton married Mike L. Easton, and they had two children. Daughter Melissia Miller Norrell married Stephen Wayne Norrel, they have no children except me and Millie, their dog. Daughter Jackie Miller Allen Williams married James Dwayne Allen, and they had two sons.

My father was Dee Owen Miller. He was born in Jack County in 1904. He was killed in 1935 when a trailer truck hit his car head-on where Richland Plaza Shopping Center is now. My mother was Winnie Alma Rix Miller, born in 1908 in Gordon, Texas, and died in Smithfield in 1971.

Bette Jo's father, Hiram Gregor Gerth, was born in 1876. He died in 1951. Her mother was Zanna Melissia Pemberton Gerth who was born in 1884 and died in Smithfield in 1969. Bette Jo had five sisters and three brothers. The girls were Iva Kirk, Gladys Rose, Edna Jeannet, Alta Mae Oxford, and Martha Nell Rapp. The boys were Thurmond, Marvin, and Doris Raymond Gerth.

Submitted by Dee Owen Miller Jr.

ROY AND ANN MILLER

Roy and Ann Miller moved with their family from San Antonio to North Richland Hills in 1957. Since the Miller family moved to North Richland Hills, growth and change in the city have been monumental.

Roy Miller was born in 1926, the third child of Roy King and Kathryn Jane Miller. He attended Dallas schools and graduated from Woodrow Wilson High School. During World War II, from 1943–1946, he served in the South Pacific with the Marine Air Corp.

Roy Miller, 1987

After returning from the service, he began his insurance career as a clerk with a company in Dallas, a position with the State Board of Insurance in Austin, and a field representative for a large insurance company from 1972 until his death.

Ann Miller was born in 1927, the older of two daughters of John T. and Maurita Fay Luther. She attended Dallas schools and graduated from Woodrow Wilson High School. She then attended Southern Methodist University where she was a business major and a member of Kappa Alpha Theta Sorority.

Roy and Ann met at a school dance in 1946, and dated until their marriage in 1949. David, the oldest of their five children, was born in 1950, followed by Deborah in 1952, and Paul in 1956. In 1959, Van was born and Alan came along in 1964.

The Miller family lived on Vance Road for 30 years. They raised their children across the street from the Hubert Joyner and George Riddle families. The 12 children of these families are married with children of their own, and they all remain close friends.

Many wonderful memories were born in the years the families were neighbors, with backyard cookouts, coffee get-togethers, children playing in the yards, and swimming in the Riddle's pool on summer afternoons.

Snow Heights Elementary School was a block from their home, and North Richland Junior High was just another block away. All of the Miller children attended these schools and later Richland High School. Alan attended both Richland and Haltom High schools.

Perhaps what is best remembered about the Miller sons is basketball. All of the boys were tall and played basketball through junior high and high school and were on all-district and all-regional teams. Through the years, there were countless, heated two-on-two games played on the goal in the Millers' front driveway.

Basketball was a big part of the Miller family's life for 20 years. There were many weeks when Roy and Ann attended seven or eight games.

Ann Miller (center); L/R-Alan, Deborah, David, Paul, and Van Miller, 1997

Deborah, the Miller's only daughter, graduated from Richland in 1970. She was chosen to be on an area department store teen board for three years, where she was a teen model. She attended Stephen F. Austin State University and Tarrant County Junior College.

After the children were grown and married, Roy and Ann moved just one mile west of Vance Road to a home on Cliffside Drive. Roy passed away in August 1987, and Ann continues to live there.

She is a member of First United Methodist Church of Fort Worth, where she is a volunteer at the church mission in the Infant Formula Program. She is a member of the Fort Worth Woman's Club. She enjoys traveling, playing bridge, reading, and most of all, her 10 grandchildren.

David is cofounder of EnCap Investments, an oil and gas investment firm with offices in Dallas and Houston. David and his wife, Mary Lee, met while they were at SMU and married. They have two children, Kyle and Meredith.

Deborah has been an American Airlines flight attendant for 21 years. She is married to Tom Sanford, a California native and UCLA graduate. Tom was an Air Force fighter pilot flying the F-15 before becoming an American Airlines pilot. Tom and Deborah have two children, Audrey and Andrew.

Paul continues to live in North Richland Hills. He and his wife, Jodi, an Ohio native who attended Akron University, live in Meadow Lakes. They have two sons, Matthew and Christian.

Van and his wife, Melissa, met while attending Southwest Texas State University, where they both graduated. They live in Keller with their two children, Brooke and Lance.

Alan, the youngest son, married Meg Rodgers, also a North Richland Hills native. They both attended UT Austin, and graduated in 1987. Alan received his bachelor's degree from UT Austin and his master's from SMU. He and Meg have two little girls, Hayley and Lindsey.

Ann feels very blessed that all of her children and grandchildren remain nearby, and she is able to see them often.

Submitted by Ann Miller

DENVER L. AND JACQUELINE L. MILLS

The Mills family—parents, Denver Laverne and Jacqueline Louise, and their children, Nancy Gail and Susan Louise—moved into their new home on Nancy Lane in North Richland Hills in March 1959. We

Denver and Jackie Mills, 1976

moved into our new Johnny Sandlin-built home on Carol Court in May 1962. Johnny was principal of Snow Heights Elementary and moonlighted building homes.

Denver was active in city affairs until 1980, serving on the Planning and Zoning Board, Zoning Board of Variances, and later the City Council for two terms. Some of the highlights encountered in office were getting the old worn-out streets repaved, bringing a firm water supply to NRH from Trinity River Authority and the City of Fort Worth, building a new City Hall, also home to the library and Police Department, developing a park system, approving new subdivisions, and getting our own mall so that we wouldn't have to go to Hurst to shop, and we could derive all of that much needed tax revenue.

We moved to California in 1964 in order for Denver to obtain a master's degree in economic engineering from Stanford; and again in 1968 for Denver to have a year's experience at the Corps of Engineers Laboratory in Sacramento. During each move, we rented out our home on Carol Court so we could return home to our friends and neighbors.

In May 1984, the Corps of Engineers transferred Denver to Little Rock, Arkansas, as chief of engineering for the district. It was a tearful move, since we had to sell our Carol Court home. Nancy and Susan cleaned out the attic because Jackie would cry and couldn't throw anything away. We are still wondering about certain items.

Nancy and Susan Mills, 1976

Upon Denver's retirement from the Corps, we moved to Salado, Texas to be near our children.

Nancy, her husband John Mackey, and their two children, Charlotte, 11, and Price, 13, reside in Temple. Nancy is editor of the Quarterly Magazine for Scott and White Hospital. John is an insurance broker.

Susan and her daughter, Erin Louis Miller, also reside in Temple. Susan is principal of Belton High School.

Denver served on the NRH City Council from 1976-1980, and both he and Jackie have been very active in the Salado-Temple/Belton area since moving there. Jackie has been involved with the "Salado Legends" play since 1993, both in writing and directing.

HUGH AND JOY MINGLE

Hugh and Joy Mingle arrived in North Richland Hills from Vienna, Austria, in August 1984. Our youngest son, Jeffrey Bach Mingle, was a sophomore in high school, and we entered him into Fort Worth Christian School. He graduated in 1987. Hugh Rice Mingle was born in 1927 in Detroit, Michigan. Marion Joy Smith Mingle was born in 1928 in Logan County, Kentucky. Jeffrey Bach Mingle was born in 1969 in Abilene, Texas. Our three older children, Timothy Hugh, Beth, and Bonnie, were born in Germany and are married with families.

We met at Harding College, Searcy, Arkansas, and married in 1951. Immediately after our marriage, we were called to Germany as missionaries where we worked with the Churches of Christ and started our own family. We have lived in Michigan, then Texas, California, then Texas, Austria, and back to Texas. We think we have found a great retirement home here in NRH! Our current address is Redondo. Joy is retired from American Airlines, and Hugh has reentered the full-time work force at the World Bible Translation Center after retiring from Horace Mann Insurance Company. We have 13 grandchildren and with eight of them living in the area, we are very busy grandparents!

We are members at Richland Hills Church of Christ. We also attend services at Lakewood Retirement Center. Hugh is a World War II Army veteran. We enjoy traveling, singing, gardening, biking, walking, and entertaining (grandchildren, mostly!).

RUSSELL AND HOLLY MITCHELL

When Russell (Russ) was born in 1953 his family was living in a home located just yards from where Cuco's Restaurant now sits on Glenview Drive. It was considered Richland Hills at that time but is now a part of North Richland Hills. This officially makes him a true native of North Richland Hills.

Standing-Holly, Amanda, Russ, and Shannon Mitchell

Russell spent the majority of his growing up years in Haltom City. During high school he worked in Montgomery Ward's lawn and garden department in the old Richland Plaza. He graduated from the original Haltom High School, attended Tarrant County Junior College, Howard Payne University, and Northwood University in Dallas majoring in business. While attending college he worked in the insurance industry for several companies before establishing his present business with Farmers' Insurance in 1991.

Holly was born and reared in Miami, Florida. She graduated from the University of Florida with a bachelor's degree in early childhood education in 1978. Holly moved to Texas in 1979 after being hired by American Airlines for flight attendant training. She was based at Dallas/Fort Worth Airport upon graduation and has just completed her 19th year as an American Airlines flight attendant.

Russell and Holly met in 1983 through mutual friends. They married in October 1984 and moved into their newly built home on Post Oak Drive in NRH. Their first daughter, Shannon, was born in 1986, and their second daughter, Amanda, was born in 1991. They also have a son, Shane, age 23, from a previous marriage.

Russell became interested in local politics in early 1990. He entered and ran in several council and mayoral races throughout the '90s. He won council seat place two in May 1998. He has served on the NRH Park and Recreation Board, North East Transportation Committee (NETS), is a member of the Northeast Tarrant County Chamber of Commerce, Lions Club, and Tarrant County precinct chairman and election judge.

Shane Mitchell, 1993

In 1995, Russell and his family moved four blocks from Post Oak Dr. to their current home on Old Hickory Drive in NRH. They love the unhurried lifestyle and country atmosphere that part of the city offers while still being close to all the amenities of North Richland Hills.

Aside from politics, Russell and his family enjoy traveling, camping, swimming, and spending time together as a family. They are active members of Harvest Baptist Church in Watauga where Russell is currently a deacon and Sunday school teacher. Holly sings in the choir and also teaches Sunday school.

Their daughters attend Harvest Christian Academy (church affiliated) where both Russell and Holly are very involved in school activities and the Parent Teacher Fellowship.

The family truly enjoys living in North Richland Hills. It is a great city to live in and raise a family. They look forward to being a part of NRH's bright future.

WALTER MONTGOMERY
MEMORIES OF SMITHFIELD - 1930 TO 1946

Walter "Monty" and Eda Montgomery moved to Smithfield from Fort Worth in 1929, along with a daughter, Juanita, and son, G. R. "Jiggs." Another daughter, Lavelle, was born in 1934. Walter Montgomery was a welder at Swift & Co. on Fort Worth's North Side.

Their home was located atop a small hill on 10 acres (now the site of the North Richland Hills Post Office). Looking due south from the home, you could see the cars turning off the Grapevine Highway (known then as Four Points) in late evening or night by their headlights. There was little traffic, but if you were expecting someone to arrive at that time, it was easy to see them coming. The road from Four Points to downtown Smithfield made an "S" curve around the Montgomery property. The curve is no longer there having been replaced by the direct route of busy Davis Boulevard.

They attended Smithfield Methodist Church. The Montgomery family was active in all aspects of the community, school, and Smithfield Methodist Church, which was a small country church served by ministers every other Sunday during its early days. On "preaching" Sunday the minister always had open invitations from the ladies of the church for dinner with the family—a really sumptuous feast, but usual Sunday fare for most families on the Sabbath. Home-grown vegetables, meats, and rich desserts were served. Summer revival services and Bible school held by the Methodist and Baptist churches were shared and enjoyed by all the community together, regardless of church affiliation.

Rev. Charles Johnson and his wife, Nell, a very young couple of a Baptist church, started the first Boy Scout and Girl Scout troops in the mid-1930s for anyone who wanted to join.

I, Juanita Montgomery Tandy, recall many facets of my life in Smithfield. Many memories recalled involve those days at Smithfield school. Sometime in the early or mid-1930s, high school students were sent by bus to Riverside High School (which became Amon Carter-Riverside) in Fort Worth. First grade was in a small white building just south of the red-brick, two-story school building. This later was a small cafeteria, which served plate lunches for 5 cents.

In early March, the school bus took the children to the Fat Stock Show on Exchange Avenue in North Fort Worth for the day, leaving from the school in the morning and returning home in the afternoon. In later years, this became today's Southwestern Exposition & Live Stock Show at the Will Rogers complex in west Fort Worth.

Teachers were required to live in the community (residing with a local family if they did not have their own residence there) and were expected to attend one of the local churches at least twice each month. School board members required each teacher hired to have a teaching degree/certificate. They were quite proud of this, as it was not always a requisite in small country schools during those days.

There were many families who played caring and important roles in the lives of Smithfield residents and the community—the Amundsons, Parkmans, Autreys, Hays, Lewises, Gilberts, Hightowers, Sniders, Scotts, Cardwells, Walkers, and Montgomerys. Particularly during Depression years and World War II time, everyone cared, shared, and looked after others.

The family, whose name is at the front of all, was that of Mr. and Mrs. A. G. Meacham (Guy and Madge) and their daughter, Margaret, my close and dear friend at school and away. Mrs. Meacham's mother and sister, Mrs. Smyth, and her daughter, Lois, had the town's telephone switchboard in their home. There were few telephones scattered across the area; but as well as providing telephone service, the switchboard was the source of important news, both good and tragic. Mrs. Guy Meacham played the piano at the Methodist Church, taught the Intermediate Class (following primary age and before junior high age), and was active in the PTA and all community affairs. Guy Meacham taught the young people's class in Sunday school. It was made up of the young single adults. His wonderful deep bass voice was always in the choir section. Their daughter, Margaret, was an accomplished violinist who studied under Brooks Morris of Fort Worth. Her special music presentations were indeed a wonderful treat on many Sundays, even after she went away to college and to a life away from Smithfield.

These are only a few of my memories of my early life

in Smithfield from 1929 to 1946. Friends and family members still live in that area, now North Richland Hills. You have to close your eyes to remember the little town that is today a large growing town, growing larger each day. It is impossible to list all those so important in the life of Smithfield, and I am sure there are many others who will cover more than I.

Submitted by Juanita Montgomery Tandy

G. R. MONTGOMERY FAMILY

G. R. Montgomery and Billie Montgomery, 1985

My name is Nola Myrene Montgomery Sanders. My parents and most of my relatives have been lifelong Smithfield residents. I lived in the same house in Smithfield that my dad also grew up in, from my birth in 1953 until I began a travel career as an American Airlines flight attendant in 1974. After being based in New York City for 18 long months, I was thankful when I was able to transfer to Dallas/Fort Worth Airport, and appreciated Texas more than ever.

My parents, G. R. Montgomery and Billie Autrey Montgomery, met when they were in the first grade together at Smithfield School. Apparently, their romance began when G. R. (Jiggs) ran Billie into the ditch in the first grade and kissed her!

My father's parents were Walter Lee Montgomery, who was born July 1885, and Eda Laura Storie Montgomery, born in July 1886.

The Montgomerys moved from Fort Worth to Smithfield in 1929, when G. R. was 6 years old. They bought 14 acres of land about a mile south of Main Street. A fire burned their home in June of 1934. That fall, they built another house that became the family home place where Eda and Walter raised their children, and also where G. R. and Billie later raised their family. My parents sold the property in 1984, and in 1987 we had the house moved to my land near Weatherford, where it sits once again in a rural area. I had the house restored, and jokingly call it our family "museum." The North Richland Hills Post Office on Davis Boulevard now occupies the site of our old home place.

Both of my mother's parents grew up in Smithfield. Her father, Walter Napoleon Autrey, was born Nov. 1883. He worked for the county, guarding prisoners in his younger years, and then, later, driving a maintainer doing road work. In 1920, he married Etha Mae Swain who was born in October 1897. They bought several acres next to the railroad track on the east side of Smithfield Road, where a lumber company is at present. They had eight children: Ruby Lee (Jansky), a son, W. M., who died just a month before his second birthday after his clothing caught fire from a stove; my mother, Billie Louise (Montgomery); Mildred Lucille (Burton); Welton Cantrell; May Jean (Hamilton); Mary Helen (Koonce); and Oren Swain, "O. S." All of the children were born at home, and if the doctor was not available, neighborhood women came to help with the delivery.

My parents attended Smithfield School through seventh grade, then went to high school at Riverside High School.

After G. R. completed his service in the U.S. Army, he and Billie married on October 16, 1948. I was born on November 18, 1953, and my brother, George Robert Martin Montgomery III (George or "Nubbin"), was born on June 12, 1956. George married Janelle Rogers in 1977. They live in Springtown now, and they have three sons, George Robert Martin Montgomery IV (Marty), Joshah Michael Roger Montgomery, and Philip Daniel Ryan Montgomery.

Mother quit her job as a bookkeeper at the Star-Telegram when I was born and did not return to a paying job until after my brother was in school. She spent the next 20 years working for Birdville school cafeterias, where she began as a substitute and then became a cafeteria manager.

Daddy worked at the Swift & Co. meatpacking house in Fort Worth and had a welding business at home called Montgomery's Welding Shop. He was often called upon to do everything from small repair jobs to building fences and cattle gates. My brother and I were very proud of the fact that Daddy built the bleachers at Green Valley Raceway when it opened.

We lived at the "Y" of "old" and "new" Smithfield roads. I remember the big trucks making and paving the "new" Smithfield Road, which is now known as Davis Boulevard. There was a small gas station built at the intersection in the early 1960s, and I remember my parents talking about a "gas war" (I could picture it!) and gas being 19 cents a gallon.

G. R. Montgomery and Billie Louise Autrey (Montgomery) and their first grade class, Smithfield, 1930. First Row- Jimmie Ray Scott, Opal Garrett, Kenneth Mahaffey, Leora Autrey, Billie Louise Autrey, Harry McCarmick, Wendell Zartman, G. R. Montgomery, Jimmie Lou Camel, Marzell Elston: Second Row- Jack Marvin Palmer, Glenn Walker, Grace Rumfield, Lane Davis, Geraldine Sturch, Wilma Zartman, Lucille Parkman, Jean Tennison: Third Row- Elizabeth Brooks, Charles Fisher, R. B. Watts, Marvin Reynolds, L. J. Palmer, P. H. Corbet, Ollie May Autrey.

There were three churches—Methodist, Baptist, and Church of Christ—and all were a very important part of the community. My family went to Smithfield Methodist, but we would also sometimes attend revivals or other activities at the Baptist church. The smell of honeysuckle and gardenia reminds me of those summers at church. When I was in high school, I played the piano and organ for Sunday night services and sometimes for Sunday morning. Jack Pemberton and King Bell were choir directors, and as my musical education was in progress, and my experience limited, they let me choose my favorite songs for the singing. I always picked happy, lively songs like "When the Roll is Called Up Yonder," "Showers of Blessings," and "Love Lifted Me." My daddy played the mandolin and sang.

The Smithfield Masonic Lodge was also a big part of life in the community, and Daddy was a member for 44 years. He was a past master, a district deputy grand master, and the Smithfield Masonic Lodge secretary for about 25 years.

My grandfather, Walter Autrey, lived next to the railroad tracks on old Smithfield Road, and he had several acres of pasture with horses, and a barn with a hay loft. The family, with all my aunts, uncles, and cousins, met there at PaPa's every Sunday for dinner, and the kids always ate in the kitchen. There were big glasses of sweet iced tea, and I remember there were lots of pies and cakes safely out of reach on top of the buffet hutch until after the meal. After dinner, the women did the dishes, and the men played cards or board games. The children played in the barn or in the yard, climbed trees and the water tower, had chinaberry "wars," and dropped things in the well. My uncles enjoyed practicing "bucking bulls" on a barrel that they had strung up with springs. Sometimes Aunt Juanita would play the piano, and everyone would sing hymns.

When I was growing up in the 1950s and '60s, there were no restaurants in the area. In the 1960s, Fred Morrow opened Fred's Bar-B-Q about a half-mile south of our house, and that is the first cafe that I remember in town.

My uncles were members of the Smithfield Volunteer Fire Department. Whenever a fire call came in, there was a relay type of notification. The men left to answer the fire call, and the wives had a list of other firemen to be telephoned. The first man to arrive at the station would sound the siren to notify others available within hearing distance. If the fire call went on for several hours, the wives would bring sandwiches and beverages to refresh the firemen.

In some ways, our city has evolved very carefully and deliberately. Perhaps that conservative approach is what has kept the hometown atmosphere and pride alive in North Richland Hills, in spite of its phenomenal growth.

I'm proud of the city that North Richland Hills has become (although we "old-timers" still often call it Smithfield). We daily take for granted all the conveniences that we have today, with police and fire protection, "city water," a library, shopping, restaurants, and movies. But every time I walk into the North Richland Hills Post Office, I think back to a more intimate town and a slower time. I have fond memories of growing up on that hill, and I am thankful for the wonderful foundation that my parents and all the townspeople of Smithfield gave to me.

Submitted by Myrene Montgomery Sanders

BILLIE T. AND LORIE T. MOORE

Billie T. Moore and Lorie T. Moore reside on Havana Drive, in the Holiday Heights section of North Richland Hills. They moved to NRH in 1993 from Atlanta.

Lorie was born in Griffin, Georgia, a small, but growing, town near Atlanta. She is a graduate of Florida A&M University in Tallahassee, Florida, and has worked in public school systems half-way around the world. She is currently employed with the Fort Worth Independent School District as an elementary school teacher.

Bill was born in a small town called Ozark, Alabama, but was raised in north Florida. Bill earned his master of arts degree in criminal justice administration at the Atlanta University in Atlanta. He retired from the U.S. Air Force in 1982 after 21 years of faithful service. He is currently employed with the Department of Defense. He is an appointed member of the NRH City Council, serving on the Teen Court Committee. He is also a member of the Northeast Tarrant County United Way steering committee.

The Moores are members of the Richland Hills Church of Christ. Bill enjoys golfing, while Lorie enjoys working with culturally deprived kids, preparing them for a brighter future.

JAMES AND GLADYS MORAN

The family of Gladys and James Moran moved from Fort Worth to North Richland Hills in 1958, building a house on Redondo Drive.

All our children attended newly built Snow Heights Elementary.

Our children went horseback riding in the area south of where the loop is now, west of Rufe Snow to Fossil Creek. The only pool for recreation swimming in the area was at Barrbrook Park in Haltom City. It was a very nice large pool. One of the highlights of the day for our children in the summer was to visit the snow-cone stand on Blaney Street near Mott's. The snow-cone stand remained in that location for many years. In talking to our children about their memories of growing up in NRH, they mentioned these things; playing and riding bikes in the open fields around our house, catching crawfish in the drainage ditch behind our house on Redondo, and taking hikes and exploring the gravel pits near Fossil Creek. Many times they went jogging on Rufe Snow toward Watauga because there was very little traffic.

Standing, L/R-David Rick, Rob, Dr. James (Randy), Cliff, Brenda, Lance; Seated-James, Gladys, Sherry Moran Gehring

Our family first began attending the Richland Hills Church of Christ when it was at the Grapevine Highway location. James' mother, Myrtle Moran, was a charter member. The church is now located near the golf course along Loop 820.

James Reuben Moran was born in 1925, to Myrtle (Cooper) Moran, and George Buford Moran. James' family moved from Oklahoma to New Mexico when he was 5 years of age.

He had one sister, Georgia Lee (Moran) Stephens (deceased April 12, 1988). He graduated from Albuquerque High School in 1943. From high school, he went into the Army Air Force Engineers. He fought in the Pacific during World War II, starting in Australia and ending up in Tokyo. He was overseas about two years.

Following discharge, he attended the University of New Mexico, graduating in 1950.

His parents moved to Fort Worth about 1946. They owned and operated a skating rink on N. Main Street in Fort Worth for about 15 years. James married Gladys Eva Anderson in 1950, and operated his parents' skating rink for a couple of years. He went to work for Bell Helicopter as an engineer in 1953. He retired in January 1989 after 37 years of service.

Gladys Eva (Anderson) Moran was born in 1925 to Mettie May (Smyth) Anderson, and Causen Alexander Anderson. Soon after her birth, her family moved to Wichita Falls, then Keller.

Gladys Moran lived in Keller during her years of schooling. She had four brothers and one sister. Her father was a farmer. Gladys' parents, grandparents, brother, and two aunts and uncles are buried at Bourland Cemetery in Keller. She graduated from Keller High School in 1943. She remembers the years her brothers played football at Keller, and that Birdville High School (now Haltom) was their biggest rival. She remembers going to the games and being in the Keller Pep Squad.

We moved to Cylinda Sue Circle in 1970 and have resided there since that time. Our four children grew up in the North Richland Hills area.

James Randall (Randy) born in 1950, David Ricky born 1954, Sherry Lynne, born 1956, and Robbin (Rob) Kent, born 1959. The boys were all active in little League, Boy Scouts, and school sports. Randy graduated from Richland in 1968, later married Brenda Lou Daniels, and is a dentist in Hurst. They have two sons.

Rickey graduated from RHS in 1972, married Michelle Ann Pawelek from Poth, Texas. He works as a geophysist for Tesoro Petroleum Company in San Antonio. They have two children.

Sherry graduated in 1974. She works in a management position for Frito-Lay, married Jay Gehring, and lives in Carrollton. They have a daughter.

Rob graduated in 1978 and is an active attorney in the Fort Worth-Arlington area. He lives in the TCU area of Fort Worth.

Many changes have taken place in the North Richland

Hills area since the Morans moved here. We used to always see friends when we went out into the community. Now it is a big part of the Metroplex. We are proud to live in the great city of North Richland Hills.

Submitted by Gladys E. Moran

STANLEY AND MARGARET MORRIS

Stanley Burton Morris was born March 6, 1921, in Dallas. Margaret Elizabeth Walker was born November 9, 1924, in Stone County, Missouri. They met during World War II when Stanley was stationed at Camp Shelby, Mississippi. He was a master sergeant in the 69th Infantry Division. Margaret was a civilian employee for the Quartermaster Corps.

Stanley served our country in England, France (where his feet froze), and Germany, where he witnessed the linkage of the United States with Russia.

After the war ended, Stanley settled in Fort Worth with his family. Almost immediately, he was employed by

Back-Gary and Carey; Front-Stanley, Mark, Margaret, 1963

Southwestern Bell Telephone Company, retiring in 1978 as a repair supervisor.

Margaret had moved to Oklahoma City where her family lived, later accepting a job with the Veterans Administration in Washington, D.C. Margaret and Stanley were married April 6, 1947, in the First Baptist Church, Oklahoma City.

Fort Worth became their home, and the place where their children were born. Twins Carey Lynn and Gary Gwyn were born on December 7, 1948, and Mark Allan on December 12, 1954.

With a desire for suburban life, they found a house in "little" North Richland Hills, which had a grocery store, post office, and school nearby. Tabor Street was only one long block, a rugged, undeveloped trail, with a dead end at Rufe Snow Road, in poor condition. To the north and west, there were only wooded areas and wild animals. They thought they would have "space" forever. They moved there Oct. 15, 1956.

Stanley and Margaret joined the Richland Hills Baptist Church, where their membership remains today. Carey and Gary were choir members.

Carey and Mark both played Little League and Bronco League baseball sponsored by the Northeast Optimist Club. For their family this began many years of pleasure and community service, perhaps thousands of hours of work involving baseball.

As third graders, Carey and Gary entered the North Richland Elementary talent show, winning first place with Carey playing piano and Gary singing. Today, Carey is pianist and music coordinator in her church, while Gary remains a singer.

Carey played in the band in junior high, high school, and college and was a majorette in junior and senior high school. She attended Tarleton State University and graduated from Howard Payne University with a degree in elementary education. She lives in Tucson, Ariz., and is administrative assistant in the Department of Communication at the University of Arizona. She has two lovely daughters, Kristi and Heather.

With a great enthusiasm for sports and a desire to excel, Gary was the first person to letter in four sports at Richland High School. At Cisco Junior College, he also played baseball, football, and basketball.

Gary has enjoyed a very successful career in the entertainment industry. He has traveled all over the world sharing his talents. He appeared in the television specials, "The All-Star Salute to our Troops" and "Welcome Home of the Troops Returning from Desert Storm." Gary entertained the troops during the Bosnia-Sarajevo crisis.

He has four wonderful sons, Samuel (Sam) Alexander, Matthew (Matt) Burton, Hunter Drake, and Garon Hurley. Garon was born November 14, 1997, in New York.

Mark, the youngest Morris son, is a born salesman. As a sales manager, he travels over a large territory. He is a great outdoorsman and could have survived well as an early settler in our country. He would enjoy living in a year-round climate of 35 to 40 degrees, arising at 4 A.M., and heading for the "hunting ground." He especially enjoys bow and arrow season. If a hunting season is not open, he can be found at his lake where he enjoys fishing, or with his family taking a horseback ride or maybe just picking wildflowers. Fortunately, Mark lives in the "Hills of Oklahoma" and can do things he and his family enjoy. He has three beautiful daughters, Melissa, Brittani, and Shana.

Submitted by Margaret Morris

MELVIN AND ESTELLE MORROW

Melvin Morrow and his wife, Estelle Willis, have lived on Arnold Terrace since 1966. Melvin is the grandson of a cir-

Back, L/R-Melvin, Sam, Doyle, Estelle; Front, L/R-Carolyn Morrow Hicks, Donnie

cuit riding Methodist minister. He is retired from the city of Fort Worth where he was equipment director. During his long employment there, he worked with Rodger Line (later a city manager for North Richland Hills).

Estelle worked as secretary to the administrator of Glenview Hospital. They have four children, eleven grandchildren and twenty great-grandchildren. They are active members of Christian Temple Church in North Richland Hills.

During their retirement, they have enjoyed camping and traveling with church friends and family.

Submitted by Betty Leslie

M. E. MUSGROVE AND FAMILY

The M. E. Musgrove family established their home in North Richland Hills in 1960, the first to live on Standley Drive. At that time the family consisted of M. E., his wife Barbara, their son Michael Lynn, born July 1957, and one on the way, Kimberly Kay, born October 1960. Six years passed before their youngest was born, Pamela Gay, in 1966.

Back-Mike and Kim; Front-M. E., Barbara, and Pam

M. E. started that same year, 1960, at Bell Helicopter where he is still employed as an aeronautical experimental engineer. Barbara is a landlord to six rent houses—also a "domestic engineer."

Their oldest child, Mike, started elementary school at Smithfield until Holiday Heights was built. He then attended the new Watauga Junior High, where he voted on the school colors and mascot. He went on to Richland High School, was very active in track and received many medals, graduated in 1975. He graduated from the University of Texas at Arlington in 1979. Mike bought his first home in NRH at the corner of Topper Court and Noreast Drive. There he began his family with his wife, Laura Abbott-Musgrove, and daughter, Casey Lynn, born September 20, 1992. They now live in Southlake and are still active with the Richland Hills Church of Christ.

M. E. and Barbara's eldest daughter, Kim, attended the same schools. At Richland High, she was active in Basketball Goaltenders and was an honor student, graduating in 1979. She graduated from University of North Texas with a bachelor of business administration in 1983. She married Richard Thut and moved to Maryanna Way, also in NRH. They welcomed two girls, Chelsea Ann, born in June 1989, and Linsey Catherine, born in 1992. They now reside in Bedford.

The youngest daughter, Pam, attended the same schools as Kim. Graduating in 1985, Pam was active in

her church youth group at Midtown Church of Christ. She then went to Abilene Christian University, receiving a bachelor of science degree in 1989. After returning from college, she married Kevin Burnett, who, as it should be, lived in NRH all of his life within five miles of the Musgrove's home. Pam and Kevin live in NRH on Timberline Court and on April 10, 1996, welcomed a son, Joshua Lee, to their home.

After nine years on Standley Drive, M. E., Barbara, and family moved in 1969 down the street to Joreen Drive. Here they lived and loved for 26 years. Their life has been NRH baseball, Boy Scouts, Girl Scouts, and other activities. M. E. and Barbara have been members of the PTA from the beginning, 1963. Most of that time they were involved with all three children's classes at once.

M. E. and Barbara live in Southlake, and have for the past two and one-half years. They are very proud to be a part of the history of NRH. Yes, it has been a "wonderful life" in NRH.

MARVIN AND VERN MYERS

Marvin, Vern, and David Myers moved to North Richland Hills in February 1968 from Lubbock. Marvin had just joined the staff of North Richland Hills Baptist Church as minister of education and administration. His wife, Vern, was librarian of Lubbock High School. Shortly after moving here Vern became the first librarian of the new Trinity High School in the Hurst-Euless-Bedford School District, beginning in August 1968. David, 10 years old, was in the fourth grade at Snow Heights Elementary School. The family resided on Marilyn Lane. Later David attended North Richland Junior High and Richland High School, where he graduated in 1976.

In 1968 Airport Freeway was under construction from North Richland Hills to Euless. Vern drove on the dirt access road to her work in Euless. The only shopping center nearby was the Richland Plaza center on Belknap. If we couldn't find what we needed there, we had to drive to Seminary South or Dallas. But everything else was convenient. The old Buddies Super Market and Town and Country Drug were frequent stops for us.

In 1976, Marvin accepted a job in Nashville, Tennessee with the Baptist Sunday School Board, where he worked until 1981. Then he became executive director of the National Association of Church Business Administration and moved its national offices from Kansas City to the Northeast National Bank Building in NRH. The family rejoined the North Richland Hills Baptist Church, where we are still members. Marvin

Marvin, Vern, and David Myers

retired from NACBA in July 1998. He is an avid collector of fishing collectibles and church offering plates.

Marvin was born in Jackson, Mississippi, but came to Texas as soon as he could in 1955. He graduated from Southwestern Baptist Theological Seminary in Fort Worth in 1957. He was music and education director for the Main Street Baptist Church in Grand Saline, Texas, where he met Vern Caperton. They were married June 14, 1956. Vern was born in Grand Saline and is a graduate of East Texas State University in Commerce.

David was born in Dallas. He graduated from the University of Texas in Arlington in 1981, and then entered the U.S. Marine Corps, presently holding the rank of major. He is now a pilot with Northwest Airlines and a Marine Reserve Pilot. He lives in Virginia Beach, Virginia, with his wife Joselyn and daughter Jesseca. When asked where he is from, he always says North Richland Hills.

In 1984 Vern became an elementary librarian with the Birdville schools, and retired from that position in 1992. She is still active in church work and enjoys traveling and reading.

We have lived in Dallas, Odessa, Lubbock, and Nashville, but North Richland Hills is a community we are proud to call home. This community has grown tremendously and has made so many improvements. But it still has a small town atmosphere, good government, and best of all, most of our friends live here.

KENNETH B. "ACE" AND DAYLE NACE

There was a big move of American Airlines employees into the northeast Tarrant County area in the early 1950s. "Ace" and Dayle Nace were part of that immigration of families in October 1952 when they moved into one of only six houses on Turner Terrace in what would soon become the new town of North Richland Hills. These first houses were built on Daley, Cummings, Turner Terrace, and the first block of Vance Road. Their daughter, Diana, was born in Buffalo, New York, August 13, 1949, but had the privilege of growing up in NRH. They were the 19th family in the area.

Ace was born in Wilmington, Delaware, where he began his aviation career as an airport operator and flying instructor. He flew domestic flights with the Air Transport Command during World War II, both flight training and transporting cargo.

Dayle was born in Denton, Texas, reared in Fort Worth and worked at Meacham Field.

Ace became a pilot for American Airlines and soon after moving to NRH, he was working on his fourth million

"Ace" and Dayle Nace

miles of flying for American. From 1940 to 1978, he flew from Dallas to Los Angeles, with the last several years spent flying to the Caribbean, South Pacific, Australia, and New Zealand. He enjoyed the two-day layovers in Hawaii, and when he had trips to the South Pacific, he was gone from home one week, then at home for one week.

The year 1929 began a life-long passion for Ace Nace. His father was a telegrapher for the Pennsylvania Railroad, and Ace got his ham radio license when he was 11 years old. One of his first calls was to a ship that foundered off the Atlantic Coast with only the ship's captain left on board. One time he made contact with Gen. Curtis LeMay. The conversation was: "Hi, Curt"—"Hi, Ace." He has worked special events stations such as the carrier Yorktown and Brooklyn Navy Yard. He has more than 1,000 QSL contacts. This is the acknowledged international code designating operator's location, and he has exchanged QSL cards with operators from all over the world.

Ace's second hobby was motorcycles. He owned a Honda Goldwing, traveled the lower 48 states, all the Canadian provinces, and the John Cabot trails in Nova Scotia. He made the "Four Corners Tour" of the U.S. twice with neighbor, Gene Berrier. Ace was 65 years old the first time he made the trip, 68 the second time.

His goal was to ride until he was 80, but on May 19, 1998, he gave it up at age 79.

Dayle taught piano for 10 years. She enjoyed bowling and took up roller skating when she was in her 40s. She decided that a Saturday afternoon at Holiday Roller Rink was taking your life into your own hands. Both Ace and Dayle were involved in the NRH Civic League, and Dayle was a charter member of the NRH Garden Club.

Ace served five years as a member of the NRH City Council and served as mayor in 1957.

Ace remembers getting a phone call late one night. It seems a poker game had been enjoyed at the Rapid Mart after hours, but nonetheless, not "appropriate." He told the players to just go home.

Ace and Dayle continue to enjoy their home on Turner Terrace. Diana, a 1967 Richland High graduate, lives in Hurst and is employed by Ernst and Young Accounting Firm in Los Colinas.

Submitted by Evalyn Lochridge from interviews with Ace and Dayle Nace

PATRICIA NEIGHBORS

Patricia Neighbors, a native Oklahoman, moved to the Fort Worth area in 1978 to become the choral director at Richland High School. The daughter of two school teachers, Don and Nancy Neighbors, she and her sister, Debra and brother, David, all grew up with a love and aptitude for music. All three children were active in band and choir in school and all played the piano. Singing was a favorite family activity whether at church, at home or in the car going on family vacations. Patricia began piano lessons at age four, and playing the piano for church as a sixth grader and by the time she was in junior high was the regular church pianist and later organist. She graduated from Choctaw High School in Choctaw, Oklahoma and received a Bachelor of Music Education Degree from Central State University in Edmond, Oklahoma, where she was president of Sigma Alpha Iota, a professional music fraternity for women. She was also named outstanding woman music student, was listed on the Dean's and President's Honor Roll, was listed in Who's Who in American Colleges and Universities.

Patricia Neighbors

In 1974 Miss Neighbors was hired for her first teaching job as choral director at Harrah Junior–Senior High School in Harrah, Oklahoma. Under her leadership the choirs grew in enrollment and began to qualify for the state contest. In addition to teaching, Patricia was simultaneously working on her master's in music education at the University of Oklahoma, taking course work in the summer and studying voice and conducting during the year. She received her master's degree in 1979.

In 1978 she was hired to become the choral director at Richland High School. Richland High choirs began receiving the highest awards in University Interscholastic League competition. The school recorded numbers of students being named to the Texas All-State Choir (the single most significant achievement of any high school choir student) and they were invited to sing at National American Choral Directors Association Convention in Nashville in 1983. On the local campus, she was directly involved with drama teachers in producing a musical each year. Everything from an extravaganza like *Hello, Dolly* or *Music Man* to a small ensemble–like *Godspell* and *Working* were among the fare.

One of the joys of teaching for her was investing in her students and having former students come back to visit always reporting on what was going on in their lives. As students married and had families she lovingly referred to new babies as "my grandstudents." She says that it was not unusual for former students who had gone on to major in music in college to call her about half way through their first semester just to talk to a kindred spirit for a little advice.

After 10 years at Richland High School the doors began to open for a new opportunity of service in North Richland Hills. The church where Miss Neighbors had attended since 1978, North Richland Hills Baptist Church, offered her a full-time position as music associate. This position would allow her to continue her ministry to people in the community and as she noted, "They never graduate!" as music associate she works directly with every age group in the church. She plays the organ for the adult choir, the Praisingers, and directs the Senior Adult Choir. Now known as Patricia or "Miss Patricia," she is still investing in people and their families. Her children's choirs are full of "grandstudents" as she enjoys teaching

the next generation how music can be a tool for personal development as well as a pathway for them to come to know God and His Gift of Love.

After 20 years of involvement in North Richland Hills, grown men and women who serve in this community as business owners, salesmen, school and community leaders, ministers and parents are referred to as "my little boys or girls" as many strike a note of joy and pride for Patricia. "I hope that maybe one small thing I said or did helped influence them in a positive way."

EARL AND ADA NEWMAN

Ernest Earl Newman was born November 28, 1911, in Fort Worth. He was the son of Otto Franklin Newman and Myrtle Brewster Newman of the Riverside area of Fort Worth. Earl had two brothers and seven sisters. Earl attended Riverside School and lived in that area until he married Ada Leta Howard on February 7, 1931, in Marietta, Oklahoma.

Earl and Ada Newman

Ada Howard Newman was born June 3, 1914, in Granbury. She was the daughter of Frank Howard of Fort Worth and Bessie Stacy Howard of Lipan. She had one sister and one brother. Ada attended school in Lipan and the Riverside area.

Earl and Ada had four sons. Charles Ray Newman, born March 31, 1932, married Gail Willis and presently lives in Granbury. The second son, James Harold Newman, was born August 25, 1933, married Shirley Brown, and presently lives in Newark. The next son, Billy Don Newman, was born July 5, 1935, married Carole Kuhn, and presently lives in Santo. The youngest son, Ronnie Earl Newman, was born July 6, 1942, married Frieda Rhine, and presently lives in North Richland Hills.

Earl and Ada bought 60 acres in Smithfield in 1949 and moved to what was then a very rural area. This property is east of Davis Boulevard on Shirley Drive and south of Newman Drive. Earl Newman developed part of this property as a subdivision in the early 1960s. The streets in the subdivision were named for the Newmans' four daughters-in-law:

Sons and daughters-in-law of Earl and Ada Newman; Back, L/R-Charles, Harold, Bill, Ronnie; Front, L/R-Gail (Willis), Shirley (Brown), Carole (Kuhn), and Frieda (Rhine)

Shirley, Gail, Carole, and Frieda. The Newmans gave each son half an acre of land in the subdivision on which to build a home and raise their families.

The Newmans have a total of 12 grandchildren: Debbie Vogt, Jan Brock, Karen Newman, John Newman, Cindy Clines, Joanne MacPherson, James Harold Newman Jr., Michael Newman, Steven Newman, Douglas Newman, David Newman, and Teresa Newman. They have 24 great-grandchildren: Shelly Miller, Kristi Vogt, Aaron Vogt, Austin Brock, Jae Brock, Amy Foley, Miranda Nichols, Chad Pool, John Robert Newman, Ashley Newman, Jace Newman, Haley Clines, Lucas Clines, Jessie MacPherson, Abby MacPherson, Gary Newman, Stephanie Newman, Rachel Newman, Jacob Newman, Jared Newman, Brittany Freeman, Shane Freeman, David Earl Newman Jr., and Shana Newman. There are two great-great-grandchildren: Chandler Miller and Braeden Miller.

Earl's first job was with Fort Worth Sand and Gravel in 1927. He started Abbott and Newman Sand and Gravel in 1948 with a partner, Foy Abbott, also of Smithfield. The two men later started a concrete business together, Abbott and Newman Concrete Company. They sold this business to Gifford-Hill Concrete. In 1961, Earl started Newman Sand and Gravel, and then in 1962, he and his sons started Newman Brothers Materials Company. While still in this business, they bought a trucking company and started Newman Brothers Trucking Company in 1965. Earl retired in 1970, but the sons continued in the trucking business until selling out in 1985.

Ada Newman was a devoted wife, mother, and grandmother. She was happy being a homemaker. She enjoyed taking her 12 grandchildren to the movies and out to eat. The Newmans had a farm in Lipan where they took their grandchildren on weekends to hunt and fish. Earl, his sons, and grandsons enjoyed many hunting and fishing trips all over Texas.

Earl and Ada have been members of the Smithfield Church of Christ for 47 years, and Earl served as treasurer of the church for several years. Earl was also a cofounder of Fort Worth Christian School. He was on the Board of Directors of Haltom City State Bank for 17 years and belonged to the Smithfield Masonic Lodge.

Earl and Ada celebrated their 50th wedding anniversary February 7, 1981. They were married 62 years. Earl died August 9, 1993, and is buried in Mt. Olivet Cemetery in Fort Worth. Ada is still a resident of North Richland Hills.

Submitted by Shirley Newman

JAMES HAROLD AND SHIRLEY NEWMAN

James Harold Newman was born August 25, 1933, in Fort Worth, to Earl Ernest Newman and Ada Howard Newman of Smithfield. He lived in the Haltom City area until he was 16 and graduated from the old Birdville High School. In 1949, the family moved to a 60-acre farm on a hill in Smithfield. This had been the home of Shirley

James Harold and Shirley Brown Newman, 1987

Brown, whom Harold later married. Shirley's father, Burney Brown, traded the Brown farm for the Newman home on North Haltom Road in Haltom City.

Shirley was born August 14, 1935, in Fort Worth. When she was 2 months old, she moved with her father, Burney C. Brown, and her mother, Louise Quayle Brown, to Smithfield to live with her paternal grandparents, Louia B. Brown and Halcie Calloway Hightower Brown. Shirley's only sister, Linda Kay Brown Alread, was born in Smithfield where she still lives. Shirley attended Smithfield Elementary School and Amon Carter-Riverside High School, graduating in 1953. She and Harold married in Smithfield May 28, 1955, at the Smithfield Methodist Church where they are still members.

Shirley and Harold have three children. Cynthia Diane Newman was born in Fort Worth on March 6, 1956. Joanne, was born March 27, 1958, and James Harold Newman Jr., was born April 28, 1962. All three children attended Smithfield Elementary. Cindy attended Richland Junior High for one year while Watauga Junior High was being built. Cindy and Joanne both attended Watauga Junior High, but Jimmy was in the first class to attend the new Smithfield Junior High. All of the children graduated from Richland High School.

L/R–David, Cindy and Lucas Clines, Shirley Brown Newman, Haley Clines, Joanne (Newman) and Gordon MacPherson, Harold and Jimmy Newman

Cindy is now employed by Camp Fire Boys and Girls. She married David Wallace Clines, vice president of a security firm. They have two children, a daughter, Haley Diane Clines, born November 27, 1983, and a son, Lucas Adam Clines, born October 8, 1987.

Joanne graduated from the University of Texas in Austin. While touring in Europe she met her future husband, Gordon Archibald MacPherson, on a train in France. She joined the Peace Corps, serving two years in

Niger, West Africa. Joanne married Gordon on April 15, 1989. They made their home in Canada where Gordon is a corporate travel agent. They have two daughters.

James Harold Newman Jr. ("Jimmy") has lived in Kona, Hawaii, for the last 10 years working in construction. He has just recently moved back to Texas to start a business in construction and masonry. He is a member of the Smithfield United Methodist Church.

When Harold and Shirley married, Harold had his own gravel truck. He worked for Abbott and Newman Concrete and stayed on as a supervisor when Abbott and Newman sold the business to Gifford-Hill Concrete.

Harold, with his three brothers, Charles, Bill, and Ronnie, and their dad, Earl Newman, started Newman Brothers Materials in January, 1968. The company operated rock crushers, producing crushed stone and other road building materials. In 1965, they also started Newman Brothers Trucking, which they owned until 1985. After the trucking company was sold Harold retired. However, when his brother Ronnie, and Ronnie's son David, went back into the trucking business three years later Harold bought a truck and worked for them for seven years.

In 1989, Shirley and Harold moved to Newark, Texas, 25 miles northwest of Fort Worth, where they currently live.

Submitted by Shirley Newman

THOMAS EDWIN AND JEAN NEWMAN

Tom and Jean Newman and their three sons, James Jennings Newman, Thomas Edwin Newman Jr., and William George Newman, moved to North Richland Hills in 1962. They thought they had moved to the country when they purchased their home on Palomar Drive. Within months after moving to Palomar, Holiday Heights Elementary School and new homes were being built all around.

Thomas E. and Jean Newman

With their young sons, Tom Newman became very active in the Richland Youth Association. He not only coached, but served in all capacities to promote the youth association.

In 1970, Tom Newman was elected to the North Richland Hills City Council. He served on the City Council until 1976, and was elected mayor in April 1976, serving one term. During his terms in office he saw new business developments like, Sanger-Harris, Steak and Ale, and Furrs Cafeteria all being built in NRH. The city began to grow.

Tom and Jean Newman's three sons, Jimmy, Eddy, and Billy Newman, all graduated from Richland High School. The eldest son, James Jennings, is now a radiologist in Tulsa and lives there with his wife Alicia, daughter Liz, and son Clayton. The middle son, Thomas Edwin Newman Jr., is a

Eddy, Billy, Jimmy Newman

planner for Knowlton-English-Flowers Civil Engineering firm in Bedford. He lives in North Richland Hills with his wife Sheila and sons Seth Alan and Thomas Edwin Newman III (Trey). The youngest son, Billy Newman, is an inspector at Ling-Temco-Vaught in Grand Prairie. He lives in North Richland Hills with his wife, Brenda, and two sons, Brandon and Scott.

EMMA PEARL AND ROWENA BALLEW NEWTON

My name is Emma Pearl Newton. I moved to Richland Hills in 1989 from Monahans, Texas, to take care of my sister, Rowena Ballew, who was ill with lymphoma. In 1990 we decided to buy a home together and found a lovely house in the Meadow Lakes Area of North Richland Hills.

Rowena and I were born in Lewisville, Texas, to W. C. M. and Willie Pearl Shepherd Saunders. Our lives always seemed to mirror each other. We both graduated from high school in Lewisville, both received our bachelor's degree in home economics from Texas Woman's University in Denton, and our master's degree from North Texas University.

Rowena Ballew spent her entire 42-year career as an educator teaching homemaking. She taught in Putnam, the Waco Children's home, Grapevine, and Carrollton before joining the Birdville District. She began teaching at the junior high level and taught five years at Richland Junior High School. In 1961 she moved to Richland High School upon its opening. The building was not complete when the school bells rang in September, and the homemaking classes met in the faculty teachers' lounge for some time. She loved teaching, and it showed in her students work. She was always ahead of her time with new sewing and decorating tricks. Rowena died in 1991.

I taught school for 40 years, teaching homemaking, the third grade and last, being promoted to be the elementary coordinator of the Monahans-Wicket-Pyote School District. I have one daughter, Elaine, who teaches school in Sonora. She will soon complete her 30th year of teaching. She was born in Brownwood and graduated from Monahans High School and Texas Tech University in Lubbock with both bachelor's and master's degrees in elementary education.

Rowena and I both became members of St. Luke United Methodist Church, the Theta Theta Chapter of the Delta Kappa Gamma Society, Retired Teachers Association, Fort Worth China Decorators Club, and the

Fort Worth Porcelain Art Club. We both also shared the same hobbies including sewing, knitting, crocheting, and china painting. I continue to enjoy these hobbies and taking care of a bobbed-tailed cat named Panda.

It has been my privilege and pleasure to live in this area. The people are so friendly, nice and helpful, and I have made many new friends.

Submitted by Emma Pearl Newton

C. E. AND JEAN NEYLAND

C. E. and Jean Neyland and their two children moved into their new home on Briley Drive December 13, 1953. The children were 5-year-old Barbara and 1-year-old Norman. Barbara was transferred from the Crestwood Elementary School in Fort Worth to the Birdville school system. Richland Elementary School had just opened the previous fall, but the classes were already overcrowded, so our daughter had to attend an elementary school (Central Elementary, I think) on the grounds of Haltom High School at Carson and Belknap streets. Before North Richland Hills Elementary was built, she attended Glenview Elementary, then transferred to North Richland. She went to Richland Junior High School followed by Richland High School, from which she graduated in 1965. Norman attended North Richland Elementary, North Richland Junior High School, and Richland High School, graduating in 1971. I, Jean Neyland, began substitute teaching in the Birdville District in 1961 and was hired as a full-time teacher at Haltom Junior High School in 1964. I retired just before the death of my daughter from cancer in the fall of 1990.

During the early '50s, North Richland Hills was not yet a city. Mail was delivered to mailboxes fastened to curbside posts. Phone service involved multiple lines. A security person provided police protection, but fortunately there was little crime at that time.

There were no supermarkets in the area. Homemakers drove to Haltom City on Wednesdays (double S&H stamp day) for grocery shopping, because the only nearby store was a small one in Richland Hills named Wehring's. There was only one gasoline station, a Humble station, run by Mr. L. C. Akins.

At the time we moved in, most of the houses had septic tanks. Shortly before our house was built, a sewer line was placed in the alley, and we connected to it thus avoiding having a septic tank.

Home milk deliveries were made at that time, and a bakery truck came by every week to sell all sorts of baked goods. The first large shopping center in the area was Richland Plaza. In 1970 North East Mall opened with Leonard's Department Store as an anchor.

The City Hall and community meeting facilities were in a building at the corner of Glenview Drive and Morgan Circle. As our city expanded, so did crime and taxes, but the good outweighs the bad, and I do not wish to move anywhere else.

Submitted by Jean B. Neyland

RAYMOND RICHARD AND BETTE LEE RUDD NOLEN

The Nolen household at the present time is composed of Raymond and Bette. Their daughters: Mona, born in Dallas, and Georgia, born in Fort Worth, attended North Richland Elementary and Junior High Schools and graduated from Richland High School.

Ramona (Mona) Anne Nolen Kerby lives in New Windsor, Maryland, with her husband, Steve, in an 18th century home. She has a bachelor's degree from Texas Wesleyan University, master's degrees from Texas Christian University and Texas Woman's University, and a doctorate in library science from TWU in Denton. She writes children's books, teaches graduate library science courses, and coordinates library media technology at Western Maryland College.

Georgia Anne Nolen Gann lives with her husband, Greg, and children

Bette and Raymond Nolen

April, Kyle, and Jonathan in Park Ridge, Illinois. Georgia, a graduate of Texas Christian University, taught hearing-impaired children while Greg attended law school. She is involved with the activities of their children and is a director and lecturer for the international Community Bible Study.

Raymond, a native of Fort Worth, served in the Marines from 1943 to 1946, graduated from the University of North Texas with a major in business administration, and later studied at Texas Christian University. A licensed Interstate Commerce Practitioner and Certified Association executive, he retired after spending 25 years as the executive vice president of Texas Grain and Feed Association.

He received the Paul Harris award from the Rotary Club and various other awards from professional and civic organizations for his work as an officer and/or board member. For several years, he was a member of the Dean's Advisory Committee for Texas Tech's College of Agricultural Science. Currently, he serves as a Silver-Haired Legislator. Since retirement, he has become addicted to golf.

Bette, born in Denton, majored in biology and received bachelor's and master's degrees from the University of North Texas. She completed postgraduate work with certifications in school administration and counseling. She worked for 29 years in Birdville schools as a teacher, counselor, assistant principal, and principal.

As a member of the Theta Theta chapter of Delta Kappa Gamma, she cherishes an achievement award from that organization. Bette and Raymond, members of Richland Hills United Methodist Church, attend Fidelis Sunday

School Class. Bette is a life member of Texas Retired Teachers Association and PTA, and at this time is president of the Birdville Association of Retired School Personnel.

Her hobbies include sporadic "dabbling" in crafts, sewing, reading, family history research and writing, yard work, travel, and antique appreciation.

Submitted by Bette Nolen

JAMES T. AND MABLE NORMAN

James T. and Mable Norman were pioneer residents in North Richland Hills, moving into one of the first houses built on Cummings Drive in 1952. Open fields of rye grass, septic tanks, and muddy streets, which were rivers when it rained, were memories of Mable.

It didn't take long for the Norman family to become involved in the community. They were very involved in the organization of the NRH Civic League and the foundation of the city from incorporation and the first council-mayor election in April 1953. James entered the political arena and served as a councilman on the first City Council. To broaden his community involvement, he was an initial director of the Greater Richland Chamber of

James and Mable Norman, 50th wedding anniversary, 1991

Commerce after its formation in December 1957. He also served as third president of the chamber. He was president of Tarrant County Water Supply Corporation and was a trustee, then president, of the Birdville Independent School District Board, serving BISD for seven years.

Mable Norman served as chairwoman of the Birdville chapter of the American Field Service, Birdville PTA Council, and many civic committees, including enrollment of NRH residents for the first sewer and drainage project.

James and Mable Norman were married June 8, 1941. They moved to the NRH community from Meadowbrook area of Fort Worth, having moved to Fort Worth from Kentucky. There were two children, James Curtis Norman, born November 7, 1942, and Anne, born June 11, 1947.

James held various management positions with the world's largest manufacturer of work clothes, Williamson-Dickie Manufacturing Company, until his retirement.

The Normans celebrated their 50th wedding anniversary in 1991. James passed away September 5, 1992.

Interview with Mable Norman

Submitted by Evalyn Lochridge

PHILLIP AND EILEEN NORRIS

In 1949, at the end of World War II, Phillip and Eileen Norris "migrated" to Fort Worth, Texas. Phillip had been employed at the Curtiss Airplane Division of the Curtiss-Wright Corporation in Columbus, Ohio, since graduation

L/R-Mark, Danny, Eileen, Nancy, Phil Norris

in 1942 from the University of Iowa. We came to Texas as soon as we could! Phillip was hired at Consolidated Vultee as an engineer.

Mark was 4 years old. Daniel Phillip was born in 1950. Nancy was born the following year.

At that time, Ira McMurray was building houses about six miles east of Oakhurst where we were living. In December 1954 we bought one of Ira's new homes and moved in on New Year's Eve. Our house was surrounded with pasture land or empty lots. Deville Drive was unpaved. There were no stores except the Rapid Mart on Grapevine Highway, no shopping center, no Loop 820. The only elementary school was in Richland Hills, and the junior and senior high school were in Haltom City. We felt like pioneers. Closest shopping was in busy downtown Fort Worth.

Mark graduated from the new Richland High School in 1965. Danny followed in 1970 and Nancy in 1971. Phillip continued to work at the plant, now General Dynamics, until 1984.

The family joined Richland Hills United Methodist Church in 1957. Phillip and Eileen continue to live in their house in North Richland Hills, still a pretty residential neighborhood in spite of Loop 820 rushing by to the north and east, and North Hills Mall looming its head adjacent to the loop on the west.

Eileen was born in Perry, Iowa. Phillip was born in Webster City, Iowa. They both graduated from the University of Iowa in 1942 and were married May 11, 1942, and moved to Columbus, Ohio.

HARVEY AND LUCILLE NORTON

Harvey and I, Lucille Norton, were married in 1939 in Fort Worth. We were both reared in the Rhome community. We met when his sister, who was my best friend, introduced us. We dated two years before we married.

At that time, I was working for Montgomery Ward, and he worked for Hobbs Trailers. Our first home was in Saginaw.

Harvey took a job with Civil Service, and we went to Vallejo, California,

Lucille and J. M. "Harvey" Norton

where he worked in the shipyards. We were there during Pearl Harbor, and it was a very tense and frightening time. Our first child, Judy, was born there.

Two years later, we came back to Texas and settled in Saginaw, where our second child, Jane, was born.

Harvey was called by the Navy to Bremerton, Washington, to work on wrecked warships. He was there about six months then he was drafted into the Army.

When he came home, he went to work at Consolidated, now Lockheed-Martin. I was busy with our growing family, and soon, our third child, Joyce, was born. I worked in the post office, and then I owned and operated a dry cleaners in Saginaw.

After about four years, Harvey decided we would start our own business. We worked very hard, and later began Norton Metals Inc. in Saginaw. During this time, we moved to Sunnybrook Addition in the Smithfield area of North Richland Hills in 1961. Our home was the first house built in what was then a large grassy area of pastureland.

Harvey was one of the first board members of Fort Worth Christian School, and in the early 1990s, we were honored for our service at the school's annual Harvest Dinner.

I worked as secretary of Norton Metals several years with Harvey until I retired. He was in the business 40 years before retirement in 1996. All our daughters and sons-in-law have worked in the company.

Judy married Larry Dunlap. They have one son, Coyt. He and his wife, Michele, have three daughters: Shelby and twins, Morgan and McKenzie. All live in North Richland Hills. Larry is still with Norton Metal Inc.

Jane married Dale Scott, a minister of the Nocona Church of Christ, and she teaches elementary school there. They have three children: Timothy, Kimberly, and Joel, and six grandchildren: Clayton, Christopher, Marissa, Amanda, Chelsa, and John William.

Joyce married Larry Yates, who also still works for the company. They have three children: Cory, Kristi, and Jody, and two granddaughters.

Harvey and I enjoy traveling, and we have made one trip around the world and many trips to Europe, Africa, Canada, South America, and the Far East. Our latest journey was an interesting cruise across the icy, 4,000-mile-long Northwest Passage from Greenland to Alaska.

We now live in the Meadow Lakes Addition and love North Richland Hills. Our city is like a village in the midst of a city. It is so friendly. We see our neighbors at the grocery store, post office, church, school, and shopping.

It is a wonderful place to live.

Submitted by Lucille Norton

CHARLIE AND MARTHA NULL

Hurrying to the thin shade of the old mesquite tree by the side of the road, the two small girls set the heavy milk bucket down and rubbed the pressure marks on their palms left by the handle. The younger sister inched a bare toe toward a tar bubble made by the summertime heat on the blacktop road. They were on their way to Sam Snider's General Store in Smithfield. The year was about 1944. The milk bucket was full of chicken eggs carefully placed on a thick cup towel in the bottom. A couple of times a week they carried out this chore of taking the eggs to the store to be sold for 20 cents a dozen. When Mr. Snider emptied the bucket, they could each have a nickel from the egg money if there wasn't a broken egg. The thought of trying to decide just what piece of candy or "soda water" they would select made them at once anxious to get there and also to be ever so careful with the breakable eggs.

The children, Dorothy and Loraine, were the daughters of Charlie and Martha Null, and they lived on what is now Chapman Road. The family had moved to the area in 1937 and built a two-room house on the site of the old cotton gin long before the old dirt road had a name. The two-acre piece of land had a huge surface well on it. The well was 16 feet across and was fed by three springs. It was the original well dug to service the gin. Over the years the family had built a chicken house and barn and, of course, there was the outdoor privy. Coal oil lamps provided light for homework. The weekly wash was done at the well in a huge black cast-iron pot with water hand drawn from the well and heated over a wood fire. The detergent was shaved pieces of white lye soap made from lye, grease, and wood ashes. The clothes, hung on barbed-wire fences, were dried by the sun. Dresses, shirts, and dresser scarves were starched, sprinkled, and ironed with a sad iron heated on a burner of the coal oil stove. The precious rinse water was carefully poured along the rows of vegetables in the neat little garden. Farm animals included two Jersey milk cows, several pigs, about a hundred chickens, and a dog named Amos.

Electricity, and finally phone service, became available to the rural area. Our first phone had an eight-party line, and lots of times I was told by an "adult" to get off the line. There was one family car, and it seemed that Daddy worked on it every weekend, just to keep it going. He was a good mechanic, and lots of people in the neighborhood brought their car to his shade tree garage to be fixed. Years later he operated a lawnmower repair shop from the home site. He was known as the Lawnmower Man of North Richland Hills.

Halloween Carnivals at the school and revivals at the churches provided the adults and children of the community with activities. There was a weekly Play Night at the Methodist Church started by their pastor, Gilbert Ferrell. This was outside when the weather was good. We played volleyball and had Kool Aid (then it was called Polly Pop) and cookies, before walking home under the stars. Women gathered for quilting bees at each other's houses. It seems as if a quilting frame with a half-finished quilt hung from the ceiling of our house all my childhood. Impromptu games of scrub softball and hopscotch vied with making a playhouse down in the woods for passing long, languid summer afternoons. Once in a great while, picture shows were shown behind the school gym. The whole family went along, sitting on old quilts and sharing local gossip with neighbors while we waited for it to get dark enough for the show to start. We were especially lucky if the snow-cone man was there.

Gradually, the community, along with the country, climbed out of the long-term effects of the Great Depression. World War II was a mixed bag of blessings. Many families sent sons and husbands to places they had only seen in a geography book to fight an enemy whose language they could not even understand. But the war years also brought The Bomber Plant, and men and women of the little town joined Tillie the Toiler on the assembly line. Regular paychecks began to find their way into the households. Now, a washing machine or a radio or a car could be "bought on time" with the confidence of being able to pay for them.

We finished high school at Amon Carter in Riverside. My older sister married and had four children. She worked for awhile for an insurance company and then for the Birdville School District in the cafeteria service. Her husband worked in air-conditioning. They have both retired and now live in Weatherford. I became a registered nurse, becoming the first person in my family to complete college. I taught nursing at the University of Texas at Arlington for many years, married, and had two daughters. My husband owned a commercial refrigeration company for many years before his retirement.

Sunrise. Sunset. Swiftly go the years. Little barefoot girls carrying eggs to the store grow up overnight to become mothers, nurses, and grandmothers, and the little bucolic town of my childhood nestles in the corners of my mind. It was a wonderful free-spirited place where we flew paper kites on windy March days and drove the cows home to be milked as the shadows lengthened and swallows darted over our heads. It was an enchanting time, and I love to go there in my memories for solace and refuge in these hectic and impersonal days.

Submitted by: Dorothy Lee Null Parker

NAT AND LYNN O'DAY

In May 1970, Nat and Lynn O'Day, with their three children, Robin, Steve, and Tim, settled in North Richland Hills. Nat, a lieutenant colonel in the U.S. Army, was preparing for a second tour to Vietnam before retiring from a military career. The O'Days had spent the three previous years stationed in Hawaii but decided to retire in North Richland Hills to be near Lynn's mother, Alliene Mullendore, and her sister, Kay Granger.

In 1970 Alliene Mullendore had just been named principal of North Richland Elementary School, later to become Alliene Mullendore Elementary. Alliene began her career with the Birdville School District in 1942 as the first teacher hired by Superintendent Wylie G. Thomas. Following retirement in 1973, after a long and distinguished career as an educator and administrator, she became the first woman member of the BISD School Board.

Front, L/R-Chelsea Granger, Alliene Mullendore; Middle, L/R-Lynn O'Day, sister Kay Granger, Brandon and J. D. Granger; Back, L/R-Steve, Tim and Nat O'Day, Robin Dettmer

After retiring from the Army, Nat began a second career with the City of Fort Worth, retiring in 1997 as a finance administrator. His last years were enjoyable, as he became known as the "first brother-in-law" to Mayor Kay Granger. He now stays busy volunteering in Congresswoman Granger's office with special projects. On Saturdays, he can be found playing with children at Cook Children's Medical Center in Fort Worth. He was Volunteer of the Year in 1992. He is a docent at the Amon Carter Museum and gives lectures and tours for Performing Arts Fort Worth, the administrative arm of the Bass Performance Hall.

Lynn worked at the North Richland Hills Public Library from 1986 to 1997. Her volunteer efforts center on the arts, having served as president of the Symphony League of Fort Worth and chairwoman of its fundraiser, Oktoberfest. She currently serves on the Board of Directors of the All Church Home for Children. Prior to her employment at the library, she served on the North Richland Hills Library Board for eight years. Nat and Lynn are members of Richland Hills United Methodist Church.

All of the O'Day children live in the area. Their two grandchildren, Kelly Lynn and Michael Hans Dettmer, also are nearby. Robin graduated from Texas A&M in 1982 and the University of Texas Law School in 1985. She is a partner in the law firm of Shannon, Gracey, Ratliff & Miller. Robin married Jorg Dettmer from Unterluss, Germany, in 1970.

Steve graduated from Sam Houston State University in 1985 and has worked for Blackmon Mooring Steamatic Catastrophe since 1988. He recently bought a home on 10 acres in Azle. Steve hopes to turn a reptile hobby into a small business using his marketing background.

Tim graduated from Sam Houston State University in 1986 and has been manager of Leslie Pool Supplies on South Hulen Street since 1991. He recently bought a home in Bedford. In his spare time he is lead guitarist in a band that plays in local clubs and private parties.

MILTON AND JOHNNIE MARIE O'NEAL

Milton was born October 15, 1932, in Fort Worth, Texas, and has lived in this area all of his life. He graduated from Trimble Tech High School in 1953. He attended Brantley Draughon Business School. He was employed by Continental Grain Company for 10 years, and he worked for Carter & Burgess Engineering for 13 years. He has belonged to the Church of God most of his life. He has served the church in many areas, singing in the choir, ushering, and serving on councils and committees, acting as Sunday school superintendent, and helping in a Sunday morning service in a rest home for 14 years.

He has always enjoyed doing yard work. Milton now works with the "Bill Glass Prison Ministries." He has gone to several of their crusades. He is thrilled to tell those men about Christ.

Milton married Johnnie Marie Barber February 23, 1957. She was born March 31, 1935, in Ladonia, Texas. Her family moved to Sweetwater, Texas, in 1948. She graduated from Nolan High School in Sweetwater in 1953 and moved to Fort Worth in 1956. She worked for Johnson & Johnson Medical for 24 years and took early retirement on Feb. 1, 1994. Her hobbies are: reading, sewing, quilting, and crocheting. She has belonged to the Church of God most of her life. She has served as a Sunday school teacher, youth leader, and has held various other offices.

Milton and Johnnie Marie have two children: Karen Marie, born October 12, 1960, and Milton Keith, born February 10, 1962. Both were born at Harris Hospital, and both attended schools in Riverside.

Karen married David Davis, and they had two children. Karen is now married to Craig Franek and they enjoy living in NRH.

Keith married Michele Elliott in 1982. They have two children. He is employed by Channel 5-Lin Productions. He is technical director and editor. They live in the Park Glen area between Keller and Watauga.

Milton and Johnnie Marie moved to NRH in 1985 from Riverside. They moved here because they liked the neat, peaceful, quiet neighborhoods. They also liked the beautiful homes and friendly people.

Milton retired from Carter & Burgess Engineering in 1979. After they moved to NRH, he began volunteering at Botanic Gardens. He enjoyed that very much.

Milton now has a very large flower garden by the side of his home. It started with just a few lilies, cannas, and iris, and he has added to it every year. He has outlined the beds in rock. Now he is making walkpaths out of brick all through it. He works at least 40 hours a week out there, has received the Yard of the Month award from the NRH Beautification Committee, and enjoyed being featured in a *Fort Worth Star-Telegram* feature story about his gardens.

There are a lot of people who stop to look at the garden. They often ask to take pictures and walk through it. He welcomes anyone who wishes to share the beauty of the garden.

PHILIP E. AND GERALDINE ORR

Forty years ago on June 16, 1958, our family, Philip Jr., Jerry, and our 4-year-old daughter, Cynthia, made the big move to Blaney Avenue in North Richland Hills from Fort Worth. We were so impressed (even if we couldn't afford it) to be able to move into this new, growing area and getting a home with three bedrooms, two baths, a two-car garage, and lots of closets on a half-acre lot. Philip had made another big move. He had opened his first pharmacy in 1957: Orr's Pharmacy in the

Cynthia, Karen, Geraldine "Jerry," and Philip Orr

Richardson Building on the Grapevine Highway in North Richland Hills. Being young and with big dreams, he operated his pharmacy from 8 A.M. to 10 P.M. six days a week, and 1–6 P.M. on Sunday. So by living near his business, his wife and daughter could come see him at the pharmacy and bring his dinner every evening.

We were welcomed by wonderful neighbors on Blaney—the Daniels, Walkers, Sims, Grammers, Davises, Segers, Carrs, Edwards, Haglers, and the Smiths. Our neighborhood has remained very stable, and several of the original owners are still on Blaney Avenue. Our world on Blaney ended at Riviera Drive. Undeveloped open fields and only a few trees were beyond Riviera. We felt fortunate to have the post office on Blaney (I still miss it) plus a Buddies Grocery Store and the Mott's store.

In 1959, Philip purchased the old 7-Eleven building on the Grapevine Highway and operated his pharmacy under Bench and Orr Pharmacy. He opened a second store in Riverside in 1959. He spent the remaining years of his retail pharmacy career as owner and pharmacist at Hurst Pharmacy in Hurst, retiring in 1993. He spent more than 40 years as the "corner druggist."

Philip Orr, son of Philip Edward and Fannie Noland Orr, was born July 19, 1926, in Natchitoches, Louisiana. He was educated at the parish schools in Natchitoches, graduated in 1948 from Louisiana State University with a bachelor's degree in chemistry, and worked for Texas A&M as a research chemist at Grand Isle, Louisiana. In 1952 he received his bachelor's degree in pharmacy from Oklahoma University. Philip served as a pharmacist mate in the Navy in World War II.

Philip's memberships include Richland Hills Methodist Church, Lion's Club, Sertoma (past president), American Pharmaceutical Association, Texas Pharmaceutical Association, Tarrant County Pharmaceutical Association (past president and recipient of Lifetime Achievement award), National Association of

Retail Druggist, and American College of Apothecary (national board member). He is the recipient of the Carnegie Hero Award.

Philip married Geraldine Tompkins in June 1952. Geraldine (Jerry), the daughter of Ted Troy and Edith Morrow Tompkins, was born June 4, 1933 in Oklahoma City. She attended the Oklahoma public schools, graduating from Central High in 1950. She attended Oklahoma University and received a bachelor's degree (magna cum laude) in chemistry and biology from Texas Christian University in 1956. She worked as a medical technologist for Terrell Labs, taught in the Hurst-Euless-Bedford School District, and worked in the family pharmacy for 25 years.

I, Jerry Orr, taught Sunday School at Richland Hills Methodist Church. I taught kindergarten for a couple of years, then was promoted to fourth grade and taught those wonderful 9-year-olds for 25 years. The family has been members of Richland Hills Methodist since 1958.

I was the leader of Cynthia's Blue Bird, Camp Fire, and Horizon Club organizations. I know my neighbors on Blaney remember the camping trips because it always rained on us, so I would end up back home in my front yard with all that wet, muddy equipment, trying to clean it up. The group stayed together nearly 10 years with girls coming and going. Best of all, I remember the wonderful girls and their mothers that I worked with.

Cynthia was born September 30, 1953, in Fort Worth. She started to kindergarten at Richland Private School on Glenview Drive in 1958. The next fall, 1959, Snow Heights Elementary had been constructed, and Cynthia started as a first-grader on the first day of a new school. North Richland Junior and Richland High were built and ready for her. Cynthia was active in school activities, played the piano, was a member of the band, and an honor student. She was active in Blue Birds, Camp First Girls, and Horizon Club. She and many of her friends learned to swim at Barrbrook Park. Cynthia graduated from Texas Wesleyan University (summa cum laude) and the University of Texas at Arlington with a master's degree in marketing. Cynthia is employed by American Airlines as a systems planner/analyst in the Sabre Division. Cynthia has one daughter, Karen Rollow, born November 17, 1986. They live in Dallas.

Over the years, our closets have shrunk, and the half-acre has grown larger, especially at lawn-care time, but we know we made a good decision to move to North Richland Hills in 1958. We enjoy family activities and gatherings, genealogy, and travel. By attending pharmacy conventions, we were able to see much of America. We have traveled to Europe several times.

Submitted by Geraldine Orr

CARL AND BETTY ORTON

Carl Frederick Orton was born April 4, 1954, in Red Bank, Monmouth County, New Jersey. He grew up in Keyport, New Jersey, where he lived in a house that was built in 1831. His parents are Frances Ogden Orton of North Richland Hills, Texas and William Francis Orton of Phoenix, Arizona. Frances Orton moved from New Jersey to NRH in 1995. Carl attended the Keyport High School and graduated in 1972. He graduated from Kean College of New Jersey in May 1982 with a bachelor's degree in computer science.

Betty Jan Woodward Orton was born August 19, 1955, in Fort Worth and lived most of her life in NRH. She is the daughter of H. E. and Daisy Woodward of NRH. Betty attended Fort Worth Christian School from kindergarten through the 12th grade and grad-

Back-Carl and Betty Orton; Front-Tim, James, "Maggie" the dog

uated in 1973. She went to Harding University, Searcy, Arkansas, for one year. She also attended North Texas State University and University of Texas at Arlington.

Even though Betty grew up in NRH, she met Carl in New Jersey while staying with her brother, Gary, and his family. She and Carl were both working for J. C. Penney while Carl was in school. They married in Middletown, N. J., on May 29, 1982, and moved to Fort Worth two weeks later, following Carl's acceptance of a position with General Dynamics (currently Lockheed-Martin). He worked there for 14 years. Presently he works for Motorola Cellular Infrastructure Group.

Betty has been a homemaker since they married. She does volunteer work and substitute teaching in the Birdville schools. Betty does family history and genealogy and is a member of several genealogy societies, including Mid-Cities Genealogical Society. Betty and Carl are members of the Richland Hills Church of Christ and have two children, Timothy William, born in 1983, and James Richard, born in 1987, both in Fort Worth. Carl and Betty and boys have lived in the northern part of NRH for nine years.

JOSEPH RAY OUJESKY

Ray Oujesky was born in Fort Worth on December 5, 1959. He is the son of Joseph (Buddy) and Joy Ray Oujesky. He has one brother, Robert and one sister, Suzy. Ray grew up in Hurst, Texas and attended L. D. Bell High School and graduated from the University of Oklahoma. His special interests were student government, football, and playing guitar with "Backroads."

Ray married Rita Wright on November 22, 1986, at the St. Theresa Church in Austin. Rita's parents were Gary and Kay Wright of Ada, Oklahoma. She grew up in Enid, Oklahoma and attended Enid High School and the University of Oklahoma. Her special interests were the Chi Omega Sorority and retail clothing sales. Rita has been a financial consultant for 10 years.

Madeline Oujesky, daughter of Ray and Rita Oujesky

Ray and Rita have one child, Madeline Grace Oujesky, born August 27, 1995 at the Columbia North Hills Hospital in North Richland Hills.

Because of the affordable housing and familiarity with the area, Ray and Rita moved to NRH in 1990 from Austin. They have attended the St. Elizabeth Ann Seton Church for seven years. Ray and Rita hold church positions and also are members of the Northeast Richland Lions Club and the Northeast Tarrant Chamber of Commerce.

Ray served on the NRH City Council from 1992 until 1996. He has been the city's municipal judge since 1996.

Ray and Rita enjoy going to Adventure World, NRH2O, Chuck E. Cheese and taking walks in the neighborhood. Many memorable things have happened since they have been in North Richland Hills; the birth of their daughter, being elected to public office and meeting more friends than they ever imagined. They admire and appreciate the men and women who give their time and talents to make NRH a superb place to live and work.

JOHNNIE "BUDDY" AND EVA PANNELL

Johnnie "Buddy" A. Pannell Jr. was born December 9, 1919, in Denton County. I, Eva Densmore Pannell, was born May 14, 1923, in Dallas. We married March 15, 1941, at Lewisville. Buddy served in the U.S. Army during World War II, from June 11, 1942, to December 28, 1945, with the rank of sergeant. He served in the Aleutian Islands off the coast of Alaska and in Germany until discharged. During World War II, the Aleutian Islands were heavily contested by the Americans and the Japanese because of their significant strategic importance. Now, Aleutian military stations are vital links in the air defense of North America. After the

Back, L/R-Martha, Kathy, Mike, Tonya; Front L/R-Buddy, Eva

war, we began our life in Fort Worth, where Buddy got a job with General Dynamics. He worked there from February 1947 to January 1982. Buddy passed away March 23, 1995, and is buried at Bluebonnet Hills Memorial Park in Colleyville.

We moved to our home on Ken Michael Court in North Richland Hills on October 5, 1956, with our four children, Kathy, Martha, Mike, and Tonya. Kathy, then 8 years old, began the third grade, and Martha, 6, began the first grade at North Richland Elementary. Mike was 5 and Tonya was 1.

The family joined North Richland Hills Baptist Church in May 1957, where all four children were saved and baptized. North Richland Hills was a small city then. Bill Perry was mayor. There was very little "law and order" (not much was needed), and Buddy became a volunteer deputy. The "inner loop" is still like a small town, where everybody knows each other and cares.

Kathy graduated from Richland High School in 1966 and married James L. Masten in January 1969. They have two daughters, Gina and Jeanette. Kathy graduated from Sam Houston State University in Huntsville and now lives in Richmond, Texas.

Martha graduated from Richland High School and attended Tarrant County Junior College. In August 1966, she married Gerald D. Andrews. They have two daughters, Teresa and Bethany, and twin granddaughters, Emily and Colleen Abdo. Martha and Gerald now live in Hurst.

James Michael (Mike) graduated from Richland in 1969. He married Diane Farmer of North Richland Hills. They have two daughters, Nicole and Jennifer. Mike passed away December 6, 1994.

Tonya graduated from Richland in 1973. She married David L. Stevenson. She has three sons, Cory, David, and Johnny, and one grandson, C. J., and now lives in Burleson.

Living in North Richland Hills has been like paradise on earth.

Submitted by Eva Densmore Pannell

WILLIAM HALY AND GLADYS PARCHMAN

William Haly Parchman was born January 16, 1894, in Little Fossil Community, Tarrant County. Gladys Rone was born August 5, 1897, in Mansfield. They met in church in Fort Worth when Haly was 17 and Gladys was 14. They dated for four years and were married September 4, 1915.

Haly went to work at Armour Packing Company in Fort Worth in 1908 at the age of 14. He was paid 7.5 cents per hour to skin calves, which along with full-grown cattle, were skinned by one person. He retired from Armour in 1956, and the couple traveled throughout the United States.

After their marriage, they lived in several places in Tarrant County and decided to buy land and build a home. In 1925 they purchased 13 acres of a cotton patch that had been a part of the Hardisty farm outside the Birdville community. They paid $150 an acre for the prop-

Haly and Gladys Parchman, 1976

erty. This block was originally 25 acres located between Pipeline Road (Glenview Drive) and Grapevine Highway. One acre was designated school land, which is now Daley Avenue. Later, the J. J. Hurleys and the Gregorys bought the remaining acreage between the present Vance Road and Daley. The 13 acres bordered Will Snow's property on the west, Pipeline Road on the north, and Grapevine Highway on the south.

The Parchmans found the country property ideal. They had been living on the north side of Fort Worth, but needed more room to take care of their cow and several chickens. Haly raised a Mediterranean breed of chickens, Anconas, which won many red, white, and blue ribbons for him in the Southwestern Exposition and Fat Stock Show in Fort Worth. One year he entered 17 chickens and won eleven ribbons. He both showed the chickens and sold their eggs. They always cultivated a garden to raise their own vegetables.

There were no utilities at all in 1925. Their electricity was furnished by a Delco system until about 1936, when the electric company brought power to that area. For water, they had cisterns for everyday use, except for drinking, and that water was hauled from Will Snow's water well. A well was dug by Luther Brooks in about 1938. The well was in the Paluxy sand and was 650 feet deep.

Parchman home—originally faced Grapevine Highway. Later turned to face Parchman Street.

The Parchman house at the beginning was three rooms and was remodeled several times until it finally had eight rooms and two baths. This house faced Grapevine Highway until the late 1950s, when it was moved to face Parchman Street, which they built. They remained there until 1973 when they moved to Haltom City where they lived until their deaths, his in 1986 and hers in 1987. This was just two months before their 71st wedding anniversary.

When the area started to build around them, they sold the land along the Grapevine Highway for businesses. The first was developed for the Rapid Mart, owned by their son, Stanley, a Dairy Kreem, Evergreen Thumb Nursery,

and Joe Hicks Service Station. This acreage, except for one lot, is now the property of North Richland Hills Baptist Church. The Parchmans also built the first swimming pool in NRH. It was behind these businesses, accessible from the side road, and leased out each summer, usually to the YMCA. Many NRH children learned to swim here.

Three Parchman children grew up on this place, and all three attended Birdville schools and graduated in the years 1936, 1947, and 1955. Anita married Julius Bussey in 1943, and they now live in Sunset, Texas. They have five children and 13 grandchildren. Julius Bussey was an educator in the Birdville School District for 42 years, serving as teacher and principal of several schools, including being the first principal of Richland Elementary School.

Stanley G. is married to Vontilla Bell and lives in Westlake, Texas. They have four children, eight grandchildren, and two great-grandchildren. He built and operated the popular Rapid Mart grocery, along with partner Tully Angle, for many years. It was located on the corner of Vance Road and Grapevine Highway, part of the original Parchman 13 acres.

Gayle Parchman Gunther lives in Granbury and had five children (one deceased) and five grandchildren.

Haly Parchman served on the Birdville School Board for many years, and the Parchmans were members of North Richland Hills Baptist Church. Julius and Anita Bussey, Stanley and Vontilla Parchman, and Gayle Gunther were honored guests of the church at its 40th anniversary in May 1996.

JOHN ALLEN AND BILLIE FAYE TODD PARISH

I, John Allen Parish, was born July 18, 1926, in Santa Anna, Coleman County, Texas, to Lillian Freeman and Ratio Preston Parish. I have a brother, Royce Parish, now of Dallas, and sister, Vi Peterman, of Fort Worth. During my childhood, I attended schools in Coleman and Waxahachie, continuing my studies at Texas Christian University and North Texas State College in Denton. For 23 years I taught school and was an elementary principal in the Birdville Independent School District, retiring in 1970. During this period for 26 years, I was also a home builder, and retired from that profession in 1988.

My wife, Billie Faye, was born in Paragould, Arkansas, to Idell Myhan and Charles Ed Todd. She grew up with one sister, Doty Todd Dudley, now deceased. Billie Faye attended schools in Memphis, Tennessee, Paragould, Arkansas, Waxahachie, and Texas Woman's University in Denton. We married June 29, 1947, in Waxahachie. Billie Faye said she will never retire as she has been a homemaker, mother, and wife for these 50 years we have shared.

We have two children, Annette Parish Hunt and Charles P. (Chip) Parish. Annette married Philip Hunt of North Richland Hills after they both graduated from Richland High School and the University of Texas at Arlington. They presently live in Arlington and have three beautiful daughters, Rachel, Jessica, and Stephanie.

L/R-Annette (Parish) Hunt, John, Billie Faye, Chip Parish

Chip also graduated from Richland High School and the University of Texas at Arlington, and has been a teacher at Richland High School the past five years. He has given us two wonderful grandsons, Chuck and Joey.

Billie Faye and I moved to Haltom City in 1961, then to Harrell Street in North Richland Hills. Our family has enjoyed boating, skiing, and fishing, while I have enjoyed playing golf at both Diamond Oaks and Woodhaven country clubs. Billie Faye and I play tennis, and regularly play bridge and dominoes with friends, many of whom we met through PTA, church, and neighborhoods where we have lived. Both children have played in the junior and senior high school bands, so the entire family has enjoyed football games, especially the halftime activities! Our family has also been active in the Assembly of God Church for many years where Billie Faye and I have been Sunday school teachers.

We have been active in many community organizations. Billie Faye has been a member of the Builders Auxiliary of Fort Worth and Tarrant County and held various offices in the PTA while the children were attending school. I am a past president of the Builders Association of Fort Worth and Tarrant County; member of the Board of Directors of the Haltom-Richland Chamber of Commerce; member of the Board of Directors of the National Association of Home Builders, and was president of the Northeast Lions Club.

One memory that will never fade concerns the Fossil Creek flood, when another principal and friend, B. J. Stigler, called to say he had students stranded on the roofs of their homes. I took our boat to the flooded area, and he and I rescued families from their roofs and into our boat. It was always neighbor helping neighbor in NRH.

In 1969, I developed a melanoma cancer, and my good friends in the Birdville Council of PTAs had a prayer for me. They must have been pretty powerful prayers, because here it is 28 years later, and I am still going strong (well, pretty strong).

We moved away from North Richland Hills in 1974 to east Fort Worth but find ourselves coming back for shopping and visiting friends. Thank goodness Loop 820 will take us back to familiar territory so quickly. It is still home to us.

Submitted into story form by Nancy Dowler

FRED AND ALINE PARKER

The Parker family, Fred, Aline, and two-year-old Fredric Forest, moved from Fort Worth to Richland Hills in February 1951. David William was born May 21, 1952, making our family complete.

We were charter members of Richland Hills Baptist Church where Fred sang in the choir, was in the first group of deacons ordained in the church and was the first church treasurer. I, Aline Parker, was superintendent of the Cradle Roll Department and also was president of the Richland Park Garden Club. Though we were happy with our church and good neighbors, we moved to North Richland Hills in March 1955. Our street, Ken Michael Court, had no streetlights, and the city did not have a police department. We joined our neighbors in paying a private security man to drive by once a night and shine a spotlight on our house.

Fred Parker

We joined the North Richland Hills Baptist Church in 1957 when Jimmy Hester was pastor. Fred sang in the choir as long as his health permitted, and son, Forest, sang with the church Choraliers. We moved to Marilyn Lane in September 1959. We continued to lead busy lives, as the boys participated in Scouts, church activities, band, drama, and football. I did volunteer work including serving on the Fort Worth YWCA executive board as secretary, vice president, and chairman of the Long Range Planning Committee, held offices, including president, of the Ridglea Rejebian Book Review Club. Fred was a 20-year member of the Fort Worth Lions Club and president of the Texas Credit Men's Association. I continued community involvement serving on the Mayor's Advisory Committee and Parks Commission during Cal Luper's term as mayor; helped organize the North Richland Hills Library, and was a member of the first Library Commission when Marion Massey was mayor.

Aline Parker

Fred suffered a second heart attack, and following heart surgery, died November 30, 1974.

In the ensuing years, I have continued service in the schools and community, including chairman of the cancer drive for Northeast Tarrant County; chairman of the March of Dimes for the NRH area; was election judge for NRH during Dick Faram's years as mayor, was a member of the first Town Hall Committee in 1966, and continued to be a member of the present Town Hall Commission, (reactivated during Mayor Tommy Brown's administration) and currently serve on the NRH Historical Committee.

David Parker

F. Forest Parker

The boys were very fortunate to be in school during W. G. Thomas' years as superintendent. They attended schools in the Birdville District from first grade through high school. During these years I served 11 years as a PTA president along with most other offices and 10 years on the Texas PTA Executive Committee and Board of Managers. I received a Texas Life membership from North Richland Elementary PTA and a National Life membership from the Birdville Council of PTA.

In high school, Forest was active in drama productions, played trumpet in the school band and the Rebel Brass, a self-directed brass ensemble. He attended the University of Texas at Arlington and the University of Texas at Austin, receiving his degree in communications. Forest and Marna Altman, who attended North Carolina State University, were married July 16, 1988. They live in Southlake with their 7-year-old, Caitlin Jessica and William Forest, born February 7, 1998. They attend White's Chapel United Methodist Church where Forest plays in the band for the contemporary service.

In high school, David was active in drama productions, chorus, was a member of Rebelaires and the football team. He graduated from Texas Christian University and received his master's degree from University of North Texas. He and Terry Hendrickson, a graduate of Texas Woman's University in Denton, were married May 20, 1972. After 22 years in the BISD, David accepted the position of principal of Splendora High School in 1997. Terry and David live in Kingwood with their two daughters, Paige Briggs, a sophomore at TWU in Denton, and Brooke Leigh, a junior at Splendora High School. They are members of the Methodist Church and are active in the church's Stephen Ministry program.

Submitted by Aline Parker

JAMES BERNARD AND CORDIA ADELINE PARKMAN

James Bernard Parkman, the son of James Madison and Genie M. Jones Parkman, was born October 9, 1889, at Cusetta, Georgia. James died December 26, 1976, at the Boulevard Manor Nursing Home in Richland Hills. James and Cordia Adeline Green were united in marriage

Back, L/R-Margie Parkman Branch, Bill Parkman, Ann Parkman Gilbert, J. C. Parkman, and Earl Parkman, Front - James and Cordia Parkman

August 6, 1916. Cordia Green was born September 8, 1894. She died at their home near Smithfield on January 13, 1971. Cordia was the daughter of Walter Winfred and Sarah Deborah Matlock Green. James B. and Cordia A. Parkman were buried in the cemetery at Smithfield.

James B. worked several years on the farm of James Madison Parkman, about five miles north of Grapevine. In 1919, James and Cordia moved to a farm about one and one-half miles east of Smithfield where he farmed a few years before going to work at Burrus Mills in Fort Worth and later at Universal Mills where he worked until he retired in 1954. The Parkmans' original home burned on February 28, 1942, and they rebuilt at the same location.

James and Cordia had seven children. Elmer Earl was born at Grapevine, Denton County, May 17, 1917. Earl served as a Seabee with the U.S. Navy, taking two tours of duty in the South Pacific without injury. Jake served as a B-17 pilot flying some 40 missions over Germany without injury. He was the eldest. He married Lillian Elizabeth Moore on March 11, 1939. Lillian was born May 23, 1918. They had four children: Lillie Lue, Susan Jane, Cynthia Ann, and Bryan Earl, born April 7, 1954.

Raymond Edward was born at Smithfield April 2, 1919. He died May 5, 1919, and is buried at Smithfield.

Frank Lloyd, was born March 26, 1920, at Smithfield. Frank was killed in a mill accident just prior to World War II on May 28, 1941; he was buried at Smithfield.

James Carrol (Jake, J. C. or Jim) was born May 3, 1922. Jake married Nellie Mae Gunn in 1950. Jake was stationed at Langley Field, Hampton, Va., and Nellie Mae died while they were there. Jake married Lois Elaine Hollaway April 14, 1956. Lois Elaine was born April 27, 1932. Jake and Lois have two children, Lisa Ann and James Carrol Jr. (Jamie). Jake died June 9, 1985.

Ann Lucille was born at Smithfield, June 1924. She married Clarence (Sirpie) Leon Gilbert July 21, 1944. Clarence Gilbert, served with the U.S. Army in the European sector during World War II, receiving a wrist wound. They had three children, one a stillborn girl, and Leah Jane, and Lue Ann. Lue Ann was killed in an auto accident in February 1984.

William Sandy was born July 27, 1928, at Smithfield. Billy served in the U.S. Army as an athletic and recreation noncommissioned officer during the Korean conflict, but he did not leave the United States. He married Eva Coleen Dunn July 31, 1960. They have three children, Penny Lynn, Beth Frances, and Craig Alan.

Margie Nell was born at Smithfield, May 25, 1931. She married Billy Albert Branch September 11, 1953. They have two children, Sondra Gail and Karen Sue.

All of the children of James and Cordia Parkman received their elementary education at Smithfield Elementary School. Earl graduated from Grapevine High School. Frank, Jake, Ann, Billy, and Margie graduated from Carter-Riverside High School in Fort Worth. Earl, Frank, Jake, and Billy all participated in football in high school. Earl played football and basketball at Grapevine

High. Frank, Jake, and Billy played football at Carter-Riverside. Jake played basketball as well and was named All-City his senior year. Billy went to New Mexico State University and played football for four years. He also coached football and baseball teams in Las Cruces.

This family history of James B. and Cordia A. Parkman was compiled by their children from family records and conversations with their mother and father. Some of this information was first recorded in the early 1960s and has been updated through the years until the latest information was added in 1997.

Submitted by Margie Parkman Branch

ELZIE AND WANDEAN PARKS

Elzie and Wandean Garrison Parks moved to North Richland Hills on Marilyn Lane in 1968, with their daughters, Phyllis Lynne and Nancy Anne. Elzie was born in Temple, Oklahoma and was raised in Holliday and Iowa Park, Texas. He graduated from Iowa Park High School in 1942, entered the U.S. Army and served in the Signal Corps and the Military Police. Upon his return from World War II, he entered Midwestern University in Wichita Falls and graduated in August 1949 with a bachelor's degree in business administration. He joined Texas Electric Service Company in Odessa and spent 36 years with them, retiring in the Fort Worth office in 1987. Some of his years of service were in Odessa, Midland, and Andrews. He completed his service with TU as a plant accountant in the Fort Worth office from 1968 to 1987. Elzie is an active member of North Richland Hills Baptist Church and Texas Utilities Retirement Club.

Wandean Garrison Parks, born in Matador, Texas, to a pioneer Motley County family of ranchers, graduated from Matador High School in 1941 and entered Wichita General Hospital School of Nursing in Wichita Falls. After her graduation in 1944, she enlisted in the U.S. Army Nurse Corps as an officer and was sent immediately to the South Pacific during World War II. She was dis-

charged as a first lieutenant after the war ended. This was the first of her long career in nursing, all of which was in surgery. Upon her return from the South Pacific, she was with the Wichita Falls Clinic Hospital, and for several years in the Andrews Hospital in Andrews. Upon their arrival in North Richland Hills, she worked at Harris Hospital and then with Glenview Hospital in NRH and its successor HCA North Hills Hospital. She was director of surgical services for about 20 years before her retirement in 1989. Wandean is a member of the North Richland Hills Baptist Church, the Association of Operating Room Nurses, charter member of Women in Military Service of America, and is listed on the Women of Military Service of America Memorial Monument at the gateway to Arlington National Cemetery in Washington, D.C.

Their daughter, Phyllis Lynne, graduated from Richland High School in 1970 and is married to Ronnie Landes. They currently live in west Fort Worth. Their daughters are Terri Landes and Julie Alsobrooke, both graduates of Haltom High School.

Their daughter, Nancy Anne Rhoten, is a 1975 graduate of Richland High School and is the mother of Katie Lynne Warrick and Jeremy N. Thornton. Katie is a 1994 graduate of Keller High School and is currently attending Tarrant County Junior College. Jeremy is a 1996 graduate of Azle High School and attended McMurray College in Abilene on a basketball scholarship and is currently enrolled at TCJC. Katie has a son, Brandon Riley Warrick.

PAUL AND JUDY PASCHALL

Our relationship with North Richland Hills began in January 1967 when my wife, Judy, and I led the music at NRHBC for the January Bible conference. At the end of that week NRHBC issued an invitation to us to come on staff, and later that month we came, along with our 3-month-old daughter, Paula Kaye.

Our first home was on Vance Road, just two doors from the church. It had been a parsonage for Brother Hal, Dr. Jack Terry, the former minister of music and youth, and then our family. The house was taken down years ago to make room for parking.

We are now working on our 30th year here at NRHBC.

One of the greatest contributions we have been able to make to our city has been the Greater Fort Worth Christmas Pageant, begun in 1974. That first year we had 3,000 people to attend the two performances held at Richland High School. More than 200 people participated in the production. Forty-five hundred attended the next year, and 6,000

Back, L/R-Ronnie and Phyllis (Parks) Landes, Brandon Warrick, Julie Landes, Nancy (Parks) Rhoten, Katie Thornton Warrick; Front, L/R-Elzie and Wandean Parks, Jeremy Thornton, Terri Landes

Paul and Judy Paschall

attended the next four years. Just as we realized our production had outgrown the school, we received a call from the director of the Tarrant County Convention Center. He invited us to come to the theatre with our production, and we have been there for the past 17 years. More than 600 people are now involved in the production that in 1997 reached more than 11,000 children, youth, and adults. It has become one of the best-attended theatre events all year and allows our church to minister to almost 10,000 people outside our own church family. They come from nearby communities, cities, and states. The silver anniversary of the pageant will be celebrated with the 1998 production.

In 1969, our family welcomed a son, Clint Brooks. Paula Kaye and Clint had wonderful experiences at Holiday Heights Elementary, North Richland Junior High, and Richland High. We

Caleb, Paula Kaye (Paschall) holding Lindsey, Odus, and Blake Compton

were blessed through the years with godly teachers and wholesome activities to plug into—sports programs, music programs, drama.

We began building a new home in Meadow Lakes in April 1998, but we will miss our corner at Holiday Lane and Lola Drive when we move. We enjoy working in our yard, having won on two occasions NRH's Yard of the Month award. It's a joy to work in the yard and was as person after person honks while driving by. It's a busy corner, but it has been a prosperous one as well, as we have held garage sales, both personally and for our church's mission projects. We have made as much as $9,000 on our corner, as we raised money for mission trips to Honduras. My record for selling something is 37 seconds.

Judy told me, as she was dusting a silk ficus tree, that she was tired of it in our home. I asked her if she was sure, and she knew what that meant. I was out the door, placing the tree on our corner when someone yelled out, "How much?" Fifteen dollars was the answer I gave, as they slowed to a stop, loaded it in their car, and 37 seconds later we were ordering a pizza to be delivered for Saturday night supper! Three thousand coke cases, antiques, school furniture, estate sales, and unwanted accessory items are just a few of what has been sold through the years.

All that will probably stop when we build a home on a cul-de-sac next to Iron Horse Golf Course. A few golf balls and some fresh lemonade will probably be the main things for sale in our yard, and those will be sold by our grandchildren. Surely an occasional garage sale will still be allowed as well. After all, it doesn't take much brains to work in the yard, but it sure is fun to sell while you work!

We've seen malls constructed, streets widened, freeways enlarged, schools built, and churches built and enlarged. But with all the changes, the city of NRH still

remains our home. We love the people and the atmosphere of a community on the grow but still is made up of people that you would like to meet one at a time.

And I guess that's why we've enjoyed our church, which allows us to minister to, and be a part of people's lives and to live on our corner, where we get to wave at, and to know so many wonderful people.

Our plans include seeing me build a home for my wonderful wife. She's an awesome interior decorator, and I look forward to seeing her express her unique gifts in a new home. We look forward to our grandchildren coming to see us in Meadow Lakes, walking on the golf cart paths in the evening, and waving at golfers from the two swings that will be installed on our 80-feet of porch. And our goal is at age 100 we will be our church's chief greeters, hugging and welcoming every child, young person, and adult who comes to worship at the North Richland Hills Baptist Church . . . the church that we refer to our friends in the ministry as First Baptist, World!

Clint, Tonia, Annah Jane Paschall

Paula Kaye, an accomplished harpist and vocalist, is married to Odus Compton. They live in Shawnee, Oklahoma, with their children: Blake, Caleb, and Lindsey. Odus is director of the Baptist Student Union at Oklahoma Baptist University.

Clint married Richland High classmate Tonia Williams. They live in Katy, Texas, and have one daughter, Annah Jane. Clint is minister of youth at Bear Creek Baptist Church.

Submitted by Paul Paschall

DAVID LYNN AND KATHRYN JANELLE PATTERSON

Kathryn Janelle Schmidt and David Lynn Patterson were married in Hurst in 1994. Kathryn grew up in North Richland Hills. She attended Snow Heights Elementary, North Richland Middle School, Richland High School, and Oklahoma Baptist University. She is the daughter of Paul and Kay Schmidt of North Richland Hills.

David was born in Wichita, Kansas, and grew up in Pryor, Oklahoma where he attended Pryor High School. He also attended Oklahoma Baptist University. He is the son of Donald Lee and Mary Ann Patterson of Pryor.

The Pattersons lived for a short time

David and Kathryn (Schmidt) Patterson

after college in North Richland Hills but moved in 1995 to Tulsa where they currently live. Kathryn is employed as a telecommunications project manager where she finds the global aspects of her work in international sales to be especially interesting. David is with the U.S. Postal Service.

Kathryn has an interest in music and the flute, and in crafts. David enjoys Mopar cars and history, especially the military history of the world wars. The couple also likes to jet-ski and care for their two cats—a golden and a gray tabby.

Submitted by Kay Schmidt

FRED AND ANN PERCHARD

Fred Perchard and I, Ann Perchard, were both born and raised in San Antonio, Texas. We both attended high school there. Fred went to Highlands, and I went to Harlandale. After high school, Fred went into the service, U.S. Navy Construction Battalion. I went to work for Southwestern Bell Telephone as an information operator.

We married in 1968. Our first child, Steven, was born in February 1971. In May 1972, we moved to Euless. We lived in an apartment several months then moved to a rent house in Benbrook.

In May 1973 we moved into our first home on Holiday Lane in North Richland Hills. Fred went to work for Continental Trailways as a bus driver, and I was a homemaker.

Our second child, Clint, was born in November 1979. Both of our children attended Holiday Heights Elementary School, North Richland Middle School, and Richland High School.

In 1984 my husband went into the trucking business. After Steven graduated he went to work for Delta Air Lines. Clint wants to be an auto mechanic. He has worked part-time at an automotive repair shop and is presently working at a local dealership.

In 1991, we moved to Caracas Drive in NRH. While my children were in school I did PTA work and volunteer work for the school. I currently serve on the NRH Parks and Recreation Board.

Submitted by Ann Perchard

BENNY AND REBA PERRY

Reba Maxine Anderson Olsen Perry was born January 21, 1930, to Causen Alexander Anderson and Mettie May (Smyth) Anderson in Keller. There was a record cold spell when she was born. She was born at home, and the doctor had trouble getting through the ice and snow. This was the January they drove cars out on Lake Worth.

Reba had five siblings: Causen Aubrey Anderson, Leroy Anderson, George Alton "Pat" Anderson, Gladys Eva Anderson, and Coy Rudolph (Rudy) Anderson.

Reba and siblings grew up in Keller where they finished high school. Today they all live in the Fort Worth/Keller/NRH area. The parents lived in Keller until their deaths.

Reba graduated from Keller High School in May 1947.

Front, L/R-Presley Olsen, Reba Perry, Ashley Olsen; Second row-Crissy Olsen, Benny Perry, T. J. Olsen, and Adam Olsen; Third row-Russell Moyer, Marlene and Beth Olsen; Back row-Terry, Chris, and Loyd Olsen

She married Gerald (Jerry) Elmer Olsen June 5, 1954, in Fort Worth. They had three sons: John Christopher (Chris) Olsen, Loyd Alvin Olsen, and Terry Lee Olsen.

Reba and her three children moved to Watauga in the summer of 1971. Chris was in high school, and he enrolled in Haltom High School because he could ride the bus at that time. They did not bus the children to Richland High School from Watauga. Loyd was entering junior high school, and he attended Watauga Junior High. Terry was beginning fourth grade and went one year to Watauga Elementary School. The following year Grace E. Hardeman was completed and he finished his elementary years there. Following this time he attended Watauga Junior High and Richland High School. Loyd and Terry both played the trumpet in the school band in junior high.

Our house was the first to be built in a two-block area on Whispering Lane. The only grocery store anywhere near our home was Harold's Grocery & Meat Market on the corner of Denton Highway (Texas 377) and Watauga Road. They did not stock very many groceries, so we had to drive to Safeway (which is long gone now) on the corner of Davis Boulevard and Grapevine Highway. We shopped at Richland Plaza, and the Northeast Mall was just being built. We also went to the movies at Richland Plaza. Other landmarks we patronized that are no longer there were the Belknap Drive-In, Richland Bowling Alley, and the swimming pool at Barrbrook Park. Holiday Skating Rink, located on Carson Street, was a favorite of the boys. Chris spent quite a lot of time in the Carnation Ice Cream shop in the Richland Plaza Shopping Center, since it was so close to Haltom High School.

Chris graduated from Haltom High School and now resides in Arlington. Loyd graduated from Richland High School and now lives in Grapevine. Terry worked at the Waffle House on Grapevine Highway while he was going to Richland High School.

Reba married Benny Joe Perry May 25, 1980. Benny and Reba now live on Pearl Street in NRH. We have seen Davis Boulevard change from a little two-lane road to a much wider, heavily traveled highway lined with businesses. We really felt we lived in the country in 1980. The area behind our home was just woods. Now we have a six-lane highway (Mid-Cities Boulevard) running behind our home. We no longer come home to find quail in our backyard or hear owls "hooting" at night. North Richland Hills has grown so much in the past 25 years. We have a lot of wonderful memories of our family and friends and watching it grow into the city it is today.

Both Benny and Reba retired from Bell Helicopter Textron in Hurst in 1990. Benny enjoys woodworking, the internet, and attending to his rock garden and pond in the back yard. Reba likes ceramics and hand sewing (crochet, cross stitch, etc.). Both enjoy traveling but are always glad to get back home to North Richland Hills.

Submitted by Reba Perry

WILLIAM (BILL) PERRY
MAYOR OF THE CITY OF NORTH RICHLAND HILLS
APRIL 7, 1959–1960

William (Bill) Perry was the only child born to William Andrew and Alva Odell Perry on November 9, 1925 in Neptune, Tennessee.

During World War II, he served in the U.S. Army and was stationed in Boston for a while. After the war, Bill owned and managed service stations in Tennessee and later in Texas. At one time, he owned an automotive garage on the Grapevine Highway.

Bill and his wife, Christine, and Bill's parents moved to the small community of North Richland Hills in the early 1950s to their first home on Kris Street.

They later built a home off Holiday Lane on Riviera Drive where they lived until their deaths. When they built their house in 1958, there was nothing north of Riviera but fields. Bill and Christine had five children, three of whom still live in the Metroplex. He enjoyed taking his family on trips to Tennessee to visit friends and family and to hunt and fish. Bill's favorite sport was deer hunting.

Bill was very active in the early years of the city of North Richland Hills and took great pride in serving as mayor from 1959–1960.

William (Bill) Perry passed away March 29, 1975 and is buried at Bluebonnet Hills Cemetery in Colleyville near his wife and parents.

ED AND FAYE PEWITT
"NOT FAR FROM THE NEST"

In the fall of 1955, when the Pewitt family moved to Flory Drive in North Richland Hills into one of the few subdivisions north of Grapevine Highway, little did they know what the next four-plus decades would bring. They never could have predicted a five-lane Rufe Snow Drive, 3,000 students at Richland High School, nor did they really know how God would bless them, their children, and their grandchildren in the years to come.

The following is just one brief historical review of what life can be like and rewards that can come as a result of raising a family in a town which has been centered around family bonds and community involvement.

Faye and Ed Pewitt moved from the Riverside area of Fort Worth to NRH with their three children, Carol, Gary, and Cindy in 1955. They moved across the street from what was then called North Richland Elementary and later renamed Alliene Mullendore Elementary. One of their first orders of business was to become members of North Richland Hills Baptist Church in order to lay a foundation for their children's spiritual life. Ed was employed by Southwestern Bell, where he later retired in 1980. Faye went to work in the Birdville schools' cafeteria system where she worked until retiring in 1973. Still today, Faye is a "staple" of Flory Drive, and many who drive up and down nearby Glenview Drive still look for her smiling face and friendly wave. Ed died in December 1993.

Not falling far from the nest though are the Pewitt's three children. Carol Pewitt Hallows, who graduated from Richland High School in 1966, married Gary Hallows (RHS 1964), and has resided on Hovenkamp in Richland Hills for more than 25 years. Carol is an escrow officer for Stewart Title Co. in Arlington. Her husband, Gary, has been with American Airlines for over 30 years. Carol attended North Richland Elementary, Richland Junior High (North Richland Junior High not being built yet) and Richland High School.

Gary Pewitt is the family member who truly came "full circle." Gary, a graduate of Richland High School in 1968, married his college sweetheart, Louise Trammell, in 1970, and they have one child, Coby, a policeman for the city of Richardson and former president of the National Honor Society of North Texas State University. Many remember Gary for his athletic ability and God-given talents exhibited on every type of playing field, from a Little Leaguer playing shortstop, all through his exciting high school football career as the *Fort Worth Star-Telegram's* 4A-4 Player of the Year in 1967. He also attended North Richland Elementary, Richland Junior High, and even North Richland Junior High the first year it opened; and, of course, Richland High School. Gary, a Hurst resident, can continue to be seen on the playing field as a coach at Richland High School and sometimes even playing, although on the computer, in his classroom at Richland High School.

The youngest of the Pewitt children, Cindy Pewitt Guerrero, was only 1 year old when the Pewitts moved to NRH. Cindy also went through the North Richland schools and graduated from Richland High School in

1972. While still a cheerleader at Richland High School, Cindy also began her 26-year career at Educational Employees Credit Union and continues her employment there today.

The tradition of "not far from the nest" is still prevalent in the Guerrero household today. Cindy continues to live in NRH with her children, Jason and Courtney. Jason, a Richland High School graduate in 1994, is a fireman for the city of Dallas and continued the traditions set by his father, Henry Guerrero (RHS Class of 1970), and Uncle Gary, of providing excitement on a football playing field. The youngest of the Pewitt and Guerrero clan is Courtney, currently a high-kicking, fast dancing, Dixie Belle senior at Richland High School. Courtney will carry on the tradition of Richland High School graduates in 1998 when she becomes the ninth in the Guerrero family (also from the North Richland-Smithfield area) to graduate from Richland High School.

DON AND DEBORA KAY PHIFER

Don Phifer and Deborah (Debbie) Haidusek both grew up in Haltom City and attended Haltom High School. After graduation, Don attended TCJC and the University of Texas in Arlington, where he earned a BBA in Real Estate and Finance. Deborah, upon graduation from high school, went to East Texas State and then North Texas State University, where she earned a degree in Vocational Home Economics and Early Childhood Development.

Don and Deborah Phifer were married in August 1986, shortly after graduating from college. They bought their first home in North Richland Hills in 1987 and moved to their current home in 1997. In April 1991, Don and Deborah were blessed with their first child, a little girl, Alexis Marie. Their son, Andrew Daniel, was born in April 1995.

In January 1993, Don started Don Phifer and Associates, a commercial real estate company that later evolved into Phifer and Associates Inc. The company specializes in selling undeveloped commercial real estate in Tarrant and Denton counties.

In August 1985, Deborah went to work for Arlington ISD, teaching kindergarten. She taught

Debbie, Don, Alexis with Andrew in front

three years at Rankin Elementary and the last 10 years at Roquemore Elementary.

After several years of interest in local politics, Don was prompted to run for City Council by Council Member Mark Wood and Mayor Tommy Brown. In May of 1996, Don was elected to the North Richland Hills City Council, to fill an unexpired term for Place 5. In 1997, Don was reelected to the same position in an unopposed race.

While serving on the City Council, Don has served on many committees, such as the CIP Committee, Park Development Committee, North Richland Hills Crime Control and Prevention District. He was a representative to the North Texas Commission and elected mayor pro tem in June 1998 by the City Council. In addition to the aforementioned committees, Don represents North Richland Hills and five neighboring cities on the Regional Transportation Commission. He served two years on the St. John School Advisory Council and chair of its Finance Committee. He also serves on the Texas Municipal League Committee on Utilities and the Environment, and a subcommittee on electric deregulation. Don is a member of the Liberty Bank Advisory Council, Northeast Chamber of Commerce, and the Northeast Richland Lions Club, where he also serves on the Board.

DAVID AND BETH PHILLIPS

The David S. Phillips Family moved to North Richland Hills from Houston in August 1984. We moved to Lincoln Drive, a new street—so new it was not on the school district map when we went to register our children for school.

Our family is David Samuel Phillips, born in Hartford, Conn. 1951, and Beth Mingle Phillips, born in Frankfurt, Germany in 1953. We met at York College, York, Nebraska in 1971 and married in 1972.

Back, L/R-Beth, David S., Marijoy; Front, L/R-Timothy, David R., Bethany

Marijoy Phillips was born in Thousand Oaks, California in 1976; David Reynolds-Rice Phillips was born in Webster, Texas, in 1977; Bethany Ruth Phillips was born in Webster, Texas, in 1981; and our NRH native, Timothy Joseph Phillips, was born in 1990.

We are members at Mid-Cities Church on Precinct-Line Road. We own two small businesses: Employee Administration Specialists Inc. and Administrative Staffing Inc. We are members of the Fort Worth Chamber of Commerce, Cowtown Executive Association, National Association for Alternative Staffing, Concerned Women for America, National Rifle Association, the Heritage Foundation, and we support Texas Right to Life.

We have volunteered in the Birdville schools beginning when our two older children entered Smithfield Elementary. Our children attended Foster Village Elementary, Watauga Junior High, North Ridge Middle, Haltom High, and Green Valley Elementary. Our high school graduates went on to four-year universities receiving academic and leadership scholarships. Our third child is a student at Fort Worth Christian School, and the youngest is in Birdville Independent School District at

Green Valley Elementary. Beth has served as president of Foster Village Elementary PTA, North Ridge Middle School PTA, and Birdville Council of PTAs. Beth, Donna Stewart, and Paula Good were founders of the Birdville Volunteer Partnership established through the Council of PTA for the BISD.

We currently reside on Oak Court. As parents, we received the highest honor when our daughter nominated us, and we were selected Parents of the Year at Abilene Christian University. We enjoy camping, biking, fishing, walking, target shooting, crafts, horse riding, antiquing, and softball.

Submitted by Beth Phillips

DELMA AND MARY ANN PHILLIPS

Delma Phillips was born December 6, 1920, in Honey Grove, Fannin County, Texas. He married Mary Ann Haywood in Fort Worth on November 3, 1941. Mary Ann was born June 7, 1924, in Wolfe City, Texas.

"Phil" was employed by Swift & Company in January 1942, and on September 2, 1943, entered the U.S. Army. He crossed the English Channel into France. He was a corporal in charge of an anti-aircraft crew with the 386th Anti-Aircraft Artillery from February 2, 1944, to November 1945.

1944 - Corporal Delma Phillips

Following graduation from Brantley-Draughon Business School in 1942, Ann went to work as secretary for Zweifel, Floore & Hicks, Fort Worth attorneys. After separation from the Army in 1945, Phil returned to their home in Fort Worth where Anita Sharon was born November 4, 1943, and where Peggy Ann would be born July 21, 1947.

Ann Phillips holding Sharon, 1944

Phil returned to Swift & Company as foreman, and their family soon moved to 38 acres near Smithfield, purchased through the third application processed by the new Veteran's Land Board in Austin. Their son, James Ralph, was born January 17, 1951. All three children graduated from the Keller School District. After graduation from East Texas State University, Sharon worked for Delta Airlines for a few years before marrying an English national, Christopher Burfield.

The Burfields reside in Georgia where they have been with both the airline industry and aircraft manufacturing for many years. They have a daughter, Jennifer, who recently graduated with a degree in international business and a minor in French.

Peggy attended East Texas State University and Texas Woman's University, and married Stanley Campbell of Sulphur Springs, who earned a degree at ETSU. After a stint in the U.S. Marines, he became a manager for

Montfort of Colorado. They have a daughter, Kristen, and a son, Boone.

Peggy is big on volunteerism, as was her sister, and beginning some years ago read for the blind over the radio in Greeley, Colorado. Peg has been involved with the Colorado Governor's Committee in reacquainting schoolchildren with that state's ranching heritage. She worked for several years with the Cattleman's Ball, as well as taking pets once a week

Peggy Phillips - 1964

to a nursing home. She celebrated her "Big Five-O" birthday in 1997 by climbing Longs' Peak at 14,000-plus feet. She has donated one of her original sculptures to the annual Cattleman's Ball to be auctioned off for the benefit of the Cancer Fund. Both Peggy and her mother became interested in sculpture during the 1950s after Ann had three semesters of sculpture under nationally known Evaline Sellors, whose favorite medium was clay.

After 27 years with Swift's, Phil left to go into business for himself. In 1972, he and Ann visited Moscow and Leningrad, and in 1985, Ann spent one month in York, England, doing research for her minor on a master of fine arts degree. She also holds a master's degree in history-government, and is Phi Alpha Theta. She wrote a weekly historical column for three years and has recently copyrighted "Fletcher Warren Reporting for Duty, Sir," the life-story of a Texas ambassador from Wolfe City.

The Phillips' son, James, after attending Tarrant County Junior College, spent four years in the U.S. Air Force before marrying Carolyn Denise Carter, on Nov. 3, 1973. Carolyn also attended TCJC. She and James have two children, Chelsea Leigh, a freshman premed student, and Casey James, a freshman in high school, who loves golf. James now has the family business in North Richland Hills, but spends as much time as possible at Eagle Nest, New Mexico. Carolyn is a medical encoder with a major hospital in Fort Worth.

The James Phillips family, L/R: Casey, James, Carolyn and Chelsea, a first year Pre-Med student.

DR. DAVID AND ANNABEL PILLOW

Dr. David J. Pillow, his wife Annabel, and their four children Kathy, David Jr., Charles, and Carolyn moved to North Richland Hills from the Texas Christian University area in 1956. The new house on Vance Road, purchased with GI Bill financing, was very small compared with her parents house, where they were living, complete with a "full dining room."

The Pillows visited the NRH area one Sunday afternoon with Dr. Charles and Helen Rush, who would become their neighbors on Vance Road. The Rushes lived in Haltom City, and since the Pillow-Rush Medical and Surgical Clinic had been established in 1955 in the NRH Shopping Center, Dr. Rush was having to take most of the "on call" messages.

Back, L/R-Dr. David and Annabel Pillow; Seated, L/R-Kathy (Pillow) Hudson, David Jr., Charles, Carolyn (Pillow) Riggs, John

The decision to move was made, and Annabel literally cried, "Leave a large house for a much smaller one, leave our beloved University Baptist Church, all the children's activities in Cub Scouts, Bluebirds, and squeeze a family of six into a much smaller, although new, house!!" The rooms were so small that one bedroom wouldn't accommodate twin beds, so they had to be stacked into bunk beds. There was no den, so the living room was the center of all family activities, other than eating which was done in the kitchen. Carolyn's chair was wedged in a small space between the refrigerator and the cabinet. It was a good thing she was small.

Another "move shock" came when the Pillows realized the move must be complete with a change of churches. The desire to become totally involved in the community was important, and so the decision was made to visit NRH Baptist Church on the first Sunday after the move. But one problem occurred to Annabel—she hadn't brought a hat. One wouldn't think of not wearing a hat at University Baptist Church in 1956. The result was positive because no one wore a hat on that Sunday.

The house was small, but the lot was huge. One day Annabel was ready to go to a meeting, and Carolyn was playing in the neighborhood. Annabel got on the bicycle, good dress, high heels and all, to go look for her. That evening Dr. David said he thought they had a pretty good reputation in the area, but now he wasn't sure.

After a year and a half the family moved to Richland Hills to a house on Brooks Avenue that had four bedrooms. John was born in 1963 at Glenview Hospital during this time. The four older children graduated from Richland High School.

Kathleen (Kathy) Hudson, Ph.D., born 1945, returned to Richland High School to teach, now teaches at Shreiner University in Kerrville. She heads the freshman orientation, enjoys her horses on eleven acres, heads up the Texas Heritage Music Foundation which sponsors festivals, coffee shops featuring artists on campus, etc.

David James Pillow Jr. M.D., born 1947. Emergency Medical Services based at Saint Paul's Hospital in Dallas, works through various hospitals. Lives in Plano.

Charles Foster Pillow, born 1950, CPA, Source Finance Inc., Dallas. His oldest son recently graduated from University of Texas. Charlie lives in Grapevine. He was an outstanding football player at Richland High School and later Texas Christian University.

Carolyn Lea Riggs, born in 1952, Certified Registered Nurse Anesthetist (CRNA). Recently shattered her wrist while rollerblading.

John K. Pillow, M.D., born 1963 at Glenview Hospital. Graduated Grapevine-Colleyville High School, now emergency medical doctor at Brownwood Regional Hospital.

David and Annabel Pillow celebrated their 50th wedding anniversary September 13, 1994, with all of their children. There are now eleven grandchildren and one great-granddaughter, ages 29 years to 3 months. Their home has been in Colleyville for many years.

ARNOLD AND LIL PITCHFORD

After growing up in communities near Weatherford, Texas, Arnold Pitchford and Lil Campsey met while attending college in North Texas State in Denton and married April 7, 1950.

They moved to Cummings Drive in North Richland Hills in November 1957 and have four children. In 1978, the family moved to Mobile, Alabama, but moved back to NRH in July 1987. In 1994, they moved to Arnold's home place on a farm near Weatherford. They have nine grandchildren ranging in age from 4 to 22.

L/R-Harold, Arnold, Karen (Johnson), Lil, Carol (Eberly), Frances (Peck)

The Pitchfords' children:

Harold Pitchford, born July 22, 1951, in Natchez, Mississippi, is married to Donna Jones Pitchford, and they have three children. Harold works for Fort Worth Parks and Recreation Department;

Frances Pitchford Peck, born September 9, 1952, in Natchez, is married to Steve Peck, and they have one son. Frances teaches in the Grapevine-Colleyville Independent School District;

Carol Lee Pitchford Eberly, born March 9, 1956, in New Orleans, is married to Jerry Eberly, and they have two children. Carol teaches in the Hurst-Euless-Bedford ISD;

Karen Pitchford Johnson, born April 17, 1961, is married to Steve Johnson and they have three children. Karen teaches in the Lamar ISD in Paris, Texas.

Arnold Pitchford spent 37 years in the oil and gas industry and three years as a church business manager before spending his retirement years raising Beefmaster cattle. He is an elder in the Richland Hills Church of Christ.

Lil Pitchford taught seven years at Bell High School. Besides working with Arnold in his church ministry, she does farm chores and enjoys hobbies of playing tennis, volleyball, softball, and teaching aerobics.

Interview by Pat Riddle

PRYOR FAMILY

Sherman Pryor and Kathryn Pryor moved to Circular Drive in North Richland Hills September 10, 1957. They were the parents of eight sons.

Walter "Buddy" Pryor was the first of five sons to be born in Hugo, Oklahoma. He was born in 1934, and attended Diamond Hill High School in Fort Worth. He died September 20, 1997.

Johnnie E. Pryor, born in 1935, worked at Bell Helicopter and was a member of the Glenview Baptist Church. He refereed football, and on the way back from a game in 1974, he had a heart attack. He left two small boys (5 and 6 years old) who still live in this area.

Kathryn Pryor Creamer on her 80th Birthday, 1996

Joe Mack was born in 1937, attended Diamond Hill High School, and won a football scholarship at North Texas State University. He has been a coach for 37 years and has coached at Smithfield Middle School for the past seven years.

Frank Pryor, born in 1939, attended Diamond Hill High School but moved to a school in Haltom City in 1957. He coached boxing for 30 years at the Panther Boys Club. His wife is still the president of the Golden Gloves Club. Frank has worked at Bell Helicopter plant for 32 years. They live in Watauga.

Sammy Pryor was born in 1941 and moved to NRH in 1957 where he attended Birdville High School. He died in 1981 from a heart attack, leaving four children.

The next three sons were born in Fort Worth. Alvin Pryor, born in 1945, finished school at Haltom High and worked 15 years for Bell Helicopter. When caught in a layoff at the plant, he opened his own business. He and brother Walter developed the roads and streets in Hugh White's Estates on Highway 156. He married Brenda Eddleman, who has a business on the Grapevine Highway in a shopping center near Tarrant County Junior College, Northeast Campus. Alvin has coached boxing at the Golden Gloves for many years. His teams have been in the nationals every year since 1978. The most important thing Alvin and his wife did in their lives was to adopt a beautiful baby girl in 1979. Their daughter likes horses so the Pryors moved to Wise County where she has been involved with the Northwest High School rodeo team for the past four years. She was rodeo queen one year. She is a beautiful cowgirl.

Dwight Pryor, born in 1947, has worked for Bell Helicopter for 25 years. Dwight has one son and one adopted daughter. Dwight attended North Texas State University and is a teacher at a Haslet school. His wife has worked for J. C. Penney for many years.

Ted Steven Pryor, born in 1951, moved to NRH when he was 6 years old and went through schools in Haltom City. Ted has two sons, Andy and Brandon. Andy won the North Texas Champion Bull Rider contest and went to college in Vernon, Texas. Brandon played football and baseball for Richland High School and attended Weatherford Junior College. Ted is the owner of Pryor Floor Covering on Crites Street in Richland Hills and lives in NRH.

Sons of Kathryn Creamer: L/R, Walter Ed, Ted, Joe, Kathryn, Frank, Dwight, Alvin Pryor

Sherman Pryor died in 1996. Kathryn (Pryor) Creamer was married in 1968 to Loyce Creamer, and he was a wonderful step-dad to all the family for 28 years. He died in 1995.

"The Pryor family has seen NRH grow from Richland Hills to Smithfield and all the shopping centers in between," said Kathryn Creamer, who was 82 on March 26, 1998.

Submitted by Kathryn (Pryor) Creamer

LARRY AND MARIAN RAMSEY
THIRTY YEARS IN "ELDORADO"

There is a South American legend about a fabled city of opportunity called "Eldorado." In North Richland Hills there is a street named Eldorado Drive in the Richland Oaks Addition between Bedford-Euless Road and Texas 26 via Strummer Drive.

Larry and I, Marian Woolard Ramsey, moved onto

Eldorado in 1967 from Euless. Today, we still have many of the same neighbors we had in 1967. In some cases, children and grandchildren of former homeowners occupy the homes. In other cases, young families have purchased the homes of deceased neighbors. In 1967, Eldorado could be described as "bucolic," because Bedford-Euless Road was a hard-topped, two-lane country road. There was no North East Mall in Hurst (a block away) and no Loop 820. There was no Airport Freeway (Texas 121) and no place to dine out except Grandma's Chicken Shack on the Grapevine Highway. Instead of restaurants, shops, traffic, and constant construction, there was a beautiful pond and white fence at the southern tip of Strummer Drive.

In 1969, we welcomed to our home the only child who has ever lived in this house. Daniel Tyson Ramsey loved to fly kites and play ball in the vacant fields south of Eldorado and Bedford-Euless Road. "Restaurant Row," from Bennigan's to Red Lobster, was once the home of countless quail, doves, rabbits, snakes, an iguana, and other creatures.

In the early 1970s, NorthEast Mall, with a huge Leonard's Department Store, changed the quiet residential area forever. Soon came the construction of Loop 820, Airport Freeway (121), restaurants, businesses, and traffic. In 1978, there was snow every week for six weeks, and the neighborhood children and a few parents turned an incline off Loop 820 into a great place for dishpan sledding.

In 1981, Bennigan's was built at the intersection of Strummer Drive and Bedford-Euless Road. Today, on the south side of Bedford-Euless Road, is a string of restaurants, a warehouse, pawn shop, and a motel. By the time Ty was a teenager, he worked at several of the restaurants. After graduating from Richland High School in 1988 and the University of Texas at Austin in 1992, Ty entered the business world and is now an account executive with Office Depot Business Services.

Larry retired in 1995 after 32 years at Bell Helicopter as a buyer and property disposal specialist. I retired in 1994 from a teaching career that included Dallas, Hurst-Euless-Bedford, and Birdville schools, as well as Tarrant County Junior College. Larry and I were college sweethearts at North Texas State University in Denton in 1959.

Today we tell people we live in "downtown" North Richland Hills. We have seen no reason to move, for every few years downtown keeps getting constructed around us. Even the post office moves more frequently, for I recall the construction of the post office on Blaney Drive and the dismantling of the facility for a new location on Davis Boulevard. Within walking distance of our home, we have Bennigan's, Leonardo's, Shrimp Pot, Ernie's, Chili's, Olive Garden, Red Lobster, TGI Friday's, Haverty's, Pier 1, Old Navy, Blockbuster, Barnes and Noble, MJ Designs, Ross, Oshman's, Garden Ridge, and other shops.

Because the Airport Freeway (121) exit for Bedford-Euless Road and the Loop 820 Exit for North Richland Hills (eastern section) is within a block of Eldorado, I dream that some day a major hotel chain will want to turn our neighborhood into a Dallas Galleria-type area with a first-class hotel and maybe even a retirement complex, complete with an indoor golf course and whatever it takes to make all of our neighbors happy.

Submitted by Marian Woolard Ramsey

RAY FRANKLIN AND MAXINE RAMSEY

Ray Franklin Ramsey was born December 10, 1921, in Pleasant Hill, Louisiana, to Laverna Currie and Jesse Ray Ramsey. He grew up in Pleasant Hill, attending schools there before entering Louisiana State University at Baton Rouge. His special interests were math and history. Ray has one brother, Harold Ramsey of Fort Worth, and one sister, Wanda O'Kelley of Richland Hills.

Back, L/R-John, Tammy, Kim, Jesse, Maxine, and Ray; Front, L/R-Sheila and Logan Clippard, Lexi, Abbi, Jessica

Ray married Maxine Maley September 24, 1943, in Weatherford. She was born May 12, 1922, the daughter of Hattie Hall and Charlie Maley in Woodson, Texas, and spent her youth there. Maxine attended schools there and continued her education at Texas Woman's University in Denton. Her favorite activities and studies during this time included sports, crafts, art, and home economics. She grew up with three brothers, John Earle and Charles (both deceased) and Barton Maley of Fort Worth.

Both Ray and Maxine enjoyed careers at the General Dynamics plant. Ray was employed there 38 years and Maxine 11 years. Both retired the same day in May 1987. Since their retirement, Ray enjoys stamp and coin collecting, while Maxine devotes her spare time to gardening and collecting antiques.

Matthew Ramsey

The Ramseys moved to Steven Street in North Richland Hills 43 years ago. Their two sons are Jesse Ray Ramsey II, born December 27, 1946, and John Weldon, born May 28, 1959. Both boys attended Richland Elementary School and Richland Junior High School. Jesse attended Ardmore High School in Ardmore, Okla., but returned to this area and graduated from Richland High School. He entered Tarleton State

Maci and Teri Ramsey 1997

College on a football scholarship and later transferred to Texas Wesleyan University in Fort Worth. He also attended Texas College of Osteopathic Medicine, completing his intern and residency at William Beaumont Hospital and El Paso. John attended Graham High School, continuing his studies at Tarleton State and San Angelo State Colleges. Ray and Maxine have six grandchildren and one great-grandchild, Logan Clippard.

Jesse is married to Kimberly Wallace, and they live in Jackson, Missouri, where Jesse is an emergency room doctor in Cape Girardeau. They have six children.

John married Tamera Tuckey, and they have one son, Matthew. John entered the Department of Public Safety Academy in Austin, graduating as an officer of the Department of Public Safety. He is stationed in Georgetown, where the family presently lives.

The Ramsey family were members of Richland Hills Baptist Church for 43 years before moving their membership to North Richland Baptist Church. Ray is a charter member of Richland Hills Masonic Lodge, the Boy Scout program, and Richland Youth Association. Maxine was active in the Cub Scouts, Richland Youth Association, the PTA, and the Richland Hills Garden Club.

BERNICE C. AND VERA ABBOTT REDDING

Vera Abbott worked her way through college during the Great Depression. She was studying to be a teacher at Commerce State College in Commerce, Texas. After she earned her teaching certificate, Vera moved to Smithfield to live with her brother, E. Foy Abbott and his family.

At the time, Smithfield was a small town surrounded by a large rural area. There were no conveniences. Five to 10 people used the same telephone party line. The streets were just dirt, with the exception of Smithfield Road, which was hot-topped. It still had plenty of chugholes, however. Water from a well at the schoolhouse was piped through very small pipes into the homes. When someone on the north side of the school took a bath, the people on the south side had no drinking water. There was no form of transportation or fire protection, except for the "tow-sack brigade." There was a post office, a grocery store, a barbershop, and a telephone office. The fire that ravaged the city earlier burned the rest of it. The city

B. C. and Vera Abbott Redding

of North Richland Hills had not yet been born.

Vera's first teaching position was at Glade Elementary. Her $70-a-month salary added to the family income. In 1934, A. D. Roach, the county school superintendent, got Vera a place in Bedford to teach. It was there Vera fell in love with teaching. Vera taught in Bedford nine years. While teaching in Bedford, Vera also fell in love with Bernice C. Redding, a native son. After five years of stormy courtship, she married him. That meant moving out of the Abbott family home to the other side of the tracks, as B. C. built a grocery store on Main Street across from where they lived in Smithfield. Vera kept on teaching.

B. C. was christened Bernice C. Redding in 1902. When his family moved to Fort Worth, he and his father, Eugene, worked for Armour's Meat Packing Company. But Uncle Sam called Eugene to service, so B. C. moved with his family to the country where he supported his mother by growing tomatoes and milking cows. Armour's didn't pay a boy of 15 very much.

B. C. with a flock of feathered friends

In 1937, the family moved to Smithfield where B. C. met Vera; they were married in 1941. B. C. remodeled the old blacksmith shop, making it into a grocery store. When the economy improved, he bought more property, at the corner of Main Street and Smithfield Road, from the Lewis family where he built the cream brick store, still standing, and a new home just east of the store.

Although Vera had married, she was still deeply involved with her Abbott family, and B. C. had his own parents to be concerned about. Vera was called by Birdville School Superintendent Wiley G. Thomas to come to Birdville to teach. That meant $100 per month. "I don't want to interview you," Mr. Thomas told her. "I want you to go to work!" She did, taking her brother Foy's two boys, Tommy and Don, with her. As the boys progressed grade-wise, Vera moved up a grade. When asked why, she told people, "Eula is not well. Foy works from light to dark. Someone has to keep up with Tommy and Don." Vera spent the next 25 years teaching in Birdville.

With his marriage, B. C.'s interest in Smithfield grew. After his dog, Bozo, and his wife, Vera, B. C.'s greatest love was the Smithfield Volunteer Fire Department, which he, with the combined efforts of the volunteers, helped to organize from scratch. With sheer grit and a determination that Smithfield would never burn again, the volunteers stretched their credit to buy a fire engine, which they dubbed "Old Red," and built "The Smithfield Volunteer Fire Station No.1." With barbecues, races, public rallies, and other activities, they paid off their debt. College professors came in and taught the volunteers how to fight fires and give first aid. The community was knitted together by their loyalty to the Fire Department. B. C. gave 23 of the best years of his life to the Fire Department and to the upbuilding of Smithfield. In return, he received many honors. When he retired from the Fire Department in 1972, he was made Honorary Chief for Life.

Vera Abbott Redding and brother, E. F. "Foy" Abbott

Vera Redding was active in Smithfield Church of Christ for 50 years, and she taught the church's young people for most of that time. Vera, who still lives in her home on Main Street in the Smithfield section of NRH, retired from Birdville schools in 1969 to care for her ill mother. B. C. passed away in 1980.

Submitted by Vera Redding

BILL REEVES

The current effort to record the history of North Richland Hills is commendable. It is good to see the formation of historical societies throughout northeast Tarrant County. Perhaps, the most historical site in the county, Birdville, has the least physical evidence of its existence and tremendous impact on the genesis of the Metroplex. Birdville, as a development of Bird's Fort, was where it all began, and now it is but a fading memory.

I am proud that I was born in the town of Birdville in 1925 when it still boasted a business district on Broadway. At that time, the Birdville School District was located entirely in one location, at Carson and Belknap streets. We considered Birdville, at that time, to include areas now comprising Haltom City, Richland Hills, and North Richland Hills, with the exception of the proud little town of Smithfield. I was very familiar with Smithfield since this was the home of my maternal grandparents, Ed and Mattie Walker. They lived directly across from the depot, and Ed was a blacksmith and ran a Gulf station for many years on Main Street. They are at rest in the Smithfield Cemetery.

W. O. Reeves (1869–1924)

My family has deep roots in the North Richland Hills area. My great-grandparents, George Franklin and Carolyn Elizabeth Brewer Reeves, moved to Tarrant County in 1865 or 1866. They built a log house where Richland Plaza is located. My great-great-grandparents, Osborn and Rebecca Osborn Reeves later joined them. After my great-grand-

Mary Bell Reeves (1872–1950)

parents moved to Handley, my grandfather continued to live in the log home. My father, John Franklin Reeves, was born there in 1896, as well as four sisters. Two of these sisters were early teachers in Birdville. The tennis coach at Haltom High School, George Angle, is the grandson of one of these teachers, Leona Angle.

My grandfather, William Osborn Reves (Reves is the old spelling of the family name) built a large two-story house, at the corner of Carson and Edwards Street, in Birdville in 1913. It accommodated a growing family that ultimately numbered nine daughters and three sons. My grandfather was a dairy farmer and county commissioner. After his death in 1924, Granny Reeves continued to operate the dairy and built a number of rent houses. Granny sold the land between Baker Boulevard and the Grapevine Highway that permitted the rapid development to the east of Big Fossil Creek. I remember, as a kid, riding a horse from her home on Birdville Hill to round up her cattle grazing on this land. Reeves Street is now located in this development.

I was born in the last house on Birdville

W. O. Reeves Home in Birdville, circa 1913

Hill, across from where Thomas Coliseum is now located. My father built the home where I was born. My home was just up the hill from Big Fossil Creek, which was where I spent many hours as a youth.

The town of Birdville, as I knew it, ceased to exist in 1932 when the businesses relocated to take advantage of the traffic flow on the new highway on East Belknap. Prior to this, Birdville had a small business district, about a block long, on Broadway, at the top of Birdville Hill, stretching to Carson Street. Thomas Coliseum now occupies most of the area where the old businesses were located

A man living in Baird, Texas, owned the telephone company. The telephone office (switchboard) was located in a four-room house owned by Granny Reves. It did not have a bathroom and inside toilet facilities. At one time, it housed the telephone operator and her sister, in two rooms, which included the switchboard and kitchen.

Earl West gave me my first haircut, which cost a quarter at that time. He later moved his shop to Haltom City, and I think he continued to use the same board to cut the hair of youngsters that I sat on for my first haircut.

Many of the Birdville teachers roomed and boarded at Granny Reves' house. You would understand why they wanted to stay there if you ever ate a meal prepared by her; each one was a feast.

I started school in the first grade in a one-room frame building (located across from the Birdville Baptist Church) rented from the Bewleys. My first-grade teacher was Bessye Clark, and the superintendent was W. T. Francisco.

This was during the Depression and times were hard. We were all so poor that we didn't recognize it. When I got in the fourth grade, my father told me that I was old enough to buy my own school clothes. So, each summer, I would do farm work to earn money to buy my school clothes. Before school started, my mother would take me to Engler's Department Store, near the Fort Worth Courthouse, to buy my khakis for the year. This was a big step up from the blue overalls I wore when I first started to school.

I was attending Birdville School when it started playing football. Early opponents included adversaries like Sanger, Valley View, and Alvord. The school won its first two district championships before I graduated in 1943.

J. C. McCurry and I enlisted in the Navy in March 1943, and were allowed to graduate before being called to active duty. The Class of 1943 paid a heavy price in the war. Ben Angle, my first cousin, and two very good friends, John Cox and J. C. McCurry, would not survive the war.

One of the better known streets in North Richland Hills is Rufe Snow Drive. I knew Rufe Snow when I was a youngster. Granny owned some land, where she baled hay, close to Mr. Snow's farm. Some of my classmates lived on what is now Rufe Snow Drive. Their last names were Parker, Killingsworth, and Rose. I often went to Will Snow's house on Grapevine Highway, located on the hill on the Grapevine Highway, just east of Rufe Snow Drive, to play with his son Lonnie Ray. Lonnie Ray was nicknamed "Charge It" because of his habit of purchasing candy at M. H. Portwood's Grocery, in old Birdville, and telling them to "charge it." The Parchmans lived just east of Will Snow, and Guy Reeves, my dad's first cousin, later had a farm at Four Points, where Hudiburg Chevrolet is now located.

I realize that I must bring this rambling epistle to a close. I also recognize that I have mainly talked about old Birdville, whereas this is for the North Richland Hills history. But to me, the history of this area cannot be cleanly separated by present political boundaries.

Submitted by William Osborn (Bill) Reeves

WILLIE AND GUY REEVES

Willie Hazel Anderson married Minter Guy Reeves May 26, 1918 . . . from the Trinity River Bottom, to the prairie

lands, which abounded with native Buffalo grass (present site of Hudiburg Chevrolet) . . . this couple was fortunate to celebrate 50 years plus of a happy marriage as farmers and dairymen, raising feed crops for their cattle and food for the family.

Guy and Willie Reeves ready for Christmas Eve with the family, 1955

The family story that follows was collaborated on by their daughters Georgia Reeves Duncan and Mary Ruth Ellis, sons-in-law Herman Hardy Duncan Jr., now deceased, and Dr. Norman Dean Ellis, as well as grandchildren Deana Lynn Ellis Hoffman and David Wayne Ellis.

As we tell and relive our family story in the late 1990s we are humbled by the memories of a caring and hard-working farm family in rural Northeast Tarrant County.

We have chosen to share the following personal diary, with location updates, as recorded by Willie Reeves. The diary was found in some of her personal belongings after her death.

As this diary is read it is truly amazing to see the change that has occurred in the northeast section of Tarrant County. How the Anderson Arwine-Reeves family has seen the barbed-wire fences disappear for the thundering freeways.

The mid-1940s brought change as Willie and Guy moved to the prairie at Four Points. Willie and Guy were charter members of the Richland Hills United Methodist Church. Reeves Hall at the church bears the family name. Guy also served on the School Board for Birdville Schools. Willie enjoyed the homemaker role in the home, maintaining an active membership in the Hurst Home Demonstration Club as well as a very active role in gardening and a strong helpmate on the farm.

Four Points was a busy intersection in this rural area in the '40s and '50s. The '60s brought about a giant earth-mover and a major intersection change. As depicted in home movies—grandchildren Deana and David watched the giant earthmover from the front yard of their grandparent's home, which is the present site of Hudiburg Chevrolet.

Now in the late '90s, Deana and Bill Hoffman with their daughter, Haley, and David and Debra Ellis, with their children Danielle and Duncan, are again experiencing change and watching the progress of the area and rebuilding of Loop 820.

As descendants of early pioneer families, Hattie Arwine and Jim Anderson and Adean Deason and G. Press Reves, we cherish our memories and look forward to a strong, prosperous future forging into the next millennium and beyond.

PERSONAL DIARY AS RECORDED BY WILLIE HAZEL ANDERSON REEVES

MINTER GUY REEVES—WILLIE HAZEL ANDERSON MARRIED MAY 26, 1918

*Rented 2 rooms from Aunt Pet White; * lived there 2 weeks. * Hauled water in wagon with Nick's red mules. Corn perished in 4 days from hot weather. * Finished chopping cotton; made 4 bales cotton * Guy was discharged from service, moved that day over on Grapevine Highway on Daddy Anderson's place, 106 acres.

*Georgia was born June 19, 1919. * Guy worked by the day down at his dad's "dollar a day shop" where he got $2.00 a day. * Moved in August 1919 to Dad Reeves place on river, 268 acres. Handley-Ederville Road. * Farmed Dad Reeves', dug well with digger $75.00. We boarded with Mother & Daddy Anderson. * Had 1 cow, 2 horses and 1 mule Dad Reeves gave us. * Sold milk to Alta Vista dairies, picked up in 5 gal. cans.

* Uncle Doc gave Guy a horse (George). * We paid $318.00 cash rent. * Moved January 19, 1929 to Mrs. Womack's place in bottom on river. * Mary Ruth was born May 25, 1933. * Farmed on 1/3 grains and hay. * Milked cows and sold milk to Metzger's Creamery. * Moved to 4 points on Grapevine Highway and Smithfield Road. * Dairyed there until 1958; sold 120 acres and bought Mrs. Rodgers place West Watauga; 250 acres, still dairying August 1968. * Sold place at Four Points to Hudiburg in October 1966, moved to Richland Hills December 1966.

WILLIAM OSBURN AND MARY BELL REEVES
BY E. F. CRITES JR.

I did not know my grandfather, William Osburn Reeves, born March 16, 1869, as he died March 22, 1924, but I have fond memories of my grandmother, Mary Bell Pelley Reeves, who was born Nov. 16, 1872 and died Oct. 22, 1950. We called her Granny. We always enjoyed going to her house because there were always so many activities and people there and many good things to eat. Some of my mother's sisters and their children were always there, and we enjoyed running and playing.

The house was a large, two-story white house located a block off Broadway at Edwards and Carson streets in Birdville. My grandmother, with help from the family, farmed several hundred acres just north of Birdville Coliseum and football field. The land ran east across Big Fossil Creek and took in a portion of what is the former Richland Plaza Shopping Center at the corner of Broadway and Texas 26.

Near the center of this property, when I was probably 7 or 8 years old, I remember stories of an old log cabin that was located near the Grapevine Highway where my mother and some of her brothers and sisters were born. I can remember on hot summer days when my cousins, Bill Reeves, Ben Angle, and I would enjoy swimming in the "old blue hole" on Big Fossil Creek. During those days, none of us had the luxury of a swimsuit.

The farm was large, but I have no idea how many acres. There was some acreage away from the main place. My grandmother raised wheat and oats, which were used for their own cattle as well as sold for profit. They also operated a large dairy. I remember one occasion when I was playing with

Mary Bell "Granny" Reeves at old well house, Birdville, circa 1948 Grandmother of Bill Reeves and E. F. Crites Jr.

my cousins around some old machinery and cut off the end of my finger. I ran to the house, and Granny looked at it and said not to worry. She got a can and put some coal oil in it and had me put my finger in it, and then she wrapped it in a coal oil rag, which seemed to take care of the pain and the problem.

Granny always tried to help schoolteachers who needed a place to live and rented rooms to several teachers over the years. One of these teachers I recently talked to was Mozelle Phelps, the daughter of John Bussey. Mozelle started teaching in the Birdville School District in 1928 at the age of 18 and taught there for 42 years. Her starting pay was $80 per month. Granny rented a room or two to Mozelle in 1929, and when she got married in 1935, Granny added a kitchen and another room, and Mozelle and her husband, Doyle Phelps, lived there.

I also have fond memories of hog-killing time when the hogs were slaughtered and processed for the coming year. I can still see the pots of water boiling and the tremendous amount of food that was prepared for the workers. It seemed there was always something cooking in Granny's kitchen.

Christmas was a very special time when the whole family got together, and it seemed as though there were hundreds of people there. All the kids anxiously awaited Santa Claus (R. M. or W. O. Reeves in full Santa Claus suit) to show up, and he always did on Christmas Eve with some kind of present for all the kids, and there were many.

I enjoyed riding the horses, but they were there to work the cattle and do other work on the farm. Granny would let me ride behind my older cousin, Leslie Angle, or another older cousin. Granny would tell Ben and me to go to the barn loft and get a few squab pigeons for supper, and she would make pigeon pie. What a treat!

ANGELA MCGOWAN RENFRO

When James and Vivien McGowan moved our family to North Richland Hills in the early 1950s, little did I, Angela McGowan Renfro, know I would live and/or work here for the rest of my life. We moved from Fort Worth to our new home on Marie Street, where my sister Elizabeth (O'Neal), and I had to walk to Rufe Snow Drive to a row of mailboxes to get our mail. We also could walk to Mr. Ford's grocery store where 5 cents would buy a lot of candy! We were not allowed to ride our bikes on Rufe Snow, because it was too busy!

We started to school while living on Marie Street. Because of the explosive growth in this area, we transferred to a new elementary school almost every year, though we continued to live in the same house! First and second grades: Richland Elementary (Mrs. Clover and Mrs. Scott;) third, fourth, fifth grades: beginning at Glenview Elementary until North Richland Elementary (now Mullendore) could be finished (Mrs. Trotter, Mrs. Niendorff, Miss Shannon).

We moved to the North Hills area in 1957 on Sheridon, but memories of early North Richland Hills abound. For example, our mother was a charter member of Richland Hills Methodist Church. (I believe the members met at Richland Elementary until the sanctuary was completed.) I also remember the opening of the Safeway Store, going to Virgil's Beauty Shop, and eating at Jay's Grill—the best chicken-fried steak!

I have worked at Richland High School my entire adult life, always thankful that my parents moved our family to this area.

Submitted by Angela McGowan Renfro

MELTON AND HAZEL RHINE

Melton and Hazel Rhine lived in many places when they were a young married couple, but then they found Hewitt Street in Smithfield and they have been there ever since. Both Melton and Hazel were born on a farm, Melton in Wise County in a little town called Sycamore in 1920, and Hazel in Brumbelow, 10 miles north of Decatur in 1918. The couple met when Melton's brother started going with a girlfriend of Hazel's. Sometimes, when the creek was up, Melton had to ride a horse to visit Hazel. They lived a long way apart, and Melton couldn't see her every day. They went together about four years before they were married in 1937.

The Rhines started married life in Decatur where he worked at a dairy. Their son, Ray, was born in 1939 while they lived there. After two years in Decatur, they moved to Fort Worth's Northside. Next, they moved to Handley where their second child, Frieda, was born. Later, they moved to Bedford and rented farmland.

After a time, the Rhines moved again, this time to Smithfield where they lived next door to Barber Cobb. They rented 38 acres from a friend. At this place, they had cows, horses, and hogs. Their third child, Barbara, was born here. Melton continued to work for Armour, 34 years in all, until he had heart surgery in 1972.

In 1951, the family was able to buy some land of their own. They bought six acres of vacant land on Hewitt Street. The land cost $100 an acre, and the Rhines had six

$100 bills saved to buy their six acres. Mr. Rhine didn't believe in the bank, so Hazel sewed herself a little pocketbook thing out of sugar-sack material to keep their savings in, and she kept the pocketbook inside her bra. On Hewitt Street, the Rhines built their home and raised their children. They have lived there 46 years.

The first thing the Rhines did on Hewitt Street was build a cement-block barn on the place. It was their intention to keep living in their rented house until they were able to build a home on their own land. However, after a year and a half, the family moved into the barn because Hazel didn't like the idea of paying rent when they didn't have to. Melton and Hazel did much of the work on the house themselves. Of course, they still had all their other work to do, too, so it took them about 18 months to complete the house.

All the Rhine children, Ray, Frieda, and Barbara, attended Smithfield School. They remember the day a tornado came through and destroyed the school's gymnasium. Children had been playing ball in the gym minutes before the storm hit. The gym was never rebuilt.

Ray and Frieda went to Carter-Riverside High School. Barbara graduated from Richland High.

When the family moved to Hewitt Street, it was not paved or named. It was named later for the Hewitt family that lived around the corner from the Rhines. Two other streets in the area were named for the Hewitt children, Buck and Frankie B.

Since moving to Smithfield, the Rhines have attended Smithfield Baptist Church. They were active in the church's programs for children and teens.

Hazel milked nine cows and separated the milk by hand, and churned and molded about 40 pounds of butter a week. Melton would take the butter with him on his delivery rounds to different grocery stores and sell it for about 75 cents a pound.

Mr. Rhine was also a volunteer fireman. The Smithfield Volunteer Fire Department was formed in 1948, and there were a lot of members because not everyone was nearby all the time. If there was a fire, whoever was around would answer the call. At various times, Melton was the department's chaplain and assistant fire chief. Their son, Ray, was the first paid fire chief in North Richland Hills. The Smithfield volunteers would answer calls for help throughout the county. They were the only fire protection North Richland Hills had in its early years.

There were some unusual people living in Smithfield at various times. Dr. H. C. Allison owned some property on Starnes Road where he had a sort of sanitarium. He was supposed to be a medical doctor, but many thought he was a peculiar kind of guy. He cared for people who had something the matter with their minds. There was a big, high fence around his place so the patients couldn't wander off. The waters from the spring that fed his tank were supposed to have healing powers. Ray Rhine worked for him some, and the Rhines remember that Dr. Allison had a big patch of sweet potatoes. He would hire the boys to dig the sweet potatoes, and he paid them pretty good.

One time Ray came home with some rotten, smelly sweet potatoes that he and the Hudlers and the Starnes boys were throwing at each other and making a big mess. The Rhine kids were scared of Dr. Allison, and they wouldn't dare go in his house. Hazel Rhine used to work the elections, and she and the other workers would get aggravated at Dr. Allison. He asked lots of questions about how many people were voting, and as the election counts were all done by hand, the questions posed by Dr. Allison slowed down the process. He was curious about the elections the same way he was about everything. Some thought he wanted to run everything. The Rhines believed he was the one that started the idea to get North Richland Hills to take in Smithfield, and that there were four or five others with him in that effort. The Rhine family was not in favor of the annexation because of city taxes, and they feared Smithfield would lose its identity, which is exactly what happened.

The volunteer fire department had asked all residents to pay 25 cents a month to support the department. It was called a tax, but it wasn't, really. It was just a contribution, but people objected to it. Dr. Allison went around talking to people, warning them about what could happen, and how it would improve everything if North Richland Hills took over. And although the Rhines never did understand how it happened, they lived in Smithfield one day, and then by 7 A.M. the next morning, the city had the signs up for North Richland Hills, and Smithfield was gone.

There have been lots of changes since then, some good, some not so good. There are more conveniences now, and the things you need are not so far away. But what was lost was the sense of community, of being close neighbors. Everybody used to work together, but as the city began to grow and get bigger, it seemed to the Rhines that people grew apart.

Melton Rhine died Jan. 21, 1998.

Submitted by Melton and Hazel Rhine

GENE AND CONNIE RIDDLE

Morris E. (Gene) Riddle and Constance (Connie) Riddle were married in Los Angeles on September 26, 1948.

Connie was born in Detroit, February 15, 1929. She was the daughter of Antonio Palazzolo and Vita Pollaccia. The family moved to California in 1947 after she graduated from high school. Connie worked as a private secretary, bookkeeper, and bank teller.

Gene was born in Fort Worth on May 4, 1928, the son of Lonnie Morris Riddle and Juanita Mae Brown. Gene attended Fort Worth Technical High School where he played football and competed in Golden Gloves. He has a sister, Doris Jean Harmon, who lives in North Richland Hills. Gene was in the U.S. Navy from 1946 to 1950. He served on the USS Pasadena. It was while his ship was in port at Long Beach, California, that he met Connie.

Gene and Connie have two sons. Mark Edward was born in Houston on October 5, 1950, and Richard Eugene was born at the San Diego Naval Hospital on December 7, 1951. In 1965 the family left the hectic pace

of California for the quiet rural setting in the Smithfield area of North Richland Hills. They purchased five and one third acres of land, built their home, raised a few head of cattle, and had horses for the boys. At that

Back-Gene Riddle; L/R-Rick, Mark, Connie

time, the roads in their area were in poor condition. There were no sewer facilities, and water was scarce. The population was approximately 16,000.

Mark attended Richland High School and then entered the University of Texas at Arlington. He is a licensed civil engineer employed with the firm of Knowlton, English and Flowers, Inc. Mark married Debra Ann Outlaw in 1971. She is a registered nurse and the daughter of Jefferson Davis and Jean Outlaw. They have one daughter, Staci Susan, born in 1976.

Richard graduated from Richland High School where he enjoyed playing football. He attended Navarro Junior College in Corsicana, Tarrant County Junior College, and UTA. He loves music, both writing and playing. He is married to Kim Stewart, the daughter of Dick and Arlene Hackbarth of Granbury. They live in Evergreen, Colorado, and are self-employed. Their first child was born in March 1998.

Gene and Connie are active members of St. Paul Methodist Church in Hurst. Gene has served as chairman of Administrative Council, chairman of Pastor-Parish Relations, and chairman of trustees. Connie has served as president of the United Methodist Women, circle leader, and chairman of Health and Welfare. Gene was a member of the NRH City Council from May 1968 to May 1971, then was employed by the city as assistant street superintendent, made acting city manager in February 1972, then city manager in May 1972 to August 1978, then director of public works and utilities. He has worked in city administration for the cities of NRH, Keller, and Hillsboro. While NRH city manager he was instrumental in getting the original section of the present City Hall built. It was opened in 1976, debt-free.

Gene has been an active member of the Northeast-Richland Lions Club since 1972. He has served in all offices, including president and district offices. Since retirement in 1988, he has been spending more time enjoying his workshop, fishing, and traveling.

GEORGE AND PAT RIDDLE

George Riddle, a native of Pennsylvania and veteran of World War II, and Patricia (Pat) Nimmo Riddle, who grew up in the Riverside area of Fort Worth, met during the war and married October 18, 1945. They first moved to North Richland Hills in 1949 to a rent house on the Grapevine Highway next to the home of Pat's aunt and uncle, Vera and Will Snow, the son of NRH pioneer Rufe Snow.

They bought their first home in Richland Hills, but moved back to NRH in 1958 to their present home on Vance Road. Their four children and spouses are: daughter Patricia and son-in-law Robert Rose of Grapevine; son Mark and daughter-in-law Vickie Riddle, Arlington; daughter Glenna and son-in-law Steve Howard, who live in a home on Lake Worth; and daughter Robin and son-in-law Tony Keeble, of Grapevine. All of the Riddles' children graduated from college, and daughter Patti and her husband are Dallas psychologists. Mark is a safety engineer and his wife Vickie is a social worker. Glenna is a ticketing agent for American Airlines, and her husband works for Southwestern Bell. Robin, a recreational therapist, presently stays at home with her two young sons. Her husband, Tony, is a family practice physician at clinics in Hurst and Irving.

Back, L/R-Vickie Riddle, Robert and Pat Rose, Robin holding Geddy, Tony, Ian Keeble, Tracy and Cory Howard; Middle, L/R-Matthew and Mark Riddle, Pat and George Riddle, Glenna, Blake, and Steven Howard; Front, L/R-Renee Riddle, Heather, and Haley Howard

Grandchildren: Renee and Matthew Riddle; Heather, Cory, Tracy, and Haley Howard; and Ian and Geddy Keeble. Great-grandson: Blake Howard.

There were homes on both sides of Vance Road south of Shauna Drive when the Riddles moved to NRH. Most of the land toward Richland High was still pasture land. Rufe Snow Drive was a deserted, bumpy, crooked, two-lane road leading to Keller. The Riddles are charter members of the Richland Hills Church of Christ, which began in Richland Hills and then moved to North Richland Hills.

George Riddle operated an auto repair shop in Haltom City for many years, and Pat was a homemaker and kept the company books. She began studying oil painting in 1973 and sold many of her paintings, especially pastoral scenes of bluebonnets, covered bridges, and windmills. She graduated from Tarrant County Junior College Northeast Campus and then began attending the

University of Texas at Arlington where she graduated at age 56 in 1983 with a degree in journalism. She became a reporter for the *Fort Worth Star-Telegram Northeast* in 1984 and soon became a columnist. Although she officially retired in 1995, she continues to write a column each week called "Northeast People."

Pat was honored to be a member of the city's historical committee that prepared this book. North Richland Hills has been a wonderfully safe and stable community for the Riddle family, and they love their neighbors, their city, and the Birdville School District very much.

Submitted by Pat Riddle

JAMES WILLIAM AND ADELE RUTH ELLIS ROBERTS

Ruth Ellis Roberts was born in Whitney, Texas, to William Daus and Edith Jones Ellis on April 27, 1926. When she was 18 months old, her parents moved to the 1300 block of Lincoln Avenue on the north side of Fort Worth.

Ruth's father worked 41 years for the Fort Worth Water Department, continuing to work another 20 years at two other jobs. Both parents are now deceased.

Ruth, an only child, attended Denver Elementary, J. P. Elder Junior High, and the old Technical High School that was located next to J. P. Elder Junior High.

After living for a number of years in California, Ruth

James and Ruth Roberts

came back to Fort Worth in 1955. On November 20, 1956, the house on the corner of Mackey Drive and Briley was completed, and Robert L. Harr and Adele Ruth Harr moved in. Eleven months later, an addition was made, a baby boy named Robin Craig Harr. Robin is an only child.

The Harrs joined North Richland Hills Baptist Church on Vance Road on Oct. 5, 1958.

On November 20, 1997, the house was 41 years old. One of the residents of this home is the same, only the name has changed. The names are now Adele Ruth Roberts and James W. Roberts.

I, Ruth Roberts, cannot imagine living in a nicer city than North Richland Hills. My son never went any farther to school than maybe a mile or so to high school. I never drive over five miles to shop for anything we need or desire. I retired from the Fort Worth Federal Credit Union, which was in the bank building at Grapevine Highway and Vance Road. James retired as a watch repairman, working from home doing contract work with many of the department stores and jewelry stores in the area.

Submitted by Adele Ruth Roberts

JAMES H. AND JEAN ROBINSON

James Hartle Robinson was born June 1, 1919, in Weatherford. He was raised on Fort Worth's North Side and graduated from North Side High School in 1936. He then served in the Navy for five years. While in Los Angeles he met Gloria Margene Kimbrell, who was born October 1, 1926, in Jasper, Alabama. Jim and Jean married December 6, 1945. They resided in Haltom City until they built their new home on Holiday Lane West in North Richland Hills. Jim was part of the original board to prepare building specifications for NRH. He was employed from 1952 to 1955 by Clarence Jones as manager at Jones Lumber Co. on Belknap Street.

In 1954, the Robinson family moved to their new home with their three girls: Judy Ann, born in Dallas October 19, 1947; Janice Marie, born in Littlefield December 13, 1949; and

Back-Janice, Judy; Front-Jean, Brenda, James "Jim"

Brenda Joyce, born in Fort Worth April 22, 1952.

On September 12, 1988, Jean died of cancer. Jim continued to live at their home until July 1995 and now lives on Sierra in NRH.

In 1965, Judy graduated from Richland High School where she was one of the first Dixie Belles. She and her husband, Robert Allen Bowers, and two children, Shelley Denise and James Allen, resided in NRH for many years. Judy and Bobby now live in Boise, Idaho, as do Shelley, her husband, Donald Carter, and their three children. Judy and Bobby's son, Jay, and daughter-in-law, Trish, live in Hurst and have one daughter. Janice graduated from Richland High School in 1968. She was a Dixie Belle for three years and a lieutenant her senior year. Janice is a charter member of the Texas Girls Choir. After high school she attended Tarrant County Junior College South Campus, Texas Woman's University, Texas Wesleyn College, and graduated in 1972 from dental hygiene school at TCJC-NE. She has worked in the Mid-Cities area as a dental hygienist for 25 years.

While a junior at RHS, Janice met Roger Pete Owens. He was born in 1949 in Fort Worth. Roger graduated from RHS in 1967 and from North Texas State University in 1974 with a bachelor's degree in marketing. After dating five years, Roger and Janice were married March 25, 1972, at Richland Hills Baptist Church, by Rev. James E. Bass. They have two children, Jeffrey Matthew and Allison Janelle. Jeff and Allison are students at North Richland Middle School. The Owenses attend North Richland Hills Baptist Church where Janice has been a member since 1958. Roger is in procurement at Bell

Helicopter where he has been employed 19 years. The Owenses live on Carston Court in NRH.

Brenda graduated from RHS in 1970 and was a Dixie Belle, like her two sisters. She was married to Richard Wayne Laurence April 9, 1971, at North Richland Hills Baptist Church by Rev. Hal W. Brooks. They have two children, John Andrew and Elizabeth Ann. Brenda and Rick live on Suncrest Court in NRH.

Submitted by Janice Robinson Owens

LLOYD D. AND PATRICIA A. ROBINSON

Lloyd Darrell Robinson was born in Indiana in 1939. He entered the Air Force in 1958. He met Patricia (Pat) McClure in 1960. Pat had met Darrell's sister, Connie, at Indiana State Teachers College and had written to Darrell. He came home on leave in 1960, and met Pat in person. He proposed to Pat on Thursday, August 18, 1960, and they were married 10 days later on August 28, 1960, in Pat's church in Crawfordsville, Indiana.

Pat McClure was born in 1939, in Crawfordsville, Indiana. She graduated from Crawfordsville High School in 1957 and attended Indiana State Teachers College. Darrell and Pat traveled to several bases during the first nine years of marriage, including Glasgow, Montana; Belleville, Illinois; Peru, Indiana; Great Falls, Montana; and to Okinawa from 1965–69. On June 4, 1969, they moved to Texas and stayed with friends in Fort Worth until August 1969 when they bought their first home in North Richland Hills on Vance Road—next door to George and Pat Riddle and family. In 1973, the Robinson family moved to a larger house on Victoria Avenue where they still reside.

The four girls attended North Richland schools. Pat worked at Fort Worth State School for five years, from 1983 until 1988, and then became a foster parent for two teenage girls, who were mildly retarded. The girls lived with the Robinson family for five years and have gone on to their own lives in the community. Both girls graduated

Back, L/R-Lloyd Robinson, Brandon and Clay Jolley, Gary Hamilton, Jeff and Judy Justice, Karen, Ziad Ghaziri, Angela; Second from Back, L/R-Beth Jolley, Robin Hamilton holding LeeAnn Hamilton, Chelsy Justice; Third from Back, L/R-Whitney Jolley, Cheri Ghaziri, Pat Robinson, Najah Ghaziri; Front, L/R-Robbie Ghaziri, Patty Justice, Joey and Jeffrey Justice

from Richland High School after attending the Home Resource program. Pat was responsible, along with Fort Worth State School personnel and other Association of Retarded Citizens members, for getting the Rainbow Club started with the ARC of Northeast Tarrant County. She served on the ARC board for a couple of years, and she and Darrell are still members and support the organization.

Darrell traveled to several places around the world while in the Air Force. He left North Richland Hills in 1972 from Carswell Air Force Base and served 18 months in Guam. He returned to Altus, Oklahoma, for a tour and then served in Turkey for 18 months. After the tour in Turkey, Darrell was stationed in Lubbock at Reese Air Force Base where he ultimately retired on October 31, 1978.

The following day, he began Robinson's Sewer Service and has been in the plumbing business ever since. Darrell obtained his master's license and changed the name of the company to Robinson Plumbing and Repair. He is the master plumber and Pat helps with some of the office work. Robinson Plumbing has grown and Darrell and Pat are members of the Northeast Tarrant Chamber of Commerce. Darrell is also a Business Partner with the Birdville Independent School District through the Chamber where he is a mentor to students at North Ridge Elementary. Pat is employed at North Ridge as an educational assistant in the Physical Education Department. Darrell and Pat were recognized by the BISD Board of Directors at the July 1997 meeting.

Darrell has also been a mentor to Women's Haven, the Tarrant County home for battered women and children. He has contributed many hours and dollars to the Haven since beginning his business in 1978. Darrell was named Volunteer of the Year for Women's Haven, and later the award was named in his honor and is now presented to other outstanding volunteers each year.

Darrell has also supported the Northeast Business and Professional Women's local organization since 1988. Pat became a member at that time and has served in most offices including president. She is currently active and serves as the legislative chair for Northeast BPW as well as the BPW/Texas District 11 legislative chair. Pat served as editor for the NEBPW newsletter in the 1996–97 year. Pat and Darrell are supporters of the Northeast Tarrant Chamber, BISD, and the city of North Richland Hills.

Darrell and Pat's family has grown from four daughters to four sons-in-law, four grandsons, four granddaughters, and two foster daughters. The four daughters are Elizabeth Elaine, Robin Ann, Cheryl Lee, and Judith Lynn.

The Robinson family also were hosts to three students, two from Brazil and one from China through the Youth for Understanding program.

PAUL AND KATHERINE ROBINSON

The Paul Robinson family consisted of three members: Paul, born in Sulphur Springs November 5, 1918; Katherine, born in Hutchinson, Kansas, July 16, 1921; and Sharon Ann, born in Tucumcari, New Mexico, November

Paul and Katherine Robinson

2, 1949. Paul and Katherine were married in Dalhart, Texas, August 2, 1938. Sharon Ann came along 11 years later.

Paul, after completing World War II service in the Air Force, was employed by the Federal Aviation Agency, in the field of air traffic control. Katherine was employed by the Air Force and the Navy in an administrative capacity. Following World War II, they lived in San Antonio for 11 years. In June 1957, Paul was transferred from San Antonio to Fort Worth and assigned to FAA's Regional Headquarters. He served 11 years in that assignment before being transferred to the FAA's Washington, D.C. headquarters.

In 1957, Paul and Katherine built a home on Winnell Way in North Richland Hills. This home had 1,550 square feet in the house and cost $14,200. This was a very happy time due to the wonderful neighbors living on Winnell Way. The immediate neighbors were Norman and Mary Ruth Ellis, Grant and Geneva Linder, Royce and Lou Wilson, Bill and Skeet Jolly, Marwood and Dorothy McClelland, and Don and Sue Norris.

Upon arrival in North Richland Hills, the family joined the Richland Hills Methodist Church. Sharon Ann entered the Birdville school system in the third grade. She continued in the Birdville system until she graduated from Richland High School in 1967. In 1964, Sharon Ann was a charter member of the Dixie Belles, a drill and dance team sponsored by Richland High School. While Sharon Ann was in the elementary grades, her mother, Katherine, was active in the PTA and was president of the Snow Heights PTA in 1960–61.

Paul and Katherine moved from North Richland Hills in 1967 when Paul was transferred to the FAA's Washington, D.C. headquarters. Sharon Ann left the area at the same time to enter Texas Tech University in Lubbock.

Amy, Sharon (Robinson), Paul, and Bill Stevenson

Sharon Ann married William "Bill" Stevenson of North Richland Hills in June 1968. After they completed their education in Lubbock, they returned to North Richland Hills. Sharon Ann and Bill had two children,

Amy and William Paul. Both attended Birdville schools through grade 12. Upon completion of their college education, Amy at Texas Tech University and William Paul at Henderson State University in Arkadelphia, Ark., they returned and made their home in North Richland Hills.

After retiring from the FAA in Washington, D.C., Paul and Katherine returned to the area and made their home in Hurst, Texas.

CHARLES AND FAY ROGERS

The immediate family of Charles Rogers moved to the city of North Richland Hills and back into this area in January of 1976. Charles, a southern Baptist preacher, has spent the past 34 years traveling and preaching within the United States and among some 44 countries. Charles Rogers, the third of four children of Arlin Avery and Lorene Deaton Rogers, was born in the Pleasant Glade Community located off Farm Road 157, about four miles south of Grapevine. The Rogers family has been in the area since the 1800s. The parents of Arlin Rogers were Jesse Clark Rogers and Grace Myrtle Ingram. Jesse's parents Layton Thurman Rogers and Margaret Sparger Rogers, are buried in the Smithfield Cemetery (located in present day NRH) along with many other Rogers and Sparger ancestors and relatives.

Charles Ray Rogers married Fay Hines Rogers, the daughter of Thomas Jefferson and Maud Gentry Hines of Handley (East Fort Worth). Charles and Fay were married in August 1954 and were blessed with three children. Their oldest daughter, Sheree Gay Rogers, is now married to Imad Saberjissa, and they make their home in NRH. Sheree has one daughter, Chaliese Gay Rippey. Chaliese, a 1995 graduate of Richland High School, attended Birdville schools from kindergarten to high school. Chaliese was an honor student and won many awards representing her track and cross country teams at Smithfield Junior High and Richland High. She is now attending Southwest Texas State University in San Marcos and was inducted into the Golden Key National Honor Society.

Charles and Fay have one son, Denne Rogers, who resides in Denton. Their youngest child, Robin Celeste Rogers, is now married to John Robert Eddins, both 1981 Richland High School graduates. They also make their home in NRH with their daughter, Alexandra Elizabeth Eddins.

Charles, granddaughter Alexandra Eddins, and Fay Rogers

EDWARD "BUCK" AND RUTH ROGERS

In September 1944, Edward B. "Buck" Rogers from New York, met Ruth W. LeRoy from Massachusetts, at LaGuardia Airport in New York where they both worked

Edward and Ruth Rogers Family, 1986; Back, L/R-Edward, Robert, Thomas, Paul, David; Middle, L/R-Barbara, Connie, Douglas, Amy, Pamela; Front, L/R-Colby, Edward "Buck," Ruth holding Michael, Kellye

for an airline. They were married in 1946. The birth of two sons, Edward in 1948, and Robert in 1950 in New York, preceded Buck's requested transfer to Dallas where he continued to work for American Airlines until retirement in 1979.

After arriving in Texas, six more children were born into the Rogers family. Barbara, in 1951; Thomas, in 1952; Douglas, in 1955; Pamela, in 1957; David, in 1959; and Paul, in 1961: David and Paul were born after the family moved to their new home on Conn Drive in the Richland Heights Addition of North Richland Hills in June 1957.

The Anderson farmhouse and other farm buildings dominated the landscape until the land was sold and the area was developed. One of the most visible landmarks in this area of the city was the huge water tower between Ashmore and Booth-Calloway that was built to store water for this section of the city.

One evening of torrential rain is memorable because it involved an heroic rescue. A man clung to a tree above the flooding waters of the raging creek throughout the night hours. Residents heard his cries for help and called the fire department, which came immediately. However, the firemen could not effect a rescue because their ladders could not reach the terrified man. Through the night hours, all the neighbors called out encouragement to him and as dawn broke, a Bell helicopter lifted him from his perilous perch. Son Rob gave an account of the rescue in one of his high school classes the next day, and an astounded male classmate turned to him and said, "That was my father." It was customary for heavy rains to flood Airline Drive south of Glenview but not usual for floodwaters to rise on the north side of Glenview. However, one time the water did reach the carport of the Rogers' house. Son Doug delivered the morning Star-Telegram and after a heavy rain one morning, he arrived back home late and soaking wet. In the pouring rain he had slipped, bicycle and all, into the torrent of Calloway Creek at Booth Calloway Road. After pulling himself out of the rushing water, he retrieved his bike and headed for home and safety—a really scared paperboy.

Buck and Ruth dedicated themselves to the task of educating their family to the fullest extent. The eight children attended Glenview Elementary, Richland Junior High, and Richland High. They participated in school sports and activities from 1957 to 1979. Football, baseball, softball, basketball, track, cross country, Dixie Belles, Young Life, Boy Scouts, and Campfire were among their interests.

Buck worked with the Boy Scouts of America for more than 25 years as scoutmaster of Troop 168 sponsored by Richland Hills United Methodist Church. His dedication encompassed the troop, district, council, and national organization. Buck died in December 1989.

When the youngest child graduated from high school in 1979, Ruth chose to focus on herself and on Buck, who had retired that year. By 1981 all eight children were high school graduates, six were college graduates, and the two youngest were completing their college careers, and Ruth decided it was time for her to complete her college education. She attended Tarrant County Junior College and earned an Associate Degree in 1985. In 1991, she graduated from Texas Woman's University, exactly 50 years after her original college graduation year.

After Buck's death in 1989, Ruth changed course in order to lead a productive life in areas to which she had always aspired. She became a volunteer instructor at the Adult Education Center at the NRH Public Library where she spent several nights a week teaching reading, GED preparation, and English as a second language. She also started her own business, doing private tutoring in English, reading, ESL, French, and Spanish. Her contacts with Wellesley and Texas Woman's University alumnae also continued.

All eight Rogers children had graduated from college by 1983, and all pursued their individual goals. The first grandchild will begin her college career in the fall of 1998.

Edward L. Rogers, CFRE, Texas A&M and North Texas State graduate. He and wife Susan and son Charles Edward live in Bedford.

Robert S. Rogers, A&M graduate, is a pilot with USAir. He lives in Spring Branch, Texas, with wife Connie and children Kellye and Michael.

Barbara E. Rogers, TWU grad and former teacher, represents Blessing/White as an organizational development consultant. She and husband Herman and daughter Julia make Grapevine their home.

Thomas A. Rogers, University of Texas and UT Medical School, is a doctor in family practice in El Paso where he lives with wife Juanita and daughters Ciera and Tyana.

Douglas W. Rogers, Texas Wesleyan graduate, is a CPA and serves as accounting projects manager for TU Electric. He and wife Amy and son Colby live in Plano.

Pamela Rogers, Texas Woman's graduate, is a professor at the University of Wisconsin-Platteville. Her home is in Mineral Point, Wisconsin.

David C. Rogers, graduate of North Texas, is a teacher in Grand Prairie. He lives in North Richland Hills.

Paul R. Rogers, Texas A&M graduate, is a medical service specialist in the Vacaville State Prison hospital in California. He lives in Fairfield, California, and has two daughters, Akilah and Briana.

Over the last 40 years, many occasions arose where Buck Rogers had opportunities to move to other cities served by American Airlines, but Ruth and Buck made a decision to stay in Texas, and it is impossible for Ruth to imagine living anywhere else but in North Richland Hills. Based on the quality of life here, the opportunities available, the school system and the economic conditions, Buck and Ruth were never sorry to have made that choice.

Submitted by Ruth Rogers

VERAL AND LOIS ROY

On March 15, 1954, Veral and Lois Roy and their two children, Glenda and Charles, moved on North Onyx Drive in North Richland Hills. I, Lois Roy, still live in the same house, and hope I will live here for the rest of my days.

It was a quiet street when we moved here, not much traffic. Our closest grocery store was on Highway 183. Later, Safeway built their store at the corner of Grapevine Highway and Rufe Snow Drive. There was a cafeteria in the shopping center where Winn Dixie is now. The cafeteria was on the opposite end from North Richland Drugstore.

Lois Roy Family, 1993

The only restaurant was at the "Y" at Denton Highway and Belknap Street. It was called the Log House. You had to go to the west side of Fort Worth to find larger restaurants. On May 10, 1956 my husband was killed in a truck accident in Bakersfield, California. It was a very traumatic time for me, but I had my children and my parents, who were very supportive.

Glenda married Leonard Leimbach in 1960. They have three children and live in St. Joseph, Mo. Glenda and Leonard lived across the street from me for a couple of years. My son-in-law used to run his bird dog where the Glenview apartments are now. It was just a pasture then. Richland Plaza was our first mall, and it was nice, but when Northeast Mall was built, Richland Plaza deteriorated.

In January 1956, Richland Hills Church of Christ was started in the Glenview Elementary School in Richland Hills. We built our first church building on the Grapevine highway in Richland Hills and later built one on Rufe

Snow Drive in North Richland Hills. I am a charter member and very proud of that.

I now have seven grandchildren and 11 great grandchildren. I am so proud of all of them.

Charles and his wife, Peggy, live in Burleson. They have three boys and a girl. They have a very successful business, which is C. A. R. Transport, and all the children work in the business.

I am 85 years old now. I have enjoyed my life, and I have loved living it in North Richland Hills.

Submitted by Lois Roy

RUMFIELD FAMILY
OZIAS RUMFIELD

Ozias Rumfield was born in Athens County, Ohio, June 17, 1842, to Peleg M. and Rachel Pettit Rumfield. When he was 19 years old, he served three months as a Union soldier in the Civil War before moving to Washington Township, Independence County, Arkansas. His wife, Mary Jane Mingus Rumfield, and son, Charlie, joined him in Arkansas. By the 1870 census, there was another son, Thomas, in the family.

In October 1873, Ozias filed for 72 acres of land at Smithfield, Tarrant County, Texas—15 miles from Fort Worth. The patent was granted January 1, 1874. The land was parallel and south of what is now Rumfield Road. The 1880 Texas census lists Ozias; wife, Mary Jane, born in 1844 in Ohio; Charles, born in 1863 in Ohio; Thomas, born in 1867 in Arkansas; Hozie born in 1869 in Arkansas; William, born in 1873 in Texas; George, born in 1875 in Texas; Lydda, born in 1878 in Texas; Alice, who died in Texas when she was 6 months old; and Delia Marie, born in Texas in 1882. Mary Jane died April 7, 1883, and is buried in the Smithfield Cemetery.

Ozias married Mrs. Angelene Burnett July 12, 1883. He died Dec. 28, 1919, and is buried in the Smithfield Cemetery. He and his family lived at the "brow of the hill," in a log cabin they built at the intersection of Rumfield Road and Kirk Lane, on the south side of Rumfield Road.

CLYDE JOHN RUMFIELD

Clyde John Rumfield was born to Thomas Allen and Florence Lay Rumfield in Smithfield, July 10, 1894. He married Edith Simpson January 17, 1914. Edith was born in Eddy, Bell County, Texas, December 2, 1896, to Joseph Braxton and Susan Adeline Smith Simpson. Her father was a Christian Church preacher. She finished high school in Fort Worth where her father was pastor of the Rosen Heights Christian Church. She played the violin and piano very well and sang in a quartet with her three sisters.

Nine children were born into this family, seven girls and two boys. It was said that Clyde Rumfield "only finished the eighth grade, was an honest man, and thought all problems could be solved through loving God and getting an education." Seven children who lived to adulthood

received college degrees or business school certificates. The children of this family were Billie Florence, Betty Elizabeth, Vera Dorothy, Inez Nell, Grace, Johnny Leon, Mary Jane, Clara Jo, and Thomas Brack. The last two died in infancy.

Clyde worked

Clyde John Rumfield descendants: Back-Vera, Betty, Mary Jane, Center-Inez, and John, Grace. Front-Billie

for F. B. Porter as manager of a 10,000-laying-hens and hatchery operation and ran a 40-cow dairy until his death. F. B. Porter was a chemical engineer and president of Southwestern Laboratories. Clyde served on the Smithfield School Board until he resigned over the firing of a teacher, who was a neighbor. (Emma Ousley later had an Arlington Junior High School named after her.)

Clyde died in the Glenview Hospital February 2, 1962. Edith died July 15, 1971. Both are buried in the Smithfield Cemetery.

THOMAS ALLEN RUMFIELD

Thomas Allen Rumfield, who was born in Independence County, Arkansas, April 22, 1867, and Florence Lay, who was born in Dalton, Georgia, December 24, 1869, were married July 15, 1888, in Tarrant County. Four sons were born to this couple: Thomas Hardy, Clyde John, Buryl, and Opie. His parents were Ozias and Mary Jane Mingus Rumfield.

Tom was 5 feet, 8 inches tall and weighed 165 pounds, but when he talked he was 10 feet tall. Tough and uneducated, but with a compassionate nature, he was a pushover for his grandchildren. He believed in hard work and in helping others. He sometimes loaned money to neighbors to attend out-of-town funerals or to help with other needs. He became a Mason March 22, 1913, in the Grand Prairie Lodge at Smithfield.

Thomas Rumfield was a farmer. He raised peaches, apples, berries, corn, and cotton. He also raised hogs to butcher, and he cured the meat in smokehouses, which he built. He also built berry shacks to store picked berries. He built a house, cellar, and cistern. The concrete cellar furnished protection during storms and was a

Thomas Allen Rumfield holding Buryl, Florence (Lay) Rumfield; Standing-Thomas Hardy and Clyde John

cool place to store canned fruit and vegetables.

Florence was an excellent cook and preserver of fruits and vegetables. Pies, cakes, cobblers, and biscuits were her specialties. She raised a garden and took care of a cow and chickens. She sold cream for her spending money.

Thomas sold a small farm and retired when his health began to fail in early 1936. He died in All Saints Hospital July 7, 1937, and is buried in Smithfield Cemetery. Florence lived on the home place, on the northeast corner of Rumfield Road and Davis Boulevard until her death, August 17, 1948.

DELIA MARIE RUMFIELD

Delia Marie Rumfield was born to Ozias and Mary Jane Mingus Rumfield on February 22, 1882, in Smithfield. Aunt "Dee," as she was known by family members, worked

for Sterling Steves, a lawyer, and accumulated enough money to buy 52 acres at the Grapevine Highway and Bedford-Euless Road. She married Andrew F. Cunningham, a theology student at Texas Wesleyan College.

Delia and Andrew built a grocery store and Texaco station at the intersection known as Four Points. They kept the store open six and one-half days a week. Delia loved to go with

Andrew and Delia (Rumfield) Cunningham

Andrew to the Crazy Water Hotel in Mineral Wells and to Glen Rose to visit spas. She and Andrew enjoyed dining on Sundays at fine hotels in downtown Fort Worth, including the Texas and Blackstone hotels.

Andrew and Delia Cunningham sold their store in 1953 and moved to Fort Worth where they were displaced from their Karnes Street home by the construction of the Airport Freeway (Texas 121). They moved a few blocks to the Oakhurst Addition. Delia died March 31, 1966, and is buried at Mount Olivet Cemetery in Fort Worth.

Compiled by Evalyn Lochridge from information furnished by Johnny Rumfield.

JOHNNY AND MARY RUMFIELD

Johnny Leon Rumfield, fourth generation of Rumfields in the Smithfield area, was born September 23, 1926 near the intersection of Precinct Line and Lockett Roads. Johnny was one of nine children—seven girls and two boys—born to Clyde John Rumfield and Edith Simpson Rumfield. The Smithfield Cemetery is populated with many Rumfield family members. His heritage in the

Smithfield area dates back to 1874 when his great-grandfather Ozias Rumfield, received a patent for 72 acres of land parallel and south of what is now Rumfield Road.

Johnny attended Smithfield Elementary, Carter-Riverside High School, received a bachelor's degree from Texas A&M in 1951 and master's degree from North Texas State University in 1959. He served in the Army Air Corps during World War II, where he was known by his Buddies as "Rumfield from Smithfield."

He lived in Smithfield from 1926 to 1952 and Fort Worth from 1952 to 1982. Johnny and his wife, Mary, moved to their home on Susan Lee Lane in North Richland Hills on June 2, 1982, where they still reside. He spent his working career as a teacher, coach, counselor, vice principal, and principal for the Fort Worth School District.

Johnny is a Mason and was master of the Smithfield Lodge for the 1996–1997 year when the lodge celebrated its 120th year. It was founded in 1876. He is also president of the Smithfield Cemetery Foundation.

Johnny has two children, Ginger Burlison and John W. Rumfield. Mary has a daughter, Judy Faulkner. They have four grandsons, Jay, John, Matthew, and Joshua. Johnny was a member of Smithfield Methodist Church for many years and presently belongs to Richland Hills Christian Church. His hobbies are golf, fishing, and hunting.

Compiled by Evalyn Lochridge from information furnished by Johnny Rumfield

The Harvey E. Russell Family

Harvey E. Russell and his wife, Fidelia Gilliam Russell, grew up in Gainesville, Texas, but moved to Fort Worth after they married in November 1938. In 1941, they moved out in the country to what is now North Richland Hills and rented a small house on Glenview Drive, one or two blocks west of Rufe Snow Dr. (Now and then, they would see Mr. Rufe Snow walking along the street which now bears his name.) In 1942, they moved several blocks to the east and rented a small house from Bill Mackey at the corner of Glenview Dr. and Flory Rd.

In 1946, Mr. and Mrs. Russell bought three and one-half acres of land, for three hundred dollars an acre, at what is now 3921 Scruggs Dr. The land was bought from Will Snow, one of Rufe Snow's sons, and was a couple of blocks to the west of the W. H. Parchman home. After buying the land, Mr. Russell built their home, a little at a time. It was originally four rooms, then six, now nine. Mrs.

Fidelia and Harvey Russell

Russell remembers that their street was at one time called Calloway Rd. and that they had several rural box numbers over the years. The Russells shared the pastoral setting of the '40s and '50s with some really good neighbors: the Roland Fortenberrys, the Walter Watkinses, the B. A. Nikirks, the C. W. Smiths, and the Troops and Andersons who lived on top of the hill in the unique "rock houses."

The family raised chickens, ducks, sheep, goats, pigs, and cows. On a regular basis, Mr. Russell, with the help of a friend, would kill one of his hogs and process the meat. The homemade sausage that he made was excellent. He and his wife canned or froze many fruits and vegetables each year. Mr. Russell grew a garden every year, not only out of necessity, but also out of enjoyment and relaxation. In recent years, he has planted many flowers in his large garden plot. An article and photo featuring his flower garden was published in the *Fort Worth Star-Telegram* several years ago, and a Richland Hills artist used his beautiful poppy garden as inspiration for some of her paintings. (On one occasion, law enforcement officials also took an interest in Mr. Russell's poppies, but, after investigation, found they were legal.)

Life for the Russells in the '40s and '50s included butane gas, no telephones or television, dirt and gravel roads, ditches and culverts, rural mail delivery (with mail boxes lined up on Hwy. 26, known then as the Grapevine Hwy.), septic tanks, wire fences, and farm animals. Boswell Dairies delivered milk to the front porch, and more things were sold door-to-door, such as Watkins and Raleigh products, Fuller brushes, and Manor Bakery goods. There were no malls, so the Russell family had to go to downtown Fort Worth to shop.

Mr. and Mrs. Russell had four children: Harvey Norman (12-19-39), Elizabeth Ann (7-29-43), James David (10-25-48) and Rebecca Louise (2-6-53). The two older children rode the bus to Central Birdville for several years when there was only one campus (at the corner of Belknap and Carson). Later they walked or rode their bikes to the newer schools as they were built. As the children were growing up, they enjoyed going to Rapid Mart, at Vance and Hwy. 26, to buy candy and cokes and to the Dairy Kreem, at Parchman and Hwy. 26, for burgers and floats. They would also go to a small store called Henry's on Rufe Snow near Harmonson Rd. to buy candy. In the late '50s, they enjoyed playing miniature golf at Mrs. C. L. Douglas' golf course on Parchman St.

Harvey and Fidelia Russell have lived in their North Richland Hills home for over fifty-two years. They celebrated sixty years of marriage in November 1998. Mr. Russell worked as a manager for Leonard Brothers Dept. Store for over thirty years, then later worked for Mitchell's Dept. Store. Mrs. Russell was a licensed vocational nurse at All Saints Hospital for about fifteen years. The oldest child Harvey Norman and his wife, Diane, live in Houston. Elizabeth and her husband Garland Sheppard and their son Gary, twenty years old, live in Richland Hills. The Russells' beloved son, James David, passed away in 1992. Rebecca and her husband Walt Bunge and

their foster son Peter live in Houston.

Although life was not easy in those early days before North Richland Hills came into existence, families such as the Russells accepted the conditions of life as they were and made the best of them. Clearly, they are stronger people today for having done so.

Written by Elizabeth Russell Sheppard

WAYNE AND SANDY RUTHERFORD

Wayne and Sandy Rutherford were married December 27, 1975, and moved to their first home in January 1977. Wayne was raised in Fort Worth, graduated from Castleberry High School, and attended Texas Wesleyan College. His brother is Johnny Rutherford, who is a famous race car driver. Wayne also raced and won many races during his career.

Sandy Lankford Rutherford was a native Texan from Graham, graduated from Graham High School, and received a bachelor's degree from University of Texas at Arlington in education. After the purchase of their home, she became a realtor and has sold real estate in the area since 1979. On September 12, 1977, Tobi Jo Rutherford was born. Tobi was the first of three daughters, joined

Back, standing-Tobi, Wayne; Middle-Sandy; Front-Ragen, Sidney

by Shelby Ragen Rutherford November 22, 1982, and Sidney Randall Rutherford August 7, 1986.

All three girls attended Snow Heights Elementary and North Richland Middle School. In 1996 Tobi graduated from Richland High School and is currently a sophomore at Stephen F. Austin State University, majoring in education. Ragen is a freshman at Richland, and Sidney is a sixth grader at North Richland Middle School.

Wayne and Sandy have tried to be as active in school as work permits. Wayne enjoyed all of the children participating in the North Richland Girls Softball League. They are members of Richland Hills Christian Church on Glenview Drive.

We have loved raising our family here. We have the best neighbors, and most of them were here when we moved in 22 years ago. We've seen NRH grow and change, but it is still a friendly place to live and raise your family. We have and still are loving NRH.

Submitted by Sandy Rutherford

JACK AND ANN SANDIFER

Rufe Snow Drive was a rough, two-lane road with "borrow" ditches on each side in March 1960 when Jack Wesley Sandifer and Annie Joe Brown Sandifer moved from the Polytechnic area of Fort Worth to their present home on Cylinda Sue Circle in North Richland Hills.

Jack and Ann Sandifer

"We shopped at the Safeway Store, corner of Rufe Snow and Grapevine Highway and Rapid Mart at Grapevine and Vance Road," Jack Sandifer said. " We banked in downtown Fort Worth. Only farmland was present north of us." They watched the construction of banks, other commercial development, new schools, churches, and Northeast Loop 820.

Jack Sandifer's parents were Ruth Marie Gaston and John Leonard Sandifer. He has one sister, Shirlee Sandifer Singer. Ann Sandifer's parents were Kelton Chapman Brown and John Lawrence Brown. Her brother, now deceased, was Jessie Riley Brown.

Jack and Ann married May 3, 1941. Their daughter, Pamela Ann Sandifer was born February 21, 1949, in Fort Worth. She graduated from Richland High School in 1968, attended Tarrant County Junior College, and graduated from North Texas State University in 1972. She married Michael Wayne Stevens June 12, 1976. They live

Daughter's family-Michael and Pam (Sandifer) Stevens, with sons Daniel and Benjamin

in Tyler and have two sons, Daniel Wesley Stevens, who was born September 15, 1988, and Benjamin Tyler Stevens, born September 20, 1991.

The Sandifers have been active members of the North Richland Hills Baptist Church for 37 years. Ann was the first teacher of the church's Mother's Day Out program. She also taught a girls' class and was director of the three-year-old Sunday school department. Jack served as a deacon and was the church's Training Union director and bond program director.

Jack worked for an insurance company 40 years before retiring in 1986. He has been active in the Downtown Optimist Club, Northeast Lions Club, Northeast Tarrant Chamber of Commerce, D/FW Claim Managers Council, and is past president of Fort Worth Claim Men's Association. The Sandifers love to travel and play table games. He raises a garden every year, and Ann freezes or cans the produce.

One of the most memorable things happening to them in NRH was when their daughter graduated from NTSU and became a teacher in San Antonio.

"We moved her there, gave her a used car plus funds to open a bank account," Jack Sandifer said. "Her move away from home was with love and hugs, a very significant event we'll never forget."

Compiled by Pat Riddle

JOHNNY B. AND MARY LOU SANDLIN

Mary Lou and Johnny B. Sandlin moved to Northeast Tarrant County in 1954. Mr. Sandlin was a football coach and teacher at Birdville High School, and Mrs. Sandlin was a legal secretary. They have four children: Michael was born July 5, 1954, and graduated from Richland High School and Trinity University in San Antonio. He is married and has three daughters and one son; Terry Lee was born in 1955 and graduated from Richland High School and Trinity University in San Antonio. He is married and has three daughters and one son. Suzy (Speight) was born Aug. 26, 1959, and graduated from Richland High School and the University of Texas at Austin. She is married and has two daughters and one son. John Scott was born Feb. 14, 1965, and graduated from Bell High School and Southern Methodist University. He is married and has one daughter, born Jan. 1, 1998.

The first home built by Mr. and Mrs. Sandlin was their personal home on Venice Street in North Richland Hills in 1957. At the time, they had no idea that J. B. Sandlin Homes would eventually become one of the most recognized names in the home-building industry in Tarrant County. In 1960 they moved to a Sandlin-built home on Harrell Street in NRH. Mr. Sandlin, with the help of his wife, Mary Lou, built houses part-time from 1957 to 1966. They entered the home building industry full time in 1966. During the 40 years in the building industry, they have built over 3,500 homes and developed over 5,000 residential lots. Many of our homes and developments have

The Johnny Sandlin family, on board cruise ship, 1991. Back, L/R-Terry, Chris, Scott, Michelle, Maggie Sandlin, Suzy (Sandlin) and Matt Speight, Eve and Mike Sandlin; Middle, L/R-Melissa, Jon, Jilaine, Beth Sandlin, Maggie, Zachary Speight; Front, L/R-Stephen, Mary Lou, Johnny, Amy, and Andrew Sandlin

been in NRH such as: Holiday Estates, Holiday Heights, Holiday North, Holiday East, Holiday West, Emerald Hills, Meadowview, North Ridge, Diamond Oaks South, Thornbridge Estates I-V, Richland Hills West, and Century Oaks I-IV. The Sandlins have had their office in NRH for the past 40 years.

Today their three sons and son-in-law, Matt Speight, orchestrate the business activities of five home-building divisions within the Sandlin Companies, including a pool building company.

Mr. Sandlin was assistant principal of Birdville High School from 1957 to 1960 and principal of Snow Heights Elementary School from 1961 to 1965. He served as city councilman of North Richland Hills from 1965 to 1970. Mr. Sandlin has been a charter member of the Northeast Richland Lions Club from 1963 to the present and was president in 1966. In 1996, Mr. Sandlin was awarded the Melvin D. Jones Fellowship award for his devotion and service to Lionism.

Mary Lou retired as decorator of Sandlin Homes in 1990. Now she spends her time traveling, playing bridge, shopping, and keeping up with 10 grandchildren. Johnny is semi-retired and spends his time traveling, playing golf and tennis, and also keeping up with 10 grandchildren.

Submitted by Mary Lou Sandlin

LINDA SPURLOCK SANSOUCIE

Linda Spurlock Sansoucie was born in Dallas in 1940. She was married to Madie F. Sansoucie. She had two children, Joe Clarence Marlin Spurlock III and Allison Spurlock Morrison, and one grandchild, William Alexander Morrison. Mrs. Sansoucie served on the North Richland Hills City Council for 10 years. During her council tenure, Mrs. Sansoucie was noted

Linda Spurlock Sansoucie

for keeping a watchful eye on fiscal matters and for being an advocate of city parks.

Mrs. Sansoucie's career included working as an election consultant and teaching in the Birdville School District. She was also a horseback riding instructor for the YMCA's Camp Carter at one time. Leisure time was devoted in part to membership in several clubs, a sorority, and her church. She belonged to Delta Gamma sorority, Diamond Loch Bridge Club, Fort Worth Woman's Club, and Peace Lutheran Church.

Among her accomplishments as a City Councilwoman was the formation of the North Richland Hills Beautification Committee in 1988. Mrs. Sansoucie believed that NRH would become a better place to live, as it became more beautiful. She was an advocate for as many parks and as much green space as possible for the citizens of NRH to enjoy. She is credited with being one of the first council members to voice concerns about city beautification projects, and it was always part of her agenda to attempt to raise awareness of the importance of including planning for beautification in every city venture.

Mrs. Sansoucie died in January 1998. Glenview Neighborhood Park was renamed Linda Spurlock Park in honor of her dedication to parks and beautification projects.

PAUL AND KAY SCHMIDT

The purchase of their first house in 1971 brought Kay and Paul Schmidt to the Holiday Heights neighborhood of North Richland Hills. Diana Kay Hardin had married Paul Ralph Schmidt at Richland Hills Baptist Church in 1966. Kay, born in Fort Worth, and Paul,

1986, Back, L/R-Kathryn, Kent, Paul; Front, L/R-Kay, Kari, Karen

born in Glendale, California, both attended Richland Junior High and Richland High School. Their colleges were Arlington State for Paul and University of Texas at Arlington and Texas Woman's University for Kay.

The Schmidts have four children, all of whom have attended Snow Heights Elementary, North Richland Middle, and Richland High School. Their oldest child, Kathryn Janelle, was a Spanish education major at Oklahoma Baptist University. Now Kathryn Janelle Patterson, she lives in Tulsa with her husband David Patterson.

Kent Marshall became a veterinary technician in Watauga after studying business at North Texas State University. He is active in Texas Search Dogs and is an ice hockey enthusiast.

Karen Suzanne was a public relations and communications major at Howard Payne University where she was a member of Phi Beta Lambda national business organization, Delta Chi Rho service sorority, and Howard Payne Student Foundation. She currently is a marketing intern with the Marketing and Publications Department of Howard Payne University.

The youngest child in the Schmidt family is Kari Dianna. Kari likes sports, especially ice hockey and basketball, and collects Coca-Cola memorabilia.

Paul's work history includes being a manager of International Video Tele-communications for Electronic Data Systems Corporation and employment at the Southern Baptist Radio and Television Commission. Presently, he is director of Information Systems for Pro View Capital, LLC. He served in the Air Force in Libya and the United States, and he was chosen as an Outstanding Young Man of America in 1982. Kay, a preschool director and teacher for 25 years, is presently director of library services for North Richland Hills Baptist Church.

The Schmidt family has attended North Richland Hills Baptist Church for 32 years. Paul has served as Sunday school and Royal Ambassador teacher. Kay has been on the North Richland Hills Library Board since 1983 and has served a term as president of the board. She was a member of the Library Needs Assessment Committee and the Library Bond Committee. In his spare time, Paul enjoys several hobbies: operating a ham radio, woodworking, and building musical instruments. Kay's special interests include needlework, quilting, and libraries. A favorite activity of the family is camping.

Paul remembers a time in North Richland Hills when there was only pasture land north of Riviera Drive, when Rufe Snow Drive was a two-lane, hot-top road with tall grass growing along both sides, and shopping had to be done in Fort Worth or Dallas, as there were no local shopping malls. Kay's special memories include walking to Rufe Snow with the children to see the Sesquicentennial Wagon Train as it came through North Richland Hills on its way to an overnight camp at Green Valley Raceway off Davis Boulevard. The Schmidts think that better retail and entertainment centers, the junior college campus, and the improved library facility have added greatly to our community.

Submitted by Kay Schmidt

RALPH AND ALVA JUNE SCHMIDT

Alva June Sherk from Flint, Michigan, married Ralph Julius Schmidt of Southgate, California, at the Little Church of the Flowers in Glendale, California, in 1942. Ralph graduated from the University of California at Los Angeles with a degree in mechanical engineering. During World War II, he served in the Third Army, Fifth (Red Diamond) Division, Second Infantry Regiment in the European Theatre. June attended Glendale College and Saint Joseph Hospital School of Nursing in Fort Worth. The Schmidts and their three children moved from California to Deville Drive (where they still live) in North Richland Hills in 1957.

All the Schmidt children attended Birdville schools. The first child in the Schmidt family was Paul Ralph who married Kay Hardin, also a graduate of Birdville schools. He is director of information systems for Pro View Capital. Diane Michele Schmidt Newton married Richard Ray Newton. She was an academic language therapist and is an interior decorator at Diane's Designs. David Michael Schmidt,

Ralph Schmidt

the youngest child, married Deborah Diana Burkett. He is with ADA Designs, a residential/commercial design and planning service. Their children have blessed Ralph and June with 12 grandchildren.

Ralph Schmidt had been a mechanical engineer for 50 years when he retired at the end of 1981. He started as an apprentice at Menasco Manufacturing Company in 1940 and retired as president and chief operations officer of the company. He was listed in Who's Who in the South and Southwest in 1969–70. June was a registered nurse for 30 years at Glenview Hospital and Northeast Medical Clinic.

Alva June Schmidt

The leisure activities of the Schmidts through the years have included building model airplanes, pen and ink drawing, writing poetry, and traveling. Genealogical research is also an interest. Ralph hand-built a 1923 model street rod with an all-wood delivery-van body which won four first place awards at the Fort Worth Classic Car Show. The Schmidts have been members of North Richland Baptist Church for 36 years where June taught the ninth grade girls and young marrieds' Sunday school classes. Ralph is a lifetime member of the Society of Manufacturing Engineers.

The Schmidts remember their neighborhood as a friendly place. Twenty-six children lived on their block. They recall shopping at Buddies Grocery Store on Blaney Street, at Cox's on Belknap Street, and at Striplings, Monnigs, Leonard Brothers', and The Fair department stores in downtown Fort Worth. Ralph remembers that Leonard's would lend you money if you were short of cash.

The changes the Schmidts have noted in North Richland Hills during their long period of residence are the creation of an excellent city government and many well maintained city parks. North Richland Hills was a new community when the Schmidts moved here. It was so quiet one could hear the crickets and the frogs. There was a grocery store, a barber shop, a Mott's variety store, a cafeteria that was short-lived, and a drugstore for local shopping.

The Pillow-Rush-Jacobson medical clinic was in the shopping center also, but hospital facilities were in Fort Worth. Loop 820 was in the thinking stage. There was only one elementary school in North Richland Hills at the time, and junior high school students went to Richland Junior High. The Barrons had a small swimming pool off Grapevine Highway and Parchman Street. Now, however, there is everything needed: a fine city government, multistoried office buildings, three shopping centers plus strip centers, and numerous grocery stores to choose from. The city has retained its friendly atmosphere and is a safe and clean, progressive place to live.

Submitted by Kay Schmidt

HAL AND DORIS SCHUBERT

Harold F. and Doris J. Schubert and their children, Hal and Terri, moved to Deville Drive in North Richland Hills on April 15, 1955. There were very few houses on their street, and consequently, mail delivery for them was at the corner of Victoria and Deville Drive. They remember how exciting it was when the mail was brought to their house! Harold, from Columbus, Ohio, met Doris during World War II at a dance at Tarrant Field (later Carswell), where he was stationed in the Army Air Force (which became the U.S. Air Force). They were married October 12, 1945. After Harold's military service and college training at Ohio State University, he went to work in the Industrial Engineering Department at General Dynamics, which lasted 24 years and included five years with General Dynamics in San Diego. Employment at General Dynamics took a downturn, so he left and joined Bell Helicopter as a plant engineer and facility layout specialist. He retired from Bell in 1985. Doris' first job was with the city of Fort Worth as a secretary. Subsequently, she worked for American Airlines, for the IRS, for General Dynamics, and at the LTV facility in Grand Prairie.

Hal was born in Fort Worth in 1952. He attended Tarrant County Junior College, University of Texas at Arlington, and now lives in Rochester, New York, where he is a professional computer programmer. While in school, he played the accordion well enough to qualify to perform on the Ted Mack Amateur Hour when it came through Dallas on its last national tour.

Back, L/R-Terri Schubert Whaley, Mike Whaley, Hal Whaley; Front, L/R-Doris, Harold Schubert, Nathan Whaley

Terri was born in Fort Worth in 1953. She graduated from Texas Woman's University in Denton with a degree in home economics and kindergarten certification and now teaches at Fort Worth Christian School. Terri married Michael (Mike) Ray Whaley in 1975. He also lived in NRH on East Holiday Lane with parents, Raymond and Jo Whaley, and his sister, Deborah. Terri and Mike have two sons, Nathan and Chase. Nathan is a senior at Richland High School, and Chase is in the seventh grade at Fort Worth Christian School. Mike graduated from the University of Texas at Arlington and now works in the Equipment Engineering Department at Bell Helicopter. The family enjoys hunting and fishing.

Back, L/R-Mike Whaley; Front, L/R-Terri Schubert Whaley, Chase, Nathan Whaley

Harold was a Cubmaster at Davis Memorial United Methodist Church for two years, scoutmaster for three years, and an Explorer Scout advisor for a year while living in San Diego. During the time that Harold was a Cubmaster, Hal was in the same den with his future brother-in-law, Mike.

Terri has fun memories of riding her bike down "Mesquite Hill," as the top of Blaney Avenue was called. She also enjoyed selling Girl Scout cookies for her Brownie Troop No. 361 and walking to the "drugstore" and planning on saving her money to buy board games, a favorite pastime. She enjoyed growing up with her friends from Snow Heights Elementary, which she attended the first year it was opened in 1959, through her graduation year, 1971, at Richland High School, where she was a Dixie Belle.

Harold and Doris have been members of Richland Hills United Methodist Church and the Homebuilders Sunday School Class since 1956. Harold is teaching the class at the present time. Terri, Mike, Nathan, and Chase attend the Richland Hills Church of Christ in NRH.

Harold served on the NRH Board of Adjustment from 1982 to 1989 and the Board of Appeals from 1989 to 1990. Harold and Doris are members of the Fort Worth Elks Lodge. They also enjoy traveling.

JOHN AND LEONA SCHWARTZ

When John R. and Leona Schwartz moved into their North Richland Hills home on Catalina Court, there were no paved roads and no neighbors. It was October 1953, and the Schwartz's house was the first house built in the area north of Briley Drive and east of Holiday Lane. John and Leona both grew up in Buffalo, New York, and John, employed by Bell Helicopter, had been transferred when Bell opened a new plant in Hurst.

Living in the wide open spaces was a revelation to John, Leona, and son John R. The family discovered a very relaxed way of living, with cows from a nearby farm coming to graze on the Johnson grass, a type of grass new to the Schwartzes. The family dog discovered the fun of chasing jackrabbits. All of the family soon had the feeling they had lived in the "boondocks" forever and thought it was sheer heaven.

Construction sites began to crop up here and there, but not much attention was paid to them. Leona still remembers that fateful day and how it felt to look up Riviera Drive and see the moving van with the first family moving in. Gone was their paradise, but it would be nice to have neighbors. It was a very strange feeling.

The oldest son, John R., was born in Buffalo November 26, 1946. Two more children were born to the Schwartz family while living in NRH. James F. was born May 3, 1955, and died October 18, 1990. Mary Kathryn Schwartz Williams was born January 22, 1961, and now lives in Aledo. There are nine Schwartz grandchildren. John R., who lives in Groesbeck, has five children, Jim had two, and Mary Kathryn has two.

The elder Schwartzes were married at St. Joseph Catholic Church in Buffalo January 22, 1944. John retired after 43 years of working for Bell Helicopter. The family attended St. John the Apostle Catholic Church for 33 years, and both parents were quite active in the church. John ("Jack") was head of the Parish Council's Building Committee. Leona taught seven years at St. John the Apostle Elementary School and then became principal of the school for another 17 years, retiring June 30, 1989. Both served on the Catholic Charity Board and the Diocesan Pastoral Council.

Leona Schwartz said, "I have the best neighbors in Texas. NRH has been a very good community in which to live."

CHARLES AND ALICE SCOMA

The Charles Scoma family arrived in North Richland Hills in June 1979 when the only building on the north side of Loop 820 and Rufe Snow intersection was a Gulf station. Anthony began the second grade at Snow Heights Elementary, and Charlece was in kindergarten. We were new in the area; Charles grew up in Dallas and graduated from South Oak Cliff High School and North Texas State University. Alice grew up in the little town of Wylie in Collin County and also graduated from North Texas.

In 1983, we moved from the Diamond Loch area and built a house on Cardinal Lane in the Smithfield area. Numerous trips to City

Charles and Alice Scoma

Hall concerning such things as building permits, and later the pending location of Mid-Cities Boulevard, propelled us into active city involvement. Alice was appointed a charter member of the Beautification Commission, a very fulfilling assignment. Charles was elected to two terms on the City Council beginning in 1989. He ran and was elected to the Birdville Board of Trustees and is in his sixth year of service.

Civic involvement has been a family affair. Anthony was appointed teen advisor on the first Teen Court Advisory Board, which was both educational and a lot of fun for him. He graduated from Richland High in 1990, and then the University of Texas at Austin. He is now married, a student and employee of the Assembly of God Theology Seminary in

Anthony and Charlece Scoma

Springfield, Missouri. His wife, Deanna, also a UT graduate from Austin, is a CPA with an accounting firm. Two years after Anthony, Charlece served on the Teen Court. Charlece was also appointed to the board as teen adviser. She was also a Richland Rebel and graduated from Houston Baptist University. She is now a medical student at the North Texas Health Science Center in Fort Worth. Charlece was married in June 1997 to Michael Hughes.

Charles was employed in various management positions for over 25 years by both Sears Roebuck and Wal-Mart stores. He was later employed by an international consulting firm and the Federal Home Loan Bank before starting his own business in 1991. He is a member of the Lions Club, Chamber of Commerce, and is past board president of the Northeast Orchestra. Alice is a teacher at Richland High School. The Scoma family has been active members of Bethel Temple in Fort Worth since moving to the area in 1979. We have enjoyed being part of a progressive city with an emphasis on parks, service to the citizens, and a commitment to beautification.

Charles was elected mayor of NRH in May 1998.

JAKE AND NANCY SCOTT

Nancy James Scott moved to the Smithfield area from Fort Worth in 1936 with her mother, Mrs. James, grandmother, and two brothers. Mrs. James purchased a rock house located at the corner of Amundson and Precinct Line Road from a man named Counts. In 1937, Mrs. James married a man named Angel and they lived in that rock house for many years. Today, several ancient pear trees still can be seen on the east side of this property, although the house has been gone many years. In the springtime, the trees are covered with white blossoms followed by hundreds of pears that bend the branches to the ground.

In 1938, Nancy dated and married a young man of the community, J. L. (Jake) Scott. He was the son of Joe Scott, and his three brothers were Hugh, Willard, and Jimmy

Ray. Joe Scott was the son of Matt Scott, a circuit rider for the Methodist Church who had moved to the Smithfield area from Arkansas. Following the death of Joe Scott's mother, Matt married a woman named Dona. She and Matt Scott had three daughters who grew up to marry prominent men of the Smithfield community. Mae married R. D. Kidwell, Dorthula married Vern Lewis, and Valta married a man named Robnett.

As a young man in the Smithfield community, Joe Scott held a number of interesting jobs. In addition to his work at the Quarter Master Depot in Fort Worth, he found time to help Guy Meacham deliver the mail in Smithfield. They worked for the postmaster, Jim Turner. For awhile he worked at the Smithfield bank. A man named Ray White from Keller had sponsored the bank, which was destroyed along with the drugstore, general store, and several other structures when a fire swept the little town in the late 1920s. The fire started in the Quinn home on Main Street during the middle of the day. Mrs. Quinn's mother was an invalid, and lost her life in the devastating blaze. Jake Scott, Joe's son, later told Nancy that he was working at a Mobile Filling Station on Camp Bowie when he heard about the fire. He jumped into his car and started home. A policeman stopped him for speeding. When the policeman heard the reason for the excessive speed, he escorted Jake instead of giving him a ticket. Following the death of his first wife, Joe Scott married Ida Anderson Arthur.

Nancy's aunt was Hellen Reagan. She and her husband, Chester, had moved to the Smithfield area in the late '20s, buying many acres east of Precinct Line Road where they operated a hog farm. Later, they had a large dairy there. Still later, they developed the subdivision known as The Reagan Estates. This was one of the first planned subdivisions located today in the city of Colleyville. Nancy remembers that the Reagan's first house burned to the ground, taking with it priceless furnishings, including a French Provincial piano.

Nancy and Jake had two children, Larry and Keith. Keith and her husband live in the College Hills area of North Richland Hills. Jake died in 1984. He is buried in the Smithfield Cemetery. Nancy lives in the white house they built together on Smithfield Road just south of Main Street. She said that the pear trees lining the north side of the driveway were planted in early 1900s. Like the trees at the old Angel home place, they still bloom and bear fruit year after year.

Information from interview with Nancy Scott

CHUCK AND ZANDA SEABERG

Having married just four months before, and less than a mile away, Chuck and Zanda Seaberg moved into their North Richland Hills home in early 1996 with Chuck's sons, Chris and Jon, and Zanda's 17-year-old cat, Abby.

Zanda's parents, Lowell and Joyce Hilger, and brother, Zane, moved to NRH in 1966. Zanda graduated from Richland High School and attended and worked at Tarrant County Junior College Northeast. She graduated from Texas Wesleyan College (now University) and received a master's degree from North Texas State University (now UNT).

After having lived on the east side of Fort Worth, Euless, and Haltom City, Zanda returned to NRH in 1996 with her new family. In the fall of 1996 Chris entered Richland High School 24 years after Zanda had graduated, and Jon attended North Richland Middle School.

Chuck Seaberg was born in Lubbock and graduated from Texas Tech University. His career in sales took him to Oklahoma where Chris and Jon were born. They moved to NRH in 1987.

When Chuck and Zanda met on a blind date arranged by Fort Worth friends, they did not know that they were already practically neighbors, with Chuck living in an apartment two exits from Zanda's off Loop 820.

Chuck is a licensed chemical dependency counselor with experience working with adolescents. As an officer of the Community Supervision and Corrections Department, he is counselor for the Tarrant County Bootcamp for young offenders where he also uses certifications as a ROPES Course instructor and in acupuncture.

Zanda is a licensed professional counselor and manages the staff training department for Tarrant County Mental Health Mental Retardation where she also teaches management classes. She has taught in the Mental Health and Psychology programs at TCJC and is active in the rehabilitation community.

Chris and Jon both take honors classes and are active in school sports and choir.

Submitted by Zanda Seaberg

BOB AND MATTA LOU SHEEGOG

Bob E. Sheegog and his wife, Matta Lou (nee McPherson), along with their daughter, Margie Sue, moved to North Richland Hills in September 1960. Margie entered second grade at Snow Heights Elementary School. At that time, there was no middle school, Rufe Snow Drive was a two-lane road, and 820 was unheard of. In 1974, Margie married Greg Stone. They now live in Garland with their three children, Danny, Erin, and Andrew.

JOHN AND NINA SHELBY

North Richland Hills was mentioned in the news many times before we knew where it was or had any inkling that we would be moving there. Some of our friends bought houses there, and we visited them, but we never dreamed we could live in such a nice place.

John Alexander Shelby Jr. was born April 25, 1922 in Handley, which was the largest unincorporated area in Texas. Some of Handley still exists, but part of Handley is now known as Meadowbrook. He met Olga Nina Kjorstad in 1945 in Kirkland, Washington, and we mar-

John and Nina Shelby

ried November 2, 1946. I was born in Williston, North Dakota January 31, 1924, and lived there through high school. We moved back to Texas in 1948.

Fortunately, we both eventually found jobs in the aircraft industry. John retired from Bell Helicopter in September 1987 after 37 years, and Nina retired from General Dynamics in January 1991 after 40 years. Nina carpooled to General Dynamics most of those 40 years. We purchased our house on Catalina Court in July 1958 and still reside there. The area north of Riviera Drive was open pasture with lots of mesquite trees growing there. East Belknap was our main thoroughfare to Fort Worth, and there were no great eating places in the North Richland Hills area. "Dining out" meant driving to East Lancaster, Camp Bowie Boulevard, or downtown.

John's parents were John and Vera Shelby. He had one brother, Walter, and one sister, Gladys, both deceased. Nina's parents were John and Rena Kjorstad. Both came from Norway and homesteaded in the rural Williston area. She had four brothers and four sisters. Two brothers and two sisters are still living in Williston; the other four are deceased. Her family held a reunion in August 1997 in North Dakota where they celebrated her oldest sister's 90th birthday.

Living in NRH has been wonderful. Our street has only nine houses, and each has a great family. One neighbor, the first residents on the street, still live in their house. Another neighbor bought the home of her parents when they died. They have since retired and really enjoy "living" in the neighborhood. Several families on our block have young children, so there is a nice "mix" on our street. We wouldn't think of living on any other street or in any other city.

The city of North Richland Hills provides a center for senior citizens at Glenview Drive and Morgan Circle. Many people enjoy the Dan Echols Senior Adult Center and the varied activities and services it provides for members. What a great place to spend our free time!

The North Richland Hills area has grown as predicted when we moved here; however, we had no idea it would become as congested as it is. Road construction has been the biggest headache for the area. It's frustrating when the alternate routes are also under construction.

Submitted by Nina Shelby

RANDY AND SUSAN SHIFLET

Randy moved to the area from Mineral Wells in 1972 to attend TCJC. During his first semester he read an article in the Star-Telegram that the City of North Richland

Hills was beginning a Police Cadet program in January 1973. The program was funded for four students enrolled in Criminal Justice programs to work 20 hours a week at the Police Department. In addition to compensation for work, the federal government paid tuition and books. Randy applied for and was hired as one of these cadets.

He began his career with the City as a police dispatcher, working the weekend midnight shift. In July 1973 he was hired as a full-time police officer but remained as a dispatcher until early 1974, at which time he went through the Regional Police Academy and began patrol duties. At 18, he was the youngest police officer ever hired by the City. Randy remained in the Patrol Division for several years and was promoted to sergeant in 1978. After a year as a patrol sergeant, he was transferred to supervise the internal operations of Police Communications and Records.

In 1980 he was appointed as a commander, which was later reclassified to the title of captain. In this capacity he was the public information officer for the Police Department for 12 years. Randy attended North Texas State University part-time and received his bachelor's degree in criminal justice in 1987. In 1992 Chief Jerry McGlasson appointed him assistant police chief, and in 1993 he was appointed as assistant city manager by City Manager Rodger N. Line. In 1997, City Manager Larry J. Cunningham appointed him deputy city manager.

Susan moved to North Richland Hills in 1978 with her parents and went to work for the Hurst Police Department in 1979. While supervising communications personnel, Randy attended many area functions related to his duties. In 1980, while attending a regional communications meeting in Grapevine, he met Susan Hulsey, a dispatcher for the City of Hurst. This "chance" meeting grew into a love that resulted in marriage between Susan and Randy in July 1981. Susan continued with the City of Hurst until 1989 when she returned to school full time, obtaining her master's in accounting from the University of North Texas in 1991. She is presently a CPA for Arthur Andersen in Fort Worth.

Ryan was born to Randy and Susan in 1984 at Northeast Community Hospital in Bedford. He has lived his entire life in North Richland Hills and attended Birdville schools. He is a freshman at Richland High School and enjoys playing baseball and football. At the age of 6, Ryan awoke around 4:00 A.M. and couldn't sleep so he decided to play a video game. He looked outside to see if anyone was up

Randy, Ryan, Russell, and Susan Shiflet

and observed two men attempting to break into his father's unmarked police car. He woke his mother, who in turn woke his father. Susan called the police while Randy confronted the two subjects. Randy apprehended one and the police who were called apprehended the other a couple of blocks away. For his efforts, Ryan was named "Crimewatcher of the Year" for North Richland Hills and a mayoral proclamation issued by Mayor Brown proclaimed "Ryan Shiflet Day" for his efforts.

Completing the family lineup is Russell, born in 1987 at Columbia North Hills Hospital in North Richland Hills, making him the only native family member of North Richland Hills. He has lived his entire life in the city and also attends Birdville schools. Russell enjoys soccer and plays regularly at the Green Valley Soccer Park. He loves animals and has a knack for training them. He plans on becoming a veterinarian.

Randy and Susan look forward to enjoying many years in the city and hope to retire and remain in North Richland Hills since this has truly become their home. Randy's fondest memories of the city involve the many citizens he has met and worked with over the years. He considers his involvement in the construction of the police building in 1987 and the City Hall expansion in 1996 as highlights of his career.

"I am so honored to have been a part of this city and to have had an opportunity to serve the citizens and enjoy the friendships of fellow employees for the past 25 years as we grew from a town of 16,000 to a city of 55,000 residents," Randy said. "Either the widening of Rufe Snow Drive north of 820 to a five lane road (between cow pastures) or the day the stop signs and yield signs were replaced with traffic signals at Davis Boulevard, Grapevine Highway, and Bedford-Euless Road has to rank near the top as true progress for North Richland Hills. They were both rather historical events at the time."

BEN AND MARY SHILCUTT

Ben Shilcutt, his wife, Mary, and children, Bruce, Bryan, and Debra, moved to Rufe Snow Drive in February 1961.

Their home place, located on the west side of Rufe Snow, consisted of a brick home and four acres of land. A Mrs. Parker lived to the south of them on a 25-acre lot, which became a hangout for teenagers when she died and left the property uninhabited.

To the north of the property, there were three other homes, each on a four-acre lot. The four homes shared a large stock pond at the rear of the properties, and each home had a gas meter on one of the lots. Each home had its own water well and septic tank.

Rufe Snow Drive was a two-lane, black-top road and was widened to four lanes in 1963 when the city condemned the front 10 feet of each property and then assessed the property owners for curbs! North Richland Junior High was also opened that year.

Bruce, Bryan, and Debra all attended Snow Heights Elementary, North Richland Junior High, and Richland

Debbie, Ben, Bruce, Bryan, and in the front, Mary

Senior High School.

When the family moved to Rufe Snow, the high school was being constructed. There was no 820 freeway, no mail delivery to the door, no city water on the west side of the road. Even today, the mail is delivered to the curb mailboxes, not to the house.

Ben worked as a teacher and coach in the Birdville schools from 1956 to 1986. He served as principal at Richland High from 1970–1975. He then worked at the Birdville ISD Administration Building until he retired in 1986. Mary was a librarian at Fort Worth Christian Junior College from 1961–1965 and then served the Birdville ISD for 27 years. She was the librarian at Richland High School for 25 years before retiring in 1992.

In 1983, they sold part of their land to a company developing portions of what would be known as Meadow Lakes.

At the present time, Bruce lives in Houston, Bryan in Abilene, and Debra in North Richland Hills on Karen Drive.

JOHN THOMAS AND RUBY AUSTIN SHIVERS JOHN WILLIAM AND ALINE BOST SHIVERS

John Thomas Shivers, born in 1855 at Tuscaloosa, Alabama, came to Texas with his family in a covered wagon along with friends and their families.

After much looking, he purchased 240 acres of land, all in timber, for $13 per acre. He could have bought land "out on the prairie," as he called it, which is now Watauga and Saginaw for $3 per acre. He wanted the timber to have logs to build his house, barn, and fences. He was going to marry Ruby Austin, who came to Texas in 1871. She was born in 1859 at Trenton,

Lyndahl Shivers

Georgia, and remembered during the Civil War hearing the cannons booming and the soldiers pilfering food in the kitchen. Kitchens were built away from the main house. There were 40 families who planned the trip to Texas, but the trip was postponed a year because of sickness and crop failure with one of the families.

There were 90 covered wagons in the train. Forty wagons brought the families, and the remainder carried supplies. In this group was a man everyone called Daddy Rawhide. Having lost his wife, he and a 12-year-old daughter made the trip in a cart drawn by two oxen. Not wanting to leave his hound, he made a bed for it under the cart with rawhide. When the dog was tired, he hopped into his bed to ride. Daddy Rawhide was always two hours late reaching camp.

Aline Bost Shivers

On Friday afternoons camp was made early. Saturday was washday. Cass White, for whom White's Chapel was later named, conducted church services on Sunday. He served as pastor and mentor during the 11 months of hardship with deaths, births, and illnesses.

In the evening, camp was made in a circle to protect people and horses. The horses could graze through the night. The last circle was made in July 1871 at what is now White's Chapel.

Ruby Austin married John Thomas Shivers in 1883. There were two sons, James and Henry. James married Mabel Joyce and their son John William Shivers was born June 3, 1909. The other son, Henry, married Etta Cooper. The Coopers lost their two adopted children, Oliver, at age 6 with scarlet fever, and Tommy Jr. in an automobile accident in October 1936.

Johnny Shivers

John Thomas cleared the land and hauled logs to Smithfield Depot to ship them for sale to pay for the place. This acreage is northeast of Smithfield in the 8300 block of Davis Boulevard, which is now a five-lane highway.

The location of the log house on the hill and later the site of the frame house with the stone chimney is now covered by one of the elegant homes in the new Thornbridge Addition.

John and Ruby were very fortunate to have one of the best water wells in the country. In drought years, neighbors hauled water from this well for their use and some brought their clothes there to do their washing.

John William, known to his friends as Johnny, spent a lot of time with his grandmother when he was a little boy. His favorite story was the one his grandmother told him about her covered wagon trip to Texas. Johnny had picked up a

cigar box full of arrowheads and he could visualize the Indians roaming the woods on his granddad's place.

John married Aline Bost June 28, 1935. A baby daughter, Lyndahl, was born March 14, 1939. She attended school at Keller from beginning to graduation when she had the honor of giving the valedictory speech. As she grew up she

James (1884–1945), Mabel Joyce (1882–1972), and son Johnny Shivers

enjoyed the piano lessons given by Mrs. Madge Meacham. Later she had other teachers and also took organ lessons. She became a member of the Smithfield Methodist Church (now Smithfield United Methodist Church) at an early age. She played the piano and organ a short time for the church services.

Henry Shivers, son of John Thomas and Ruby Austin Shivers (1886–1962)

Lyndahl went to college one year at North Texas State and then to Texas Tech in Lubbock. In her senior year on March 15, 1961, one day after her 22nd birthday, Lyndahl became seriously ill with a brain aneurysm. She died March 16, 1961.

Except for a brief time when John's work took them to Henderson, Texas, and the KMA oil fields in Wichita County, Texas, John and Aline lived on the home place. John was born there and with the exception of the short time away working, spent all of his life at the present site.

Aline has lived on this place 62 years. She was born at Josephine and moved to Smithfield in November 1930 with her family. At the end of her life, the saga of John Thomas and Ruby Austin Shivers will be a closed chapter.

John Thomas Shivers died in 1923 and Ruby Austin Shivers died in 1932. They are both buried in Smithfield Cemetery.

Etta Cooper Shivers, wife of Henry Shivers, holding son, Oliver

Submitted by Aline Bost Shivers

BYRON AND JOAN SIBBET

Joan and Byron Sibbet married and moved to North Richland Hills in 1973. They have one daughter, Staci, who is a 1994 graduate of Richland High School.

Joan was born in Sherman, Texas. She is a graduate of North Texas State University. She has taught in the Birdville Independent School District since 1968. Her mother, who is now retired, worked for the Knox Insurance Company. Joan's mother's side of the family farmed in the Pottsboro,

Texas, area. Her father was in an 8th Air Force P-51 fighter escort squadron, during World War II. He later became the assistant superintendent of the Northwest Independent School District. Her father's side of the family were longtime residents of Denison, Texas.

Byron has served on the North Richland Hills City Council from 1988 to 1998. Before that, he served on the Cable Television Board and on

Byron, Joan, Staci Sibbet

the 1985 Capital Improvements Bond Committee. He was born in Fort Worth, and spent most of his youth in West Texas. He is a graduate of McMurry University. His first remembrance of what is now North Richland Hills was visiting a farmhouse on the Grapevine Highway during his childhood and playing in a field that is now the site of the North Richland Hills Baptist Church.

His mother's side of the family established themselves in the Atlanta area in the early 1800s. They served in the Confederacy during the Civil War. After the war, they moved to the Indian Territory where they were frontier merchants. In the early 1900s, they came to Fort Worth and eventually set up Echols Brothers Radiators.

On his father's side of the family, Byron's great-grandfather served in the Wisconsin Infantry of the Union Army. After the Civil War, he returned to Wisconsin where he worked as a river pilot and a lumberjack. Byron's grandfather moved to Fort Worth in the 1920s where he became a cement merchant.

BURVON AND SARA HENDERSON SIKES

In August 1963, the Sikes family moved from Albuquerque to Fort Worth. Burvon was credit operating manager for the southwest region for Montgomery Ward. We left a climate of 4 percent humidity in New Mexico and arrived here to a shocking 98 percent humidity. Texans were friendly—a cowboy at the motel greeted me with, "Howdy, Ma'am."

Our friends, Lou and Ken Hubbard, transferred by the same company, lived on Neal Street in North Richland Hills. Ken called Lutz Realty, and John Lutz leased us a house in Richland Hills. At that time, Richland Hills had flooding problems, and with water standing under the house, our children were often sick due to dampness.

Ruth Supulver, a longtime resident of NRH, helped me find a house on Redondo Street. We moved there in March 1964. When we were transferred to Kansas City in 1975, our youngest children remained in this house, not wanting to leave NRH. Burvon died of a massive heart attack in September 1978.

I returned to live with the children on Redondo Street

and went back to work at Northeast National Bank. In 1985, I left Allied Bank and joined Nations Bank. After many changes in bank names, I retired in February 1990.

After graduation from RHS in 1966, Bryan Farel Sikes attended Northeast Louisiana University, graduating in 1970. He is a self-employed freight broker and quarterhorse breeder and lives in Long Lane, Missouri. He married Susan Ann Pelton of Fort Worth. She was killed in 1995 in an automobile accident. They have four children.

Robin Harriett Sikes Mitchner graduated from Richland High School in 1972. She attended Tarrant County Junior College and Weatherford Junior College. She lives at Lake Weatherford and is a homemaker. She has been a member of North Richland Hills Baptist Church since 1963.

Russell Alan "Rusty" Sikes graduated from Richland High School in 1974 and Texas Wesleyan College in 1978. He married Leslie R. King, daughter of Henry and Phyliss King of NRH. They have three children, all students in Birdville schools. All the family are members of Birdville Baptist Church. Rusty has been employed by Layman Container of Fort Worth as purchasing agent and stock product manager since 1981.

When we moved to Redondo Street, Rufe Snow Drive was a narrow road. A friend asked, "Where did you find this quaggly road?" We could hear the dynamite blasts during the building of Loop 820.

North Richland Hills was a great city to raise our children.

Submitted by Sara Henderson Sikes

SAM AND MARJORIE SIMS

Sam Sims and Marjorie Hoke were married in February 1940 in Phoenix. They moved to North Richland Hills on Blaney Avenue in June 1955 from Santa Cruz, California. Their children, Sharlene and Stephen, were both graduates of Richland High School and attended Texas Christian University. Sharlene is married to Franklin Horak, and they have three children. Stephen is married to Eloise Pope Sims, and they also have three children. Stephen attended the University of Texas Dental School and is now a dentist with offices in Hurst.

Sims 50th wedding anniversary; Back, L/R-Kiley Horak, Stephen, Kelli, and Eloise Sims, Sharlene, Frank, and Kelly Horak; Front, L/R-Sam Sims, Kimble Horak, Bryan, Stephanie, Marjorie Sims

Sam and Marjorie attended St. Andrews Episcopal Church for 42 years. Sam was in the oil production business for many years with Kimbell Oil Co. and later Sims Oil Co.

When they moved to NRH, they were out in the country at the end of Blaney Avenue. There were barbed-wire fences, and the kids all called it Goat Hills. We had no police or fire department. The water system was very bad. One night in 1965 my son Stephen and I were just coming home from an RHS baseball game and had parked both cars in the drive. When we came inside the house, we heard this loud noise and came out to find a car had wiped out two trees and the back of both cars. It was winter time, and the city had spread gravel on the road. Luck was with us, as the trees changed the path of the car which was headed right into the house.

We have been very happy and have made many lifetime friends. There are several families still in our block who were here in 1955.

Submitted by Sam Sims

HERB AND ADELINE SLAUGHTER

Herb and Adeline Slaughter moved into their first North Richland Hills home on Vance Road February 1, 1956 with sons, Paul, Philip, Stephen, and David. Herb was born in Abilene May 22, 1924. Adeline was born in Dallas August 5, 1924, to Selma and Gus Daniels. The Daniels lived in the Oakhurst section of Fort Worth. Adeline's brother, Paul Daniels, served as mayor of Richland Hills for 18 years.

Paul Slaughter, born in Fort Worth August 28, 1948, started school in Memphis, Tennessee, when the family moved there for a few years. He graduated from Richland High School in 1965, currently lives in Seminole, Texas, with his wife Cathy and children, Christi, Meredith, and Paul Jr., and is a doctor in family practice.

Philip was born March 28, 1952, the first baby to be born in the new Baptist Hospital in Memphis. He graduated from Richland High School in 1972. He, his wife Julie, and children, Mimi and Andrew, live in Fort Worth. He is associated with Ashworth Golf Apparel.

Stephen was born January 18, 1954, in Memphis, and graduated from Richland High in 1972. He lives in

Back, L/R-Philip, Paul Jr., Kristi, Paul, Adeline, Herb, Stephen Jr., Stephen, Shaun, David; Middle, L/R-Andrew, Julie, Cathy, Brenda, Amanda, Judy holding Kailee, Colten; Floor, L/R-Mimi, Meredith

Southlake with his wife, Brenda, and children, Shaun, Amanda, and Stephen Jr. He operates the Shoe Box stores in several Texas cities.

David was born in Fort Worth May 13, 1958, and graduated from Richland High in 1976. David, his wife, Judy, and children, Colten and Kailee, live in Dallas where he has business interests in shoe design companies, and other business ventures.

The family joined NRH Baptist Church in 1959 and quickly became integrated in all the programs provided while enjoying the spiritual leadership of Pastor Hal Brooks. Hal and Paula became very close friends, as did Dr. David and Annabel Pillow. Their lives became centered in their church, community, doctors, friends, and neighbors.

Four sons created a monumental scheduling task for Adeline, as she had to coordinate church and school activities while still making time to run "taxi service" for Boy Scout activities and all sports from Peewee Leagues through high-school teams.

From the Vance Road home, the Slaughters moved into a new home on Deville Drive in 1959 where they lived for 19 years. It was here that the family suffered through a house fire in 1963. The fire started in the kitchen vent, which ignited from an accumulation of grease in the attic. The builder had failed to install a vent through the attic and roof. The kitchen and den were completely burned, and heat and smoke damaged everything in the rest of the house. Adeline's sewing machine was in the far part of the house, and it was completely destroyed. She spent weeks making trips into Fort Worth to price every item in the house for insurance claims, everything from a potato peeler and paring knife to bath and bed linens, small and large appliances, furniture, and clothing.

The Slaughters were charter members of Diamond Oaks Country Club. Herb took up the game of golf, and he still enjoys it very much. They bought a house in Diamond Loch addition in 1978, and it backs up to the golf course.

Herb retired in 1991 after 45 years in the shoe business. The couple agrees that NRH has been a wonderful place to raise a family, and the two of them are still enjoying their lives here.

Story submitted by Evalyn Lochridge from interview with Adeline Slaughter

DAVID AND VIRGINIA SMITH

The Smith family moved from Monna Street in Haltom City to Tourist Drive in the North Hills subdivision of North Richland Hills in September 1961. The entourage making the trip across the Denton Highway included father David Earnest Smith; mother Helen Virginia Smith; two sons, Brian Randal and David Ryan; a daughter, Janet Lynn Smith Gallman; and two dogs, Sandy and Koko (now deceased).

Our first born, Brian, made his appearance on June 7, 1950 in Denton followed by David on April 23, 1952 in Haltom City, then Janet on August 17, 1954 in Fort

Worth. Janet shares her August birthday with her mother and a daughter, Cari, born in 1987. Helen Virginia Smith was born in Cape Girardeau, Missouri and father Smith was born in Sadler, Texas, on September 30, 1926.

After graduating from Haltom High, all the Smith children received their bachelor of arts degrees summa cum laude from Harding University at Searcy, Arkansas. Janet was valedictorian of her graduating classes from both Haltom High and Harding. Brian was salutatorian at Haltom, and David Ryan was very close to the top of his graduating class. All received various honors and scholarships for college.

Following graduation from Gainesville High School, David joined the Navy in November 1944, serving almost two years. He received a bachelor's degree from North Texas University in 1949, and a master's degree in 1952. In September 1949, David joined the faculty at Keller School District where he spent three years teaching eighth-grade subjects, and coaching junior high sports. The Birdville School District called him in the fall of 1952, and 36 years later David retired from the teaching profession, having concluded 34 years as principal of Browning Heights Elementary School. This school was renamed David E. Smith Elementary in March 1988. He has also served as an elder in the Birdville Church of Christ for 30 years.

Helen Virginia finished high school at Cape Girardeau, Missouri and received a bachelor of arts degree from what was then Texas State College for Women (now Texas Woman's University) in 1949.

LUCIAN AND JOSEPHINE SMITH

Lucian Smith was born in Hill County on October 3, 1911, and moved to Fort Worth at the age of 12. Josie was born in Cooke County on September 29, 1912, and moved to Fort Worth at the age of 15. They met as teenagers and played baseball together as students at Diamond Hill High School. They were married April 23, 1934, in Tarrant County.

Josie and Lucian Smith, 1972

The Smiths spent some time in South Texas working for M. W. Kellogg Co., Humble Oil and Refining Co. in Baytown, and Magnolia Refinery.

The births of two sons completed this family. Sammie was born in Harris County on December 5, 1939 and Marvin was born in Tarrant County on April 7, 1947.

In 1941 Clarence Jones drove the Smiths to see a farm he had traded for (this would later be where North Richland Hills first began). Some time later they drove by and he was on a dozer cutting streets, which was the beginning of the new development. Josie called him the "father of

Marvin Smith

the city." At that same time he was building a home for the Smiths in Haltom City, which Josie designed. They later sold this home and bought a 160-acre farm on the north side of North Richland Hills. This area was taken into NRH about 1958. "There were hectic times until Rodger Line came to be the city manager, and the city became a nice place to be," Josie said.

The Smiths built a home in 1950 on Douglas Lane and did most of the work themselves. Josie has sold off most of the land, but still lives in their home on eight acres.

Lucian and Josie ran a dairy for 18 years. Boswell Dairy trucks picked up their milk every day. In 1973 they sold 69 Jersey cows and 34 more acres later and retired from dairying. They had 20 wonderful years together, fishing, traveling, enjoying friends and family. Josie still does most of her yard work, enjoys oil painting and baking cakes and cookies for people. She tries to do something for someone every day. She enjoys fishing on their 500-acre ranch in Wise County.

Josie is extremely proud of her two sons. Marvin is a successful builder of beautiful homes in NRH. He and his wife, Jill, have two children, Shane and Stacie, both in college. Sammie is a professor of accounting at Stephen F. Austin University in Nacogdoches, Texas, where he and his wife, Lynda, and their two children make their home.

Josie and Lucian were always active in the community. She continues to be a member of Smithfield Baptist Church, and Lucian served on the Smithfield School Board. The

Sammie Smith

community formerly gathered at the school to take up money to pay teachers' salaries. They prompted the School Board to get into the Birdville School District. As a result, the area began to get some nice schools.

Josie watched the building boom of the 1980s and remembers the rural atmosphere diminishing. She misses the combines and the golden grain fields she used to see from her kitchen window. She is quite sure, however, the children would not miss Sammie's chores at school when he brought in coal and helped the teacher start a fire.

Story by Josie Smith from an interview by Evalyn Lochridge

MICHAEL AND MARTHA SMITH

Michael and Martha Smith married in January 1974. Martha worked for three years, while Michael attended pharmacy school at the University of Texas at Austin. After graduation, we lived in Terrell for a year and a half before moving to Arlington. We were there less than a

Lucas, Martha, Michael, and Whitney; Front-Ashley

year before we bought our first home in North Richland Hills in February 1979. We moved to a new subdivision on Chapman Road. We had to go north of Loop 820 on Rufe Snow Drive, which was a two-lane road. There was a big hill where the railroad crossed.

Michael was a pharmacist at the time for Town & Country Drug. He worked at several locations in the area over a span of 14 years. The local chain drugstore, which originated in NRH on Grapevine Highway (first known as North Richland Drug) thrived for many years and reached a total of 14 stores before selling out to Eckerd in 1992. Mike is currently working as a compounding pharmacist at Medicine Shoppe in Arlington.

Because of a growing family, we moved to another home inside the Loop in 1987. We have three children. Ashley, born November 7, 1978, was home schooled until she graduated in 1997. Whitney, born July 1981 and home schooled until her sophomore year. Currently, she is a senior at Grace Preparatory Academy in Arlington. Lucas was born in June 1986. This is his first year at Grace, where he is in the seventh grade.

In August 1979, we joined North Richland Hills Baptist Church. Christmas pageants, Bible studies, mission programs, choirs, ballet, basketball, YMCA soccer, baseball, and Northeast Area Youth Association baseball are a few of the activities that have enriched our lives for almost two decades in our community of NRH.

Submitted by Martha Smith

RUFE SNOW FAMILY
BY PAT NIMMO RIDDLE

In interviews with the two surviving grandchildren of North Richland Hills pioneers Rufe Snow and his wife, Jessie Melbourne Snow, I talked with my two first cousins, Dorothy Snow Clopton, 82, who lives in Tucson, Arizona, and Lonnie Snow, 72, a resident of Springfield, Ore. My aunt, Vera Nimmo Snow, was married to Will Snow, Rufe's oldest son.

An 1895 map of what later became North Richland Hills shows the Rufe Snow farm, which then was beside a winding, narrow country road. The home place was located at what is now the southeast corner of Rufe Snow and Shauna

Drives (across from North Richland Middle School).

Rufe Snow (1867–1957) and Jessie Melbourne Snow (1870–1942) had the following children: Will Snow, Ruby Snow Reynolds, Mary Ellen Snow Greenfield, Claude Snow, and Katherine Snow Harrell. They also had a set of twins who died when 21 days old. Besides two grandchildren, Rufe Snow, who lived to age 90, and Jessie Snow, who died at 72, are survived by several great-grandchildren, great-greats and third greats.

Rufe Snow's eldest son, Will Snow (1890–1961), and his wife, Vera Nimmo Snow (1894–1964), built a home on the Grapevine Highway about 1919. Many years later it was moved to another location in the city, and the Will Snow home place land is now the location of a Diamond Shamrock Service Station.

In order of birth, Will and Vera Snow's children were: Louis Snow, Dorothy Snow Clopton, Nimmo Snow, Weldon Snow, and Lonnie Snow.

Rufus Snow

Dorothy Snow said Rufe Snow was the first Snow to live in the North Richland Hills area, but her great-grandfather Snow "left Grandpa Snow some land in downtown Fort Worth from Weatherford Street even past the courthouse," she said. She didn't know his first name or when he came to Tarrant County.

"Rufe Snow was a county commissioner of Precinct 3," Lonnie Snow said. "His name is on the cornerstone of the Criminal Courts Building in Fort Worth. My sister said his name was on there because he was a commissioner, but I told her it was because he was the first prisoner," he said with a chuckle. "That really got her going. Bill Melbourne was the jailer and used to run the jail down there. There was a hanging gallows in the old jail." He said his Grandma Snow ran a small dairy.

In memories of going to her grandparents' home, Dorothy Clopton said: "It was just a little road Grandma Snow would come down in her buggy, but people would also drive on it in their cars. Grandpa Snow, Grandma said, had one of the most important cars of that day with lights on the side. I don't remember ever seeing it, but I do know Grandma Snow would never ride in it. She rode in her buggy. She loved her buggy, and I would ride with her."

Near the Rufe Snow farm lived two teachers, Nell and Katie Gray, who taught at Birdville. On Broadway coming east down what was known as "Birdville Hill" that led to the old Grapevine Highway, you also could go on to Texas 183 (now Texas 10) "a little road that went to Hurst," Clopton said, to reach the farm of C. G. "Uncle Bum" and Aunt Mary Melbourne and their children Fay Bell and

Dick. They lived on a farm in what is now Richland Hills. "Fay Bell and her husband Elmer James, built a house there next to Aunt Mary," Clopton said. "Jessie Melbourne Snow was the sister of Uncle Bum Melbourne and Kate Calloway."

Previous to 1917, Harvey and Lucy Brookshire Nimmo (Pat Riddle's grandparents) had a farm at the southwest corner of Rufe Snow Drive and the Grapevine Highway. Even though the farmhouse was in what is now Richland Hills, some of their land could have extended into North Richland Hills. They moved to Godley in 1917.

Will and Vera Snow built their home on the Grapevine Highway about 1919. Besides running a dairy, Will Snow did highway work for Precinct 3. One commissioner he worked for was Frank Estill. The Snows lived there until Will Snow's death in 1961. Because they were so involved in the community, a friend of Will Snow's said his epitaph should read as a poet said, "He lived in a house by the side of the road and was a friend to man." Vera Snow died in 1964 at her daughter's home in Tucson, Ariz.

"Great sadness was caused in the family when my brother, Nimmo Snow, was killed on a motorcycle with another young man, Gene Hensen, when Nimmo was 17. He was killed at the corner of the Denton Highway and what is now Broadway Street on July 28, 1935.

"There wasn't a bit of crime. You could leave your house door open all the time. Mother never shut her door."

Lonnie Snow agreed about safety at the Will Snow home where he was born in 1925: "I never saw a key to the front door," he said.

"My mom named me after him," he said. "Uncle Bill Melbourne had a restaurant down there. That's where I got the nickname 'Chawge It.' When they asked 'Who to?' I said, 'To my daddy, and if not my daddy, then dammit, chawge it to myself.' I never lived that down."

A family named Andrews had two houses on that road, then Jim Cavender had a house. "He was the guy that got murdered at his place in 1930 when I was 5. They put him in a barn in a granary full of oats, and they covered him up. They estimated he had been dead three or four days when they found him. They never did find out who did it, but it made an impression on me, you better believe it."

He recalled a car owned by Rufe Snow's daughter, Ruby, who married Lee Reynolds. "Aunt Ruby had an old Dodge coupe—a great big thing as long as a hay wagon, but it was still a coupe," he said. "Out on the radiator, the ornament had a thermometer-type thing for a radiator cap. As the water got hot, it would come up in the glass tube. It was in the 1920s. If they still had that radiator cap, it would sure be a collector's item today."

GENE AND LAMOYNE SNYDER

Clinton Eugene Snyder was born September 14, 1930, in Bomarton, Baylor County, Texas. The third child of Charlie Daniel and Ocie Vera Snyder, he chose to enter the world in the middle of a typical West Texas sandstorm. His father was postmaster of the small, rural burg and also manager of the community co-op grain elevator. He and his wife also operated a small grocery store for several years.

After graduating with the last class of Bomarton Rural High School, a class of eight, Gene set out to make his fame and fortune. He found little fame and even less fortune. He first tried his hand at railroading with Fort Worth & Denver Railway and later as a farmhand driving a tractor and killing mesquite trees. In February 1950, he came to Fort Worth and was hired by Convair (later named General Dynamics) where he worked his way up through the ranks to become a tooling inspector. Ten years later he left General Dynamics to join Bell Helicopter.

Terry, Lamoyne, Karen, Todd, seated-Gene Snyder

I, Lamoyne Thomas Snyder, was born September 19, 1931, in Big Lake, Reagan County, Texas, to Alfred Hensler and Ruby Altus Thomas. The first of three daughters, I was christened Gwendolyn Lamoyne Thomas. It should be a sin to pin such a name on an infant, but evidently Mother liked it. And seeing the names both she and Dad had been stuck with, perhaps it was a family tradition.

At the time of my birth, Dad was working for Humble Oil Company. But farming was in his blood, and he soon moved his wife and baby daughter to a farm in Comanche County. Ten years and two daughters later, he moved the family to a farm in Baylor County.

Education for me took a new twist in 1948 when Bomarton High School consolidated with Seymour High School. A little fish in a much bigger pond, I still managed to graduate second highest in a class of 96. After two semesters of college at North Texas State University in Denton, I came to Fort Worth in May 1950 to work as a secretary at Hobbs Trailers on North Main Street.

Gene and I were married July 2, 1950. This was the Korean war era, and housing in Fort Worth was as scarce as hen's teeth. The first year of our marriage was spent in the home of an elderly lady on Bluebonnet Drive in the Riverside area of Fort Worth. Here we rented a bedroom and shared kitchen privileges with the landlady. After a year on the waiting list, we were able to rent a duplex apartment on N.E. 30th Street in north Fort Worth.

In March 1955, we purchased a small house on Charles Street in what then was known as West Richland Hills. As the family grew, more space was needed. So in 1961 we bought our present home on Shauna Drive, one block east of Snow Heights Elementary School in North Richland Hills. The three Snyder children were born in Fort Worth: Lynn Karen in 1952, Terry Eugene in 1956, and Stephen Todd in 1971. All three graduated from Richland High School, and at this writing still live in the Fort Worth area.

In 1993, Gene was diagnosed as having Alzheimer's. He continued to work at Bell as a product assurance representative, earned his 35-year pin, and was given a two-year disability leave until his full retirement in January 1997.

During the 40-plus years we have lived in North Richland Hills, we have observed many changes and major expansion in the area—all listed in the city's history section of this book.

Through the years, we have been privileged to participate in some significant community projects and activities. Both Gene and I were instrumental in the organization and charter of Birdville Association for Retarded Children (now The Arc of Northeast Tarrant County), and have served in various capacities in the organization since its inception in 1971. I served for a time on the Advisory Council for Tarrant County Mental Health/Mental Retardation Services. I also served on United Way's Northeast Human Services Committee and its After School Task Force. I am a lifetime member of Texas PTA.

As members of North Richland Hills Baptist Church since 1956, we have been active in all phases of the church's growth. Gene served as deacon chairman, building committee chairman, Sunday school director for 12 years, Sunday school teacher, church clerk, and served twice on the committees to select new staff personnel. I served as Woman's Missionary Union president, taught Sunday school classes, and was a member of the church's 40th Anniversary Committee. I also was on the first board of directors for Cornerstone Assistance Network, an organization meeting the needs of the homeless and the needy.

The family has also experienced a number of traumatic occurrences. While cycling along Fossil Creek, Todd discovered the body of a dead man in the creek. A young boy was killed by a car at the intersection by our home. Two teenagers almost lost their lives when they lost control of their motorcycle and crashed into one of our trees. Another boy broke his leg on our curb. A young man crashed his automobile into a car parked in front of our house, ramming it up into our yard. Gene's unmanned Chevy slipped out of park, rolled down the driveway and across the street, running over a neighbor's tree and narrowly missing the neighbor working under his car.

Life in North Richland Hills has been anything but dull. And the years ahead offer promise of more pleasure and probably more trauma. Even so, North Richland Hills is a great place to live and raise a family.

Submitted by Lamoyne Thomas Snyder

LEWIS H. AND BILLIE J. SOMMERMEYER

The Sommermeyer family moved to North Richland Hills in 1965. Lewis was an associate minister with St. Luke Methodist Church for four years prior to that date and was being appointed to the Arlington Heights Methodist Church. Billie was employed as a teacher in the Birdville School District's Vocational Home Economics Program.

Lewis and Billie liked the growing and progressive area of Northeast Tarrant county and especially North Richland Hills. After deciding to remain in the Birdville School District, a search for a home in the area began in earnest. We examined 133 houses before settling on the Green Meadow Drive property. Johnny Nobles, Billie's principal, helped them find the right house, one he had built.

Pam transferred to Snow Heights Elementary, located east of North Richland Junior High where Billie taught. In 1966, she became a part of the first group of students to open Holiday Heights Elementary School. Billie remembers helping with a Little Rebs Cookbook to raise funds for the fledgling PTA. Bill and Sue, when they became school age, also attended Holiday Heights.

When Holiday Heights Elementary opened, there was no bridge over Walker Branch on Lola Drive to connect the west side of the Holiday Heights subdivision. Richland High School was still new and the roads near it were not yet completed. Also, Loop 820 was under construction. Traffic to and from the schools was a mess. And to compound the issue, all the children west of Walker Branch had to use Maplewood (near all the construction and with no traffic lights), to get to and from school. On dry days, they would walk through the "low water" dirt crossing (that was not a street), for a shortcut.

Lewis decided to collect signatures on a petition from residents on both sides of the branch to ask the city, county, and builders to construct a bridge on Lola so that children could walk over safely, and cars could drive over. This

Back, L/R-Pam, Sue, Bill, Front-Lewis, Sherry holding Brittany and Billie Sommermeyer- Not pictured: Brandon Zachariah, born April 29, 1998

took a lot of organizing neighbors, getting petitions signed, and researching engineering and safety needs that would be in line with city and county specifications. Lewis went before the City Council at the old complex on Glenview Drive with statistical materials, maps, and petitions. He also had assurance from county and from of the builders in the area that they would consider the three-way payment of the cost of the bridge.

The council, delighted to see something organized and well presented, took the recommendation under study, and one month later approved building the bridge with the help of the county and the builders. In 1997, Lola, because of the bridge, (a new and wider one now), is a major east-west artery between Davis Boulevard and Holiday Lane and the two schools.

For a while there was a divided household. Pam went to Haltom High School and Bill and Sue went to Richland High School. One bedroom was "Buffalo Land" and another "Rebel Land." Lewis and Billie even had to swap school sides at halftime to be fair. There was no "loser" talk afterward at home. The peace was kept.

When Billie was hired in 1961 to teach in BISD, she had a conference with the secondary coordinator in charge of vocational homemaking. In this conference, she was told that he expected the homemaking teachers to set the standard for proper attire for the other teachers. That included wearing the "proper foundation garments."

Billie taught at Haltom High School, North Richland Junior High, North Oaks Junior High, and in the summer, she taught summer vocational homemaking every other year at Richland High School. She retired in 1988.

Lewis served at Arlington Heights Methodist Church for five years and then was assigned to First Methodist Church in Fort Worth in 1970. He retired from there in 1989. Since retirement, both have been active in the community of North Richland Hills, serving in various civic and environmental groups. They also continue to work in the church.

Pam graduated from Haltom High School in 1974, Bill from Richland in 1978 and Sue from Richland in 1984. All went to college. Bill married Sherry Kay Rodgers in 1992. They live in Plano and are the parents of Brittany, born in 1994 and Brandon, born in 1998. Pam now lives in Dallas and Sue in Atlanta, Georgia.

WILL AND HELEN SPRADLING

Will and Helen Spradling were married July 8, 1955, in Fort Worth at the home of a family friend.

Will was born on October 1, 1935, in the Indian Hospital in Lawton, Oklahoma, to Dorothy and C. W. "Bill" Spradling. His maternal grandmother was Mattie Pewenofkit, a Comanche Indian, who married Raymond Hunnington Hyde, who was Scottish, Irish, English, and Welsh. Will is very proud of his Indian heritage.

Will lived in Waurika, Oklahoma, with his parents and siblings, Leilani and Buzzy. His father worked for the Rock Island Railroad and was spending more time in Fort

Worth than in Oklahoma, so the family moved to Fort Worth in 1942. Will attended Fort Worth schools including Technical High School, where he graduated in 1953. He received a basketball scholarship from Texas Christian University and attended there for a year and a half. In March 1955, he went to work for Texas Electric Service Company.

Will, Cindy, Helen, and Steve Spradling

Helen is the only child of DeLois and Marvin Berry. She was born in Seymour, Texas. Her family moved to Fort Worth in 1942 when her dad was offered a job at Convair (later known as General Dynamics and now Lockheed). She attended Fort Worth schools including Technical High School, where she graduated in 1955. Ironically, Will and Helen attended Charles E. Nash at the same time. Although they did not know each other, Buzzy, Will's brother, was in her first-grade class. Helen lived on East Belknap Street, and Will lived on Weatherford Street, only a block apart. Little did they know that they would meet in 1952 and marry in 1955.

Will and Helen have two children, Steve and Cindy. Steve was born in June 1956, and Cindy was born in March 1960. Will and Helen moved from Fort Worth to Hurst in 1958. Helen went to work for Bell Helicopter in 1962. They moved to North Richland Hills in 1963. When they first moved to their home on Vance Road, there were no houses on either side of them. Loop 820 was under construction, and there were no businesses north of the existing Loop on the now "very busy" Rufe Snow Drive.

One of the things that attracted Will and Helen to their new home was the location of the schools. Steve and Cindy attended Snow Heights Elementary School, North Richland Junior High, and Richland High School. Steve graduated from Richland in 1974, and Cindy followed in 1978.

Steve married Jerri Lynn Evans in 1978. Jerri is also a graduate of Richland High School. They live in North Richland Hills with their two children, Stephanie Lynn and Jeremy Evan. Stephanie is a student at Richland High School. Jeremy attends Snow Heights Elementary School.

Cindy was a member of the Texas Girls Choir from 1970–1976. During this time, she toured the Orient and Great Britain with the choir. Upon graduating from high school, she received an athletic scholarship to the University of Texas at Arlington. After graduating in 1983, she went to work for American Airlines. She shares a home in Bedford with her friend, Sherryl Wanager.

After 37 years of service, Will retired from TU Electric in October 1992. He enjoys golfing with some of his retiree buddies.

Helen retired from Bell Helicopter Textron in October 1995 after 33 years of service. During 24 of those 33 years, she worked for Webb Joiner, who is presently chairman and chief executive officer. Before her retirement, she was staff assistant to the president. Will and Helen are members of Richland Hills Church of Christ.

Submitted by Helen Spradling

STARNES FAMILY

We moved to our 40 acre farm on Douglas Lane in Smithfield on Thanksgiving Day, 1949. Magnolia Petroleum Company, where my father, Bertram Starnes, worked, shut down in Fort Worth and transferred operations to Beaumont. Everyone was offered a job there, but with no seniority, so my parents decided not to move. Lucian Smith, who lived right across the street, also worked for Magnolia, and he was already living out here. That is how my parents found out about this place. After our move to the farm, my father operated a service station, feed store, and tractor rental business at Four Points where Davis Boulevard, Bedford-Euless Road, and Grapevine Highway intersected.

We didn't really farm our 40 acres. It was more of a stock farm. My father had an orchard, but mainly he raised quarter horses and Appaloosas. We also raised Angus cattle. Once upon a time, we had about 10,000 turkeys up on the hill near where the water tower on Starnes Road is today. When it rained, their droppings ran into the stock tank and killed the fish. Environmentalists would string us up today.

Bertram Lamar Starnes was born in 1908 and died in 1965. He was married in 1937 to Ita Clara Counts, who was born in 1918. She died in 1963. They had four children. Their second child, Gary, is the author of this family history.

My father was killed in a fire at the Norris place. A man who was living there was working long hours, and he would leave early in the morning and come home late at night. My father got worried because he never saw a light, so he went up to check on him. The guy evidently didn't turn the butane stove off completely, and the house was filled with gas. Nobody knows what happened, but there was an explosion and my father was burned. He died later from his injuries. Starnes Road was named in his honor after his death.

My mother was a traditional housewife when we were small. But after we were in school, she got her degree from Texas Wesleyan College. She later taught at North Richland Elementary (now Mullendore) while she worked on her master's degree in education. She later died of cancer.

The oldest of the Starnes' children was Sharon Starnes Word. She was born in 1939. She had twins from a first marriage, and two more children from her marriage to Cliff Word. She died in 1987 of complications following an auto accident.

James Milus Starnes was born in 1946 and graduated from UTA in 1968. He is presently a customs import specialist with the U.S. Customs Service. He is married to

Catherine Mina Smith of Roanoke. Cathy is a medical staff assistant at Harris Methodist H.E.B. hospital in Bedford.

Kenneth Oren Starnes was born in 1948. He was killed in a construction accident at John Peter Smith Hospital. He was in an elevator and the brakes gave way and he fell several stories.

I (Gary) was born in 1943. I married Sonja Iris Elam in 1967. We were introduced by relatives and are fourth cousins. Sonja has a master's degree in art education and has taught art in the Hurst-Euless-Bedford school district since 1966. We lived in Fort Worth for a few months after we were married, but after my father died, we moved into the old home place on Douglas Lane where we still live. We have one daughter, Emily Susan Starnes Kinsky, who teaches in Lubbock. Emily was Phi Beta Kappa at Baylor in 1993, and earned a master's degree in mass communication from Texas Tech in 1996. She was married to Edward D. Kinsky in 1993. I am a professor of history at Dallas Baptist University. Since 1991, I have been director of the master of liberal arts program. I was chosen Most Outstanding Professor by the DBU faculty in 1989 and Most Outstanding Professor by the student body in 1990. I have published several books on the early history of Texas under the rule of Mexico and Spain. Sonja was elected Teacher of the Year at Bedford Heights Elementary in 1990. She was also president of the Mid-Cities Art Education Association. Sonja and I are active at Broadway Baptist Church.

When I was young, there was a lot of hard work to do around our place and very few opportunities for fun. We would get up before the roosters, and slop the hogs and milk the cows. I would change clothes and catch the school bus and ride all over the county on the way to school. In the afternoon, I would go straight to the service station to work until it closed. When I got home from the station, there was work to do with the farm animals. I would dig post holes and string wire, etc. After I could drive, I would deliver feed. And we would mow pastures for people. My father leased us out—"slave labor"—to mow lots. If I had a dollar for every acre I've ever mowed, I would retire this minute. I remember standing up on this Ford tractor with a five-foot brush hog behind it, mowing. When the tractor would hit the weeds and grass, the pollen would just fly all over me. After all that, there wasn't much time left for fun things. We used to go to the Dairy Queen. There was a skating rink in Haltom City behind Guynn's store. And there was a swimming pool down the hill from Guynn's called Barrbrook. I went to school with Judy and Iris Guynn.

Douglas Lane is named for Marvin Douglas Smith, son of Lucian Smith who lived across the street from us. The Hightowers lived way down on Douglas, on the left. They had pigs. When the wind was right, we knew that for sure North Richland Hills has grown a lot in the last few years. Lots of Yankees are coming down. Their eyes have been opened, and they are coming to God's country. Land is cheaper. Businesses have moved here to take advantage of our friendly business climate—lower wages and fewer labor unions. Companies like American Airlines and Bell Helicopter provided jobs. After World War II, there was also a political climate conducive to growth.

The early influential leaders in the area were the pastors like Floyd Amos. He built First Baptist, Smithfield. He was a part-time carpenter, and he built the building, at least partially. Charles Brinkley, Dr. Charles Rush, J. Fred Davis were also influential, and my father, possibly, early on. In the last few years, I think one of the characteristics of North Richland Hills is the way they have tried to do top-drawer stuff. I think you can see that in the parks, in their approach to development, in better planning for roads, and transportation. Sonja went to the Police Academy and she was impressed by it. She really did appreciate the attitude and the ideas of the police chief and officers who spoke and the ideas they were putting forth for our city.

Submitted by Gary Starnes

DON STEGALL

INTERVIEW WITH DON STEGALL,
MEMBER OF A PIONEER SMITHFIELD FAMILY

Our family moved to the farm on Smithfield Road, now known as Davis Boulevard, and Grapevine Highway, on the west side of Smithfield Road. Our farm contained 150 acres of land, and it was one of three farms of that size. Our farm and the property adjoining on the north and south was originally owned by the Booth family, Ray Booth, Lloyd Booth, and another whose name I cannot recall. Their father owned the land. I was told that Mr. Booth divided the farms up into three equal parts. J. Fred Davis Sr. owned the farm on the north. My father, J. M. Stegall and wife Lila Stegall owned our farm.

There was a service station on the corner of Grapevine Highway and Smithfield Road. I remember one of the fellows who operated it was Ralph Wade. They sold gas, some small amount of groceries, and things of that sort. We bought a lot of gas from Mr. Wade.

We moved to the farm in October 1943. At that time we were living in the TCU area. My father was a practicing attorney in Fort Worth. He was too old to be drafted to go into service, but he felt he could do something to contribute to the war effort, so he said, "We are going to move to the farm and raise foodstuff and feedstuff for the war effort."

My first experience with farming that fall of 1943 was a hegari crop, planted in rows. My dad bought a row binder, and I would get up early, in the wee hours of the morning and run that row binder. I operated the binder, and sometimes the tractor, and sometimes my dad did. We cut about 25 to 30 acres and then had the joy of shocking the crop after we had it cut.

My dad planted a garden soon after we moved to the area. He doubled or tripled the recommended seed amounts in several cases and the ensuing crop was beyond everyone's imagination. We gave away vegetables, begged people to take them, filled up the deep freeze with vegeta-

bles, and Dad seemed to think it was just an ordinary crop. After that we planted oats, wheat, and hegari. Our farm had 150 acres; 100 in cultivation and 50 in pasture. Some days I plowed all day long on a tractor. We had a three-disk plow on that tractor. You would start out on the outside of the field, and it seemed to take forever to go completely around the field.

I used to fish and hunt all that entire country out there. Fishing was good on the creek and the water hole. There was a hole down there on Guy Reeves' pasture where there was a big bluff. It was pretty deep when it was full of water. I would go there, catch a grasshopper, put him on the line, and flip it into the water. You could see the bass come up under the other fish and grab it. I caught a lot of fish out there.

I used to hunt ducks over there. I killed ducks, rabbits, quail, and doves. There wasn't anything between the Cunninghams and Bedford.

We stayed on the farm until about 1954. I left to go to the University of Texas in 1950 so I was pretty much away during that time. I married the first year after college. Our first residence was that garage apartment at the farm. We went to Mineral Wells on our honeymoon. Then I got my undergraduate degree and went to law school. Mother and Father continued to live on the farm and raise cattle.

Davis Memorial United Methodist Church was built probably not more than 150 yards north of our home. The church was not built when we were out there, however. The area was pretty rural then and is now covered up in traffic and congestion. Hudiburg Chevrolet was built on the Reeves property, and possibly North Richland Middle School was also on Reeves land.

There are many pleasant memories of our time in the NRH area, laced with funny, sad, interesting, and rewarding events in my lifetime. I consider myself fortunate to have lived in the area during such a memorable period in my life.

Interview recorded and submitted by Billie Sommermeyer.

DELBERT AND MARY STEMBRIDGE

On February 13, 1960, Delbert Ray Stembridge and Mary Frances Mathis were wed at East Mountain Baptist Church in Upshur County, Texas. Delbert was attending Lamar University at the time, and Mary had completed the associate of arts degree at Kilgore College. Delbert graduated from Lamar University in June 1962 with a bachelor of science degree in civil engineering and entered the Navy.

On January 22, 1963, a daughter, Sara Lynn, was born in Longview, Texas, and six weeks later, mother and baby joined Delbert in Pensacola, Florida. The Navy took the family from Pensacola to Norfolk, Virginia, and finally to Great Lakes, Illinois, where Delbert was discharged in 1966.

In 1966, Delbert went to work for Texaco Inc. in New Orleans, Louisiana, designing off-shore drilling platforms. On January 13, 1967, Steven Reese was born in Marrero, Louisiana. He is the only nonnative Texan in the family. In

Back-Steven; Front, L/R-Delbert, Mary, Sara

April 1967, we decided Texas was where we wanted our children raised and educated. We came home on a two-week vacation, and Delbert got a job with Rady and Associates consulting firm in downtown Fort Worth. We rented a house on Scruggs Park Drive in Richland Hills.

When we were ready to build our first home, Delbert stuck a pin with a string and pencil attached on a Fort Worth map and drew a circle around Fort Worth. That is how we decided we wanted to live in North Richland Hills. At the time, Highway 121 was under construction to downtown Fort Worth, and you could be downtown in about 15 minutes or less. North Richland Hills was about a 10,000-resident, "bedroom community" at that time with very little commercial development. We moved into our first home in Holiday Heights Addition in December 1967.

Richland Plaza Shopping Center was the neatest thing since "pockets on shirts." We lived in Holiday Heights where our children went to elementary school and later attended North Richland Junior High. In January 1984, we moved up a notch home-wise and moved to the Meadow Lakes addition on Woodcreek Court. Both Sara and Steven went to Richland High School. Sara achieved the lieutenant position in Dixie Belles, and Steven played football. Both children were involved in RYA sports programs, including softball, baseball, and football. Sara attended North Texas State University and graduated with a bachelor's degree in management. Steven went to Texas A&M University, graduating with a bachelor's degree in political science.

For a brief period from 1991 to 1993, we lived in Trophy Club, Texas, but our roots ran too deep in North Richland Hills, so we moved back here in 1993 and settled in the Smithfield section of North Richland Hills.

I can remember when Rufe Snow Drive was a two-lane road, and when Steven played baseball, the park was way out in the "boondocks" on Chapman Road. I also remember the house that was on the corner of Highway 26 and Loop 820 on the corner where Hudiburg Chevrolet now stands. In the early 1970s, Delbert served on the Planning and Zoning Commission. I worked for American Airlines for 16 years, retiring in June 1995. We have attended North Richland Hills Baptist Church and North Fort Worth Baptist Church.

Submitted by Mary Stembridge

CLIFTON AND LUCILLE STEVENS

Clifton and Lucille Stevens moved to the Smithfield area in 1962. Lucille was a homemaker and Clifton retired from Menasco in 1984. Clifton (Cliff) served on the North Richland Hills City Council in the late 1960s and also on the Industrial Development Committee for several years. He served as a deacon at Haltom Road Baptist, First Baptist Smithfield, and North Fort Worth Baptist. Clifton passed away from a heart attack on April 4, 1997.

Their children include:
- Judy, who married Wayne Simmons in 1967. They live in Ponder and have two children: Sha Rene and Shawn. Judy is a librarian at Calhoun Middle School in Denton, and Wayne works at Menasco.
- Jane, who married Gary Fox in 1977. They live in Grapevine and have one daughter, Mandi. Jane is a homemaker, and Gary owns the Fox Rental stores.
- Janice, who married Frank Ross in 1973. They live in North Richland Hills and have two children: Lori and Jeremy. Janice is a homemaker and works part-time, and Frank owns Renaissance Machines Technologies.
- Rick, who married Angela Griffith in 1979. They live in North Richland Hills and have two children: Amy and Austin. Rick works at Menasco, and Angela is a homemaker.

PRATT AND ARMINTA STEVENS

Pratt and Arminta Stevens moved to the Smithfield area in November 1944 with their three children: Clifton, who was away in the Merchant Marines, Jeanelle, and Aurelia. Pratt worked for Gulf Oil Company in Fort Worth and served on the Keller School Board.

The Stevenses were members of the First Baptist Church of Smithfield where Arminta taught a ladies' Sunday school class for 30 years. Arminta died in 1980, and Pratt died in 1981. All surviving children, grandchildren, and great-grandchildren still live in the Metroplex area.

Clifton Stevens married Lucille Hargrove in 1946, and they have four children: Judy, Jane, Janice, and Rick. Clifton died from a heart attack on April 4, 1997.

Jeanelle Stevens married Ramon Giles in 1956, and they have two children: Ken and Nena.

Aurelia Stevens married Jimmy Reynolds in 1953, and they have two children: Kim and Jim. Aurelia passed away in 1972.

FOSTER AND JUDY STEVENSON

Our family moved to North Richland Hills in December 1958 from Haltom City. Our son, William Gaines (Bill), was in fifth grade and daughter, Susan Elizabeth, was in second grade. Both children attended Snow Heights Elementary the following year. It was just completed, and the principal was Billy H. Smith.

Foster and I, Judy Stevenson, lived on Holiday Lane East, and the street ended as a dead-end street where the red light is at present, at the Loop 820 bridge. North of there

The Foster Stevenson Family

was open prairie, where the children hunted rabbits. There were no streetlights in that area, and the police protection consisted of the Tarrant County Sheriff's Office. There was some building of new homes west of us, but very few between us and Rufe Snow Drive—nothing for at least two or three blocks.

Bill attended Richland Junior High, then Richland High School, which was built during that time. When the high school was built, Holiday Lane was extended, and became quite a thoroughfare. North Richland Junior High was built, and Susan attended there the first year after it opened in 1963.

In 1958, Davis Memorial Methodist Church was begun, and due to pressure from our children, we felt compelled to leave St. Luke Methodist in Haltom City, where we had been members for some time. First services for this church were held in Mr. J. Fred Davis's barn on his farm, on whose land the church was eventually built. We joined after the building was finished in 1960. Ted Spencer was the pastor.

Subsequently, Loop 820 was built, and a stop sign was placed at the access road, and Holiday Lane became busier all the time. The area between us and Rufe Snow Drive all built up with new homes and new people.

Both our children graduated from Richland High School, and Bill attended Texas Tech. In June 1969, he married Sharon Robinson at St. Luke Methodist Church. Sharon is the daughter of Paul and Kay Robinson, who lived on Winnell Way. She had attended high school with Bill. Both attended Texas Tech, and Sharon finished Methodist Hospital School of Nursing. They came back to the area upon finishing college and a stint in the Navy. They live on Shady Lake Drive at the present time.

Their children, Amy Lynn and William Paul, were raised here and continue to live in the area after finishing college. Amy finished at Texas Tech and is an elementary school teacher. Paul finished Henderson State College, is a pilot working as a flight instructor. Amy was engaged to Stacy Whitehurst of Benbrook. They were married December 30, 1997, at St. Luke's.

In high school, Susan was an officer in the Dixie Belles, and was very interested in basketball, so we attended most all of the basketball games, no matter where they played.

It was a busy time for all. She attended Tarrant County Junior College one year and later worked at Union Bank and moved to Conroe in 1976, where she was employed at First National Bank, which is now Nations Bank.

She is married to Larry Roberts, formerly of Texas City. They live in Willis near Lake Conroe. He is employed by Louisiana Pacific, and she is secretary to the principal of a Willis Elementary School. They have two children. Bryan is 14, and in the first year of high school, and Anna Beth is 10 and in the fifth grade.

We moved to Caracas Street in 1986, and Foster passed away in 1988. In 1993, I was encouraged to give up my new home and move to Panorama Village, a suburb of Conroe, near Willis, to live near Susan and her family. Here, I have made a new life and am a member of First United Methodist Church in Conroe.

All is well that ends well, and we all have very fond memories of our time in North Richland Hills, and our family will still be represented there for some time to come.

Submitted by Judy Stevenson

DUB AND LANONA STEWART

The Dub Stewart family lived on "Teachers' Row" on Dawn Drive in North Richland Hills since the fall of 1959. Dub grew up in Birdville. He participated in sports and graduated from Birdville High School. He attended Weatherford Junior College where he met his wife, Lanona. Dub and Lanona both received bachelor's and master's degrees from North Texas State University, now University of North Texas. They have taught in Weatherford and Birdville schools most of their lives.

Dub coached at Richland High from the year the school opened, so the family feels they are some of the original Rebels. Dub and Lanona had 3-year-old twin sons when they moved from Weatherford. Stan and Steve learned to walk and climb by playing on the track and the football-field "dummies" where their dad was coaching. These twins are now teachers. Stan is golf coach at Haltom High, and Steve coached for a number of years at Bell High School. Steve is presently at the Hurst-Euless-Bedford Tech Center teaching computer education. Stan

Back, L/R-Steve, Stan, Amberly, Rachel; Middle, L/R-Cheryl, Stephanie, Dub, Debbie; Front, L/R-Blair, Lanona, Rachel

graduated from North Texas and Steve from Texas A&M. Steve's master's degree is from North Texas.

Some of this family's favorite memories are of games played in the dirt road that is now the north end of Dawn Drive. Since there were nine coaches within two blocks, there were always enough "kids" ready to play ball of some kind. Dub still plays softball with a seniors' group. They play about eight to ten tournaments each year, one even in Hawaii. They play four times a week when there are no tournaments.

Johnny Nobles had a big part in building "Teachers' Row." He was athletic director for Birdville ISD at the time and would build each new coach a house for a very reasonable price. Thus all the coaches and many other teachers lived on nearby streets. John Hugh and Ida Smith, the George Conants, the Joe Sparks, the Ed Logans, the Burt Burlesons, the J. B. Sandlins, the Bob Cashions, Bessie Penick, the Joe Angells, the Jim Armstrongs, Ronnie Pipes, and Deanie Wingo Blair were all educators who lived in the close neighborhood. Johnny Sandlin also built many houses in this area.

Dub had a tiny, tiny car in those early years of Richland High School. Each morning he would pick up at least three other coaches to ride to school. They had a "game plan" as to how to get in and out of the little car. Athletes from Richland, who lined up each morning to watch this plan, also had a plan of their own—they would pick up the car and set it on the sidewalk. Getting it back on the street was not as easy.

Stan and Debbie have three girls, Rachel and Ashley Stewart and Amberly McCallon. Steve and Cheryl have a girl, Stefanie, and a boy, Blair.

Dub and Lanona are active in St. Luke United Methodist Church, Steve and Cheryl attend Mid Cities Bible Church and Stan and Debbie attend North Richland Hills Baptist Church.

LACY AND LOIS STEWART

Nathan Lacy Stewart was born in Olney, Texas, on June 22, 1925. He went to school in Jal, New Mexico, through the third grade. After his father died, the family moved to Smithfield, Texas, where he began the fourth grade.
Lydia Lois Green Cook was born in Brownfield, Texas, on March 2, 1928. Her father worked for Gifford Hill Pipe Company, and the family moved frequently.

Both Lacy and Lois worked at Convair (now Lockheed) for two years until their marriage on March 21, 1953, in Weatherford. Lacy went into the insurance business and later worked for American Manufacturing Company. He retired in 1984.

In 1958, the Stewarts began building a house in the Smithfield area. They had been living with family members, and when the house was just a shell, they moved into it. It was raining on moving day and needless to say, the road wasn't paved. Mr. Gil Bridges used a wagon and team to haul furniture and boxes from Amundson Road to the house. Lois had saved some of her grocery money from

week to week and bought new linens for her new home. When the wagon hit a stump, the chest of drawers filled with new linens was dumped in the mud. Lois made a trip to the Laundromat that night.
Grandpa Green made an L-shaped road south off Amundson and east to the house, and it was named Stewart Drive.

Lacy and Lois, center, at Smithfield Reunion

Lois's children are Janiece Cook, Ted Cook, and Mike Cook. The next five children were all born in Fort Worth. They are Liz Stewart, Ray Stewart (deceased), Nathan Stewart, Patricia Stewart, and Becky Stewart.

There are nine grandchildren and three great-grand-children.

All of the children went to Smithfield Elementary School where Mr. W. E. Walts was their principal, and each graduated from Richland High School.

The Stewart family had an old Studebaker car they were very proud of. Once Lacy went to an auction and returned home with four goats in the car. He put them in a pen with only three strands of barbed wire around it. Two of the goats went right under the wire and were never seen again. The Stewarts also had ducks, geese, pigs, and cows.

In May 1989, Lacy Stewart realized the only time he saw many of his friends was at funerals and visiting at the hospital. He decided to invite the entire community for a Smithfield reunion to be held on the Stewarts' four acres on the firstweek end of May. That first year it was a three-

Plaque honoring Lacy and Lois Stewart

day get-together, but since has been held for two days. Lacy and many friends set up tables, and everyone brought chairs and food, which was spread for the noon meal. Children enjoy just playing and adults enjoy playing horseshoes, washers, and table games, but mostly just visiting and remembering old times. There is no music to drown out the friendly chatter. Attendance is usually around 300 both days.

In 1991, all his friends honored Lacy by planting a tree in the Stewart front yard and setting a plaque at its base. There were so many friends who helped with the reunion arrangements: G. R. Montgomery, Roy Carter, Ray McCauley, King Bell, Red Harston, J. C. Harston, L. J. Palmer, James Gaddy, Harold Autrey, Leon and Billy Wiseman, Stanley Tatarevich, James Simmons, and Lee Stewart, to name a few.

Lacy Stewart died November 1, 1995. His last wishes were for his family to carry on with the reunion. They have kept that promise. The Stewart home on Stewart Drive is still a busy place with family and friends coming and going. It's a home that is full of love and family values. This is a rare trait in this decade of the '90s.

Story told to and submitted by Evalyn Lochridge

REV. T. LYNN AND THELMA STEWART

Rev. T. Lynn and Thelma Hand Stewart moved to North Richland Hills in mid-1965. Tom Stewart had retired from the ministry at First Baptist Church in Grapevine in late 1964. Tom was born in Oklahoma Territory, in what is now Norman, on March 15, 1903. His family moved to Gordon, Texas, when he was 2 years of age. His father operated a horse-and-wagon freight line between Gordon and Mineral Wells. Tom's father died when he was a boy, and the family moved to Mineral Wells. Tom played basketball for Mineral Wells High School and graduated as president of his senior class in 1921.

During this time, he had met Thelma Hand, a classmate, who was born in Mineral Wells. After the death of her mother, when Thelma was only a very young girl, she was reared by her grandmother. In August 1923 Tom and Thelma were married and had a daughter, Corrie LaVerne, on July 31, 1924. On March 10, 1926, they had a son, Thomas Willard Stewart. Shortly thereafter, they moved to Fort Worth where Tom worked for Railway Express Company. In about 1927, he enrolled in Southwestern Baptist Theological Seminary in Fort Worth to study for the ministry.

T. Lynn and Thelma Stewart

Tom's first church was a small one in east Dallas and then Field Street Baptist in Cleburne. Both of these were on a part-time basis while he was attending the seminary. His first full-time church was in the late 1920s or early 1930s in Roanoke, then to Rhome for a few years. In the middle or late 1930s, he became pastor of First Baptist Church in Hamilton. It was in Hamilton that both Corrie and Thomas Willard ("Buddy") graduated from high school. Shortly after this, Tom became pastor of First Baptist Church in Coleman. Tom was asked to serve on the board of directors of Howard Payne College in Brownwood during this period. Corrie was attending Howard Payne and graduated in the class of 1946. Buddy entered the Army and served in active combat duty in Germany in World War II. Upon his return from the service, Buddy attended and graduated from Baylor University in Waco.

In 1946, Tom was called as pastor of First Baptist Church in Burkburnett. He served there until 1955, when he was called by First Baptist Church Grapevine. Under his leadership, a new sanctuary was built at this location in 1958. Buddy met and married Frances Evans of Fort Worth shortly after his graduation from Baylor. Corrie started a teaching career in Coleman schools in 1946. In 1949, while teaching in Burkburnett, she met H. Oscar Lochridge of Iowa Park. In April 1952, they were married and later became residents of North Richland Hills.

During his ministry, one strong point of this family was the establishment of church libraries where they served. Thelma was very accomplished at this. Tom was elected chairman of the Church Library Committee of the Baptist General Convention of Texas and served in this capacity for many years.

Upon his retirement in 1964, and subsequent move to NRH in 1965, Tom and Thelma joined North Richland Hills Baptist Church. Shortly after, Rev. Hal Brooks, the pastor, asked Tom to accept a position as associate pastor of this church. His duties were to be involved in the visitation of prospective members in the greater Richland area, hospital visitation, and conducting of Sunday services in the pastor's absence. This arrangement worked to perfection in the growth of the church. These two men, working side by side, constituted one of the greatest teams of preaching pastors that one could imagine. During this period, Thelma was asked to be librarian of the church and commenced to build the library. Others have continued this work to make it one of the finest anywhere.

Tom retired again a few years later due to health problems and died in 1987. Earlier that year he had suffered the death of a grandson, Gary Lane Lochridge, and his good friend and colleague, Rev. W. Hal Brooks. Thelma died in 1996 at the age of almost 94. They were a wonderful and dedicated couple, who served for almost 60 years in the ministry of the Gospel.

Submitted by H. Oscar Lochridge

DAVID AND FRAN STOUT

The Stout Family moved to North Richland Hills on June 17, 1987, from Bedford. David Brian Stout (Dave) was born in Fresno, California, to Norma Owings Stout Russell and Jack C. Stout on March 26, 1959. In 1972, Dave made his home in Houston with his parents and younger brother. He attended Sharpstown High School, graduating in 1977, attended the University of Houston, completing two years of college, then served in the Army from 1980 to 1983 as a military policeman. He still serves in the Army Reserve as a criminal investigator. Dave has been with the Fort Worth Police Department since April 1985 and is a detective in the North Division.

Frances Sue Millichamp Stout (Fran) was born in Houston to Zoe Louise Wiley Millichamp and George Hillary Millichamp on December 5, 1959. She graduated from Sharpstown High School in November 1977. Dave and Fran married on April 16, 1983 in Houston. Fran is an educational assistant with Birdville ISD. She works in the Special Education Eepartment at Carrie F. Thomas Elementary. Fran likes to spend her time on genealogy, crafts, and watching old movies.

Their first child, Melissa Lynne Stout was born on March 5, 1984, in Houston. Melissa attends Smithfield Middle School. She is a pianist, plays bells in our church bell choir, and is a member of the youth group at Richland Hills United Methodist Church.

Their second child, David Brian Stout II (Davy) was born on January 13, 1986, in Fort Worth. He is in his last year at Carrie F. Thomas Elementary. He will attend Smithfield Middle School next year. His favorite pastime is sports. He plays basketball and baseball. In school, he is on the Students in Action Committee.

Their third child, George Robert Stout (Georgie) was born March 24, 1988, in Bedford. He attends Carrie F. Thomas Elementary. He is in the third grade and enjoys sports, playing with his cars and his action figures.

The Stout family are members of Richland Hills United Methodist Church.

GARY AND LENNIE SUGGS

Lennie Lou Cribbs and Gary James Suggs were married on July 28, 1972. Lennie is the daughter of Lewis Earl and Hattie Belle Reeves Cribbs. Gary is the son of James and Jessie Hammer Suggs.

Lennie was born in Fort Worth in 1946. She was raised in Hurst. She attended grade school at Hurst Elementary School and Richland Elementary School, Hurst Junior High School, and graduated from L. D. Bell High School in 1964. Lennie attended McMurry College in Abilene for one year and transferred to Texas Wesleyan College in Fort Worth. In 1969, Lennie completed her student teaching at North Richland Junior High. She graduated in 1970 with a bachelor's degree in physical education. After teaching one-half year at Wilshire Elementary in Euless, she taught physical education four years at Bedford Junior High School.

Today, she is a volunteer worker at Richland High School.

Gary James Suggs was born in Hobbs, New Mexico, on July 8, 1949. He lived in Eunice, New Mexico, until his parents moved to Aspermont, Texas. Gary graduated from Aspermont High School in 1967, attended Wayland Baptist College for two years, and then attended West Texas State. Soon the Army decided that they needed him to join.

After completion of his Army basic training in Ft. Leonard Wood, Missouri, he was recommended and accepted to officer candidate school in Ft. Belvior, Virginia. Upon graduation as a Second Lieutenant, he was assigned to Ft. Bliss in 1970. In 1972, he received an honorable discharge as a first lieutenant. It was that same year that he met and married Lennie Cribbs. He attended Tarrant County Junior College for one semester before transferring to North Texas State University from which he graduated in 1974 with a bachelor's degree in business education. Since 1975, Gary has been employed by NCH Corporation working with the subsidiaries, P&M Mfg. Company and Aqua Plbg. Products. He has served in various managerial positions during his 22 years with the company.

Gary and Lennie moved to North Richland Hills in 1976. They still reside in the same home in the Diamond Loch East Addition.

In 1982, the Lord blessed Gary and Lennie with a son, Jason James Suggs. He attended Mullendore Elementary and North Richland Middle School. At present, he is a sophomore at Richland High School where he is active in football and in rodeo. As a freshman, he played trumpet in the Symphonic Band. North Richland Hills is the only home that Jason has ever known.

When our family gets too much of the fast pace of the city life, we retreat west to Albany. We enjoy riding horses, tending cattle, hunting, and fishing on our small farm.

Gary, Lennie, and Jason are active members of North Richland Hills Baptist Church. As we grow older, we want to continue to give the Lord all the credit for who we are, for what He has done in our lives and for what He is going to do in our lives.

Submitted by Lennie Suggs

JAKE AND MILLIE TARWATER

The Tarwaters have been married 50-plus years. Jake is a lifelong resident of Smithfield. His parents and grandparents were early settlers of the area. He is one of six children born to Alex and Ethel Daniel Tarwater. His siblings were Alex, Jack, Nell, Dick, and Ruth. Jake describes his father as a "man of the soil" who raised cotton and corn on 160 acres of fertile black land along what is now Starnes Road. There was the usual assortment of farm animals, cows, pigs, and chickens along with the "work animals"—horses and mules used for plowing and pulling wagons. Jake's name is really John Clinton, but his father gave him the nickname, which stuck, saying that he was as deliberate as the family mule, Ol' Jake.

Jake recalls a warm, secure childhood watched over by parents who obviously loved each other and their children.

The school year was closely related to planting and harvesting. Boys would go to school the first day and stay out about six weeks or so until the crops were in. In the spring, they would attend until it was time for planting. They went to 10 grades then, and obviously the girls got to attend longer than the boys, because of the farm work. They got up at 4:00 A.M. to get all the morning chores done before setting off to walk three miles to Smithfield school. Jake's usual chore as a small lad was to keep his mother's wood box full for the cook stove. In the afternoon, he had to go to the far pasture to drive the cows up for milking. As the years passed, and the children grew up, his mother never went to bed until all of them were home safe and sound. It was not uncommon to meet his father carrying a lantern down the lane seeking a child who was a bit late getting home. He remembers the comfort of seeing the pale light in the darkness and feeling secure in his parent's concern.

The Hightowers, Brownfields, and Daniels had land adjoining theirs along Starnes Road. His grandparents, John and Margaret Boone Tarwater, bought the land for 25 cents an acre. Margaret came from Boonesville and was possibly related to Daniel Boone. Her brother, John, and John Tarwater, served together in the Civil War. Through her brother, Margaret and John Tarwater met and married. They came to the Smithfield area following the war.

Jake was born on the homestead. He jumped off the house when he was 7, breaking his arm. His dad carried him inside and summoned Dr. Gilbert and neighbors to help set the arm. Jake's Aunt Allie Daniel administered the chloroform while his dad, Uncle Merrill Daniel, and Jim Hightower held him still. All injuries did not turn out so lucky. Jake's cousin stepped on a nail while playing in the corncrib. Doctor Gilbert lanced the wound, but the child died of tetanus a short time later.

Barber Cobb helped Jake out with a $30 loan just before World War II. Jake had a job promised him in the islands building military bases. The only problem was that he had to pay his own way to New York to catch the boat to the islands. Train fare to the big city was $33. During a haircut, he was relating this sad state of affairs, saying it was the chance of a lifetime, but he just didn't have the money. Barber Cobb said, "Well, I don't think you should miss this great opportunity, and I'll lend you the money."

Jake later entered the Army, serving in the European theatre. Following the war, he pursued the building trade for more than 42 years, building such structures as the TCU theatre in Fort Worth, and the Lodge in Smithfield.

Jake and Millie have two sons and four grandchildren. Both sons, Jimmy and Johnny, live in North Richland Hills

Interview with John Clinton "Jake" Tarwater, related to
Dorothy Parker

DON AND PEGGY (BURKHART) TAYLOR

We came to North Richland Hills in June 1966 from the Polytechnic area. We bought a home on Venice Street, two blocks from Richland Plaza. House payments were less than $100 per month, and the playgrounds were a vacant, undeveloped lot one block from home, Fossil Creek behind us and the street.

Kimberly and Jeffrey were in the first and second grades at Richland Elementary on Baker Boulevard (until I learned the boundaries the next year). They enrolled at North Richland (now Alliene Mullendore) Elementary. They went to North Richland Junior High and both graduated from Richland High School in 1976 and 1977, respectively. Kevin entered Little Tyke Day Care on Baker Boulevard. Upon Nanny Bradford's retirement from Little Tyke, she took Kevin and Steven Lightford home with her to keep. She and Grandy kept the boys for several years before they started school and after school hours until they reached late elementary classes. The boys loved them and they loved the boys in return.

I worked for transport trailer manufacturing firms for about 25 years. Bob was a police officer for the City of Fort Worth for 16 years. He went to work for the D/FW Department of Safety in 1972 and retired in 1998. We divorced in 1976.

Venice Street was home for my family and our many friends until 1983. Our neighbors were like family. We carpooled to the Little League games and school functions. Little Leagues were in three different parks at that time; behind Bell Helicopter off Handley-Ederville Road, Smithfield ball park, and girls softball at Fossil Creek. Early teen and high school years were filled with playdays and rodeos. Jeff was involved in the high school rodeo functions. He kept his horse at Blackie Frazier's Stables on Grapevine Highway, across from Tarrant County Junior College.

Kim went to work as a dispatcher for the City of North Richland Hills after graduation. She is married to Jerry Killion (NRH fireman). They have two boys, William Benny "Webe" and Jesse Shan. They live in Watauga, just about a mile from Grammie's.

Jeff married Pam Cabiness, an RHS graduate. They had two children, Ryan Layne and Kristan Kay. Both are students at Richland High School and will graduate in the spring of 1999. Jeff is an electrician and Pam works for Albertson's. Ryan works for Winn Dixie and Kristan works for a cosmetic dentist in Colleyville. (Parents are divorced.)

Kevin graduated from Keller High School in 1982. He went to work in the airfreight business at D/FW. He married Donna Fisher Hughes in 1991. Donna was a Haltom graduate and works as a paralegal. She had two children, Lauren, a sophomore at Haltom High and Dylan, an eighth-grade student at Haltom Middle School. Kelci Dawn was born in 1992. She begins kindergarten this year. She and Jesse are two weeks apart in age and look like twins.

Times were so simple and nice in the "good old days" when you were not constantly worried about the safety of your children. Skateboards were the "in" thing, and as small as the children were, they could ride them in the street and down the driveways. We didn't need speed bumps to slow the traffic.

The Armstrongs, Auerbachs, Bains, Blairs, Morrows, Spradlings, Waters, and Phillips were the best of friends and neighbors.

Don Taylor and I married in 1985. He is in the insurance business, and in 1990, we were transferred to Amarillo. It was nice and a lot of new friends were made, but home is where the heart is, and NRH held my family and heart! In 1994 we were transferred back. We bought a house on Oakview Avenue.

Don's family lives in NRH. His brother, Dale and Mary Lee Taylor and his mom, Nadine, live on Parkway. His sister and brother-in-law, Jeanette and Greg Daniell live on Greendale Ct., his daughter and son-in-law, Cheryl and Jeff Griffin, Amy and Jason, live on Carolyn, and his son, Chris and friend, Michelle, live in Summerfields. Chris has two children, Jimmy and Carly, by an earlier marriage. Don's daughter and son-in-law, Dana and Don Spaulding, live in Tennessee. Dana's children, Eric and Monica, are in Memphis and Louisiana, respectively.

We both work in the city. Don's office is on Rufe Snow, and I work for the City of NRH. We are enjoying our home on Oakview Avenue in the north part of the city, in the midst of our children, grandchildren, families, and friends. We enjoy playing golf at Iron Horse Golf Course and entertaining the grandkids.

Jack and Barbara Terry

The Jack D. Terry Jr. family moved to North Richland Hills in May 1963. Jack had become the minister of music and education and youth at the North Richland Hills Baptist Church. The family consisted of Jack, Barbara Jones Terry, and son, Douglas Lloyd Terry. Their first residence was a parsonage of the North Richland Hills Baptist Church next door to the church on Vance Road. Jack was pursuing a doctor of philosophy degree at Southwestern Baptist Theological Seminary and working at the church. During the three and one-half years at the church, a beautiful little girl, Patricia Lynn, was born into the Terry household. This would complete the Terry family. The Terrys presently have four grandchildren: Ryan Terry, Jenna Terry, Garrett Spriggs, and Haylee Spriggs.

Jack was born in Houma, Louisiana, Barbara was born in Quinlan, Texas, "Doug" Terry was born in Terrell, Texas, and "Tricia" was born in Terrell. Jack was educated at Port Neches High School, Port Neches, Texas. He completed his bachelor's degree at East Texas Baptist College in Marshall; completed the master of religious education and doctor of philosophy degrees at Southwestern Baptist Theological Seminary.

Barbara and Jack Terry

Barbara was educated at Terrell High School and has completed half of a registered nurse program at Baylor School of Nursing, Surgical Division in Dallas. Doug graduated from Richland High School and Texas Christian University with a bachelor of business administration, and Southern Methodist University's Southwestern School of Banking. Tricia graduated from Richland High School and Texas Christian University with a bachelor of science in elementary education.

Jack has been employed as a professor, dean, and vice president for institutional advancement at Southwestern Baptist Theological Seminary for the past 29 years. Jack was a professor at Hardin-Simmons University (1966–1969), professor in and dean of the School of Religious Education, Southwestern Baptist Theological Seminary and since 1996 has served as vice president for institutional advancement at Southwestern Seminary. Barbara has practiced her favorite profession of being a wife and mother. Doug has been in banking since graduating from college, presently the president of Overton North East Bank. Tricia married Mark Spriggs in 1991 and has been a teacher in the Keller and Birdville School Districts.

The Terry family has been members of North Richland Hills Baptist Church, North Fort Worth Baptist Church, and presently are members of First Baptist Church in Euless. Jack is a member of the Northeast Richland Lions Club and the Haltom Richland Chamber, and was president and vice president of the Richland Dixie Belles Booster Club. He is past president of the Southwestern Baptist Religious Education Association and vice president of the Southern Baptist Religious Education Association. He is presently a member of the Texas Baptist Development Officers Association. Barbara has been active in the Seminary Woman's Club, serving twice as president and many other officer positions.

In civic activities, Jack has served on many committees in the Northeast Tarrant Chamber of Commerce. He also served as a member of the Birdville Independent School District Board of Trustees for 10 years and as the vice president and president of the Board of Trustees during his tenure.

Favorite hobbies of the Terry family are: golf, gardening, cooking, traveling, and writing. The Terrys have held major offices in many organizations and received honors including:

Jack was: Outstanding Alumni, East Texas Baptist University, Outstanding Young Men in America, Outstanding Educator of America, American Legion Outstanding Student Award.

Barbara was: Miss East Texas, 1953; Miss America Pageant, Drum major, Terrell High School Marching Band, Surgical nurse in Training, Baylor School of Nursing, President 21 Club, Abilene Women's Club, Twice president of the Seminary Woman's Club.

Douglas was: vice president of the Richland High School Student Council, Texas Christian University Honor Scholar, Phi Delta Theta Fraternity, Phi Delta Theta—

Chaplin—and chapter honor scholar at Texas Christian University, Youngest Bank President in Texas in 1985. Patricia was: captain-elect of the Dixie Belles, 1983; captain of the Dixie Belles, 1984; National Honor Society at Richland High School Magna Cum Laude, TCU, Delta Gamma Sorority.

Submitted by Barbara Terry

COLLEENE THARP

Colleene Tharp was born May 24, 1936 in Cheyenne County, Oklahoma. She and her mother, Ollie Grover Burton, moved to Haltom City when she was 16. She attended Birdville High for a semester. She lived in North Richland Hills the first time on Morgan Circle. Warren Paul Caldwell was born there on December 8, 1956. The next year, the family moved to Haltom City, just off Haltom Road. Billy Don Caldwell was born Nov. 19, 1957. The family moved into their second home in NRH just before Thanksgiving in 1966. Lawrence Wayne Tharp was born Feb. 10, 1967. Wallace Bradley Tharp was born February 10, 1972. The boys attended school at Holiday Heights, Carrie Francis Thomas, Watauga Junior High, Smithfield Junior High, and graduated from Richland High. Brad graduated from Angelo State University.

Paul and Beth Caldwell live in Aurora, Texas, with son, Daniel. Bill Caldwell lives in Dallas. Lance and Dee Ann Tharp and daughter, Chelsea, live in Grapevine. Brad Tharp lives in Arlington. Granddaughters Amanda and Barbara Caldwell, live in Mexico, Missouri, and spend summers in NRH. Amanda, Barbara, and Chelsea have all attended Carrie Francis Thomas Elementary School.

Colleene works at Winn Dixie and at Garden Ridge as a cashier. She is a member of North Richland Hills Baptist Church, and is an alumna of the Citizens Police Academy of NRH. She also takes classes at Tarrant County Junior College.

Submitted by Colleene Tharp

Colleene Tharp, Billy Don Caldwell, Lance, and Brad Tharp

THROOP (NRH PIONEER FAMILY)

This history of the Throop family was written by Minnie Anderson Mason, who grew up in North Richland Hills but has lived in Richland Hills many years.

My maternal grandmother, Minnie Ragsdale Throop, was born in Nashville, Tennessee, in 1874 and was 5 years old when she came to Texas in 1879 with her mother and baby sister. It took five days on the train. She would tell about the engineer stopping to get water for the train, and she had a small bottle that her mother would let her fill for drinking water. There were ladies at each stop selling biscuits and hard-boiled eggs. The Ragsdale family settled in Bransford (now a part of Colleyville).

Minnie married William Hardy Throop in 1896. The Throop family came to Texas in 1836. Charles Throop (grandfather of W. H. Throop) helped start Lonesome Dove Baptist Church in the Grapevine-Colleyville area. Hardy Throop and his mother, Flora Throop, donated land for Pleasant Run Baptist Church in Colleyville.

Minnie and Hardy had five children, including my mother, Myrtle Throop Anderson, 93, and my aunt, Lovie Throop Emery, 83. Hardy Throop farmed and had a work crew of men, mules, and wagons. They constructed railroad trestles. The Throop family sold out and moved into Fort Worth.

Minnie Throop and daughters moved to the Harmonson Addition on West Harmonson Road in 1937. It is a part of North Richland Hills. The daughters, Myrtle and Lovie, now live on East Harmonson Road. The family worshipped at Birdville Church of Christ until Richland Hills Church of Christ was formed, and they moved their membership there.

This area was very rural until 1952 when Bell Helicopter opened. There were no telephones, no stoplights, and no bus service. Everyone went into Fort Worth on Saturdays to shop. Guynn's Store was the place to shop in this area. We saw the first taxi cab on Harmonson Road after World War II when a neighbor's son came home from the war.

I, Minnie Anderson Mason, was 3 years old when I moved to North Richland Hills. The family above includes my maternal grandmother, grandfather, my mother, and my aunt. I married Paul Mason in 1953, and we have one daughter, Pamela Mason Machun, and twin grandsons, Kevin Todd and Clinton Cole Goodpaster, who live in NRH.

DON AND DORIS TIPPS

In 1957, Doris and I, Don Tipps, lived in an apartment in Riverside that had no air-conditioning. One hot summer Friday evening, while driving around with the car windows down trying to create a cool breeze, we realized that we had never been east of the Denton Highway. We decided to explore in that direction and see what was out that way. We traveled past Harold's Log Cabin Restaurant and east on Belknap Street. As we passed Birdville High

School and started down the hill, we saw the lights of Birdville Stadium and a small crowd watching a football game. We continued east into the darkness and became aware that there was little to see in that direction.

I turned the car around headed west, and we again approached the lights of the Birdville Stadium. Not wanting to hurry back to our hot apartment, I pulled into the entrance beside the administration building and was able to drive up to the fence on the south side of the field. As we sat there alone in the car watching the game, little did we know that in the near future our son and daughter would perform on that very field; that both Doris and I would be employed by the Birdville School District; and that we would spend our lives in this area surrounded by many wonderful friends.

In 1951, after graduating from Breckenridge High School, I joined the Marine Corps and spent 1952 in Korea. When I was discharged in 1954, I was eligible for the GI Bill and enrolled in North Texas State College majoring in art education.

Although Doris grew up in Graham only 30 miles away, we never met until we attended North Texas State College. She was Doris Walker, majoring in business education. Doris and I were married in 1956 and moved to Fort Worth because of the job opportunities for Doris and so I could continue to commute to Denton.

Later we moved to the Riverside area where the first of our two children, Donie, was born July 22, 1957, in Harris Hospital. After I graduated from North Texas State College, I was hired by Birdville to teach art and shop at Richland Junior High. We moved to Caroldean Street in Haltom City, and Doris got a job at the Federal Aviation Administration in Blue Mound. Tracye was born on May 16, 1961, at what was then called Glenview Hospital. In 1964 Doris went back to college full time.

In September 1967, I was transferred to Richland High School. Doris graduated from North Texas State University and was assigned to teach business education at Richland Junior High.

After living in Haltom City from 1960 to 1968, we moved to our present home on Tabor Street in North Richland Hills. We moved our church membership from Glenview Baptist Church to North Richland Hills Baptist Church because of the strong youth program. Loop 820 had just been completed, and the land north of the loop was mostly pastures and open fields. Rufe Snow Drive was a two-lane road and hardly a road at all north of the Loop. South of the loop there were very few houses on the west side of Rufe Snow all the way to Fossil Creek. We rode our Honda 90 motorcycles all over the fields that now have expensive homes and the Iron Horse Golf Course.

During our early years as teachers, one of our monthly pleasures was to go with a group of friends to dinner. There were hardly any restaurants in the Northeast area, so we would drive to the west side of Fort Worth and eat at Jimmy Dips, Cattlemen's, Blue Star, or the Western Hills Inn. We would then go to downtown Fort Worth to see a movie. Before we had the Richland Plaza, we did most of our shopping downtown at Leonard Brother's, Everybody's, Penney's, Cox's, Monnig's, and the Golden Goose Shoe Store.

During Donie's school years, he participated in many sporting activities and became one of the first male cheerleaders that Richland High ever had. He graduated in 1976, joined the Navy and was aboard the USS Nimitz during the Persian Gulf incident and the ill-fated attempt to free the hostages in Iran. He married Christy Dollar Cater in 1987. Christian Cater was 5 years old when they married. Landry Barrett was born March 14, 1989, and Shylea Alexis was born October 16, 1993.

Tracye was a Dixie Belle and a cheerleader at Richland High School and graduated in 1979. She later graduated from Texas A&M and taught in Birdville for a few years. She is presently a flight attendant with Southwest Airlines.

Doris later taught typing and business at Haltom High, counseled at Watauga Junior High and was an assistant principal at Haltom Junior High. She became principal at Smithfield Middle School in 1989.

Standing-Donie, Christy, Christian Cater, Tracye; Seated-Doris, Landry, Don, Shylea Alexis

I was a counselor my last 23 years at Richland High School and retired in 1994. I have been a board member of the NRH Parks and Recreation Department since January 1980.

Submitted by Don Tipps

JOHN AND KAY TOWNSEND

I, John Townsend, moved into my present home on Nancy Lane, North Richland Hills, Texas on June 8, 1958. At that time there was nothing north of Maplewood Street but Johnson grass, nothing east but Smithfield Road, and Maplewood ended at Susan Lee Lane.

In July 1959 I transferred my membership from Central United Methodist Church in Fort Worth to Davis Memorial Methodist Church which was just getting started. At that time we met in Mr. J. Fred Davis' cow barn. Rev. Ted Spencer was the pastor. Through his efforts the church was built at its present location 5301 Davis Boulevard. Rev.

Grady Brittan is the present pastor.

I am a member of Smithfield Masonic Lodge #455 and past master of Richland Hills Masonic Lodge #1348. I retired from Texas State Department of Human Services August 31, 1980.

There was no access across the

John and Kay Townsend

creek to the west, and we could get into our area only from Smithfield Road. We had to drive down Smithfield Road to the Grapevine Highway to shop for groceries at Berry Brother's Market at the new North Richland shopping center. This store later became a Buddies Super Market.

When the streets were first paved, a wide space had to be left open because a Sinclair pipeline ran east and west along Maplewood Street. When a hard rain came and water filled this opening, a car was always driving into it and had to be towed out.

In the spring of 1981, I was the first school crossing guard at Rufe Snow and Hightower. The next two years I was crossing guard at Holiday Heights Elementary, corner of Susan Lee Lane and Lola Drive. Then I was moved to North Richland Middle School, 4800 Rufe Snow where I served until 1993.

I was born August 21, 1912 in a farming community known as Hog Eye, two and one-half miles east of Celeste, Hunt County, Texas. I started to school in Mineral Wells, graduated from grade school in 1927 in Wewoka, Oklahoma, and graduated from high school in Sasakwa, Oklahoma in 1931. I served in the Army in World War II, then graduated from Texas Christian University in May 1950 with a bachelor's degree in business. I married Catherine (Kay) Wilkes March 24, 1967. She was born June 25, 1924 and graduated from A.M.I. Catholic School May 28, 1940.

I support the public schools and try to visit and eat lunch at least one meal a month at Holiday Heights and North Richland Middle School.

Submitted by John Townsend

ARTHUR AND DEBORAH TRIBBLE

Deborah Helton moved to North Richland Hills in 1968 at the age of 15. As a student at Richland High School, she recalls nothing but farmland north of the school and remembers Rufe Snow Drive as a "farm road leading nowhere." She witnessed the building of Northeast Mall and had her first job there at Striplings. She met Arthur Tribble, a graduate of Carter-Riverside High School, at

Texas Wesleyan College in 1972. They married on June 1, 1973, at Riverside Baptist Church and completed college, living on campus as "dorm parents" in the athletic dorm. Debbie received a Bachelor of Arts degree in English and speech; Art received a Bachelor of Science degree in physical education and English in 1975. They moved to NorEast Drive in NRH in 1978. Debbie taught English at North Richland Junior High for nine years, and Art taught English and history at Haltom Junior High and later Haltom High School, where he coached several state-ranked, cross-country teams.

In 1978, Debbie received a master's degree in counseling and psychology at North Texas State University. In 1982, she took a leave of absence from Birdville schools at the birth of their first child, Aaron Russell, on April 27. Elisa Denise joined the family three years later on Aug. 21, 1985. Debbie returned to Birdville as a counselor at Smithfield Junior High School and Richland High School. Debbie received a Delta Kappa Gamma International Scholarship in 1996, which aided in the completion of her doctoral degree in educational administration from the University of North Texas in 1997. Art taught and coached briefly at Colleyville Junior High and later became a coach and then an administrator in Everman ISD. Both Debbie and Art attained mid-management certifications at Texas Woman's University. In 1991 the family moved its church membership from North Richland Hills Baptist Church to its mission church, Northwood, Church for the Communities.

Debbie was an assistant principal at North Oaks Middle School for two years and then in 1992 became the principal of Watauga Middle School. In 1993 she became a member of Leadership Northeast. In 1995 she received the Chamber of Commerce Chairman's Award for initiating Vital Link in Northeast Tarrant County. At this time, she is principal of the Shannon Education Center. In 1995 the family bought a home on Riviera in Meadow Lakes.

In 1997 Dr. Tribble was named as the principal of Birdville's third high school and directed efforts toward its opening in the fall of 1999. The new campus would become a 300,000-square-foot campus nestled in an oak grove at the southwest corner of Mid-Cities Blvd. and Precinct Line

Arthur; Front-Aaron, Debbie, and Elisa

Road. In September 1997 Dr. Tribble was honored as Richland High School's Distinguished Alumni.

Written by Deborah Tribble

GEORGE AND PATSY TUCKER

George and Patsy Tucker, with their 4-year-old son, Braden, moved to North Richland Hills from Arlington on April 4, 1974. They had just completed construction of their new home in Diamond Loch. George worked at Bell Helicopter Operations, which focused on Iranian contracts. Patsy, a former Dallas secondary English teacher, was a stay-at-home mom. Braden attended the Peace Lutheran Red Apple School.

Braden, George, and Patsy Tucker

There was no such worry as traffic congestion. Areas near Diamond Loch were largely grassy fields where rabbits ran, and boys rode dirt bikes. There was not even a 7-Eleven store nearby. North East Mall was new; Richland Plaza Mall was deserted. Life was generally slow and easy. Security and safety satisfaction were commonplace commodities. Time was available to get acquainted with neighbors. Everybody was motivated to make new friendships. Diamond Loch wives sponsored monthly coffees, as well as gourmet, garden, and bridge groups.

Diamond Loch residents watched carefully, as their children grew, developed, matured, and managed the educational steps, which prepared them to leave home with their futures awaiting. Some of the moms who have been 25-year friends in this neighborhood consider that they have gone from "diapers to Depends" together.

Good neighbors make good citizens. The city has benefited from their concern. Many Diamond Loch residents have served as City Council members, commission members, and volunteers for events such as the national Bicentennial of 1976. George served on the NRH Planning and Zoning Commission for eight years. Patsy now serves on the Beautification Commission where she coordinates the Yard-of-the Month program.

The Tuckers were pleased when the NRH Economic Development Department selected their Diamond Loch home to represent a growth campaign in 1976. Their house, along with Bates Container, Sanger-Harris, and Tarrant County Junior College Northeast Campus, graced an advertisement mailer which was sent throughout the United States recommending North Richland Hills for growth and expansion. It was a great compliment to the Tuckers to have their home selected as representative of the residential community.

In November 1993, the Tuckers sold their Diamond Loch home to build a smaller, more energy-efficient home in the Woodland Oaks Estates in NRH. The neighborhood is filled with young professional families, who mirror the attitudes, ages, and expectations of the 1974 vintage Tuckers. The circle continues.

Submitted by Patsy Tucker

CULLEN AND DOROTHY TURNER

Cullen Y. Turner was born in Talpa, Texas, November 24, 1913. His formal education included a degree in civil engineering from Texas A&M. At one time, he worked for the Texas Highway Department and later worked with his father, who was a bridge builder for Luther A. Turner and Son. In later years, he was a very successful general contractor, building homes and commercial buildings. Cullen Turner married Dorothy M. Jones in 1936. Her parents were Clarence and Alma Ruth Daley Jones. Dorothy was born March 27, 1916, in Baltimore, Maryland. Dorothy graduated from Polytechnic High School in 1932 and attended Baylor University one year. Dorothy was a housewife, later became secretary of the board of Haltom State Bank. She was a member of the Order of Eastern Star and the King's Daughters. Her hobbies were traveling and sewing.

Their son, Cullen Wayne Turner, was born in Fort Worth, November 18, 1940. He graduated from Amon Carter-Riverside High School in 1958 and Texas Christian University in 1962 with a bachelor's degree in business. He and his wife, Pam, have two sons, Carey and Berry.

Cullen's other involvements included service in the Army Corps of Engineers during World War II where he reached the rank of lieutenant colonel. He was a member of the Lions Club, Texas Terrazzo Contractors Association, Riverside Methodist Church, and the Masonic Lodge. Cullen was a member of the original North Richland Hills Civic League and ran for mayor in one of the first elections in NRH.

Cullen Y. and Dorothy Turner on 25th wedding anniversary cruise-1961

Some of the accomplishments of Cullen's construction business included Hudiburg Chevrolet in NRH, the Winn Dixie Grocery store in Greater Richland Center, several homes in NRH, including the home of Dick King and the Turner home on Holiday Lane West.

L/R-Cullen, Pam, Berry, and Carey

Dorothy died February 22, 1991, and Cullen died April 4, 1995.

Submitted by Cullen Wayne Turner

ELLA WALKER TURNER

REMEMBERS OLD SMITHFIELD

Ella Walker Turner sat in her comfortable living room and leaned her head covered with beautiful white hair on the back of her chair. Eyes closed, she began to talk of her parents, Ed and Mattie Walker, her brothers and sisters and when they all lived in the little town of Smithfield.

Her dad was in the Land Rush in Oklahoma in 1889. He had farmed 620 acres and was also a blacksmith. He was sort of an adventurer and had taken his wife there after promising that their house wouldn't have a dirt floor. Mrs. Walker had her youngest son, Earl, at home in the three-room house with wooden floors. Ed had gone for the doctor, but by the time they got back, the 14-pound boy had already arrived with the help of a midwife. Earl joined his older brothers, Moody and Guy, and sister, Clara. Later on, sisters Ella and Ruth completed the family.

In 1905, the Walkers moved to the Smithfield area, buying a small farm on the site that later became the Mangham airport. Mr. Walker went into business with Mr. John Shaw who owned the local blacksmith shop.

Ella was born in 1911. Her parents moved to town, building a house at the east end of Main Street where the old cannery had been. The house had a concrete front porch where Ella whiled away long summer days playing jacks with girlfriends. There was also a baseball diamond on the lot in front of Sam Snider's store. In the winter, when a skim of water on the baseball field

Ed and Mattie Walker

froze, Ella and her friends skated on the makeshift pond.

Mrs. House was the depot agent, an appointed position with the railroad. Ella's brother, Moody, became the agent after Mrs. House. The railroad depot was just north of the Walker house, and the railroad section house, a two-story affair, was just east of the Walker home on Amundson road. The train stopped twice a day, and many times Ella and other kids rode the caboose to Bransford where the train stopped for water. Ella's mother and her friend, Mrs. Turner, would ride the train to the State Fair in Dallas each year. She usually entered her angel food cakes and bread in the cooking contest, frequently winning blue ribbons. For a fee, her father also drove people to the fair, but he would not drive anyone to a dance. "It was not the moral thing to do."

Before Barber Cobb opened his barbershop, Ella's parents took the children into Fort Worth once a month to get a haircut at Stripling's Department Store. One time, Ella had just received a pretty purse for her birthday, and she left it at Stripling's. She cried and cried, but of course, it was way too far to go back to town to look for it. She was glad to get her hair cut by Barber Cobb after the purse episode.

Ella's little sister, Ruth, became a school teacher at Smithfield School. She taught Ella's two daughters before her untimely death at the age of 25 following an appendectomy. Her pallbearer's names read like a roll call of all the prominent families of the community. Older sister, Clara, married John Reeves, and moved to Birdville. Her brothers all lived as adults in Smithfield.

Ella, now widowed, lives in Arlington, and can be seen frequently at the Smithfield reunion in the company of her brother Moody's children.

Interview with Ella Walker Turner
as told to Dorothy Parker

GORDON AND MARYBELLE WALKER

An Oregon lumber company expansion into Texas brought Gordon and Marybelle Walker and their son, Philip, to this area in March 1978. The new corporation was a manufacturing plant near Dallas/Fort Worth Airport. North Richland Hills was a city unknown to us, but we liked the proximity to the airport and the suburban neighborhood.

Gordon was corporation controller in several areas before his retirement in 1988. Then he formed his own company, Access Bookkeeping and Tax Service, and has his office in our home.

He was born in Roseburg, Oregon, and graduated from Roseburg High School. He attended college until he enlisted in the Army Air Force during World War II. After four years, he returned to Oregon State University and graduated in 1947 with a bachelor of science in business and industry.

Gordon was a longtime member of the Lions Club in Oregon and received a distinguished service award when he moved to Texas. He is a member of the Northeast Chamber of Commerce.

I, Marybelle Russell Walker, was born in Hillsboro, Oregon, and attended schools in Corvallis and Albany, graduating from Albany High School. I played piano or pipe organ for several churches, played for school and community events and radio stations KOAC and KWIL, had a scholarship to Oregon State University, and graduated in 1947 with a bachelor's degree in business and industry. I also had many elective hours in piano and choir and was a Euterpe Music Honorary member.

Gordon and Marybelle met at Oregon State University and married in 1948. We have three children and four grandchildren. Marybelle has been a private piano teacher for 30 years and is a member of Mid-Cities Music Teachers Association and of Sonata Club.

Our daughter, Chris, her husband and children moved to Texas in 1982 from Eugene, Ore. She attended Oregon State University and Lane Community College, as well as Tarrant County Junior College. She is a recruiter for Staffing Services in Dallas and was formerly with Birdville Independent School District at Smithfield Middle School.

Gene attended Treasure Valley Community College on a football scholarship. He was in restaurant management after returning from two years in Vietnam with the Army. He later went into banking. He is currently vice president of remittance processing for the southwest region for the Nations Bank in Dallas.

They have two children, Andy and Jill. Both are Keller High School graduates. The family lives in Watauga.

Our son, Norm, was working for Guyon Alloys in California when he made a trip to Texas to see his family and met his future wife, Cheri White, of Watauga. He has a bachelor's degree in business administration and international economics from Oregon State University. Norm is contracts manager for Bell Helicopter in Hurst. One of his many programs for Bell Helicopter recently won the Department of Defense, Nunn-Perry award for excellence.

Cheri was born in Fort Worth and is a graduate of Richland High School and University of North Texas. Cheri and Norm married in 1982. At the time, she was employed by Emery Air Freight and remained there until the arrival of their two children, Amy and Tyler. They live in Keller.

Our son, Phil, was born in Eugene, Oregon, and attended Junction City High School. He was a Lions Club Youth Exchange student to Australia before entering Richland High School as a senior. He returned to Oregon to graduate with his class there. He attended TCJC (NE) and later Texas Christian University while working for Texas American Bank in Fort Worth. He has a bachelor's degree in business administration.

All of the family is active at North Richland Hills Baptist Church.

JAMES M. AND LOUISE M. WALKER

James M. Walker was born February 22, 1925, in Grapevine, Texas. He and two brothers and four sisters were the children of Viola Hall and William Luther Walker. James spent his youth in Haltom City and attended Birdville schools. During World War II, he was a member of the Merchant Marines, returning to graduate from North Texas State University in 1950.

After meeting during their college days, James and Louise M. Carlisle married and settled in Kilgore, Texas. Then, in 1955, they moved to Holiday Lane in North Richland Hills, realizing construction opportunities were much greater in the Dallas-Fort Worth area. The well-known Walker Construction Company was the first large general contractor to locate in northeast Tarrant County in 1969.

During the ensuing years, the company has constructed over 623 projects, including North Hills Shopping Center, 131 schools, the original Texas Ranger Stadium, much of the major construction at Dallas-Fort Worth International Airport and Harris Methodist H.E.B. Hospital, as well as remodeling of Harris Methodist, Fort Worth hospital, and the Stouffer Hotel in Dallas. Louise was office manager of Walker Construction for 30 years until her retirement in 1986. James is now semiretired, enjoying more time to spend with his love of ranching at the family ranch in Bosque County, also reading and visiting with friends.

Louise M. Carlisle Walker was born May 21, 1926 to Florence Hattie Harrison and James Edward Carlisle in Seminole, Oklahoma, spending her childhood in Overton, Texas. She attended Overton schools, completing her education at North Texas State University in 1952.

They have two sons: Joseph M. "Joe," born June 4, 1949, and James M. "Chip," born October 21, 1955. Both attended North Richland Junior High School where Joe was the first student body president of this new school. Both graduated from Richland High School and both attended Southern Methodist University; Joseph graduating in 1971 and Chip in 1978.

Joe married Donna Atherton and later married DeLee Bradford in 1975. They presently live in the Meadowbrook area of Fort Worth. Joe has two sons, Matthew and Joseph. Chip married Elizabeth Ann Swinney in 1980 and they live in Bedford.

The family has attended St. George and St. John Catholic churches during the past 42 years, serving on the Finance Committee, ushering, and assisting with the altar, as well as heading various committees within these congregations. James and Louise have given of their time and talents to the community with active participation in the Haltom-Richland Chamber of Commerce, Lions Club, Associated General Contractors, Richland Garden Club, Woman's Club of Fort Worth, Philanthropic Educational Organization, Oakcrest Woman's Club, the Men's Club, and Shady Oaks Country Club. James has been a member of the NRH Board of Zoning and Adjustments, Chamber of Commerce, and a member of Northeast National Bank Board of Directors. He remains a director of the Associated General Contractors of America.

Submitted by James and Louise Walker

WALTER B. AND CALLIE MAE WATKINS

Walter and Callie Mae Watkins moved to what is now Scruggs Drive in North Richland Hills in February 1951. They had formerly lived on the north side of Fort Worth.

Walter was a building contractor, building houses in North Richland Hills and Westcliff, when he found the property.

He had lived on a farm in Alabama while he was growing up and always wanted to move back to the country. This was it, he thought. There was bus service, which would be necessary since Callie Mae, a native of Fort Worth, didn't drive at that time.

There were only five houses on their street, Calloway Road, which was later renamed Scruggs Drive. The street was a poor-grade, hot-topped road. The closest large grocery store, Wehrings, and a small drugstore were on Baker Boulevard in Richland Hills. There was a country store, Ford's, on Rufe Snow Drive. The closest service station was on Grapevine Highway and Pipeline Road (now Glenview Drive).

The water system was owned by the Will Snow family. The Watkins' property was on the end of a small water line. Sometimes they had very low or no water pressure, especially on the weekends. They were on a six-party phone line at first. Walter had to run the gas line from Pipe Line Road to his house (about 1.5 acres away). They were on a septic tank. They had a garden, chickens, and rabbits. Walter was very disappointed that what he had thought was good black farmland was hard black clay.

They had one daughter, Patsy ("Pat"), still living at home. She was in the eighth grade. She attended a Birdville school at first and then went to the Fort Worth School District where she graduated. Pat learned to drive on Rufe Snow. She would drive as far as the railroad tracks and back, very seldom meeting another car.

Callie Mae's mother, Nellie Donnell, also lived with them. Their two older daughters, Juanita Watkins Fondren and Roxie Watkins Turner, were married and lived in Fort Worth.

Walter built houses on Vance Road, Briley Drive, Cummings Drive, Turner Terrace, and Deville Drive in North Richland Hills. He also built in Richland Oaks, Diamond Oaks, and Richland Hills. Callie Mae worked at North Richland Drugstore in the snack bar after Walter passed away. Pat married Paul Nix in 1954. They lived in Richland Hills until 1972 when they moved to North Richland Hills. They have four children, Cindy, Susan, Jane, and Warren.

Submitted by Patsy Nix

JACK AND EVELYN WATSON

I met my wife Evelyn while I was an aviation cadet stationed at Maxwell Field, Alabama, where she was a clerk-typist in the Base Photo Section. We were married in Camden, South Carolina, on Christmas morning, 1942. I went on to serve as a pilot in the 487th BS 340th BG in Sicily, Italy, and on the island of Corsica in 1943–44, and in various training assignments upon returning to the states. Our first child, Linda, was born while I was overseas.

I was born in Fresno, California, in 1916, and had been employed before the war by an industrial painting con-

tracting firm. I returned to that company after being separated from the Air Corps in 1945. I was transferred from California to Fort Worth to manage operations of the firm in Texas and Oklahoma. Our family continued to grow with the birth of two more children, sons Jim in 1947 and Mark in 1957.

Our first Texas home was a rented house in the Riverside section of Fort Worth in 1951. In the summer of 1952, we purchased a home located on the northwest corner of Cummings Drive and Blaney Street. There were no more than 35–40 families in the development, which encompassed the streets of Blaney, Vance Road, Briley, Turner Terrace, Cummings, and Daley. The soil on the lot was black and difficult to till, and our effort to start a lawn in the fall was wasted, but we were successful the next spring. The developer had installed concrete curbs and gutters on all streets but no paving. Drought conditions prevailed and the resultant DUST from the traffic over dirt roads became an irritant to all and became a community project to eliminate.

We joined the North Richland Hills Civic League, which was formed early in 1953. This organization gave us a base from which to work out a plan to have our streets paved, and it also provided a way to defend ourselves from possible undesired annexation attempts. Bids eventually were received on the paving and a lot of doorbell ringing was done by many residents to inform all owners of their share of the costs. There were a few nonparticipants, and paving in front of their homes was skipped.

Incorporation of the city came about during this same time period, and an election was held to elect city officials. I was elected the first mayor and served a one year term.

In retrospect, I wonder where Evelyn and I found time for civic involvement. We were both involved in the Civic League, and Evelyn was active in the Garden Club, a bridge group, and Cub and Brownie Scouts. We were charter members of the Richland Hills Methodist Church, and I served some time as a steward there. We were young, however, and hoped to raise our children to be involved in both family and community activities, so we felt it necessary to provide a good example.

First mayor of NRH and family 45 years later, L/R-Linda, Mark, Jack, Jim, Evelyn

Our family moved back to California from North Richland Hills in 1961, thus ending our association with the growing city. We have made several visits back to the city over the years, however, and have always been pleased that we had that association with the city in its early years when we see the progress the citizens of North Richland Hills have made in building on what we helped start in 1953.

Submitted by Jack Watson

WILLIAM AND FLORENCE WATTS

William Thomas Watts and Florence Bailey married in Keller in 1908. They had seven children, Willis, Carl, Edgar, a baby girl that died at birth, Walter, Louise, and R. B. Watts. All were born in Smithfield.

Ricky Miller

Louise Watts Miller is the only one of these children still living. She resides on Moneda Circle in Haltom City. Willie was a rodeo participant, Carl was a little of everything, Edgar was a dairy hand and then worked at Armour and Company packing house, then later at the Smithfield School as custodian until his death in 1979. Louise was a housewife and mother of four children. She married Cecil Stowe in 1940 and Shirley Temple Stowe was born in 1941, then a son, Cecil, was born in 1945.

Louise's husband, Cecil, drove the community bus at Smithfield. The bus was owned by Sidney Redd of Haltom City. In 1953 Louise married Clyde Miller and had two children, Richard Lee Miller and Myrna Florence Miller. Myrna passed away in 1990 with cancer and is buried in the Smithfield Cemetery. Myrna was 33 years of age at the time of her death.

R. B. (Buddy) Watts married Johnny Bess Rose and worked for Sinclair Oil Company and when it moved to Beaumont, Texas, they transferred there. Buddy passed away in 1969. Johnnie and their son, David, still live in Beaumont.

Myrna Miller

All of the Watts children were born and raised in Smithfield and went to school there.

Submitted by Louise Miller

LYLE AND PALMA WELCH

Lyle E. Welch was born in Wenatchee, Washington, on July 11, 1927 and moved to Tarrant County in 1948. Lyle has four children, Wanda, Ralph, Lyle Jr., and Roger. He met his wife, Palma, in 1964, and they were married in 1968. Palma was born in Glasco, New York, on Palm Sunday, hence the name Palma. She met Lyle at a truck terminal that she visited with her sister. She also has four children, Roberta, Robert, Kathy, and Harold. In one day they became a family of 10.

Palma has been volunteering with the North Richland Hills Animal Services Center since it started the program in 1989. She has been a Warm Hugs on Wheels volunteer, making thousands of visits to area convalescent homes taking the pet therapist to work with residents. In addition, Palma volunteers at all the Animal Services special events such as Photos with Santa, Adopt-a-thon, Paws for the Cause, and NRH Critter Connection. Employees of the NRH Animal Services have said of Palma, "Palma has given much to the shelter including sponsoring adoptions for individuals and senior citizens. She is a very special person, and we are proud that she has chosen our organization as the focus of her time and energy."

Lyle and Palma Welch

Lyle has been active in politics since 1968 when he was a delegate to the national convention for the presidential election.

Lyle and Palma became active in the city about 1980, serving on the North Richland Hills Civil Service Commission. He was elected to Place 1 on the City Council in 1988 and served as mayor pro tem in 1993. He currently is chair of the North Richland Hills CIP committee and serves on the North Richland Hills Animal Control Advisory Committee, the Ad Hoc Committee for Iron Horse Golf Course, and the North Richland Hills Crime Control and Prevention District. He retired in 1991 from Lisa Motor Lines Inc. as president and chief executive officer.

L. C. "BILL" AND CLARIS WELTY

L. C. "Bill" Welty was born near Gordon in Palo Pinto County, Texas. Claris Irene Willis was born in 1920 near Decatur in Wise County, and moved to Fort Worth where she met Bill. They were married in 1937 in Fort Worth. While living in Fort Worth they became parents of two daughters, Clara Mozelle, born in 1938, and Theta Irene, in 1942.

In 1963 the Weltys purchased three acres on Smithfield Road. This was a rural area, and they had several horses roaming the property. This property was sold to be developed as a mall. However, when Mid-Cities Boulevard was planned, it was purchased for this thoroughfare, which cuts through this area east and west.

Bill and Claris Welty

The Weltys now live on Boulder Court in North Richland Hills. Bill retired from Murdock-Lockheed Aircraft March 1976. Claris retired from Burris Mills/Cargill in the summer of 1985. They are members of Pleasant Glade Assembly of God. Besides the two daughters, they now have five grandchildren and five great-grandchildren.

Mozelle Welty and Arnie Lanier married in Fort Worth and since 1971 have lived in NRH. Mozelle works in the offices of Tarrant County Junior College. Arnie works at General Motors. Daughter Vicki and Willard Hall live in NRH with their two children, Bryan and Andrea. Theta Welty and John Hall married in 1962, and they also live in NRH. They are the parents of two children, Suzanne and John Christopher. John Hall is involved in a gospel music ministry across America and has sung on several Gaither Videos. Theta works in the offices of the Dallas Mavericks.

Submitted by Bill Welty and Betty Leslie

MARION AND HATTIE WEST

I, Hattie Helm West, was 6 years old when my parents moved from Okmulgee, Oklahoma, where I was born. They rented a farm from a Mr. Cale in the Florence School District near Keller, so I went to school in this district. Later, we moved to another farm between Keller and Smithfield, which belonged to John T. White. He was Smithfield School principal, later elected county school superintendent. He made it possible for me to go to the Smithfield School. I began second grade there in 1923 and continued school at Smithfield until I quit to get married at the age of 16.

My brothers and I often walked to school or got rides with our daddy or neighbors. It was a long way to school, and it seemed farther when it was cold. We often warmed ourselves by the huge pot-bellied stove at school. It was probably a five or six mile walk.

I married Marion West of Watauga April 23, 1932. We lived with his folks, then moved to the Harmonson Addition. We moved away, then came back to Smithfield in 1940 with two children, Kenneth Roy, age 6, and Mary Sue, age 1. Marion worked for King Candy Co.,

Sunshine Biscuit Co., and Stroud Butane Co. When he delivered butane for Stroud, all the kids in Smithfield called him the "Butane Man."

We joined Smithfield Baptist Church where Marion served as a deacon, and both of us were Sunday School teachers. When Kenneth started to school, it seems we began taking part in about everything in Smithfield. Marion served on the School Board, City Council, volunteer fire department and was a Boy Scout leader. I worked in the PTA, serving as room mother many times, was in the home demonstration club, and did just about anything I was asked to do. When Sue started to school, every time something was needed, she always told them, "My mommy will do it." Both Kenneth and Sue finished high school at Carter-Riverside in Fort Worth.

Smithfield wasn't very large when we lived there. There were about a dozen houses on the Smithfield Road (now Davis Boulevard). But we knew everybody.

We moved our membership from First Baptist Church, Smithfield to North Richland Hills Baptist Church in 1956. I am still a member there, deeply involved in senior adult activities, and Marion served as an usher for many years.

Sue and her husband, Bill Mathis, live in North Richland Hills. They have four sons. Ken and his wife, Donna live in Tyler. He had two sons, one is deceased, and a stepdaughter, whom we love very much.

We've seen so many changes through the years. We love everything about our city and are happy to be a part of it.

Marion West died May 18, 1998.

Submitted by Hattie West

Standing, L/R-Ken West, Sue West Mathis; Seated, L/R-Marion and Hattie West

RAYMOND AND JO WHALEY

Raymond and Jo Whaley and their children, Deborah Jane and Michael Ray, moved to North Richland Hills in October 1956. Holiday Lane was a dead-end street. Look at it now! A high school was built on our street, then came all the traffic. Holiday Lane was the only through street to the high school. There was only one elementary school north of Glenview. Deborah attended that school, but Mike was still a preschooler.

Raymond Whaley was born in Illinois Bend Community, Montague County, to Frank and Lucy Whaley. I, Jo Whaley, was born in Dye Mound, Texas, to Elmer and Mary Wilson Dunn.

We both graduated from Saint Jo High School. Raymond graduated from North Texas State University in Denton, Texas. He taught school in Montague County for five years before moving to Fort Worth in 1943. We both worked for Consolidated Vultee Aircraft Corp., now General Dynamics. Jo worked as a draftsman and Ray in engineering supervision. Raymond worked there until retirement in 1973. He continued to operate a car wash in Everman, raised cattle on land in Montague County near the Red River. He enjoyed watching baseball and football. Raymond died April 3, 1977.

Deborah graduated from Richland High and North Texas State University in Denton. She now teaches in the Hurst-Euless-Bedford school system. She was married to John Hawkins, son of Louis and Sam Hawkins of North Richland Hills. They have two children, Laura and Markham. Laura attends Richland High, and Markham attends Snow Heights Elementary.

Mike graduated from Richland High and the University of Texas at Arlington with a degree in business. He now operates car washes and works for Bell Helicopter. Mike married Terri Shubert, daughter of Harold and Doris Schubert, of North Richland Hills. She graduated from Richland High and Texas Woman's University in Denton. She now teaches at Fort Worth

Christian School. They have two sons, Nathan and Chase. Nathan is a senior at Richland High and Chase attends Fort Worth Christian Middle School. They all enjoy a houseboat on the lake and hunting deer, turkey, and other animals on land near Red River in Montague County. Nathan killed a deer last season with a bow and arrow.

All of our family are members of Richland Hills Church of Christ. Raymond served as deacon and taught senior adults for several years until his health began to fail. Jo taught first and

Back, L/R-Laura Hawkins, Chase Whaley, Nathan Whaley. Front-Markham Hawkins

fourth grades for almost 10 years. We have met and made friends with some wonderful people in NRH.

WAYNE WHITE

The Wayne W. White family moved from Fort Worth to the present address on Harmonson Road in March of 1949. We have remodeled and rebuilt twice since then. When we came here, we had a county paved two-lane street. We had bus service on the hour during the day.

We had water and gas service furnished by Ben Harmonson. The water came from two wells. One was where Rufe Snow Drive water tower is now and the other was north of the new park between Glenview, Dawn Drive, and Harmonson Road.

We had inside plumbing. Most of our neighbors had outhouses. We had a septic tank with lateral lines running in the back patch. All these lots were 1.25 acres. We had no police or fire departments, county and school tax only. The only school was on Carson Street and Texas 121. We had two children: Betty Ann, 2, and Jimmy Wayne, 2 months, when we moved and three more since then. Their names are Rodney William Joseph, Patrick Tommy, and Albert.

There was a little store in front of McGee's garage, run by the Wallers. At the corner of Pipeline Road (now Glenview) and the Grapevine Highway, there was a service station and Red Shack Café; Marvin Richardson families ran both. Guynn's Grocery at Carson and 121 was where people shopped, except for Leonard Brothers in downtown Fort Worth. Then in 1950 Wehrings Grocery was built at the corner of 183 and Rufe Snow, and then later the Buddies opened in Greater Richland Shopping Center at Blaney and 121.

We used to hunt rabbits and quail in and around old Broadway Road, below Birdville Hill, from the end of Dawn

Standing-Deborah; Seated, Raymond, Jo, and Mike

Drive all through the woods to Fossil Creek. The bridge washed out on old Broadway Road, and the road was closed.

In 1953, the Civic League was formed. The first meeting was at Herb and Maude Arnold's office with about six members. Then we started meeting at the hall back of the Methodist Church on Glenview (in 1956). At that meeting, 21 of us were elected to be reserve police and were given two badges each. We were to help evacuate the school on the third Wednesday of each month, at 10:00 A.M. Joe Sayers was chief. Joe had to move to Fort Worth, and I (W. W. White) was appointed to take his place by Mayor Don Denney.

We had a car raffle in 1955 and 1956. In 1955, it was a Buick Special. In 1956, it was a Chevrolet Del Ray coupe. At the drawing, Mr. Clarence Jones' name was drawn. He gave the car back to the Civic League and it was sold and the money was put into a building on Glenview Drive and Morgan Circle. The lot was donated, as was most of the labor and lots of material. Roy Kelley and I put up the frame and soffit around the building. We had a meeting in the new building in October 1956.

Some of our reserve police worked in Richland Hills moving people out of the flooded area, cleaning out silt, washing walls down, and keeping looters out. Water was up to the eaves on some houses.

In the last 10 years, I have gotten older and slowed down. I don't do much civic work anymore. Rufe Snow's old home place was where the big trees are at Rufe Snow Drive and Shauna Drive. He used to ride to Fort Worth with me sometimes. He was a nice old fellow. He liked to ride in my Model-A Ford. I also knew Will Snow, his son. He worked for the county. He had four sons: Louis, Nimmo, Weldon, and Lonnie, and one daughter, Dorothy. Weldon was in the concrete business, and Lonnie sold cars.

The Wayne W. White Family in Harmonson Addition

There is a little brass plaque at the Broadway Bridge built in 1938, and it was put back in the new bridge. It names the county judge and commissioners for 1938–1940.

Submitted by W. W. White

JAMES AND LAURIE WHITT

Back-James and Laurie Butcher Whitt; Front-Hayden Austin and Haylie Autumn Whitt

James Whitt was born in Fort Worth and lived in Watauga all his life until his marriage to Laurie Butcher in 1989. The Whitt family now includes Hayli Autumn, born October 18, 1991, and Hayden Austin, born February 4, 1994. Both children were born at Harris Hospital in Fort Worth.

James graduated form Richland High School in 1982. He has an associate degree from Tarrant County Junior College and has worked for Siecor in Keller since 1986.

Laurie was born in 1967, in Washington, D.C. Her family moved to North Richland Hills in 1977, then to Hurst in 1985. She returned to North Richland Hills when she and James married in 1989, and they have made their home in the northern part of the city since that time. Laurie graduated from Richland Hills High School in 1985 and TCJC Dental Hygiene Program in 1987. She has been employed as dental hygienist since 1987 and has worked more than five years for Dr. Roberts in Euless.

ROY AND LORENE WILLIAMS

Roy M. Williams and his wife, Lorene, moved to North Richland Hills in 1960 with their three children, Bill, Linda, and Marilyn. Bill finished the sixth grade that same year at North Richland Elementary School, and Linda started first grade in the fall.

The North Richland Drug was a good spot to find kites and hot fudge sundaes, made to order. This landmark drugstore honored credit accounts on many of its customers, and to the dismay of some parents, the store would charge hot fudge sundaes on the account of unsuspecting parents if the kids said the parents had OK'd it. Kites did not normally go "on account," however, since you could find a flight-worthy kite for a nickel.

No one worried much over the whereabouts of their children back then. In fact, the whole concept of missing children was an extremely foreign thought—everyone had so many of their own. Kids were never missing for long; they could always be found at a friend's house or on the way to the drugstore.

Barrbrook Swimming Pool was a jewel for the area, although it probably was located in Haltom City. The families of NRH all claimed it as their own park, and it was the best form of entertainment to come to the area for many years. Later additions to the local entertainment scene included Richland Plaza, home of the Carnation Ice Cream Parlor, Arnold Palmer's Putt-Putt Course, and the Cinema Movie Theater. However, none of these attractions held a candle to Barrbrook.

Stories recounted by Bill, Linda, and Marilyn Williams seem like small tales compared to what happens today in a child's life, but they were ever so big at the time. The best stories that come to mind involve the Twist dance contest at Buddies grocery store, the time Bill fell off his bike entering Barrbrook and got amnesia (we thought it sounded like ambrosia), and the time we held a beautiful funeral service for Pokey Will-Sny, the pet turtle once owned by both the Roy Williams family and the Gene Snyder family. And then there was the time that Roy came home with the fireworks only to hit his head on the garage door that had been left partially extended outward. He fell straight back on the pavement, saw more fireworks than he bargained for, and remembered his two black eyes for years to come.

We remember it all and only wish we were all together to enjoy it again. Roy Williams passed away on a hot summer night, July 17, 1996. We will cherish his memory and his wise decision to make NRH our home for growing up and staying together.

DOUG AND MERLA RAE WILLIAMSON

Douglas D. Williamson and Merla Rae (Miller) Williamson and their two daughters, Dee Angelia and Deborah Ann, moved to Victoria Avenue in North Richland Hills in the summer 1969.

We had just purchased our first house which was "home" from the first time that we saw it. It had been a rent house and we were going to fix it up. We have been fixing it up for 28 years, and it's still a "work in progress."

I, Merla Williamson, met Doug while I was working at Eastland Memorial Hospital in Eastland, Texas, when he had fallen on ice and injured his back. Doug had just returned to Eastland from a four-year tour of duty with the Air Force in Germany, and he was helping run their dairy business while his dad was in the hospital.

Doug and I "ran off" and married September 2, 1963, and the minister of the Richland Hills Church of Christ, Ralph Starling, performed the service in the building that is now the Metroplex Baptist Church. It is funny how our lives together started within a mile of where we live today, 34 years later.

Angie and Debbie started preschool and kindergarten at Richland Private School so that I could go to work at Swift Edible Oil Co. Doug was working for General Dynamics and finishing his college work at night at University of Texas at Arlington, where he received a bachelor's degree in psychology and accounting. He completed his work toward his CPA in 1985.

Angie and Deb started school at Mullendore Elementary, graduated from Richland High School and went to UTA to finish with bachelor of nursing and bachelor of marketing and finance degrees respectively. Angie married John R. Fanning in December 1994, and they live in Abilene where John has his own appraisal business and Angie is nursing at Hendrick Memorial Hospital. They are active in the Mission, a church that ministers to the homeless.

Deb lives in New York City and works in event production with National Media Group. She has traveled from coast to coast producing events and is now limiting her travel to three or four times a year. She is still active in aerobic exercise and various dance classes.

Doug and I are still doing accounting and taxes at our office at 6900 Grapevine Hwy. in NRH. where we have been since 1985. We have been very blessed to attend and belong to NRH Baptist Church. I am active in my Sunday school and choir.

Submitted by Merla Williamson

CARL AND MARY EVELYN WILLIS
Memories of Mary Evelyn Crow Willis

My mother was Lela Evelyn Crow, and my father was Erskine Monroe Crow. I was born in Tarrant County in the Pleasant Run area April 1, 1918. I went to Pleasant Run School. There were seven children in the Crow family, five boys and two girls: Floyd Monroe, William F., John Harold, Mary Evelyn, Mildred Alice, David Olan, and Elijah James. All went to school at Pleasant Run

Carolyn, Mary, Carlene, Carl Willis

School. William and Harold finished school at Grapevine in 1935.

In late 1935, we moved to Nocona, Texas, for three years before moving to Tecumseh, Oklahoma in 1938. I worked in two or three places and in October 1943 I became a clerk in the Tecumseh

Pleasant Run School Reunion, 1977-Carl and Mary Willis

Post Office and worked there until I married a minister, Rev. Carl Vernie Willis in November 1948. We moved to Mulberry, Arkansas, in 1949 where he was pastor of First Baptist Church. Then a miracle happened and little Mary Carlene came along January 16, 1950. After serving there, we moved to Eureka Springs, Arkansas, and there another miracle came along, Alice Carolyn, on July 18, 1952.

From there, we moved to Hess Baptist Church in Oklahoma, then to Buckeye, New Mexico, for three years. Next we moved to Hobbs, New Mexico, where Carl became associational missionary until 1962. We moved back to Texas in March 1962 and served in Azle First Baptist Church for 10 years. Then Carl had a heart attack and two bypass surgeries and passed away August 24, 1994. During these years, Carl also taught at Haltom Junior High School for 13 years.

Carlene married Barry L. Meier December 14, 1974. On October 26, 1977, the blessed event, our only grandchild, Carolyn Elizabeth, was born. Carlene and Barry live in North Richland Hills. Carolyn worked for Motorola here and also in Albuquerque, New Mexico. She moved back to Oklahoma in August 1995. Both our girls graduated from Richland High School, and both went to Oklahoma Baptist University. Carolyn is at OBU now studying to be a therapist.

We moved to NRH in July 1962 and have been here ever since. Very few houses were on Deaver Drive then. I made quilts and quilted and sold many in our senior citizens' fairs. I also crochet.

Our family tries to be together at my younger brother's house in Marlow, Oklahoma at Thanksgiving time, having had as many as 55 or more attend. Also, my brothers and sisters get together on July 4 to enjoy one another.

Submitted by Mary Willis

RAY AND EDNA WILSON

Ray and Edna Wilson and children, Gale, 6, and Brian, 3, moved to North Richland Hills from the north side of

Fort Worth in 1963. We moved from a street where neighbors had coffee in each other's homes, and the *Fort Worth Star-Telegram* printed a story on us.

It was like the country when we moved here, not many houses, no freeways, no places to eat except one little drive-in on Grapevine Highway. Gale loved their chili-cheeseburgers. Rufe Snow was a hot-top, two-lane road with barbed-wire fencing on both sides. Archie's Doughnuts was located on the Grapevine Highway. I used to get doughnuts every Saturday morning for the kids. Good!

When Gale was 7 years old, I was a Bluebird leader. I would walk to school to meet the girls, and walk them to my home to do crafts and have a little snack. We took trips, like flying over our house in a helicopter, took gifts to kids in John Peter Smith Hospital, went to a television studio, lots of fun things!

Later, both our children took skating lessons at Holiday Roller Rink every day. When Brian was 14 years old, Shawn was born. He had the same teacher that Brian had in the first grade, and he was in the choir in junior high and high school.

All our children graduated from Richland High School, Brian in 1978, Gale in 1975 and Shawn in 1990. Shawn used to decorate the stage for choir programs at Christmas. He even went back to junior high to do this after he was in high school.. Now Brian has two stepdaughters going to high school. Ray retired after 37 years in the used car business.

My maiden name was Dacus. I was born in Rhome, Texas, and Ray was born in Crowley. Our children were born in Fort Worth.

Submitted by Edna Wilson

DON HOUSTON AND IDA LILLIAN WISEMAN

I grew up in the community of Smithfield. My parents, Don Houston Wiseman and Ida Lillian Spears Wiseman, moved to Smithfield in 1936. There were five children in the family: John William, Leon Howard, Jenelle, Billy Dan, and Gorman Lynn. When I was in the fourth grade, our family moved to Smithfield. My father received a nice bonus from the government for his years of service in World War I. The bonus gave him the opportunity to buy a farm. Our 62-acre farm was located one mile north of the Smithfield School. There were 40 acres on one side of the road, and 22 on the other.

Times were hard back then, but we settled into a happy life in the Smithfield Methodist Church and the two-story brick school we attended. We have happy memories of the many good teachers there who cared for each child. We also had a gym where we enjoyed many happy hours. I remember the little bottle of ink that rested in a hole in each desk, and the pen staff we used to practice cursive writing, making perfect circles and ovals for a good grade in penmanship.

Mother cooked on a kerosene stove. Daddy was a truck farmer, so we had all kinds of good vegetables. Daddy would raise a hog every year and have it killed and dressed out and stored in the smokehouse. He raised corn, and he would have it ground so we could have cornbread. For refrigeration, we had a box that we put a square of ice into, and the ice would melt and drip into a pan on the floor. We would have to remember to empty the pan so it wouldn't run over on the floor. What I remember most vividly was that we had a well right at the back door. Leon and John dug the well. Daddy sold the 40-acre tract of the farm to get money to build us a new house.

The church provided social life in the community. Leon remembers the boys creating their own entertainment. We didn't have money like the children do nowadays. One thing that gave much joy was when six or seven boys would go up into the woods on Amundson Hill on the weekend and bake sweet potatoes. They would dig a little hole and put a little sand over the potatoes and build a fire on top of that. It would take a couple of hours before the potatoes would be ready. And sometimes, if he was brave enough, a boy would raid a farmer's chicken house, and there would be roast chicken to go with the sweet potatoes. Also, the boys would hunt possum and coon on Friday and Saturday nights up on Amundson Hill.

In the summertime, our father would try to sell his produce. He would take the back seat out of the old Chevrolet and make a shelf there. He would take vegetables and go to the market on Jones Street in Fort Worth.

To court a young girl in Smithfield, boys would try to get their parents' car. Three or four couples would go up to a little "lover's lane," or if they had enough gas, would go to Inspiration Point on Lake Worth. There was not money for movies unless it was free. When our family finally got a car, a 1932 Chevrolet sedan, Smithfield Road was still a dirt road, and when it rained, you didn't dare let those tires get out of the ruts. If you did, you would get stuck. Dad bought the Chevy from western singer W. Lee O'Daniel, who later became the governor of Texas.

Smithfield was the only town that had a post office and did not have a city government. Hurst and North Richland Hills called their post offices subdivisions of Fort Worth. One of the biggest changes for Smithfield was the paving of the roads, and also, getting the utilities.

The first weekend of May each year, there is a Smithfield reunion at the Methodist Church. Leon is preparing to remarry soon. His wife died several years ago, and at the reunion last year, he ran into Wilma, a woman he had gone to Sunday school with when he was a young man. They did not "have eyes for one another" at that time, but were just friends. Now they are going to be married. I grew up with some of Wilma's sisters. Wilma lost her husband in 1981.

Leon remembers that one school year all he had was one shirt, and it was full of patches. Whenever he would stoop over, one of the patches would pop. That's when

Dad was out of work from his injury. But, we all stuck together. Leon, John, and Bill dropped out of school and went into the service. I graduated from high school and spent most of my life in the secretarial field. Our youngest brother, Gorman, went on to finish school and go to college. He became a teacher and has just retired, so our parents managed to keep us all together and we turned out pretty good.

Interview by Nancy Dowler with Jenelle Wiseman Tatarevich

JOE AND HAZEL WOMACK

Hazel Womack Perry has been a homemaker for 70 years and says she is not retired yet. She is 93 years old, in perfect health, and still going strong. In her later years, Hazel managed 14 rentals and restored a beautiful old home when she was 89. Hazel's parents were Marvin Smith and Louvina Dennis Smith. She was born in Bulcher, Texas, in 1905, one of seven children. One of

Joe Womack

her brothers was Lucien Smith, an early settler in Smithfield. Hazel graduated from Saint Jo High School and Brantley-Draughn Business School. She married Joe Womack from Louisiana in 1927. Joe was a gunite contractor and he died in 1961. Hazel later married Tom Fetner and then Troy Perry.

Joe and Hazel had six children, five of whom are still living. They are: Laura Louise (Lou) Doyle, who lives in Decatur; Joe Don Womack of Denton; Barbara Ann Williams, who lives next door to her mother and is the court coordinator for Judge Fender; Gloria Dale Reed, who lives in Saginaw; and Dan R. Womack of Fort Worth. One child, Betty Jo Womack, died as an infant. Hazel has 14 grandchildren and 18 great-grandchildren.

In the spring of 1948, Joe Womack built his family a home out in the country on Bursey Road. He wanted to get his children out of the city and into a healthier environment. He had multiple sclerosis, which also prompted the move. The family cultivated 40 acres of land and had cows and horses. Also, not far away was the home of Hazel's brother, Lucien Smith. The Womack children had lots of fun playing together, but they also had some responsibilities. Joe Womack had a contracting business, as well as the farm

Hazel Womack Perry

to run, and he was ill, so the children needed to help with the farm chores.

The home the Womacks built on Bursey Road was constructed of gunite cement. The cement walls of each room in the house were finished in a different pattern and in a different color. In later years, the home was sold to the Neal family, and today it houses the Bursey Road Senior Citizen Center.

Hazel, a member of North Richland Hills Baptist Church for 24 years, has served as president of her Sunday school class and of the Tuesday Bible Study Club. She also was a member of the Mid-Cities Christian Women's Club and the Senior Adult Bible Study. She was a charter member and first treasurer of the Multiple Sclerosis Society of Tarrant County and a member of the Eastern Star and Harris Hospital Auxiliary.

In their spare time, the Womacks liked to go on excursions to the Fort Worth Zoo and the Botanic Gardens. They also took part in church activities.

L/R-Dan Womack, Gloria (Womack) Reed, Barbara (Womack) Williams, Lou (Womack) Doyle, and Joe Don Womack

The Womack family can remember when the roads in Smithfield were gravel, when everyone had septic systems, when shopping was done in Smithfield or at Guynn's Store in Birdville. The children rode horses, played in the woods, and were perfectly safe anywhere they chose to roam. The Womack family has grown from its original seven members to a current 54. Hazel and her daughter, Barbara Williams, who still live in North Richland Hills, appreciate most of the changes that have taken place in the area. In particular, they enjoy never having to leave North Richland Hills for anything unless they so desire. The malls, the service businesses, the restaurants, grocery stores, and hospitals all make life easier than it once was.

Submitted by Barbara Williams

RAE AND AUDREY WOMACK

Right-Audrey and Rae Womack at their wedding in 1949, at the home of her aunt and uncle; Left-Clarence and Ruth Jones.

Audrey Womack's uncle and aunt, Clarence and Ruth Jones, purchased several hundred acres off Grapevine Highway, which eventually was incorporated and was the beginning of North Richland Hills. When Mr. and Mrs. Jones first purchased the acreage, they built a beautiful two-story colonial home, which faced Grapevine Highway. Rae and Audrey Womack were married in the Jones' home in 1949. After development of NRH had begun, the Jones' home was moved to Cummings Drive.

In 1957, the Richland Hills Chapter 1040, Order of the Eastern Star, was organized. Audrey was one of the first 13 members initiated into the chapter. In 1961, Rae and Audrey's sons were candle lighters at their cousin's (Naomi Cummings) installation as Worthy Matron. Rae had the honor of serving as Worthy Patron in 1966–67.

Rae and Audrey built a house on Redondo Street, and the fam-

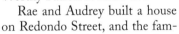

Pat Womack.

ily moved to their new home in April 1963. At that time, twins Mike and Pat completed the fifth grade at Snow Heights Elementary School. Mike and Pat attended North Richland Junior High where they were active in scholastic sports. As members of the ninth-grade basketball team, Mike and Pat helped the team win the District (basketball) Championship. Mike and Pat graduated from Richland High School in 1970.

During their tenure at RHS, Mike and Pat were varsity basketball team members. During their junior year, the RHS varsity basketball team won district, bidistrict, and competed in regional finals. Mike and Pat each attend-

Mike Womack.

ed Tarrant County Junior College and attained their respective associate degrees in applied science. Pat continued his education at the University of Texas at Arlington where he earned a bachelor's degree.

In 1974, Mike was employed by the City of North Richland Hills and Pat was employed by National Can Company. Mike became an NRH police officer in 1976. As of 1997, Mike is still with the NRH Police Department and holds the rank of captain. Pat relocated to Phoenix in 1990.

CLYDE "CORKY" AND EVALYN WOOD

Clyde H. "Corky" and I, Evalyn Nichols Wood, bought our first house and moved to the suburbs in May 1953. This area was called North Richland Hills, but we had no idea why. We only knew that pretty new homes were being built that were affordable to young couples. Our house on Vance Road was to be home for the next 10 years. It cost $18,500, it was air-conditioned, and the mortgage interest rate was 5 percent.

Corky and Evalyn met while students at Texas Wesleyan College (now University) and were married August 18, 1949. We graduated in May 1950. Donna Dee, born in Fort Worth September 26, 1950, and Randal Lee, born in Wichita Falls June 7, 1952, completed our family at that time. Mark Stephen joined the Wood family September 5, 1955, and has lived his entire life in North Richland Hills.

1971-Back-Randy, Mark; Front-Clyde "Corky," Evalyn, and Donna

Our house was situated on a corner lot at Vance Road and Briley Drive, the last streets north and west in this small community, which had just voted to incorporate in April 1953. We joined Richland Hills Baptist Church, the NRH Civic League, and quickly became active and acquainted with most of the residents. Our neighborhood was very close-knit, and we spent a lot of time visiting across the fence or street while trying to get a yard established. We were in the middle of a seven-year drought, the water system was new and inadequate, and often we couldn't get a trickle of water. The streets were unpaved, and we had no schools, doctors, or shopping facilities and couldn't get a telephone for about a year. Then we were on an eight-party line.

Corky was employed by Aircraft Investment Corporation at Meacham Field. He later helped establish an aircraft finance division for Mercantile National Bank in Dallas. His expertise was in the private aircraft sector, and this was one of few banks in the nation handling aircraft loans. Since we only had one car, he found the Bowen bus to downtown Dallas to be a very accessible mode of transportation. The Dallas bus station was just across the street from the bank. I drove him to a pickup spot in Richland Hills on Texas 183 (now Texas 10) every morning, then had the car to shuttle children to school, shop, doctor's, and other appointments. I became active in PTA at North Richland Elementary and served in various offices. I also was president of the North Richland Hills Garden Club in 1956–57.

All three children attended North Richland Elementary School (now Mullendore) and shared the same first grade teacher, Mrs. Willie Parr. After we built a new house in the Snow Heights Addition in 1963, Randy and Mark completed elementary school at Snow Heights Elementary; Donna moved from Richland Junior High to the newly completed North Richland Junior High. All three graduated from Richland High School. Donna graduated from Baylor University in 1972 with a bachelor's degree in Nursing. Mark attended Stephen F. Austin University for 2 1/2 years, graduated from University of Texas at Arlington in 1977 with a degree in banking and finance. Randy attended Tarrant County Junior College and Sul Ross University in Alpine. He died June 4, 1975 and was buried in Greenwood Cemetery, Fort Worth, on his 23rd birthday.

Corky and Evalyn were charter members of NRH Baptist Church, joining in the first service February 26, 1956. I continue to be an active member. Corky served on the NRH City Council and was mayor pro tem in 1957. He enjoyed golf, fishing, and maintaining a beautiful yard. I enjoy crafts, sewing, reading, and gardening. I am currently chairperson of the historical committee appointed by the NRH City Council, which is researching and compiling information for the publication of a history book of NRH, producing a video, and establishing an archives. I was chosen "Volunteer of the Year 1997" from NRH as a result of my work as committee chairperson.

I began teaching school full time when North Richland Junior High was built and opened in September 1963. I taught homemaking until my early retirement in June 1983. I was presented the life membership award in PTA in 1973.

Corky joined Northeast National Bank in 1976 with the establishment of the Northeast Bancorp, Northeast National Bank being the anchor bank. The first acquisition to the holding company was the First State Bank of Bedford in 1977, and he became president and later CEO, positions he held until his death December 27, 1980.

I continued teaching until the end of the school year in 1983. I married Oscar Lochridge June 11, 1983 and we have enjoyed retirement by traveling extensively, researching family histories, and enjoying our eight grandchildren.

Submitted by Evalyn Wood Lochridge

WOOD-AUSTIN FAMILIES
THE JOHN ALEXANDER WOOD AND JAMES COLUMBUS WOOD FAMILIES

John Alexander Wood and wife, Mary Ann Hendricks Wood, came to the Smithfield area in 1877 and bought 90 acres north of town. They came from Obien, Tennessee. John was born in 1837 and died in 1881. Mary Ann was born in 1843 and died in 1926. Eight children were born to this union:

- James Columbus Wood, 1861–1938 Married Mary Matilda Morgan
- Riley Winfield Wood, 1864–1904 Killed in oil field accident
- John Thomas Wood, 1866–
- Mary Magnolia Wood, 1868–1928 Married Jim Johnson
- Sam Wilford Wood, 1870–1947 Never married
- William David Wood, 1873–1954 Never married
- Paralee Isabelle Wood, 1879–1882 Married Joe Coffman
- Jennie Lou Wood, 1879-1882

James Columbus Wood and Mary Matilda Wood had five children:

- Jenny Lou Wood, 1889–1983 Married Albert Austin
- Delia Maud Wood, 1891–1975 Married Robert McFarland
- Henry Otis Wood, 1893–1917 Killed in World War I in France
- Guy Frank Wood, 1898 Married Norma Smith
- Georgia Wilma Wood, 1906–1986 Married Jack Davis

Sam and William continued to live on the old home place until their deaths. They never owned or drove a car, so they would walk to town every weekday afternoon and play dominoes and visit with their friends on the porch of the Snider General Store. They farmed and raised livestock. The water well that was dug near the house supplied water to the family and also to others who had a need. Willie told of men who came with horse and wagons and filled barrels with water. The water had to be pulled up with a rope and bucket. The well is still producing good water.

The Wood family was well respected and loved by all who knew them. Most of the family is buried in the Smithfield Cemetery. They belonged to the Smithfield Methodist Church.

Jennie Lou Wood married Albert Austin and they had four sons:

- Berle Lee Austin, 1909–1982 Married Gussie Long

- Thurman Marvin Austin, 1911–1981 Married Rosa Kidd
- Winnie Doyle Austin, 1914–1996 Married Ann Schaffer, Juanita Sanders
- Charles Estil Austin, 1920–1992 Married Margarite Russell

Thurman Marvin Austin and wife, Rosa Elizabeth, and their two children, Sharon Ann and Bobby Wayne came to the Smithfield area in November 1948. Another son, Larry Glenn was born in 1951. They bought the remaining acreage of the farm that Thurman's great-grandfather John Alexander Wood had bought when he moved his family from Obien, Tenn., in 1877. Only one member of John's family was living in 1948, William David Wood, affectionately known as "Willie." He still lived in the house that was built in 1877. Sharon, Bobby, and Larry attended Smithfield Elementary, Richland Junior High, and Haltom and Richland high schools. Sharon married Danny Cobb and they have three daughters, Elizabeth Renee, Dana Lynn, and Tessa Alise. They live in Decatur. Bobby Wayne married Marie Gallegly, and they have three children, Jordan Lee, Hillary Camille, and Jacob Philip. They live in Miami, Florida. Larry Glenn married Delinda Caldwell and they have two sons, Zachary Nathan and Benjamin Chase. They live in North Richland Hills.

Submitted by Rose Austin

MARK S. AND LISA HARPER WOOD

Mark S. Wood, son of Clyde H. "Corky" and Evalyn Wood, was born September 5, 1955. Mark was the youngest of three children, with his sister, Donna, and brother, Randy, also at home. In 1963 the family moved to the Snow Heights Addition. That was the same year North Richland Junior High (now Middle School) opened. His mother started teaching that fall at the junior high and taught there for 20 years before retiring. Mark attended North Richland Elementary (now Mullendore), Snow Heights Elementary, North Richland Junior High, and Richland High School, graduating in 1973. He then entered Stephen F. Austin University in Nacogdoches. He later transferred to the University of Texas at Arlington where he graduated 1977 with a bachelor's degree in finance. In 1985, Mark was named Richland High School Alumni of the Year.

Mark and his wife, Lisa Harper Wood, have three daughters: Ashley Nicole, born August 24, 1982; Alden Elizabeth, born July 27, 1984; and Maegan Eason, born June 24, 1984. All three attend the same schools that Mark did. They are all involved in athletics and are excellent students. Lisa was born and reared in Grapevine where she graduated from Grapevine High School in 1975. She enrolled at Texas Woman's University in Denton where she graduated with a bachelor's degree in 1979 and master's degree in library science in 1980. She has worked in public library service for 18 years, serving the last 11 years as the library director for the city of Keller. In 1996 she was honored by being named Texas Library Director of the Year.

In 1976, while attending UTA, Mark began a career in banking by becoming a drive-in teller at Texas Commerce Bank-Arlington. He quickly moved up through the ranks to become a commercial loan officer. In 1982, he transferred to Texas Commerce Bank-Hurst to head up the real estate department. In 1984, he was named president and chief executive officer of the bank and the next year was promoted to chairman of the board. In 1987, with branch banking transforming Texas banking, Mark resigned and started his own business. The following year he, along with his lifelong friend and classmate, Mark Howe, started the commercial

Standing-Maegan Eason, Lisa, Ashley; Front-Mark, "Brady," Alden

real estate brokerage and development firm of Howe/Wood & Company. Their firm specializes in Tarrant County properties primarily located in northeast Tarrant County.

In 1982, Mark was appointed to the Planning and Zoning commission of North Richland Hills, where he served for nine years. In 1991, he was elected to the City Council. He was later elected for two additional terms and also served one year as mayor pro tem. In 1997 he left the council but was then re-appointed to the Planning and Zoning Commission where he continues to serve. Some of his proudest accomplishments, while on the council, include major improvements to the city's streets, construction of the new City Hall, and greatly increasing the number and size of the city parks, including projects such as NRH2O, the Richland Tennis Center, the Green Valley Soccer complex, and several other parks around the city.

Mark was 5 months old when his parents became charter members of the North Richland Hills Baptist Church in February 1956. To this day he is reminded that he had the distinction of being the first baby in the church's nursery. He has attended North Richland Baptist Church all his life, serving in numerous positions including deacon, finance committee chairman, and building committee chairman through two major building pro-

grams. While in high school, he worked on the construction of the present church auditorium. Lisa is a Sunday school teacher in the Youth Department.

Fond memories of growing up in NRH include watching the construction of Loop 820 and wondering if cars would ever use the vacant stretch of road. It was always fun to follow area creeks for miles north through undeveloped areas without seeing many houses, and to ride bikes to Richland Plaza to play in and around this new, modern shopping center, play miniature golf, and buy turtles at Kresge's. Later, when the Cinema opened at Richland Plaza, it was fun to go to the movies on Friday nights and then walk over to the Carnation Ice Cream Shop.

He, like a lot of other kids in town, learned to swim at the old YMCA pool on Parchman Road, now the site of a parking lot owned by the North Richland Hills Baptist Church. The first job Mark remembers having was, at age 10, delivering circulars door to door for the North Richland Drugstore. Later, he enjoyed taking his daughters back to the drugstore to eat lunch at their coffee shop.

BILLY J. AND IRIS WOODALL

Billy J. and Iris Corinne Sousae Woodall moved to Briley Drive in North Richland Hills on April 1, 1958, from the Polytechnic area of Fort Worth. At this time Rufe Snow Drive was only a two-lane street, and there were no city taxes.

Bill was born January 2, 1931, in Fort Worth to Winnie Pennington and Henry William Woodall. He has two sisters.

Iris was born October 20, 1931, in Shidler, Oklahoma. to Edna Clyona Attebery and Daniel Matthew Sousae. She has a sister and a brother.

Bill and I, Iris, graduated from Polytechnic High School in Fort Worth, Bill in January 1949, and I in May 1949. Bill started working for the Texas and Pacific Railroad in Fort Worth in 1949, as a car apprentice, then as a car inspector. He was a wrecker engineer for 20 years. This later became Union Pacific Railroad.

I worked for Retail Merchants Credit Bureau for three years. We were married May 13, 1950, in Polytechnic Christian Church in Fort Worth by Bill's uncle, Andy Franklin Cash.

Bill served 16 months of his two-year military service in Korea with the U.S. Army in the railroad battalion. I was a

Iris and Billy J. Woodall, 1989

timekeeper at Convair for three years. I was also a secretary for Baldwin Mechanical Contractors in Watauga for 10 years.

We are members of Richland Hills Christian Church.

We have two children, Debra (Debbie) Lynne Woodall Dubberly of Bedford, born in Fort Worth in 1957, and Donald Glen Woodall of Annetta South, Parker County, born in Fort Worth in 1959. Debbie has been an executive secretary for Texas Utilities for 16 years. Donald is a certified public accountant and controller at Lubrication Engineers.

We have five grandchildren of whom we are very proud. We enjoy keeping them and doing things with them.

Bill is past master of Richland Hills Masonic Lodge No. 1348 and is still very active in the lodge work. He is also a member of Hurst Chapter No. 492 and Hurst Council No. 407, Worth Commandery No. 19, and the Moslah Shrine.

I am a member of the Mid-Cities Genealogy Society, treasurer of Pennington Research Association, Tarrant County Junior College Computer User's Group and Special Interest Group (computer genealogy).

Bill retired from the Union Pacific Railroad January 6, 1993, with 44 years of service. We are active at the Dan Echols Senior Adult Center, teaching pinochle, playing bridge, crafts, and crocheting and taking senior citizen classes at Tarrant County Junior College Northeast in bridge, water exercise, "42," genealogy, and computer. Bill also plays bridge at Bursey Road Senior Citizens' Center. We have been gardening in the Texas Utilities easement behind our house for about 17 years. Bill also enjoys hunting and fishing.

Submitted by Iris Woodall

DONALD AND JUDIE WOODALL

I, Donald Glen Woodall Sr., was born June 17, 1959 in Harris Hospital, Fort Worth. My parents are Iris Corinne Sousae and Billy J. Woodall, who live on Briley Drive in North Richland Hills. I have one sister, Debra (Debbie) Lynne Woodall Dubberly, of Bedford, who was born in Fort Worth February 18, 1957.

I attended North Richland Hills schools and graduated from Richland High School in 1977 where I was in the marching band and the stage band, playing the alto and baritone saxophones. I was president of the chess club and a member of the National Honor Society.

I played baseball in the Richland Youth Association when they played off Handley Ederville Road, south of the railroad tracks in Richland Hills.

I remember Rufe Snow Drive being a narrow country road, especially at the northeast corner of Rufe Snow and Loop 820 where there was a cotton field with a pretty brick house out in the middle of the field.

I lived on Briley Drive until I graduated from the University of Texas at Arlington with a degree in accounting. I received my master's degree in finance at North Texas State College in Denton. I am a certified

Back, L/R-Judie and Don Woodall Sr.; Front, L/R-Donald Jr., Daryl, Daniel

public accountant and controller at Lubrication Engineer's in Fort Worth.

Judie went to Lindsay School in Lindsay, Texas, where she graduated in 1982. She earned a degree in engineering at the University of Texas at Arlington and has been an engineer at Bell Helicopter since 1987.

I married Judith (Judie) Ann Marie Felderhoff May 21, 1988, in St. Mary's Catholic Church in Gainesville, Cooke County, Texas.

We bought our first home on Doris Court in North Richland Hills in 1988, living there until 1995. We bought our present home in Annetta South, which is in Parker County.

We have three sons, Daniel Joseph Woodall, Daryl Anthony Woodall, and Donald Glen Woodall Jr.

H. E. AND DAISY WOODWARD

Hanson Elroy "Woody" Woodward was born February 23, 1920, in Glasco, Kansas. He was the only child of Hanson S. and Mary W. (Lampert) Woodward. Woody married Daisy Belle Lyles from Justin, in Denton County. Daisy was born April 15, 1923, in Decatur but moved to the Dooley farm where her mother, Mary Emma Dooley Lyles, had grown up. Daisy's father, Willis E. Lyles, lived in Alvord before moving to Justin.

Woody and Daisy were married in June 1945, in Kansas City. Woody attended radio school and was working with Bendix, which was working on the cutting edge of television in the 1940s. Daisy was a registered dietitian. In 1949, they moved to Fort Worth where Woody worked for Leonard's Department Store as the manager of the Radio and TV Service Dept. Later, he left Leonard's and

1989, Back-Gary, Mary Kay, Mark, and Betty; Front-Ken, Daisy and H. Elroy Woodward

went to work for Pride (Carwash) Manufacturing. There he introduced solid state circuitry to replace the more fallible electronic relays.

Woody and Daisy had five children: Hanson Mark, born in 1947 in Kansas City; twins Gary Jay and Mary Kay, born in 1950; Betty Jan, born in 1955; and Kenneth Bruce, born in 1961. All but Mark were born in Fort Worth.

In 1958, Woody and Daisy moved to the College Hills Addition of North Richland Hills, because they wanted to send their children to the new Fort Worth Christian School. There were only four or five houses in the addition at that time. In fact, they had to open barbed-wire fences to get to the addition when they were looking at the lots.

Daisy started teaching school at Fort Worth Christian. She taught homemaking, science, chemistry, and biology. Later, she taught in the Northwest School District. She retired in 1990.

Woody and Daisy were members of the Eastridge Church of Christ, which later became Midtown Church of Christ. Woody was an elder for many years. Daisy taught classes, and both were very serious students of the Bible.

Music was one of the many hobbies of Woody. He played the guitar, banjo, dulcimer, and violin, and he loved to read. Raising children and teaching school were all that Daisy had time for. Now she loves to garden and go to garage sales.

Woody died of cancer June 12, 1989. Daisy still lives in NRH, and three of her children live in the area. She still substitutes for the Birdville ISD, is involved in church work, and works part-time for a local department store.

Submitted by Betty Woodward Orton

CARL AND SUE YATES

Carl and Sue Yates met and married in Wichita Falls on September 12, 1958. Carl was born in West Virginia. Sue, the former Sue Snyder, was born in Itasca, Texas.

Carl was in the Air Force and stationed at Wichita Falls where Sue was working. A son, Jim, was born in Wichita Falls, July 1959. Carl, Sue, and Jim moved to North Richland Hills in 1961. A daughter, Carla, was born in Fort Worth in 1962. Carla and Jim attended schools in North Richland Hills, both graduating from Richland High School.

Jim and wife, Olivia, live in Houston. Carla and husband, Rex, live in Grand Prairie with their two sons, Shane and Brock.

Carl, who is semiretired, was a car dealer in Fort Worth for many years. Sue's brother and sister-in-law, Gene and Lamoyne Snyder, live in NRH and attend North Richland Hills Baptist Church, as does Sue. Sue has been a member of this church since 1961, most of this time teaching a Sunday school class and working in the nursery.

There have been many changes in the past 30 years for Carl and Sue. The Meadow Lakes and Iron Horse Golf Club area is where Carl formerly hunted dove. Sue shopped at Winn Dixie when it was a Buddies store. The first mall was Richland Plaza, and the NRH library used to be there.

W. ALVIN AND FAY YATES

This story begins on December 5, 1954, when I, Al Yates, was transferred by the Civil Aeronautics Administration from Dallas Love Field to the Air Route Traffic Control Center. I commuted from Dallas to Fort Worth for six months before moving the family to North Richland Hills in June 1955. I bought a house on Mackey Drive. My family consisted of my wife, Beverly Fay, and our children, Beverly Ann and Charles Arthur. Our house was the fourth house on our block with open fields to the west. My children were age 11 and 9, respectively. They had their schooling in the Birdville school system, both graduating from Richland High School.

Beverly met and married Joseph David Sanders, also an NRH resident on June 12, 1964, at North Richland Hills Baptist Church, the Rev. Hal Brooks officiating.

L/R-Charles, Beverly, Fay, Alvin Yates

They now live in Aubrey, Texas. They have two children, Susan Rae and Joe David.

Charles received his bachelor's degree from Baylor University. While at Baylor, he attended a church camp at Falls Creek, Okla., and met Mary Lee Brouer from Arlington. They were married, January 24, 1970, on Mary's birthday, by the Rev. Hal Brooks at North Richland Hills Baptist Church. They live in NRH. They have two children, Kristin Freeman and Josh Yates.

Charles holds a master's degree in counseling from the University of Texas at Arlington, and he has an office in Hurst. He serves on the Birdville School Board and is a past president of the board. Mary has taught in the BISD schools and is a legal secretary for a law firm in the area.

Fay was born in Port Arthur October 14, 1924. She was very active at North Richland Hills Baptist Church, especially with the youth. She was loved by everyone who knew her. She worked with several government agencies before passing away with cancer in 1990. We were happily married 46 years.

I was born in Farmersville, Texas on December 12, 1918. My family moved to Dallas when I was an infant. I received my primary education in the Dallas schools and a bachelor's degree from Southern Methodist University. My first flight training was through the Civilian Pilot Training Program at SMU in the fall of 1941, where I received my private pilot's certificate. Flying became my favorite hobby.

In 1942 I enlisted in the Army Air Corps and served four years as an Army Airways Communications Specialist—Control Tower Operator. Most of the time was spent in Florida and the Aleutian Islands. After my discharge, I continued my hobby of flying and received my commercial pilot certificate, and later my airline transport certificate. In addition, I hold several ratings and certifications.

One of the most rewarding things I've accomplished was being written into the Guinness Book of Records. In 1976, my partner and I broke the record for the most takeoffs and landings at unduplicated airfields. After our first record was broken, we made a second attempt and were successful. We continue to hold the record for the most take-offs and land-ings in a "day-light" day. We made 193 take-offs and day-light landings at unduplicated airfields in 14 hours, 57 min-utes in a Piper Seminole on June 15, 1979.

After retir-ing from the

Bob Phoenix, left, and Alvin Yates check the Guinness Book of World Records

Al and Lou Yates

FAA as a team supervisor on January 1, 1977, with 28 years in government service, I was appointed as a designated pilot examiner for the FAA. In that capacity, some of this work was done from Mangham Airport in NRH. I have enjoyed teaching others to fly, piloting small company planes for their executives, giving check flights to other pilots, and flying my own plane for pleasure.

On May 29, 1993, I married a former resident of NRH, Lou Hubbard. Her husband, Ken, had also passed away. Fay and I had been friends of Ken and Lou Hubbard since we were neighbors and friends in the '50s. We lived on the same street, were members of North Richland Hills Baptist Church, and had many common interests. We believe that Fay and Ken would be very happy that we have found happiness together. Now our family has doubled. Since our children have known each other most of their lives, they were happy to unite our families.

Lou is an accomplished porcelain artist who has won many awards for her work. She teaches two regular class-es each week and gives seminars throughout the country. She is vice president of the International Porcelain Artists and Teachers Association, and has held several offices in the State Federation of China Painters as well as the China Painting Teachers of Texas. For three years, she taught at the World Organization of China Painting school at the University of Colorado in Pueblo.

Lou and I have enjoyed traveling since our marriage, especially several cruises. We think all our children, grandchildren, and great-grandchildren are the greatest.

SUSIE ANN YEATTS

Susie Ann Yeatts, who grew up in Sanger, Texas, moved to North Richland Hills in 1969. She was born February 11, 1947 in Sanger to Flora Ethel Charger Yeatts and Aaron Harvey Yeatts. She has three brothers, Clyde, Fred, and Don Yeatts, and one sister, Yvonne Yeatts Cain.

Susie Yeatts has been an educator 29 years, the first 11 in the Birdville Independent School District, the next nine in the Hurst-Euless-Bedford ISD, and has complet-ed nine more years back at BISD, where she is assistant principal at North Ridge Middle School.

She received a bachelor's degree in Spanish at the University of North Texas at Denton, studied one summer in Spain doing postgraduate work through the University

Susie Yeatts

of Dallas, attended Texas Woman's University in Denton, and has a master's degree from Texas Christian University.

Her special interests include education, music, geology, rock collecting, traveling, reading, and going to movies.

Yeatts, who is single, is especially interested in "how people think and what they think, and how to help them change negative thoughts to successful positive thoughts," she said.

She is a member of the North Richland Hills Baptist Church where she is on the counseling and finance committees, has taught Sunday school classes, and has sung in the choir 28 years.

Yeatts, who completed a course at the NRH Citizens Police Academy, remembers when "Rufe Snow Drive was a gravel road," she said. "The only close restaurant, except for Sir Loin Steakhouse and Carnation, was C. A.'s Restaurant in Hurst. My favorite dress shop was Hollie's in the North Richland Shopping Center."

"I've become friends with a lot of great people," she added.

STANLEY AND BARBARA YUCHNOVICZ

Stanley Harry Yuchnovicz and Barbara Imogene Coffer Yuchnovicz were married August 1, 1952, at Temple Baptist Church in Detroit. Both were born in Detroit; Stanley, February 16, 1925, and Barbara, February 12, 1930.

They moved from Taiwan in February 1994 to North Richland Hills. He taught one and one half years at Texas Baptist Bible College in Bedford before he had a stroke, and they have been members three years at Bedford Baptist Temple where Barbara teaches Sunday school and the Wednesday night Awanas Bible Club's Cubby Class of 2- through 4-year-olds.

They did missionary work 42 years for the Baptist Bible Fellowship in Springfield, Missouri, until they retired July 31, 1995.

They have two children, Ron David Yuchnovicz and Karen Ethyl Yuchnovicz Hader, and one grandchild, Christopher Michael Hader. Ron David attended the Christian school in Taiwan and has lived in several states in the United States. Karen is married to Michael King Hader. The Haders live in North Richland Hills.

"We were able to speak Mandarin Chinese and Taiwanese and established churches, helped build a Bible school, designed and built churches, slept on hard Chinese beds, fellowshipping with the Chinese and learning a new culture and eating their food," Stanley Yuchnovicz said. This was all in Taiwan where different groups of people spoke both Taiwanese and Mandarin.

Barbara enjoys crocheting, knitting, making things for the Awanas Cubby Class and has helped in decorating the church.

They enjoy spending time at the Bursey Road Senior Center in NRH, where both help out. They have enjoyed seeing Precinct Line Road and Mid-Cities Boulevard built from Davis to Precinct Line.

Submitted by Stanley Yuchnovicz

CLYDE AND LORENE ZELLERS

Clyde and Lorene Zellers

Clyde and Lorene Zellers and daughter, Sandra Kay, moved to North Richland Hills in 1954, living first on Blende Street, then on Venice Street. There are many good memories of the neighborhoods and good neighbors like the Frank Watts, Ray Renfro, and Joe Laine families. The Zellers family made its third move in NRH in the early 1960s, moving to the newly developed Snow Heights Addition.

Clyde was born in Weatherford, Texas, attended high school there, then attended Texas University, Texas Christian University, and Brite Seminary. He was in the general insurance business from 1946 to 1974 and served as a Methodist minister from 1974 to 1989. He became a hospice chaplain from 1989 to 1996 and is currently area supervisor for Jackson Health Care.

After moving to NRH, Clyde soon became involved in his community's affairs. He served on the NRH Zoning Commission; then was elected to the City Council in 1959, became mayor pro tem in 1960, then was elected mayor in a special election in August 1960, serving in this office until the 1961 election. This was a very turbulent period in the political scene for NRH, and Clyde, as mayor pro tem, felt the pressure on his shoulders. Mayor Bill Perry was charged with many indiscretions, hearings were held in the auditorium of North Richland Elementary School, and Mayor Perry was impeached and removed from office.

During this time of Zeller's leadership, the first Police Department was established, the first police chief was hired, and the first Fire Department was organized.

Clyde served in the Army Air Force from 1941–1946, most of that time being spent overseas, mainly in England, Italy, and India. He was selected as outstanding minister of the Central Texas Conference of the United Methodist Church in 1980. This area comprises some 400 churches. He is presently serving on the Tarrant County Senior Citizens Committee.

Lorene Zellers was born in Truscott, Knox County, Texas. She graduated from Goree High School. In NRH, she served as a Girl Scout assistant leader and has been an active member of Richland Hills United Methodist Church along with her family.

Sandra Zellers Billings graduated from Richland High School in 1967 where she was in the original Dixie Belles drill team, organized in 1964. She was also active in the choir and drama club, performing in *Oklahoma* and *Bye-Bye Birdie* under the direction of Dub Fisher. Sandra and her husband, Rick Billings, own and operate a bed and breakfast in Wimberly, Texas. Her daughter, Sunny Heimbecker, recently graduated from Southwest Texas State University in San Marcos.

Clyde, granddaughter Sunny Heimbecker, Lorene, daughter Sandra Zellers Billings, 1994

Clyde said, "It is especially amazing to watch the rapid growth of this city and watch how quickly dirt roads were paved and shopping centers have sprung into view. I shall always remember serving on the City Council and the honor of being mayor of our great city; also being a part of hiring the first police chief and organizing the Fire Department. My wife and I are delighted to be a part of the Star of the Metroplex—NRH."

Lorene Zellers died August 14, 1998.

Index